LITTLE
FAMILIES

From records compiled by

BENJAMIN FRANKLIN WILBOUR

VOLUME II

LITTLE COMPTON, RHODE ISLAND

CLEARFIELD

First Edition originally published
Little Compton, Rhode Island, 1967
Second Edition, with corrections and additions, 1974
Third Edition, 1983
Fourth Edition, 1985
Fifth Edition, 1997

Reprinted with permission of
Little Compton Historical Society
Little Compton, Rhode Island

Reprinted for
Clearfield Company by
Genealogical Publishing Co.
Baltimore, Maryland
1997, 1998, 2000, 2003, 2005, 2007

Volume II ISBN-13: 978-0-8063-4705-9
Volume II ISBN-10: 0-8063-4705-8
Set ISBN-13: 978-0-8063-4703-5
Set ISBN-10: 0-8063-4703-1

Made in the United States of America

LITTLE COMPTON

FAMILIES

VOLUME 2

LITTLE COMPTON
FAMILIES

Published by

LITTLE COMPTON HISTORICAL SOCIETY

From records compiled by

BENJAMIN FRANKLIN WILBOUR

LITTLE COMPTON, RHODE ISLAND
1967
With corrections and additions
1974
Soft Cover Edition
1985

MANCHESTER'S STORE, ADAMSVILLE, R. I.

THE MANLEY FAMILY

1. JOHN[1] MANLEY of Providence, probably born in England.
He married TEMPERANCE TURNER, born in 1737 (?), died in 1803.
Residence: Providence.

From Deed Book three, page 190 in Providence: "I Temperance
Manley of Providence, widow, relict of John Manley of Providence.
To son William Manley of Providence, gentleman, one half of a certain
undivided tract of land in Westport, of 110 acres bounded north formerly
by Thomas Howland, east by Pardon Brownell, south by Benjamin Duval
and Wing Durfee, west by Isaac Wilbor and Rescomb Palmer with half of
the buildings, also salt marsh in LC 10 acres bounded north on Quicksand
Pond, east and south by William Whitridge and west by Benjamin Head.
29 March 1788. . . "

Her will, recorded in book 1, page 7, made 7 May 1802 and proved
5 Jan. 1803: ". . . To son William Manley use of all real estate and
personal estate. To two grandsons, John and William Moore Manley,
after death of William, the above estate. To granddaughter Temperance,
large silver spoon . . . To grandson John Manley. . . rest and residue to
Sally Burr Manley. . . "

Children:
2. i.   William, b. 23 Jan. 1767 (?).

2. **WILLIAM[2] MANLEY** (John[1]), born 23 Jan. 1767, died in LC 30 Sept. 1841. Residence: LC.

He married first 3 Oct. 1787 SALLY BURR, born 15 Oct. 1761, died in LC 3 April 1789. He was married second in LC 16 Aug. 1789 by Thomas Palmer, justice, to JUDITH SNELL, daughter of Job and Ruth (Davenport) Snell of LC, born in LC 29 Oct. 1769, died there 6 June 1849.

They lived in the east part of town, probably on the Westport line near John Hoxie and Wilbor Palmer, around Pottersville.

His will, recorded in LC Probate book 9, page 30, made 5 Feb. 1841 and proved 8 Nov. 1841: ". . . One dollar each to daughters Sally Burr Hoxie, Hailey Turner Pearce, Temperance Turner Tompkins and Ruth Head; to son John my mahogany desk; to grandson Benjamin Turner Head my watch; to wife my comb and all my wearing apparel, all my wheels and reels; to son William Moore all my stock and he to be sole executor. . . "

Children by first wife:
i.   Amey, d 4 April 1789.

Children by second wife, recorded in LC:
3. ii.   John, b. 5 May 1790.
   iii. Sally Burr, b. 15 July 1791; m. (1) in Westport 25 Sept. 1812 Calvin Manchester; m. (2) about 1825 John Hoxie, son of Peleg and Francis (Pittman) Hoxie.
   iv.   Haley Turner, b. 17 Dec. 1792; m. (--) Pearce.
   v.   Armida, b. 20 March 1795; m. (intention 30 March 1814) John Snell.
4. vi.   William Moore, b. 19 Oct. 1796.
   vii. Temperance Turner, b. 11 May 1798; m. in LC 15 June 1817 Seabury S. Tompkins.
   viii. Ruth, b. 23 Jan. 1800; m. in LC 18 Oct. 1818; m. Palmer Head, son of Benjamin and Abigail Head.

3. **JOHN[3] MANLEY** (William[2], John[1]), born in LC 5 May 1790, died 4 Nov. 1845 ae 55. Residence: LC. He was married in LC 26 Jan. 1812 by Peleg Sisson to BETHANIA BRIGHTMAN, daughter of Israel and Bethany (Palmer) Brightman, born in Westport 13 Jan. 1792.

Children, recorded in LC:
i.   Job Turner, b. 1 Nov. 1812; m. 28 July 1833 Hannah A. Bessey of Westport.
ii.   John Alexander, b. 1 Dec. 1813.
iii. William, b. 15 Sept. 1815, according to the Dartmouth census.
4. iv. Clarke Davenport, b. 29 Aug. 1818.
   v.   Edwin, b. 2 Feb. 1820.
   vi. Thomas Tucker, b. 18 May 1821, according to the Dartmouth census; m. Ann (--), b. in 1824. They had two children, John, b. in 1847 and Willa, b. in 1839.
   vii. Aroet, b. 8 Sept. 1823; d. 1909; m. in Dartmouth 28 Aug. 1849 Malvina Eldridge, daughter of Simeon and Deborah

Eldridge of Dartmouth, b. in 1829, d. in 1903. They had
a daughter Deborah, b. in South Dartmouth in 1850, m.
in LC in August 1869 Ephraim Manley, son of William and
Abby Manley.

viii.   Bethany, b. in 1826; m. in Westport 31 Aug. 1845 William
Manchester, son of Hercules and Abby Manchester, mariner.

4. WILLIAM MOORE[3] MANLEY (William[2], John[1]), born in LC 9
Oct. 1796, died there 24 Oct. 1861. Residence: LC. In 1850 they were
living near Quicksand Pond, close to the Westport line.

He married in LC 12 Sept. 1830 ABIGAIL BROWNELL, daughter
of Stephen and Cynthia (Wilbor) Brownell, born 30 April 1813; died
in 1909. They are buried in Beech Grove cemetery in Westport.

Children, all recorded in LC:
i.   Oliver Perry, b. 10 Dec. 1831; d. 9 Nov. 1832.
ii.   Judith Maria, b. 11 Aug. 1833.
iii.   Mary Elizabeth, b. 12 April 1835; m. in LC 27 June 1855
Samuel P. Palmer, son of Wilbor and Hannah (Brownell)
Palmer.
iv.   William Moore, b. 12 April 1835; d. 26 May 1906.
v.   Abigail Niles, b. 11 May 1837.
vi.   Oliver Perry, b. 11 May 1837; d. in 1859; m. Hannah G.
(--).
vii.   Stephen Wright, b. 24 Oct. 1839.
viii.   (--), b. 24 Oct. 1839.
ix.   Daniel Dwelley, b. 3 Oct. 1841; d. in 1861.
x.   Charles Howland, b. 14 March 1843; d. in 1874.
xi.   Seabury Turner, b. 1 March 1844.
xii.   Ephraim Gifford, b. 1 March 1844; m. 16 Aug. 1869 Deborah
Manley, daughter of Aroet and Malvina Manley, b. in
South Dartmouth in 1850.
xiii.   Rachel Gifford, b. 1 March 1845.
xiv.   Sylvester Cooley, b. 6 Sept. 1846; m. Hannah A. (--), b. in
1846, d. in 1884.
xv.   Sarah Nickerson, b. 11 May 1848; m. 23 Sept. 1883 Horatio
N. Hart, son of Rubin and Phebe Hart of Tiverton.
xvi.   Francis Napoleon, b. 21 Oct. 1850.
xvii.   Susan A., b. 29 April 1855; m. (--) Hart.

5. CLARKE DAVENPORT[4] MANLEY (John[3], William[2], John[1]),
born in LC 29 Aug. 1818, died 6 April 1871. Residence: LC. He
married AMEY ALMEY, born 25 June 1823, died 2 April 1875.

They were listed in the LC census, at which time they lived in
the east part of the town near George L. Dyer, John Hoxie and Palmer
Head at Pottersville. They are buried in the Elm Street cemetery,
Padnarum, South Dartmouth.

Children:
i.   Thomas G., b. 27 June 1846.
ii.   John, b. in 1846; d. in 1923; m. Elizabeth W. (--), b. in 1849,
d. in 1923.
iii.   William H., b. in 1839.

iv.   Almy, b. in LC 19 Nov. 1850; d. 13 Jan. 1851.
v.   Susan, b. in LC 19 Nov. 1850; d. 13 Jan. 1851.

❧

THE MANTON FAMILY

HENRY MANTON (colored), born in North Carolina, married DORA (--). Residence: LC.

    Children, recorded in LC:
i.   Bertha Isabel, b. 4 May 1886; d. 18 Nov. 1890.
ii.   Son, b. 24 Oct. 1887.
iii.   Ida May, b. 1 Jan. 1896.
iv.   LeRoy, b. 15 Feb. 1899.
v.   Everett, b. 8 March 1901.

❧

THE MARTIN FAMILY

ANDREW MARTIN, married in LC 6 July 1737 MARY LYND, daughter of Jonas and Abigail (Elliot) Lynd, born in LC 6 July 1713. Residence: LC.

    Children, born in LC:
i.   Lynd, b. 27 May 1740.

. . . .

1. ADELBERT ALLEN MARTIN, son of David Franklin and Sarah A. (Macomber) Martin of Tiverton, born 8 April 1888 in Tiverton. He married in LC 14 Oct. 1916 DOROTHY WILBOUR, daughter of Philip H. and Grace (Ropes) Wilbour, born in LC 1 Jan. 1891. Residence: LC.

    Children:
i.   Philip Wilbour, b. 9 Sept. 1918.
ii.   Adelbert Allen Jr., b. 7 June 1920.
2. iii.   David Lincoln, b. 23 Feb. 1922.

2. DAVID LINCOLN[2] MARTIN (Adelbert), born in Fall River 23 Feb. 1922/3. He married in LC 21 Feb. 1948 GERALDINE ANN BETTENCOURT, daughter of Joseph and Geraldine (Costa) Bettencourt, born in LC 20 June 1927. Residence: LC.

    Children:
i.   David Lincoln Jr., b. in Fall River 6 Sept. 1949; d. there 10 Sept. 1949 ae 4 days.

THE MIAS FAMILY

1. NICHOLAS[1] MIAS, married in LC 3 March 1708 ELIZABETH
NICHOLAS, possibly the daughter of Richard and Phebe Nicholas, born
14 June 1688 (?). Residence: LC.

His will, recorded in Taunton book 5, page 58, made 4 Sept. 1727
and proved 16 Jan. 1727/28: ". . . To wife Elizabeth use of all real
estate while she remains my widow. To son Gitto all housing and lands
after the decease of my wife; if he dies then to my two daughters Phebe
and Alice. To son Oliver 25 pounds and all silver buttons, two silver
spoons and all silver money. To daughter Phebe one feather bed. . . To
daughter Alice one feather bed. . . Rest and residue to two sons Gitto
and Oliver at decease of wife. . . " Inventory of his estate, taken 2
Jan. 1727: total 119 pounds-16 shillings-no pence.

      Children, recorded in LC:
- i.   Phebe, b. 30 Aug. 1708; m. (intention 7 March 1736) Jeremiah
Rogers.
- ii.   Alice, b. 13 Feb. 1710; m. in LC 30 April 1735 Jonathan
Grinnell.
- 2. iii. Gitto, b. 10 June 1713.
- 3. iv. Oliver, b. 21 March 1715.

2. GITTO[2] MIAS (Nicholas[1]), born in LC 10 June 1713, married
about 1738 SARAH (--).

      Children, recorded in LC:
- i.   Elizabeth, b. 8 Dec. 1739.

3. OLIVER[2] MIAS (Nicholas[1]), born 21 March 1715, baptized at
St. Michael's in Bristol. He married 13 May 1736 at St. Michael's
in Bristol MARY MUNROE, daughter of Joseph and Mary (Bowerman)
Munroe.

He had land located on the highway north of Elisha Clapp which
he gave to his son Barnabus in 1777. There is also record of a Capt.
Oliver Mias living in Exeter, R.I., in May 1756.

      Children:
- i.   Oliver Jr., m. Elizabeth Niles, probably at East Greenwich,
R.I.
- ii.   Gideon, m. Marcy (--). Residence: Pownal, Vt.
- iii. Barnabus.

It is believed that there were also other children in this family.

THE MOORE FAMILY

ARTHUR E. MOORE, born in Bridgewater, Mass., 20 Dec. 1853, died in LC 23 Dec. 1914. He married LILLIAN AMELIA MANCHESTER (BRIGGS?), daughter of Charles F. and Ann Eliza (Manchester) Briggs, born in LC 9 Oct. 1860, died in East Providence 14 Dec. 1922 ae 62. Residence: LC.

Children, recorded in LC:
i.   William Remington, b. 29 Oct. 1894.
ii. Henrietta, b. 26 March 1896; m. John F. Almy.

ဆ⊷ၣ

THE MORSE FAMILY

ANTHONY MORSE, born in 1800, married HANNAH C. (--), born in 1812. This family was listed in the census of 1850, but not in the census of 1865. Residence: LC.

Children:
i.   John V., b. in 1833.
ii. Selecta, b. in 1839.
iii. Fernando, b. in 1841.
iv. Ardella, b. in 1847.
v.   Alvarado, b. in 1850.

ဆ⊷ၣ

THE MOSHER FAMILY

1. HUGH[2] MOSHER (Hugh[1]), born in 1633, died in 1713. Residence: Newport and Dartmouth.

He married first REBECCA HARNDELL, daughter of John Harndell. He married second SARAH HARDING, born in 1652, died in 1716.

He appears in several legal records of his time: In 1660 he and others bought certain land in Westerly, R.I. In testimony of 1663 he called himself 30 years old, and was listed as a freeman in 1664. In 1684 he bought from Thomas Lawton part of his homestead farm in Dartmouth.

He was a blacksmith, and also was ordained as pastor of the First Baptist Church. This church soon grew to include families living in Dartmouth, Tiverton and LC. In his will he lists himself as coming from Newport, but before his death he had moved to Dartmouth.

His will, made 12 Oct. 1709 and proved 7 Dec. 1713: ". . . In the
8th year of reign of our Lady Ann, Queen of Great Britian. . . To son
James all land in Newport with house . . . and land in Dartmouth and
Westerly; to grandson Hugh, son of Nicholas Mosher, 100 acres of
land and to other grandsons of the surname of Mosher 50 acres each;
to wife Sarah all movables I had with her at marriage; to son James
rest of land; to each grandchild not of my name 10 shillings; to sons
John, Nicholas, Joseph and Danile 12 pence each; to each daughter
10 shillings or 20 shillings as estate holds out. . . "

Children:
i.   Nicholas, b. in 1666; d. 14 Aug. 1747; m. 12 Aug. 1687
     Elizabeth (--).
ii.   John, b. in 1668; d. 1 Aug. 1739; m. 5 March 1692 Experience
     Kirby, daughter of Richard and Patience (Gifford) Kirby.
iii.   Joseph, b. in 1670; d. in 1754; m. Lydia Tabor, b. in 1673,
     d. in 1743.
iv.   Mary, d. in 1748; m. 19 May 1691 Joseph Rathbone.
v.   James, b. in 1675; m. (1) 9 July 1704 Catharine Tosh; m.
     (2) 22 May 1714 Mary Devol.
2.   vi.   Daniel, d. in 1751.
vii.   Rebecca, m. John Kirby.

2. DANIEL³ MOSHER (Hugh², Hugh¹), died in Dartmouth in 1751.
Residence: Dartmouth. He married about 1704 ELIZABETH EDWARDS.
His will, made 22 July 1751 and proved 19 Sept. 1751: ". . . To
wife best bed, half of household goods, cow and riding beast for rest
of life or during her widowhood, and she to be provided for by my son
George with 6 bushels of indian corn, 100 pounds of good meat, five
cords of firewood yearly. . . to son George 10 acres of marsh land
and half of the land where he lives and a grindstone; to son Roger one
half of certain land. . . to son Benjamin 10 acres of land, he paying
son Hugh 40 shillings; to sons Constant and Ephraim rest of lands
given to Roger and Benjamin; to son Ephraim land where he formerly
lived; to son Daniel 40 shillings paid by son George; to daughter Mary
Trafford an iron pott; to three daughters rest of personal at death of
wife. . . "

Children, recorded in Dartmouth:
i.   Benjamin, b. 19 April 1706; m. in Dartmouth 12 Sept. 1728
     Abigail Maxfield.
ii.   Daniel, b. 1 July 1709.
iii.   Michael, b. 27 Sept. 1711.
3.   iv.   Constant, b. 11 Sept. 1713.
v.   Rachel, b. 14 June 1715; m. Corey Herendeen.
vi.   George, b. 9 May 1717; m. Hannah Wing.
vii.   Ephraim, b. 8 Dec. 1718.
viii.   Roger, b. 30 March 1720; m. in Dartmouth 26 May 1746
     Phebe Sherman, daughter of Nathan Sherman.
ix.   Hugh, b. 17 March 1721/2; m. 7 Dec. 1740 Elizabeth
     Butts.
x.   Patience, b. 29 June 1724; m. (--) Brownell.

xi.   Mercy, b. 12 Oct. 1726; m. in Dartmouth 17 Sept. 1749
       Philip Trafford, son of Thomas Trafford.

3. CONSTANT[4] MOSHER (Daniel[3], Hugh[2], Hugh[1]), born in Dartmouth
11 Sept. 1713, died there in 1791. Residence: Dartmouth. He married
there 6 Oct. 1737 SARAH SHERMAN, daughter of Timothy and Dorothy
or Deborah (Russell) Sherman.

A division of the estate was taken in Dartmouth 3 Jan. 1792 in
which his eleven children were listed as below, and his estate was
itemized with 5 acres and three fourths with a dwelling house. The
estate was appraised at 24 pounds. On 23 Feb. 1792, Michael, Seth
and Ebenezer, for three pounds and 18 shillings, sold to John Mosher
seven acres and buildings "the homestead farm of our father Constant
Mosher, late of Dartmouth, bounded east on the highway, west on the
river, south on James Mosher, and a swamp near Shingle Island, said
land being given to our mother Sarah by her father Timothy Sherman. . . "

Children, recorded in Dartmouth:
i.   Zilpha, b. 28 July 1738; m. in Dartmouth (intention 24 Dec.
       1757) Stephen Russell.
ii.   Ebenezer, b. 25 Oct. 1739; m. 10 Feb. 1763 in Dartmouth
       Jane Craw, daughter of Richard and Joanna Craw.
iii.   Lusannah (Susannah?) (Lurana?), b. 17 Nov. 1741; m. 26
       Dec. 1765 in Dartmouth Thomas Wilkie.
iv.   John, b. 31 May 1744; m. 8 Jan. 1767 in Dartmouth Rebecca
       Chase.
v.   Constant, b. 17 Nov. 1746; m. in Dartmouth 16 Dec. 1769
       Mary Reed.
4. vi. Michael, b. 6 Jan. 1749.
vii.   Lemuel, b. 13 March 1752; m. 24 March 1772 in Dartmouth
       Elizabeth Sherman, daughter of Joshua Sherman.
viii. Seth, b. 26 March 1754; m. in Dartmouth 22 April 1774
       Susannah Sherman.
ix.   Timothy, b. 28 May 1757; m. (21 Oct. 1784) in Dartmouth
       Chloe Hollis.
x.   Deborah, b. 16 Aug. 1759; m. in Dartmouth 6 Sept. 1776
       Benjamin Sims.
xi.   Sarah, b. in 1761; m. in Dartmouth 25 Sept. 1778 Gideon
       Rogers.

4. MICHAEL[5] MOSHER (Constant[4], Daniel[3], Hugh[2], Hugh[1]), born
in Dartmouth 6 Jan. 1749, died before 26 Oct. 1807 when his inventory
was taken. Residence: Dartmouth. He married there 28 July 1774
JUDITH KIRBY.

The inventory of his estate listed an old house and five acres and
57 rods of land. . . total, 69 dollars and 37 cents.

In a deed recorded in Dartmouth, Constant Mosher Jr., and his
wife Mary sold to Michael Mosher, hooper, on 18 May 1774, 30 acres
on eastward of swamp in Dartmouth, bounded each by Christopher Mason's
land. Michael Mosher and his wife Judith sold the above to Jonathan
Clarke 6 Oct. 1774.

Children, recorded in Dartmouth:

    i.   Joseph, b. 25 June 1775.
    ii.   Anna, b. 23 May 1777.
    iii.   Thomas, b. 15 April 1779.
5. iv.   Michael, b. 27 Sept. 1781.
    v.   William, b. 28 May 1783.
    vi.   Robert, b. 14 Feb. 1786.
    vii.   Paul, b. 18 Feb. 1791.
    viii. Pardon, b. 18 Feb. 1791; d. in LC 27 Feb. 1841.

     5. MICHAEL[6] MOSHER (Michael[5], Constant[4], Daniel[3], Hugh[2], Hugh[1]), born in Dartmouth 27 Sept. 1781, died in LC 21 May 1865. Residence: Dartmouth and LC.
     He married in Dartmouth 31 Oct. 1805 LEVINA SEEKELL, daughter of Peter and Jane (Claghorne) Seekell, born about 1788, died 21 Nov. 1847. She is buried in the Old Commons cemetery. They lived on Goose Wing Beach, at that time called Head's Beach.
     His will, recorded in LC Wills, book 11, page 302, made 18 Oct. 1852 and proved 6 Dec. 1854: ". . . To daughter Mary Ann Morse. . . to daughter Emily Manchester one dollar. To son William one dollar. To daughter Phebe one dollar. To granddaughter Mary Augusta, daughter of my son William, 5 dollars. To two grandsons Thomas and Edward, sons of William, one dollars each. To Almira, daughter of Caleb, one bed and bedstead. To son Caleb, use of all real and all personal except what I have otherwise given away and then to his heirs all estate after him. . . "

      Children:
    i.   Mary Ann, b. in Dartmouth 25 Dec. 1812; m. there 11 July 1830 Henry Morse.
    ii.   William, b. in Dartmouth 13 Sept. 1814; m. in Newport 9 Nov. 1841 Rebecca Manchester of Westport.
    iii.   Emily, b. 1 June 1818; m. in Dartmouth 26 Aug. 1833 Capt. Richmond Manchester.
6. iv.   Caleb Sekell, b. 6 Aug. 1822.
    v.   Phebe, b. in LC 14 Dec. 1828; d. in 1910; m. 5 April 1846 in Dartmouth Beriah Manchester, b. in 1815, d. in 1907.

     6. CALEB SEEKELL[7] MOSHER (Michael[6], Michael[5], Constant[4], Daniel[3], Hugh[2], Hugh[1]), born in Dartmouth 6 Aug. 1822, died in LC 21 Feb. 1905. Residence: LC.
     He was married in LC 27 March 1847 by the Rev. Richard Davis to MARY MARIA CROSBY, daughter of John and Elizabeth (Pearce) Crosby, born in LC 20 Aug. 1832, died there 22 Feb. 1905.
     They lived at the end of the Long Highway on the west side of the road, where the late Lemuel Sisson lived.

      Children, recorded in LC (names not always given, but obtained from census of 1865):
    i.   Almira, b. 14 June 1848; d. 11 May 1936; m. Samuel Palmer, son of Wilbor and Hannah (Snell) Palmer.
    ii.   Ida, b. in LC 31 March 1852; d. 2 Feb. 1931; m. George C. Simmons.
    iii.   Ella, b. in LC 7 Dec. 1853; m. Jason Ballou.

iv.   Eudora, b. in LC 5 Sept. 1855; d. young.
v.   Child, b. 6 Nov. 1856; d. young.
vi.   Miranda Amelia, b. in LC 6 Nov. 1856; d. 30 March 1935;
         unmarried.
vii.   Nora, b. 8 Jan. 1859; d. in LC 11 Jan. 1940; m. George V.
         Snell, son of George and Sarah (Pierce) Snell.
viii. Elizabeth Rose, b. in LC 20 May 1860; d. 8 Nov. 1929; m.
         Samuel Slocum Field, son of Henry and Ann (Slocum) Field.
ix.   Son, b. in December 1862; d. 4 Feb. 1863.
x.   Gibbs Peleg, b. 4 Jan. 1864; d. 29 July 1931; unmarried.
xi.   Cornelia M., b. 13 Dec. 1868; m. 2 April 1891 Charles F.
         Manchester, son of Charles and Comfort (Lake) Manchester.

. . . .

Miscellaneous records of the Mosher family in LC:

A daughter, born 23 Nov. 1863 to Sherman W. and Clarinda M.
Mosher.
William R., born in LC 5 Aug. 1873 to William and Emma Mosher
of Westport.
Charles Frederic, born 10 Sept. 1874 to William H. and Emma
Mosher.
Marcellina, born 2 Dec. 1875 to Andrew and Emma Mosher.

Patience, wife of Daniel A. Mosher, died 12 Sept. 1878 ae 56-1-6,
buried in the Old Commons cemetery.
Levina, wife of Michael Mosher, died 21 Nov. 1847 ae 59, buried
in the Old Commons cemetery.

OSCAR E. MOSHER, born in Fairhaven, Mass., in 1880, died in
1937, buried in Pleasant View cemetery. Residence: LC. He married
IDA M. WILKIE, born in 1882.

        Children, recorded in LC:
i.   Lloyd Merritt, b. 11 Sept. 1905.
ii.   Everett Borden, b. 11 Dec. 1907.
iii.   Charles Rodman, b. 11 March 1910; m. (?) Ellen Hanson.
         They had a son Charles Rodman Mosher Jr., b. in Fall
         River 5 June 1937.
iv.   Merle, b. 29 May 1912.
v.   Janice, b. 2 July 1922.
vi.   Alice Mae, b. 10 July 1925.

THE NEGUS FAMILY

GEORGE B. NEGUS, perhaps son of William and Hannah A.
(Slocum) Negus of New Bedford, born in New Bedford (?) 21 Nov.
1846. Residence: LC, where they were listed in the census of 1880.
He married SARAH E. (--), born in 1848.

Children, recorded in LC:
i.   Child, d. in LC 2 Oct. 18--.
ii.   George Franklin, b. in LC 20 April 1871.
iii. Eliza M., b. in LC 15 Sept. 1873.
iv. Cora J., b. in LC 24 Oct. 1877.
v.   Son, b. in LC 16 Oct. 1878; d. 16 Oct. 1878.

THE NEWTON FAMILY

JAMES EDWARD NEWTON, son of James and Elizabeth S. (Anthony)
Newton of Fall River, born in Fall River 3 Dec. 1866, died in Providence
13 May 1947. Residence: Fall River and LC.
He married 10 Nov. 1896 HETTY BAKER WHITE, daughter of
Andrew M. and Allie M. (Brown) White, born in Fall River 9 July 1872.

Children:
i.   Dorothy, b. 10 Dec. 1897; d. 1 Feb. 1927; m. 5 June 1923
     Dr. Clifton Leach.
ii. Elizabeth Anthony, b. 28 June 1903; m. 10 Oct. 1936 Nelson
     Cabot, son of F. Elliot and Ethel (Cunningham) Cabot,
     b. 18 Jan. 1901.

THE ORMSBY FAMILY

1. DANIEL[1] ORMSBY of Dartmouth, married in LC 19 Sept.
1751 by Daniel Searles, justice, to MARTHA BROWNELL, .daughter
of John and Mary (Carr) Brownell, born in LC 17 Feb. 1723. Residence:
LC.

Children, recorded in LC:
i.   John, b. 3 July 1752.
ii.   Olive, b. 21 Dec. 1754.
2. iii. Thomas, b. 19 Aug. 1755.

2. THOMAS[2] ORMSBY (Daniel[1]), born in LC 19 Aug. 1755. He
married in LC 4 Feb. 1779 SUSANNAH WILBOR, daughter of William
and Mary (Babcock) Wilbor, born in LC 22 Oct. 1749.

Children, born in LC:
i.   Daniel, b. 28 March 1781.
ii. Martha, b. 15 Oct. 1782.

THE PABODIE FAMILY

From the Pabodie Genealogy by Selim Hobart Peabody, 1909.

1. JOHN[1] PABODIE, born in Nosely Parish, Leicestershire, England. He married ISABELL HARPER.

He came to Plymouth in New England on the ship Planter in 1635, and became a freeman 7 March 1636/7. He received a grant of 10 acres of land on the Duxborrow side lying betwixt the land of William Tubs and Experience Mitchell. It was bounded on the southwest by the sea and on the east by the Blew Fish River. He also had a 30 acre tract of land at North River.

His will, proved 27 April 1667: "In and upon the 16th of July in the yeare of our Lorde 1649, I John Paybodie of Duxbrook in the Colonie of New Plymouth, planter being in perfect health and soud in memory, God be blessed for it, doe ordaine and make this my last will and testament in maner and forme as followeth: My soule to God that gave it hopeing to be saved by merit of Christ my blessed Saviour, Redeemer, and as for my worldly goods as followeth: Item. I give and bequeath unto Thomas my eldest son one shilling. I give and bequeath unto Francis Paybodie my second son one shilling. I give and bequeath unto William Pabodie my youngest son one shilling. I give and bequeath unto Annis Rouse my daughter one shilling. Item. I give and bequeath unto John Rouse and son of John Rouse my lands at Carswell in Marshfield after my Wife's decease. Item. I give unto John Pabodie son of William my lott of land att the new Plantation. Item. I give all the rest of my goods that are mine living and dead unto my wife Isabel Paybodie whom I make my sole executrix and all the legacies are to be paid by William Paybody my youngest son, when they shall be demanded. . . "

    Children:
    i.   Thomas.
    ii.   Francis.
2. iii.   William, b. about 1619.
    iv.   Annis, d. about 1688; m. about 1639 John Rouse of Marshfield, Mass., d. 16 Dec. 1684.

2. WILLIAM[2] PABODIE (John[1]), born about 1619, died in LC 13 Dec. 1707. Residence: LC.

He married in Duxbury, Mass., 26 Dec. 1644 ELIZABETH ALDEN, daughter of John and Priscilla (Mullins) Alden of Plymouth, born in 1623, died in LC 31 May 1717. She is said to have been the first white woman born in New England, although this legend has been denied. Both are buried in the Old Commons cemetery. William Pabodie grew up in Duxbury with his father and then took for himself various occupations. He has been identified as yeoman (1648), boatman (1672), and planter. He was also a land surveyor and surveyed the land in LC with Constant Southworth.

He acquired by purchase with others a share of land in LC and moved there about 1684. He purchased most of the three quarters of a mile square in LC, which was formerly laid out to 32 different purchasers. The bounds of his land were as follows: bounded east on the great main road, west on the Sakonet River, south on Col. Benjamin Church, which land now belongs to the Benjamin F. Wilbour heirs, and north on the John Wood farm which was made up of the northernmost lots from the road to the river and one lot wide, bounded on the north by Taylor's land. William Pabodie owned most of the three quarters of a mile square, formerly the reservation of Awashonks, queen of the Sogonates, excepting the lots that border on Taylor's land and the lots on the other side of the road, one lot wide. There has been much controversy as to where he lived and for a long time it was claimed that he lived in the so called Betty Alden house, the property of the late Lizzie Gray. This was however, claimed by people who did not know that besides owning this land he also owned the Isaac C. Wilbour place and the present David Brayton place. (It is the belief of the editor that he lived in what in 1890 was the Isaac C. Wilbour house.) He also bought land in Mettapoisett and Sepecan which he later sold.

Also a school teacher, he taught in LC, as well as serving as secretary and record keeper of the first proprietors of LC.

On 1 Aug. 1654 he was elected to the General Court which met at Plymouth, and he served there until 1663, and again from 1668 to 1682.

His will, recorded in Taunton Probate, book 2, page 193, made 13 May 1707 and proved 27 Feb. 1708: "Executors, wife Elizabeth and son William. . . To wife, east end of house in LC and part of the land given formerly to son William, all to be hers while widow, and also to her all household goods, cattle, bills due and money, but if she choose to claim her thirds of my land and house at Duxbury and make use of them, then my son William to have the whole of housing and lands in

WILLIAM PABODIE

1707

(Old Burial Ground)

LC and to pay Samuel Barlett 50 shillings per year during the time his mother makes use of her thirds at Duxbury. To son William after death of his mother, the part of house and land bequeathed her for life. To son William other land and all my books, tools. . . To three grandsons, namely Stephen Southworth, son of daughter Rebecca, deceased, and John and William Pabodie, sons of son William, land and Westquadnaug, part purchased by son-in-law William Fobes of Shubael Painter and assigned by William Fobes to my son-in-law Ichabod Wiswall. . . To daughters Mary, Mercy, Martha, Priscilla, Ruth, Sarah, Hannah and Lydia, each one shilling. To daughter Lydia Grinnell a set of green curtains, she having already received her part. . . " Inventory: 407 pounds-14 shillings. 70 acres of land at 315 pounds, dwelling house and half of barn 30 pounds. Two feather beds . . .

On 17 June 1717, the Boston Newsletter printed the following account of the death of Elizabeth Alden Paybodie: "Little Compton May 31. This morning died here Mrs. Elizabeth Paybody, late wife of Mr. William Paybody in the 93d year of her age. She was the daughter of John Alden Esq. and Priscilla his wife, daughter of Mr. William Mullins. This John Alden and Priscilla Mullins were married at Plymouth in New England, where their daughter Elizabeth was born. She was exemplary, virtuous and pious, and her memory is blessed. Her grand-daughter Bradford is a grandmother. "

Children, born in Duxbury:

i. John, b. 4 Oct. 1645; d. 17 Nov. 1669. A coroner's jury, in a finding on his death, noted that "hee, riding on the road, his horse carried him underneath the bow of a tree, violently forcing his head into his body, there of broke his skull which wee doe judge was the cause of his death." The previous year he had sold his grandfather's legacy.

ii. Elizabeth, b. 24 April 1647; d. in 1707; m. in Duxbury 16 Nov. 1666 John Rogers Jr., son of John and Ann (Churchman) Rogers.

iii. Mary, b. 7 Aug. 1648; m. 16 Nov. 1669 Edward Southworth, son of Constant and Elizabeth (Collier) Southworth.

iv. Martha, b. 2 Jan. 1649; d. in LC 25 Jan. 1712; m. (1) in Duxbury 4 April 1677 Samuel Seabury; m. (2) Lt. William Fobes, son of John and Constant (Mitchell) Fobes.

v. Mercy, b. 25 Feb. 1650; m. 16 Nov. 1669 in Duxbury John Simmons, son of Moses and Sarah Simmons.

vi. Priscilla, b. 15 Jan. 1653; d. in Kingston, Mass., 3 June 1724; m. 24 Dec. 1677 in Duxbury the Rev. Ichabod Wiswall, son of Thomas and Elizabeth Wiswall.

vii. Sarah, b. 7 Aug. 1656; d. in LC 27 Aug. 1740; m. 10 Nov. 1681 John Coe, d. 10 Dec. 1728.

viii. Ruth, b. 17 June 1658; d. in Duxbury; m. there in December 1673 Benjamin Bartlett, son of Benjamin and Sarah (Brewster) Bartlett.

ix. Rebecca, b. 15 Oct. 1660; d. in LC 3 Dec. 1702; m. about 1680 William Southworth, son of Constant and Elizabeth (Collier) Southworth.

x. Hannah, b. 15 Oct. 1662; m. 3 Oct. 1683 Samuel Bartlett.

3.   xi.   William, b. 24 Nov. 1664.
     xii. Lydia, b. 3 April 1667; m. about 1683 Daniel Grinnell, son of
           Daniel and Mary (Wordell) Grinnell.

Here lyeth the body
of ELIZABETH the wife
of WILLIAM PABODIE
who dyed May ye 31st
1717: and in the 94th
year of her age.

The original stone is incorporated
in the newer monument. She was the
daughter of John Alden and Priscilla
Mullins, the first white woman born
in New England.

Old Burial Ground

3. WILLIAM³ PABODIE (William², John¹), born in Duxbury 24 Nov.
1664, died in LC 17 Sept. 1744. Residence: LC.
     He married first JUDITH (--), born in 1669, died in July 1714. He
married second ELIZABETH (--), born in 1672, died in LC 14 Dec.
1717. He married third MRS. MARY (MORGAN) STARR.
     He moved with his father to LC and spent the remainder of his
life there. He was admitted a freeman in the Massachusetts Bay Colony
1 May 1722.
     His will, recorded in Taunton Probate, book 10, page 447, made
7 Aug. 1743 and proved 12 Nov. 1744: ". . . To wife Mary one feather
bed, furniture, all household goods that were hers before I married her
and she to have meat and drink. . . from my son William. To son John
four score acres of land from the south side of my farm adjoining the
farm of Thomas Church Esq. From the northwest corner of said Church's
farm to extend north by the highway until a west line from the highway to
the river shall make four score acres with buildings. To son William and
son Joseph rest of my farm; William's shall be two hundred pounds better
than Joseph's. To son Benjamin one fourth part of a four and twenty
acre lot the eighth in number together with additions now in possession
of Samuel Tompkins. To daughter Elizabeth, wife of Edward Gray, 25
pounds. To daughter Rebecca, wife of Joseph Irish, 8 pounds. To
daughter Priscilla, wife of William Wilcox, 20 pounds. To daughter
Judith, wife of Benjamin Church, 20 pounds. To daughter Mary, wife

of Nathaniel Fish, 25 pounds. Rest and residue to the eldest sons John
and William. . . "

Children by first wife, recorded in LC:
- i.   Elizabeth, b. 10 April 1698; m. in LC 9 May 1716 Edward³ Gray,
  (Thomas², Edward¹).
- 4. ii.   John, b. 7 Feb. 1700.
- 5. iii.   William, b. 21 Feb. 1702.
- iv.   Rebecca, b. 29 Feb. 1704; d. in Fairfield, Conn., 27 Oct. 1783;
  m. in LC 6 Dec. 1732 the Rev. Joseph Fish, son of Thomas
  and Margaret (Woodworth) Fish.
- v.   Priscilla, b. 4 March 1706; m. (intention 13 Jan. 1727/8)
  Gideon Southworth, son of William and Martha (Kirkland)
  Southworth.
- vi.   Judith, b. in LC 23 Jan. 1708; m. there 21 May 1732 Benjamin⁴
  Church (John³, Joseph², Richard¹).
- 6. vii.   Joseph, b. 26 July 1710.
- viii.   Mary, b. 4 April 1712; m. in LC 28 Nov. 1736 Nathaniel Fish.

Children by second wife:
- ix.   Benjamin, b. 25 Nov. 1717; d. in 1792; m. 7 Aug. 1745 Abigail
  Lyon. Residence: Newport.

4. DEACON JOHN⁴ PABODIE (William³, William², John¹), born in
LC 7 Feb. 1700, died there 12 Jan. 1767. Residence: LC.

He married in LC 7 Feb. 1723 REBECCA GRAY, daughter of Thomas
and Anna (Little) Gray, born in LC 1 Aug. 1704.

They sold their homestead farm called the Betty Alden place to
Pardon Gray of Tiverton 2 April 1762. This farm had been left to
him by his father.

Children, recorded in LC:
- i.   Elizabeth, b. 5 Dec. 1723; d. in LC 5 Sept. 1802; m. there
  in June 1743 John Bailey.
- ii.   Anstress, b. 5 July 1726; d. 24 Oct. 1726.
- iii.   Anna, b. 20 Aug. 1728; d. 15 Nov. 1728.
- iv.   Judith, b. 20 July 1730; m. 19 April 1750 Gamaliel Richmond.
- v.   Mary, b. 21 March 1732; d. 30 Sept. 1732.
- vi.   John, b. 14 March 1733; m. Mary Stoddard. Residence:
  Providence.
- vii.   Abigail, b. 16 Jan. 1735; m. in LC 13 Dec. 1753 Isaac Southworth.
- viii.   Ephraim, b. 9 Dec. 1736. Residence: Providence.
- ix.   Sarah, b. 18 Aug. 1738.
- x.   Mercy, b. 30 June 1740; d. ae 81; unmarried.
- xi.   Comfort, b. 9 Dec. 1744; m. 14 April 1793 Jedediah Grinnell.
- xii.   Ruth, b. 10 June 1746; m. 16 March 1780 Peleg Barker of
  Portsmouth.

5. WILLIAM⁴ PABODIE (William³, William², John¹), born in LC
21 Feb. 1702, died in North Stonington, Conn., 3 July 1778. Residence:
Stonington and LC.

He married in LC 30 July 1724 JERUSHA STAR, daughter of

Thomas and Mary (Morgan) Star, born in New London, Conn., 8 Feb. 1702/3.

Children, all recorded in LC except the last two:
i.   Rachel, b. 1 June 1725; m. in LC 16 Aug. 1746 Joshua
       Stoddard.
ii.   Thomas, b. 3 Nov. 1727; d. in Stonington 24 March 1815;
       m. 16 Aug. 1761 Ruth Babcock, d. in Stonington 6 Oct.
       1813.
iii.   Hannah, b. 3 Dec. 1729.
iv.   William, b. 16 April 1733.
v.   Lydia, b. 7 June 1735.
vi.   Samuel, b. 31 Aug. 1738. Residence: Stonington.
vii.   Lemuel, b. 12 July 1741.
viii. James, b. in Stonington 14 Dec. 1745.
ix.   Mary, b. in Stonington 14 Dec. 1745; d. 12 March 1826.

6. JOSEPH[4] PABODIE (William[3], William[2], John[1]), born in LC
26 July 1710, died in Cannan, N.Y., 7 April 1790.
He married in LC 23 Dec. 1733 ELIZABETH BRIGGS, daughter
of William and Deborah (Church) Briggs, born in LC 10 Oct. 1714.

Children, recorded in LC:
i.   Nathaniel, b. 17 June 1734; d. in Lebanon, N.Y., 24 June
       1800; m. about 1760 Elizabeth Smith.
ii.   Parker, b. 6 Nov. 1735; d. 27 Aug. 1818; m. in 1765 Mary
       Spofford.
iii.   Mary, b. 8 June 1737.
iv.   Rebecca, b. 9 May 1739; d. 7 July 1765.
v.   Isaac, b. 9 Dec. 1740; d. in Westmoreland, N.Y., in 1826.
vi.   Aaron, b. 9 May 1742; m. (--) Fitch. Residence: Lebanon,
       N.Y.
vii.   Benjamin, b. 19 April 1744.
viii. Elizabeth, b. 16 Nov. 1745.

. . . .

EASTON PABODIE of Middletown and SARISSA TOMPKINS of LC,
daughter of Benjamin and Deborah Tompkins, were married 13 Aug.
1849 by the Rev. Samuel Beane. They are buried in the Old Commons
cemetery. According to their gravestones Easton Pabodie died 8 July
1875 ae 78-9-0, and Sarissa Pabodie died 18 April 1883 in her 79th
year.

THE PAINE FAMILY

For further information on the Paine family, see the New England
Genealogical Register, No. 69, page 252.

1. WILLIAM[1] PAINE, son of William and Agnes (Neves) Paine of
Lavenham, Suffolk County, England, baptized 20 Feb. 1596/7, died in
Boston 10 Oct. 1660.

He and his wife, ANNA (--), came to New England from London in
the ship Increase.

In his will, made in Boston 2 Oct. 1660, he left to his wife his
dwelling house in Boston, mill in Watertown and household effects, 20
pounds to the college at Cambridge, and various bequests to children
and grandchildren.

Children, baptized at Lavenham:

	i.	William, bapt. 9 Nov. 1624.
	ii.	Anna, bapt. 5 Dec. 1626; buried 9 March 1626/7.
	iii.	Anna, bapt. 11 Feb. 1629/30; m. 2 April 1651 Samuel Appleton Jr.
2.	iv.	John, bapt. 2 May 1632; m. 2 March 1659 Sarah Parker.
	v.	Daniel, bapt. 6 Feb. 1634; d. without children.
	vi.	Susan, b. in 1624.

2. JOHN[2] PAINE (William[1]), baptized in Lavenham County, Suffolk,
England, 2 May 1632, died at sea. Residence: Boston. He married
2 March 1659 SARAH PARKER, daughter of Richard Parker.

Children:

3.	i.	William, b. 15 March 1664.
	ii.	Sarah.
	iii.	Hanah.
	iv.	Anna.

3. WILLIAM[3] PAINE (John[2], William[1]), born 15 March 1664, died
in Malden, Mass., 14 April 1741. Residence: Malden, Mass.

He married in Malden 9 March 1691/2 RUTH GROVER, born in
1667, died 11 April 1722.

Children:

4.	i.	William, b. probably 16 Nov. 1692.
	ii.	John, b. in 1701; d. 14 April 1741.

4. WILLIAM[4] PAINE (William[3], John[2], William[1]), born probably
16 Nov. 1692 in Malden, Mass., died in Northern, Mass., 29 Jan. 1784.

He married first in Malden 18 April 1717 TABITHA WAITE, born
in 1692, died 7 April 1721. He married second in Malden 6 Nov. 1722
ELIZABETH SWEETSTER, widow.

Children by first wife:

5.	i.	William, b. 26 June 1720.
	ii.	Edward, b. in 1724.
	iii.	Thomas, b. 27 March 1726; d. young.
	iv.	Elizabeth, b. in 1723; m. Deacon Benjamin Williams.

    v.   Ruth, m. Eleazer Fisher.
   vi.   Susannah, m. (--) Puffer.

   5. WILLIAM⁵ PAINE (William⁴, William³, John², William¹),
born 26 June 1720, died 17 July 1811. He married in 1743 MARY
BULL of Foxboro, Mass., died in February 1810.

        Children:
    i.   William, b. 13 Nov. 1743.
   ii.   Mary, b. 10 June 1745; d. young.
  iii.   John, b. 20 Aug. 1746; m. Rhoda Wellman.
   iv.   Lemuel, b. 4 April 1748; m. Rachel Carpenter.
    v.   Jacob, b. 7 Feb. 1750; m. 5 June 1754 Hannah Morse.
   vi.   James, b. 30 Sept. 1751; m. Anna Richards.
  vii.   Mary, b. 8 May 1753; m. Amos Boyden.
6. viii.   Abiel, b. 20 Nov. 1754.
   ix.   Isaac, d. young.
    x.   Asa, b. in 1758; m. Patty Bacon.
   xi.   Jerusha, b. 10 March 1760; d. ae 91.
  xii.   Hannah, b. 9 Aug. 1763; d. ae 90.

   6. ABIEL⁶ PAINE (William⁵, William⁴, William³, John², William¹),
born 30 Nov. 1754, died 3 Jan. 1840. He married CYNTHIA ROBINSON
of Foxboro, Mass., died 30 Oct. 1826.

        Children, born in Foxboro:
    i.   Cynthia, b. 25 Oct. 1779; m. 22 Oct. 1805 in Foxboro Joseph
          Tiffany Jr.
   ii.   Catharine, m. George Briggs.
  iii.   Lucinda, b. 5 Sept. 1782; d. 25 April 1851.
7. iv.   Emerson, b. 5 Dec. 1786.
    v.   Appolos, m. in 1824 (--) Harding.
   vi.   Daniel, m. in 1824 Sarah Brown.
  vii.   Zinus G., m. Mary Tompkins of LC.

   7. THE REV. EMERSON⁷ PAINE (Abiel⁶, William⁵, William⁴,
William³, John², William¹), born in Foxboro, Mass., 5 Dec. 1786,
died 25 April 1851. Residence: Foxboro, Middleboro, LC and
Halifax, Mass.
   He married 30 April 1816 LYDIA R. PENDLETON, born 20 Sept.
1792, died 24 March 1876.
   He graduated from Brown University in 1815. During high party
times which existed during 1812, he delivered an address of political
character which gave very great offense to his opponents and largely
affected all of his subsequent life. For awhile he served as a preacher
in Abington and later, for six years, in Middleboro. Then he preached
in LC for 14 years and finally in Halifax, Mass. for 10 years. As his
health began to fail in later years, he was able to preach only occa-
sionally.

        Children:
    i.   Charles E., b. 20 Oct. 1817 in Middleboro; m. 23 Nov. 1862
          Eliza P. Glover.

ii.   Charles H., b. 5 Jan. 1820; m. Cordelia Bryant of Halifax,
      Mass.
iii. Horatio, b. 11 June 1822; m. Sarah Atherton.
iv.   Mary, b. 27 Nov. 1823; m. Oliver Holmes.
v.   Sarah, b. 24 Sept. 1830; d. ae 12.

ॐ

THE PALMER FAMILY

1. WILLIAM[1] PALMER (first of this family in America), born about
1585, died in 1638. Residence: Plymouth and Duxbury.

He married first FRANCES (--), who came to America in the ship
Ann in 1623. He married second MARY TRINE, who came in the ship
Fortune in 1623.

There are two versions of his will, made 4 Dec. 1637 and proved
in Plymouth 5 March 1638. First: ". . . To my young wife one third
of my estate. . . To possible heir one third of estate and if said heir
does not appear, deal leniently with my granddaughter Rebecca and
also Moses Rawley, whom I love, and legacies to Stephen Tracy. . .
To the meeting house at Plymough and tô John Willis 40 shillings also.
To Henry and Bridgett 40 shillings, they being my children, if they
are living and demand it. . . " Moses Rawley was his apprentice.

Another version of the same will: ". . . Whereas I married a
young woman who is dear unto me, I desire that she have not less than
a third of my estate. To Rebecca my grandchild and Moses Rawley,
whom I love, but not so to put it into their father's or mother's hands . . .
I desire my executors to give something to Stephen Tracy, something
to the Plymouth church, and also wish that young Rawley may be put
with Mr. Partridge, that he may be brought up in the fear of God, and
to that end, if his father suffer it. I give to Mr. Partridge 5 pounds.
To my son Henry and daughter Bridgett 40 shillings . . ." Mr. Partridge
was the minister of Duxbury.

The expected heir appeared, for the old records show that: "Know
all men by these presents, that I William Palmer of Plymouth, cooper,
son of William Palmer of Duxburrow, Naylor, deceased, release
William Bradford, Edward Winslow and Thomas Prence for 51 pounds,
mare, cattle, goods under my father's will, received by me William
Palmer, 19 April 1659. . . " At this date William Palmer would have
been just 21 years old.

For further information on the early Palmer family, see the New
England Register, Volume 4, page 35, and the Boston Transcript, 21
July 1924 and 3 Jan. 1927.

      Children by first wife:
2. i.   William Palmer, b. 1613.
    ii. Henry, who probably never came to America.
    iii. Bridgett, who probably never came to America.

      Children by second wife:
3. iv. William, b. in 1638.

2. **WILLIAM² PALMER** (William¹), born in England about 1613, came to Plymouth in 1621 ae 8 with his father, in the Fortune, died in Duxbury in 1636.

He married in Scituate 27 March 1633 ELIZABETH HODGKINS. She married second 2 Jan. 1637 John Willis.

He had no will but inventory of his estate is found, filed 25 Aug. 1636, in which are mentioned children Thomas, William and Rebecca. There is also record of a legal action in which John Willis of Duxbury complained on behalf of his daughter-in-law Rebecca Palmer against Tristram Hull and his wife in an action of assault and battery, to the damage of 50 pounds.

Children:
i.   Thomas.
ii. William, b. 27 June 1634; m. (1) Mary Paddock (?), daughter of Robert Paddock; m. (2) Susannah Hathaway (?).
iii. Rebecca.

3. **WILLIAM² PALMER** (William¹), born in Duxbury in 1938, married SUSANNA COOK, daughter of John Cook. Residence: Dartmouth.

He was killed by the Indians when on his way home on Fort Street in Fairhaven, after visiting his father-in-law John Cook in the garrison there. He was buried under a pear tree in Fairhaven at the corner of Washington and Walnut Streets in the rear of the annex to the school. He left a will.

There is also record of a legal action taken by John Willis and his wife Elizabeth, in a complaint against Mr. William Bradford, Mr. Edward Winslow and Mr. Thomas Prence, executors of the will of William Palmer Sr., deceased. They sought damages for 20 pounds for a lot of land which complainant pretended he had right to by the marriage of his wife, who had formerly been the wife of William Palmer the younger, son of said William the elder. The jury found for the defendants and gave them 12 pounds in damages and the charges of the court, according to Plymouth Colony records, Judicial Acts, page 7, 2 Jan. 1637/8.

Children:
4. i.   William, b. in 1663.
5. ii. John, b. 6 Dec. 1665.
   iii. Joseph. Residence: Tiverton.

4. **WILLIAM³ PALMER** (William², William¹), born in 1663, probably in Dartmouth, died in LC in 1746. He married about 1685 MARY RICHMOND, daughter of Capt. Edward and Abigail (Davis) Richmond, born in 1668. Residence: LC. They lived on the east part of the town where he had much land, around Pottersville and Quicksand Pond, where many of his descendants continue to reside. He and his brother John were the first two settlers of the name in LC, their father being from Dartmouth and their grandfather from Plymouth.

His will, Taunton Probate, book 11, page 209, made 13 Jan. 1745/6 in the 19th year of the reign of George the 2d, and proved 4 Nov. 1746: ". . . To son William 5 shillings. To son Joseph one half tract of land I formerly gave to my son William and since bought of him; bounded east on the pond, south and west on land of Charles

Brownell, north on land I bought and gave to my son Joseph, northerly
half of said land and all that part of homestead farm which I have
already given my son Joseph. To son John 5 shillings. To son Thomas
all that part of my homestead farm I have given my son Thomas. To
son Sylvester all that part of my homestead farm that I have already
given him. To my sons Thomas and Sylvester, the south half of land
I formerly gave to my son William by deed, which since I rebought,
bounded east by the pond, south and west by land of Charles Brownell,
north on land which I have given my son Joseph. To daughters Elizabeth
Head and Abigail Shaw 5 shillings each, and to grandson Gamaliel Richmond, son of daughter Patience Richmond, 5 shillings. To daughter
Susannah Southworth 20 shillings. My son Joseph to be sole executor. . . "

    Children, recorded in LC:
6. i.   William, b. 17 Jan. 1686.
    ii.   Elizabeth, b. 12 Nov. 1687; m. in LC 29 June 1709 Henry
          Head.
    iii. Joseph, b. 19 June 1689; d. in 1764; unmarried.
    iv.   Susannah, b. 24 Oct. 1692; m. (1) (--) Blackman; m. (2)
          Benjamin Southworth.
7. v.   John, b. 13 Nov. 1694.
8. vi.   Thomas, b. 7 Jan. 1697.
    vii. Mary, b. 10 Jan. 1699; d. young.
    viii. Benjamin, b. 3 Nov. 1700; d. young.
    ix.   Abigail, b. 5 April 1702; d. in September 1790; m. in LC
          10 Aug. 1721 Israel Shaw.
    x.   Patience, b. 19 Feb. 1704; m. in LC 14 Dec. 1727 Peleg
          Richmond.
9. xi.   Sylvester, b. 2 May 1706.
    xii. Peleg, b. 8 March 1708; d. young.

    5. JOHN³ PALMER (William², William¹), born in Dartmouth 18
May 1665, died in LC 13 Oct. 1753. Residence: LC, on Willow Avenue
on the west side of the road.
    He married first ELIZABETH RICHMOND, daughter of Edward
and Abigail (David) Richmond, born in LC 6 Dec. 1666, died there 9
Feb. 1717. He was married second in LC 28 Aug. 1718 by Thomas
Church, justice, to SARAH BLOOD, born in 1682, died in LC 25 July
1766. All are buried in the Old Commons cemetery.
    His will, recorded in Taunton, made 10 April 1745 and proved
27 Nov. 1752: ". . . To wife Sarah two Negroes and all household goods.
To son John two 18 acre lots that he now lives on. To sons Edward,
Job, Aaron, William, Henry, 10 pounds each old tenor. To son Moses
40 acres of my homestead farm lying on north side near to Carr's land
on the west side of highway. To son Simeon my executor, my now
dwelling house and all land on the west side of the highway excepting
40 acres to son Moses, and two ten acre lots east of highway east from
my house that I now live in. To daughters Sarah Wilbor and Elizabeth
Southworth 10 pounds each. . . "

    Children, recorded in LC:
10. i.   John, b. 24 Nov. 1687.
    ii.   Sarah, b. 29 Sept. 1689; m. in LC 22 June 1710 John Wilbore,

son of William and Martha Wilbore of Portsmouth.
iii.   Elizabeth, b. 17 Nov. 1691; m. in LC 11 Oct. 1716 Edward
       Southworth.
iv.   Edward, b. 29 Aug. 1693.
11. v.   Job, b. 17 Sept. 1695.
vi.   Aaron, b. 19 Dec. 1697.
vii.   Anna, b. 24 March 1699; d. 18 Feb. 1716.
viii. Isaac, b. 14 Jan. 1701; not named in the will, probably died
       young.
ix.   William, b. 18 March 1703.
x.   Esther, b. 31 Aug. 1706; d. 27 April 1723.
xi.   Henry, b. 11 Oct. 1709; d. 27 April 1723.

       Children by second wife:
xii.   Gideon, b. 29 June 1719.
12. xiii. Moses, b. 8 May 1721.
13. xiv.   Simeon, b. 13 July 1723.

6. WILLIAM⁴ PALMER (William³, William², William¹), born in
LC 17 Jan. 1686. He was married there 9 Feb. 1715 by Richard
Billings, justice, to MARY IRISH, daughter of John and Elizabeth
Irish, born in LC 9 April 1695.
    Residence: LC. They lived for a time in the vicinity of Quicksand
Pond in the east part of town, and then probably moved away.

       Children:
i.   Jerusha, b. 1 June 1716.
ii.   Mary, b. 28 Feb. 1719.
iii.   William, b. 7 March 1721.
iv.   David, b. 17 Nov. 1722.
v.   Lawton, b. 24 Nov. 1727.
vi.   Patience, b. 28 Jan. 1730.
vii.   Micah, b. 10 May 1732.
viii. Priscilla, b. 5 July 1734.
ix.   Content, b. 13 Sept. 1736.
x.   Elizabeth, b. 13 Dec. 1738.

7. JOHN⁴ PALMER (William³, William², William¹), born in LC
13 Nov. 1694, died in 1785. He left no will, but his estate was administered 3 May 1785 by his son John. Residence: LC.
    He was married in LC 23 Feb. 1716 by Richard Billings, justice,
to ALICE SHAW, daughter of Israel and (--) (Tallman) Shaw, born in
LC 17 Nov. 1695.
    From records of the Taunton Probate: ". . . Know ye that we
Perez Palmer, yeoman, and Alice Palmer, spinster, both of Dartmouth,
appoint our trusty friend Wilson Soule, attorney, for suit brought
against us by our brother, John Palmer, administrator of the estate
of our father John Palmer, deceased. 28 July 1785. . ." There is a
later record to the effect that "Alice and Perez Palmer have conceded.
. ." and signed John Palmer.

       Children, recorded in LC:
i.   Peleg, b. 21 Nov. 1716.

ii.   Bathsheba, b. 4 June 1718; m. in LC 27 Nov. 1737 Joseph
Head.

iii.   Judith, b. 28 March 1719; m. in LC in October 1742 William
Brown.

iv.   Dudley, b. 13 Sept. 1720; d. 15 Jan. 1724.

v.   Alice, b. 15 Jan. 1722; d. 30 June 1726.

vi.   Elizabeth, b. 1 Oct. 1723; m. 12 Oct. 1746 Robert Brown.

vii. Alice, b. 15 Oct. 1725; d. in September 1805. Her will was
made 15 March 1805.

viii. Benjamin, b. 4 Feb. 1728; m. (intention 28 Oct. 1758) in
Dartmouth Sarah Davenport, daughter of John and
Elizabeth (Taylor) Davenport.

14. ix.   John, b. 22 Sept. 1731.

x.   Perez, b. in 1733; m. in Westport 7 June 1781 Mary Palmer
of LC.

8. THOMAS[4] PALMER (William[3], William[2], William[1]), born in
LC 7 Jan. 1697, died there 13 May 1768. He is buried in the Old Commons cemetery No. 1. Residence: LC, in the vicinity of Quicksand
Pond in the east part of town.

He was married in LC 5 April 1742 by Richard Billings, justice,
to ABIAL WILBORE, daughter of Samuel and Mary (Potter) Wilbore,
born in LC 27 May 1707.

Children, recorded in LC:

15. i.   Joseph, b. 3 May 1742.

16. ii.   Thomas, b. 5 Sept. 1743.

17. iii. Elkanah, b. 3 Aug. 1745.

iv.   Mary, b. 10 June 1747; m. (intention 19 May 1781) Perez
Palmer, son of John and Alice (Shaw) Palmer.

18. v.   William, b. 21 May 1749.

19. vi. Benedict, b. 29 Oct. 1753.

9. SYLVESTER[4] PALMER (William[3], William[2], William[1]), born
in LC 2 May 1706, died there in 1756. Residence: LC.

He was married in LC 9 June 1740 by Richard Billings, justice,
to AMEY WAIT, died in July 1776.

His will, recorded book 1, page 209, made 6 Aug. 1756 and proved
13 Dec. 1756: ". . . To wife Amey household goods and she to be executor. To son Rescomb when age 25 years all my land in the neck
called Houghes neck, 51 acres bounded north by my brother Thomas and
partly on the cove that falls in Quicksand Pond, south and west by Quicksand Pond. To son Sylvester, land I bought, 8 acres at west of Quicksand
Pond, south on brother Thomas and west on Charles Brownell, north on
my brother Thomas. To son Samuel 200 pounds. . . "

Her will, recorded book 2, page 349, made 4 March 1776 and proved
6 Aug. 1776: ". . . To son Rescomb 6 dollars. To son Lemuel one bed,
bolster and two pillows, my great stilliards and my best meat tub. To
grandson Amaziah Wilcox all the household goods which were in possession of his mother, Ruth Wilcox, deceased. To daughters Mary
Earle, Patience Gifford and Eunice Palmer 8 pounds, 8 shillings
equally divided among them. To daughter Eliphal Head one pound, 16

shillings. To daughter Bethany Brightman 18 shillings. To daughter
Esther Palmer one bed and twelve shillings. To daughter Eunice all
household goods which I have not given away. To granddaughter Almey
Head one silver spoon marked N.P. Son Lemuel Palmer to be executor. . ."

Children, recorded in LC:
20. i.   Rescombe, b. 25 Aug. 1742.
     ii.   Mary, b. in 1744; m. 14 Nov. 1765 Lawton Earle.
     iii. Ruth, b. about 1746; m. (--) Wilcox.
     iv.   Patience, b. 21 April 1749; m. in LC 27 April 1774 Joseph
           Gifford, son of Enos and Phillis Gifford.
21. v.   Sylvester, b. 7 April 1752.
22. vi.   Lemuel, b. 1 Aug. 1753.
     vii. Eunice, b. about 1756; m. in LC 8 Jan. 1778 William Brownell,
           son of Stephen Brownell.
     viii. Eliphal, b. about 1758; m. (?) Benjamin Head.
     ix.   Parthenia, b. about 1760; d. young.
     x.   Esther, b. about 1762; d. young.
     xi.   Deborah, b. about 1748; d. 1 Sept. 1770; m. in LC 25 May
           1769 Charles Manchester.
     xii. Bethaney, m. in Westport 15 Oct. 1772 Israel Brightman,
           son of Henry and Hannah Brightman.

10. JOHN[4] PALMER (John[3], William[2], William[1]), born in LC
24 Nov. 1687. Residence: LC.
     He was married 25 Dec. 1705 in LC by Richard Billings, justice,
to MARY HILLIARD, daughter of William and Deborah Hilliard, born
in LC 3 April 1681, died there 16 Feb. 1716. She is buried in the Old
Commons cemetery. He was married second 12 July 1777 in LC by
Richard Billings, justice, to ELIZABETH CHURCH, daughter of
Joseph and Grace (Shaw) Church, born in LC in February 1699.

Children by first wife, recorded in LC:
     i.   Bridgett, b. 17 March 1706.
     ii.   Amey, b. 24 May 1708.
     iii. Deborah, b. 30 July 1710.
     iv.   John, b. 30 Oct. 1712.

Children by second wife:
     v.   Elizabeth, b. 12 April 1718.
     vi.   Grace, b. 18 Jan. 1720; m. 31 May 1741 Daniel Grinnell.
     vii. Israel, b. 15 June 1722.
     viii. Esther, b. 2 Sept. 1724.
     ix.   Phebe, b. 4 April 1730.
     x.   Mary, b. 14 Dec. 1732.
     xi.   Isaac, b. 8 June 1735.
     xii. Aaron, b. 22 March 1738; m. Mary Reed. Residence:
           Plainfield, Conn.
     xiii. Israel, b. 13 March 1741.

11. JOB[4] PALMER (John[3], William[2], William[1]), born in LC 17
Sept. 1695. Residence: LC.
     He was married in LC 1 Sept. 1725 by Richard Billings, justice,

to PRISCILLA HILLIARD, daughter of David and Joanna (Andros)
Hilliard, born about 1706, died before August 1784.

> Children, recorded in LC:
> i.   Lois, b. 18 July 1726.

12. CAPT. MOSES⁴ PALMER (John³, William², William¹), .born in
LC 8 May 1721, died there in November 1759.

He was married 25 (?) 1745 in LC by William Richmond, justice,
to SUSANNA TAYLOR, daughter of Philip and Comfort (Dennis) Taylor,
born in LC 30 March 1724. Residence: LC.

> Children, born and recorded in LC:
> 23. i.   Capt. Richard, b. 19 Aug. 1747.
> ii.   Philip, b. 2 July 1749.
> iii.   Gideon, b. 23 June 1751.
> iv.   Mercy, b. 1 Jan. 1753; m. in Tiverton 17 March 1774 Samuel
>   Dennis, son of John and Hannah Dennis.
> v.   Moses, b. 19 Feb. 1755; d. in January 1784.
> vi.   Comfort, b. 9 Feb. 1757.
> vii.   Ruth, b. 14 Nov. 1758; m. in LC 21 Dec. 1780 Israel Shaw,
>   son of Israel and Sarah Shaw.

13. SIMEON⁴ PALMER (John³, William², William¹), born in LC
13 July 1723. He was still living in 1774 when he was listed in the LC
census. He was married first in LC 25 (?) 1745 by Richard Billings,
justice, to LYDIA DENNIS, probably the daughter of Robert and Susanna
Dennis of Tiverton, born in 1719, died in LC 26 Dec. 1754. He was
married second in LC 5 Sept. 1755 by the Rev. Jonathan Ellis to
ELIZABETH MORTIMER, born in 1712, died in LC 10 Aug. 1776.
Both wives are buried in the Old Commons cemetery. Elizabeth's
stone bears the famous (and mysterious) inscription identifying her
as the woman "who should have been the wife of Simeon Palmer."

He lived on Willow Avenue, once called Pudding Bag Lane, on
the place owned by Dr. James Peckham in 1850.

> Children, recorded in LC:
> i.   Susannah, b. 11 Jan. 1746.
> ii.   Gideon, b. 13 June 1747; d. 24 Oct. 1749.
> 24. iii. Humphrey, b. 28 Oct. 1748.
> iv.   Sarah, b. 24 May 1750; m. in LC 6 Jan. 1771 Jeremiah
>   Davenport, son of Joseph and Elizabeth Davenport.
> 25. v.   Walter, b. 27 March 1752.
> vi.   Patience, b. 8 Aug. 1753; m. in LC 16 Jan. 1774 Richard
>   Grinnell, son of Richard and Comfort Grinnell.
>
> Children by second wife:
> vii.   Lydia, b. 23 Sept. 1757; m. in LC 11 Feb. 1776 John Pearce,
>   son of James and Sarah Pearce.

14. JOHN⁵ PALMER (John⁴, William³, William², William¹), born
in Dartmouth 22 Sept. 1731, died 14 Aug. 1815 (?). He married (intention 7 Nov. 1767) in Dartmouth MARY STODDARD, daughter of Israel
and Elizabeth (Brownell) Stoddard, born in LC 30 July 1737.

Residence: Dartmouth, in that section which later became Westport, near the LC line. He was the only John Palmer living in Westport in 1790 and was living next to his brother, Perez, and Sylvester Brownell.

Children:
26. i.   John Stoddard.
     ii.   Isaac, b. 11 April 1784; m. in Westport 15 Sept. 1814 Rhoda Sherman.
     iii.   Alice, m. in Westport 13 Dec. 1792 Hezekiah Wilbor.
     iv.   Susannah, m. (1) John Macomber; m. (2) 25 Aug. 1805 Thomas Simmons.
     v.   Hannah, m. in Westport 5 Dec. 1800 (?) Mason Davis.
     vi.   Judith.
     vii.   Dudley, m. 6 Nov. 1803 Martha Wilbor, daughter of Brownell and Esther Wilbor.
27. viii.   Gideon.
     ix.   Falley, b. in 1794.
     x.   Israel.
     xi.   Nancy, b. 28 Sept. 1797.

The most unusual epitaph in Little Compton graveyard . . .

15. JOSEPH⁵ PALMER (Thomas⁴, William³, William², William¹), born in LC 3 May 1742, died there 17 March 1791. Residence: LC. He lived at Ocean Echo or the George Howard place of 1774.

He married about 1767 HANNAH BRIGGS, daughter of Joseph and Ruth (Coe) Briggs, born in LC 28 Nov. 1746, died there 4 March 1835. Both are buried in the Old Commons cemetery.

Children, recorded in LC:

  i.   Abigail, b. 13 June 1768; d. 27 Dec. 1850; m. 16 July 1795 William Wilbor 5th, son of Samuel and Phebe Wilbor.
  ii.   Ruth, b. 20 Jan. 1771; d. 20 Sept. 1778.
28. iii. Thomas, b. 12 March 1773.
  iv.   Mary, b. 20 March 1776; d. 22 Jan. 1850; m. 20 June 1820 Capt. Owen Grinnell, son of Malachi and Lydia Grinnell.
  v.   Hannah, b. 19 Dec. 1777; d. 7 Dec. 1842; m. 22 Jan. 1805 Elias Brownell, son of James and Hannah (Manchester) Brownell.
  vi.   Ruth 2d, b. 27 March 1779; m. Phillip Donald.
  vii. Priscilla, b. 6 Nov. 1781; m. in LC 16 Nov. 1817 Col. Joseph Pearce, son of Nathaniel and Sarah Pearce.
29. viii. Simeon, b. 14 Oct. 1785.
  ix.   Anna, b. 7 July (?).

16. THOMAS⁵ PALMER (Thomas⁴, William³, William², William¹), born in LC 5 Sept. 1743, died there in April 1803. They lived in the east part of town near Pottersville.

He was married in LC 16 June 1771 by the Rev. Othniel Campbell to PHEBE SHAW, daughter of Jeremiah and Phebe (Wilbor) Shaw, born in LC 28 May 1747.

His will, recorded book 4, page 108 LC Wills, made 14 Nov. 1798 and proved 2 May 1803: ". . . To wife Phebe use of all my lands in LC. To son Isaac one dollar. To sons Jediah and Joseph all my homestead land with buildings, that piece of land I bought of Thomas Ormsby and all the buildings. To son Jediah two thirds of above. To son Joseph one third of above. To son Moses my carpenter and joyning tools and my gun. To wife Phebe use of household goods. To three daughters Mercy, Sarah and Prudence, 10 dollars apiece. To daughter Lucy Peckham. . ."

Children, recorded in LC:

  i.   Samuel, b. 12 Oct. 1771; d. in March 1797.
  ii.   Lucy, b. 17 Dec. 1773; d. 17 Feb. 1850; m. 3 Aug. 1794 Peleg Peckham, son of John and Elizabeth (Wilbor) Peckham.
30. iii. Isaac, b. 29 Feb. 1776.
  iv.   Jediah, b. 30 Aug. 1778.
  v.   Ruth, b. 13 March 1781.
31. vi. Moses, b. 9 Nov. 1783.
  vii. Mercy, b. 28 April 1786; m. 17 Feb. 1805 Sisson Taylor, son of James and Lydia Taylor.
  viii. Sally, b. 12 March 1789.
  ix.   Joseph, b. 18 July 1791.
  x.   Prudence, b. 12 Sept. 1795.

17. ELKANAH⁵ PALMER (Thomas⁴, William³, William², William¹),

-452-

born in LC 3 Aug. 1745, died there 19 March 1806. They lived in the vicinity of Quicksand Pond in the east part of town.

He was married in LC 28 Dec. 1769 by Aaron Wilbore, justice, to EMBLIM WILBOR, daughter of Walter and Catharine (Davenport) Wilbor, born in LC 17 Nov. 1749, died there 2 Oct. 1843. They are buried in Union cemetery.

His will, recorded in LC Wills, Volume 4, page 235, made 1 July 1798 and proved 2 April 1806: ". . . To wife Emblim two feather beds and bedding and a pillion. To son Jonathan Palmer all my land and buildings that I shall die seized of. To daughter Catharine one cow and 10 dollars. To grandson Elkanah my gun. To son Jonathan all my stock. . . "

Children, recorded in LC:
32. i.   Jonathan, b. 12 Aug. 1772.
   ii.   Wilbor, b. 25 June 1775; d. young.
  iii.   Benjamin, b. 9 Dec. 1777; d. young.
   iv.   Catherine, b. 26 June 1781; d. 16 May 1850.

18. WILLIAM[5] PALMER (Thomas[4], William[3], William[2], William[1]), born in LC 21 May 1749.

He was married first in LC 8 Aug. 1779 by the Rev. Jonathan Ellis to MARY SAWDRY, daughter of John and Mary Sawdry of LC. He was married second in Newport 23 Oct. 1803 by the Rev. Michael Eddy to WAIT LAKE, daughter of William Weaver of Middletown.

Children by first wife:
    i.   Abiel, b. 2 Nov. 1779.
   ii.   Ezra, b. 2 Oct. 1781.
  iii.   Lemuel, b. 7 May 1783 (?).
   iv.   Anna, b. 29 June 1785.

19. BENEDICT[5] PALMER (Thomas[4], William[3], William[2], William[1]), born in LC 29 Oct. 1753, died there 22 July 1837.

He was married in LC 17 June 1784 by the Rev. Jonathan Ellis to DEBORAH WILBOR, widow of Lemuel Palmer and daughter of Isaac and Mary (Brownell) Wilbor, born 24 Feb. 1744. She married first 10 Oct. 1776 in LC Lemuel Palmer.

Residence: LC. They lived on or near Amesbury Lane in the east part of town.

His will, recorded in LC, book 8, page 120, made 25 Dec. 1833 and proved 11 Sept. 1837: "Benedict Palmer. . . carpenter. . . To son Wilbor all my wearing apparel and my small Bible. To daughter Edith rest and residue and she to be executrix. . . "

The will of his daughter, Edith Palmer, made 12 Nov. 1849 and proved 14 Jan. 1850: ". . . To friend Angelina Grinnell, wife of Thomas Grinnell, one feather bed and one half wearing apparel. To Martha Palmer, widow of Horatio Palmer one feather bed. I order that my executor get a pair of gravestones for my grave. The rest and residue to friend Martha Palmer and she to be sole executrix. . . " She is buried in the Old Commons cemetery near the wives of Simeon Palmer.

Children, recorded in LC:

    i.   Edith, b. 13 Jan. 1785; d. 27 Nov. 1849.
    ii.   Richmond, b. 20 Oct. 1786.
    iii.   Sybil, b. 27 July 1788; d. 19 Nov. 1827; m. Nathaniel Woodman,
           son of William and Priscilla (Brownell) Woodman.
    iv.   Wilbor, b. 5 April 1792. Residence: perhaps New York State.
    v.   Elizabeth, b. 8 April 1794; d. in October 1824.

20. **RESCOME⁵ PALMER** (Sylvester⁴, William³, William², William¹),
born in LC 25 Aug. 1742, died there in September 1792. Residence: LC.

He was married in LC 19 June 1766 by Nathaniel Searle, justice, to
HOPE BROWNELL, daughter of Pearce and Ruth (Thurston) Brownell,
born in 1750, died in New York State.

His will, recorded book 3, page 258 of LC Wills, proved 2 Oct. 1792:
"Rescome Palmer of LC, yeoman, 10 July 1792, in the 17th year of
American Independence. . . To wife Hope all household goods. To son
Joseph my land and buildings where I now live, he to support all of my
children under age of 14 years. . . " He also left 50 dollars to his son
Rescome, and one silver dollar each to his sons George, Sylvester and
Lot, and to his six daughters.

        Children (only Sarah, Deborah and Rescome recorded in LC):
    i.   Sarah, b. 9 Nov. 1766; m. Thomas Tabor of Westport.
    ii.   Joseph, b. in 1768; moved to New York State.
    iii.   George, b. about 1770; m. Elizabeth (--).
    iv.   Lot, b. about 1772; moved to Nantucket.
    v.   Elizabeth, b. about 1774; m. (--) Potter.
    vi.   Deborah, b. 1776; m. in Westport 1 May 1796 John Allen,
           son of Daniel and Betsey Allen.
    vii.   Rescome, b. 14 Nov. 1777; m. 19 March 1801 Ruth Wilbor,
           daughter of Capt. Aaron and Ruth (Hunt) Wilbor.
    viii. Sylvester, b. 19 Aug. 1779.
    ix.   Ruth, b. about 1781; m. Seth Benson of New York State.
    x.   Mary, b. about 1783; m. Jonathan Greene.
    xi.   Bethania, m. William Shaw of New York State.

21. **SYLVESTER⁵ PALMER** (Sylvester⁴, William³, William²,
William¹), born in LC 7 April 1752, died there in April 1775. Residence: LC.

He was married in LC 8 July 1773 by Aaron Wilbore, justice,
to REBECCA BRIGHTMAN, daughter of Henry and Hannah Brightman.

His will, recorded in book 2, page 318 LC Wills, made 30 March
1775 and proved 18 April 1775: ". . . To wife Rebecca all household
goods and livestock and use of all real estate to enable her to bring up
my child until he comes of age. To little son Henry all rest estate when
he come to the age 21 and all silver buckles. If my wife proves to be
with child then son Henry to pay it 12-1/2 silver dollars. If said Henry
dies then all property to the second child. . . "

        Children, first recorded in LC:
    i.   Henry, b. 4 Feb. 1774; m. in Westport 8 April 1798 Mary
           Cornell, daughter of Christopher Cornell, deceased.
    ii.   Hannah, b. in 1775; m. 23 Nov. 1791 Enos Gifford.

22. LEMUEL⁵ PALMER (Sylvester⁴, William³, William², William¹),
born in LC 1 Aug. 1753, died there in May 1783.

He was married in LC 10 Oct. 1776 by Enos Gifford, justice, to
DEBORAH WILBOR, daughter of Isaac and Mary (Brownell) Wilbor,
born in LC 24 Feb. 1744.

His will, recorded book 3, page 46 LC Wills, made 20 March
178- and proved 3 June 1783: ". . . To wife Deborah use of lands in LC
with all housing. . . To my two little daughters, Amey and Deborah,
all land in LC with all housing after their mother. To wife Deborah
all livestock and she to be the executor of this my will. . . "

Children, recorded in LC:
i.   Almy, b. 27 July 1779; m. Peleg Wood, son of Reuben and
       Ruth (Wilbor) Wood.
ii.   Deborah, b. 27 Sept. 1781; m. in 1801 Joseph Gifford, son
       of Enos and Mary (Wilbor) Gifford.

23. CAPT. RICHARD⁵ PALMER (Moses⁴, John³, William²,
William¹), born in LC 19 Aug. 1747, died there 10 Feb. 1783 ae 36.
Residence: LC.

He was married in LC 1 June 1775 by the Rev. Jonathan Ellis to
FALLEE GRAY, daughter of Samuel and Deborah (Peck) Gray, born
in LC 8 April 1754, died 8 Sept. 1836. They are buried in the Old
Commons cemetery.

Children, recorded in LC:
i.   Amaziah, b. 24 June 1777; d. 15 Sept. 1778.
ii.   Susanna, b. 3 May 1779; d. 24 March 1717; m. in LC 29 June
       1800 Thomas Palmer, son of Joseph and Hannah (Briggs)
       Palmer.
iii.   Gideon, b. 1 May 1781; m. (?). He had a son, John Simmons
       Palmer of Newport.
iv.   Richard, b. 21 Dec. 1782.

24. HUMPHREY⁵ PALMER (Simeon⁴, John³, William², William¹),
born 28 Oct. 1748 in LC, probably moved away.

He was married in LC 20 Oct. 1774 by the Rev. Jonathan Ellis to
SARAH WILCOX, daughter of Jeremiah and Sarah (Bailey) Wilcox,
born in LC 1 Jan. 1757.

Children, recorded in LC:
i.   Simeon, b. 7 June 1775.
ii.   John, b. 30 May 1777.
iii.   Walter, b. 2 March 1779.

25. WALTER⁵ PALMER (Simeon⁴, John³, William², William¹),
born in LC 27 March 1752, died there 27 Dec. 1777. He married in
LC about 1774 RUTH BROWNELL.

Children, recorded in LC:
i.   Betsey, b. 22 July 1775.
ii.   Isaac, b. 10 April 1777.

26. JOHN STODDARD⁶ PALMER (John⁵, John⁴, William³,

William², William¹). He was living in LC in 1814, but died before
1823. He married in Dartmouth 29 April 1784 MARGARET MACUMBER,
daughter of William Macumber 2d. She died in LC 25 April 1845.

The children of John and Margaret Palmer made a deed in 1823
in which they sold John S. Palmer the land "which belonged to our
honored father, John S. Palmer, deceased. . . In consideration of the
sum of 750 dollars to us in hand paid by John Palmer, son of the said
John Palmer. . ." It was bounded north on the highway, east on Peleg
Hoxie, south on Israel Palmer and west on William Palmer, Cornelius
Brightman and Peleg Hoxie.

Children, not recorded in LC, but some given in LC death
records.

33. i.   Wilbor, b. 25 Jan. 1791.
34. ii. Israel.
35. iii. William, b. about 1794.
    iv. Elizabeth, m. in Westport (intention 18 April 1807) Canaan
         G. Dyer.
    v.   Mary, m. Joshua Dwelly.
    vi. Nancy, b. 28 Sept. 1797; d. 23 Feb. 1882; m. 20 Oct. 1819
         James Hervey Tabor.
    vii. Sarah or Sally, d. in LC 1882; m. George Potter.
36. viii. John S.

27. GIDEON⁶ PALMER (John⁵, John⁴, William³, William²,
William¹), estate administered 4 Aug. 1840. He married in Westport
3 Aug. 1806 LOIS HEAD, daughter of Daniel and Hannah (Davenport)
Head, born in LC 9 April 1787. Residence: LC, Westport and Fall
River.

Children, born in Westport:
i.   Betsey, b. 6 Dec. 1806.
ii. Gideon, b. 3 Feb. 1812.
iii. Cordelia, b. 25 April 1814.
iv. Almira, b. 25 April 1816.
v.   Thomas Davenport, b. 10 Oct. 1818.
vi. Lorinda, b. 19 Jan. 1821.

28. THOMAS⁶ PALMER (Joseph⁵, Thomas⁴, William³, William²,
William¹), born in LC 12 March 1773, died there 25 June 1857. They
lived at Ocean Echo on the place owned by J. Briggs in 1850.

He was married first in LC 29 June 1800 by the Rev. Mase Shepard
to SUSANNAH PALMER, daughter of Richard and Fallee (Gray) Palmer,
born in LC 3 May 1779, died there 24 March 1817. He was married
second in LC 13 May 1817 by the Rev. Mase Shepard to MARY (BAILEY)
RICHMOND, widow of Joshua Richmond and daughter of Isaac and Sarah
(Manchester) Bailey, born in LC 4 March 1778, died there 17 April 1854.

Children by first wife:
i.   Richard Addison, b. 20 May 1801.
ii. Julius Aboyne, b. 14 June 1803.
iii. Angeline, b. 2 Nov. 1805; d. 4 Jan. 1899; m. 31 Jan. 1827
     Thomas Bailey Grinnell, son of Capt. Owen and Rhoda
     Grinnell.

37. iv. Ray, b. 12 Nov. 1808.
    v.   Asher, b. 28 Feb. 1811.
    vi. Dewitte, b. 17 June 1813; d. 6 Nov. 1814.
    vii. Amanda, b. 26 April 1815.
    viii. Susanna, b. 9 Feb. 1817; d. 27 March 1817.

         Children by second wife:
    ix. Henry Kirke White, b. 23 Sept. 1819.

    29. SIMEON[6] PALMER (Joseph[5], Thomas[4], William[3], William[2], William[1]), born in LC 14 Oct. 1785, died in Boston 17 July 1853. He married in Boston 28 Jan. 1812 MARY CALDWELL, daughter of Thomas[4] (William[3], John[2], John[1]), and Elizabeth (Greenwood) Caldwell of Ipswich, Mass., born in Ipswich 19 Sept. 1790, died in Boston 26 July 1853.

    They lived on Myrtle Street in Boston, where he joined the Park Street Church 3 Dec. 1813. She joined the same church 2 June 1827. He was in the clothing business and amassed quite a fortune.

    They died of typhoid fever within a few days of each other. He seems to have left no will. They are buried in the Forest Hills cemetery lot 656, of Chrysanthemum Path, where there is a large monument with several gravestones. There are about eight names on the lot, but the cemetery office lists the names of about twenty persons, with the date of their burial, including Dr. Horatio A. Palmer.

         Children, born in Boston:
    i.   Horatio, b. in 1814; d. ae 5 months.
38. ii. Horatio Albert, b. in 1815.
    iii. Simeon, b. in 1816; d. in 1880; m. Maria Spencer.
    iv. Mary Elizabeth, d. 23 Oct. 1867; m. Timothy W. Hoxie.
    v.   Emeline F., b. 1 Nov. 1823; d. in Boston 24 Feb. 1891; m.
         19 Nov. 1844 the Rev. Henry M. Dexter.
    vi. Frances Ellen, b. 16 May 1831; d. 26 July 1896; m. Henry
         Isaac Richmond.
    vii. Sophia Briggs, b. 5 June 1828; d. 25 Dec. 1891; m. in 1858
         Asa French. They had five children and lived in Braintree,
         Mass.
    viii. Thomas C. (?).

    30. ISAAC[6] PALMER (Thomas[5], Thomas[4], William[3], William[2], William[1]), born in LC 29 Feb. 1776, died there 2 Sept. 1850. Residence: LC. He married there 6 Oct. 1799 MARY BRIGGS, daughter of Richard and Anna (Ware) Briggs, born in LC 19 Sept. 1775, died there 7 March 1811. Both are buried in the Old Commons cemetery.

         Children, recorded in LC:
    i.   Richard Briggs, b. 20 June 1802.

    31. MOSES[6] PALMER (Thomas[5], Thomas[4], William[3], William[2], William[1]), born in LC 9 Nov. 1783. He married there 20 July 1809 ELIZABETH SEABURY, daughter of William and Deborah Seabury, born in LC 14 June 1786.

         Children, all recorded in LC:
    i.   Mary (Polly) Briggs, b. 25 March 1811; m. Isaac Fleetwood.

ii.   Prudence, b. 13 April 1812; m. Abraham Broadbent.
39. iii.   Thomas 2d, b. 5 Nov. 1813.
iv.   Phebe, b. 18 March 1815; m. (1) (--) Manchester; m. (2)
      Isaac Bradlt.
v.   William, b. 18 May 1817.
vi.   Sion Seabury, b. 1 Aug. 1819; m. Elizabeth Butts.
vii. Peleg Peckham, d. unmarried.
viii. Lucy, m. Philip Eltz.
ix.   Sarah Church, b. 1 Nov. 1827; d. in 1902; m. Parker Barden.

32. JONATHAN DAVENPORT[6] PALMER (Elkanah[5], Thomas[4],
William[3], William[2], William[1]), born in LC 12 Aug. 1772, died there
29 Oct. 1861. Residence: LC. He married in Westport 27 April 1794
DEBORAH WOOD of Westport, daughter of John and Sarah Wood, born
20 May 1776, died in LC 9 Feb. 1859. They are buried in the Union
cemetery.

Children, first two recorded in LC:
i.   Fanny, b. 4 Oct. 1794; d. 21 April 1855; m. Charles
      Manchester, son of Edward and Esther (Church) Man-
      chester.
40. ii.   Elkanah, b. 24 Aug. 1797; d. 2 July 1881; m. (1) Fanny
      Taylor; m. (2) 12 Dec. 1847 Eliza S. Manchester.
iii. Benjamin, m. (?) in LC.
iv.   Lois.
v.   Prudence, b. in 1813; d. 16 March 1895; m. 17 April 1845
      George Manchester, son of Thomas and Abigail Manchester,
      d. 19 July 1889.

33. WILBOR[7] PALMER (John[6], John[5], John[4], William[3], William[2],
William[1]), born in LC 25 Jan. 1791, died there 11 Dec. 1881. Residence: LC. He married in LC 8 Sept. 1815 HANNAH SNELL, daughter
of Benjamin and Phebe Snell of Westport, born in Westport 7 May 1794,
died in LC 15 Dec. 1881. They are buried in back of the school house
in Adamsville.

Children, born and recorded in LC:
i.   Lydia A., b. 22 May 1816; d. 22 Nov. 1877; m. Ephraim
      Soule.
ii.   Clarinda R., b. 27 May 1818; m. 8 May 1839 James Brownell.
41. iii.   Loring, b. 17 March 1820; m. 24 Sept. 1843 in Dartmouth
      Sarah Lincoln.
iv.   Phebe Ann, b. 22 July 1822; d. 2 July 1856.
42. v.   David Darius, b. 3 Sept. 1824; m. 9 Dec. 1849 Mary A.
      Manchester.
43. vi.   Jesse Abel, b. 11 June 1828; d. 27 May 1893; m. in LC 26
      Oct. 1851 Abby C. Manchester, daughter of Ephraim and
      Ann M. Manchester.
44. vii. Samuel P., b. in LC 3 Jan. 1830; d. there 30 April 1911;
      m. (1) 27 June 1855 in LC Mary E. Manley, daughter
      of William and Abigail (Brownell) Manley; m. (2)
      Almira Mosher, daughter of Caleb and Mary (Crosby)
      Mosher.

    viii.   Sarah E. S., b. 7 April 1835.
    ix.   Hannah B., b. 8 Sept. 1838; d. 22 Dec. 1838.

    34. ISRAEL[7] PALMER (John[6], John[5], John[4], William[3], William[2], William[1]), died in LC 28 Feb. 1845. He was married in LC 6 April 1815 by the Rev. Mase Shepard to MARTHA CHURCH, daughter of Caleb and Hannah (Wilbor) Church, born 23 May 1794.

        Children:
    i.   Esther Wilbor, b. in 1823; d. in LC 31 Dec. 1884; m. (1)
            (--) Brightman; m. (2) 21 May 1848 Solomon Wilbor,
            son of Nathan and Phebe (Simmons) Wilbor.
    ii.   Margaret, d. 19 Nov. 1894; m. (--) Brownell.

    35. WILLIAM[7] PALMER (John[6], John[5], John[4], William[3], William[2], William[1]), born in LC 29 June 1794, died there 1 Jan. 1876. He married MARY (POLLY) TABOR, daughter of Benjamin and Abigail Tabor, born 27 March 1797, died in LC 27 June 1860. They are buried in the Hoxie Tabor cemetery No. 12, near Pottersville.

        Children:
    i.   John B., b. 9 May 1823; d. 30 Sept. 1853.
    ii.   Susanna, b. in 1832; d. in 1833.
    iii.   William, b. in 1833; m. Mary E. (--) of Westport.
    iv.   Abby, b. in 1838.
45. v.   Henry, b. 27 May 1822.

    36. JOHN STODDARD[7] PALMER JR. (John[6], John[5], John[4], William[3], William[2], William[1]), born about 1805, died in LC 3 July 1880. They lived in the east part of town near Pottersville.
    He married SUSANNAH WILBOR, daughter of Joseph and Hannah (Brown) Wilbor, born in LC 14 Nov. 1805, died there 23 Jan. 1881. She is buried in the Wilbor cemetery on the road south of the Commons.

        Children, not recorded in LC:
    i.   Hannah B., b. 11 Aug. 1840; d. 2 April 1915 in Somerset,
            Mass.; m. (1) Jonathan Wardell; m. (2) 26 Feb. 1884 in
            LC Benajah A. Borden, b. in 1820.

    37. RAY[7] PALMER (Thomas[6], Joseph[5], Thomas[4], William[3], William[2], William[1]), born in LC 12 Nov. 1808, died in Newark, N. J., 29 March 1887. He married 3 Oct. 1832 ANN MARIA WAUD, daughter of Maj. Marmaduke Waud, born 2 Aug. 1814, died 8 March 1886 in Newark.
    He was a celebrated Congregational minister and was the author of "My Faith Looks Up to Thee."

        Children:
    i.   Charles Ray, b. 2 May 1834; m. 10 Feb. 1869 Mary Chapin
            Barnes.
    ii.   Mary Helen, b. 18 Aug. 1836.
    iii.   Edward E., b. 24 July 1838.
    iv.   William A., b. 16 April 1840.
    v.   Henry L., b. 23 April 1842.

vi.   Mary Patten, b. 13 Feb. 1844.
vii.   Harriet S., b. 1 Aug. 1845.
viii. Maria Waud, b. 20 May 1848.
ix.   Edward N., b. 22 April 1852.
x.   Francis, b. 10 July 1853.

38. DR. HORATIO ALBERT[7] PALMER, M.D. (Simeon[6], Joseph[5], Thomas[4], William[3], William[2], William[1]), born in 1816 in Boston, died in LC 29 Aug. 1849 ae 33. He is buried in Forest Hills cemetery on the lot of his father.

He married about 1837 MARTHA WELLS, born about 1814 on the Isle of Wight, died in Colorado in 1888.

His father, Simeon Palmer, was born in LC on land granted to the Palmer family, direct from the crown, in 1630. His parents were married in Boston 31 Oct. 1812.

He was a student at Yale in 1831-2, and from 1833 to at least 1836 studied medicine under Dr. George B. Doane of Boston, while also attending lectures at Bowdoin College in Maine. He graduated from Dartmouth College in 1837, and came to LC to practice medicine. He lived on what later became the Nathaniel Church place on the Commons, directly opposite the old town house. He was known as "Albert" and the son who was named for him was known as "Briggs."

Neither of his sons married. Simeon Palmer attended Judge Hoar's private school in Concord from age 12 to 17. By the time he was 22 he was farming in Alabama, and later operated a hotel in Massachusetts. He then moved to Colorado where he was associated with the Greeley Company. For one year he had a sanatarium in Elkhorn Run, followed by a business venture in Wyoming. He moved to Yakima County, Wash., where he became a prominent citizen.

"Briggs" Palmer ran away from home at age 16 to become a soldier in the Civil War. He spent five months in Andersonville as a prisoner of war. After he contracted malaria in the south, he moved to Denver for his health. There he became an assayer, and was joined by his mother and sisters. Mary Susanna married Charles Reed, vice president of the Kinsey Agricultural Co., and Frances Sophie married Henry M. Houghton.

Children:
i.   Simeon, b. 28 Jan. 1838.
ii.   Mary Susanna, b. in 1842; m. Charles Reed.
iii.   Frances Sophie, b. in 1845; m. Henry Merriam Houghton of
       Denver.
iv.   Horatio A. Briggs, b. in 1846.

39. THOMAS[7] PALMER (Moses[6], Thomas[5], Thomas[4], William[3], William[2], William[1]), born in LC 5 Nov. 1813, died there 15 Sept. (Aug.) 1867. Residence: LC, on the road south of the Commons.

He was married first in LC 25 Aug. 1839 by Joseph B. Browne to DEBORAH GIFFORD, daughter of Joseph and Deborah (Palmer) Gifford, born in LC 3 Aug. 1814, died there 4 April 1847. Both are buried in the Old Commons cemetery. He married second CORNELIA P. (--).

In his will, recorded book 11, page 479 of LC Wills, made 8 March 1867, he left 15 dollars each to his daughter Betsey; his daughter Mary

Jane, wife of Horatio N. Wilbor; and to his son, George. To his wife
Cornelia he left the rest and residue.

Children by first wife, recorded in LC:
i.   Betsey Seabury, b. 2 June 1840; d. 19 Sept. 1908; m. 24
       April 1867 James Irving Bailey, son of James and
       Abigail Bailey.
ii.   Mary Jane, b. in LC 15 May 1842; d. 8 Aug. 1936; m. 31
       Oct. 1866 Horatio Nelson Wilbor.
iii.   George Seabury, b. 19 March 1847; d. 1 Aug. 1914; m.
       Sarah Carr.

40. ELKANAH[7] PALMER (Jonathan[6], Elkanah[5], Thomas[4], William[3],
William[2], William[1]), born in LC 24 Aug. 1797, died there 2 July 1881.
He lived on the east side of Main Road in district No. 2.

He married first FANNY TAYLOR, daughter of John and Elizabeth
(Bailey) Taylor, born in LC 15 Oct. 1798, died 20 Oct. 1846. He married
second in LC 12 Dec. 1847 ELIZA S. MANCHESTER of New Bedford,
daughter of Thomas and Abbie (Briggs) Manchester, born in 1824, died
in LC 27 Feb. 1907.

41. LORING[8] PALMER (Wilbor[7], John[6], John[5], John[4], William[3],
William[2], William[1]), born in LC 17 March 1820, died there 12 April
1897, buried in Pleasant View cemetery. Residence: LC.

He married in Dartmouth 24 Sept. 1843 SARAH W. LINCOLN of
Dartmouth, born in 1820.

Children, born in LC and recorded there:
46. i.   Loring A., b. 19 Sept. 1844.
ii.   Obed N., b. 13 March 1849; d. 13 July 1876 ae 27.
iii.   Sarah W., b. 28 March 1851; d. 20 Oct. 1856 ae 5.
iv.   Sophia J., (?), b. 8 May 1853.
v.   Samuel S., b. 11 April 1855; d. 12 Oct. 1856 ae 1.
vi.   Harriett W., b. 7 June 1857.

42. DAVID DARIUS[8] PALMER (Wilbor[7], John[6], John[5], John[4],
William[3], William[2], William[1]), born in LC 3 Sept. 1824. Residence:
LC and Westport.

He married in LC 9 Dec. 1849 MARY ANN MANCHESTER, daughter
of Jethro and Ann (Young) Manchester, born in Dartmouth 13 Sept.
1830, died in LC 18 July 1914.

Children, born in LC (Daniel, David and Sarah recorded in LC):
47. i.   Daniel Dearborn Page, b. 29 Sept. 1850.
ii.   David, b. 9 Sept. 1852.
iii.   Mary Etta, b. in Westport 12 Dec. 1853; d. in LC 31 Oct. 1930;
       m. there 24 Jan. 1877 Robert G. Brownell, b. 2 March
       1852 in LC.
iv.   Chester, b. in 1854 (?).
v.   Sarah, b. 14 Dec. 1855.
vi.   Fred, who became a contractor in Fall River.
vii.   Wilbor.
viii. Abby, m. (1) (?); m. (2) William Howland.
ix.   Emma, b. in 1861; d. 20 June 1895; m. (--) Sylvia.

43. JESSE ABEL[8] PALMER (Wilbor[7], John[6], John[5], John[4],
William[3], William[2], William[1]), born in LC 3 Sept. 1828, died there
27 May 1893. Residence: LC.

He married in LC 26 Oct. 1851 ABBY C. MANCHESTER, daughter
of Ephraim and Ann (Young) Manchester, born in Westport in 1832. She
married second William Howland.

       Children:
48. i.   Jesse Leeson, b. 18 Oct. 1852.
    ii.   Ephraim Church, b. 1 Jan. 1857; m. (1) in New Bedford
           Emma Higgins (?); m. (2) Laura E. Tilton. He had a
           son, James, of New Bedford.
    iii.   Frank A., d. young.
    iv.   John, went to sea.

44. SAMUEL P.[8] PALMER (Wilbor[7], John[6], John[5], John[4], William[3],
William[2], William[1]), born in LC 16 Jan. 1830, died there 30 April 1911.
Residence: LC.

He married first in LC 27 June 1855 MARY E. MANLEY, daughter
of William and Abby, born in 1846. He married second ALMIRA MOSHER,
daughter of Caleb and Mary (Crosby) Mosher, born in LC 14 June 1849,
died there 11 May 1936.

       Children by first wife, recorded in LC:
    i.   Willis, b. 29 March 1856; m. in Tiverton.

       Children by second wife:
49. ii.   Valentine, b. 7 Oct. 1868.
    iii.   Mary E., b. 11 March 1874.
    iv.   Herbert C., b. 22 Jan. 1877; d. 25 Oct. 1896 ae 19.
    v.   Lydia Almira, b. in 1878; m. in LC 11 March 1899 Manuel
           DeAsvedo of LC, son of Antone and Mary DeAsvedo, b.
           in the Azores in 1872.
    vi.   Eudora M., m. (1) 25 Dec. 1899 in LC Elmer Z. Brayton,
           son of Thomas and Mary (Borden) Brayton of Westport;
           m. perhaps (2) Arthur Edwin Davis, son of John and Abigail
           (Walker) Davis of Barnstead, N.H., d. 18 Feb. 1945 in
           New Bedford.
    vii. Wilbur.
    viii. Sidney.
    ix.   Daughter, b. in February 1883.

45. HENRY[6] PALMER (William[7], John[6], John[5], John[4], William[3],
William[2], William[1]), born 27 May 1822, died in LC 18 Dec. 1900.
Residence: LC, in the vicinity of Adamsville.

He married in Westport 3 June 1847 MARY ALLEN BRIGHTMAN,
daughter of Cornelius and Rachel Brightman, born 11 Oct. 1827,
probably in Westport, died in Westport 26 Dec. 1886.

       Children, born in LC:
    i.   Franklin J., b. in Westport 1849; m. in LC 26 Jan. 1870
           Amanda M. Cornell, daughter of Joshua and Angeline
           Cornell.
    ii.   George H., b. in Westport 30 April 1858; d. in LC 1 Sept.

1922; m. Alice Athington, b. in 1859, d. in 1931.

Children:
    i.   Mary Brightman, b. in 1880; d. in 1948; m.
          in LC 21 June 1908 Edwin Warren Greene
          of LC, son of Edwin and Sarah (Morse)
          Greene, b. in 1871, d. in 1942.
    ii.   (?) Sarah Alice, b. in 1882 in LC; m. in Tiverton
          18 Jan. 1903 Arthur Chester Almy, son
          of Frank and Ann (Westgate) Almy, b.
          in Tiverton in 1881.

    46. LORING A.[9] PALMER (Loring[8], Wilbor[7], John[6], John[5], John[4], William[3], William[2], William[1]), born in LC 19 Sept. 1844, died there 5 Feb. 1909, buried in Pleasant View cemetery. Residence: LC.
    He married HARRIET B. GRINNELL of Tiverton, daughter of Stephen and Abigail Grinnell, born 11 Sept. 1843, died in LC 27 March 1888.

    Children:
i.   Adelbert, b. 30 May 1870; d. in LC 6 April 1900 ae 29.

    47. DANIEL D.[9] PALMER (David[8], Wilbor[7], John[6], John[5], John[4], William[3], William[2], William[1]), born in LC 29 Sept. 1850. He was living there at the time the census was taken in 1880.
    He married first SARAH A. (--), born in 1855. He married second in LC 26 April 1913 MARY ELIZABETH BURNS, daughter of Lorenzo and Harriet (Wardwell) Burns, born in Andover, Mass., 7 Dec. 1858,.

    Children, born in LC:
i.   Annie, b. 26 Feb. 1872.
ii.   George, b. in 1874.
iii. Daniel Page, b. 19 Feb. 1875.
iv. Robert, b. in 1877.
v.   Flora, b. in 1879.

    48. JESSE LEESON[9] PALMER (Jesse[8], Wilbor[7], John[6], John[5], John[4], William[3], William[2], William[1]), born in LC 18 Oct. 1852, died there 17 March 1941.
    He married in LC 16 Oct. 1871 ARDELIA MARIA PERCY, daughter of Samuel (of England) and Eliza (Clarke) Percy, born in Fall River 9 Feb. 1855, died 1 April 1944. They are buried in New Bedford.
    They lived on Snell Road in the east part of town in a house owned by Isaiah Snell in 1850.

    Children, some recorded in LC and others in New Bedford:
i.   Franklin Henry, b. 12 May 1872 in LC; d. there 3 Sept. 1874.
ii.   Lillian Maria, b. in LC 10 Nov. 1877; m. George H. Wilcox.
iii. William Howland, b. in LC 26 Aug. 1879; d. young.
iv. Emma Elizabeth, b. in 1880; m. Wallace W. Allen.
v.   Grace Jessie, b. 1 April 1881 in LC; m. John Heuston.
vi. Cora Ardelia, b. in New Bedford 29 May 1885; m. Frank
       Main.
50. vii. Ephraim Church, b. 29 Oct. 1888.

viii. May Edna, b. 1 Nov. 1889 in New Bedford; m.Myron H.
        Bertram.
ix.   Ethel Vincent, b. 11 May 1892 in New Bedford; m. in LC
        15 Oct. 1914 LeRoy Howland Wordell, son of Gershom
        and Emma (Potter) Wordell.
x.   Ruth Sarah, b. 27 March 1895 in New Bedford; m. in LC 13
        Dec. 1919 Benjamin Robert Ratner, son of Louis and
        Celia (Benjamin) Ratner, b. in Cheslea, Mass., 13 Nov.
        1896.
xi.   Jesse Leeson Jr., b. in New Bedford 13 Oct. 1897.

49. VALENTINE[9] PALMER (Samuel[8], Wilbor[7], John[6], John[5],
John[4], William[3], William[2], William[1]), born in LC 7 Oct. 1868, died
there 11 April 1939. He married there 25 Dec. 1892 LUCRETIA F.
GRIFFIN, daughter of Joseph and Eliza Griffin, born in 1866 in
Portland, Maine.

        Children, born in LC:
i.   Mabel S., m. Thomas (--).
ii.   Douglas J., b. 22 May 1895.
iii.   Valentine Samuel, b. 23 June 1896.
iv.   Ada Frances, b. 29/30 Nov. 1898.
v.   Annie Marion, b. 19 Dec. 1900 or 9 June 1900.
vi.   Eudora Lydia, b. 19 Nov. 1901.
vii.   Violet Hathaway, b. 19 March 1903 (?).
viii. Herbert Theodore, b. 20 July 1904.

50. EPHRAIM CHURCH [10] PALMER (Jesse[9], Jesse[8], Wilbor[7],
John[6], John[5], John[4], William[3], William[2], William[1]), born in New Bedford
29 Oct. 1888, died in LC 23 July 1943.
    He married first in LC 2 Sept. 1917 ANNA PEARL COREY, daughter
of Arthur F. and Bertha (Chace) Corey, born in LC 22 Aug. 1899, died
there 16 May 1927. He married second in LC 12 July 1931 MARY
FRANCES CASE, daughter of Henry F. and Annie (Fraits) Case, born
in LC 5 Oct. 1909.
    Residence: LC. They lived on Snell Road at the place owned by
Isaiah Snell in 1850.

        Children, born in LC:
i.   Church Corey, b. 20 March 1918; m. Alice Reynolds.
ii.   Anna Virginia, b. 21 May 1919; m. 14 Oct. 1939 in LC
        Abraham Stout Quick, son of Joseph and Susan W. (Gibbs)
        Quick, b. in LC 3 July 1915.
iii.   Barbara Winona, b. 24 May 1921; m. Waldemar Gydesen.
iv.   Hope Priscilla, b. 12 Aug. 1922; m. in LC 14 Sept. 1940 LeRoy
        Eugene Durkee, son of LeRoy and Elsie (Crosby) Durkee,
        b. in Nova Scotia 9 March 1919.
v.   Lydia, b. 2 April 1925.
vi.   Leeson Forest, b. 9 March 1926.

        Children by second wife:
vii.   Claudia Joan, b. 17 Jan. 1935.
viii. William Henry, b. 17 Oct. 1940.
ix.   Robert David (twin), b. 17 Oct. 1940.

THE PALMER BAKERY, LITTLE COMPTON, R. I.

. . . .

1. PHEBE[1] PALMER.

Children, recorded in LC:
2. i.   Job, b. 14 Jan. 1756.
   ii.   Ruth, b. 24 Feb. 1763.
   iii. Mary, b. 19 Oct. 1769; m. in LC 16 June 1785 David Fish,
         son of Isaac Fish of Portsmouth.

2. JOB[2] PALMER (Phebe[1]), born in LC 14 Jan. 1756. He was
married in LC 19 Aug. 1784 by Jonathan Ellis to LYDIA GRINNELL,
daughter of Stephen Grinnell. Residence: LC.

Children, recorded in LC:
i.   Phebe, b. 15 April 1785.
ii.   Sarah Palmer, b. 27 Nov. 1786; d. in LC 20 Sept. 1855; m.
       (1) 1 June 1806 in LC William Briggs; m. (2) in LC 9 April
       1822 Caleb Church, son of William and Parnell (Southworth)
       Church, b. 5 July 1759, d. 30 Sept. 1825.
iii.   Deborah, b. 8 Feb. 1788 (?).
iv.   Demageus, b. 26 Feb. 1789.
v.   Stephen, b. 1 May 1791.
vi.   Lydia, b. 7 Dec. 1796; m. Joseph Church. He m. (2) 30
       Sept. 1844 Lindall Simmons.

. . . .

Another Palmer record: BETSEY PALMER, a son Isaac, born in
LC 3 Jan. 1752.

BENJAMIN PALMER, born in 1802, died 9 Dec. 1849 ae 47. Residence: LC.

He married CLARINDA WILBOR, daughter of Isaac and Lydia (Stoddard) Wilbor, born in 1810, died in LC 29 April 1884. They are buried in the Old Commons cemetery. She married second John Ward, born in England, keeper of the poor farm in 1865.

Children, not recorded in LC:

i. Thomas W., b. in 1833; d. 15 Dec. 1849 ae 16.
ii. Alfred G., b. in September 1838; d. 21 April 1839 ae 8 months.
iii. Emma C., b. 19 Feb. 1842; d. 22 March 1911 in New Bedford; m. Alfred R. Buckley.

THE PEARCE FAMILY

1. RICHARD[1] PEARCE, born near Waltham Abbey, Essex County, England, died in Portsmouth, R.I., in 1678.

He married in Waltham Abbey 5 May 1642 SUSANNAH WRIGHT, daughter of John and Mary (Dell) Wright, baptized 5 Aug. 1627 in Waltham Abbey, died in Portsmouth, R.I., in 1678.

For further information on the Pearce and Wright families in England, see an article by Benjamin F. Wilbour in the New England Genealogical and Historical Register, volume 84, page 427.

In his will, made 22 April 1677 and proved 28 Oct. 1678 in Portsmouth, he left to his son Richard his dwelling house and land, one pair of oxen with a cart and wheels, etc. To his six sons and four daughters, he left one shilling each.

Children, given in Austin's Rhode Island Dictionary:

i. Martha, b. 13 Sept. 1645; d. 24 Feb. 1744; m. Mahershallahasbaz Dyer.
ii. John, b. 8 Sept. 1647; d. 5 Dec. 1707; m. Mary Tallman, daughter of Peter and Ann Tallman.
iii. Richard, b. 3 Oct. 1649; m. Experience (--).
iv. Giles, b. 23 July 1651; d. 19 Nov. 1698; m. Elizabeth Hall, daughter of William and Mary Hall.
v. Susannah, b. 20 Nov. 1652; d. 24 Dec. 1743; m. 4 Dec. 1673 George Brownell.
vi. Mary, b. 6 May 1654; d. 4 May 1736; m. in 1678 Thomas Brownell.
vii. Jeremiah, b. 17 Nov. 1656.
viii. James, b. 6 Dec. 1658.
ix. (?), b. 7 July 1661.
2. x. George, b. 10 July 1662.
xi. William, b. 22 Dec. 1664.

2. GEORGE[2] PEARCE (Richard[1]), born in Portsmouth 10 July 1662, died in LC in September 1752.

He married first in LC 7 April 1687 ALICE HART of Portsmouth, daughter of Richard and Hannah Hart, born in 1669, died in LC 11 March 1718. He married second in LC 22 March 1721 TEMPERANCE KIRBY, daughter of Richard and Patience (Gifford) Hart, born 5 May 1670, died 5 Feb. 1761 in LC.

His will, recorded in Taunton and proved 3 Oct. 1752: ". . . To wife Temperance 100 pounds and all household goods. To son James 30 pounds. To son George Pearce 1/2 my . . . 30 acre lot bounded southerly on Moses Butts. To grandson George Thurston 72 pounds. To daughter Mary Simmons 60 pounds. To three children James, George and Mary, rest and residue. . . I confirm deeds of gift to sons James and George Pearce. . . "

Children by first wife, recorded in LC with the exception of Samuel:

    i.   Susannah, b. 21 Aug. 1688; d. 5 Aug. 1711; m. in LC 19 Dec. 1706 Edward Thurston.

3. ii.   James, b. 4 Sept. 1691.

    iii. Samuel, b. 3 Feb. 1695; d. 29 Jan. 1705.

4. iv. George, b. 2 March 1697.

    v.   Mary, b. 16 May 1700; d. 3 Jan. 1755; m. in LC 3 Dec. 1721 William Simmons.

3. JAMES[3] PEARCE (George[2], Richard[1]), born in LC 4 Sept. 1691, died there 24 Sept. 1755. Residence: LC.

He married first in LC 5 March 1712 MARTHA WILBORE, daughter of Samuel and Mary (Palmer) Wilbore, born in LC 22 Oct. 1690, died there 2 Sept. 1760.

His will, recorded in Taunton, made 1 Feb. 1755 and proved 7 Oct. 1755: ". . . To wife Martha 100 pounds old tenor, my Negro woman named Ann and all household goods and use of the best room in my dwelling house. To son William all land I bought of Samuel Crandall, John Church, William Wilbor, son of Joseph, east of Cole Brook, where he now lives, and the housing. To son Giles land I bought of Thomas Gray and Edward Gray among the 24 acre lots in LC and part of 24 acre lot I bought of William Wilbor lying west of Cole Brook and part of the 20th lot among the 24 acre lot called Ward Lot and 700 pounds. To daughter Susannah bed and furniture. To daughters Martha Tompkins, Mary Woodman and Alice Luther 50 pounds apiece. . . To daughter Phebe one bed and 120 pounds. . . "

Children, recorded in LC:

5. i.   William, b. 19 Jan. 1713.

    ii.   Susanna, b. 24 May 1714 (?); d. unmarried.

    iii. Martha, b. 14 Aug. 1717; m. 20 March 1741 in LC Joseph Tompkins.

6. iv. James, b. 24 Sept. 1719.

7. v.   Giles, b. 23 March 1722.

    vi. Mary, b. 17 Oct. 1724; m. in LC 23 March 1749 William Woodman.

8. vii. George, b. 12 Sept. 1727.

    viii. Alice, b. 7 June 1730; m. in LC 1 Jan. 1749 Jabez Luther.

     ix.   Phebe, b. 21 Sept. 1731; d. 20 Sept. 1755; unmarried.
9. x.   Samuel, b. 29 Jan. 1734.

    4. GEORGE³ PEARCE (George², Richard¹), born in LC 2 March
1697, died there 22 Feb. 1764. Residence: LC.
    He was married in LC 20 Feb. 1717 by Richard Billings, justice,
to DEBORAH SEARLE, daughter of Nathaniel and Sarah (Rogers)
Searle, born in LC 17 Nov. 1695, died there 16 May 1776.
    His will, made 23 Nov. 1763 and proved 6 March 1764: ". . . To
wife Deborah one hundred pounds of old tenor bills, and my Negro
woman Phillis. To son Jeptha Pearce, one half of 15 acre lot, the 5th
in number in the westerly tier of lots. To son Nathaniel Pearce all
my homestead farm that I now live on, also my Negro man and my
Negro woman named Cate, said Nathaniel to be the executor of my
will. To son Richard one half of a 30 acre lot, the 32nd in number,
he to have the south side of said lot and all right I have in a 24 acre
lot. To daughters Alice Dwelly, Temperance Seabury, Sarah Sawyer,
Ruth Horswell, Antrace Tabor, Deborah Pearce, 100 pounds apiece
in bills of public credit. . . "
    Her will, made 8 Oct. 1770 and proved 4 June 1776: ". . . To son
Jepthah Pearce. . . To son Nathaniel my iron trammell. To son Richard
my desk. To daughter Alice Dwelly the bed and furniture that belonged
to my honored mother. To daughter Sarah Sawyer my great looking
glass. To daughter Ruth Horswell. . . To daughter Deborah Manchester
my tea kettle and teaspoons. To my six daughters my wearing apparel.
To four daughters Sarah, Ruth, Deborah and Alice my gold beads and
rest and residue. My Negro woman named Phillis is to be free of all
my children and any other person at my decease. . . "

               Children, recorded in LC:
     i.   Alice, b. 4 Nov. 1718; d. 28 March 1796; m. (--) Dwelly.
     ii.   Sarah, b. 11 Nov. 1720; d. 20 July 1721.
10. iii.   Jepthah, b. 20 Feb. 1722.
     iv.   Temperance, b. 20 Jan. 1724; d. 16 March 1793; m. (1) 9
               Oct. 1745 Thomas Gibbs; m. (2) Ichabod Seabury.
     v.   Jeremiah, b. 22 Dec. 1725; d. in London, England, 13 Oct.
               1750.
11. vi.   Nathaniel, b. 13 Oct. 1727.
     vii. Sarah, b. 14 Jan. 1729; d. 28 Aug. 1780; m. in Tiverton in
               1746 Josiah Sawyer Jr.
     viii. Ruth, b. 20 Oct. 1731; m. in LC 24 Oct. 1750 John Horswell Jr.
     ix.   Antrace, b. 12 Nov. 1733; m. in Tiverton 24 June 1753 Thomas
               Tabor Jr.
     x.   Deborah, b. 23 Feb. 1735; d. 25 April 1795; m. Christopher
               Manchester.
     xi.   Richard, b. 19 April 1736; d. in Tiverton 15 March 1817.

    5. WILLIAM⁴ PEARCE (James³, George², Richard¹), born in LC
19 Jan. 1713, died leaving no will. Residence: LC.
    He married first in LC 2 Nov. 1735 ELIZABETH WOODMAN,
daughter of John and Elizabeth (Briggs) Woodman of LC, born there
10 Sept. 1713. He married second ANNA (--).

Children by first wife, recorded in LC:
  i.   John, b. 30 Jan. 1736.
12. ii.   James, b. 9 Oct. 1740.
13. iii. Richard, b. 26 May 1744.
  iv.   Elizabeth, b. 14 Sept. 1749; d. young.

Children by second wife:
  v.   Peter, b. 10 Nov. 1752.
  vi.   Elizabeth, b. 23 Aug. 1755.
  vii. Thomas, b. 5 April 1758.
  viii. Susannah, b. 2 Aug. 1759.
  ix.   John, b. 3 Aug. 1760.

6. JAMES[4] PEARCE (James[3], George[2], Richard[1]), born in LC 24 July 1719, died there 14 Sept. 1767, leaving no will. Residence: LC.

He married 14 Sept. 1749 SARAH SIMMONS, daughter of John and Comfort (Shaw) Simmons, born in LC 26 Jan. 1730, died there 24 Dec. 1785. Her will, made 2 June 1756 and proved 7 Oct. 1760: ". . . To son William my Bible. To son James my square table. . . to son Giles my new iron cittle. To son George hand iron and trammell. To son Samuel my case of bottles. To daughter Susannah my Negro woman and child. To daughter Martha my chest of drawers. To daughter Mary the cullerd chest with drawer in it. To daughter Alice Luther my white chest without a drawer. To daughter Susanna all my money. . ."

Children, recorded in LC except Job, Ezekiel and Simeon:
14. i.   Wright, b. 26 July 1750.
15. ii.   Stephen, b. 20 Dec. 1753.
16. iii. John, b. 24 Aug. 1755.
  iv.   Job, b. 30 Sept. 1758; d. 26 Oct. 1782.
17. v.   Ezekiel, b. 27 March 1760.
  vi.   Ezra, b. 21 March 1761; d. young.
18. vii. Ichabod, b. 24 Nov. 1762.
  viii. Simeon, b. 27 Jan. 1764.

7. GILES[4] PEARCE (James[3], George[2], Richard[1]), born in LC 23 March 1722, died there in July 1792. Residence: LC.

He married there 23 Aug. 1744 MERCY ROUSE, daughter of George and Elizabeth (Horswell) Rouse, born 13 Jan. 1727.

His will, made 14 July 1792 and proved 7 Aug. 1793: ". . . To wife Mercy all household goods, improvement of my great room in my dwelling house and bedroom adjoining as long as she is my widow. . . To my sons Rouse and James all my land, buildings that I have in this world. To wife Mercy 100 pounds of good beef. . . Two silver dollars apiece to daughter Hannah Taylor, to grandchildren, daughter of daughter Martha Church, to daughter Sarah Seabury, to daughter Rachel Pearce, to daughter Abigail Gifford, to daughter Rebecca Seabury. One silver dollar apiece to daughter Mary Tabor and to granddaughter Edith Brownell. To daughter Lydia Bowen 12 dollars. To daughter Rachel the privilege of living in my new house as long as she is single. To son Rouse my wearing apparel. To son James my loom. . ."

Children, recorded in LC:
i.   Hannah, b. 18 Oct. 1745; m. 1 Dec. 1771 Peter Taylor, son
      of John and Joanna (Wilbor) Taylor.
ii.   Martha, b. 18 Jan. 1747; m. in 1766 Caleb Church.
iii. Sarah, b. 22 April 1748; m. Philip Seabury.
iv.   Rachel, b. 14 April 1750; m. Josiah Seabury.
v.   Elizabeth, b. 19 Oct. 1751; m. 14 Feb. 1771 William
      Brownell, son of Stephen and Edith (Wilbor) Brownell.
19. vi.   Rouse, b. 4 July 1753.
20. vii. James, b. 15 Aug. 1755.
viii. Mercy, b. 11 Dec. 1757; m. Job Taber.
ix.   Lydia, b. 29 July 1760; m. 25 July 1779 William Bowen, son
      of Nathaniel and Esther Bowen.
x.   Abigail, b. 3 March 1763; m. 30 Oct. 1791 Isaac Gifford,
      son of Enos and Mary (Wilbor) Gifford.
xi.   Rebecca, b. 13 May 1766; m. Peleg Seabury.

8. GEORGE⁴ PEARCE (James³, George², Richard¹), born in LC 12
Sept. 1727, died there in November 1780. Residence: LC.
He married first 25 Oct. 1750 DEBORAH WOODMAN, daughter of
John and Elizabeth (Briggs) Woodman, born in LC 21 Oct. 1726, died
there 30 March 1760. He married second 4 Feb. 1762 PRISCILLA
WOODMAN, daughter of Robert and Deborah (Paddock) Woodman,
born in LC 1 July 1721, died there 6 May 1791.

Children, recorded in LC:
i.   Jeremiah, b. 26 Oct. 1751; d. 25 Dec. 1751.
ii.   Isaac, b. 28 Aug. 1756; d. 3 Nov. 1756.
iii. Deborah, b. 26 June 1758; d. 26 Feb. 1759.

9. SAMUEL⁴ PEARCE (James³, George², Richard¹), born in LC
29 Jan. 1734. Residence: LC. He married there 12 Nov. 1755 BETTY
SIMMONS, daughter of Joseph and Rebecca (Wood) Simmons, born in
LC 8 March 1733.
According to the Pearce book by F. C. Pearce, published in 1888:
After living in LC he moved to Warren, R.I., where he ever afterwards
lived. He was a master mechanic, contractor and builder. Several of
the larger buildings in Warren which he built are standing to this day.
Among that number is the Baptist Church.

Children, the first four recorded in LC:
i.   Phebe, b. 18 Sept. 1756.
ii.   Priscilla, b. 1 Feb. 1758.
iii. Jeremiah, b. 17 March 1760; m. Nancy Brown.
iv.   Joseph, b. 18 Dec. 1761.
v.   Samuel, b. 19 March 1764; m. Ruth Martin.
vi.   James, b. 10 Dec. 1765.
vii. John, b. 16 Feb. 1768; m. Patience Arnold.
viii. Mary, b. 2 March 1775; d. 13 Nov. 1798.
ix.   Abigail, b. 10 June 1776.

10. JEPTHA⁴ PEARCE (George³, George², Richard¹), born in
LC 20 Feb. 1722, died there in November 1770. Residence: LC.

He married in LC 23 Nov. 1749 ELIZABETH (ELIZA) ROUSE, daughter of George and Hannah (Horswell) Rouse, born 23 Feb. 1724.

Children, recorded in LC:
i.   Elizabeth, b. 22 April 1751; d. 22 June 1753.
ii.   Ruth, b. 7 April 1753.
iii.   Elizabeth, b. 17 Oct. 1756; d. 15 July 1849.
iv.   Jeremiah, b. 15 Jan. 1758.
21. v.   Isaac, b. 15 Nov. 1759.
vi.   Deborah, b. in 1760; d. 22 Jan. 1778.
vii.   Hannah, b. 22 Oct. 1761.

11. NATHANIEL[4] PEARCE (George[3], George[2], Richard[1]), born in LC 13 Oct. 1727, died there 19 Feb. 1801. Residence: LC.

He married 1 Dec. 1751 SARAH ROUSE, daughter of George and Hannah (Horswell) Rouse, born in LC 14 Jan. 1728, died there 23 Nov. 1812.

His will, made 7 June 1800 and proved 4 March 1801: ". . . To wife Sarah all household goods and improvement of great room, bedroom and the use of the cellar, one cow. . . To son John the westerly end of my homestead farm. . . To son Joseph the easterly end of homestead with all the buildings . . . To daughters Phebe Tompkins, widow, Mary Briggs, wife of Arnold Briggs, and Betsey Seabury, wife of Gideon Seabury, 20 silver dollars each. To granddaughter Sarah Pearce, daughter of son George, deceased, 10 silver dollars. To son Joseph my cider mill. My sons John and Joseph Pearce to be executors. . ."

Her will, made 10 Jan. 1811 and proved 2 Dec. 1812: ". . . To son John 4 dollars. To son Joseph 1 silver dollar. To daughter Mary Briggs, wife of Arnold Briggs, 1 silver dollar. To daughter Bettey Seabury, wife of Gideon Seabury, that half of my pew in the Little Comptom meeting house. To daughter Sarah Pearce, wife of Ezekiel Pearce, my gold necklace. To grandson Nathaniel Tompkins 1 silver dollar. To granddaughter Sarah Brown, daughter of George Pearce, deceased, 1 silver dollar. To granddaughter Salome Saxon, daughter of Ezekiel Pearce, one silver spoon. . ."

Children, recorded in LC:
i.   Valentine, b. 14 Feb. 1751; d. at sea in 1775.
ii.   Phebe, b. 21 March 1752; m. 16 Jan. 1774 Nathaniel Tompkins.
iii.   Mary, b. 20 April 1754; m. about 1776 Arnold Briggs.
iv.   Bettey, b. 14 Nov. 1756; d. 25 April 1889 (?); m. Gideon Seabury.
v.   John, b. 26 April 1758; d. 13 Nov. 1827; m. 1 July 1784 Deborah Hix, daughter of Joseph and Elizabeth Hix.
vi.   George, b. 26 April 1758; d. at sea in 1779; m. 8 Oct. 1780 Margaret Simmons, daughter of Aaron and Abigail Simmons.
vii.   Nathaniel, b. 17 Dec. 1761; d. at sea in 1779.
viii.   Sarah, b. in 1762; m. 13 April 1786 Ezekiel Pearce.
22. ix.   Col. Joseph, b. 26 Jan. 1764.

12. CAPT. JAMES[5] PEARCE (William[4], James[3], George[2], Richard[1]), born in LC 9 Oct. 1740, died there 2 March 1821. Residence: LC.

He married 14 July 1762 DEBORAH HUNT, daughter of William and Elizabeth (Dring) Hunt, born in LC 6 May 1739. He is buried in the Old Commons cemetery.

His will, recorded in LC, made 8 Nov. 1820 and proved 9 July 1821: ". . . To son Samuel one dollar. To son William my plow and harrow. To son John all carpenter tools. To son Loring my two handled saw. To daughter Elizabeth Hilliard my largest pewter platter marked T.H.R. To daughter Sarah Wilbor, wife of Owen Wilbor. . . To daughter Abigail Hammond, wife of Christopher Hammond, my two hitchells. To wife Deborah all real and personal estate not given away and she to be sole executrix. . . "

Children, recorded in LC:
i. Samuel, b. 13 Feb. 1763; d. in New Bedford 21 Nov. 1827.
ii. Elizabeth, b. 1 July 1764; m. 19 March 1786 Samuel Hilliard.
23. iii. William, b. 7 June 1766.
iv. Sarah, b. 12 Nov. 1768; m. 30 Jan. 1791 Owen Wilbor.
v. Loring, b. 19 March 1774.
24. vi. John, b. 24 Aug. 1775.
vii. Abigail, b. 3 May 1778; m. Humphrey Hammond.

13. RICHARD[5] PEARCE (William[4], James[3], George[2], Richard[1]), born in LC 26 May 1744, died there 15 March 1718. He married MARY ELLIS, daughter of Jonathan and Patience (Blackwell) Ellis, born in LC 27 April 1744. Residence: LC.

Children, recorded in LC:
i. James, b. 2 Jan. 1778.

14. WRIGHT[5] PEARCE (James[4], James[3], George[2], Richard[1]), born in LC 26 July 1750, died there 8 April 1829. Residence: LC.

He married in 1771 ANTRACE SAWYER, daughter of Josiah and Sarah Sawyer of LC, born in LC 30 Oct. 1751, died there 12 Oct. 1835. They are buried in the Pearce cemetery north of the stone school house, way in from the road, on the west of the Long Highway.

His will, made 16 Nov. 1819 and proved 11 May 1829: ". . . To wife Antrace use of great room and chamber above, little northeast bedroom in my dwelling house, household goods, my clock and my young sorrel mare. To son Godfrey all lands I deeded to him with the buildings, Tripp lot of wood of 8 acres, and he to be executor with son Abraham. To son Thomas 800 dollars. To son Timothy 25 dollars. To son Abraham all that farm with buildings I bought of the Rev. Mase Shepard and my Irish wood lot. To daughter Sarah Pearce, wife of Capt. Benjamin Pearce, house and land where she now lives that I bought of Fortune Gray and 6 acres I formerly deeded to son Abraham. To granddaughter Sophia Pearce, daughter of my daughter Sarah Pearce, bed and bedding, in northeast corner of great chamber. To my wife 1/2 of the pew in the Congregational Church or meeting house. To grandsons Abner, George and Frederick Pearce my wearing apparel. Rest and residue of estate to sons Godfrey and Abraham. . . "

Her will, made 17 April 1832 and proved 8 Nov. 1835: ". . . To son Godfrey my corner cupboard, brass clock. . . To son Timothy one great silver spoon and two dollars. . . To son Thomas one great spoon.

To respected daughter Sarah Pearce all wearing apparel, brass kettle, large iron pot, all my pewter, great Bible. . . and after her to her daughter Sarah. To son Abraham one great Silver spoon, blue chest, fire shovel and one half flag bottomed chairs. . . To grandson James Pearce, son of my son Godfrey, one great silver spoon. To grand-daughter Antrace Pearce, daughter of Godfrey Pearce, my bed where-on I now lie, one pair of sheets . . . To granddaughter Hannah, daugh-ter of Timothy Pearce, one great silver spoon. To granddaughter Betsey Pearce, daughter of son Timothy, two dollars. To grand-daughter Sophia Pearce, daughter of Benjamin Pearce my narrow bed and largest looking glass. . . To granddaughter Phebe Pearce, daughter of Benjamin Pearce, one bed lying under that I gave to Sophia, filled with coarse feathers. To granddaughter Sarah Pearce, daughter of Benjamin Pearce. . . To granddaughter Louisa Pearce, daughter of Thomas Pearce, one great wheel. To granddaughter Antrace Pearce, daughter of Timothy, three tea spoons. To daughter-in-law Sarah Pearce, wife of Godfrey, my black silk gown. To sons and daughter of Godfrey Pearce, use of bed pan, flax hatchel, wool combs and the same to be kept at my son Godfrey's. . . "

Children, all recorded in LC except Priscilla:

25. i.   Godfrey, b. 3 Oct. 1772.
    ii.   Priscilla, b. 28 Sept. 1776; d. 25 Sept. 1778 in LC.
    iii.   Sarah Antrace, b. 29 April 1778; d. 31 Jan. 1866; m. 19 Aug. 1810 Benjamin Pearce.
    iv.   Timothy, b. 17 July 1779; m. (1) in LC 14 Sept. 1805 Hannah Dennis; m. (2) (--) Wilbor.
26. v.   Thomas, b. 6 Sept. 1784.
    vi.   Priscilla, b. 23 July 1790; d. 17 Sept. 1790.
    vii.   Abraham, b. 12 April 1792; d. 6 Sept. 1862; m. Ruth Bailey.

15. STEPHEN[5] PEARCE (James[4], James[3], George[2], Richard[1]), born in LC 20 Dec. 1753; died in Paris, Oneida County, N. Y., 14 May 1843. Residence: LC.

He married in LC 18 Feb. 1776 ABIGAIL TAYLOR, daughter of Gideon and Mary (Brownell) Taylor, born in LC 12 Nov. 1758, died in Paris, N. Y., 28 Oct. 1856.

From the Pearce book: In 1776 he entered the Revolutionary Army as ensign in the second company of infantry from Little Compton, and was soon after promoted to first lieutenant; he served during the war and at its close he retired from the service with the rank of captain in the second company of the second battalion, Newport County troops. In 1791, with his wife and four children, he removed from LC to Paris Hill, Oneida County, N. Y., where he became a pioneer settler in a wild region. He lived to see that area populous and prosperous. He served also in the War of 1812, notwithstanding his age.

Children, first five recorded in LC:

    i.   James, b. 7 Nov. 1776.
    ii.   George Taylor, b. 31 Aug. 1779; d. 25 Aug. 1848; m. Mercy Simmons.
    iii.   Lucy Simmons, b. 29 Aug. 1782; d. 15 Aug. 1867; m. 8 Nov. 1800 Simeon Walker.

iv.   Deborah Taylor, b. 6 July 1785; d. 30 Dec. 1864; m. 15 Feb.
        1808 Reuben Tower.

v.   Mary Taylor, b. 16 Dec. 1790; d. 2 Jan. 1849; m. 22 June
        1808 Eleazer Tompkins.

vi.   Andrew, b. 16 June 1793; d. 22 June 1840; m. Harriet S.
        Hale.

vii.   Emma, b. 8 April 1796; d. 22 Feb. 1878; m. 26 June 1815
        Zeriah F. Rowell.

viii.   Nancy, b. 30 Sept. 1798; d. 25 May 1854; m. Joseph Grinnell.

ix.   James, b. 30 Nov. 1803; m. Lucy Barnes; m. (2) Joanna Polley.

16. JOHN[5] PEARCE (James[4], James[3], George[2], Richard[1]), born
in LC 24 Aug. 1755, died in 1793.

He was married in LC by the Rev. Jonathan Ellis 11 Feb. 1776 to
LYDIA PALMER, daughter of Simeon and Elizabeth (Mortimer) Palmer
of LC, born 23 Sept. 1756.

Children, recorded in LC:
i.   Elizabeth, b. 25 Nov. 1776.
ii.   Walter, b. 9 March 1779.
iii.   Benjamin, b. 12 May 1781; m. Esther Hazard.
iv.   Sarah, b. 22 Nov. 1783; m. (--) Tompkins.

17. EZEKIEL[5] PEARCE (James[4], James[3], George[2], Richard[1]),
born in LC 27 March 1760, died there 10 May 1838. Residence: LC.

He married in LC 13 April 1786 SARAH PEARCE, daughter of
Nathaniel and Sarah (Rouse) Pearce, born in LC 4 Feb. 1766, died
there 24 July 1848.

Children, the first three recorded in LC:
i.   Salome, b. 11 May 1787; d. 7 Feb. 1867; m. 17 Jan. 1804
        James Sexton.
ii.   Val, b. 28 Jan. 1791; m. (1) 4 Feb. 1815 Mercy Simmons;
        m. (2) in July 1820 Catharine Boss; m. (3) 26 Sept. 1846
        Antrace Pearce, b. 3 May 1804, d. 16 April 1890.
iii.   Joshua, b. 20 Oct. 1792; d. 7 April 1816.
iv.   Mary, b. 11 Oct. 1796; d. 15 Jan. 1866; m. 9 June 1825
        George Brownell.
v.   Nathaniel, b. 12 April 1800; m. 26 Jan. 1825 Clarissa
        Simmons.
vi.   George B., b. 12 April 1800; d. 10 July 1890; m. 1 Nov.
        1821 Sally Simmons.
vii.   Ezekiel, b. 1 Nov. 1805; m. 14 Oct. 1829 Phebe Simmons.

18. ICHABOD[5] PEARCE (James[4], James[3], George[2], Richard[1]),
born in LC 24 March 1762, died there 11 Dec. 1844.

He married in LC 3 Dec. 1789 LUCY SIMMONS, daughter of John
and Hannah (Brightman) Simmons, born in LC 29 May 1771, died
there 26 Nov. 1859. Both are buried in the Pearce cemetery north
of the stone school house and west of the Long Highway.

Children, the first three recorded in LC:
i.   Jonathan, b. 31 March 1790.
ii.   Pardon S., b. 3 Dec. 1792; m. E. Allen.

iii.   Clarinda, b. 23 March 1795; d. 12 June 1864; m. 12 March
       1823 William Bartlett Wilbor, son of Jonathan and
       Priscilla (Wilbor)Wilbor.
iv.   Cinderella, m. 22 Jan. 1826 Elisha Brownell, son of Isaac
       and Betsey (Wood) Brownell.
v.   Cynthia, b. in 1804; d. 20 Oct. 1852 ae 48.

19. ROUSE[5] PEARCE (Giles[4], James[3], George[2], Richard[1]),
born in LC 4 July 1753, died there 24 Dec. 1831. Residence: LC.
He married there 19 Dec. 1776 MARY BROWNELL, daughter
of Stephen and Edith (Wilbor) Brownell, born in LC 5 July 1754,
died there 16 April 1851. Both are buried in the Pearce cemetery
near the stone school house.

       Children, recorded in LC:
i.   Giles, b. 2 Feb. 1778; m. Sarah Champlin.
ii.   Stephen, b. 5 July 1780; m. 19 Jan. 1803 Nancy Crandall.
iii. George R., b. 21 March 1782; m. 17 Jan. 1802 Lucy Graves.
27. iv. Benjamin, b. 19 May 1784.
28. v.   Cornelius, b. 27 April 1787.
29. vi. Ellery, b. 25 July 1789.
30. vii. Bradford, b. 25 Dec. 1791.
viii. Sally, b. 27 Oct. 1793; m. (1) Abraham Willcox; m. (2)
       William Proctor.
ix.   Mary, b. 25 May 1796; m. Samuel Corey, son of William
       Corey.

20. JAMES[5] PEARCE (Giles[4], James[3], George[2], Richard[1]), born
in LC 15 Aug. 1755, died there 22 July 1820. Residence: LC.
He married in LC 3 July 1783 PHEBE WOOD, daughter of George
and Desire (Gray) Wood, born in LC 9 March 1763, died there 25 June
1842.

       Children, recorded in Tiverton:
i.   Deborah, b. 26 Jan. 1786; m. (--) Dennison.
ii.   Sally, b. 28 Dec. 1787; m. (--) Jaynes.
iii. John, b. 8 Feb. 1790.
iv.   Susannah, b. 17 March 1792; m. (--) Tripp.
v.   Giles, b. 1 April 1794; m. Content Hall.
vi.   George W., b. 11 July 1797.
vii. Desire, b. 1 April 1800.
viii. Lydia, m. (--) Dodge.
ix.   Abel, b. 7 Feb. 1805; m. Sarah Herring.
x.   Phebe, b. 13 Oct. 1807; m. 14 Sept. 1833 Amos A. Hale.

21. ISAAC[5] PEARCE (Jeptha[4], George[3], George[2], Richard[1]),
born in LC 15 Nov. 1759, died there 22 May 1805. Residence: LC.
He married 1 Aug. 1784 in LC SUSANNAH STODDARD, daughter
of Nathaniel and Emlin (Wilbore) Stoddard, born in LC 9 March 1760,
died there 31 March 1825. They are buried in the Old Commons
cemetery.
They lived on Snell Road in the house once owned by Elliott Snell
(1918). This was the home of a Windmill, later moved to the Wilbour

cemetery on West Road, now a part of the Herbert Taylor house.

Children, recorded in LC:
i.   Deborah, b. 1 April 1785; m. 17 June 1804 Thomas Sanford.
31. ii. Nathaniel, b. 30 June 1787.
iii. Elizabeth, b. 27 Nov. 1789; d. 20 March 1867; m. 23 Aug.
     1818 John Crosby, d. 28 April 1852.
iv. Hannah, b. 19 Dec. 1790; d. 1 Nov. 1824; m. 5 Dec. 1819
     George Wilbor.
v.   Walter Wilbor, b. 14 May 1792; d. 7 Nov. 1811.
vi. Lydia, b. 22 Dec. 1794; d. 15 March 1862; m. 5 Dec. 1819
     Abel Simmons.
32. vii. Jonathan D., b. 15 April 1801.

22. COL. JOSEPH[5] PEARCE (Nathaniel[4], George[3], George[2],
Richard[1]), born in LC 26 Jan. 1764, died there 6 Aug. 1836. Residence:
LC.
He was married first about 1789 by the Rev. Mase Sheppard to
ANNA HILLIARD of LC, daughter of David and Ann Mercy (Irish)
Hilliard, born in LC 18 Aug. 1769, died there 27 June 1816. He was
married second by the Rev. Mase Shepard 16 Nov. 1817 to PRISCILLA
PALMER, daughter of Joseph and Hannah (Briggs) Palmer of LC, born
there 6 Nov. 1781, died there 27 Feb. 1823.

Children, recorded in LC:
i.   Phebe, b. 14 June 1792; d. in May 1812.
ii. Benjamin, b. 3 Dec. 1796; d. 2 Oct. 1822.
33. iii. Val, b. 14 Oct. 1799.
iv. Nancy, b. 16 May 1802; d. 28 July 1856; m. 12 Oct. 1822
     James Pearce, b. 6 July 1802.
34. v.   Joseph, b. 4 Nov. 1804.
vi. Nathaniel, b. 23 April 1807; m. (?); d. at sea.
vii. Ann Mercy, b. 23 April 1807; d. 5 April 1860; m. Thomas
     Records.

Children by second wife:
viii. Phebe, b. 6 June 1820; d. 30 April 1880; m. 10 Feb. 1841
     Josiah S. Pearce, b. 22 April 1818, d. 16 Nov. 1869.
ix. Priscilla, b. 13 Feb. 1823; d. 5 Feb. 1887; m. George
     Hubbard.

23. WILLIAM[6] PEARCE (James[5], William[4], James[3], George[2],
Richard[1]), born in LC 7 June 1766, died there 15 May 1846. Residence: LC.
He married 8 Aug. 1790 in LC ELEANOR PEARCE, daughter
of Jeremiah Pearce of Portsmouth, born in LC 5 Jan. 1769, died
there 22 Jan. 1834.
He served in the Revolutionary War and became a corporal.

Children, recorded in LC:
i.   Jonathan, b. 28 May 1791; d. 7 June 1814.
ii. Henry Lawton, b. 30 April 1793; d. 13 June 1861; m.
     Haity T. Pearce.
iii. Parker Hall, b. 11 Dec. 1794; d. 25 June 1874; m. Hannah

Withington.
iv. Harriet, b. 14 June 1799; d. 7 Sept. 1861; m. Harvey
  Brownell, son of James and Hannah (Manchester)
  Brownell.
v. Benjamin Franklin, b. 2 July 1801; m. 10 Dec. 1822
  Rowena Hills.
vi. Cyrus.
vii. Cyrus E., b. 24 Feb. 1809; d. in 1864. Residence: Chile,
  South America.

24. JOHN[6] PEARCE (James[5], William[4], James[3], George[2],
Richard[1]), born in LC 24 Aug. 1775, died in 1835. He married in
LC 7 Feb. 1793 ANNA TAYLOR, daughter of Robert and Abigail
(Jamison) Taylor, born in LC 22 Nov. 1778. His will, made 1 May
1835 and proved in LC 8 Oct. 1849: ". . . To daughter-in-law Mary
Ann Pearce, wife of son Robert, one turn up bedstead, cord and
bed under. To grandson William Taylor, my wooden clock. To four
granddaughters, Abigail Taylor, Prudence Wilbor, Eliza Ann Pearce
and Maria Wilbor, one dollar each. My carpenter tools and carpenter
shop to sold by my executor. To son Robert the rest and residue. . . "

  Children, recorded in LC:
i. Abigail, b. 15 Dec. 1793; m. 1 Feb. 1818 Mase Taylor, son
  of Jonathan and Martha (Briggs) Taylor, b. 13 March
  1793.
ii. Robert T., b. 14 Oct. 1796; d. in LC 7 April 1873.
iii. Prudence, b. 30 April 1798; d. in 1878; m. 26 Dec. 1822
  Hervey Wilbour, son of Daniel and Deborah (Taylor)
  Wilbour.
iv. Eliza Ann, b. 13 Dec. 1807; d. 5 May 1854; unmarried.
  See her will below.
v. Maria, b. 20 Jan. 1811; d. 13 June 1851; m. 1 April 1832
  Daniel Wilbor, son of Daniel and Deborah (Taylor)
  Wilbor.

The will of Eliza Ann Pearce, made 16 May 1850 and proved 10
July 1854: ". . . To sister Prudence Wilbur one bed. To nephew
William Taylor my best bed and my largest trunk. To nephew Daniel
Wilbur my best chest and second sized trunk. To sisters Abby Taylor,
Prudence Wilbur and Maria Wilbur my bedding. The rest and residue
to sister Prudence Wilbur. . . "

25. GODFREY[6] PEARCE (Wright[5], James[4], James[3], George[2],
Richard[1]), born in LC 3 Oct. 1772, died there 13 July 1849. Residence:
LC.
He was married 1 Sept. 1799 by the Rev. Mase Shepard in LC to
SARAH SIMMONS, daughter of George and Lucy (Davis) Simmons,
born in LC 21 Dec. 1775, died 2 April 1856. Both are buried in the
Pearce cemetery near the stone school house in LC.
His will, made 5 Feb. 1848 and proved 10 Sept. 1849: ". . . To
wife Sarah that use of one half of dwelling house, either end and all
household furniture. To son James all lands lying in LC and Tiverton
with buildings, also my desk. To son George, property at Station

Island and my silver watch. To daughter Antrace Pearce, wife of
Val Pearce, 500 dollars. To granddaughter Harriet Pearce, daughter
of James Pearce, 160 dollars. Rest and residue to son James
Pearce. . . "

Children, recorded in LC:
35. i.   James, b. 6 July 1802.
    ii.   Antrace, b. 3 May 1804; d. 16 April 1890; m. 26 Sept. 1846
           Val Pearce.
    iii.   George S., b. 14 March 1809; d. 2 April 1892; m. (1) 1 May
           1830 Harriet Barney; m. (2) 12 July 1846 Susannah F.
           Gore; m. (3) Mary L. Gordridge.

26. THOMAS[6] PEARCE (Wright[5], James[4], James[3], George[2],
Richard[1]), born in LC 6 Sept. 1784, died there 24 July 1847. Residence:
LC.

He was married 26 Feb. 1811 in LC by the Rev. Mase Shepard to
ELIPHAL TOMPKINS, daughter of John and Comfort (Seabury)
Tompkins, born in LC 15 March 1790, died 1 Feb. 1868. Both are
buried in the Old Commons cemetery.

His will, made 6 April 1841 and proved 8 Nov. 1847: ". . . To
wife use of real and personal estate excepting what is given in the
following and all furniture. But if she remains not my widow then
one third of real estate. To sons John and George Pearce my wearing
apparel. To daughter Maria Pearce one bed that is now in the east
room. Unto my children all estate both real and personal at the
decease of my wife. . . "

Children, recorded in LC:
    i.   Abner T., b. 4 Oct. 1811; m. Sarah R. Briggs.
    ii.   Frederic, b. 30 March 1813; m. 11 Nov. 1839.
    iii.   Louisa, b. 22 Oct. 1815; m. Barber (--).
36. iv.   Josiah, b. 22 April 1818.
    v.   Franklin, b. 19 June 1820; m. Elizabeth Najac.
    vi.   John T., b. 25 Aug. 1824; d. 24 July 1843.
    vii.   George T., b. 28 July 1826. Residence: San Francisco.
    viii. Maria, b. 24 Aug. 1828; m. 24 Sept. 1848 David Grinnell.

27. BENJAMIN[6] PEARCE (Rouse[5], Giles[4], James[3], George[2],
Richard[1]), born in LC 19 May 1784, died there 10 Aug. 1869.

He was married 19 Aug. 1810 in LC by the Rev. Mase Shepard
to SARAH A. PEARCE, daughter of Wright and Antrace (Sawyer)
Pearce, born in LC 29 April 1788, died there 7 Jan. 1766. They
are buried in the Pearce cemetery near the stone school house.

Residence: LC. In 1850 they lived on Willow Avenue next to
Abel Simmons, and, according to the census of 1865, they were
living at that time in district no. 5.

Her will, made 13 Aug. 1863 and proved 12 March 1866: "Sarah
Pearce, wife of Benjamin Pearce of LC of advanced age. . . To husband
Benjamin Pearce use of all real and personal estate. To sons Wright
and James P. Pearce five dollars each. To three daughters Sophia
Hilliard, Phebe Pearce and Sarah Snell, all wearing apparel. To
children Wright, Benjamin Jr. and Sarah Snell one large silver spoon

each. To daughter Sophia Hilliard my earrings and finger ring. To daughter Sarah Snell my gold necklace and great iron kettle. To granddaughter Emma Corilla Pearce, one bed and six small teaspoons. To granddaughter Estella Pearce one bed and six silver teaspoons. To grandson Albert C. G. Pearce my clock, picture of T. W. Dorr and the family register. To son Rouse Pearce my best looking glass and picture of General Washington. To sons Benjamin Jr. and Rouse, the rest and residue of my estate and they to be executors. . . "

Children, recorded in LC:
- i. Sophia, b. 14 Aug. 1811; m. (--) Hilliard.
- ii. Phebe, b. 22 May 1813; d. 13 Feb. 1910 in LC; m. Joseph Pearce.
- iii. Benjamin, b. 18 Nov. 1815; d. 4 Dec. 1815; unmarried.
- 37. iv. Wright, b. 9 Feb. 1818.
- v. James Peckham, b. 4 May 1819; m. (1) Lucy Blake, b. in 1822, d. 1 Jan. 1866; m. (2) Margaret Palmer.
- vi. Sarah, b. 3 Nov. 1820; m. 6 Dec. 1841 George W. Snell.
- 38. vii. Benjamin, b. 9 Nov. 1822.
- viii. Mary, b. 20 Aug. 1824; d. 3 Oct. 1824; unmarried.
- 39. ix. Rouse, b. 4 June 1826.
- x. Harriet S., b. in 1830.

28. CORNELIUS[6] PEARCE (Rouse[5], Giles[4], James[3], George[2], Richard[1]), born in LC 27 April 1787. Residence: LC.

He married 16 Dec. 1810 PRISCILLA BROWNELL, daughter of George and Elizabeth (Peckham) Brownell, born in LC 22 Oct. 1788.

Children, recorded in LC:
- i. Eveline, b. 24 June 1810.
- ii. George Rouse, b. 13 Nov. 1812.

29. ELLERY[6] PEARCE (Rouse[5], Giles[4], James[3], George[2], Richard[1]), born in LC 25 July 1789. He married in Tiverton 18 July 1815 HOPE NEGUS, daughter of Stephen Negus. Residence: LC.

Children, recorded in LC:
- i. Stephen Durfee, b. 20 Dec. 1815.
- ii. Eliza Brownell, b. 31 July 1817.

30. BRADFORD[6] PEARCE (Rouse[5], Giles[4], James[3], George[2], Richard[1]), born in LC 25 Dec. 1791, died there 28 June 1869. Residence: LC.

He married 22 Jan. 1818 FANNY TOMPKINS, daughter of Uriah and Mary (Taylor) Tompkins, born 18 Jan. 1796.

In his will, made 18 June 1868 and proved 14 June 1869, he left to his daughter Lydia Oliver all household furniture, to grandson H. Oliver and to Charles H. Mitchell, 100 dollars apiece, and to son Charles the rest and residue.

Children, recorded in LC:
- i. Mary Taylor, b. 16 March 1819.
- ii. Frances Bradford, b. 10 March 1820; m. 12 Nov. 1843 Albert

Manchester, son of Thomas and Cynthia Manchester.
iii.   Ann, b. 5 April 1822.
iv.   Lydia Mariah, b. 13 Feb. 1824.
v.   William Bradford, b. 26 April 1826.
vi.   Abby, b. 19 April 1828.
vii.   Harriet K., b. 30 Aug. 1830.
viii.   Henry H., b. 15 Jan. 1833.
40. ix.   Charles, b. 3 Nov. 1835.

31. NATHANIEL⁶ PEARCE (Isaac⁵, Jeptha⁴, George³, George²,
Richard¹), born in LC 30 June 1787, died there 28 March 1868, leaving
no will. Residence: LC. He married in LC 2 Nov. 1809 SUSANNAH
SIMMONS, daughter of Peleg and Eliphal (Sanford) Simmons, born in
LC 2 Nov. 1788, died 12 Oct. 1845.

Children, recorded in LC:
i.   Fallee S., b. 26 Nov. 1810; d. 9 March 1856.
ii.   Mary S., b. 16 Feb. 1813; d. 28 Dec. 1828.
iii.   Edwin, b. 17 Jan. 1815; m. in LC 6 April 1884 Susan L.
          Simmons, daughter of Taber and Betsey (Wardell) Simmons,
          born in Westport.
iv.   Benjamin C., b. 5 Oct. 1819; d. 10 May 1830.
v.   Ann M., b. 19 June 1821; m. 14 May 1879 the Rev. James
          Burlingame.
vi.   William S., b. 25 June 1824; m. Amelia McDonald.
vii.   Nathaniel S., b. 13 May 1828; d. 22 June 1830.

32. JONATHAN D.⁶ PEARCE (Isaac⁵, Jeptha⁴, George³, George²,
Richard¹), born in LC 15 April 1801, died there 3 Aug. 1866.
He married in LC 16 Feb. 1823 HANNAH PHILLIPS HEAD, daughter
of Daniel and Hannah (Davenport) Head, born in LC 4 April 1803, died
there 3 Dec. 1879. They are buried in the New Wilbour cemetery on West
Road, or the Seaconnet cemetery.
He was a blacksmith. They lived on the road at the east of the
Commons, which touches Peckham Road at the north, and lived on the
old John Peckham farm.

Children, recorded in LC:
i.   Miranda, b. 22 Feb. 1824; d. 17 Nov. 1905; unmarried.
ii.   George W., b. 12 Feb. 1826; d. 7 Oct. 1851; m. in LC 21 Jan.
          1850 Harriet Atwell White, daughter of David and Patience
          (Brown) White.
iii.   Hannah, b. 8 March 1828; m. 15 Jan. 1849 Chester Gifford.
iv.   Frederick Horatio, b. 29 Nov. 1830; d. 4 Nov. 1899; unmarried.
v.   Mary D., b. 2 Oct. 1832; m. (1) 17 Oct. 1857 Asath P. Tabor;
          m. (2) 25 March 1865 Benjamin C. Borden.
41. vi.   Abel H., b. 29 June 1834.
vii.   Julie, b. 2 Aug. 1837; m. (1) 28 Sept. 1858 Aaron Bradford; m.
          (2) 8 Nov. 1880 Joshua Cole.
42. viii.   Jonathan, b. 6 Dec. 1839.
ix.   Susan E., b. 20 Nov. 1841; m. 20 April 1869 Wiley M. Huykendall.
          Residence: Texas.
x.   Isaac B., b. 20 Nov. 1841; d. 4 Aug. 1846.

33. VAL⁶ PEARCE (Joseph⁵, Nathaniel⁴, George³, George², Richard¹), born in LC 14 Oct. 1799, died there 21 Dec. 1852.

He was married in LC 26 Dec. 1821 by Thomas Burgess, justice, to ELIZABETH (ELIZA) WOODMAN, daughter of William and Priscilla (Brownell) Woodman, born in LC 13 Sept. 1800, died 9 March 1870. Both are buried in the Union cemetery.

Residence: LC. They lived on the Long Highway. Their son Oliver was a soldier in the Civil War, serving as a private in company B, 4th Massachusetts cavalry, enlisted 14 Sept. 1863 in New Bedford, discharged 31 May 1865.

      Children, recorded in LC:
43. i.   Benjamin Seabury, b. 30 Aug. 1826.
    ii.   Nathaniel Woodman, b. 28 Aug. 1830; d. in May 1832.
    iii. George Warren, b. 7 July 1833; d. 14 Jan. 1853 ae 19.
    iv. Oliver Val, b. 3 May 1839; d. 13 July 1866.

34. JOSEPH⁶ PEARCE (Joseph⁵, Nathaniel⁴, George³, George², Richard¹), born in LC 4 Nov. 1804, died 4 July 1874. He married 29 Feb. 1832 PHEBE PEARCE, daughter of Benjamin and Sarah (Pearce) Pearce, born in LC 22 May 1813, died there 13 Feb. 1910. Both are buried in the Union cemetery.

      Children, possibly born in Tiverton, last two recorded in LC, all listed in the 1865 census:
    i.   Henry, b. 11 Jan. 1834; m. in LC 16 Aug. 1866 Catharine C. Chester, daughter of James and Arcksie (?) Chester.
    ii.   Emerson Paine, b. 24 April 1836; d. 21 March 1919; m. 3 May 1863 Kate McLeod, b. 29 Dec. 1840. Residence: Providence.
    iii. David H., b. 6 May 1838; m. 20 Nov. 1873 Lillian E. Rice, b. in June 1850. Residence: Providence.
    iv. Alfred G., b. 20 Dec. 1840; m. 3 Oct. 1870 Julia A. White, b. 11 May 1849.
    v.   Joseph B., b. 28 Aug. 1843; d. 30 Aug. 1908 in Providence; m. 15 Dec. 1864 Cynthia R. Wilbour, daughter of William and Clarinda Wilbour, d. in LC 15 June 1888. Residence: Adamsville.
    vi. Ellery A., b. 18 July 1846; m. Leah Freeborn.
44. vii. James Nelson, b. 5 Nov. 1849.
    viii. George W., b. 21 Nov. 1853; m. 3 Dec. 1885 Ida D. William, b. 4 Sept. 1856.
    ix. Nancy Anna, b. in LC 6 May 1865; d. 20 Sept. 1938; m. 7 March 1889 Charles Richmond Wilbur.

35. JAMES⁷ PEARCE (Godfrey⁶, Wright⁵, James⁴, James³, George², Richard¹), born in LC 16 May 1802, died there 3 Nov. 1896. Residence: LC.

He married in LC 12 Dec. 1822 NANCY PEARCE, daughter of Col. Joseph and Anna Pearce, born in LC 16 May 1802, died there 28 July 1856. Both are buried in the Old Commons cemetery.

      Children:

i.   Harriet A., b. 13 Dec. 1832; m. 1 July 1862 Horatio W.
      Richmond, son of Isaac and Abigail Richmond.
      Residence: Fairhaven.
ii.   Sarah Ann, d. 14 Nov. 1845 ae 14.

36. JOSIAH S.[7] PEARCE (Thomas[6], Wright[5], James[4], James[3],
George[2], Richard[1]), born in LC 22 April 1818, died there 16 Nov. 1867.
Residence: LC. He was married 10 Feb. 1841 by the Rev. Alfred
Goldsmith in LC to PHEBE PEARCE, daughter of Col. Joseph and
Priscilla (Palmer) Pearce, born in LC 6 June 1820, died there 30
April 1880. Both are buried in the Old Commons cemetery.

      Children:
i.   Sarah A., b. 3 Nov. 1846; m. 1 June 1886 William S. Liscomb.
      Residence: Providence.
ii.   Nancy James, b. 13 Feb. 1849; d. in LC 28 March 1918; m.
      in LC 11 June 1872 Asa R. Howland, b. 19 Aug. 1845.
iii. John T., b. 17 Oct. 1851; d. 25 Jan. 1911.
iv.   Isabel M., b. 29 May 1854; d. 19 May 1899; m. (1) Clarence
      O. Gray; m. (2) 28 Feb. 1886 George E. Cobb.

37. WRIGHT[7] PEARCE (Benjamin[6], Rouse[5], Giles[4], James[3],
George[2], Richard[1]), born 9 Feb. 1818, died in LC 1 Dec. 1883.
      He married 25 Aug. 1844 JULIA A. FRANCIS, daughter of Cook
and Hannah Francis, born in November 1823 in LC, died there 4 Sept.
1900. Both are buried at the Adamsville School House.
Residence: LC. In 1850 they lived on the Miranda Pierce Road.

      Children, not recorded in LC:
i.   James F., b. 5 Dec. 1845; drowned in Vineland 24 May 1864
      ae 19.
ii.   Edwin W., b. 23 June 1847; d. 18 Feb. 1863 ae 5.
iii. Caroline A., b. in 1848.
iv.   Wright, b. in 1849 (?).
v.   Charles H., b. 16 April 1849; d. 7 Oct. 1883.
vi.   George R., b. in May 1852.
vii. Orlando G., b. 31 May 1855; d. in 1914; m. Susan F. Lake,
      b. in 1855, d. in 1941.
viii. Son, b. 24 June 1857.
ix.   Amanda M., b. 26 June 1860; d. 13 Feb. 1863 ae 3.
x.   Amanda M., b. 19 May 1866; d. 12 June 1907 ae 39.
xi.   James Edmund, b. 27 March 1867.

38. BENJAMIN[7] PEARCE JR. (Benjamin[6], Rouse[5], Giles[4], James[3],
George[2], Richard[1]), born in LC 9 Nov. 1822, died there 22 Feb. 1901.
      He was married in LC 25 March 1850 by the Rev. Elihu Grant to
HARRIET S. MANCHESTER of Tiverton, daughter of Gardner and
Betsey (Hambley) Manchester, born 9 Feb. 1833, died in LC in 1904.
They are buried in Pleasant View cemetery near Adamsville.
      In the census of 1865, they were listed as living in LC district no.
8, on Nigger Lane, the road east of the Commons.
      Children:

i.   Albert Gardner, b. in 1851; d. 13 May 1911 in Warwick, R.I.
ii.   Gardner M., b. in April 1854; d. 24 Dec. 1856 ae 2.
iii.   Betsey J., d. 13 Nov. 1856 ae 3 months.
iv.   Edward W., b. 12 April 1859; d. in LC 17 July 1938; m. 7
       March 1899 in LC Ella S. Hambley, daughter of William
       and Sarah Ann (Carr) Hambley, d. 14 Aug. 1945 ae 87 in
       Cranston.
v.   Harriet B., b. 26 Nov. 1870; d. 12 Dec. 1873.
vi.   Henry G., b. 21 Feb. 1874 in LC; m. 22 Oct. 1903 in Fall
       River Catharine Hardy. They had a daughter, Gladys,
       b. 21 July 1918 in Fall River, m. 23 Nov. 1943 in New
       York City Kenneth Sutcliffe, d. 4 April 1945 in Fall River.

39. ROUSE[7] PEARCE (Benjamin[6], Rouse[5], Giles[4], James[3], George[2],
Richard[1]), born in LC 18 June 1826, died 5 May 1915, buried in the
Pearce cemetery.
He was married first in the stone church by James McKenzie 25
Nov. 1849 to COMFORT MARIA GRINNELL of Tiverton, born in 1832,
died in LC 19 Oct. 1862. She is buried in the Pearce cemetery north
of the stone school house. He married second 2 Jan. 1865 DEBORAH
BOWER, born 22 Aug. 1839.

       Children:
i.   Anne, b. in 1852; d. 29 Nov. 1853 ae 1.
ii.   Franklin A., b. 22 April 1851; d. 27 Jan. 1857.
iii.   Estella, b. 27 June 1858; d. 27 Aug. 1884; m. 2 June 1878
       Charles Richmond Wilbur, b. 3 Oct. 1838.

40. CHARLES[7] PEARCE (Bradford[6], Rouse[5], Giles[4], James[3],
George[2], Richard[1]), born in LC 3 Nov. 1835, died 30 Dec. 1914.
He married DIANNA A. BRIGGS, daughter of Charles and Ann (Man-
chester) Briggs, born in 1848, died in LC 8 Aug. 1896.

       Children, not recorded in LC:
i.   Frank Borden, b. in LC 27 May 1867; d. 25 Nov. 1948; m.
       9 April 1890 Louise F. Dobbs, daughter of Charles Dobbs
       of Providence.
ii.   Fannie Holmes, b. 15 July 1870 in LC; m. 21 Feb. 1900 Henry
       Athington, son of William and Mary (Hargrave) Athington,
       born in England in 1854.
iii.   Charles Lyman, b. 20 May 1874; d. 20 Dec. 1945 at Cranston.
iv.   George W., b. in 1876.

41. ABEL[7] PEARCE (Jonathan[6], Isaac[5], Jeptha[4], George[3], George[2],
Richard[1]), born in LC 29 June 1834. He married first 27 Sept. 1865
FANNY LACY, born 5 Feb. 1839, died in December 1870. He married
second in October 1875 HARRIET JAMES. He became a Texas rancher,
well known as "Shanghai" Pierce of Pierce Station, Texas.

       Children:
i.   Mamie F., b. 19 July 1867.

42. JONATHAN[7] PEARCE (Jonathan[6], Isaac[5], Jeptha[4], George[3],

George[2], Richard[1]), born in LC 6 Dec. 1839. He married 2 May 1866
NANNIE LACY, born 11 Aug. 1845. Residence: Dennings Bridge,
Metagoda County, Texas, where he owned a very large tract of land.
Children:
i.   Jonathan P., b. 5 Nov. 1868.
ii.   Pearl, b. 26 Dec. 1873.
iii.   Abel, b. 4 Dec. 1875.
iv.   Grace, b. 1 Sept. 1879.

    43. BENJAMIN SEABURY[7] PEARCE (Val[6], Joseph[5], Nathaniel[4],
George[3], George[2], Richard[1]), born in LC 30 Aug. 1826, died there 7
Aug. 1899. He married in LC 27 Nov. 1851 PHEBE A. BRAYTON,
daughter of Preserved and Nancy Brayton of Tiverton, born there 12
Feb. 1831/3, died in LC 1 April 1905. They are buried in Pleasant
View cemetery.
        Children, all recorded in LC:
46. i.   Annie Benjamin, b. 5 Oct. 1864.
    ii.   Philander Records, b. in LC 10 Aug. 1866.
47. iii.   Herbert Warren, b. 7 Sept. 1870.

    44. JAMES NELSON[7] PEARCE (Joseph[6], Joseph[5], Nathaniel[4],
George[3], George[2], Richard[1]), born in LC 5 Nov. 1849. Residence:
LC. He married there 13 April 1899 ISABELLA McARTHUR of
Providence, daughter of John and Isabella (Campbell) McArthur of
Nova Scotia, born in 1864.
        Children:
i.   James Nelson Jr.

    45. JAMES EDMUND[8] PEARCE (Wright[7], Benjamin[6], Rouse[5],
Giles[4], James[3], George[2], Richard[1]), born in LC 27 March 1867, died
there 27 April 1941, buried in Pleasant View cemetery.
    He married first in LC 13 Nov. 1894 LYDIA ESTHER SOULE,
daughter of John and Mary (Wilbur) Soule, born in LC 10 Aug. 1871,
died there 23 March 1933, buried at Pleasant View. He married
second in LC 29 Oct. 1933 ABBIE ELIZABETH GODFREY SOULE,
daughter of Zoeth and Julia M. (Dyer) Soule, born in East Greenwich,
R.I., 11 June 1870, died in LC 10 March 1943.

    46. ANNIE BENJAMIN[8] PEARCE (Benjamin[7], Val[6], Joseph[5],
Nathaniel[4], George[3], George[2], Richard[1]), born in LC 5 Oct. 1864.
        Children:
i.   Stewart Fuller, b. 25 July 1885; d. in 1943; m. in LC 9 Nov.
       1910 Hellen Richards Simmons, daughter of David and
       Grace (Grinnell) Simmons, b. in 1886 in Tiverton, d. in
       1946.
ii.   Eliza Woodman, b. 31 Aug. 1889; m. in LC 12 Dec. 1907
       Abel Wilbur Jennings, b. in 1886, son of Samuel and
       Nancy (Wilbor) Jennings.

    47. HERBERT WARREN[8] PEARCE (Benjamin[7], Val[6], Joseph[5],

Nathaniel[4], George[3], George[2], Richard[1]), born in LC 7 Sept. 1870, died 27 Aug. 1933. He married SOPHIA M. HILLIARD, daughter of David and Ellen LeRoy (Thayer) Hilliard. Residence: LC. They lived on Maple Avenue where his father lived in 1890.

Children:
i. Edith Gertrude, b. 10 Nov. 1901; m. 28 June 1930 Otho Edmund Wordell, son of Gershom and Emma (Potter) Wordell.

. . . .

1. ELIJAH[1] PEARCE, born in Freetown, Mass., in 1787, died 15 June 1877. Residence: LC. He married first SARAH (--). He was married second in LC by the Rev. Alfred Goldsmith 17 May 1842 to DESIRE GRINNELL, daughter of Billings and Comfort Grinnell, born in LC 1 Oct. 1788, died there 8 Oct. 1866. They are buried in back of the school house at Adamsville.

Children, not recorded in LC:
i.   Andrew, b. in 1825.
2. ii.   Luther P., b. 24 Jan. 1626.
iii. William, b. in Fall River in 1828; m. in LC 27 Nov. 1850 Mary A. Hunt, daughter of Dennis and Mary Hunt, b. in

2. LUTHER P.[2] PEARCE (Elijah[1]), born in Fall River 4 Jan. 1826, died in LC 7 Aug. 1867. Residence: LC.
He married 19 Jan. 1851 in LC JANE T. IRISH, daughter of John and Lydia (Grinnell) Irish, born in LC 30 May 1831, died in Westport 18 April 1920. Both are buried in the cemetery back of the Adamsville school.
A soldier in the Civil War, he was in Company D, 12th Regiment, Rhode Island volunteers, enlisted 11 Sept. 1862, discharged 29 July 1863 at Providence.

Children, all recorded in LC:
i.   John Elijah, b. 4 July 1853.
ii.   Luther Winfield, b. 9 Dec. 1857.
iii. Emma Lincoln, b. 3 June 1861.
iv.   Edward Sheridan, b. 1 Jan. 1867.
v.   Frank Andrew, b. 1 Jan. 1867; d. 20 May 1868.

JOHN FRANKLIN PIERCE, son of John and Sarah (Hathaway) Pierce, born in Freetown, Mass., 18 Aug. 1856, died in LC 15 March 1926. Residence: LC.
He married in LC 10 Nov. 1880 ROSETTA MARIA WILBOR, daughter of Jonathan[6] (Jonathan[5], William[4], William[3], Samuel[2], William[1]) and Rosetta Crowell (Young) Wilbor, born 29 Jan. 1853 in LC, died there 12 Sept. 1937. They are buried in Hillside cemetery.

Children, born in LC and recorded there:
i.   Emma Wilbor, b. 30 Jan. 1882.
ii.   Mabel, b. 26 April 1890; d. 27 April 1890.
iii. John Franklin, b. 13 Feb. 1892; m. Madeline Field, daughter of Samuel and Elizabeth (Mosher) Field.

Other Pearce births of which there are records in LC:
Benjamin, son of Hannah Pearce, born 13 April 1763, died 27 Aug. 1778.
Sarah, daughter of George and Margaret Pearce, born 29 May 1781.
John W., son of Robert T. and Mary Ann Pearce, born 17 July 1829.
Rebecca, daughter of Rachel Pearce, born 26 April 1788.

࿊

THE PECKHAM FAMILY

1. JOHN[1] PECKHAM, residence: Newport. He married first
MARY CLARKE, the sister of John Clarke. He married second ELEANOR
(--).

According to Stephen Farnam Peckham in his Genealogy: "John
Peckham no doubt came to Boston with Sir Henry Vane in 1634 and he
probably met there Mary Clarke who accompained her brother John
Clarke to Boston at about the same time. The acquaintance resulted
in marriage of which no record can be found. He probably was one of
the party called the Ann Hutchinson party, who founded a settlement on
the north end of Rhode Island, which became the town of Portsmouth.
In 1640 the bounds of his land were established."

On 20 May 1638 his name appeared on a list as one of those
admitted as an inhabitant of Portsmouth. He became a freeman in 1641.
In 1648 his second wife Eleanor was baptized.

His residence was in that part of Newport which is now Middletown,
and a stone marked J. P. is supposed to mark his grave.

Children by his first wife:
- i.   Mary, m. Tobias Saunders.
- 2. ii.   John.
- 3. iii.   William.
- 4. iv.   Thomas.
- v.   James, d. 26 Feb. 1711; unmarried. On 21 March 1712 the inventory of his estate in LC was taken by Mr. Peckham of Newport and Capt. Thomas Gray of LC, when power was granted William and Philip Peckham and John Taylor to sell real estate of deceased.
- vi.   Rebecca, m. John Spooner.
- vii.   Stephen, m. Mary (--).
- viii.   Clement, m. Lydia (--).
- ix.   Deborah, m. Robert Taylor, son of Robert and Mary (Hodges) Taylor.
- x.   Phebe, b. in 1666; d. in 1746; m. Thomas Gray, son of Edward and Dorothy (Lettice) Gray of Plymouth.
- xi.   Elizabeth, d. 24 May 1714; m. Peter Taylor, son of Robert and Mary (Hodges) Taylor.
- xii.   Sarah, m. William Weeden.

2. JOHN[2] PECKHAM (John[1]), married in 1667 SARAH NEWPORT.
Residence: Newport. It has been said that he lived in LC, but the

-486-

records do not support this.

Children, born in Newport:
- i.   Elizabeth, b. 17 Sept. 1668; m. James Weeden.
- 5. ii.   John, b. 9 June 1671.
- iii.   Mary, b. 30 Sept. 1674; m. (1) (--) Kenyon.
- iv.   Reuben, b. 3 Feb. 1676.
- v.   Peleg, b. 11 Dec. 1677; d. in 1715; m. Ann Holmes.
- vi.   Joseph, b. 8 March 1679; m. (1) in 1705 in Newport Mary Evans, daughter of Richard and Patience Evans; m. (2) Wait Gould.
- vii.   Sarah, b. 5 Sept. 1680; d. young.
- viii.   Timothy, b. 5 Aug. 1681; d. 5 Aug. (?); m. (1) Rachel Weaver; m. (2) Content Drake.
- ix.   Benjamin, b. 9 June 1684; m. 23 Sept. 1708 Mary Carr.
- x.   Isaac, b. 11 April 1688; m. (1) 8 Nov. 1711 Rebecca Phillips; m. (2) in 1727 Jane Sisson.

3. REV. WILLIAM[2] PECKHAM (John[1]), born about 1647, died in Middletown 2 June 1734. Residence: Newport.

He married first SUSANNA or ELIZABETH CLARKE, daughter of Joseph Clarke. He married second PHEBE WEEDEN, daughter of William Weeden, died in 1745.

He was the fourth minister of the Baptist church in Swansea.

Children, probably by first wife:
- 6. i.   William, b. 30 Aug. 1675.
- 7. ii.   Samuel.
- iii.   Mary, m. (1) Thomas Barker; m. (2) (--).
- iv.   Phebe, m. (1) (--) Tripp; m. (2) William Weeden.
- v.   Deborah, m. (1) (--); m. (2) Jeremiah Clarke.

4. THOMAS[2] PECKHAM (John[1]), died in 1709. He married first (--). He married second HANNAH (WEEDEN) CLARKE, daughter of William Weeden, died after 1722. Residence: Newport.

In his will, dated 16 Nov. 1708 and proved in 1709, he left to his son Thomas one shilling, he having had his share previously; his son Daniel 30 pounds; his daughter Sarah Underhood 5 pounds; his son James his dwelling house and land; to his wife Hannah all his cash and 3 pounds yearly and the use of his house and land given to son James.

Children by first wife:
- i.   Thomas.
- 8. ii.   Philip.
- iii.   Sarah.

Children by second wife:
- iv.   Daniel.
- v.   James.

5. JOHN[3] PECKHAM (John[2], John[1]), born in Newport 19 June 1671, died in LC in 1722. Residence: LC. He married 6 June 1696 MARY BENNETT, daughter of Joseph and Margaret Bennett of Newport, born

in 1671, died in 1756 ae 85.

In 1714 he sold the land that had been willed to his minor son, Joseph, by Joseph Bennett. In 1712 he signed in the administration of the estate of his uncle, James. He lived on the acres inherited from his father. For many years he was elected deputy to the legislature from LC. After 1703 he was not returned. Family tradition says that he and his wife are buried in the Peckham burial ground on the old farm in LC, but he was a Quaker, and according to the Friends record: "John Packom of Seconnet aged, he departed this lif at his own house in Seconnet, the 4 day of ye 10 month 1722 and was bureyed in Friends bureying place neare the meeting house in Seconnet."

His will, recorded in LC wills, book 4, page 159, made 1 Dec. 1722 and proved 7 Jan. 1722/3: "To wife Mary Peckham four cows and the use of the west chamber in the west end of my dwelling house. To son John 40 shillings. To son Joseph west end of dwelling house and all land west of the highway where I now live, bounded west by the highway, east by the highway, north by Ezek Carr and Mr. Richard Billings, and south by David Hilliard and highway. Part of land east of highway where I now live from the east end of stone wall by great swamp, north land of Richard Billings, south on Indian Bridge so called and south by highway. To son Reuben Peckham remainder of lands east of highway by my house and meadow land, the eighteenth and nineteenth lots at Barker's Neck. To three children, Lydia, Margaret and Ruth, 20 pounds each."

> Children, all recorded in LC with the exception of Reuben and Ruth:

9. i.   John, b. 27 July 1696.
    ii.   Lydia, b. 8 May 1698; d. 28 June 1778; m. 12 Feb. 1728 John James, son of William and Susan (Martin) James.
10. iii. Joseph, b. 18 Feb. 1701/2.
    iv. Mary, b. 3 Oct. 1704; d. young.
    v.   Margaret, b. 30 June 1707; m. 4 Feb. 1729 Benjamin Chandler.
    vi. Ruth, b. in 1710.
    vii. Reuben, b. in 1712; d. in 1736; m. Sarah (--).

6. WILLIAM³ PECKHAM (William², John¹), born in Newport 30 Aug. 1675, died there 18 Jan. 1764.

He married in Newport 10 June 1703 MARY TEW, daughter of Henry and Dorcas Tew of Middletown, born 10 Oct. 1680, died 3 May 1753.

He was a farmer in Middletown. He became a freeman of Newport in 1704. He is known to have been a member of the first Baptist Church of Newport in 1751.

> Children, born in Newport:

    i.   Mary, b. 7 Sept. 1704; d. 12 June 1728; m. 21 Jan. 1724 James Barker.
11. ii.   William, b. 3 Sept. 1706.
    iii. Dorcas, b. 3 July 1709; d. 17 March 1785; unmarried.
    iv. Henry, b. 26 Feb. 1711; m. 27 Sept. 1742 in Newport Hart Sewell.
    v.   Elisha, b. in Newport 8 May 1716; d. 17 July 1758; unmarried.

7. SAMUEL³ PECKHAM (William², John¹), died in 1757. Residence: Middletown.

He married first (--) CLARKE. He married second ELIZABETH
WEEDEN, daughter of James and Mary Weeden.

  Children, probably born in that part of Newport which is now
  Middletown:
 i. Phebe, b. 21 June 1715; m. in Newport 10 Oct. 1751 John
    McNear.
 ii. Elizabeth, b. 6 Feb. 1717.
 iii. Samuel, b. 7 Oct. 1719; m. Mary (--).
 iv. James, b. 13 Nov. 1721; m. 28 Jan. 1745/6 Sarah Greene.
 v. Mary, b. 13 April 1723; d. in 1811; unmarried.
 vi. Freelove, b. 30 Dec. 1725; m. 10 Dec. 1741 Jonathan Lawton.
12. vii. William 3d, b. about 1727.

  8. PHILIP[3] PECKHAM (Thomas[2], John[1]).

   Children:
13. i. Joshua, b. 20 July 1718.

  9. JOHN[4] PECKHAM (John[3], John[2], John[1]), born in LC 27 July
1696, died in LC 7 Jan. 1772. Residence: LC.
  He married in LC 24 Sept. 1723 MARY HART, daughter of
Richard and Hannah (Williams?) Hart, born in LC 16 Jan. 1697.
  He lived on the 30 of the Peckham acres bequeathed to him by his
father in LC, and appears to have spent his life there.

   Children, not recorded in LC:
 i. Joseph, d. 4 March 1726 ae 4 in Newport.
 ii. Ruth, m. 15 Aug. 1763 John Borden.
 iii. Reuben, b. 15 May 1741.
 iv. Lydia, m. in LC 12 Jan. 1755 Robert Crossman.
 v. Margaret, m. in LC (intention 22 Feb. 1746) John Briggs.

  10. JOSEPH[4] PECKHAM (John[3], John[2], John[1]), born in LC 18 Feb.
1701/2, died there 8 Oct. 1780. He lived on the Miranda Pierce place.
  He married first in LC 5 Nov. 1723 ELIZABETH WILBOR, daughter
of Samuel and Mary (Potter) Wilbor of LC, born in LC 23 Dec. 1702.
He married second 7 Dec. 1752 ANN (SLOCUM) GOULD, widow of Jacob
Gould and daughter of John and Barbara Slocum, born 15 Oct. 1711, died
15 Sept. 1763. She is buried in the Gould burial ground.
  His will, recorded in LC Probate, book 2, page 442, made 3 March
1775 and proved 7 Nov. 1780: "To wife Ann one bed, bedstead and
furniture, choice of any room in west end of my house to live in as long
as she remain my widow, my son John to find and provide for her. To
son John all real estate in this world that I possess except the west end
of house, farming tools, livestock and he to be sole executor. To
son Samuel one dollar. To daughters Mary Irish and Martha Brownell
eight shillings each. To daughters Sarah and Ruth Peckham 8 dollars
each. To three grandchildren, children of my daughter Elizabeth
Greenell, deceased, 8 shillings. To two grandchildren, children of
daughter Rhoda Mitchell, deceased, 8 shillings. To two daughters
Sarah and Ruth Peckham the privilege to live in the west end of my
house as long as unmarried."

Children, the first six recorded in LC:

i. Mary, b. 28 Nov. 1724; d. in 1799; m. in May 1764 John
    Irish, son of Jedediah.
ii. Elizabeth, b. 28 Aug. 1726; m. (1) 21 July 1746 Samuel
    Coe; m. (2) in LC 4 June 1748 Aaron Grinnell.
iii. Hannah, b. 13 Oct. 1728; m. (--) Lawton.
iv. Martha, b. 28 May 1730; m. in LC 17 March 1750 Joshua
    Browne 2d.
14. v. John, b. 30 Sept. 1733.
15. vi. Samuel, b. 20 Nov. 1735.
vii. Ruth, b. in 1737; d. in October 1815; m. about 1778 Thomas
    Brown, son of John and Sarah Brown.
viii. Sarah, b. in 1739.
ix. Rhoda, b. in 1741; m. 6 Nov. 1766 James Mitchell, son of
    James and Ann Mitchell.
x. Reuben, b. in 1743; d. in July 1770, perhaps at Poughkeepsie,
    N.Y.

11. WILLIAM⁴ PECKHAM (William³, William², John¹), born in
Newport 3 Sept. 1706, died in Middletown 12 April 1784. Residence:
Newport, probably in that part which later became Middletown.
    He married in Newport 22 Jan. 1736 PHEBE BARKER, daughter
of James and Mary (Cook) Barker, born 14 Nov. 1717, died 10 Nov.
1757.

Children:

i. William, b. 3 Feb. 1737; m. in Middletown 20 March 1760
    Lydia Rogers.
ii. Elisha, b. in 1738; m. in LC 12 Oct. 1769 Mary Smith, daughter
    of Thomas and Susanna Smith.
iii. Mary, b. in 1741.
iv. Phebe, b. in 1743; m. in Middletown 8 Nov. 1767 Elisha Barker.
16. v. Peleg.

12. WILLIAM⁴ PECKHAM (Samuel³, William², John¹), born about
1727, died in 1808.   Residence: Middletown. He lived on the farm
adjoining land owned by his cousin, William Peckham (known as
Mushquash William).
    He married in Middletown 5 Oct. 1758 SARAH PECKHAM, daughter
of Joshua and Ruth (Peckham) Peckham, born in Middletown 24 Oct.
1741.

Children:

i. Joshua, b. 18 June 1759; m. 8 March 1779 Rebecca Horswell.
ii. Augustus, b. 6 Jan. 1761; m. Esther Pratt.
17. iii. Felix, b. 21 July 1763.
iv. William, d. young.
v. William.
vi. Lydia, m. Pardon Sherman.
vii. Ruth, m. Christopher Barker.
18. viii. Gideon, b. 8 Nov. 1781.

13. JOSHUA⁴ PECKHAM (Philip³, Thomas², John¹), born 20 July

1718, died 31 Oct. 1741.   He married 29 Sept. 1739 RUTH[4] PECKHAM
(Isaac[3], John[2], John[1]),

Children:
i.   Sarah, b. 24 Oct. 1741; m. William[4] Peckham (Samuel[3],
       William[2], John[1]).

14. JOHN[5] PECKHAM (Joseph[4], John[3], John[2], John[1]), born in LC
30 Sept. 1733, died there 25 May 1812. Residence: LC.

He married 12 March 1757 MARY WOOD, daughter of John and
Mary (Burgess) Wood of LC, born in LC 1 Feb. 1739, died in Westport
20 Dec. 1815.

They were members of the Friends Society. They are buried on
the old Peckham farm in LC, east of the Commons. This farm, the
home of Peckhams for many generations, was owned by Mrs. Jonathan
Pierce in 1890.

His will, recorded LC Probate, book 4, page 395, made 10 March
1806 and proved 3 June 1812: "To wife Mary east end of house where I
now live except the bedroom of my sister Sarah Peckham. To son
Peleg one third of wearing apparel and one third of my books. One third
of pasture bounded east by Abner Woods, south by the common road,
west by a brook and north by John Bailey. To grandson Jonathan Peckham
my loom. To daughter Elizabeth Brownell, wife of George, 50 dollars.
My son Isaac to be executor."

Children, recorded in LC:
i.   Elizabeth, b. 9 Jan. 1761; b. in 1851; m. in LC 26 March
        1780 George Brownell, son of Stephen and Elizabeth Brownell.
19. ii.   Isaac, b. 22 Oct. 1763.
20. iii. George, b. 13 May 1768.
21. iv.   Peleg, b. 12 Feb. 1774.

15. SAMUEL[5] PECKHAM (Joseph[4], John[3], John[2], John[1]), born in
LC 20 Nov. 1735, died in Nine Partners, Dutchess County, N.Y., 15
June 1812. Residence: LC and Nine Partners, where he kept a tavern
during the Revolutionary War.

He married AVIS WOOD, daughter of John and Mary (Burgess) Wood
of LC, born in LC 21 Aug. 1740, died there 12 July 1793. They were
Quakers.

Children:
i.   Joseph, b. 20 June (or July) 1762; m. Ann Brownell.
ii.   Seth, b. 17 Dec. 1763; m. Mary Osborne.
iii.   Jerusha, b. 27 April 1765; d. 28 Feb. 1845; m. Joseph Wilbor,
       son of Jonathan and Sarah (Fones) Wilbor.
iv.   Benjamin, b. 17 April 1766; m. Mary Hoag.
v.   Hannah, b. 11 Oct. 1768; d. 10 May 1819; unmarried.
vi.   Reuben, b. 22 Jan. 1769; m. Judith Jenkins.
vii.   Samuel, b. 28 Feb. 1770; m. (1) Desire Osborne; m. (2) Mary
       Lamb.
viii. Nathan, b. 4 April 1771; m. Lydia Osborne.
ix.   John, b. 15 Sept. 1775; b. 20 Feb. 1832; m. 1 March 1810 Hannah
       Wilbore, daughter of Joseph and Mary (Pratt) Wilbore.
x.   Job, b. in March 1777; m. (1) Sarah Carman; m. (2) Jane Haight.
xi.   Avis, b. 10 Oct. 1782; d. 22 May 1849; m. Stephen Townsend.

16. **PELEG[5] PECKHAM** (William[4], William[3], William[2], John[1]), born in Middletown 1739-48, died there 12 April 1833. Residence: Middletown.

He married 25 Oct. 1772 in Middletown ELIZABETH SMITH, died in Middletown 13 Dec. 1833.

Children, born in Middletown:

i.	Edward Smith, b. 1 Aug. 1773.	
ii.	Henry, b. 27 Dec. 1780; m. Esther Gould.	
iii.	Mary, b. 4 April 1783; m. 11 Dec. 1803 Nathaniel Barker.	
22. iv.	Peleg, b. 3 Oct. 1785.	
v.	Elizabeth, b. 10 Sept. 1788.	
vi.	Elisha, b. 5 May 1790; m. Elizabeth Dunham Sylvester.	
vii.	Phebe, b. 21 June 1792.	

17. **FELIX[5] PECKHAM** (William[4], Samuel[3], William[2], John[1]), born 21 July 1763 in Middletown, died 10 Nov. 1844. Residence: Middletown.

He married 19 Nov. 1786 TRYPHENA STOCKMAN, daughter of Jacob and Anna (Wilbor) Stockman, born in Newport 9 Sept. 1765, died 16 Feb. 1851.

Children:

i.	Nancy, b. 3 Sept. 1787; m. Johnson Whitman.	
ii.	Hannah, b. 17 Oct. 1788; m. Benjamin Smith.	
iii.	Abner, b. 5 April 1790; m. in Middletown 13 March 1813 Rachel Barker, daughter of David Barker.	
23. iv.	Samuel Stockman, b. 27 Aug. 1792.	
v.	Tryphena Stockman, b. 20 June 1794; m. 4 Feb. 1813 Jethro Peckham.	

18. **GIDEON[5] PECKHAM** (William[4], Samuel[3], William[2], John[1]), born in Middletown 8 Nov. 1781, died 24 April 1854. Residence: Honeymoon Hill, Newport.

He married in Middletown 2 Jan. 1806 CYNTHIA BARKER, daughter of Gideon Barker, born 10 Feb. 1787, died 2 March 1856. They had 49 grandchildren.

Children:

i.	Benedict, b. 19 Oct. 1806; m. Hannah Clark.	
ii.	John C. B., b. 23 April 1808; d. 29 Jan. 1892; m. 14 April 1831 Barbara Rider, daughter of William Rider.	
iii.	Ezra, b. 8 Jan. 1810.	
iv.	Elizabeth, b. in 1811; d. 9 Feb. 1869; unmarried.	
v.	Cynthia Ann, b. 16 Jan. 1813; m. Louis Thurston.	
vi.	Malinda Barker, b. 24 May 1815; d. 18 June 1841; m. Samuel Cummings.	
24. vii.	Gideon Barker, b. 16 May 1817.	
viii.	Hosea, b. in 1819; d. in 1821.	
ix.	Hosea, b. 14 Dec. 1821; d. 27 June 1888.	
x.	Nathaniel, b. 27 Aug. 1823; m. Jane Tucker.	
xi.	Sarah, b. 13 June 1827; d. 2 March 1849.	
xii.	Ardelia, b. 3 May 1830; m. Elisha Clarke Peckham.	

xiii. Philip Mason, b. 1 Jan. 1833; d. 21 Jan. 1888; m. 13 Jan.
       1854 Mary D. Tucker.

19. ISAAC[6] PECKHAM (John[5], Joseph[4], John[3], John[2], John[1]),
born in LC 22 Oct. 1763, died there 18 June 1821. Residence: LC.
     He married in Dartmouth 29 Sept. 1785 PHEBE WILBOR,
daughter of Charles and Hannah (Borden) Wilbor, born in LC 28 Oct.
1764, died there 29 Nov. 1827. Her brother was Governor Isaac
Wilbor. They were members of the Society of Friends.
     His will, recorded LC Wills, book 5, page 255, made 9 June 1821
and proved 9 July 1821: ". . . Considering the certainty of death and
desiring to preserve that harmony which now exists among my connections. . .
To wife Phebe Peckham use of west great room and bedroom adjoining.
All my household goods, one half of chaise and one half of black mare.
To daughters Hannah and Ruth use of west end of my dwelling house and
one fourth of milk room. To them 150 dollars each. To sons Jonathan and
James 5 dollars each. To wife and two daughters use of garden at west
end of house. To son Benjamin my best suit of wearing apparel except
one. To son John the rest and residue. I also desire that my Head Farm,
so called, be sold for paying of note to Sanford Almy, Isaac Wilbor,
Joshua Austin, Thomas White, William White and Ephraim Gifford. My
friend William Howland and son John executors . . ."
          Children:
     i.   Jonathan, b. 24 Dec. 1786.
     ii.   John, b. 4 Jan. 1789; m. 28 Oct. 1828 Judith Foster, daughter
           of John and Ruth Foster of Charlestown, R. I.
     iii. Hannah, b. 15 April 1791.
     iv.   Ruth, b. 4 Oct. 1793, according to Westport church records.
25. v.   James Davis, b. 5 Jan. 1801.
26. vi.   Benjamin, b. in 1805/6.

20. GEORGE[6] PECKHAM (John[5], Joseph[4], John[3], John[2], John[1]),
born in LC 13 May 1768. Residence: LC.
     He was married in LC 6 Aug. 1796 by the Rev. Mase Shepard to
LYDIA HEAD, daughter of Jonathan and Ruth (Little) Head of Westport,
born in Westport 19 Dec. 1769.

          Children, recorded in LC:
     i.   Samuel, b. 16 June 1793; m. Abigail Sanford.
     ii.   Jerusha, b. 30 Nov. 1795; m. William Seabury.
     iii. Sarah, b. 13 Dec. 1799; m. John Sanford.
     iv.   Otis, b. 25 Jan. 1805.
     v̇.   Ruth, b. 31 Sept. 1807, m. William Clarke.
     vi.   Mary, b. 23 April 1810; m. Otis Rankin.

21. PELEG[6] PECKHAM (John[5], Joseph[4], John[3], John[2], John[1]),
born in LC 12 Feb. 1774, died there 10 April 1862 ae 88. Residence:
LC.
     He was married in LC 3 Aug. 1794 by the Rev. Mase Shepard to
LUCY PALMER, daughter of Thomas and Phebe (Shaw) Palmer, born
in LC 17 Dec. 1773, died there 17 Feb. 1850. Both are buried in the
Old Commons cemetery.

Children, first three recorded in LC:

i.   Abraham, b. 10 March 1796; d. 29 Jan. 1880; m. Lucinda
     Blackwell, b. in 1806, d. 19 Sept. 1874 ae 68.
27. ii. Wilbor, b. 27 Dec. 1798.
iii. Stephen, b. 17 Nov. 1800.
iv. Sophia, b. 17 Nov. 1805; d. in 1888 (according to family
     Bible); m. by Rev. Emerson Paine 19 Oct. 1823 to
     Newell Ambler.

22. PELEG[6] PECKHAM (Peleg[5], William[4], William[3], William[2],
John[1]), born in Middletown 3 Oct. 1785, died in LC 4 March 1872 ae
86.

He married in Middletown 28 July 1810 FREELOVE SOPHIA
HAZARD, daughter of George and Jane (Tweedy) Hazard, born in
Newport 24 Feb. 1783, died in LC 9 June 1861. She also had a brother,
William Tweedy.

Children, born in Middletown and the first three recorded
there:
28. i.   George Hazard, b. 22 June 1813.
29. ii. Peleg, b. 19 Feb. 1815.
iii. Jane Elizabeth, b. 3 Sept. 1824; d. ae 80; m. (1) (--) Barker;
     m. (2) Elijah Pierce.
iv. William, m. Lucy Healey.
30. v.   Nathan Carter, b. in 1826.

23. SAMUEL STOCKMAN[6] PECKHAM (Felix[5], William[4], Samuel[3],
William[2], John[1]), born in Middletown 27 Aug. 1792, died in Newport
21 Feb. 1870.

He married first SABRINA DEWEY, daughter of Christopher and
Margaret (Brown) Dewey of Stonington, Conn. He married second LYDIA
RYDER. He married third AMELIA S. DEWEY. He married fourth
MARY ANN FRINK.

Children by first wife:

i.   Charlotte, b. 11 Nov. 1817; m. Gideon Barker Peckham, her
     second cousin.
ii. Julia Ann, b. 10 Sept. 1819; d. 29 Nov. 1861; m. 5 Nov. 1840
     Robinson Potter Barker.
iii. Jacob Stockman, b. 30 Dec. 1820; d. 29 Dec. 1822.
iv. Amos, b. 19 May 1823.
v.   Sabrina, b. 25 April 1825.

24. DEACON GIDEON BARKER[6] PECKHAM (Gideon[5], William[4],
Samuel[3], William[2], John[1]), born in Middletown 16 May 1817, died 7
Dec. 1874 ae 57. They were living in Westport at the time of the 1870
census.

He married 13 Nov. 1838 CHARLOTTE S. PECKHAM, daughter
of Samuel Stockman and Sabrina (Dewey) Peckham, born 11 Nov. 1817,
died 16 April 1874. Both are buried in Pleasant View cemetery. She
was descended from Samuel[6], Felix[5], William[4], Samuel[3], William[2],
John[1].

Children:
31. i.   Albert, b. 1 Feb. 1840.
    ii.   Jacob S., b. 10 Dec. 1841; d. in Fairhaven, Mass., 22 May
          1904; m. Annetta W. (--), b. 22 Sept. 1848, d. 21 Nov.
          1918.
    iii. Margaret Sabrina, b. 1 May 1843; residence: Lewiston,
          Maine.
    iv.   Samuel Stockman, b. 6 May 1845; d. in 1904. Residence:
          Fairhaven.
    v.   Frederick Henry, b. 22 Feb. 1846; d. in Lewiston, Maine.
    vi.   Joseph Crocker, b. 12 March 1848; d. in Adamsville 15 May
          1895.
    vii. Julia Ann, b. 3 Aug. 1849; d. 6 July 1889; unmarried.
    viii. Charlotte Amanda, b. 8 March 1853; m. Zoeth Stubbs.
    ix.   Edith Maria, b. 5 March 1854; m. Robert Olds.
    x.   Willard B., b. 11 Aug. 1857; d. 10 Feb. 1925; m. Delia
          Jordan, b. 30 June 1850, d. 3 April 1932. Residence:
          Long Plains, Mass.
    xi.   Amelia Dewey, b. 6 March 1861; m. Fred S. Chapman of
          Lewiston, Maine.
    xii. Amos Lincoln, b. 1 March 1861; m. Harriet Walker or
          Harriet Clarke.

25. DR. JAMES DAVIS[7] PECKHAM (Isaac[6], John[5], Joseph[4],
John[3], John[2], John[1]), born in LC 4 Jan. 1801, died there 22 Dec. 1849.
Residence: LC. They lived on the west side of Willow Avenue, formerly
named Pudding Bag Lane.
    He was married in LC 22 Dec. 1824 by the Rev. Emerson Paine to
HARRIET BYRON BROWNELL, daughter of Edmund and Priscilla
(Briggs) Brownell, born in LC 14 March 1803, died there 17 March
1847. Both are buried in the Old Commons cemetery.
    His will, recorded in LC Probate, book 10, page 207, made 17 Dec.
1849 and proved 11 Feb. 1850: "James D. Peckham of LC, physician.
To son James Edmund my Cole Brook wood lot which I purchased of
Ezra Brownell. Also the Greenhill land east of house and highway. . .
and all of the buildings west of the highway called Carr land. . .
unmarried daughters Phebe, Mary and Charlotte shall have the use
and improvement of the west part of the dwelling house. To daughters
Sarah White, Phebe, Mary and Charlotte Peckham, the rest and residue."

        Children, none recorded:
    i.   Sarah A., m. Christopher White.
    ii.   Phebe Wilbour, m. Warren Seabury.
    iii. Mary B., b. 2 Nov. 1829; m. 9 March 1891; m. Borden Wordell.
    iv.   Charlotte S., b. 17 May 1834; d. 17 Feb. 1900; m. 1 Jan. 1855
          Arthur T. Wilbur, son of Peleg and Elizabeth (Gifford)
          Wilbur.
32. v.   James Edmund, b. 6 March 1839.

    26. BENJAMIN[7] PECKHAM (Isaac[6], John[5], Joseph[4], John[3], John[2],
John[1]), born in 1805/6, died in LC 21 Dec. 1854. Residence: LC. He
married ELIZA TOMPKINS, daughter of Benjamin and Deborah (Simmons)

Tompkins of LC, born in LC 13 April 1803, died there in 1897. She is
buried in the Old Commons cemetery next to her parents.

Children:
i.   Isaac Borden, b. in LC 10 July 1829.
ii.   Charlotte A., b. about 1834; m. in LC 10 Feb. 1857 Richard
      · W. Sisson, son of Benjamin and Elisa Sisson.

27. WILBOR[7] PECKHAM (Peleg[6], John[5], Joseph[4], John[3], John[2],
John[1]), born in LC 27 Dec. 1798, died there 14 July 1871 ae 73.
Residence: LC.

He was married in LC 13 Nov. 1824 by the Rev. Emerson Paine to
PRISCILLA WILBOR, daughter of Joseph and Hannah (Brown) Wilbor,
born in LC 9 March 1801, died there 22 March 1874 ae 73. They are
buried in the Wilbor cemetery south of the Commons.

In her will, recorded LC Probate, book 11, page 692, made 21
Aug. 1871 and proved 11 May 1874, Priscilla Peckham, widow, left
one dollar each to sons Oliver and Alanson, and to son George all
the rest and residue of her estate.

Children, born in LC and recorded there:
33. i.   Oliver Perry, b. 7 Aug. 1828.
34. ii.   Alanson Wilbor, b. 30 July 1832.
35. iii. George Wilson, b. 18 Dec. 1838.

28. GEORGE HAZARD[7] PECKHAM (Peleg[6], Peleg[5], William[4],
William[3], William[2], John[1]), born in Middletown 22 June 1813, died
in LC 13 May 1897. Residence: LC. They lived on the south side of
the swamp road.

He was married in LC 24 Nov. 1847 by the Rev. Samuel Beane to
MARY WILBOR BROWN, daughter of Pardon and Sophia (Wilbour)
Brown, born in Ledyard, Cayuga County, N.Y., 14 Jan. 1822, died in
LC 11 July 1900 ae 78. They are buried in Hillside cemetery,
Tiverton four corners.

Children, recorded in LC:
i.   Pardon George, b. 26 Nov. 1848; d. in LC 1 March 1900;
      m. 22 Dec. 1874 Augusta Brown, daughter of Humphrey
      and Deborah (Gray) Brown.
ii.   Sophia Elizabeth, b. 15 March 1851; moved to Fall River
      where she died, unmarried.
36. iii. William Tweed, b. 12 Aug. 1855.
iv.   Mary Lena, b. 7 July 1863; m. in LC 6 July 1899 William
      Haynor, son of Joseph and Elizabeth (Hutchett?) Haynor
      of Cambridge, Mass., born in Canada in 1858.
v.   Sarah Olivia, b. 14 June 1866; m. in LC 13 June 1892
      Christopher J. Barlow, son of Morris and Susie Barlow,
      b. in Newport.

29. PELEG[7] PECKHAM (Peleg[6], Peleg[5], William[4], William[3],
William[2], John[1]), born in Middletown 19 Feb. 1819. He married in LC
2 Nov. 1841 SARAH ANN GRAY, born in Tiverton in 1822.

Children:

37. i.   John Peleg, b. in 1844.
    ii.   Sarah F., d. in LC 8 Feb. 1873 ae 15-10-21.
    iii. Josephine, b. in 1859 (?); m. (--) Manchester.
38. iv.   Joseph, b. 27 Sept. 1859.
    v.   William G., b. 31 March 1865 ae 2-9-0.
    vi.   Jane E. (possibly), b. in 1866 (?).

30. NATHAN (NATHANIEL) CARTER[7] PECKHAM (Peleg[7], Peleg[6], William[5], William[4], William[3], William[2], John[1]), born in Middletown in 1826, died in LC 21 Nov. 1892 ae 66. Residence: LC. They lived on the east side of the main road opposite Coval Osborn.

He married in LC 21 March 1852 ABBY G. BROWN, daughter of Humphrey and Deborah (Gray) Brown, born 22 Sept. 1831, died in LC 11 Jan. 1915 ae 83. Both are buried in the Old Commons cemetery, next to the children of his brother, Peleg Peckham.

    Children, probably born in LC:
    i.   Edward Jesse, b. 8 Dec. 1855 or possibly 18 May 1854; m. in LC 22 Dec. 1881 Eudora S. Hardy, daughter of Holder and Tabitha Potter.
    ii.   Lizzie Dora, b. 2 April 1861; d. 19 March 1863.
    iii. Abby Sophia, b. in LC 23 Dec. 1862; d. in New Bedford 24 Sept. 1911; m. in LC 25 Dec. 1884 Charles Dean Sisson, son of James and Vilroy Ann (Dean) Sisson, b. in North Dartmouth 11 July 1860, d. in LC 29 Dec. 1927.
    iv.   Nathaniel Carter, b. 19 Jan. 1869; d. 1 July 1886 ae 17.

31. ALBERT[7] PECKHAM (Gideon[6], Gideon[5], William[4], Samuel[3], William[2], John[1]), born in Middletown 1 Feb. 1840, died in LC 2 Jan. 1906 ae 65. He is buried in Pleasant View cemetery.

He married CHARLOTTE F. BRIGHTMAN, daughter of Rufus and Phebe (Barker) (Allen) Brightman, born in Providence 28 Sept. 1842, died 28 Jan. 1908.

Residence: LC. They lived on the West Road, near Peckham's corner. A farmer and flower grower, he had many green houses.

    Children, recorded in LC:
    i.   Laura Frances, b. 27 Feb. 1864; d. 8 Feb. 1846 in Swansea; m. in LC 5 April 1894 Lemule Sisson, son of Levi and Mary (Tabor) Sisson.
39. ii.   Gideon Barker, b. 30 Oct. 1866.
40. iii. Rufus Franklin, b. 3 July 1868.
41. iv.   William Albert, b. 17 July 1870.
    v.   Lidora Louise, b. 2 Sept. 1872; m. in LC 4 Nov. 1897 William Northupp Sisson, son of John and Eudora (Almy) Sisson.
    vi.   Walter Everett, b. 22 Oct. 1874; m. 8 June 1898 Carrie B. Rogers.

32. JAMES EDMUND[8] PECKHAM (James[7], Isaac[6], John[5], Joseph[4], John[3], John[2], John[1]), born in LC 6 March 1839, died there 3 June 1923 ae 84.

He married in LC 31 Jan. 1860 HANNAH BORDEN SOULE, daughter of Ephraim and Lydia (Palmer) Soule, born in LC 2 May 1839, died there

10 Jan. 1939, less than four months before her one hundredth birthday. Both are buried in the Old Commons cemetery.

They lived on Willow Avenue in LC, just opposite where his father, Dr. Peckham, lived and on the east side of the avenue.

> Children, recorded in LC:
> i.   Harriet James, b. in LC 17 Feb. 1863; d. there 18 July 1946 ae 83; m. (1) 29 Nov. 1883 William Bennett Brownell, son of Galen and Harriet Brownell; m. (2) in LC 15 March 1893 Abram Wordell, son of Gardner and Olive Wordell.
> ii.   Charles Ellsworth, b. 23 Aug. 1865; m. Sarah Stoddard.

33. OLIVER PERRY[8] PECKHAM (Wilbor[7], Peleg[6], John[5], Joseph[4], John[3], John[2], John[1]), born in LC 7 Aug. 1828, died there 22 June 1896. Residence: LC. They lived in the house near the blacksmith shop near Christian Corner.

He married in LC 7 March 1854 JULIANNA MANCHESTER, daughter of Wanton and Hannah (Brownell) Manchester, born 24 Dec. 1832, died in LC 14 Oct. 1911. They are buried in the Wilbor cemetery on the road south of the Commons.

> Children, recorded in LC:
> i.   Sarah, b. 19 March 1855.
> 42. ii.   Edgar Spencer, b. 20 Oct. 1858.
> iii.   Sarah Louise, b. 18 March 1861; d. in LC 28 Sept. 1941; unmarried.
> iv.   Julianna, b. 12 Jan. 1862; d. 1 Nov. 1924; m. in LC 13 Dec. 1882 George T. Howard, son of Thomas and Lucy (Hayward) Howard, b. 10 Sept. 1858, d. in LC 6 Oct. 1924.

34. ALANSON WILBOR[8] PECKHAM (Wilbor[7], Peleg[6], John[5], Joseph[4], John[3], John[2], John[1]), born in LC 30 July 1832, died there 4 Dec. 1907 ae 75. Residence: LC. They lived on Peckham Road on the north near the Albert Peckham place.

He married PRISCILLA WOODMAN, daughter of Humphrey and Rhoda (Wilbor) Woodman, born in LC 21 May 1831, died there 16 Sept. 1887. They are buried in the Woodman cemetery.

> Children, recorded in LC:
> i.   Charles H., b. 27 March 1860; m. in LC 1 July 1890 Jennie M. Bone, daughter of John and Euphemia Bone, b. in Scotland in 1871; no children.

35. GEORGE WILSON[8] PECKHAM (Wilbor[7], Peleg[6], John[5], Joseph[4], John[3], John[2], John[1]), born in LC 18 Dec. 1838, died there 7 Jan. 1889. Residence: LC.

He married in LC 30 June 1875 RACHEL ANNIE RATHBURN, daughter of George and Adelaide Rathburn, born 15 Jan. 1856 in Providence, died in LC 3 Sept. 1923.

> Children, recorded in LC:
> i.   George Nelson, b. 17 June 1876; d. in Cranston 15 Dec. 1945; m. Catharine McDougall of Fall River.
> ii.   William Wilbor, b. 5 March 1880 in LC; d. there 4 March 1943;

unmarried.
iii.   Bessie B., b. 14 July 1882.
iv.   Ardelia Maria Priscilla, b. 7 May 1889.

36.   WILLIAM TWEED[8] PECKHAM (George[7], Peleg[6], Peleg[5],
William[4], William[3], William[2], John[1]), born in LC 12 Aug. 1855, died
there 1 March 1933. Residence: LC. They lived on the Swamp Road
on the old William Southworth place.
He married first in LC 25 Feb. 1890 CLARABELLE HORTON
JENNINGS, daughter of Samuel Mosher and Nancy (Wilbor) Jennings,
born in LC 29 Nov. 1871, died there 5 June 1900. He and his first
wife are buried at Hillside cemetery at Tiverton Four Corners. He
married second in Fall River 16 Jan. 1902 JENETTE MARIAN
(SINCLAIR) RASSELYE of Providence, daughter of John and Gladys
(Draper) Sinclair, born in Great Forkes, Maine.

Children by first wife, recorded in LC:
i.   Ada Belle, b. 5 Aug. 1891; m. John Kirkwood.
ii.   Bernice, b. 6 April 1896.

Children by second wife:
iii. Wilhelmina, b. in LC 21 Nov. 1902.

One of these daughters married Walter Hopewell.

37.   JOHN PELEG[8] PECKHAM (Peleg[7], Peleg[6], Peleg[5], William[4],
William[3], William[2], John[1]), born in Middletown in 1854. He married in
LC 26 July 1877 SARAH ELIZABETH WILLISTON, daughter of Pardon
and Sarah Coe (Hart) Williston, born in Tiverton in 1858.

Children:
i.   Dora, b. in 1879.
ii.   Lillian, b. 14 June 1881; m. in Tiverton Harry MacFarland.
iii. Sarah, b. 25 Dec. 1883; m. in Tiverton James Wordell.
iv.   Elma, b. 1 March 1894; m. in Portsmouth Rachel Peckham.
v.   Emma (twin), b. 1 March 1894; m. in Tiverton George
      Anthony of Portsmouth.

38.   JOSEPH VALENTINE[8] PECKHAM (Peleg[7], Peleg[6], Peleg[5],
William[4], William[3], William[2], John[1]), born in Tiverton 20 Sept. 1859,
died in LC 21 March 1933 ae 73. He is buried in Beech Grove cemetery.
He married in LC 29 Nov. 1883 EMMA CALISTA GIFFORD,
daughter of Barney and Rebecca (Tripp) Gifford, born in LC 6 May
1862, died there 2 April 1933 ae 70. She is buried in Hillside cemetery,
Tiverton.

Children, recorded in LC:
i.   George Barney, b. 21 Nov. 1884.
ii.   Helen, m. (--) Lake.

39.   GIDEON BARKER[8] PECKHAM (Albert[7], Gideon[6], Gideon[5],
William[4], Samuel[3], William[2], John[1]), born in Westport 30 Oct. 1866,
died in 1950. He is buried in Pleasant View cemetery.
He married in LC 20 Dec. 1892 LILLIAN MAY TABOR, daughter
of Theodore and Betsey Rounds (Hart) Tabor, born in LC 18 Dec. 1874,

died in 1945.

Children:
i.   Charlotte Brightman, b. 25 March 189-.
ii.   Theodore, b. 14 Sept. 1900.
iii.   Elizabeth (possibly), b. in 1901; d. in 1933.
iv.   Bessie Louise, b. 2 Aug. 1904.
v.   Everett Barker, b. 30 July 1906.

40. RUFUS FRANKLIN[8] PECKHAM (Albert[7], Gideon[6], Gideon[5], William[4], Samuel[3], William[2], John[1]), born in LC 3 July 1868, died there 23 Dec. 1917. Residence: LC.
He married in LC 4 Nov. 1892 ESTHER IDELLA HAMBLY of Tiverton, daughter of James and Margaret (Negus) Hambly, born in Tiverton 2 July 1870, died in LC 28 July 1904 ae 34. They are buried in the stone church cemetery in Tiverton.

Children, born and recorded in LC:
i.   Rufus Brightman, b. 1 June 1894 in LC; d. 9 July 1957 ae
        63; m. 16 Dec. 1928 Theodora Millicent Wilbour, daughter
        of Daniel and Hannah (Soule) Wilbour.
ii.   James Otis, b. 5 March 1896; d. in LC 28 Nov. 1925.
iii.   Esther Idella, b. in LC 21 May 1900; m. there 22 June 1929
        Vincent Rose, son of Charles Edward and Mabel (Healey)
        Rose of Tiverton, b. 14 Jan. 1896 in Tiverton.

41. WILLIAM ALBERT[8] PECKHAM (Albert[7], Gideon[6], Gideon[5], William[4], Samuel[3], William[2], John[1]), born in LC 17 July 1870, died there 1 Sept. 1942 ae 72. Residence: LC.
He married in LC 16 Sept. 1897 INEZ E. MAXWELL, born in Rindge, N.H. He is buried in Pleasant View cemetery in Tiverton.

Children, born in LC:
43. i. Raymond Maxwell, b. 31 July 1899.
ii.   Frances Gertrude, b. 3 Feb. 1902; m. in LC 29 June 1929
        Ian McLean Walker of Providence.
44. iii. Bernard Morris, b. 31 May 1903.

42. EDGAR SPENCER[9] PECKHAM (Oliver[8], Wilbor[7], Peleg[6], John[5], Joseph[4], John[3], John[2], John[1]), born in LC 20 Oct. 1858, died there 31 Dec. 1929 ae 71. Residence: LC. They lived on the north of Meeting House Lane, on land now owned by the town.
He married in LC 19 March 1885 ELMA DAME BARKER, daughter of Edwin and Rebecca (Sherman) Barker of Tiverton, born in LC 17 Dec. 1858, died there 23 May 1934 ae 75. They are buried in the cemetery south of the Commons.

Children, recorded in LC:
i.   Rheba Sherman, b. 22 March 1886; d. 3 Oct. 1942; unmarried.
ii.   Howard Spencer, b. 31 March 1891; d. in LC 12 Feb. 1945;
        m. Helen Stevens.
iii.   Marjorie Barker, b. in LC 22 Aug. 1896; m. in LC 11 Oct.
        1919 Leo Albert Robinson, son of Melville and Blanche
        (Getchell) Robinson of Woonsocket.

43. RAYMOND MAXWELL[9] PECKHAM (William[8], Albert[7], Gideon[6], Gideon[5], William[4], Samuel[3], William[2], John[1]), born in LC 31 July 1899. Residence: LC.

He married in LC 20 Nov. 1926 CLARA JESSIE BALLINGER, daughter of Albert and Ida (Clark) Ballinger, born in Newark, N.J., 20 Nov. 1906.

Children, born in Fall River:
i.   Eleanor, b. 18 Sept. 1927; m. Donald Gavin.
ii.   Albert Raymond, b. 14 Jan. 1929; m. in Warwick 15 Sept. 1951 Mary (or Marjorie) Jane Barry of Greenwood, R.I., daughter of Richard and Mary (Gillis) Barry, b. in Providence 19 Sept. 1931. They had a daughter, Kathy A., b. in Fall River 12 April 1953.
iii. Norman M., b. 22 June 1930.
iv.   Gordon Philip.

44. BERNARD MORRIS[9] PECKHAM (William[8], Albert[7], Gideon[6], Gideon[5], William[4], Samuel[3], William[2], John[1]), born in LC 31 May 1903, married FEROL JOHNSON. Residence: LC and Tiverton.

Children, recorded in LC:
i.   Janice Johnson, b. in Providence 20 Sept. 1931.
ii.   Jason Maxwell, b. in Fall River 21 Sept. 1939.

1. CYRUS[1] PECKHAM, born in Middletown 1821, married MARY (--), born in Massachusetts in 1823. They were listed in the census of 1865 in LC.

Children, given in the 1865 LC census:
i.   Sarah B., b. in Middletown in 1847.
2.   ii.   Robert L., b. in 1849.
iii. Annie Louise, b. in April 1852; m. in LC 6 Dec. 1871 Charles Otis Wilcox, son of Charles and Priscilla (Gray) Wilcox of Tiverton.
iv.   Lois, b. in LC in 1855; d. there 1 Aug. 1881.
v.   Leonice, b. in LC 14 July 1857; m. (--) Davis.
vi.   Jenny, b. in LC in May 1861; d. there 23 March 1863.
vii. Kate, m. 16 Nov. 1864 Edward A. Coggeshall, son of Edward and Nancy Coggeshall, b. in Portsmouth in 1839.

2. ROBERT[2] PECKHAM (Cyrus[1]), born in Middletown in 1849, died in Westport in 1942. Residence: LC.

He married first ELIZA B. HUNT, daughter of Samuel E. and Lucy B. (--) Hunt, born in LC 9 April 1851, died there 1 Aug. 1881. He married second CYNTHIA FIELD, born in 1852. She is buried in the Old Commons cemetery.

Children, born in LC:
i.   William Leslie, b. 27 July 1874.
ii.   Elizabeth Borden, b. 5 June 1881; d. 27 Jan. 1885.

. . . .

LEANDER PECKHAM, son of George W. and Eliza Peckham, born in Middletown in 1827. Residence: LC.

He married in LC 25 Nov. 1858 PATIENCE S. GRAY, daughter of Amasa and Phebe (Irish) Gray, born in LC 13 Jan. 1839.

   Children, recorded in LC:
i. Esther, b. 25 Dec. 1859.
ii. Leander Amasa, b. 28 Jan. 1863.

CHARLES H. PECKHAM, born in 1835, married MARGARET J. (--), born in 1850.

   Children:
i. Alvin A., b. in 1880.

SAMUEL ARTHUR PECKHAM, born in Middletown 6 March 1845, died 8 Feb. 1900. He married CAROLINE B. BRIGHTMAN, daughter of Rufus Ward and Phebe (Allen) Brightman, born in Providence 18 Feb. 1846, died in LC 5 Feb. 1920. They are buried in Pleasant View cemetery next to the stone church in Tiverton.

   Children:
i. Carrie Walker, b. in LC 21 Dec. 1866; d. 25 Dec. 1890.
ii. Julia A. M., b. in LC 10 June 1868; d. in Cranston 2 April 1926.
iii. Ida, b. 27 Jan. 1877; d. 10 Dec. 1904.

❧

THE PERKINS FAMILY

PAUL FRANKLIN PERKINS, son of Charles F. and Cynthia L. (Hopkinson) Perkins, born in Brookline, Mass., 26 Jan. 1887. He married in LC 2 Sept. 1922 AGNES LEEDS BURCHARD, daughter of Rozwell and Edith Russell (Church) Burchard, born in Boston 26 Feb. 1900.

❧

THE PHILLIPS FAMILY

Additional information on the Phillips family may be found in the New England register No. 16, page 325.

1. WILLIAM[1] PHILLIPS, born about 1584, married ELIZABETH (--). Residence: Taunton. His will was dated 16 April 1654, in which it was declared that he was aged at least three score and ten at that time.

   Children:
2. i. James.
  ii. Elizabeth, m. James Walker.

-502-

·2.   JAMES² PHILLIPS (William¹). Residence: Taunton.

     Children:
i.   James, b. in January 1661.
ii.   Nathaniel, b. 25 March 1664.
iii.   Sarah, b. 17 March 1667; m. in Taunton 19 Dec. 1688 Samuel
       Wilbore Shadrach, son of Samuel Shadrach, b. 1 April
       1663.
iv.   William, b. 21 Aug. 1669.
3. v.   Seth, b. 14 Aug. 1671.
vi.   Daniel, b. 7 May 1673.
vii.   Ebenezer, b. 16 Jan. 1674.

   3. SETH³ PHILLIPS (James², William¹), born in 1675, married
ABIGAIL (--), born in 1680, died in 1744.
   He was living in Taunton during King William's War and made
an expedition to LC during that time on his own horse, according
to notes made in 1691. He afterwards settled in LC.

     Children, recorded in LC:
i.   Elizabeth, b. 26 Sept. 1700; m. in LC 9 July 1722 John
       Sanford Jr., son of John and Content (Howland) Sanford.
ii.   Elisha, b. 21 Jan. 1702; m. in LC 30 Sept. 1736 Innocent
       Butts.
iii.   John, b. 1 Nov. 1703.
iv.   Hannah, b. in 1707; d. in LC 9 Jan. 1738; m. (intention 7
       May 1728) in LC Eliphalet Davenport, son of Thomas
       and Catherine (Woodworth) Davenport of LC.
v.   Mary, m. 7 Oct. 1734 Ephraim Davenport, son of Thomas
       and Catharine (Woodworth) Davenport of LC.

THE POPE FAMILY

   COL. SETH POPE, son of Lemuel and Elizabeth Pope, born in
Dartmouth 4 March 1719/20.
   He married first in LC 30 July 1741 ABIGAIL CHURCH, daughter
of Nathaniel and Innocent (Head) Church of LC, born in LC 8 Oct.
1719, died 8 May 1778. He married second in LC 25 Nov. 1779 MARY
(CHURCH) SIMMONS, widow of Isaac Simmons and daughter of Caleb
and Deborah (Coe) Church of LC, born in LC 6 Jan. 1728, died there
3 Sept. 1815. His second wife is buried in the Old Commons cemetery.

     Children, recorded in Dartmouth:
i.   Richard, b. 22 Dec. 1742.
ii.   Alice, b. 8 Jan. 1744; m. in Dartmouth (intention 9 Feb. 1764)
       Eleazer Hathaway.
iii.   Nathaniel, b. 22 June 1747.
iv.   Innocent, b. 8 Dec. 1749.
v.   Ephraim, b. 20 July 1752.
vi.   Seth, b. 15 April 1755.

THE POTTER FAMILY

1. NATHANIEL[1] POTTER. Residence: Portsmouth. He was admitted to the Island of Aquidneck in 1638.

He married DOROTHY (--), born in 1617, died 19 Feb. 1696. She married second John Albro.

Children:
2. i.   Nathaniel, b. in 1637.
   ii.   Ichabod, d. in 1676; m. Martha Hazard, daughter of Thomas and Martha Hazard.

2. NATHANIEL[2] POTTER (Nathaniel[1]), born in 1637, died in Portsmouth 20 Oct. 1704. Residence: Portsmouth and Dartmouth.

He married ELIZABETH STOKES, who died after 1704.

His will, dated 18 Oct. 1704 and proved 20 Nov. 1704: "To wife all movables, her living in the house for life and a third of estate. To son Stokes one half of my land in the south side of the highway. To son Nathaniel one shilling. To son William four pounds. To son Benjamin three pounds. To daughter Mary Wilbor two pounds and a cow. To daughter Rebecca Kerby two pounds and a cow. To daughter Elizabeth Potter three \pounds. To daughter Katherine Potter four pounds at age. To son Ichabod two acres of land."

Children:
   i.   Stokes, d. in 1718; m. Elizabeth (--).
   ii.   John, d. in 1764; m. Mary (--). Residence: Dartmouth.
   iii. Nathaniel, b. about 1669; d. 16 Nov. 1736; m. about 1688 Joanne Wilbore, daughter of William and Martha Wilbore of Portsmouth.
   iv.   William, d. after 1720; m. Anne Durfee, daughter of Thomas Durfee.
   v.   Benjamin, d. in 1709; m. Mary (--).
3. vi.   Samuel, b. in January 1675.
   vii. Mary, m. Samuel Wilbore, son of William and Martha Wilbore.
   viii. Rebecca, m. Robert Kirby, son of Richard and Patience (Gifford) Kirby, b. 10 March 1674.
   ix.   Elizabeth, m. 3 July 1707 Benjamin Tripp, son of John and Susanna (Anthony) Tripp.
   x.   Katharine, m. Thomas Cornell, son of Samuel Cornell.
4. xi.   Ichabod.

3. SAMUEL[3] POTTER (Nathaniel[2], Nathaniel[1]), born in January 1675 in Dartmouth, died in 1748. Residence: Dartmouth.

He married MARY BRENTON, born in 1681.

His will, made 5 March 1738 and proved 17 Aug. 1748: "To wife improvement of all real estate for life; to sons Nathaniel and Aaron five shillings each; to son Benjamin ten acres at death of wife and like legacy to son Samuel; to son Job 20 acres at death of wife; to daughters Fear Halliday, wife of William, Mary Tripp, wife of Othniel and Elizabeth Day, wife of Richard, all household goods at death of wife and one half of stock and outdoor movables; to sons Benjamin, Samuel and Job, one half of stock and outdoor movables."

Children, all recorded in Dartmouth:
5.   i.   Aaron, b. 26 Sept. 1701.
    ii.   Nathaniel, b. 9 Sept. 1703 in Dartmouth; m. there 10 March
          1725 Zerviah Cudworth of Freetown, Mass.
    iii.   Fear, b. 3 May 1705; m. in LC 25 Dec. 1723 William Halliday.
    iv.   Mary, b. 11 Feb. 1709; m. Othniel Tripp.
    v.   Elizabeth, b. in Dartmouth 10 Aug. 1711; m. Richard Day.
    vi.   Benjamin, b. 23 Sept. 1714; m. in Dartmouth 11 Nov. 1736
          Ruth Brownell of Dartmouth.
    vii.   Samuel Jr., b. in Dartmouth 23 Sept. 1714; m. there 23 Sept.
          1730 Elizabeth Maxfield.
    viii. Job, b. 29 Nov. 1717 in Dartmouth.

4. ICHABOD[3] POTTER (Nathaniel[2], Nathaniel[1]), died in Dartmouth
in 1755. Residence: Dartmouth. He married ELEANOR (--).
    His will, made 15 March 1754 and proved 4 Nov. 1755: "To son
Jonathan part of homestead farm; to son Ichabod part of homestead
farm where I now live, he paying all legacies; to grandson Thomas
Potter, son of George, deceased, land; to son Stokes, certain land;
to daughter Rebecca a bed and privilege to live with her mother while
unmarried, and at her marriage 10 pounds by son Jonathan; to daughter
Sarah Wood four pounds; to granddaughter Elizabeth Potter, daughter of
George, deceased, . . . to wife Eleanor all household goods, all money
in the house, a cow and privilege of dwelling house while widow, and
maintenance by sons Jonathan and Ichabod; to son Jonathan, Stokes·and
Ichabod, rest of live stock and husbandry tools; to daughters Rebecca
Potter and Sarah Wood all household goods left at death of wife; to son
Jonathan all wearing apparel."

Children, born and recorded in Dartmouth:
    i.   Rebecca, b. 29 March 1710.
    ii.   George, b. 3 Jan. 1714; m. in LC 21 April 1740 Martha
         Case.
    iii. Jonathan, b. 14 Nov. 1716; m. 28 Sept. 1740 Rebecca
         Southworth.
    iv.   Elizabeth, b. 16 Dec. 1718.
    v.   Stokes, b. 16 Dec. 1720; m. in Dartmouth 22 Nov. 1740
         (1744?) Phebe Durfee.
6. vi.   Ichabod, b. 9 Feb. 1722.
    vii. Sarah, b. 13 March 1725; m. in LC 19 Sept. 1745 Henry
         Wood, son of Henry and Content (Thurston) Wood.

5. AARON[4] POTTER (Samuel[3], Nathaniel[2], Nathaniel[1]), born in
Dartmouth 26 Sept. 1701. Married HOPESTILL (--). Residence:
Dartmouth.

Children, born and recorded in Dartmouth:
    i.   John, b. 5 Sept. 1723; d. in Dartmouth 27 March 1778; m.
         there 21 March 1741 Margaret Gifford, daughter of
         Jeremiah Gifford of Dartmouth.
    ii.   Stoughton (Stephen), b. 17 April 1725; m. in Dartmouth 8
         March 1751 Ruth Weaver of Swansea.
7. iii. Champlin, b. 23 May 1727.

iv.   Thomas, b. 5 Feb. 1730.
v.   Sarah, b. 7 Feb. 1733.

6. ICHABOD[4] POTTER (Ichabod[3], Nathaniel[2], Nathaniel[1]), born in Dartmouth 9 Feb. 1722. Residence: Dartmouth.

He married in LC 26 Dec. 1751 HOPE THURSTON of LC, daughter of Edward and Sarah (Carr) Thurston, born in LC 8 Sept. 1727.

Children:
i.   Thurston, b. in Westport 25 Oct. 1757; d. 16 June 1744; m. 16 May 1782 in Dartmouth Deborah Nye.
ii.   Barney, m. Lucy (--).
iii. Edward, d. 26 April 1845; m. in Westport 22 April 1798 Betsey S. Potter of Taunton.
8. iv.   Ichabod, b. in 1758.

7. CHAMPLIN[5] POTTER (Aaron[4], Samuel[3], Nathaniel[2], Nathaniel[1]), born in Dartmouth 23 May 1727. Residence: Dartmouth and LC.

He married first in Swansea 20 April 1749 HEPZIBAH GIBBS of Swansea. He married second in LC 15 Dec. 1750 (intention in Dartmouth 19 Oct. 1750) ABIGAIL HILLIARD, daughter of David and Susannah (Luther) Hilliard, born in LC 11 Oct. 1732, died 3 July 1753 ae 21. She is buried in the Old Commons cemetery.

Children:
i.   Henry.
ii.   David, b. in LC 24 April 1752; d. in 1815; m. Ruth Briggs.
iii. John, m. in LC 3 Oct. 1776 Mrs. Rebecca Brownell of LC.
iv.   Samuel, b. in 1757; d. 6 March 1846; m. 21 Nov. 1782 in Dartmouth Deborah Ricketson, daughter of John and Phebe Ricketson.
v.   Patience, b. 14 Nov. 1765; d. in March 1853; m. in Dartmouth 29 Jan. 1786 Noah Russell of Dartmouth.

8. ICHABOD[5] POTTER JR. (Ichabod[4], Ichabod[3], Nathaniel[2], Nathaniel[1]), born in Westport in 1758, died there in 1821. Residence: Westport and LC.

He married in Westport 9 March 1794 CYNTHIA SHERMAN (or Cynthia Macumber) of Westport.

His will, recorded book 5, page 193, made 30 March 1820 and proved 14 Aug. 1820: ". . . To wife Cynthia all household goods and use of one third of all real estate; to son Stokes who is now absent 500 dollars and if he does not return to his wife Cassandra 100 dollars; unto daughter Phebe 100 dollars; to son Pardon 300 dollars when 21 years of age. . . To son George rest and residue. . . "

Children:
9. i.   George, b. 27 Nov. 1792.
ii.   John, d. in 1820; m. about 1819 Ruth Coggeshalle.
iii. Stokes, b. in (?) in LC; d. in 1837; m. Cassandra Reed.
iv.   Phebe, b. in LC in (?); d. in 1850; m. Melvin Borden.
v.   Pardon, b. in LC 15 Dec. 1811; d. in 1832; m. Eliza B. Mathews, daughter of Jeremiah and Sarah Mathews.

9. GEORGE[6] POTTER (Ichabod[5], Ichabod[4], Ichabod[3], Nathaniel[2], Nathaniel[1]), born in Westport in 1792, died in LC 1 March 1878 ae 85.

He married about 1823 SALLY PALMER, daughter of John Stoddard and Margaret (Macomber) Palmer, born in LC in February 1815, died there 28 April 1882.

Children:
- i. Cynthia, probably m. Samuel Woodworth.
- 10. ii. John Barney, b. 11 Oct. 1827.
- iii. William, b. in LC 18 Sept. 1834; d. 1 April 1876; m. 15 June 1857 L. L. Kelly.
- 11. iv. George Mowrey, b. 13 Feb. 1839.

10. JOHN BARNEY[7] POTTER (George[6], Ichabod[5], Ichabod[4], Ichabod[3], Nathaniel[2], Nathaniel[1]), born in LC 11 Oct. 1829, died there 30 Nov. 1912. He is buried in Pleasant View cemetery. He married in LC 14 Oct. 1850 SARAH WILCOX, daughter of Joseph and Rhoda (Lake) Wilcox of Tiverton, born in Tiverton 1 April 1830, died in LC 19 Aug. 1924 ae 94.

Residence: LC. This family was listed in the census of 1865 and again in 1880. They lived at the corner in Pottersville.

Children, recorded in LC:
- i. Grafton, b. in LC 30 June 1851; d. there 15 Nov. 1851 ae 5 months.
- ii. Grafton 2d, b. in LC 27 May 1852.
- iii. Clifton Fremont, b. in LC 4 June 1856; d. there 3 Jan. 1931; m. Elizabeth Grinnell, daugher of William and Ella (Hindle) Grinnell, b. in Tiverton 9 March 1872, d. in LC 7 March 1925.
- iv. A daughter, b. in LC 26 Sept. 1859; d. 27 Sept. 1859 ae 1 day.

11. GEORGE MOWREY[7] POTTER (George[6], Ichabod[5], Ichabod[4], Ichabod[3], Nathaniel[2], Nathaniel[1]), born in LC 13 Feb. 1839, died in LC 19 Dec. 1921.

He married in LC 21 Oct. 1864 HANNAH GRAY WILBOR, daughter of John Gray and Susan (Crosby) Wilbor, born in LC 15 June 1845, died there 7 Sept. 1917. They are buried in Pleasant View Cemetery near the Stone Church in Tiverton.

Residence: LC. They lived on the corner in Pottersville. He was a stone mason.

Children, recorded in LC:
- i. Emma Frances, b. in LC 2 June 1865; d. there 10 Oct. 1950 ae 85; m. in LC 22 June 1882 Gershom Wordell, son of Gideon and Sarah (Grinnell) Wordell.
- ii. Susan Alida, b. in LC 22 Aug. 1868; d. there 25 Feb. 1925 ae 56.
- iii. Nellie Fuller, b. 17 Sept. 1876 in LC; d. there 30 July 1943; m. 25 Sept. 1898 William Hazard Wilbor, son of Oliver and Mary (Field) Wilbor, d. in 1929.
- iv. A daughter, b. in LC 29 April 1875.

THE PRICE FAMILY

1. **JOHN[1] PRICE**, son of John and Mary (Rouse) Price, born about 1681. Residence: LC.

He was married in LC 8 Jan. 1702 by Joseph Church, justice, to MARTHA GRAVES, daughter of John and Martha (Mitton) Graves of Cascoe, Maine, born in 1680.

He was a cordwainer. His mother was Mary Rouse, daughter of John and Anna (Pabodie) Rouse. She died in 1698 and is buried in LC in the Old Commons cemetery.

His wife, Martha Graves, was the daughter of John Graves and Martha Mitton, who was the daughter of Michael Mitton and his wife, Elizabeth Cleves, who was the daughter of George Cleves, the founder of Portland, Maine. Martha Graves's sister came to LC also and married William Bailey, son of John, and grandson of the first settler, William Bailey. See the Genealogical Dictionary of Maine and New Hampshire for further information.

At the settlement of the estate of James Rider of LC in 1715/6 Rider's goods or part of them were at the house of John Price and part were at the house of Capt. Rouse. In the Old Commons cemetery there is a grave marked "Here lyeth John ye son of John Price and Martha his wife. He died November ye 29th 1718 aged 18 dys." Next to this grave is the grave of his grandmother Martha (Mitton) Graves, but only the foot stone is now in existence. It says, "Martha Graves 1700."

        Children, recorded in LC:
- i.   Mary, b. 15 Nov. 1703.
- ii.   John, b. 2 Feb. 1706; d. 23 Feb. 1718.
- 2. iii.   William, b. 12 Jan. 1708.
- iv.   Elizabeth, b. 11 Jan. 1710.
- 3. v.   Oliver, b. 1 Sept. 1713.
- vi.   Simeon, b. 23 May 1717.
- vii. John, d. 29 Nov. 1718 ae 18 days.
- viii. Martha, b. 8 Nov. 1719.
- ix.   Keturah, b. 23 Feb. 1722.
- x.   John 2d, b. 10 Sept. 1724.

2. **WILLIAM[2] PRICE** (John[1]), born in LC 12 Jan. 1708. Residence: LC.

He was married first in LC 24 Dec. 1731 by Richard Billings, justice, to SUSANNA SALISBURY, daughter of Joseph and Mary (Padduck?) Salisbury of LC, born 7 April 1713. He married second in LC in March 1743 DEBORAH GIBBS, daughter of Warren and Abigail (Hilliard) Gibbs of LC, born there 19 Dec. 1717.

        Children by first wife:
- i.   Nathaniel, b. in LC 18 April 1732.
- ii.   John, b. in Tiverton 24 April 1735.
- iii.   Joseph, b. in Tiverton 18 March 1737/8.

        Children by second wife, recorded in LC:
- iv.   Susanna, b. 2 Dec. 1743.

    v.   William, b. 13 April 1745.
    vi.   Seth, b. 23 Oct. 1746.
    vii.   Mary, b. 24 Dec. 1747.
    viii. Warren, b. 26 Dec. 1749.
    ix.   Deborah, b. 3 Nov. 1751; m. in LC 25 July 1784 Thomas
             Kempton, son of Thomas and Mary Kempton.

    3. OLIVER[2] PRICE (John[1]), born in LC 1 Sept. 1713. Residence:
LC.
    He married in LC 20 Dec. 1738 PHEBE GIBBS, daughter of Warren
and Abigail (Hilliard) Gibbs of LC, born there 11 Nov. 1714.

          Children, born and recorded in LC:
    i.   Benjamin (twin), b. 6 Dec. 1739.
    ii.   Phebe, b. 6 Dec. 1739.
    iii.   Isaac, b. 25 Aug. 1741.
    iv.   Oliver, b. 21 June 1743.
    v.   Simeon, b. 6 March 1745.

THE RECORDS FAMILY

    1. JONATHAN[1] RECORDS, born in 1684, died in LC 1 June 1742
ae 58. He is buried in Old Commons cemetery.
    He was married in LC 28 Feb. 1706 by Richard Billings,
justice, to MARY WILBORE, daughter of John and Hannah Wilbore
of LC, born there about 1686, died there in 1771.
    Residence: LC. They lived on the road that goes to South Shore.
They lived at the corner of Swamp Road and the road now called Wilbor
Sisson Boulevard. He was a cooper.
    His will, recorded book 10, page 163, made 10 May 1742 and
proved 15 June 1742: "To wife Mary a bed with furniture and one cow.
To son Jonathan my desk, oval table, two chests, in my great room
below, all my cattle, horses, working tools, my pew in meeting house,
great long table, my great chair and he to be executor. To daughter
Hannah Wilbor, one good bed. To daughter Mary Church, 10 pounds
and . . . cupboard. To daughter Martha Wilbor, high case of drawers
and great looking glass. To daughter Comfort Tabor, my loom and
weaving tackling that belongs to it. To daughter Abishag Briggs, all
my pewter, brass and iron. To John Records if he be in the land of
the living ten pounds if he ever returns home again. The rest and
residue to son Jonathan and his mother. . . "

          Children, all recorded in LC:
    i.   Hannah, b. 24 Nov. 1706; m. in LC 20 June 1728 Jeremiah
             Wilbor; son of William and (--) (Tallman) Wilbor and
             grandson of Peter Tallman.
    ii.   Mary, b. 23 April 1709; d. 16 Feb. 1784; m. in LC in
             September 1731 Richard Church, son of Joseph and
             Grace (Shaw) Church.

  iii. Martha, b. 23 April 1709; m. in LC 12 Aug. 1729 Joseph
     Wilbor, son of William and (--) (Tallman) Wilbor.
  iv. Judith, b. 15 Jan. 1711; d. 13 Jan. 1729.
  v. John, b. 5 Nov. 1714.
  vi. Comfort, b. 5 Nov. 1714; m. in LC 23 Nov. 1738 Thomas
     Tabor.
2. vii. Jonathan, b. 20 May 1720.
  viii. Abishag, b. 16 Feb. 1716; d. 17 May 1790; m. 16 July 1739
     William Briggs, son of Job and Mary (Tallman) Briggs.

  2. JONATHAN² RECORDS (Jonathan¹), born in LC 20 May 1720,
died there in April 1777.

  He was married in LC 11 Aug. 1741 by William Hall, justice, to
MARY BRIGGS, daughter of William and Deborah (Church) Briggs,
born in LC 12 Aug. 1719.

  His will, recorded LC wills, book 2, page 415, made 11 March
1775 and proved 8 April 1779: ". . . being something infirm as to
bodily health. . . To my wife Mary improvement of best room in my
now dwelling house, best bed and furniture, one cow, four sheep and
all my geese and to be kept by my executor both in winter and summer,
and also improvement of all household goods as long as she remains
my widow. To son Owen my old gun, silver buttons for breeches and
a living in my house as long as he is single. To son William whole of
my real estate where I now dwell both housing and land and all shop
tools. To daughter Rhoda one bed stead, bed and cord, my high cupboard, being in my house and a living in my house as long as she is
single. To daughter Rachel one bed, bed stead and great oval table
and a living in my house as long as she is single. To daughter Ruth
one bed, bed stead, my great chest and a living in my house as long
as she is single. To three daughters, Rhoda, Rachel and Ruth, all
the rest of my household goods. My son William shall provide for
his mother as long as she remains my widow and live in the house with
her. My pew in the Congregational Meeting House to all my children,
son William to have the rest and residue and to be my executor. . . "

    Children, the first three and last recorded in LC:
  i. Jonathan, b. 22 Aug. 1743; d. in 1771.
  ii. Judith, b. 13 Feb. 1745.
  iii. Rhoda, b. 4 Jan. 1747; d. February 1785.
  iv. Thomas.
  v. Owen.
3. vi. William, b. 8 Jan. 1758.
  vii. Rachel, m. Nicholas Underwood.
  viii. Ruth, m. in LC 24 Feb. 1785 Champlin Wilbor, son of Walter
     and Catharine (Davenport) Wilbor.

  3. WILLIAM³ RECORDS (Jonathan², Jonathan¹), born in LC 8 Jan.
1758, died there 8 Sept. 1825. Residence: LC. He was given a place
on the Swamp Road where both his father and his grandfather lived before him.

  He was married in LC 12 Dec. 1778 by the Rev. Jonathan Ellis to
JUDITH BROWNELL, daughter of Paul and Deborah (Dennis) Brownell,

born in LC 23 Jan. 1758, died there 18 Feb. 1820.

Children:

i.   Jonathan, b. in LC 27 Feb. 1780; m. (1) in LC 15 Feb. 1807
      Priscilla Hilliard, daughter of Samuel and Elizabeth
      (Pearce) Hilliard; m. (2) in LC 7 Jan. 1816 Mary Brownell,
      daughter of George and Elizabeth (Peckham) Brownell.
ii.   Dennis, b. in LC 13 June 1782; d. 15 Nov. 1809; m. (intention
      2 Sept. 1804) Thankful Wilbor, daughter of Brownell and
      Esther (Wilbor) Wilbor, b. in LC 21 Dec. 1781, d. there
      5 Jan. 1806.
iii. Owen, b. 21 May 1784; m. in LC 11 Dec. 1808 Sally Wilbor,
      daughter of William Jr. and Sarah (Carr) Wilbor, b. 19
      July 1784, d. 16 June 1835 in LC. Residence: Dartmouth.
iv.   Rhoda, b. 14 June 1786; m. in LC 7 Nov. 1806 William Hilliard,
      son of Jonathan and Susanna (Wilbor) Hilliard of LC.
v.   Hannah, b. 1 Oct. 1788; d. 26 Aug. 1825; unmarried.
vi.   Priscilla, b. 22 Jan. 1794.
vii. Thomas, b. 15 March 1797; d. in LC 22 March 1881; m. Ann
      Pearce, daughter of Col. Joseph and Anna (Hilliard) Pearce.
viii. Mary, b. 28 Aug. 1799; m. Asa Davoll.

THE RICHMOND FAMILY

1. JOHN[1] RICHMOND, born in 1594. He came from Wiltshire,
England, probably from the town of Amesbury. Mr. Harry Richmond
of LC found in Bristol, England, a ship's passenger list on which it
said that John Richmond of Amesbury in Wiltshire bound for Virginia
on a ship sailing in 1635.
    John Richmond was one of the purchasers of Taunton, Mass., in
1657. Undoubtedly he was married before he came to this country, but
neither the name of his wife nor the date of his marriage have been
discovered. He died in Taunton 20 March 1664 ae 70.

Children:

i.   John, b. about 1620; m. Abigail Rogers, daughter of John
      Rogers of Duxbury, Mass.
2. ii.   Edward, b. about 1632.
iii. Sarah, b. about 1638; m. (1) Edward Rew; m. (2) James
      Walker.
iv.   Mary, b. about 1639; m. William Paul of Berkely, Mass.

2. CAPT. EDWARD[2] RICHMOND (John[1]), born about 1632, prob-
ably before his father came to this country. He died in LC in 1696.
    He married first ABIGAIL DAVIS, daughter of William and Mary
Davis of Boston. He married second AMEY BULL, daughter of
Governor Henry and Elizabeth Bull.

Before coming to LC, he owned a place in Newport, in that part now called Middletown. A gunsmith, he bought two great lots in LC. He lived on the place known as the Father Richmond place, which is slightly north of the entrance to Meeting House Lane, on the other side of the West Main Road and is buried in this place, where his gravestone (the next to the oldest in town) may still be seen in the small Richmond cemetery. He was the first settler by the name of Richmond in LC.

He was one of the incorporaters of LC in 1674. The deed of the town was made out to the following first settlers:

Joseph Church	Samuel Gray	Thomas Ward
William Southworth	John Irish	John Shearman
John House	Peter Gilmore	Isaac Woodworth
Nathaniel Warren	John Washburn	William Pabodie
Benjamin Woodworth	Benjamin Church	John Rogers
Edward Richmond	William Fobes	Simon Rouse
Joseph Woodworth		Josiah Cook

These men came primarily from Duxbury, Plymouth and other Massachusetts towns, but they were soon joined by a much larger flood of people who came over from the Island of Rhode Island and the towns of Newport and Portsmouth.

Capt. Richmond's inventory is on record in Taunton.

GRAVESTONE OF CAPTAIN EDWARD RICHMOND
Richmond Cemetery, Little Compton, R. I.

From the book of Little Compton Records, is this copy of the listing of the estate of Capt. Edward Richmond:

Edward Richmond administrator of the estate of his father Capt. Edward Richmond late of LC deceased exhibited an account May 19 1697 of debts, "Which I have payde, and stand engaged to pay since his decease." Items paid.

To Doctor Arnold for his help in my father's sickness.
For drinke at the funerall.
To Mr. William Foabs and Daniel Eatton for taken an Inventory.
Pyde Weston Clark.
To Saml Crandall for keepeing a payr of oxen.
For three quarts of rum when we divided the estate.
To Daniel Howland.
Twife Goeing to Bristol and Christopr, Charges.
Joseph Blackman for three paire of shoose.
Ezeck Carr for Triming of Caske.
Mr. Jones in money which was due by him by bond.
Simon Rouse for mending a Gunn lock.
John Iriish for half a c of Clabords.
John Peckham for mowing.
Daniel Greenel for Expence when the land was lotted.
Daniel Eatton for Father's expence.
Tom the Indian for digging the grave and a debt due to him before.
John Briggs for keeping of rams and 5s for boot for horfs.
John Smith the taylor for work done.
Brother Henry and Ann.
Mr. Pabodie for the allotment and going with us.
Ebenezer Allen
Thomas Waite.
Doctr Talmon for cureing Amos his legg.
William Simmons for smith Worke.
Zachariah Allin.
Mr. Natha payde for a debt upon booke.
Mr. Collings for rent of sheep.
Mr. Codington for book debt.
Daniel Thirston for money lent and Book Dt.
Mr. Homsbye for expence.
Mr. Pabodye and Mr. Foabs for laying out land.
Jonathan Danford for makeing a Coff.
Aunt Northway for a winding sheet.
Joseph Church Jr.
To Mr. William Foabs 8s wch he pd for father for the Purchase of land.
Aron Davis for keeping a calfe and one Board lent.
And for funerall, parts of ye sd Estat delivered to the several children. 351 pds 19 s 10 p May 19 1697.

Children by first wife:
i.   Abigail, b. in 1656; d. in 1744; m. (1) about 1679 John
      Remington, son of John and Abigail Remington, d. in
      1688; m. (2) Henry Gardiner, b. in 1645, d. in 1744.
3. ii.   Edward, b. in 1658.
iii. John, d. in 1738 or before; m. Elizabeth (--).
iv.   Mary, m. William Palmer.
v.   Elizabeth, b. 6 Dec. 1665; d. 9 Feb. 1717; m. John Palmer.
vi.   Esther, b. in 1669; d. 12 Nov. 1706; m. Thomas Burgess,
      son of Thomas and Lydia (Gaunt) Burgess, b. in 1668,
      d. 1 July 1743.
4. vii. Sylvester, b. in 1672.
viii. Sarah.

Children by second wife:
ix.   Henry.
x.   Ann.

3. EDWARD[3] RICHMOND (Edward[2], John[1]), born in 1658, died
in 1682 in LC. He married about 1682 SARAH (--), died 14 Feb. 1743.
Residence: LC.
He was the fourth town clerk in LC; his father Edward was the
second town clerk.

Children, recorded in LC:
i.   Abigail, b. in 1683; m. John Simmons.
5. ii.   Edward, b. 3 Dec. 1689.
iii. Anna, b. 22 Jan. 1692/3; m. 3 May 1711 William Wilbore.
iv.   Elizabeth, b. in 1694; d. young.
6. v.   Benjamin, b. 10 Jan. 1695/6.
vi.   Amey, b. 22 Nov. 1697.
vii. Mary, b. 15 March 1700; m. Peter Crandell.
viii. Esther, b. 3 Feb. 1703.
ix.   Abigail, b. 25 Nov. 1704; m. George Manchester.
x.   Elizabeth, b. in November 1707.

4. COLONEL SYLVESTER[3] RICHMOND (Edward[2], John[1]), born
in LC in 1672, died there 20 Nov. 1754. Residence: LC.
He married first about 1693 ELIZABETH ROGERS, born in 1672,
died in LC 21 Oct. 1724. She was the daughter of John Rogers of
Duxbury, who married Elizabeth Pabodie and was granddaughter of
John Alden and his wife, Priscilla Mullins. He married second 18
Feb. 1728 DEBORAH CUSHING, daughter of John and Sarah (Hawks)
Loring, born in September 1674, died 18 Oct. 1770.

Children by first wife, recorded in LC:
7. i.   William, b. 10 Oct. 1694.
ii.   Elizabeth, b. 10 May 1696; m. 8 July 1716 (?) Nathaniel
      Fisher.
8. iii. Sylvester, b. 30 June 1698.
9. iv.   Peleg, b. 25 Oct. 1700.
10. v.   Perez, b. 5 Oct. 1702.
11. vi.   Ichabod, b. 27 Feb. 1704.

vii.   Ruth, b. 7 March 1705/6; m. 27 Aug. 1724 Ephraim Atwood.
viii. Hannah, b. 9 July 1709.
ix.   Sarah, b. 31 Oct. 1711; m. 19 Nov. 1730 Peleg Heath.
x.   Mary, b. 29 Nov. 1713; m. the Rev. Nicholas Loring.
xi.   Rogers, b. 25 May 1716; m. Mrs. Susannah (Vial) Lee.

5. EDWARD[4] RICHMOND (Edward[3], Edward[2], John[1]), born in LC
3 Dec. 1689.

He married 6 May 1711 REBECCA THURSTON, daughter of Jonathan
and Sarah Thurston, born 28 Nov. 1689. He was a freeman of Newport.

    Children, recorded in LC:
i.   Sarah, b. 20 Dec. 1711.
ii.   Mary, b. in 1714.
iii. Priscilla, b. 27 Feb. 1718; m. 19 March 1793 Samuel Hart.
iv.   Eunice, b. 23 Sept. 1722.

6. BENJAMIN[4] RICHMOND (Edward[3], Edward[2], John[1]), born in
LC 10 Jan. 1695, married about 1719 MARY (--). Residence: LC.

    Children, recorded in LC:
i.   Elizabeth, b. 16 April 1718; m. Benjamin Hathaway (?).
ii.   Mary, b. 16 June 1720.
iii. Sarah, b. 26 Nov. 1721; d. 2 June 1726.
iv.   Edward, b. 17 July 1723; m. Elizabeth Powell.
v.   Priscilla, b. 3 March 1725; d. 14 Sept. 1726.
vi.   Sarah, b. 2 Nov. 1726.
vii. Priscilla, b. 26 Feb. 1729.
viii. Rebecca, b. 26 Feb. 1729.

7. JUDGE WILLIAM[4] RICHMOND (Sylvester[3], Edward[2], John[1]),
born in LC 10 Oct. 1694, died there 22 Feb. 1770.

He married in LC 8 July 1724 ANNA GRAY, daughter of Dr. Thomas
and Anna (Little) Gray, born in LC 29 Jan. 1702, died in Bristol 9 Oct.
1762.

He was one of the assistants to the Governor from 1753 to 1755. He
was a judge, and instrumental in locating the line securing Little
Compton to Rhode Island. He was named town clerk 15 March 1731.

His will, dated 5 July 1765 and proved 3 April 1770 in LC: ". . . To
son Barzilla 500 Spanish milled dollars. To son Ephraim 150 Spanish
milled dollars. To son William Richmond northerly part of ye farm I
now live on, from the highway to the sea from a straight line in the
middle of said farm, and what right I have in Dye lot with my dwelling
house and one half of my Collamer land. To son Perez the other half
or remaining part of said farm with the other half of Collamer land.
To son Thomas 5 Spanish milled dollars. To son Sylvester 300 milled
dollars. To daughters Elizabeth Brownell, Mary Ware and Sarah
Walker 50 dollars each. To daughter Abigail Fitts 100 dollars and my
silver tankard. To all my daughters my remaining household goods.
To daughter-in-law Hannah Richmond, wife of son William, my great
Bible and my books to be divided among my daughters. To grandson
Gilbert Richmond, son of my son Ichabod, 100 dollars. To grand-

children, children of my son Ephraim, excepting Anna, 100 dollars equally. To granddaughter Anna, one daughter of my son Ephraim, 50 dollars. To son William Richmond my Negro man named Solomon and my Negro woman named Amey, he to take care of her during her life and she to be obedient to him. To son Ebenezer. . . Sons William and Perez to be executors. . . "

Children, born in LC:
	i.	Barzilla, b. 13 April 1721; m. 24 Nov. 1743 Sarah Knight.
12.	ii.	Ephraim, b. 5 May 1723.
	iii.	Elizabeth, b. 26 Feb. 1725; m. Jonathan Brownell.
13.	iv.	William, b. 20 Aug. 1727.
14.	v.	Perez, b. 13 Oct. 1729.
	vi.	Icabod, b. 18 Oct. 1731; m. (1) Martha (--); m. (2) 15 Nov. 1753 Mary Vunis.
	vii.	Thomas, b. 13 Dec. 1733.
	viii.	Marcy, b. 26 Dec. 1735; m. (1) Dr. George Ware; m. (2) 10 Sept. 1772 Thomas Church.
	ix.	Sarah, b. 8 Jan. 1738; m. 25 March 1758 David Walker.
	x.	Sylvester, b. 7 Oct. 1740; m. (intention 14 Nov. 1762) Lusanna (Cook) Whitmarsh.
	xi.	Abigail, b. 26 Feb. 1744; m. (intention 14 Nov. 1762) 29 Dec. 1764 Capt. Peter Pitt Jr.

8. COL. SYLVESTER[4] RICHMOND (Sylvester[3], Edward[2], John[1]), born in Dartmouth 30 June 1698, died 14 Jan. 1783. He married ELIZABETH TALBUT, daughter of Jared and Rebecca Talbut of Dighton, Mass., born 14 June 1699, died 23 June 1772. He moved from LC to Dartmouth.

Children, first two born in LC, the balance born in Dighton:
	i.	Ezra, b. 20 Jan. 1721; m. Mary Baylies.
	ii.	Rebecca, b. 12 Feb. 1723; m. 15 Aug. 1751 Constant Southworth.
	iii.	Elizabeth, b. 22 Dec. 1726; m. Thomas S. Searles.
	iv.	Sylvester, b. 20 Nov. 1729; m. Abigail Nightingale.
	v.	Hannah, b. 17 Sept. 1731; m. Joseph Andrews.
	vi.	Mary, b. 10 March 1733/4; m. (1) Samuel Buckman; m. (2) Col. Jonathan Loring.
	vii.	Ruth, b. 18 March 1736/7; d. in Dighton, Mass.
	viii.	John, b. 12 March 1738/9; m. (1) Margaret Lee; m. (2) Mrs. Atwood.
15.	ix.	Nathaniel, b. 12 March 1738/9.

9. PELEG[4] RICHMOND (Sylvester[3], Edward[2], John[1]), born in LC 25 Oct. 1700. He married first 14 Dec. 1727 PATIENCE PALMER, born in LC 19 Feb. 1704, died 27 Dec. 1728. He married second MRS. MARY VIOL.

Children by first wife:
	i.	Gamaliel, b. 24 April 1728; m. Judith Peabodie, b. 20 July 1730. They had five children.

10. CAPT. PEREZ[5] RICHMOND (William[4], Sylvester[3], Edward[2], John[1]), born in LC 5 Oct. 1702, died there 15 Sept. 1770.

He married 11 March 1731 DEBORAH LORING, daughter of Thomas and Deborah (Cushing) Loring, born in Duxbury 9 Dec. 1710, died in LC 14 April 1782. Both are buried in the Old Commons cemetery.

They lived in that part of LC which later became a part of Westport Harbor.

Children, recorded in LC:

   i. Hannah, b. 15 Jan. 1732; m. 2 June 1759 David Jacobs.
16. ii. Joshua, b. 1 July 1734.
   iii. Edward, b. 5 Aug. 1736; m. 25 Oct. 1770 Elizabeth Throop.
   iv. Loring, b. 27 Dec. 1738; d. 20 Sept. 1754.
   v. Perez*, b. 1 Feb. 1741; m. 28 Dec. 1770 Hannah Brightman.
   vi. Deborah, b. 30 June 1742; m. 19 March 1772 James Jacobs.
   vii. Elizabeth, b. 21 Nov. 1745; m. 12 July 1763 Capt. Joshua Jacobs.
17. viii. Benjamin, b. 7 Aug. 1747.
   ix. Mary, b. 26 Aug. 1749; m. 11 Sept. 1777 Ephraim Simmons.
   x. Lucy, b. 26 July 1751; m. 7 June 1770 George Brownell.

*Perez, his son, lived in the house which was on the place recently owned by Frederick R. Brownell, at the head of Meeting House Land on the west side of the road. His commission from King George II was dated 1 Sept. 1742. He inherited the bulk of his father's property and was prominent among the men of his time. His will was dated 29 May 1765 and proved 24 Sept. 1770. His homestead was partly in LC and partly in Westport, and in that part of Westport which is now Westport Harbor. He and his wife are buried in the LC cemetery. Her stone has the following inscription: "In memory of Deborah, relict of Capt. Perez Richmond of Dartmouth. She departed this life 24 April 1782 in the 72d year of her age. Farewell, vain world, thou hast been to me, dust and a shadow, these I leave with thee."

11. DR. ICHABOD[4] RICHMOND (Sylvester[3], Edward[2], John[1]), born in LC 27 Feb. 1704, died 29 Sept. 1762.

He married first about 1753 MARY (--). He married second (banns published 20 July 1757) ABIGAIL FORD of Pembroke.

He was a physician, practicing in Dartmouth in 1733, in Bristol in 1737, and in LC in 1746. He bought the homestead of Henry Head of Dartmouth.

Children by his first wife:

   i. Gilbert, b. 27 April 1754.
   ii. Nathaniel, m. (1) Sally Mann; m. (2) Susannah Greene.

12. EPHRAIM WILLIAM[4] RICHMOND (Sylvester[3], Edward[2], John[1]), born in LC 5 May 1723. He married 19 Jan. 1744 ELIZABETH COOK of Tiverton, died in April 1797 in Tiverton.

He settled with his family in LC in 1743, and his first three children were baptized there. He had a slave who was a hatter, who would go to Providence and work there at his trade. The slave helped to support his owner in his old age.

Children, born in LC but only two recorded there:

i. Jeremiah, b. 9 Aug. 1744; m. Elizabeth Warner.
ii. Lillis, b. in March 1746; m. 2 Nov. 1768 David Simmons.
iii. Alice, b. in 1749; m. (intention 7 Nov. 1770) Daniel Witherell.
iv. Anna, b. in 1749; m. 1 July 1770 William Simmons.
v. Gamaliel, b. about 1751.
vi. Ichabod, b. about 1754.
vii. Thomas, b. about 1757.
viii. James, b. about 1760; m. Mary Tompkins.
18. ix. William, b. 10 July 1763.
x. Mary, b. 20 Sept. 1765; d. 20 June 1847; m. 13 June 1784 James Tompkins.

13. COL. WILLIAM[5] RICHMOND (William[4], Sylvester[3], Edward[2], John[1]), born in LC 20 Aug. 1727, died there 23 Sept. 1807.

He married HANNAH GRAY, daughter of Samuel Gray, born in 1738, died 5 Jan. 1812. He owned the Capt. Edward Richmond place and is buried there. He had no children.

The following biography of Col. Richmond is taken from the Genealogy of the Richmond family by Joshua Richmond.

At the convention of the Governor's Council as supreme ordinary of the English colony of Rhode Island and Providence Plantations at Newport, May 1760, William Richmond Esq. was one of the ten assistants of Gov. Stephen Hopkins. He was one of the Representatives of the town in 1779, was first deputy in 1780, '81, '88, '90 and '93. He was moderator of town meetings in 1777, '82, '83, '86, '87, '88 and '91, and on the committee of safety for the county of Newport. He served in one or two campaigns in the Canadian war, as lieutenant under his brother, Colonel Barzillai; was lieutenant of a company sent against Crown Point in 1755, and Captain in Colonel Champlin's regiment in 1756. He had a command as Colonel in the Revolutionary War and was Colonel of the State Brigade in 1776. He was Military Governor of Newport at one time during the War. He went on a military expedition to Long Island. The British had penetrated on the east part of the Island and he went with a detachment of soldiers, from the Connecticut shore, and dispersed them. Colonel Richmond and General Barton, who surprised and took Prescott prisoner, were on terms of closest intimacy. The General was accustomed to spend a part of the summer with Colonel Richmond.

The Richmonds freed their slaves before the Revolution, and settled them in Dartmouth woods. The Richmond farm, owned and occupied by Col. William Richmond, lies north of the farm now owned by Frederic Brownell Esq. (which formerly was the property of Judge Perez Richmond and extends from the road to the Seaconnet River.) Here Capt. Edward Richmond (first of the name) settled, died and was buried. His tombstone is still visible in the old family burying ground. This farm was in the possession of the family continuously until within a few years. Rev. William Richmond of New York bought two and a half acres of land of Primus Collins, given to him by Colonel Richmond, tore the old house down and made the Richmond farm complete as it was in the beginning before the Colonel's gift to Collins.

There is a noted historical place on the farm called Awashonks

Rock, or Treaty Rock (named after Awashonks, the Queen of the Sogonate Indians) where Col. Benjamin Church made his treaty with Awashonks, the Queen, in King Philip's War. It was through his means and negotiations that the Indians of Seaconnet were induced to break with Philip.

The following inscription is upon the tombstone in the old family burial place, located near the house: "Col. William Richmond, who having served his country in several public stations for many years, departed this life Sept. 23, 1807, 81 years of age."

Colonel Richmond was a large man with very white hair in his old age. He was a gentleman of the old school, but jocose, liberal and greatly beloved by his family and kindred. He was wealthy for the times and one of the first men in the town, very active and public spirited in all its affairs. Many anecdotes are told of him and his slaves, of which the following may be interesting:

Once, in high party times, Colonel Richmond was told by the presiding officer that his vote would be taken out of the ballot box (though he was well known since boyhood to every man in the town) because he had not registered his name; the Colonel replied, "If you touch my vote, I shall come down with this cane on your head," at the same time holding the vote in his left hand and the rebellious cane in the right hand. The officer attempted to extract the vote, and the cane came down and hindered the operation. A row ensued, in the midst of which an unexpected combatant appeared. Primus Collins, who had been honored with election to the Negro governorship of Rhode Island (an ancient custom in the state) and who was always called Governor Collins, was in the gallery. The white of his eyes and of his teeth were soon visible; and exclaiming, "It is about time for

RICHMOND CEMETERY
on Treaty Rock Farm
--probably the oldest
cemetery in town.

In includes,
among others,
the graves of:

Capt. Edward Richmond
    (d. in November 1696)
William Richmond
    (d. 22 Feb. 1770)
Perez Richmond
    (d. 23 Nov. 1800)

this darkey to drop, " he leaped from the gallery into the midst of the
combatants and by means of his black face, sudden appearance, and
vigorous blows, scattered the opponents of "Old Master" right and
left and the vote remained undisturbed.

Primus Collins had been a slave of the Colonel, and was subject
to twenty five years service but he liberated him and afterwards gave
him a farm. This farm was called the Primus Flat Iron. When he
became a free voter, by the ownership of land, Colonel Richmond took
him to the polls and told him to put in his vote. The moderator forbade
it, and said he had no right. Colonel Richmond drew up his cane and
with a loud voice declared, "That man shall vote," and Collins became
a voter until his death. Afterwards, however, Isaac Wilbour (who was
Chief Justice and member of Congress) of LC got the word white in-
serted in the statute respecting voting. Colonel Richmond had another
slave named Saul, who had the entire supervision and control of his
farm. He found a Negro woman and bought her, and had Saul marry
her. They had children, one of whom he gave to the Rev. Mase Shepard,
his minister, and others to some of his friends. Saul was complete
master of ceremonies and affairs about the farm. An ox could not be
bought without his presence and counsel. Mr. Shaw, a member of the
Senate of Rhode Island from LC, said of the Richmonds in LC, "Damned
proud family, they esteem their Negroes better than common folks."

The Colonel was an ardent patriot and Revolutionist. He resided
at one time about the commencement of the Revolutionary struggle at
the house of his brother Barzilla in Providence, who was a good Deacon,
but timid and peace loving, if he did not in his heart sympathize with
the Tories. The good man had family worship regularly every morning.
Three days passed. The following morning the Deacon, as usual, had
read the Scripture and was rising in order to pray, when the Colonel
caught up his famous and trusty cane and, raising it above his head,
exclaimed, "Stop," and added, "I have been here now three days,
and every morning you have prayed and haven't mentioned the American
Congress, nor prayed for the success of the American arms. Now by
God, if you don't this morning, I will knock you down with the cane
when you say Amen." It is said the Colonel was not religious, but he
certainly believed in the efficacy of prayer, and his patriotism was
beyond a doubt.

Primus Collins lived in LC many years, and died in February
1858 aged eighty one years. He was highly esteemed and was a worthy
and pious man. His daughter married Charles Simmons, and lived
one time at the head of Middle Street, New Bedford, Mass.

14. JUDGE PEREZ[5] RICHMOND (William[4], Sylvester[3], Edward[2],
John[1]), born in LC 13 Oct. 1728/9, died 23 Nov. 1800/1.

He married 3 Feb. 1754 MERCY CHURCH, daughter of Thomas
and Edith (Woodman) Church, born 18 Sept. 1734, died 24 Oct. 1813.

He was appointed to enlist Minute Men in LC in June 1775, and
held various offices in the town. He was a leading and influential
man; auditor of town accounts, moderator of town meetings in 1784,
'85, '89, '90, '93 and '94. He was also judge of probate court and
president of the town council. A mild old gentleman, he was fond of
children and popular. He lived 50 or 60 years opposite the head of

Meeting House Lane, the place later owned by Fred R. Brownell.
In 1759 he was quarter master and enlisted officer for LC and
was one of a committee "Who shall use diligence to procure arms and
accoutrements" in 1776. He was killed by a fall from his horse.

Children, born and recorded in LC:.
i.   Sarah, b. 24 Aug. 1756; m. 27 April 1776 Job Clapp.
ii.   Ruth, b. 6 Sept. 1758.
iii. Elizabeth, b. 9 March 1760; m. Isaac Hathaway.
iv.   Mary, b. 29 Sept. 1761; d. 23 Nov. 1765.
19. v.   Thomas, b. 5 Sept. 1764.
vi.   Benjamin, b. 11 July 1765.
vii. Anna, b. 24 March 1767; m. 17 Jan. 1792 George Atwood
      of Dighton, son of Ephraim and Abigail Atwood.
viii. Charles, b. 28 Sept. 1768; d. 23 Jan. 1769.
ix.   Mary, b. 5 April 1770; m. in 1800 George Codding.
x.   Charles, b. 9 July 1773; ship wrecked 18 Oct. 1803.
xi.   Hannah, b. 17 Dec. 1775; m. Cyrus Ellis of Providence.

15. NATHANIEL[5] RICHMOND (Sylvester[4], Sylvester[3], Edward[2],
John[1]), born in Dighton, Mass., 12 March 1739, died 1 Jan. 1808.
Residence: Westport.
He married first (intention 28 Sept. 1765) ANNA BROWNELL,
daughter of Jonathan and Elizabeth (Richmond) Brownell. He married
second (intention 14 July 1792) REBECCA SHAW, daughter of David
Simmons of Dighton.

Children, born in Westport:
i.   Samuel Buckman, b. 14 April 1767; m. Eunice Mack.
ii.   Elizabeth, b. 5 Feb. 1769; m. Isaac Jones.
iii. Sylvester, b. 13 April 1771; m. Sarah Tyler.
iv.   Jonathan, b. 3 July 1774; m. Rebecca Almy.
v.   Mary, b. 19 March 1776; m. Silas Tuttle.
vi.   Ruth, b. 16 April 1780; m. (1) Loring Gray; m. (2) Deacon
      Thomas Burgess.
vii. John, b. 16 April 1780; m. Maria (--).
viii. Nancy, b. 11 Feb. 1783; m. Isaac Hathaway.
ix.   Fallee, b. 11 May 1785; m. Henry Dow Giffor.

20. iv.   Joshua, b. 27 April 1770.
v.   Deborah, b. 29 Oct. 1772; d. in Providence 27 March 1802.
vi.   Sally, b. 4 Feb. 1775; d. in Easton 15 May 1847; m. James
      Wiswell.

16. JOSHUA[5] RICHMOND (Perez[4], Sylvester[3], Edward[2], John[1]),
born in LC in that part which is now Westport Harbor 1 July 1734,
died 1 March 1778. He married 26 Nov. 1761 ELIZABETH CUSHING,
daughter of John and Deborah (Barker) Cushing of Scituate, Mass.,
born 9 April 1744, died 25 Oct. 1780. They are buried in the Old
Commons cemetery.

Children:
i.   Deborah, b. 8 June 1764; d. 12 Jan. 1772.
ii.   Cushing, b. 2 March 1766; d. on board the Jersey prison ship

in New York ae 14.
iii.   Elizabeth, b. 6 May 1768; m. 6 Sept. 1796 William Gay.

17. DR. BENJAMIN[5] RICHMOND (Perez[4], Sylvester[3], Edward[2], John[1]), born in LC in that part which is now Westport Harbor 7 Aug. 1747, died in LC 20 Feb. 1814.

He married 14 Oct. 1770 SARAH CHURCH, daughter of Thomas and Ruth (Bailey) Church, born 24 May 1751, died 7 March 1817. They are buried in the Old Commons cemetery. Her father was the son of Thomas Church by his third wife, Sarah, and he was the son of Col. Benjamin and Alice (Southworth) Church.

Many stories are told of Dr. Benjamin Richmond, of his kindness of heart and generosity, of his low fees for medical attendance, his eccentricities and quaint speeches. He was a surgeon in the Revolutionary War and a doctor in LC for many years. He lived and owned the place later owned by Samuel Soule which is on the Long Highway north of Snell Road, on the west side of the Long Highway. It is said that there are·many herbs still growing there, which were planted by him to be used in his profession. He and his wife are buried in the Old Commons cemetery.

Children, born in LC:
i.   Charlotte, b. 5 Jan. 1773; d. 9 March 1773.
ii.   John Wilkes, b. 25 Sept. 1775; m. (1) 7 Nov. 1804 Mary
            Sheffield; m. (2) 7 April 1815 Henrietta (Shaw) Bours.
iii.   Clarissa, b. 13 Jan. 1778; m. 16 Oct. 1805 Ichabod Richmond
            Jacobs.
iv.   Braddock, b. 19 Feb. 1780; m. (1) 30 May 1805 Nancy Lindsey;
            m. (2) in November 1814 Mrs. Ruth (Sheffield) Taylor.
v.   Sophia, b. 16 Dec. 1785; m. 15 Nov. 1809 Ebenezer Simmons.
vi.   Galen, b. 8 Jan. 1785; m. 28 Aug. 1809 Elizabeth Wheeler.
vii.   Arouet, b. 11 Aug. 1786; m. 10 Feb. 1811 Clarinda Ware.
viii.   Clarinda, b. 2 March 1789; m. (1) 18 Aug. 1818 James
            Donaldson; m. (2) 24 May 1824 Dyer Pearl.
ix.   Horace, b. 1 May 1790; m. 4 Oct. 1814 Eliza Waldron.
x.   Franklin, b. 14 July 1792; m. 2 June 1817 Elizabeth Coy.
xi.   Barton, b. 17 Dec. 1793; m. 2 June 1817 Deborah Briggs.
xii.   Harriet, b. 3 June 1796; m. 8 Jan. 1829 Joseph H. Johnson.

18. WILLIAM[6] RICHMOND (Ephraim[5], William[4], Sylvester[3], Edward[2], John[1]), born in LC 10 July 1763, died there 19 Jan. 1833.

He married 6 Aug. 1785 DEBORAH SEARLES, daughter of Nathaniel and Lucy Searles, born in November 1766, died in Pawtucket, R.I., 31 May 1828.

He was a sea captain and lived with his uncle, Col. William Richmond, who intended to make him his heir and leave him the homestead of the first Capt. Edward Richmond. For good reasons he changed his mind, and gave the farm to William Richmond of Providence.

Children, born in LC:
i.   Lucy Ellis, b. 20 Dec. 1786; m. Simeon Gray.
ii.   Betsey Cook, b. 24 Jan. 1788; m. 11 Feb. 1815 Rufus
            Alexander.

iii.   Lois Grey, b. 14 Jan. 1790; m. John Helm.
iv.   George William Augustus, b. 19 Jan. 1794; d. at sea.
v.   Eliza Searle, b. 25 July 1797; m. William Dutcher.
vi.   Charlotte Searle, b. 4 Jan. 1800; m. William Miller.
vii.   Mary White, b. 2 March 1801; m. (1) Alpheus R. Pierce;
     m. (2) Isaac Linderman.
viii.   Sarah Church, b. in November 1803; m. Marvin Byington.
     Residence: Dundee, N.Y.

19. THOMAS[6] RICHMOND (Perez[5], William[4], Sylvester[3], Edward[2], John[1]), born in LC 5 Sept. 1764, died in Ponfret, Conn., 25 Sept. 1840. He married LUCY SIMMONS, daughter of Adam and Deborah Simmons, died in July 1835. In 1803 they moved from LC to Pomfret.

Children, born in LC:
i.   Deborah Simmons, b. 15 Feb. 1786; m. Benjamin Morris.
ii.   Benjamin Church, b. 15 Dec. 1788; m. Rhoda Thornton.
iii.   Sarah, b. 8 Aug. 1790; d. in Orleans County, N.Y., in 1858.
iv.   Isaac Simmons, b. 17 May 1792; m. Sarah Billingham.
v.   George Attwood, b. 30 Sept. 1793; m. 1 Dec. 1814 Myra
     Levens.
vi.   Betsey, b. 3 Aug. 1795; m. Archelaus Upham.
vii.   Gilbert, b. 25 Sept. 1798; m. Clarissa Billingham.
viii.   Charles, b. 12 Oct. 1799.
ix.   Perez, b. 6 May 1801. Residence: Washington County, N.Y.
x.   Sylvester, b. 14 April 1803; m. Lucy (--).

20. JOSHUA[6] RICHMOND (Joshua[5], Perez[4], Sylvester[3], Edward[2], John[1]), born in LC in that part which is now Westport Harbor 27 April 1770, died 31 March 1812.
He married 10 Sept. 1797 MARY BAILEY, daughter of Isaac and Sarah (Manchester) Bailey of LC, born there 4 March 1778, died 17 April 1854.
He was a prosperous merchant in Providence and was interested in navigation and in business with the southern states. While absent in the south caring for the business of the firm, his partner defrauded him of his property. He never recovered from this severe blow, and died at the age of forty-two. It is said that he possessed many noble qualities, was a handsome, courtly gentleman of the old school, and was always most elegantly attired.

Children:
21. i.   Isaac Bailey, b. 14 June 1798.
ii.   Mary, b. in Providence 3 Aug. 1800; d. 12 Aug. 1802.
iii.   John Cushing, b. 10 Jan. 1803 in Providence; m. (1) 6 Dec.
     1826 Louisa Jenks.
iv.   Joshua, b. 19 June 1805 in Providence; m. (1) 27 May 1834
     Hannah Hussey; m. (2) 27 June 1839 Lydia Hussey.
v.   Mary, b. in LC 23 Oct. 1807; d. 17 Sept. 1808.
vi.   William, b. in LC 25 Nov. 1809; d. 29 Sept. 1834; unmarried.

21. ISAAC BAILEY[7] RICHMOND (Joshua[6], Joshua[5], Perez[4], Sylvester[3], Edward[2], John[1]), born in LC 14 June 1798, died there 2

Oct. 1888. He married 30 Sept. 1823 ABIGAIL BROWN, daughter of
the Honorable John and Lois (Taylor) Brown of LC, born there 15
Sept. 1803, died 14 July 1884.

He was apprenticed in Providence at the age of fourteen to one of
the foremost architects and builders of the country, and was appointed
to superintend the erection of the Independent Presbyterian Church in
Savannah, Ga., when nineteen years old. He engaged in business in
Savannah soon after, as architect, contractor and merchant, and remained there twenty years.

He returned to LC on account of the health of his wife, and lived
in the old homestead of the Rev. Mase Shepard, which he had purchased for a summer residence while living in Savannah. When
leaving the south, he gave his slaves their freedom and brought
several of them to his northern home, where they were household
servants for many years. He soon after engaged in business in New
Bedford, Mass., as agent and proprietor of whaling vessels, and continued these commercial relations for thirty years, LC still being his
home.

Aside from his private business, he was interested in many cor-
porate enterprises. He was projector, and for nineteen years president
of the Tiverton and LC Mutual Fire Insurance Company, and director
of the Commercial Insurance Company of New Bedford.

He was a Whig and Republican in politics. He represented his
district in the State Senate in 1870 and '71, was Notary Public, President of the Town Council and filled other township offices.

For fifty years deacon of the United Congregational Church, and
one of its most staunch and generous supporters, he was remembered
for his firm, undeviating loyalty to truth and justice, and honorable
methods in all things. He was a liberal contributor to many religious
and charitable societies, and a life member of many of them. He
established the Richmond Academy in town, erected a suitable building
and sustained the school for a period of years, for the benefit of his
own and other children.

It is said that it was indeed a beautiful sight when Deacon Richmond
and his wife drove up with their carriage and span of horses on Sunday
morning before the church.

Children:
22. i.   Henry Isaac, b. 22 Nov. 1824.
    ii.   Horatio Whitridge, b. 20 June 1827; m. (1) 1 July 1862
           Harriet N. Pierce, daughter of James and Nancy Pierce;
           m. (2) 27 Feb. 1873 Emma Akin.
23. iii.   Georgianna, b. 12 Oct. 1829.
24. iv.   Preston Baker, b. 5 April 1832.
25. v.   William Brown, b. 28 Feb. 1835.
    vi.   Charles Cushing, b. 17 May 1837.
    vii.   Abby Elizabeth, b. 1 Jan. 1840; m. 17 Feb. 1869 Timothy
           Wright.
26. viii. Joshua Bailey, b. 15 July 1843.

    22. HENRY ISAAC[8] RICHMOND (Isaac[7], Joshua[6], Joshua[5], Perez[4],
Sylvester[3], Edward[2], John[1]), born in LC 22 Nov. 1824, died there 13

April 1899.

He married 4 Jan. 1859 FRANCES ELLEN PALMER, daughter of
Simeon and Mary (Caldwell) Palmer of Boston, born 16 May 1831, died
in LC 26 July 1896.

He spent several years in Benicia, Calif., in the mercantile
business. After 1859 he was for several years in Boston, engaged in
the South American and Manila trade. He retired to LC and purchased
his grandfather's farm, which had been in the Bailey family since the
settlement of the town.

      Children:
i.   Henry Isaac, b. 27 Sept. 1865; d. in LC in 1956.

    23. GEORGIA ANNA[8] RICHMOND (Isaac[7], Joshua[6], Joshua[5],
Perez[4], Sylvester[3], Edward[2], John[1]), born in Savannah, Ga., 12 Oct.
1829, died in LC 29 Jan. 1899.

She married 20 Nov. 1855 STEPHEN BOWEN, son of Stephen and
Sarah Bailey (Irish) Bowen of Newport, born 31 Oct. 1829, died 3 Oct.
1888. Her husband was a merchant in Boston. They resided in Roxbury,
Mass.

      Children (Bowen):
i.   Lillian Richmond, b. 6 Sept. 1856; d. 4 Oct. 1863.
ii.   Georgiana, b. 8 June 1859; m. 20 Sept. 1883 Dr. Charles
        Francis Withington, b. in Brookline, Mass., 21 Aug.
        1852. He graduated from Harvard College with an A.B.
        degree in 1847, and an M.D. degree in 1881.
        Children (Withington) born in Roxbury:
        i.   Sidney, b. 7 June 1884.
        ii.   Robert, b. 7 June 1884.
        iii. Margaret, b. 1 Aug. 1888.
        iv. Paul Richmond, b. 21 June 1890.
        v.   Eliot, b. 27 March 1896.
iii.   Stephen, b. 14 May 1869; m. 14 Sept. 1696 Annie Cushing,
        daughter of George and Mary (Rose) Cushing. Residence:
        Jamaica Plain.

    24. PRESTON BAKER[8] RICHMOND (Isaac[7], Joshua[6], Joshua[5],
Perez[4], Sylvester[3], Edward[2], John[1]), born in Savannah, Ga., 25 April
1832, died in Providence 12 Sept. 1883. Residence: LC.

He married first in LC 5 April 1855 ELIZA GRAY BROWN,
daughter of Christopher and Eliza (Church) Brown, born 30 Oct. 1837
in LC. He married second in Tiverton 8 June 1870 MARIA MACIE
DURFEE, daughter of the Honorable Gideon and Emeline (Seabury)
Durfee of Tiverton, born there 13 Sept. 1838, died in 1922.

He was a merchant in Benicia, Calif., and afterwards engaged
in the grocery business in the store later occupied by the Charles R.
Wilbur Company. He was in business in LC for many years. He
served the town several years in the capacity of treasurer and col-
lector and with the exception of a few months, was the only secretary
of the Tiverton and LC Mutual Fire Insurance Company, until the
time of his death. He was also for many years treasurer of the United
Congregational Church and Society.

During President Buchanan's administration he held the office of Postmaster, and at the breaking out of the War of the Rebellion, he attempted to raise a company, having had the promise of a captain's commission under Colonel Sayles. Not succeeding in this as soon as he desired, he reported to the front and served as a private in the Battle of Fredericksburg, in which his intimate friend and commander, Colonel Sayles, was killed. The night after the battle he, with two or three others, returned to the battlefield to secure the body of Colonel Sayles, which--at great personal peril--they succeeded in doing.

Soon after he had entered the ranks, in the Seventh Rhode Island Infantry, he was promoted to regimental postmaster, and at the time of the formation of Burnside's division, he was promoted to postal agent of that division, which office he held until he was honorably discharged at the end of the War. He was in service more than four years.

Children by first wife, recorded in LC:
i.   Willard Preston, b. 15 April 1856; m. Mary Helen Shearer.
ii.   Isaac Lester, b. 12 Jan. 1862; d. 16 April 1876.

Children by second wife:
iii. Gideon Henry, b. 13 March 1871; m. 8 Feb. 1900 Elizabeth
      Louise Parks. Residence: Providence.
iv.   Charles Durfee, b. 23 Sept. 1875. Residence: Providence.

25. WILLIAM BROWN[6] RICHMOND (Isaac[7], Joshua[6], Joshua[5], Perez[4], Sylvester[3], Edward[2], John[1]), born in LC 28 Feb. 1835, died 21 May 1893. He was a chemist and druggist in Boston, but moved to LC for the sake of his health and lived at the homestead for many years. He was one of the projectors and president of the Seaconnet Steamboat Company, and also treasurer for many years of the United Congregational Church.

26. JOSHUA BAILEY[8] RICHMOND (Isaac[7], Joshua[6], Joshua[5], Perez[4], Sylvester[3], Edward[2], John[1]), born in LC 15 July 1843, died there 7 Aug. 1931.

He married 22 Dec. 1880 JOSEFA RUBIRA, only child of Eladio and Francesca (Ardizzi) Rubira of Santander, Spain, born in Havana, Cuba, 4 Jan. 1853, died in Boston 30 June 1931.

He was an importer, manufacturer and sugar refiner in Boston, and a director in various corporations, but retired from active business in 1890 and devoted his time to the care of estates held in trust and to the compilation of the genealogy of the Richmond family. He spent part of many consecutive years abroad and was familiar with several languages. He was a member of the Boston Athletic Club, the Boston Art Club, The Country Club, and various other societies.

In 1882 he was decorated by Pope Leo XIII, commander Des Croises Du Saint Sepulcre de Jerusalem, a military order founded by Pope Alexander VI in 1492. This is an honor rarely conferred upon a Protestant.

Children:

    i.   Corinne, b. 26 Oct. 1881; m. Stuart Burchard.
    ii.   Ralph Sumner, b. 13 Dec. 1883; m. Edith (--).
    iii. Carleton Rubira, b. 13 Feb. 1887; m. Helen Cook.

. . . .

REV. WILLIAM[8] RICHMOND (James[7], William[6], Sylvester[5], William[4], Sylvester[3], Edward[2], John[1]), born 11 Feb. 1846, died in Fall River 28 June 1928. He married 14 July 1891 GRACE FAY THROOP, daughter of William and Caroline (Collins) Hooker.

A graduate of Harvard with the class of 1874, he served as a priest in St. Mark's Church in Orange, N. J., in 1878, and became rector of All Saint's Church in Orange in 1885. He lived on the old Edward Richmond place in LC in the summertime.

    Children:
    i.   Grace Angela, b. in Orange, N.J., 21 March 1895.
    ii.   William, b. in Orange, N.J., 12 July 1896.

CARLETON RICHMOND COTTAGE, 1750
Little Compton, R. I.

THE ROBINSON FAMILY

NATHANIEL ROBINSON, born in Swansea 17 Nov. 1802, died
in LC 9 May 1851. He married in LC 23 Nov. 1828 JULIA ANN
BROWNELL, daughter of Humphrey and Sally (Head) Brownell, born
in LC 21 Jan. 1810. They were living in LC at the time the census
was taken for the year 1850.

Children, born in LC:
i.   Malvina, b. 9 April 1831.
ii.   John, b. 18 March 1833; m. in LC 8 Dec. 1857 Charlotte E.
        Brownell, daughter of James and Lydia (Church) Brownell
        of LC.
iii.   Maria, b. 10 Aug. 1835.
iv.   William F., b. 8 April 1841.
v.   Sarah H., b. 15 Nov. 1844.

ᏫᏬ

THE ROUSE FAMILY

1. JOHN[1] ROUSE, died 16 Dec. 1684 in Marshfield, Mass. He
married (license 7 Jan. 1638/9) in Marshfield ANNIS PABODIE,
daughter of John and Isabel Pabodie, died slightly before 12 Sept.
1688 when her will was proved.

Residence: Marshfield. He was a servant of Thomas Prence,
a proprietor of the town in 1640, and a town officer in 1645.

Children:
i.   Mary, b. 10 Aug. 1640; d. in LC in 1698; m. John Price.
        Her gravestone is the oldest in cemetery 1.
ii.   John, b. 28 Sept. 1643; m. Elizabeth Doty. He died in Marsh-
        field in 1717, leaving to his sister Elizabeth and his brother
        Simon the rest and residue of his estate.
2. iii. Simon, b. 14 June 1645.
iv.   George, b. 17 May 1648.
v.   Elizabeth, m. 10 April 1681 Thomas Bourne.
vi.   Ann, m. Isaac Holmes.

2. SIMON[2] ROUSE (John[1]), born in Marshfield 14 June 1645, died
in November 1721. He married CHRISTIANNA (--).

Residence: Dartmouth and LC. According to some records, he
moved to LC in 1674, but this is uncertain. It is known that he kept
a house of entertainment in LC (then called Seaconnet) in 1681.

His will, dated 19 Dec. 1723 and proved 28 Nov. 1724, mentioned
his wife and children. Of the 100 acre great lots, he was allotted No.
15, which is just north of the Quaker Meeting House.

Children:
i.   William, b. in 1673; m. (1) Mary (--) of Taunton; m. (2) 18
        Nov. 1739 Sarah Sampson, daughter of Abraham and Laura

(Standish) Sampson, b. in 1700/03. They moved to
Pennsylvania and had a son, George.

3. ii.   James, b. in 1678.

     iii.   Mary (Mercy), b. in 1681; m. in LC in January 1701 by
            Joseph Church, justice, to John Stephens.

     iv.   Barbara, b. in 1683; d. in 1700.

     v.   Simon Jr., b. in 1685, d. in 1702.

     vi.   Christianna, b. in 1687; d. in 1703.

     vii. John, b. in 1690; m. 29 June 1720 Ann Lathly (?), daughter
            of Philip and Mary (Bishop) Lathly, b. in 1701, d. in 1738.

3. JAMES[3] ROUSE (Simon[2], John[1]), born in 1678, died in LC
24 Feb. 1742. Residence: LC.

He was married first in LC 15 March 1703 by Joseph Church,
justice, to JOANNA FISHER, died in LC 2 Nov. 1707. He was married
second in LC 25 Oct. 1709 by Richard Billings, justice, to MARGARET
ANDROS or ANDREWS.

Children by first wife, recorded in LC:

4. i.   George, b. 9 Jan. 1704.

     ii.   Rebecca, b. 29 Nov. 1705; m. in LC 21 May 1732 Robert
            Taylor, son of John and Abigail (--) Taylor.

     iii.   Joanna, b. 12 Sept. 1707.

Children by second wife:

     iv.   Mary, b. in LC 7 Nov. 1710; d. 8 July 1736; m. 28 Feb. 1731
            William Jamison.

4. GEORGE[4] ROUSE (James[3], Simon[2], John[1]), born in LC 9 Jan.
1704, died there 15 Oct. 1775. He is buried in the Old Commons
cemetery.

He was married in LC 19 Sept. 1723 by Richard Billings, justice,
to HANNAH HORSWELL, daughter of Peter and Elizabeth Horswell,
born 1 April 1706 in LC.

Residence: LC. They lived north of John Hunt and Joanna Rouse,
his wife. According to the census of 1774, the Rouse family was living
in the next house north.

His will, recorded in LC book 2, page 328, proved 5 Dec. 1775:
". . . To wife Hannah all real and personal during her widowhood. One
good cow to each of my daughters, Joanna Hunt, Lydia Cook, Rebecca
Simmons, and to daughter Mary Rouse one good cow and one good
feather bed and furniture. All my estate to be sold after my wife's
death and divided into shares. . . "

Children, recorded in LC:

     i.   Elizabeth, b. 23 Feb. 1724; m. in LC 23 Nov. 1749 Jeptha
            Pearce, son of George and Deborah (Searl) Pearce.

     ii.   Mercy, b. 13 Jan. 1727; m. (1) in LC 28 Dec. 1742 Tetaman
            Schreech; m. (2) in LC 23 Aug. 1744 Giles Pearce.

     iii.   Sarah, b. in LC 14 Jan. 1728; d. in November 1812; m. 1 Dec.
            1751 Nathaniel Pearce, son of George and Deborah (Searl)
            Pearce.

     iv.   Joanna, b. 31 May 1734; m. in LC 29 April 1753 John Hunt,

son of William and Elizabeth (Dring) Hunt.
v.   Lydia, b. 28 April 1736; m. in LC 25 Dec. 1757 David Cook of
      Tiverton.
vi.   Mary, b. 3 March 1738. There was a Benjamin Rouse born
      in LC 14 Oct. 1758 to a Mary Rouse. This Mary Rouse is
      probably the daughter of George and Hannah (Horswell) Rouse.
vii. Rebecca, b. 17 Jan. 1744; m. in LC 6 Oct. 1760 Peter Simmons,
      son of Benjamin and Mercy (Taylor) Simmons.

છ෯૭

THE SABINS FAMILY

CHARLES E. SABINS, born in 1855 in Westport. He married
LYDIA JANE HUNT, daughter of Fobes and Almira (Devol) Hunt, born
in 1851, died 3 April 1920. This family was listed in the LC census of
1880.

Children:
i.   Almira, b. in 1873.
ii.   Sarah Ann, b. 2 April 1875 in Westport; d. 25 Dec. 1946; m.
      Ahira S. Nickerson.
iii. Charles, b. in 1878; d. in LC 24 Sept. 1882.
iv.   Charles Albert, b. in Tiverton 3 Jan. 1885; d. 21 Sept. 1938.

છ෯૭

THE SALISBURY FAMILY

1. WILLIAM[1] SALISBURY, born in Denbigshire, Wales, died in
Swansea 24 June 1675, married SUSANNA (--).
In 1653 he was serving as a herdsman, taking care of cattle in
Dorchester, Mass., in that part that in 1662 became Milton, Mass.
He moved to Swansea as early as 1671, when he received a grant of
land there, and was prospecting in Swansea when the Indians made
an attack. Both he and his son John were killed, and a tablet marks
the spot where they fell.
On 30 July (?) the selectmen of Dorchester voted to grant the
Widow Salisbury liberty to get 2100 clapboards out of the common
swamps. On 7 May 1677, Widow Salisbury was admitted to full
communion in the Dorchester church, and on 1 July 1677 her children
were baptized there.

Children, the first two recorded in Dorchester and the
others in Milton:
i.   William, b. 14 June (or Aug.) 1659; perhaps m. 30 July
      1684 in Swansea Hannah Cole.
ii.   Susanna, b. 27 Feb. (or April) 1662 in Boston.

iii.   Hannah, b. 18 May 1665; d. 29 June 1665.
iv.   Samuel, b. 17 May 1666; m. (1) 21 Aug. 1698 Mary (--);
        m. (2) 28 Nov. 1699 Jemima Martin.
v.   Cornelius, b. 7 Oct. 1668; m. Mary (Mercy) (--) in Swansea.
vi.   Hannah, b. 20 April 1671; d. ae 1 month.
2. vii.   Joseph, b. 5 May 1675.
viii.   Abigail, m. John Williston of Milton.
ix.   John, killed by Indians 24 June 1675.
x.   Elizabeth.

2. JOSEPH² SALISBURY (William¹), born in Milton, Mass., 5 May 1675, died in LC 22 June 1714. He married (?) MARY PADDOCK.
Residence: Dorchester, Milton, Mass., and LC. He probably came with his minister, the Rev. Richard Billings, who was from Dorchester.
In his will, recorded book 3, part 1, page 191, Joseph Salisbury, cordwainer, left to his wife Mary use of all estate both real and personal as long as she remained a widow, to each of his sons, John, William and Joseph, he left one third of his real estate and homestead, and to his three daughters, Hope, Susanna and Mary, 10 pounds each. The inventory of his estate listed housing and land worth 250 pounds, total 384 pounds, 9 shillings, 11 pence.

    Children, recorded in LC:
i.   Mary, b. 5 Aug. 1699; m. 21 Aug. 1716 Daniel Shrieve, son
        of Daniel and Martha Shrieve of LC.
ii.   Hopestill, b. 12 April 1702.
3. iii.   John, b. 2 Oct. 1704.
4. iv.   Joseph, b. 30 June 1707.
v.   William, b. 22 Sept. 1710; m. 27 Dec. 1731 Deborah Palmer.
vi.   Susanna, b. 7 April 1713; m. 24 Dec. 1731 William Price,
        son of John and Martha (Graves) Price.

3. JOHN³ SALISBURY (Joseph², William¹), born in LC 2 Oct. 1704. Residence: LC. He was married there 6-7 March 1728 by Sylvester Richmond, justice, to ABIGAIL HEAD, daughter of Henry and Elizabeth (Palmer) Head of LC, born there 24 Dec. 1710.

    Children, born and recorded in LC:
i.   Henry, 8 Oct. 1730.
ii.   Jonathan, b. 4 Oct. 1732; d. in November 1768.

4. JOSEPH³ SALISBURY (Joseph², William¹), born in LC 30 June 1707. He married (intention 22 Jan. 1732) in LC INNOCENT HEAD, daughter of Henry and Elizabeth (Palmer) Head, born in LC 13 March 1713. This family appeard to have moved from the town.

    Children, recorded in LC:
5. i.   Gideon, b. 20 Aug. 1732.
ii.   Abigail, b. 16 Oct. 1733; m. 20 June 1751 Canaan Gifford,
        son of Enos and Phillis (Allen) Gifford.
iii.   Mary, b. 5 July 1736.
iv.   Elizabeth, b. 30 March 1739.

v.   John, b. 18 May 1740.
vi.   Henry, b. 15 March 1742.
vii.   Joseph, b. 6 Sept. 1744.
viii.   Ezekiel, b. 6 Sept. 1744.

For further information see the Genealogical Register 65-379-80.

5. GIDEON⁴ SALISBURY (Joseph³, Joseph², William¹), born in
LC 20 Aug. 1732. Residence: LC. He married there 22 April 1757
PRISCILLA SHAW, daughter of Jeremiah and Phebe (Wilbor) Shaw,
born in LC 11 March 1733.

Children, recorded in LC:
i.   Hope, b. 20 Aug. 1757.
ii.   Bemanuel, b. 21 Nov. 1760.
iii.   Abigail, b. 18 Jan. 1765.

. . . .

ANTHONY SALISBURY, married HANNAH (--). Residence: LC.

Children, recorded in LC:
i.   John, b. 12 July 1781.
ii.   Elcy, b. 9 Dec. 1789.
iii.   Jonathan, b. 10 Oct. 1792.
iv.   William, b. 12 July 1787; d. in LC 11 June 1862.
v.   John Allamander, b. 27 Nov. 1797.
vi.   Hannah.

See the will of John Salisbury, listed under Alice Brown, daughter
of Robert Brown.

✂

THE SANFORD FAMILY

1. JOHN¹ SANFORD, son of Samuel and Eleanor Sanford of Alford
in Lincolnshire, England. His will was proved in 1653 in Portsmouth,
R.I.
He married first ELIZABETH WEBB of Boston, sister of Henry
Weed. He married second BRIDGETT HUTCHINSON, daughter of
William and Ann (Marbury) Hutchinson, baptized 15 Jan. 1618/9 in
Alford, Lincolnshire, England, died in Boston in 1698. She was
whipped in Boston for attending Quaker meetings. She married second
William Phillips of Boston.
He and 18 others signed the Portsmouth compact 7 March 1638,
the year after he was expelled from Boston for being a follower of
Ann Hutchinson. On 20 May 1638 he was allotted six acres of land on
the north side of the great cove. He was a freeman in 1641, and became
a constable and a lieutenant there. In 1653 he was president of Portsmouth and Newport.
His will, made 22 June 1653 and proved in the same year: "Execu-

trix, wife Bridgett, overseers, brother-in-law Edward Hutchinson of
Boston and friends Richard Tew of Newport, Richard Borden, Philip
Sherman, Edward Fisher of Portsmouth. . . To wife my new dwelling
house in which I now live with all and every chamber therein and half
the cook room and all the house on the north side of the aforesaid cook
room, all my right in the great orchard and land on north side of my
dwelling house, meadow and one third of all cattle and movables for
life. To son John half the cook room, the old house and the ferry and
two houses on south side of a certain path, a Negro man and wife. . .
To son Samuel 40 acres at Black Point, four oxen, two cows. . . To son
Peleg at age, 20 acres in Black Point, second Roan mare, five ewes, 5
ewe lambs, French gun and sword. To son Rescomb at age, 40 acres at
Black Point and a mare and like legacies to son William, Esborn and
Elisha. To daughter Eliphal Sanford 100 pounds. To daughter Ann 60
pounds at marriage. To all sons the rest and residue. . . "

His wife's will was made 29 Sept. 1696 and proved 18 Aug. 1698.

Children by first wife:
2. i.   John, b. 4 June 1633.
    ii.   Samuel, b. 14 July 1635; d. 18 March 1713; m. (1) Sarah
          Wordell, daughter of William and Mary; m. (2) 13 April
          1686 Susannah Spatchurst.

Children by second wife:
    iii. Eliphal, b. 9 Dec. 1637; d. 18 Jan. 1724; m. Bartholomew
          Stratton.
    iv.   Peleg, b. 10 May 1639; d. in 1701; m. (1) Mary Brenton;
          m. (2) Mary Coddington.
    v.   Endcome, b. 23 Feb. 1640; d. in 1667.
    vi.   Restcome, b. 29 Jan. 1642; d. in 1667 or 1671.
    vii. William, b. 4 March 1644.
    viii. Ebson, b. 25 Jan. 1646; d. before 1726.
    ix.   Frances, b. 9 Jan. 1648; d. young.
    x.   Elisha, b. 28 Dec. 1650.
    xi.   Ann, b. 12 March 1652; d. 26 Aug. 1654.

2. JOHN[2] SANFORD (John[1]), born in Boston 4 June 1633, died
in East Greenwich, R.I., or Portsmouth, R.I., 25 Jan. 1687. Residence:
Portsmouth. He married first 8 Aug. 1654 ELIZABETH SPATCHURST
of Bermuda, died 6 Dec. 1661. He married second 17 April 1663 MARY
GREENE, widow of Peter Greene and daughter of Samuel and Susanna
(Burton) Gorton of Warwick, R.I.

He was named a freeman 17 May 1653, general treasurer 1655,
and was appointed a member of the Council of Sir Edmund Andros by
Andros himself.

Children, born in Portsmouth:
    i.   Elizabeth, b. 11 July 1655; d. 27 Aug. 1718; m. (1) Henry
          Dyer; m. (2) Daniel Remington; m. (3) Simon (--).
    ii.   Mary, b. 18 Aug. 1656; d. in 1658.
    iii. Susanna, b. 31 July 1658.
    iv.   Rebecca, b. 23 June 1660.
    v.   Mary, b. 30 March 1664; m. (1) Robert Durfee; m. (2)

(--) Thomas.
  vi.   Eliphal, b. 20 Feb. 1666.
3. vii.   John, b. 18 June 1670.
  viii. Samuel, b. 5 Oct. 1677; d. 3 Sept. 1738.

3. JOHN[3] SANFORD (John[2], John[1]), born in Portsmouth 18 June 1670. Residence: Portsmouth and LC.

He married first in 1698 CONTENT HOWLAND, daughter of Samuel Howland and granddaughter of Henry Howland. He married second in LC 9 Oct. 1722 PATIENCE LANGWORTHY, widow of Andrew Langworthy and daughter of Robert and Mary (Ladd?) Brownell.

Children, first three born in Portsmouth, the others in LC:
4. i.   John, b. 5 May 1699.
- ii.   Abigail, b. 20 June 1701; m. in LC 17 April 1728 Melitiah Martin of Swansea.
  iii. Joshua, b. 17 Dec. 1702.
  iv. Mercy, b. 19 Jan. 1703; m. in LC (intention 22 Jan. 1726) George Grinnell, born in LC.
  v.   Mary, b. 4 June 1705; m. in LC 18 Sept. 1726 William Grinnell, b. in LC.
  vi. Ruth, b. 7 Aug. 1707; m. Aaron Mason, b. in LC.
  vii. Content, b. 9 Dec. 1708; m. Thomas Langworthy, b. in LC.
  viii. Elizabeth, b. 24 June 1711.

4. JOHN[4] SANFORD (John[3], John[2], John[1]), born in Portsmouth 5 May 1699. He lived in LC, but moved to Stonington, Conn., before 1740.

He was married in LC 9 July 1722 by Richard Billings, justice, to ELIZABETH PHILLIPS, daughter of Seth and Abigail Phillips, born in LC 26 Sept. 1700.

Children, all recorded in LC:
  i.   Lois, b. 6 Sept. 1722; m. in LC 9 Oct. 1742 Edward[4] Irish (John[3], John[2], John[1]).
  ii.   Joshua, b. 12 Feb. 1724.
  iii. Content, b. 28 Jan. 1726.
  iv. Abigail, b. 24 April 1728; d. 19 July 1731.

. . . .

1. PELEG[1] SANFORD, son of George and Deborah Sanford of Tiverton, born in 1801, died in LC 30 March 1877. Residence: LC.

He married first (intention 5 Oct. 1822) in Westport DEBORAH GIFFORD, born in 1804, died 22 May 1840. They are buried in the Pleasant View cemetery at the Stone Church in Tiverton. He married second RUTH G. (--), born in 1806, died 15 Oct. 1841.

Children, not recorded in LC, but listed in the census of 1850:
2. i.   George, b. in 1825.
  ii.   Deborah.
  iii. Susan.
  iv. Betsey, b. in 1839; m. in LC 28 April 1859 Albert T. Brownell, son of Charles and Susan Brownell of LC.

2. GEORGE W.² SANFORD (Peleg¹), born in Tiverton in 1825, died 8 Dec. 1899. Residence: LC. He married first in LC 7 Oct. 1850 ELIZABETH G. HOWLAND, daughter of Benjamin and Hannah Howland, born in 1825, died in LC 18 Nov. 1851. He married second AMANDA M. (--), born in 1830, died 17 Dec. 1896. All are buried in the Pleasant View cemetery in Tiverton.

      Children, born in LC:
i.   Son, b. 22 Sept. 1853.
ii.   Ella, b. 8 June 1855.
iii.   Elizabeth, b. 16 June 1857.
iv.   John S., b. 4 Feb. 1859.
v.   Peleg B., b. in LC in 1855; m. 5 Oct. 1887 Mary E. King, daughter of Cornelius and Cynthia King of Tiverton.

. . . .

WILLIAM SANFORD, married MARY (--). Residence: LC and Tiverton.

His will, recorded Book 4, page 466, made 9 July 1808: ". . . To wife Mary all household goods she had when I married her, one good cow and the use of the dwelling house and one half of the farm where I now live. . . also a sage flat in Westport. To son William one dollar. To daughter Eliphal Simmons one bed and furniture. To granddaughters Lydia Hart, Abigail Hart and Mary Hart, one half of household goods. To son Joseph and to daughter Eliphal my pew in the Tiverton Congregational Church or Meeting House. To grandson Samuel Sanford all rest and residue. . . "

      Children, all born in Tiverton:
i.   Joseph, b. 15 June 1746.
ii.   Abigail, b. 23 Nov. 1748; m. Aaron Hart.
iii.   Peleg, b. 23 Oct. 1751; m. in October 1774 Lillis Wilcox.
iv.   Eliphal, b. 22 April 1755; m. in LC 25 Aug. 1776 Peleg Simmons.
v.   William, b. 27 Sept. 1757.
vi.   Thomas, b. 30 June 1761.

THOMAS W. SANFORD, son of Samuel and Susan Sanford, born in LC in 1826, died there 10 July 1901. Residence: Adamsville.

He married CATHARINE L. FRASER, daughter of Joseph and Mary Fraser of Boston, born in 1830 in Clifton, England, died in LC 28 Dec. 1905.

      Children:
i.   Samuel, b. 7 Nov. 1853.
ii.   Susan, b. 20 Dec. 1854; m. 9 July 1876 Theodore Dewolf Gifford, son of Philander and Content Gifford.
iii.   Harriet.
iv.   Daughter, b. 8 Dec. 1856.
v.   Mary A., b. 12 May 1858.
vi.   Silas, b. 5 Dec. 1859.
vii. Thomas W., b. 9 April 1861 in LC; d. there 25 June 1885.

viii. Fannie F., b. 17 Nov. 1862.
ix.   Adeline, b. 25 Nov. 1864.
x.   Rachel, b. 30 Sept. 1866.
xi.   Catharine, b. 28 Aug. 1868; d. 25 March 1898.
xii.   Catharine Fraser, b. 28 June 1870.
xiii. Lillias.

∽⧟∾

THE SAWYER FAMILY

1. JOSIAH² SAWYER, son of John¹ and Mercy Little Sawyer, died in 1733. His mother was the daughter of Thomas and Ann (Warren) Little.

He was married in Tiverton 20 Dec. 1705 by Richard Billings, justice, to MARTHA SEABURY, daughter of Samuel and Martha (Paybody) Seabury, born in Duxbury 23 Sept. 1679.

Children, first four recorded in Tiverton and others in LC:
i.   John, b. 20 Feb. 1707.
ii.   Hannah, b. 27 Nov. 1710; m. (intention 27 Aug. 1730) John
          Williston, son of Ichabod and Dorothy (Gardner) Williston,
          b. in 1706, d. in 1736.
iii.   Mercy, b. 28 Jan. 1711 in Tiverton; m. 6 Feb. 1741/2 Samuel
          Reed.
iv.   Mary, b. 28 Aug. 1714; bapt. in LC 24 July 1715; unmarried
          in 1733.
v.   Abigail, b. 4 Oct. 1716; bapt. 1 June 1720; m. 1 Nov. 1743
          Joseph Tabor.
vi.   Priscilla, bapt. in 1719.
2. vii.   Josiah, b. in May 1725.

2. DEACON JOSIAH³ SAWYER (Josiah², John¹), born 15 May 1725 and baptized 11 July 1725, died in 1792.

He married about 1746 in Tiverton SARAH PEARCE, daughter of George and Deborah (Searles) Pearce, born in LC 14 Jan. 1729, died there 28 Aug. 1780. He was married second 27 Jan. (?) in LC by Lemuel Taber, justice, to MRS. ANTRACE WILCOX of Tiverton.

Children, recorded in Tiverton:
3. i.   Lemuel, b. 13 Nov. 1748.
ii.   Antrace, b. 30 Oct. 1751; m. Wright Pearce, son of James
          and Sarah (Simmons) Pearce.
iii.   Priscilla, b. 20 March 1754.
iv.   Josiah, b. 26 June 1756; d. in January 1800; m. 14 July 1782
          in LC Betsey Pearce, daughter of Jeptha and Elizabeth
          (Rouse) Pearce.
4. v.   John, b. 19 Sept. 1759.
vi.   Sarah, b. 17 Sept. 1761.
vii.   Isaac, b. 25 Nov. 1772; d. in January 1804.

3. LEMUEL[4] SAWYER (Josiah[3], Josiah[2], John[1]), born in LC 13 Nov. 1748, died there 4 March 1804. Residence: LC.

He married in LC 2 Nov. 1777 BETSEY WOODMAN, daughter of William and Mary (Pearce) Woodman, born in LC 23 March 1755.

Children:
i.   Thomas, b. in LC 31 Oct. 1779.
ii.   Sarah, b. 17 June 1781.
iii. Cynthia, b. 22 June 1783; m. 23 June 1812 Thomas Manchester.
iv.   Stephen, b. 14 Feb. 1785.
v.   Ruth, b. 27 Feb. 1787.
vi.   Thomas, b. 6 Feb. 1789.
vii. John, d. in 1847. See his will below.
viii. Lemuel.

The will of John Sawyer, son of Lemuel, recorded book 10, page 12, made 6 Jan. 1845 and proved 8 Nov. 1847: "John Sawyer of LC, wheelwright. . . To sister Cynthia Manchester use of my dwelling house a part of that I bought of my brother, Thomas Sawyer, as long as she remains single. . . My great Bible, then to my grand nephew John Sawyer Manchester, son of my nephew Andrew Manchester. Also all household goods. To brother Thomas all my wearing apparel. To brother Lemuel my farm whereon I now live and all other real estate in this town and Tiverton and all rights in the Congregational Society old meeting house, chisels butts. . . To nephew Albert Manchester one half my money in the Savings Bank of Fall River. . . and my carpenter tools. To niece Ruth Head the other one half of my money. To niece Phebe Manchester 5 dollars and pew in the Free Will Baptist Church in Tiverton with her mother, Cynthia Manchester and cousin Ruth A. Head. . . "

5. JOHN[4] SAWYER (Josiah[3], Josiah[2], John[1]), born in LC 19 Sept. 1759, died before 9 April 1797. Residence: LC and Tiverton.

He married in LC 3 May 1787 RUTH STODDARD, daughter of Benjamin and Phebe (Brownell) Stoddard, born in 1759. She married second 9 April 1797 in LC Capt. Gideon Simmons.

Children, recorded in LC:
i.   Phebe, b. 5 Oct. 1788.
ii. John, b. 22 Oct. 1790.

. . . .

JOHN SAWYER, married MARTHA FOBES.
Children, born in LC:
i.   John, b. 2 Feb. 1707.
ii.   Hannah, b. 27 Nov. 1710.
iii. Mercy, b. 28 Jan. 1711.

JAMES SAWYER.
Children, born and recorded in LC:
i.   Lydia, b. 17 Oct. 1803.
ii.   Mary, b. 9 April 1805.
iii. Betsey, b. 22 July 1807.
iv.   James, b..16 March 1809.

ANDREW SAWYER, born in 1861 in Tiverton, died in 1931. He is buried at Pleasant View cemetery. He married ELIZABETH (--), born in LC. He had a brother, William, born in 1857, died in 1904.

   Children, recorded in LC:
  i. George, b. 2 Aug. 1888 in Westport; d. in LC 20 Sept. 1890.
  ii. Gladys, b. in 1892; d. in 1924; m. (--) Borden.
  iii. Millicent R., b. in 1894; d. in LC 17 May 1895.
  iv. Edward, b. in LC 8 Feb. 1900; d. there 23 Dec. 1900.

THE SEABURY FAMILY

1. JOHN[1] SEABURY, died prior to 1662, married GRACE (--). A mariner, he was living in Boston in 1639 when he bought a house lot there and was admitted as an inhabitant. He moved later to the Barbados, and was joined there by his wife. Before February 1650, she had married, second, Anthony Lane. On 16 April 1662 his two sons made claim to certain land which had belonged to their father.

   Children:
  i. John, moved to the Barbados.
2. ii. Samuel, b. 10 Dec. 1640.

2. SAMUEL[2] SEABURY (John[1]), born in Boston 10 Dec. 1640, died in Duxbury 5 Aug. 1681. Residence: Duxbury. He was a physician.
  He married first 16 Nov. 1660 in Duxbury PATIENCE KEMP, daughter of William Kemp of Duxbury, died there 29 Oct. 1676. He married second in Duxbury 4 April 1677 MARTHA PABODIE, daughter of William and Elizabeth (Alden) Pabodie of LC, born in Duxbury 25 Feb. 1650, died in LC 5 Jan. 1712. She married second after 1681 William Fobes of LC, son of John and Constant (Mitchell) Fobes.
  In his will, he left to his son Samuel his land and property in Duxbury. To son Joseph "Those great silver buttons which I usually wear," and to son John his birding piece and musket. He willed that his Negro servant Nimrod be disposed of by sale, in order to support the "bringing up of my children, especially the three youngest born."

   Children by first wife, born in Duxbury:
  i. Elizabeth, b. 16 Sept. 1661.
  ii. Sarah, b. 18 Aug. 1663.
  iii. Samuel, b. 28 April 1666; m. in Duxbury 13 Dec. 1688
     Abigail Allen. Residence: New London, Conn.
  iv. Hannah, b. 6 July 1668.
  v. John, b. 7 Nov. 1670; d. 18 March 1672.
  vi. Grace, b. 1 March 1673; d. 16 March 1673.
  vii. Patience, b. 1 March 1673; d. 16 March 1673.
  viii. John, m. 9 Dec. 1697 in Duxbury Elizabeth[3] Alden (David[2],
     John[1]), d. 4 Jan. 1771. Residence: Groton and Lebanon,
     Conn.

Children by second wife:
3. ix.   Joseph, b. 8 June 1678.
     x.   Martha, b. 23 Sept. 1679 in Duxbury; m. 20 Dec. 1705
          Josiah Sawyer, son of John and Mercy (Little) Sawyer,
          d. in 1733.
     xi.   Child, b. after father's death.

3. LIEUT. JOSEPH³ SEABURY (Samuel², John¹), born in Duxbury
8 Jan. 1678, died in LC 22 Aug. 1755. Residence: Duxbury and LC.

He was married in LC 25 Sept. 1701 by Joseph Church, justice, to
PHEBE SMITH, widow, daughter of Lt. William and Elizabeth (South-
worth) Fobes, born in 1679, died in LC 21 April 1715. Both are buried
in the Old Commons cemetery. He married second, according to the
Ladd Genealogy, MARY LADD, daughter of William and Elizabeth
(Tompkins) Ladd, born in LC 5 March 1699.

Children by first wife:
4. i.   Samuel, b. 5 June 1702.
     ii.   Martha, b. 7 Feb. 1704; d. in Bristol, R.I., in 1780; m. in
          LC 16 Aug. 1723 Benjamin Manchester, d. 15 May 1760.
     iii.   Joseph, b. 2 Dec. 1705.
5. iv.   Benjamin, b. 20 Jan. 1708.
6. v.   Sion, b. 27 March 1713.
     vi.   Mary, b. 17 April 1715; m. in LC 19 Oct. 1738 Fobes South-
          worth, son of Edward and Mary (Fobes) Southworth.

Children by second wife:
     vii.   Phebe, b. 2 May 1723; m. (--) Lawton.
     viii. Hannah, b. 7 Feb. 1724; m. Charles Cadman.
     ix.   Gideon, b. 16 March 1726; d. young.
     x.   John,
     xi.   Elizabeth, b. 2 Feb. 1730; m. Daniel Allen.
     xii.   Sarah, b. 4 Dec. 1732; m. 3 June 1753 Edward Cadman.
     xiii. Ichabod, b. 18 Jan. 1734.

4. SAMUEL⁴ SEABURY (Joseph³, Samuel², John¹), born 5 June
1702 in LC, died there in March 1768. Residence: LC.

He was married in LC 2 March 1732 by Thomas Church, justice,
to LYDIA LADD, daughter of William and Elizabeth (Tompkins) Ladd,
born in LC 1 March 1711.

His will, recorded book 2, page 109 LC Probate, dated 20 Nov.
1767 and proved 4 April 1768: ". . . To wife Lydia use of all real
estate til son William comes of age. To son William all lands I now
live on in LC with buildings. To four oldest daughters, Lillis Cornell,
Patience Devil, Comfort Wilcox and Pheby Pearce, above what I have
already given them one silver dollar each. To daughter Mary Seabury
enough of my household goods to make her equal with her sisters.
To daughter Hannah Manchester and daughter Abigail Seabury also
part of household goods. To my daughter Abigail the use and improvement of my bedroom and kitchen until her marriage. . . "

Children, all recorded in LC with the exception of Hannah:
     i.   Barnabus, b. in LC 2 June 1732; d. there 13 Nov. 1753.

ii.   Lillis, b. 7 May 1734; m. (intention 29 April 1758) in Dart-
      mouth Philip Cornell of Dartmouth.
iii. Patience, b. 14 May 1736; m. (intention 19 Dec. 1754) in
      Dartmouth John Devoll of Dartmouth.
iv.   Comfort, b. 4 July 1738; m. (intention 24 Jan. 1761) in
      Dartmouth 5 Feb. 1761 Samuel Wilcox.
v.   Nathaniel, b. 27 June 1740; d. 6 Jan. 1754.
vi.   William, b. 2 May 1742; d. 19 Dec. 1753.
vii. Phebe, b. 15 March 1744; m. Richard Pearce.
viii. Mary, b. 15 March 1744; m. William Corey.
ix.   Hannah, b. in 1746; m. (intention 1 Nov. 1766) in Dartmouth
      James Manchester.
x.   Abigail, b. 7 Feb. 1749, recorded in Westport; m. in LC
      12 Aug. 1781 William Watkins.
xi.   Deborah, b. 12 Aug. 1752; d. 20 Nov. 1753.
7. xii. William, b. 24 Jan. 1755.

5. CAPT. BENJAMIN[4] SEABURY (Joseph[3], Samuel[2], John[1]), born
in LC 20 Jan. 1708; died there 11 Sept. 1773.
       He married about 1733 REBECCA SOUTHWORTH, daughter of
Edward and Mary (Fobes) Southworth, born in LC 22 Dec. 1708, died
there 12 Dec. 1789. They are buried in the Old Common cemetery.
Residence: LC. They lived on the Tiverton line near Windmill Hill.
       His will, recorded book 2, page 241 LC Wills, made 2 March
1773 and proved 5 Oct. 1773: ". . . To wife Rebecca the bed we now
lodge on and a satisfied maintenance to be provided by my executor
and have household goods if she remains my widow. To three daughters,
Marcy, Mary and Ruth. . . To son Benjamin my new gun and silver
beaker and 15 good dollars. To son Isaac Seabury my sword, old gun
and 15 good dollars. To son Gideon my lot of land being part on the
7th lot among the 15 acre lot above Cole Brook of about 9 acres. To
daughter Rebecca one dollar. To daughters Mercy, Mary and Ruth
one bed, bedding or the beds they call their own. To son Constant
Seabury my dwelling house, my tan yard being partly in LC and partly
in Tiverton and my part of a boat. My son Constant to be executor.
And my daughters to have a good lot of leather fit for their gloves.
All of my children to have my pew in the meeting house. . . "

            Children, recorded in LC:
i.   Mercy, b. 13 Aug. 1734.
ii.   Mary, b. 25 Jan. 1736.
iii. Rebecca, b. 25 Jan. 1736; m. (--) Almy.
iv.   Ruth, b. 26 Nov. 1739.
v.   Benjamin, b. 24 Jan. 1743.
vi.   Fobes, b. 29 March 1745; d. 4 June 1746.
8. vii. Gideon, b. 1 March 1747.
9. viii. Constant, b. 19 June 1749.
ix.   Isaac, b. 3 Nov. 1751.

6. SION[4] SEABURY (Joseph[3], Samuel[2], John[1]), born in LC 27
March 1713, died there 10 Aug. 1801. Residence: LC and Tiverton.
       He married in LC in May 1733 ANNA BUTTS, daughter of Moses

Butts and granddaughter of Thomas Butts, born in LC 28 March 1709.

> Children, all recorded in Tiverton, the first also recorded in LC:
>
> i.   Aaron, b. 6 Aug. 1733.
> ii.   Joseph, b. 20 June 1736; m. in Tiverton 4 March 1802 Rachel Pearce, daughter of Giles and Mercy (Rouse) Pearce of Tiverton.
> 10. iii. Philip, b. 6 Dec. 1740.
> iv.   Alice, b. 8 Dec. 1742.
> v.   Peleg, b. 13 June 1745.
> vi.   Dorcas, b. 9 Jan. 1748; m. Abner Soule.

7. WILLIAM[5] SEABURY (Samuel[4], Joseph[3], Samuel[2], John[1]), born in LC 24 Jan. 1755, died there 3 March 1837. Residence: LC.

He married DEBORAH SNELL, daughter of Isaac and Sarah Snell of LC, born there 16 Aug. 1757.

His will, recorded LC Wills, book 8, page 172, made 3 June 1835 and proved 3 April 1837: ". . . To son Pindar my wood lot in Tiverton bounded east by Mathew Manchester, south by Robert Seabury, west by Gideon White and north by Asa Davol, also to him my homestead farm . . . " He also left to Pindar half of his personal estate. He left bequests of 10 dollars each to sons Samuel and Isaac, and 20 dollars each to son William, and to all of his daughters and granddaughters. To his daughter Mariah he also left the use of the northeast bedroom of his house.

> Children, all recorded in LC:
>
> i.   Samuel, b. 4 Jan. 1777; m. in LC 11 July 1802 Patty (Mary) Seabury, daughter of Philip and Sarah (Pearce) Seabury of Tiverton.
> ii.   Isaac, b. 11 Dec. 1778.
> iii.   Sion, b. 7 Nov. 1780.
> iv.   Sarah, b. 23 Sept. 1782; m. Job Manchester.
> v.   Lydia, b. 15 July 1785; m. (intention June 5 1812) in Westport John Manchester.
> vi.   Elizabeth, b. 14 June 1786; m. Moses Palmer.
> vii.   Herzilla, b. 10 May 1790; m. William Durfee.
> viii. William, b. 19 Feb. 1792; m. Jerusha Peckham, daughter of George and Lydia (Head) Peckham, 30 Nov. 1795. They had Otis Seabury, b. in 1821, d. in 1906, buried in the Graham cemetery in Hubbardsville, N. Y., m. Hannah Tripp, b. in 1820, d. in 1909. Otis had four children: Sarah, b. in 1845; Emma, b. in 1847; Frances, b. in 1849 and m. Edward L. Hunt; Georgianna, b. in 1852 and m. Francis Smith.
> 11. ix. Pindar, b. 17 Dec. 1793.
> x.   Sally, b. 7 Dec. 1795 (probably the one who had Hannah Seabury, who married Horace Almy.)
> xi.   Maria, b. 18 Oct. 1801; d. in LC 6 Dec. 1863.
> xii.   Mary, m. Anson Tallow.

8. GIDEON[5] SEABURY (Benjamin[4], Joseph[3], Samuel[2], John[1]),

born in LC 1 March 1747, died there 29 Oct. 1827. Residence: LC.

He married ELIZABETH (BETSEY) PEARCE, daughter of Nathaniel and Sarah (Rouse) Pearce, born in LC 14 Nov. 1756, died there 25 April 1839.

   Children, recorded in LC:
12. i. Benjamin, b. 20 Oct. 1776.
 ii. Alden, b. 24 March 1779.
 iii. Frederick. His estate was administered by Gideon Seabury
     (possibly his son) 9 Dec. 1822.
 iv. Sally, possibly the daughter of Gideon and Betsey, was married
     about 1845 by Thomas Burgess, justice, to Henry Brightman,
     son of Stephen and Priscilla Brightman.

  9. CONSTANT[5] SEABURY (Benjamin[4], Joseph[3], Samuel[2], John[1]), born in LC 19 June 1749, died there 26 Dec. 1806. Residence: LC.

He married, according to Tiverton church records, 19 Dec. 1771 SUSANNAH GRAY, born in 1751, died 13 May 1816. They are buried at the foot of Windmill Hill, on the northeast side of the old road.

His will, recorded LC, book 4, page 253, made 6 April 1805 and proved 4 Feb. 1807: ". . . To wife Susannah all personal estate not otherwise disposed of, improvement of all real estate until son Robert arrives at age of 21 years, then she to have as long as she remains my widow. . . To sons Isaac, William and Ichabod 25 dollars apiece. . . To daughters Phebe Seabury, wife of George Seabury, and Hannah Wilcox, wife of Joseph Wilcox, one dollar each. To daughter Bridget Seabury all household goods. To son Robert all real estate in LC and Tiverton at the age of 21. . . "

Her will, recorded book 5, page 49, made 2 March 1816 and proved 5 Aug. 1816: ". . . widow, in poor health. . . son Isaac to have one dollar. Son Robert my great stilliards. Son Ichabod one dollar. To daughter Phebe Seabury, wife of George Seabury, a blue and white coverlid. To daughter Hannah Wilcox, wife of Josiah Wilcox, a calico bed quilt. To daughter Bridget Cook, wife of Isaac Cook, one pair of sheets and one thick blanket. To granddaughter Catharine Seabury, · daughter of Elizabeth Seabury, 7 silver teaspoons. To four daughters, Phebe, Hannah, Bridget and Elizabeth my wearing apparel. My daughter Elizabeth to be executor. . . "

   Children, recorded in LC:
13. i. Isaac, b. 19 March 1776.
 ii. Phebe, b. 13/23 May 1778; m. George Seabury.
 iii. William, b. in LC 23 May 1780; m. (1) 12 April 1807 in LC
     Rhoda Woodman, daughter of Edward and Priscilla
     (Negus) Woodman; m. (2) 16 Feb. 1834 in Dartmouth
     Sally Woodman, daughter of Edward and Priscilla (Negus)
     Woodman. Residence: New Bedford.
 iv. Hannah, b. 29 July 1782; m. 2 Nov. 1800 in LC Josiah Wilcox,
     son of Gideon and Phebe (Davenport) Wilcox of Tiverton.
 v. Bridget, b. 14 Sept. 1784.
 vi. Ichabod, b. 18 Nov. 1786.
14. vii. Robert, b. 10 July 1789; m. 3 Jan. 1813 in LC Caroline

Woodman, daughter of Edward and Priscilla (Negus)
Woodman.
viii.   Elizabeth, b. 16 Nov. 1792.

10. PHILIP[5] SEABURY (Sion[4], Joseph[3], Samuel[2], John[1]), born in
Tiverton 6 Dec. 1740, died 10 Jan. 1878. Residence: Tiverton.
According to the church records at Tiverton Four Corners, he
was married 7 Jan. 1767 in Tiverton to SARAH PEARCE, daughter of
Giles and Mercy (Rouse) Pearce, born in Tiverton 22 April 1748, died
12 Dec. 1796. They are buried in the Congregational cemetery, Lake
Road, Tiverton.

Children, recorded in Tiverton:
i.   David, b. 31 May 1767; m. Lydia Wood, daughter of George
        Wood.
ii.   Cornelius, b. 2 May 1769; m. in Tiverton 16 March 1714 Mary
        Gray, daughter of Pardon and Mary (Brown) Gray.
iii.   George, b. 27 July 1771.
iv.   Pearce, b. 7 Jan. 1773.
v.   Mary, b. 6 April 1777.
vi.   Job, b. 23 June 1781; d. in LC 7 Jan. 1861; m. in LC 5 June
        1803 Betsey Hunt, daughter of William and Betsey
        (Little) Hunt.

11. PINDAR[6] SEABURY (William[5], Samuel[4], Joseph[3], Samuel[2],
John[1]), born in LC 17 Dec. 1793, died there 29 Jan. 1866. Residence:
LC, where they lived on the Tiverton line.
He was married in LC 18 June 1839 by the Rev. Orrin J. Wait to
POLLY BROWNELL of Westport, daughter of Nathaniel Brownell of
Westport.
This couple evidently did not leave any children. On 19 March
1866, Charles Seabury and Charles Manchester were named his heirs
at law, on petition of Simeon Manchester.

12. BENJAMIN[6] SEABURY (Gideon[5], Benjamin[4], Joseph[3], Samuel[2],
John[1]), born in LC 20 Oct. 1776, died there 5 April 1857. Residence:
LC. He was married in LC 5 Oct. 1800 by the Rev. Mase Shepard to
RUTH MANCHESTER, daughter of John and Sarah (Bailey) Manchester,
born in LC 10 Nov. 1776, died there 21 Nov. 1786.

Children, born and recorded in Westport:
i.   George M., b. 11 June 1802; d. 6 Oct. 1821 ae 19.
15. ii. Capt. Benjamin, b. 27 Dec. 1803.
16. iii. John, b. 8 Dec. 1805.
iv.   Sarah B., b. in 1809; d. in LC 1 Sept. 1841.
17. v.   Alexander, b. 8 July 1821 in Westport.

13. ISAAC[6] SEABURY (Constant[5], Benjamin[4], Joseph[3], Samuel[2],
John[1]), born in LC 19 March 1776, died there 20 Oct. 1850. He was
married in LC 3 Dec. 1797 by the Rev. Mase Shepard to ABIGAIL
SIMMONS, daughter of Zarah and Phebe (Brownell) Simmons, born
in LC 18 Feb. 1776, died there 10 March 1859. Residence: LC.

They lived on the place in district no. 2, just south of the Swamp
Corner, where his son Andrew and grandson George A. Seabury later
lived.

His will, recorded LC Probate, book 10, page 301, made 4 Oct.
1850 and proved 9 Dec. 1850: ". . . To wife Abigail Seabury all real
estate with all the buildings. To granddaughter Susanna Gray Seabury
Woodworth, daughter of Zebedee Woodworth, by second best bed. One
dollar each to daughters Phebe Chase, Lydia Jones and Susanna Woodworth, and to son Andrew Seabury. . . "

Children:
i.   Phebe Brownell, b. 12 March 1798 in LC; m. (?) Chase.
18. ii.   Andrew G., b. 2 June 1806.
iii.   Susanna, m. (--) Woodworth.
iv.   Lydia, m. (--) Jones.

14. ROBERT[6] SEABURY (Constant[5], Benjamin[4], Joseph[3], Samuel[2],
John[1]), born in LC 10 July 1789. Residence: Tiverton. He was married
in LC 3 Jan. 1813 by the Rev. Benjamin Peckham to CAROLINE WOOD-
MAN, daughter of Edward and Priscilla (Negas) Woodman, born in LC
27 Sept. 1789, died 13 Dec. 1857. She is buried in the old cemetery at
the stone church.

On 27 Sept. 1861 he deeded to his sons Oliver and Alexander in
Tiverton 33 acres bounded west on river, north on Sapowet Avenue, and
to his son Warren and daughter Caroline his homestead farm, bounded
east on Pindar Seabury.

Children:
i.   Oliver Perry, b. in 1814.
ii.   Alexander, b. in 1815.
iii.   Caroline, b. in 1816 (?).
iv.   Frederick, b. in 1817.
v.   Caroline 2d, b. in 1819.
vi.   Warren, b. in 1826.
19. vii.   Albert, b. 8 July 1829.
ix.   Harriet C., b. in 1831.
x.   Infant.

15. CAPT. BENJAMIN[7] SEABURY (Benjamin[6], Gideon[5], Benjamin[4],
Joseph[3], Samuel[2], John[1]), born in Westport 27 Dec. 1803, died in LC 26
July 1892.

He married (intention 9 Feb. 1830) in New Bedford ELIZABETH
BROWNELL TOMPKINS, daughter of Gideon and Cynthia (Brownell)
Tompkins, born in LC 14 March 1807, died there 24 Sept. 1893. They
are buried in Union cemetery.

Residence: LC. They lived on the road south of the Commons, on
the west of the road opposite the old Wilbor cemetery. It was formerly
the Tompkins place, later owned by Stuart Burchard.

When 12 years old he went to sea and began working for two dollars
a month. At age 23 he was master of a vessel. He left the sea at 35
and two years later came tb LC, where he built a store, which he
carried on for nearly forty years. He was a member of the town

council for about 17 years, was a state senator one year and a state representative three years.

Children, first three born in Westport:
i.   Infant, b. 4 Aug. 1836; d. ae 4 days.
ii.   Charles Henry, b. 16 Sept. 1837; d. 14 Sept. 1896; m. 12 Jan. 1864 Mary E. Talbot, b. 15 Aug. 1842, d. 14 June 1920 in LC. He was a druggist in Providence.
iii. Edwin Tompkins, b. in Westport 7 April 1840; d. in LC 22 April 1911; m. in LC 31 Dec. 1867 Susan E. Sisson, daughter of Lemuel and Comfort (Simmons) Sisson, b. 16 March 1836, d. in LC 15 June 1910.
21. iv. Albert Theodore, b. 10 Oct. 1843.
v.   Elizabeth, b. 18 Aug. 1848; d. 3 Jan. 1879.
vi.   Lucia Newman, b. 19 June 1851 in LC; d. there 19 Jan. 1905; m. there 6 Dec. 1893 Isaac Wilbor Howland, son of Charles and Mehitable (Hicks) Howland.
vii. Benjamin, b. in May 1845; d. 10 April 1848 ae 2.
viii. Benjamin 2d, b. 17 Feb. 1853; m. 16 May 1876 Sarah Bacheller. He was a member of Taylor Symonds and Co., a drygoods company.

16. JOHN[7] SEABURY (Benjamin[6], Gideon[5], Benjamin[4], Joseph[3], Samuel[2], John[1]), born in Westport 8 Dec. 1805, died in LC 3 July 1865.

He was married in LC 26 Feb. 1836 by the Rev. Samuel Coleman to MARIA SHAW, daughter of Jediah and Rhoda (Manchester) Shaw of LC, born there 17 Nov. 1815, died there 1 June 1901. Both are buried in the Shaw cemetery, district no. 10, cemetery no. 6A.

Residence: LC. They lived on the Shaw land that belonged to the Shaws from the beginning of the town and is on the road that goes south to the water from Shaw road.

In his will, LC Probate, book 11, page 399, made 8 Nov. 1860 and proved 11 Sept. 1865, he left to his wife Maria all real and personal estate and named her executor.

Children, all recorded in LC:
i.   Capt. George M., b. 21 March 1837; d. in LC 12 Dec. 1895; unmarried. He was a sailor and began in 1852 in the bark Sacramento of Westport. From that time until 1884 he followed the sea. He was in the vessel Elizabeth Swift of New Bedford, the merchant ship Comet and was captain for nine voyages on the barks President and Morning Star.
20. ii. John Alden, b. 13 May 1844.
iii. Harriet E., b. 30 July 1848; d. 14 July 1871; m. 17 Sept. 1866 in LC Charles S. Davis, son of Charles and Susan Davis. They had two children, Hattie, born in South Dartmouth in 1871, m. in LC 17 July 1902 Francis Otis Tripp, b. in New Bedford in 1869, son of Holder and Ruth (Sabins) Tripp; also a baby, b. 23 June 1904 in LC.
iv. Mary Catharine, b. 20 July 1856; m. (the third wife of) Isaac W. Howland, son of Charles Wilbor and Mehitable (Hicks) Howland.
v.   Maria Cornelia (Nellie), b. in 1852; d. 8 Nov. 1933; unmarried.

17. ALEXANDER[7] SEABURY (Benjamin[6], Gideon[5], Benjamin[4], Joseph[3], Samuel[2], John[1]), born in Westport 8 July 1821, died in Brooklyn, N. Y., 29 Feb. 1896. Residence: Brooklyn. He was a painter.

He married in Westport 22 Oct. 1848 LYDIA BRIGGS MANCHESTER, daughter of Abraham and Lydia (Shaw) Manchester, born in Westport 15 Dec. 1826, died in Brooklyn 22 June 1896. They are buried in the Union cemetery.

Children:
i.   Frederick Franklin, b. 2 July 1849; d. 26 Sept. 1924.
ii.   Erastus Franklin, b. 2 Nov. 1850; d. 19 July 1852.
iii. Alexander, b. 16 Dec. 1851 (?); d. 2 Feb. 1859.
iv.   Caroline Louise, b. 3 Dec. 1852; d. in Brooklyn 11 Jan. 1916.

18. ANDREW G.[7] SEABURY (Isaac[6], Constant[5], Benjamin[4], Joseph[3], Samuel[2], John[1]), born in LC 2 June 1806, died there 18 July 1893.

He married JULIA E. KNOWLTON, daughter of James and Mary A. Knowlton, born in Hollister, Mass., 1 Feb. 1830, died in LC 28 April 1859.

Residence: LC. They lived in district no. 1 south of Swamp Corner.

Children, recorded in LC:
i.   Clara, b. 30 Jan. 1857; d. in Fall River; unmarried.
22. ii.   George A., b. 30 Jan. 1858.

19. ALBERT[7] SEABURY (Robert[6], Constant[5], Benjamin[4], Joseph[3], Samuel[2], John[1]), born in Tiverton 8 July 1829, died in LC 21 Dec. 1882. He married 8 Sept. 1852 EMELINE FRANCES ALMY, daughter of John and Levinia (Manchester) Almy of LC, born there 3 Feb. 1835, died there 3 Feb. 1910. They are buried in the cemetery at Tiverton Four Corners.

Residence: Tiverton and LC. In 1872 he purchased a farm which his widow continued to occupy and which was his homestead farm.

Children:
i.   Charles Albert, b. 16 Jan. 1854; d. 19 Dec. 1942.
ii.   Harriet E. D., b. in LC 23 Oct. 1855; m. 11 Aug. 1881 in Tiverton Albert (?) Lake of Tiverton, son of Abner and Elvira Lake.
iii.   Benjamin C., b. 18 May 1861; m. in LC 3 Dec. 1882 Jennie C. Peckham, daughter of Peleg and Sarah Peckham.
iv.   John E., b. 25 Nov. 1864; m. in LC 1 Feb. 1888 Ella L. Grinnell, daughter of Thomas and Hannah (Wilbor) Grinnell.
23. v.   William Henry, b. 30 Jan. 1867.
vi.   Flora Louise, b. 9 Jan. 1869 in Tiverton; m. in LC 2 Jan. 1893 Ezra P. B. Manley, son of Sylvester and Hannah Manley of Westport.
24. vii. Lester Almy, b. 16 March 1870.
viii.   Emma, b. 5 Nov. 1874.

ix.   Cora Belle Elizabeth, b. 22 Sept. 1878; m. in LC 12 Sept.
       1903 Anderson Dickens Allen, son of Simon Ray and
       Zilpha (Crandall) Allen of New Shoreham.

20. JOHN ALDEN[8] SEABURY (John[7], Benjamin[6], Gideon[5],
Benjamin[4], Joseph[3], Samuel[2], John[1]), born in Westport 13 May 1844,
died in New Bedford 14 Oct. 1918. He married in LC 25 Dec. 1877
NANCY GEORGIANNA GRAY, daughter of George and Charlotte
(Morgan) Gray, born in Calais, Vt., 13 Dec. 1849, died in New
Bedford 31 March 1928. She is buried in the Shaw cemetery.

       Children, born in LC:
i.   Charlotte Maria, b. 7 Nov. 1878; d. in New Bedford 1 Feb.
       1905; m. in LC 25 Dec. 1902 Dr. John Gael Hathaway of
       New Bedford, son of Benjamin and Susan (Brown)
       Hathaway. He married second Claudia Church, niece
       of Thadeus H. Church.
25. ii. Arthur Gray, b. 20 July 1884.
iii.   Allen Oscar, b. 22 Aug. 1888; d. 2 April 1933 in New Bedford;
       unmarried.

21. ALBERT THEODORE[8] SEABURY (Benjamin[7], Benjamin[6],
Gideon[5], Benjamin[4], Joseph[3], Samuel[2], John[1]), born in LC 10 Oct.
1843, died there 24 Dec. 1922. Residence: LC. They lived in district
no. 2 opposite the millhouse of Thomas R. Slicer.
     He married in LC 22 Dec. 1864 SUSAN ALICE BURLINGAME,
daughter of Henry and Susan (Sisson) Burlingame and granddaughter
of Henry and Nancy (Updike) Burlingame of North Kingstown, R.I.,
born 17 Feb. 1841, died in LC 27 March 1924.
     They had two children who died young. Only the first was recorded
in LC, a son born 21 Jan. 1875.

22. GEORGE A.[8] SEABURY (Andrew[7], Isaac[6], Constant[5], Benjamin[4],
Joseph[3], Samuel[2], John[1]), born in LC 28 Jan. 1858, died in Tiverton.
He married in LC 2 Nov. 1889 CARRIE JANE BRIGGS, daughter of Alfred
C. and Elizabeth (Brownell) Briggs, born in LC in September 1868, died
in Tiverton.
     Residence: LC and Tiverton. They lived on the place formerly owned
by his father, Andrew Seabury, in district no. 1, south of Swamp
Corner.

       Children:
i.   Elizabeth H., b. in LC 2 Oct. 1898; m. (--) Bishop of Ports-
       mouth.
ii.   Alice Jennings, b. 5 June 1900; d. in Tiverton.

23. WILLIAM HENRY[8] SEABURY (Albert[7], Robert[6], Constant[5],
Benjamin[4], Joseph[3], Samuel[2], John[1]), born in Tiverton 30 Jan. 1867,
died in LC 7 March 1941. He married there 26 Feb. 1904 JOSEPHINE
PEARCE BURLINGAME, daughter of James and Mary (Sisson) Burlingame of LC, born there 24 May 1877.

       Children, born in LC:

    i.   Grace Almy, b. in LC 12 June 1905; m. in Tiverton 28 Sept.
           1927 Milton Barker Simmons, son of Giles H. and Sarah
           (Gray) Simmons, b. 31 Dec. 1899.
    ii.   Beatrice, b. in LC 20 Oct. 1909; m. in Tiverton 26 April
           1932 Knowlton Francis Rounds, son of George and Eva
           (Snell) Simmons (?), b. in Tiverton 24 Sept. 1912.
    iii.   William Henry Jr., b. 7 May 1911.
    iv.   Susan Elizabeth, b. in LC 1 Nov. 1917; m. in Tiverton 10
           June 1944 Elmer Zephinia Brayton, son of Elmer and
           Eudora (Palmer) Brayton, b. in Westport 8 Sept. 1906.

    24. LESTER ALMY[8] SEABURY (Albert[7], Robert[6], Constant[5],
Benjamin[4], Joseph[3], Samuel[2], John[1]), born in Tiverton 16 March 1870,
died in Fall River 31 Oct. 1934. Residence: LC. He married there
13 Jan. 1893 HARRIET MARTHA JENNINGS, daughter of Samuel and
Nancy (Wilbor) Jennings, born in LC 5 Oct. 1873.

          Children, recorded in LC:
    i.   Nancy Emeline, b. 4 May 1894; m. 28 Aug. 1925 William H.
           Carnoe.
    ii.   Gladys Almy, b. 27 Feb. 1896; m. 11 May 1917 in Warren, R.I.,
           James Henry Haggarty, son of William and Margaret
           (Murphy) Haggarty.
    iii.   Wilton Jennings, b. 25 July 1899; d. 20 Dec. 1913 ae 14.
    iv.   Frederic Arthur, b. 22 Nov. 1902; d. 18 Feb. 1903 ae 3 months.
    v.   Harriet Lestena, b. 25 Feb. 1904; m. 12 Sept. 1925 in LC
           Norman Everett McKay, son of Daniel and Elizabeth
           (Bannerman) McKay, b. in Providence 12 Sept. 1900.
    vi.   Franklin, b. 11 June 1908; m. in Newport 24 Dec. 1930 Dorothy
           McClure Child, daughter of George Johnson and Jenette
           (Adams) (McClure) Child.
    vii.   Martha, b. 3 Jan. 1916; m. in Killingly, Conn., 29 Oct. 1934
           Francis B. Manchester of Ardsley, N.Y., son of Giles
           and Etta (Harrington) Manchester, b. in Tiverton Four
           Corners.

    25. ARTHUR GRAY[9] SEABURY (John[8], John[7], Benjamin[6], Gideon[5],
Benjamin[4], Joseph[3], Samuel[2], John[1]), born in LC 20 July 1884. Resi-
dence: LC and New Bedford. He married (license 29 May 1909)
MARJORIE ANTHONY GOFF, daughter of Rufus and Eva (Anthony)
Goff of Providence, born in 1888 in East Providence. They were the
parents of one child, a daughter.

. . . .

    CAPT. ALEXANDER SEABURY, born 31 March 1822, died in LC
10 June 1866. He married CAROLINE (--), born in 1821. They are
buried in the cemetery at the old stone church. They had one child,
Caroline, who may have died 14 Dec. 1854 ae 14.

    ALBERT SEABURY, married MARY A. (--), and had one child
born in LC, Abby L. P., who died 6 Oct. 1856 ae 1 year and 5 months.

A. T. SEABURY HOME, LITTLE COMPTON, R. I.

THE SEARLES FAMILY

1. ROBERT[1] SEARLES, born in Dorchester, England about 1640. He married DEBORAH SALTER and settled in Dorchester, Mass. Administration of his estate was taken there. He died 7 Feb. 1717 in Dorchester, where he had been town clerk for 16 years. His wife died in Dorchester 2 March 1713/14.

Children, born in Dorchester, Mass.:
2.   i.   Nathaniel, b. 9 June 1662.
     ii.   Salter, b. 26 June 1664.
    iii.   Esborn, b. 24 Feb. 1669; d. young.
     iv.   Robert, b. 2 July 1671; m. 4 Dec. 1695 Rebecca Evans.
      v.   Esborn, b. 18 March 1674.
     vi.   Deborah, b. 4 April 1677.
   vii.   Jabez, b. 13 March 1679.

2. NATHANIEL[2] SEARLES (Robert[1]), born in Dorchester, Mass., 9 June 1662, died in LC 5 Feb. 1750. He married in 1794 SARAH ROGERS, daugher of John and Elizabeth (Pabodie) Rogers, born in LC 4 May 1677, died there 19 Jan. 1769. He was town clerk of LC and also first teacher at the peaked top school house in LC.

Children:
     i.   Deborah, b. 17 Nov. 1695; m. 20 Feb. 1717 George Pearce.
     ii.   John, b. 12 March 1698; d. 20 March 1714.
    iii.   Sarah, b. 2 April 1700; m. 28 June 1725 Thomas Dring.
3.   iv.   Nathaniel, b. 26 April 1703.

3. NATHANIEL³ SEARLES (Nathaniel², Robert¹), born in LC 26
April 1703, died there 8 Dec. 1781. He married in December 1725
ELIZABETH KINNICUT, born in 1701, died in LC 11 Dec. 1781. They
are buried in the Old Commons cemetery and have a large flat tomb,
on which is inscribed the following:

"In life he was amiable and discreet and with strict integrity, he
discharged the several duties of a Christian magistrate and friend.
At death his steady confidence and hope in the mercy of God and
Savior supported him with that manly fortitude which ever becomes
a sincere and faithful servant of the Redeemer."

"Here lieth the precious remains of Elizabeth Searle the amiable
consort of the Hon. Nathaniel Searle Esquire. She departed this life
on the 11th day of December A.D. 1781 in the 80th year of her age.
In life her universial benevolence endeared her to all. Her virtues
as a wife and a parent and friend and the becoming lustre and her
hope being steadfastly fixed on God our Savior."

Children:
i.   John, b. 24 Aug. 1726; d. 24 March 1801.
4. ii.   Constant, b. 17 June 1728.
5. iii. Daniel, b. 8 Sept. 1730.
iv.   Betsey, b. 3 June 1732; m. 19 Nov. 1754 Amos Atwell.
v.   Sarah, b. 28 Jan. 1733; m. 30 Jan. 1758 Grindle Runnells.
6. vi.   Nathaniel, b. 25 Dec. 1735.
7. vii. James, b. 5 Oct. 1737.
viii. Ruth, b. 12 Sept. 1740; d. 22 Oct. 1740.
ix.   Comfort, b. 11 June 1742.

4. CONSTANT⁴ SEARLES (Nathaniel³, Nathaniel², Robert¹), born
17 June 1728, died in 1778. He married 18 May 1751 HANNAH MINOR,
daughter of Simeon and Hannah (Wheeler) Minor. Residence: Stonington,
Conn.

Children, the first four born in Stonington, Conn.:
i.   William, b. 2 Dec. 1751; m. 17 Oct. 1773 Philura Frink.
ii.   Hannah, b. 25 Jan. 1754; m. Nathan D. Minor.
iii. Constant, b. 17 March 1756; d. young.
iv.   Elizabeth, b. 4 March 1757; m. 13 July 1773 Capt. Dethie
      Hewitt.
v.   Constant, b. in LC 1759.
vi.   Rev. Roger, b. in Preston, Conn., 13 Aug. 1762; m. Catharine
      Scott. Their son, Leonard Searle, b. in Pittston, Pa., 7
      Nov. 1808, d. 31 Dec. 1880, m. 23 Oct. 1832 Lydia Dimoct.
vii. Ruth, b. in Preston, Conn., 1 March 1765; m. Nathan Crary
      of Groton, Conn.

5. LT. DANIEL⁴ SEARLES (Nathaniel³, Nathaniel², Robert¹), born
in LC 8 Sept. 1730, died 31 May 1779, buried in the Old Commons
cemetery. He married MARY (--).

Children, recorded in LC:
i.   Betsey, b. 15 June 1755.
ii.   Sarah, b. 5 May 1757.

iii.   Joel, b. 6 Feb. 1759.
iv.   John, b. 1765; d. 12 June 1779 ae 13.

6. NATHANIEL[4] SEARLES ESQ. (Nathaniel[3], Nathaniel[2], Robert[1]), born in LC 25 Dec. 1735. He married LUCY ELLIS, daughter of the Rev. Jonathan Ellis of LC, born in LC 4 April 1642, died 22 Nov. 1806, buried in the Old Commons cemetery.

Children:
i.   Lucy Ellis, b. in 1781; d. 15 April 1786.
ii.   Daughter.
iii.   Daughter.

7. JAMES[4] SEARLES ESQ. (Nathaniel[3], Nathaniel[2], Robert[1]), born 5 Oct. 1737, married MARY (--).

Children:
i.   Cynthia, b. in 1765; d. 28 April 1784.
ii.   Charlotte, b. in 1771; d. 25 June 1799; m. 30 Oct. 1791 Samuel Wilbor, son of William and Mary (Babcock) Wilbor.

THE SEIBEL FAMILY

WILLIAM HENRY SEIBEL, born in Tiverton 1 Feb. 1877, died in LC 16 Aug. 1935, married MARTHA YOUNG. Residence: LC.

Children, recorded in LC:
i.   William Richmond, b. in LC 28 May 1915.
ii.   Florence Marguerita, b. 14 June 1920.

THE SHALEY FAMILY

EBENEZER SHALEY of Tiverton, born in 1666. Residence: LC.

Children, recorded in LC:
i.   Sarah, b. 11 Dec. 1692.
ii.   Joseph, b. 20 Aug. 1694.
iii.   Ebenezer, b. 17 April 1696.
iv.   Joan, b. 7 March 1699.
v.   Benjamin, b. 2 March 1701.
vi.   Susanna, b. 7 May 1702.
vii.   Mary, b. 8 Aug. 1703.

THE SHAW FAMILY

1. **ANTHONY[1] SHAW**, died 21 Aug. 1705. Residence: Boston, Portsmouth and LC. He married in Boston 8 April 1653 ALICE STONARD, daughter of John and Margaret Stonard. In the Boston records, his wife's name is listed as Alice Stanare. He may have been born in 1628, the son of John Shaw, who came to Salem, Mass., in 1627 from a town near Halifax, Yorkshire, England.

In Portsmouth 20 April 1665, he bought from Philip Tabor a house and ten acres of land for 40 pounds and 300 good boards. His inventory, dated 1 Oct. 1705, listed 213 pounds, 12 s, 2d, a cow, grindstone, silver money 9 pounds, Negro man 30 pounds, etc.

        Children, the first three born in Boston:

	i.	William, b. 21 Jan. 1654; d. in March 1654.
	ii.	William 2d, b. 24 Feb. 1655.
	iii.	Elizabeth, b. 21 May 1656.
2.	iv.	Israel, b. about 1660.
	v.	Ruth, b. 10 Oct. 1660; m. John Cook, son of John and Mary (Borden) Cook, b. in 1656.
	vi.	Grace, d. 1 March 1737; m. Joseph Church, son of Joseph and Mary (Tucker) Church.

2. **ISRAEL[2] SHAW (Anthony[1])**, born about 1660. Residence: LC. He married about 1689 (--) TALLMAN, daughter of Peter Tallman of Portsmouth.

According to local records, he sold to his brother-in-law, John Cook of Tiverton, two parcels of land in Portsmouth, a right to Hog Island, buildings, orchards, etc. for 202 pounds 10 s.

        Children, all recorded in LC:

3.	i.	William, b. 7 Nov. 1690.
	ii.	Mary, b. 17 Feb. 1692; d. in LC 2 April 1713; m. 22 May 1712 Jonathan Blackman, son of Jonathan and grandson of John Blackman.
4.	iii.	Anthony, b. 29 Jan. 1694.
	iv.	Alice, b. 17 Nov. 1695; m. in LC 23 Feb. 1716 John Palmer.
5.	v.	Israel, b. 28 Aug. 1697.
	vi.	Hannah, b. 7 March 1699; m. in LC 16 July 1719 William Wood.
6.	vii.	Jeremiah, b. 6 June 1700.
	viii.	Ruth, b. 10 Feb. 1701.
7.	ix.	Peter, b. 6 Oct. 1704.
	x.	Elizabeth, b. 7 Feb. 1706; m. in LC 19 May 1726 Giles Brownell.
	xi.	Grace, b. 20 Oct. 1707; m. in LC 2 Oct. 1729 Edward Shaw.
	xii.	Comfort, b. 9 Aug. 1709; m. 6 April 1728 John Simmons.
	xiii.	Deborah, b. 15 July 1711; m. (?) 2 Oct. 1729 George White (?).

3. **WILLIAM[3] SHAW (Israel[2], Anthony[1])**, born in LC 7 Nov. 1690, died in 1767. Residence: LC.

He was married in LC 28 Sept. 1710 by Benjamin Church, justice, to CONTENT IRISH, daughter of John and Elizabeth Irish of LC, born there in September 1691. He married second ANN (--).

His will, recorded LC Wills, book 2, page 81, made 7 Feb. 1763 and proved 3 Feb. 1767: ". . . This 7th of February in the 3rd year of the reign of King George III of Great Britain. . . William Shaw of LC, far advanced in years, yeoman. . . To eldest son William Shaw all my land in the township of Dartmouth. To granddaughter Content, daughter of son William, three dollars. To second son Israel all my land in LC with buildings, all stock of every kind and my gun. To daughter Elizabeth Chase one good milch cow. To two sons William and Israel all wearing apparel. To granddaughter Content, daughter of Israel Shaw, one bed and furniture. To granddaughter Content Chase a pair of large tongs and looking glass. To my now wife Ann Shaw, all books, all household goods she brought with her when I married her. . . "

Children of William and Content Shaw, all recorded in LC:
i.   Elizabeth, b. 9 Jan. 1712; m. in LC 29 April 1731 Nathan
      Chace of Tiverton.
8. ii.   William, b. 1 Jan. 1714.
9. iii. Israel, b. 9 April 1715.

4. ANTHONY[3] SHAW (Israel[2], Anthony[1]), born in LC 29 Jan. 1694, died there in March 1759. He was married there 14 Aug. 1718 by Thomas Church, justice, to REBECCA WOOD, daughter of Thomas and Content Wood, born in LC 17 April 1696, died there in January 1766.

Her will, recorded LC Wills, book 2, page 64, made 6 Oct. 1759 and proved 4 Feb. 1766: ". . . Rebecca Shaw, widow, being something weak and low of body but of perfect mind. . . To son Benjamin my great iron kettle and farming tackling. To son Anthony and he to be executor, choice of two cows. To son Arnold one cow. To son Thomas bed and bedstead. To son John bed and bedstead in lower room. To daughters Ruth Wood, Elizabeth Wilbour and Rebecca Potter, each a spoon marked R.S. To grandson Anthony Wilbour 10 pounds. All my wearing apparel to my four daughters. . . "

Children, recorded in LC:
10. i.   Benjamin, b. 5 Oct. 1720.
    ii. Mary, b. 24 Feb. 1722; m. in LC 4 Dec. 1744 John Wood of
         Middletown.
    iii. Ruth, b. 29 Sept. 1723; m. in LC 17 Dec. 1746 Peleg Wood.
    iv. Anthony, b. 30 Nov. 1725.
    v.   Elizabeth, b. 10 Jan. 1728; d. in January 1804; m. in LC 15
         Dec. 1748 Samuel Wilbore, son of William Wilbore.
    vi. Rebecca, b. 27 Jan. 1730; m. Stokes Potter.
    vii. Arnold, b. 13 Nov. 1732.
    viii. Thomas, b. 26 Jan. 1735.
    ix. John, b. 5 May 1737.

5. ISRAEL[3] SHAW (Israel[2], Anthony[1]), born in LC 28 Aug. 1697, died in 1746. He married there 10 Aug. 1697 ABIGAIL PALMER, daughter of William and Mary (Richmond) Palmer, born in LC 5 April 1702, died there in September 1790.

His will, recorded in Taunton, book 11, page 162, made 2 March 1744 and proved 1 July 1746: ". . . in the 18th year of the reign of

George II. . . To wife Abigail all estate both real and personal excepting
what I give my children. To sons. . . and daughters. . . 5 pounds each.
Wife Abigail sole executrix. . . "

Her will, recorded LC Wills, book 3, page 198, made 8 March 1776
and proved 5 Oct. 1790: ". . . To son Blake 6 shillings. To son Israel
all real estate with buildings, my great chair and fire tongs and to be
executor of this will. To son Seth 30 pounds. To daughter Parthenia
Blackwell 6 shillings. To daughter Eunice Wood 12 shillings. To daughter
Merebah Shaw 4 pounds 10 shillings. . . "

Children, recorded in LC:
- 11. i.   Lemuel, b. 6 Sept. 1722.
- ii.   Blake, b. 21 Feb. 1723; m. in LC 1 Aug. 1745 Sarah Wait.
- iii. Parthenia, b. 19 March 1725; m. in LC 15 Dec. 1748 John
        Blackwell of Dartmouth.
- iv.   Eunice, b. 7 Oct. 1728; m. in LC 27 Nov. 1747/8 John Wood.
- v.   Lois, b. 16 Oct. 1730.
- vi.   Lillis, b. 26 March 1733.
- vii. Merebah, b. 2 Nov. 1736; may have m. (1) Gideon Shaw and
        (2) Stephen Monroe of Bristol.
- viii. Israel, b. 28 May 1739.
- ix.   Lillis 2d, b. 7 Jan. 1742.
- 12. x.   Seth, b. 6 Nov. 1745.

6. JEREMIAH[3] SHAW (Israel[2], Anthony[1]), born in LC 6 June
1700, died there in July 1764. Residence: LC. He was married there
1 April 1725 by Richard Billings, justice, to PHEBE WILBOR, daughter
of William and (--) Tallman Wilbor of LC, born there 1 Oct. 1704.

Children, all recorded in LC except Alse and Fallee:
- i.   Jedediah, b. 25 Jan. 1726.
- ii.   Ruth, b. 26 May 1728.
- iii. Jeremiah, b. 2 Feb. 1730; m. 11 Dec. 1751 Esther Southworth.
- iv.   Priscilla, b. 11 March 1732; m. 22 April 1757 Gideon
        Salisbury, son of Joseph and Innocent (Head) Salisbury.
- v.   Bemanuel, b. 1 Dec. 1738.
- vi.   Prudence, b. 15 Sept. 1744; d. 10 Jan. 1823; m. 22 Feb. 1765
        Pardon Brownell, son of John and Elizabeth.
- vii. Alse, b. 28 May 1747.
- viii. Phebe, b. 28 May 1747; m. in LC 16 June 1771 Thomas
        Palmer, son of Thomas and Abial (Wilbor) Palmer.
- ix.   Fallee.

7. PETER[3] SHAW (Israel[2], Anthony[1]), born in LC 6 Oct. 1704, died
there in January 1775. He married there in January 1734 SARAH BROWN
of Tiverton, died in May 1785 in LC.

They lived on the north side of Shaw Road on a place owned by
Thomas Wilbor in 1850. He went to Nova Scotia and bought land there,
but returned to LC, and later gave the land in Nova Scotia to his sons
Antipus and David, who settled there.

His will, recorded LC Wills, book 2, page 299, made 24 Oct.
1774 and proved 7 Feb. 1775: ". . . To wife Sarah all bed and bedding,
use of house and land where I now dwell, which land contains about 30

acres. . . To son Antipus of Amherst land in Nova Scotia, one silver
dollar. . . and my gun. To son Peter the house and farm where he now
dwelleth. . . bounded north of the highway, east on Joseph .Wilbur, south
on the sea and west on Benjamin Shaw, and also land that I bought of
Samuel Pearce. To son David of Nova Scotia all land and buildings in
west Falmouth County. . . and five sheep. To daughter Mary Shaw one
silver dollar. To daughter Hannah Tabor 30 dollars. To daughter Alice
Briggs one silver dollar. To daughters Ruth, Elizabeth and Grace, 25
dollars each. To son Peter house and land where I now live. To daughter
Innocent 200 silver dollars, if she is not restored to her reason, and
comfortable support. . . "

       Children, recorded in LC:

13. i.   Mary, b. 7 June 1735.
   ii.   Antipus, b. 27 Jan. 1737. He went to Amherst, Nova
         Scotia, before 1774.
14. iii.   Peter, b. 3 Sept. 1738.
   iv.   Alice, b. 12 Dec. 1740; m. 14 March 1767 Nathaniel Briggs.
   v.   Hannah, b. 5 May 1743; m. (--) Tabor.
   vi.   David, b. 16 April 1745. He went to West Falmouth, Nova
         Scotia, before 1774.
   vii. Ruth, b. 4 Oct. 1747; m. 16 March 1775 Moses Brown.
   viii. Noah, b. 16 July 1749; d. young.
   ix.   Sarah, b. 1 June 1751; m. in LC 2 May 1775 Samuel Hunt.
   x.   Innocent, b. in August 1753; d. in September 1778.
   xi.   Elizabeth, b. 31 Aug. 1755; m. in LC 29 Aug. 1776 John Head,
         son of Benjamin and Judith Head.
   xii. Grace, b. 24 Dec. 1757; m. in LC 8 Nov. 1778 Anthony Wilbor,
         son of Samuel and Elizabeth Wilbor.

     8. WILLIAM[4] SHAW (William[3], Israel[2], Anthony[1]), born in LC 1 Jan.
1714.
     He was married in LC 24 June 1737 by Richard Billings, justice, to
MARY HILLIARD, daughter of Capt. David and Joanna (Andros) Hilliard,
born in LC 23 June 1718, died 8 Aug. 1740 ae 22. She is buried in the Old
Commons cemetery, next to her parents. He married second in LC 22
Dec. 1743 SUSANNA BROWNELL, daughter of John and Mary (Carr)
Brownell, born in LC 15 Dec. 1716. He married third in LC 22 Aug.
1756 ANN EASTON of Newport, died in LC in August 1776.

       Children, recorded in LC:
   i.   Mary, b. 14 Sept. 1745.
   ii.   John.
   iii. Content.

     9. ISRAEL[4] SHAW (William[3], Israel[2], Anthony[1]), born 9 April
1715. He married in LC 1 June 1740 SARAH WILBORE, daughter of
John and Sarah (Palmer) Wilbore, born in LC 22 June 1715, died
there in 1785. Residence: LC.

       Children, recorded in LC:
   i.   Elizabeth, b. 15 Sept. 1740; m. 25 Sept. 1759 Arnold Campbell.
15. ii.   Gideon, b. 26 Feb. 1743.

	iii.	Cornelius, b. 24 Nov. 1744.
	iv.	William, b. 22 March 1747; d. young.
	v.	Jedediah, b. 13 Feb. 1748/9; d. young.
	vi.	Content, b. 6 Feb. 1750/1; m. 22 Feb. 1770 in LC Charles Brownell, son of Charles and Mary (Wood) Brownell.
16.	vii.	William 2d, b. 1 July 1752.
17.	viii.	Israel, b. 7 Feb. 1754.
	ix.	Uriah, b. 15 May 1758.

10. BENJAMIN[4] SHAW (Anthony[3], Israel[2], Anthony[1]), born in LC
5 Oct. 1720, died there in September 1794. He married ELIZABETH
POTTER, daughter of (--) and Mary Devol Potter, born in Dartmouth
in 1731. They owned the place on the south side of Shaw Road where
his grandson Benjamin was living in 1850.

His will, recorded LC Wills, book 3, page 293, made 10 Sept.
1784 and proved 5 Aug. 1794: ". . . To wife Elizabeth all household
stuff. To son Barnabus 80 milled silver dollars. To son Nathaniel
one silver dollar. To son Benjamin 80 silver dollars, my loom,
wearing apparel and case of bottles. To son Noah the farm. To son
Asa 100 Spanish milled silver dollars. To son Bemanuel my meadow
which I bought of Enoch Briggs. I give to my grandson John, son of
Sylvanus, deceased, land lying near land belonging to Benjamin Sherman.
To John Shaw. . . To Brownell Shaw. . . To daughter Rhoda White my
warming pan. To daughter Lucy Briggs large dripping pan. To daughter
Elizabeth Sisson two hitchels and my looking glass. To three daughters,
Rhoda White, Lucy Briggs and Elizabeth Sisson. . . To son Noah to
provide for his mother's livelihood. . . "

Children, recorded in LC:

	i.	Capt. Sylvanus, b. 4 May 1750; d. 22 Oct. 1777. He was a soldier in the Revolutionary War.
	ii.	Nathaniel, b. 24 Feb. 1752.
	iii.	Rhoda, b. 2 Oct. 1753; d. young.
	iv.	Rhoda 2d, b. 1 Jan. 1756; m. in LC 16 March 1777 Noah White, son of Christopher and Elizabeth (Thurston) White.
18.	v.	Noah, b. 2 Feb. 1758.
	vi.	Susannah, (Lucy), b. 25 March 1760; m. in LC 10 May 1778 Thomas Briggs.
	vii.	Barnabus, b. 24 Oct. 1761.
19.	viii.	Benjamin, b. 24 July 1763.
	ix.	Elizabeth, b. 5 Oct. 1764; m. in LC 13 Oct. 1783 Benjamin Sisson.
	x.	Asa, b. 4 March 1766.
	xi.	Bemanuel, b. 21 July 1768.

11. LEMUEL[4] SHAW (Israel[3], Israel[2], Anthony[1]), born in LC 28
Aug. 1697. He married there in January 1742 SARAH BRIGGS, daughter
of William and Deborah (Church) Briggs, born in LC 5 June 1721.

Children, recorded in LC:

	i.	Ezekiel, b. 1 April 1746.
	ii.	Phebe, b. 1 Feb. 1748.
	iii.	Caleb, b. 30 June 1749.

12. SETH[4] SHAW (Israel[3], Israel[2], Anthony[1]), born in LC 6 Nov. 1745, died there 17 Jan. 1835.

He married ELIZABETH (--). He was married second in LC 5 March 1772 by the Rev. Jonathan Ellis to PRISCILLA CHURCH, daughter of William and Parnell (Southworth) Church, born in LC 23 Sept. 1749. He was married third in LC 24 Nov. 1776 by the Rev. Othniel Campbell to MARY DAVENPORT, daughter of John and Elizabeth (Taylor) Davenport, born in LC 1 May 1741.

Children by first wife, recorded in LC:
i.   Elizabeth, b. 9 Nov. 1769; m. there 14 March 1799 Job Head, son of Benjamin and Fallee Head.

Children by second wife:
ii. Lemuel, b. 23 March 1774.

Children by third wife:
iii. Seth, b. 2 July 1778; d. 31 May 1797 ae 18.
iv. Priscilla, b. 22 Sept. 1780.
20. v.   Timothy, b. 14 April 1782.

13. MARY[4] SHAW (Peter[3], Israel[2], Anthony[1]), born in LC 7 June 1735, died there 26 Feb. 1801, buried in Old Commons cemetery. She was unmarried.

In her will, recorded LC Wills, book 3, page 443, made 20 March 1794 and proved 1 April 1801, she left all her personal estate and clothing, her gold necklace and rest and residue to her son.

Children (Shaw):
21. i.   Zebedee, b. 25 July 1759.

14. PETER[4] SHAW (Peter[3], Israel[2], Anthony[1]), born in LC 3 Sept. 1738, died there 10 Jan. 1795. He was married there 28 Oct. 1770 by the Rev. Jonathan Ellis to LYDIA BRIGGS, daughter of Joseph and Ruth (Coe) Briggs, born in LC 8 Feb. 1753, died there 16 March 1842.

Residence: LC. They lived on the place given him by his father, across the road from the Shaw cemetery, which is on the road that goes almost to the ocean from Shaw Road. This place was owned by Jediah Shaw in 1850.

Her will, recorded LC Wills, book 9, page 49, made 18 March 1840 and proved 11 April 1842: ". . . Lydia Shaw of LC but now resident of Westport. . . To son Jediah my iron pot. To his wife Rhoda my black silk gown. To their daughter Harriet one pair of sheets. To their son Jediah my small mahogany trunk. To daughter Mary Wilbor use of my house in LC. To grandson Bennet Wilbor my house in LC at the death of his mother. To daughter Ruth Brownell my rocking chair. To daughter Prudence Manchester my pongee dress. To Abraham Manchester my great brass kettle and my mahogany pipe box. To his wife Lydia my dining table, wearing stays and hatchel. To their daughter Rhoda one pair of sheets. To their daughter Lydia my side saddle. To granddaughter Sarah Shaw my mahogany bureau. All the rest and residue to children. . . "

Children, recorded in LC:

      i.   Mary, b. 2 Dec. 1770; d. in LC 21 June 1852; m. there 16
                 Aug. 1792 Bennett Wilbor, son of Joseph and Rachel
                 (Bailey) Wilbor.
      ii.   Ruth, b. 11 Jan. 1775; d. 12 April 1856; m. in LC 9 Feb.
                 1800 Henry Brownell, son of Gideon and Phebe
                 Brownell.
21. iii. Jediah, b. 3 April 1777.
      iv. Prudence, b. in April 1789; m. 6 June 1818 Philip Manchester,
                 son of Philip and Mary Manchester.
22. v.   David, b. 1 Nov. 1782.
      vi. Joseph, b. 6 March 1785.
      vii. Peleg, b. 12 May 1787.
      viii. Lydia, b. 25 July 1789; m. 17 April 1817 Abraham Manchester,
                 son of Philip and Mercy (Coggeshall) Manchester.

    15. GIDEON[5] SHAW (Israel[4], William[3], Israel[2], Anthony[1]), born in
LC 26 Feb. 1743, died there in November 1771. He married in Tiverton
MEREBAH GRAY, daughter of Thomas and Abigail (Brown) Gray of
Tiverton, and granddaughter of John and (--) Brown. She married
second in Bristol Stephen Monroe of Bristol.

      Children, all recorded in LC:
      i.   Borden, b. 9 June 1766.
      ii.   Ellery, b. 25 May 1768.
      iii. Lydia, b. 18 March 1771.

    16. WILLIAM[5] SHAW (Israel[4], William[3], Israel[2], Anthony[1]),
born in LC 1 July 1752. He married there 21 Jan. 1779 HANNAH WILBOR,
daughter of Charles and Hannah (Borden) Wilbor, born in LC 2 Dec. 1761.
This family apparently moved out of town.

      Children, recorded in LC:
      i.   Urius, b. 1 Oct. 1779.
      ii.   Andrew, b. 1 Aug. 1781.
      iii. Jedediah, b. 6 April 1783; m. Harriet Bower.
      iv. Israel, b. 8 Sept. 1785.
      v.   Charles, b. 27 July 1788.
      vi.   Isaac, b. 20 Oct. 1792.
      vii. Sally, b. 24 April 1794.
      viii. Hannah, b. 13 Jan. 1797.
      ix.   William, b. 19 Jan. 1799.
      x.   Matilda, b. 8 Sept. 1800.

    17. ISRAEL[5] SHAW (Israel[4], William[3], Israel[2], Anthony[1]), born
in LC 7 Feb. 1754. He married there 21 Dec. 1780 RUTH PALMER,
daughter of Moses and Susannah (Taylor) Palmer, born 14 Nov. 1758.
Residence: LC.

      Children, recorded in LC:
      i.   Moses, b. 18 Aug. 1781.

    18. NOAH[5] SHAW (Benjamin[4], Anthony[3], Israel[2], Anthony[1]), born
in LC 2 Feb. 1758, died there 8 Feb. 1844. He married first in LC

11 Feb. 1787 RHODA PALMER of Taunton, born 8 Sept. 1762.   He
married second ESTHER (--).

He lived on the old Shaw place where his son Benjamin was living
in 1850. This farm was also owned by his father, Benjamin Shaw,
and he was living there in 1774.

His will, recorded LC Wills, book 9, page 133, made 15 Aug.
1840 and proved 11 March 1844: ". . . To son Noah 100 dollars and
all my wearing apparel. To son John 100 dollars. To daughter
Elizabeth all household goods except what I otherwise give away.
To granddaughter Elizabeth Wilbor one bed, bedstead. . . To grandson Albert Shaw 25 dollars. To granddaughter Emeline Kirby 25
dollars. To son Benjamin the homestead farm given to me by my
father with dwelling house. To grandson David Shaw my lot of land
called the Davenport land. It is 30 acres bounded north by the road
that runs by my dwelling house, he to maintain daughter Elizabeth
during her life or as long as unmarried. . . "

> Children, recorded in LC:
23. i.   Benjamin, b. 18 Jan. 1788.
   ii.   Elizabeth, b. 16 Oct. 1789; d. young.
   iii. Sarah, b. 17 Dec. 1791; m. about 1800 David Shaw, son of
       Peter and Lydia Shaw.
   iv.   Hannah, b. 30 Oct. 1793; d. in LC 7 March 1839; m. in LC
       1 Jan. 1825 Thomas Wilbor.
   v.   Elizabeth 2d, b. 4 Feb. 1796.
   vi.   Rhoda, b. 14 May 1799; d. young.
   vii. Anna.
   viii. Noah, b. 25 March 1804.
   ix.   John, b. 25 March 1804; d. 26 March 1804.

> Children by second wife:
   x.   John, b. 21 July 1805.

19. BENJAMIN[5] SHAW (Benjamin[4], Anthony[3], Israel[2], Anthony[1]),
born 24 July 1763, died in Falmouth, Nova Scotia, 28 Sept. 1810. He
married LUCY AKIN, daughter of Stephen and Elizabeth (King) Akin,
died 1 Dec. 1852 in Falmouth, Nova Scotia.

> Children:
   i.   Benjamin, b. 2 May 1802 in Falmouth; d. in Hantsport,
       Nova Scotia, 8 April 1870; m. (1) 13 Nov. 1825 Rebecca
       Trefrey, daughter of Benjamin Trefrey, b. 15 Nov.
       1805, d. 26 Aug. 1847; m. (2) Olivia (Kelly) Bradshaw.
   ii.   Abigail, m. David Smith of Mount Denson, N.S.

20. TIMOTHY[5] SHAW (Seth[4], Israel[3], Israel[2], Anthony[1]), born in
1782. He was married in LC 4 March 1804 by the Rev. Mase Shepard
to CLARISSA ALLEN, daughter of William and Lucy Allen, born in
1784.   Residence: LC.

> Children, recorded in LC:
   i.   Seth, b. 18 May 1805.
   ii.   Mary Taylor, b. 12 March 1807.
   iii. Allen, b. 24 June 1809.

iv.   Maj. Willis, b. 16 Sept. 1811.
v.   William Pitt, b. 15 Feb. 1814.
vi.   Bradford Cornhill, b. 15 July 1817.
vii. Abigail Palmer, b. 4 July 1822.
viii. Ann Elizabeth, b. 28 March 1826.

21. ZEBEDEE[5] SHAW (Mary[4], Peter[3], Israel[2], Anthony[1]), born in
LC 25 July 1759, died 23 Dec. 1826. He is buried next to his mother.
He was married in LC 20 May 1801 by the Rev. Mase Shepard to ABIGAIL
WILBOR, daughter of John and Eleanor (Tripp) Wilbor, born in LC 27
May 1766, died there 24 July 1852. Both are buried in the Old Commons
cemetery.

   Children, recorded in LC:
  i. Mary, b. 19 July 1807; d. 2 Aug. 1882; m. in November 1837
    Otis Wilbor, son of Joseph and Hannah (Brown) Wilbor,
    b. 12 Jan. 1803, d. in LC 15 Jan. 1859. He was LC town
    clerk for many years and took much interest in the genealogy
    and history of the town.

22. JEDIAH[5] SHAW (Peter[4], Peter[3], Israel[2], Anthony[1]), born in LC
3 April 1777, died there 19 July 1852. He was married there 7 Feb. 1813
by the Rev. Benjamin Peckham to RHODA (MANCHESTER) SLOCUM,
widow, daughter of Philip and Mary (Coggeshall) Manchester, born 24
May 1786, died in LC 21 Nov. 1842. Both are buried in the Shaw cemetery
in district no. 10, on the west side of the road leading to the ocean.
  Residence: LC. They lived on the place owned by Peter Shaw Jr.,
down near the water across the road from the cemetery.

   Children, recorded in LC:
24. i. Jediah, b. 24 Nov. 1813.
  ii. Maria, b. 17 Nov. 1815; d. 1 June 1901 in LC; m. there 26 Feb.
    1836 John Seabury, b. 8 Dec. 1805; d. 3 July 1865.
  iii. Peter Greene, b. 6 Jan. 1818; d. 4 Jan. 1894.
  iv. Mary Ann, b. 29 July 1819.
  v. Harriet Slocum, b. 24 Dec. 1821; d. 3 June 1902; m. in LC
    28 Feb. 1843 Ephraim B. Sisson.
  vi. Mary Ann, b. 7 June 1827.
  vii. Peleg, b. 19 Sept. 1829; d. 17 June 1881; unmarried.

22. DAVID[5] SHAW (Peter[4], Peter[3], Israel[2], Anthony[1]), born in
LC 1 Nov. 1782, died there in February 1819. He married about 1800
SARAH SHAW, daughter of Noah and Rhoda (Palmer) Shaw, born in
LC 17 Dec. 1791.

   Children, all recorded in LC:
  i. Albert, b. 29 Aug. 1812.
  ii. Emiline, b. 20 Feb. 1814.
  iii. Sarah, b. 14 July 1816.
25. iv. David, b. 3 July 1818.

23. BENJAMIN[6] SHAW (Noah[5], Benjamin[4], Anthony[3], Israel[2],
Anthony[1]), born in LC 18 Jan. 1788, died there 17 Jan. 1864.

He married in LC 28 Sept. 1823 MARY ANN DAVENPORT,
daughter of Jeremiah and Anna (Burroughs) Davenport of Tiverton,
born in Tiverton 6 Sept. 1800, died in LC 26 June 1882. Both are
buried in the New Stone Church cemetery.

They lived on the place owned by his grandfather, Benjamin
Shaw, on the south of Shaw Road.

His will, recorded LC Wills, book 11, page 352: ". . . To wife
Mary all household furniture and use and improvement of dwelling
house, bounded east by land conveyed to me by my son Augustus,
south by the barnyard, west by garden wall and north by the highway.
One room in house for daughter Esther Davenport. My son James
shall keep a good cow for his mother. Son Augustus, I give him nothing,
he already having had his share. . . "

> Children, recorded in LC:
>
> i.   Rhoda Ann, b. 8 Nov. 1824; d. in LC 19 Feb. 1911; m. there
> 12 Aug. 1845 George Taylor Brownell, son of Christopher
> and Sarah (Taylor) Brownell.
>
> ii.   Sarah, b. 19 Nov. 1826; m. 3 Dec. 1845 Charles (?) Smith.
>
> iii.   Esther Burroughs, b. 20 Nov. 1828; m. 11 July 1852 Charles
> (?) Davenport; m. (2) Nathaniel Boomer.
>
> iv.   Benjamin Augustus, b. 20 Sept. 1830; m. in Providence in
> February 1858 Amanda M. (--).
>
> v.   Mary Adams, b. 12 Jan. 1833; m. in LC 19 Jan. 1854 George
> Sistare, son of Burr and Abby Sistare.
>
> 26. vi.   James H., b. 26 March 1835.
>
> vii.   George Wallace, b. 6 Nov. 1840; d. in Fall River 4 March 1915;
> m. in 1865 Charlotte E. Windsor, or Mabel F. Harlow.

24. JEDIAH[6] SHAW (Jediah[5], Peter[4], Peter[3], Israel[2], Anthony[1]),
born in LC 24 Nov. 1813, died there 31 Oct. 1885.

He married in LC 1 April 1837 FALLEE P. GRAY, daughter of
Nathaniel and Lydia (Coe) Gray, born in LC 24 Feb. 1818, died there
26 April 1854. Both are buried in the Old Commons cemetery.

He was a school teacher in LC for 50 years. They lived on his
father's place.

> Children, first three recorded in LC:
>
> i.   Horace Gray, b. 18 June 1840. He was a prominent druggist
> in New York City.
>
> ii.   Rhoda Harriet, b. 25 Nov. 1842; d. 4 Aug. 1848 ae 5.
>
> iii.   Lydia Coe, b. 6 March 1846; d. 4 Aug. 1848 ae 2.
>
> iv.   Annie Wood, b. 27 Jan. 1854; d. in Adamsville 19 Nov. 1905;
> m. in LC 13 Nov. 1881 Frank Brownell, son of Albert and
> Amey Brownell.

25. DAVID[6] SHAW (David[5], Peter[4], Peter[3], Israel[2], Anthony[1]),
born in LC 3 July 1818, died there 9 April 1861 ae 42.

He married MARY B. TAYLOR, daughter of John and Elizabeth
(Bailey) Taylor, born in LC 24 Feb. 1819, died there 17 Feb. 1899,
ae almost 80 years. Both are buried in the Old Commons cemetery.
She married second in LC 8 Jan. 1863 Orrin W. Simmons, son of Abel
and Lydia (Pierce) Simmons.

Children:
i.   Abby Maria, b. in 1849; d. in New Bedford 12 Oct. 1929; m.
in LC 19 Oct. 1869 William Henry Bailey, son of Isaac
and Phebe (Pendleton) Bailey.

26. JAMES HERVEY[7] SHAW (Benjamin[6], Noah[5], Benjamin[4],
Anthony[3], Israel[2], Anthony[1]), born in LC 26 March 1835, died in Fall
River in September 1909. He married in June 1857 HARRIET ELONA
CLARK of Fall River. Residence: LC.

Children, born in Fall River:
27. i.   Frederick Merrick, b. 23 Dec. 1862.

27. FREDERICK MERRICK[8] SHAW (James[7], Benjamin[6], Noah[5],
Benjamin[4], Anthony[3], Israel[2], Anthony[1]), born in Fall River 23 Dec.
1862, died there 29 Dec. 1903. He married there 12 June 1884
FLORENCE MAY PIERCE, daughter of George D. W. and Julia
Augusta (Kingsley) Pierce, born 18 May 1863, died in Dartmouth
22 Jan. 1932.
He built Shaw's Wharf in LC at Seaconnet, which was used by him
for his boat to Fall River in connection with his ice cream business
there. He took milk and cream to Fall River and brought back grain,
which he sold to the farmers of LC.

Children:
i.   Julia Elona, b. in LC 13 May 1889; m. 30 June 1915 the Rev.
Alwyn J. Atkins.
28. ii.   Inez Winnifred, b. in Fall River 3 June 1895.
iii.   Bernard Clark, b. in Fall River 4 Aug. 1899; m. 27 June
1925 Phyllis Klingee.

28. INEZ WINNIFRED[9] SHAW (Frederick[8], James[7], Benjamin[6],
Noah[5], Benjamin[4], Anthony[3], Israel[2], Anthony[1]), born in Fall River
3 June 1895. She married in Fall River 15 Dec. 1915 THEODORE B.
WILDES.

Children (Wildes), first four born in New Bedford and the
others in Dartmouth:
29. i.   Horace Bradstreet, b. 18 May 1918.
30. ii.   Merrick Kingsley, b. 9 Dec. 1919.
31. iii.   Winnifred Hilger, b. 5 Jan. 1922.
32. iv.   Mildred, b. 11 June 1923.
v.   Frances Elizabeth, b. 9 Jan. 1926; m. in LC 26 June 1948
Paul Wilber, son of Bernard and Janet (Goodwin) Wilber,
b. in Fall River 19 July 1925.
vi.   Glen Knyvett, b. 25 May 1932.
vii.   Richard Winslow, b. 3 Nov. 1936.

29. HORACE B.[10] WILDES (Inez[9] Shaw, Frederick[8], James[7],
Benjamin[6], Noah[5], Benjamin[4], Anthony[3], Israel[2], Anthony[1]), born in
New Bedford 18 May 1918. He married in Dartmouth in July 1942
ELIZABETH SMITH.

Children (Wildes):
i.   Frederic, b. 26 Aug. 1943.
ii.   Peter Warren, b. 27 Feb. 1945.
iii.   Stephen Drury, b. 21 July 1947.

30. MERRICK KINGSLEY[10] WILDES (Inez[9] Shaw, Frederick[8], James[7], Benjamin[6], Noah[5], Benjamin[4], Anthony[3], Israel[2], Anthony[1]), born in New Bedford 9 Dec. 1919. He married 17 April 1943 HILDA MARGUERITE PERRY.

Children (Wildes):
i.   Meredith Kay, b. 2 Nov. 1943.
ii.   Emerson Perry, b. 12 May 1945.
iii.   Everett Kingsley, b. 11 Dec. 1947.

31. WINNIFRED [10] WILDES (Inez[9] Shaw, Frederick[8], James[7], Benjamin[6], Noah[5], Benjamin[4], Anthony[3], Israel[2], Anthony[1]), born 5 Jan. 1922. She married in LC 1 June 1946 LEON ALLAN MUNGER.

Children (Munger):
i.   William Shaw, b. 23 Feb. 1948.

32. MILDRED[10] WILDES (Inez[9] Shaw, Frederick[8], James[7], Benjamin[6], Noah[5], Benjamin[4], Anthony[3], Israel[2], Anthony[1]), born 11 June 1923. She married in LC 1 June 1946 ALFRED JOSEPH LIVECCHI.

Children (Livecchi):
i.   Alfred Joseph Jr., b. 25 Feb. 1948.

. . . .

JOSIAH CROCKER SHAW, son of William Shaw, married in LC in September 1798 LYDIA BROWN, daughter of William Brown.
He is probably the one who, on 4 July 1798, delivered an oration on request of the people of the town. See the bulletin printed in Newport (MDCCXCVIII).

Children, recorded in LC:
i.   John, b. 29 Nov. 1799.
ii.   Philander, b. 6 Aug. 1801.

WILLIAM SHAW, born in England in 1792. He married MARY A. (--), born in Rhode Island in 1795. Residence: LC.

Children:
i.   William, b. in 1834.
ii.   James E. M., b in 1836.
iii.   Clarissa, b. in 1838.
iv.   Clarke, b. in 1840.

GEORGE M. SHAW, born in Scotland, married ANNA D. (--).
Living with George Shaw was Agnes McLean, daughter of William

and Margaret (MacDonald) McLean, born in Kilath, Scotland, 14 Feb. 1830, died in Providence 16 May 1921.

Little Compton Death Records also show a Margaret Shaw, widow, daughter of John and Janet MacDowell, born in Scotland, died a widow in LC 11 Nov. 1884. She was, perhaps, mother of the above George M. Shaw.

Residence: LC.

Child, recorded in LC:
i.   Robert Forrester, b. in LC 19 Jan. 1888.

THE SHEEHAN FAMILY

EDMUND FRANCIS SHEEHAN, son of Edward and Harriet (Johnston) Sheehan, born 5 March 1906. He married in LC 23 Feb. 1947 FRANCES FALLY CASE, daughter of George H. and Emma (Davis) Case, born in LC 3 March 1925. Residence: LC.

Children, recorded in LC:
i.   Karen, b. in Fall River 17 Dec. 1947.
ii.   Anette, b. in Fall River 26 Dec. 1948.

THE SHEPARD FAMILY

1. REV. THOMAS[1] SHEPARD, son of Ralph Shepard of Colney Engaine, Essex County, England, born in 1632, died in Milton, Mass., 29 Sept. 1719 ae 86.

He married first in Malden, Mass., 19 Nov. 1658 HANNAH ENSIGN of Scituate, Mass., daughter of Thomas and Elizabeth (Wilder) Ensign, born in 1639, died in Malden, Mass., 14 March 1698. He married second JOANNA (--), died in Milton 1709.

Residence: Malden and Milton, Mass. He also lived in Charlestown, Mass., for one year. He was called Thomas Shepard of Malden to distinguish between two Thomas Shepards, both of whom had the title of Reverend. See Ralph Shepard, Puritan (1893) by Ralph Hamilton Shepard.

Children:
i.   Thomas, b. about 1660/62; d. 18 April 1726; m. 7 Dec. 1682
      (or 11 Sept. 1681) in Charlestown, Mass., Hannah
      Blanchard, daughter of George Blanchard.
ii.   Ralph, b. in Malden in January 1666/7; d. 26 Jan. 1722; m.
      Mary (--).
iii. John, b. about 1668/69; d. 9 March 1691; m. 26 March (or
      May) 1690 Persis Pierce.
2. iv. Jacob, b. about 1675/77.
   v.   Hannah, m. 13 April 1681 Joseph Blanchard.
   vi. Isaac, b. in May 1682; bapt. 23 July 1682; d. 4 June 1724;
        m. 31 Dec. 1702 Elizabeth Fuller.

2. JACOB[2] SHEPARD (Thomas[1]), born about 1675/77, died in December 1717. He married in Medford, Mass., 22 Nov. 1699 MERCY CHICKERING, daughter of Dr. John and Elizabeth (Hagburne) Chickering of Charlestown, Mass., born 13 March 1668, died about 1717.

Residence: Medford and Foxboro, Mass. He moved from his father's home and purchased a farm between Dedham and Seekonk, Mass., then known as Wading River farm and later called Shepard's farm.

Children:
i.   Jacob, b. 22 Aug. 1700; d. about 1718.
ii. John, b. 25 Feb. 1704; d. 5 April 1809 ae 105; m. (1) 24 Aug.
     1726 Eleon Pond; m. (2) 8 Aug. 1728 Abigail Richardson;
     m. (3) 22 June 1731 Martha Bacon.
3. iii. Thomas, b. 24 March 1706.
iv. Joseph, b. 9 Feb. 1708; d. 28 Aug. 1773; m. (1) Mary (--);
     m. (2) 14 Aug. 1754 Keziah Mann.
v.   Benjamin, b. 24 Dec. 1710; d. 20 May 1777; m. 14 Dec. 1737
     Hepzibah Blake.

3. THOMAS[3] SHEPARD (Jacob[2], Thomas[1]), born in Foxboro, Mass., 24 March 1706, died in Norton, Mass., 19 Oct. 1774. He married 5 June 1735 CONTENT WHITE, daughter of Cornelius and Mehitable (Walker) White of Taunton, born in 1715, died 7 April 1790. Residence: Norton.

Children, born and recorded in Norton:
. i.   Sarah, b. 5 May 1736; m. 25 Jan. 1757 John Bassett.
ii.   Jacob, b. 7 Dec. 1737; d. 3 Nov. 1737.
iii.   Phebe, b. 4 April 1739 (?); d. 15 Sept. 1775.
iv.   Jacob, b. 30 Nov. 1741; d. 18 Sept. 1816; m. 11 Jan. 1781
        Lydia (Wild) Clapp, d. 11 Jan. 1822.
v.   Thomas, b. 29 Nov. 1743; d. 29 Dec. 1743.
vi.   Jemima, b. 22 Dec. 1744; d. 27 Nov. 1793; unmarried.
vii.   Rachel, b. 18 Jan. 1746.
viii.   Thomas, b. January/February 1748; d. in February 1748.
ix.   Seth, b. 21 Jan. 1750; d. 5 Nov. 1812; m. 28 May 1776 Rachel
        Dunham.
x.   Olive, b. 10 March 1752; d. 7 April 1752.
xi.   Olive, b. 3 June 1754; m. 6 April 1776 Noah Clapp.
xii.   George, b. 2 Jan. 1757; m. 6 Sept. 1781 Eunice Makepiece.
4. xiii. Mase, b. 28 May 1759.

4. REV. MASE[4] SHEPARD (Thomas[3], Jacob[2], Thomas[1]), born in Norton, Mass., 28 May 1759, died of lung fever in LC 14 Feb. 1821. He married 6 July 1788 DEBORAH HASKINS, daughter of John and Hannah (Upham) Haskins of Boston, born in Boston 5 Nov. 1765, died 11 Feb. 1841. Residence: LC.

He graduated from Dartmouth College in 1785 and was ordained in the Congregational Church, coming to LC as pastor 19 Sept. 1787. In one year he received 125 persons into his church.

His wife had a sister, Mary, born 22 Dec. 1766, who married William Ladd, son of William and Sarah (Gardner) Ladd of LC. Another sister, Ruth, married the Rev. William Emerson and they became the parents of Ralph Waldo Emerson, the writer. John Haskins, her brother, married 5 June 1791 Elizabeth Ladd, daughter of William and Sarah Ladd of LC.

Children, born and recorded in LC:
i.   John Haskins, b. 3 Sept. 1789; d. 16 Sept. 1807.
ii.   Thomas, b. 26 Jan. 1793.
iii. Hannah, b. 2 June 1795.
iv.   Mary, b. 2 May 1797.
v.   Ralph, b. 24 May 1799.
vi.   George Champlin, b. 7 Feb. 1802; d. in April 1869 in Amherst, Mass.; m. 24 May 1827 Sally Inman.
vii. Charles Upham, b. 29 June 1804.
viii. Fanny Haskins, b. 23 March 1807.
ix.   Ann Elizabeth, b. 24 June 1810; m. Hon. Edward Southworth.

5. CHARLES UPHAM[5] SHEPARD (Mase[4], Thomas[3], Jacob[2], Thomas[1]), born in LC 29 June 1804, died in Charlestown, S. C., 1 May 1886. He graduated from Amherst College in 1824 and spent a year at Cambridge, Mass., studying botany and mineralogy with Thomas Nuttall and at the same time gave instructions in Boston in these subjects. In 1827 he was invited to become Professor Silliman's assistant and continued there until about 1830, when he was appointed lecturer on natural history at Yale.

From 1834 until 1861 he filled the chair of chemistry in the medical college of South Carolina which he relinquished at the beginning of the Civil War. In 1865 he resumed those duties for a few years, after which he became professor of chemistry at Amherst. He continued to deliver lectures there until 1877 when he was made professor emeritus.

He acquired a large collection of meteorites and his cabinet, long the largest in the country, became the property of Amherst. It is now in the United States National Museum at Washington, D. C. He acquired a large collection of minerals which at one time was unsurpassed in this country and which in 1877 was purchased by Amherst College; three years later it was partially destroyed by fire. In addition to many other papers, he published a treatise on mineralogy in New Haven in 1855.

THE SHETHAR FAMILY

PRENTICE SHETHAR . He married first (?). He married second in Paris, France, 4 July 1924 SUSAN CHURCH BURCHARD, daughter of Roswell and Edith Russel (Church) Burchard, born 25 March 1903. She married second (?).

Children by first wife:
i.   Prentice Jr.

Children by second wife, recorded in LC:
ii.   Norman, b. in Fall River 30 July 1925.

THE SHERER FAMILY

JOSEPH FORREST SHERER, born in Newtonville, Mass., 5 March 1879. He married MARION OSBORN, daughter of James Edward and Delia (Carr) Osborn, born 21 July 1881. Residence: Worcester, Mass., and LC.

Children:
i. Osborn, m. Josephine W. Cassidy. They had Marion Osborn Sherer, b. in Fall River 29 Oct. 1941.
ii. Edith Osborn, b. in Worcester 7 March 1926; m. in LC 6 Aug. 1949 Thomas McClintock Whitin, son of Richard and Ina (Watson) Whitin, b. in Worcester 12 Jan. 1923.
iii. Jeanette.
iv. Charles T., m. Helen R. (--).
v. Joseph F. Jr., m. Mary M. (--).
vi. (?).

THE SHRIEVE FAMILY

From the Shreive Book of 1901 by Luther P. Allen.

1. THOMAS[1] SHERIFF (SHREIVE), born before 1649, died in 1675. Residence: Plymouth and Portsmouth. He married MARTHA (--), died after 1691. She married second Thomas Hazard, and married third Lewis Hewes.

His inventory, made 11 June 1675: House and land 15 pounds, horse and mare 7 pounds, two cows, three calves, five ewes, five lambs, eight shoats, a feather bed, six pillows, two bolsters, six blankets, ring, flock bed, fifty-six pounds of pewter, warming pan, silver dram cup, looking glass, etc. Total 218 pounds and 12 shillings.

Children:
i.   Thomas, b. 2 Sept. 1649.
ii.   John, d. 14 Oct. 1739; m. in Portsmouth in August 1686 Jane Havens, daughter of John and Ann Havens.
iii. Caleb, b. about 1652; m. about 1680 Sarah Areson of Long Island.
iv.   Mary, m. 12 Feb. 1685 Joseph Sheffield, son of Ichabod and Mary (Parker) Sheffield, b. 22 Aug. 1661, died in 1706.
v.   Susannah, d. after 1719; m. (--) Thomas.
2. vi. Daniel.
vii. Elizabeth, d. 5 June 1719; m. Edward Carter.
viii. Sarah, d. 24 June 1732; m. John Moon.

2. DANIEL[2] SHRIFF (SHREIVE) (Thomas[1]), died in 1737, married about 1688 JANE (--). Residence: LC.
His will, made 8 June 1737 and proved 20 Dec. 1737, recorded

Taunton Probate, book 8: "Daniel Shriff of LC, husbandman, being
very aged. . . To wife Jane Shriff one third part of all estate both real
and personal. Executor son Daniel Shriff. . . " He also left 10 shillings
each to his three sons, two daughters and a grandson.

        Children, recorded in LC:
- i.   Martha, b. 2 Jan. 1690; m. in LC 30 May 1709 Dennis
  Linnekinor Lincoln of LC.
- ii.   Sutton, b. 3 Dec. 1692.
- iii. John, b. 15 Dec. 1694.
- 3. iv. Daniel, b. 15 Oct. 1696.
- v.   Elizabeth, b. 20 May 1698; m. 21 Jan. 1717 in LC Charles
  Dyer.
- vi.   Thomas, b. 20 Sept. 1699.
- 4. vii. William, b. 26 March 1701.
- 5. viii. Caleb, b. 3 March 1707.
- 6. ix. Benjamin, b. in 1709.

3. DANIEL[3] SHREIF (SHREIVE) (Daniel[2], Thomas[1]), born in LC
15 Oct. 1696, died there 10 July 1741. He married there 21 Aug. 1716
MARY SALISBURY, daughter of Joseph and Mary (Paddock?) Salisbury,
born in LC 5 Aug. 1699. Residence: LC.

In his will, recorded book 10 Taunton Probate, page 52, he left to
his son John Shreif all lands, housing, messuages. . . and to his son
Abial 10 shillings. His will was made 2 May 1741 and proved 21 July
1741.

        Children:
- 7. i. John, b. in LC 22 Sept. 1720.
- ii.   Abial.

4. WILLIAM[3] SHREIVE (Daniel[2], Thomas[1]), born in LC 26 March
1701, died there about 1750. He married FREELOVE DYER, born 21
June 1699. Residence: LC.

        Children:
- i.   William, b. 6 Oct. 1720.
- ii. Susannah, b. 28 Sept. 1722.

5. CALEB[3] SHREIVE (Daniel[2], Thomas[1]), born in LC 3 March 1707.
He was married there 24 Aug. 1729 by Richard Billings, justice, to
MERCY MOSHER of Tiverton, daughter of Nicholas and Elizabeth
Mosher of Dartmouth. Residence: LC.

        Children:
- i.   Mary, b. about 1730.
- ii. Hannah, b. about 1732.

6. BENJAMIN[3] SHREIVE (Daniel[2], Thomas[1]), born in LC in 1709.
He was married 13 Jan. 1732 by Richard Brownell, justice, to BRIDGET
BROWNELL, daughter of Thomas and Grace Brownell, born in LC 5
Dec. 1713. Residence: LC.

        Children, born and recorded in LC:
- i.   Benjamin, b. 26 June 1733.

7. JOHN[4] SHREIVE (Daniel[3], Daniel[2], Thomas[1]), born in LC 22 Sept. 1720. He was married there 30 Sept. 1741 by Richard Billings, justice, to AMEY HEAD, daughter of Henry and Elizabeth (Palmer) Head, born in LC 15 May 1727. Residence: LC.

Children, recorded in LC:
i. Daniel, b. 8 June 1742.
ii. Abigail, b. 11 March 1743/4.
iii. Nathaniel, b. 7 March 1744.
iv. Mary, b. 8 Jan. 1748.
v. Elizabeth, b. 11 Nov. 1749.
vi. Ruth, b. 15 June 1751.

. . . .

DANIEL SHRIEVE, married ELIPHAL (--). Residence: LC.

Children:
i. Amey, b. 1 Nov. 1775.

THE SHERMAN FAMILY

FREDERICK LINCOLN SHERMAN, son of Walter A. and Phebe Ann (Lawton) Sherman, born 12 March 1866, died in LC in 1957. He married EMMA JOSEPHINE WILBOR, daughter of Joseph G. and Francelia (Burgess) Wilbor, born in LC 6 April 1865, died 21 March 1935. Residence: LC.

Children, born in LC, but not recorded there:
i. Louise Francelia, b. 26 May 1888, d. in Fall River 2 May 1934.
ii. Lillian Lincoln, b. 16 Jan. 1891.

THE SHURTLEFF FAMILY

From The Descendants of William Shurtleff of Plymouth and Marshfield (1912) by Benjamin Shurtleff, and other records.

1. WILLIAM SHURTLEFF, born in England 16 May 1624, died in Marshfield, Mass., 23 June 1666. He married in Plymouth 18 Oct. 1655 ELIZABETH LETTICE, daughter of Thomas and Ann Lettice, born in England in 1636, died in Swansea 31 Oct. 1693. Residence: probably in the parish of Ecclesfield, Yorkshire, England, and Plymouth and Marshfield, Mass.

2. WILLIAM SHURTLEFF, born in Plymouth in 1657, died there

4 Feb. 1729/30. He married in October 1683 in Barnstable, Mass.,
SUSANNA LATHROP, daughter of Barnabus and Susanna (Clark)
Lathrop, born 28 Feb. 1663/4, died in Plympton, Mass., 9 Aug. 1726.
Residence: Plymouth.

3. BARNABUS SHURTLEFF, born in Plymouth 17 March 1695/6,
died there 18 May 1759. He married there 16 March 1726/7 JEMIMA
ADAMS, daughter of Francis and Mary (Buck) Adams, born in Kinston,
Mass., 12 Jan. 1706/7, died in Plymouth 26 Nov. 1773. Residence:
Plympton.

4. BARNABUS SHURTLEFF, born in Carver, Mass., 3 June 1750,
died there 23 March 1832. He married in Plympton, Mass., 18 May
1775 PHEBE HARLOW, born in Plymouth 23 Oct. 1757, died in Carver
27 Oct. 1836.

5. STEPHEN SHURTLEFF, born in Carver, Mass., 4 July 1783,
died there 29 Jan. 1841. He married there 23 Aug. 1807 LYDIA ATWOOD,
daughter of Caleb and Sarah (Shaw) Atwood, born in Plympton 20 April
1785, died in Middleboro, Mass., 8 Jan. 1841. Residence: Carver.

6. STEPHEN[6] SHURTLEFF (Stephen[5], Barnabus[4], Barnabus[3],
William[2], William[1]), born in Carver, Mass., 2 Jan. 1814, died in
Gardner, Johnson County, Kansas, 26 Aug. 1858. He married in
Jackson, Ind., 20 April 1852 LYDIA FINLEY BROOKS, born in
Richfield, Ohio, 4 April 1834. Residence: Weyauwega, Waupaca
County, Wis.

    Children, born at Weyauwega, Wis.:
i.   Evangeline Diadama, b. 24 July 1854; m. in LC 14 March
        1875 Frederic Oberlin Clark, son of Presbury and Phebe
        Harlow (Schurtleff) Clark of Carver, Mass.
7. ii.   Eugene Kossuth, b. 3 May 1856.

7. EUGENE KOSSUTH[7] SHURTLEFF (Stephen[6], Stephen[5], Barnabus[4],
Barnabus[3], William[2], William[1]), born in Weyauwega, Wis., 3 May 1856,
died in Adamsville 30 Dec. 1942. He married in LC 31 Dec. 1885 HATTIE
ELMA COOK, daughter of Isaac and Lydia (Cook) Cook of Tiverton, born
in Dartmouth, Mass., 19 Oct. 1859, died in LC 2 Feb. 1943. Residence:
Adamsville, LC.

    Children, born in Adamsville:
i.   Stephen Brooks, b. 22 June 1887; m. Lena Petty.
ii.   Leola Esther, b. 27 May 1889; d. 19 Feb. 1922; m. James
        O'Connor. They had a son, Vincent.
iii.   Roy Eugene, b. 3 July 1890; d. 3 June 1915.
iv.   Maud Alma, b. 8 Sept. 1891; d. in Adamsville 19 May 1895.
8. v.   Harry Vernon, b. 20 Oct. 1893.
9. vi.   Malcolm Chesney, b. 14 March 1895.
10. vii.   Bertrand Leslie, b. 3 Aug. 1897.
viii.   Julian Dorrance, b. 12 Oct. 1899.
ix.   Venetta Gwendoline, b. in LC 17 Sept. 1902; m. there 19
        April 1930 Clarence Royce Ellwell, son of John and

Amey (Royce) Ellwell, b. in LC 23 Oct. 1892.

8. HARRY VERNON[8] SHURTLEFF (Eugene[7], Stephen[6], Stephen[5], Barnabus[4], Barnabus[3], William[2], William[1]), born 20 Oct. 1893. Married ELEANOR TRIPP.

Children:
i.   Hazel, b. in 1913; m. Howard E. Borden.
ii. Grover.

9. MALCOLM CHESNEY[8] SHURTLEFF (Eugene[7], Stephen[6], Stephen[5], Barnabus[4], Barnabus[3], William[2], William[1]), born in LC 14 March 1895. He married there 6 Sept. 1921 FLORENCE LUELLA JEWELL, daughter of John and Henrietta (Brownell) Jewell, born in Central Falls, R. I., 6 Sept. 1895. Residence: LC.

Children:
i.   Malcolm Chesney Jr., b. in Fall River 24 June 1922.
ii. John Richard, b. 16 April 1924.
iii. Helen Elizabeth, b. 28 Feb. 1926.
iv. Donald Eugene, b. in Fall River 20 Feb. 1932.

10. BERTRAND LESLIE[8] SHURTLEFF (Eugene[7], Stephen[6], Stephen[5], Barnabus[4], Barnabus[3], William[2], William[1]), born in LC 3 Aug. 1897. He married first there 3 Aug. 1922 HOPE SEAL, daughter of Albert E. and Florence (Briggs) Seal, born in Providence 21 Sept. 1902. He married second (?).

Children by first wife:
i.   David B., b. in Fall River 1 July 1930.
ii. Jeane, b. in LC 8 July 1923.
iii. Faith, b. in 1928.

. . . .

RICHARD E. SHURTLEFF, married ISABEL CORNELL. Residence: LC.

Children:
i.   Richard E., Jr., b. in Fall River 8 July 1940.
ii. Jeffrey R., b. in Fall River 11 Nov. 1944.

THE SIMMONS FAMILY

1. MOSES SIMMONS, may have been the son of William Simmons who lived in Leyden, Holland, near the church which the Pilgrims attended. The name may have been Symonson. He came to Plymouth in the Fortune from Leyden in 1621, landing on the 9th of November.
He married about 1632, probably in Duxbury, SARAH (--), perhaps SARAH CHANDLER, daughter of Roger Chandler.

In his will he stated that he was "in full decay, but of my right mind" and left to his daughter Mary, wife of Joseph Alden, four pounds; to son Aaron four pounds; to daughter Elizabeth, wife of Richard Dwelly, five shillings; to daughter Sarah, wife of James Nash, two pounds; and to his son John, four pounds. His will was made 17 June 1689 and proved 15 Sept. 1691.

Children:
- i.   Moses, m. Patience Bastow about 1662.
- ii.   Rebecca, m. John Soule, son of George Soule.
- iii. Mary, m. Joseph Alden, possibly the son of John Alden.
- iv.   Elizabeth, m. Richard Dwelly.
- v.   Aaron, m. Mary Woodworth in 1677.
- vi.   Sarah, m. James Nash of Duxbury.
- 2. vii. John.

2. JOHN² SIMMONS (Moses¹), died in 1715. He married in Duxbury 16 Nov. 1649 MERCY PABODIE, daughter of William and Elizabeth (Alden) Pabodie, born in Plymouth. Residence: Duxbury.

His estate was settled in Duxbury and divided among his widow and children by mutual agreement. His wife Mercy made her will 26 Sept. 1728, "being sick and weak and not knowing the day of my death." As proved 8 Nov. 1728: ". . . To son John 5 shillings silver money and all my sheep. To sons William, Isaac, Benjamin, Joseph and Joshua 5 shillings each. To daughter Martha 5 shillings and my riding gown and petticoat and hood, a scarf and red silk neck cloth. To daughter Rebecca 5 shillings and my best riding hood. To son Moses a bed and bedding and my cow. To sons John and Moses to be executors. . . "

Children, all born in Duxbury:
- i.   John, b. 22 Feb. 1670; d. before 1739; probably m. (1) Abigail Richmond, daughter of Edward and Sarah Richmond, d. in LC 4 Oct. 1702; m. (2) 5 Nov. 1714 Susannah Tracy.
- 3. ii.   William, b. 24 Sept. 1672.
- iii. Isaac, b. 28 Jan. 1674; m. Martha Chandler, daughter of Benjamin and Elizabeth Chandler.
- iv.   Martha, b. 17 Nov. 1677 in Duxbury; m. (1) Ebenezer Delanoe 29 Dec. 1697; m. (2) Samuel West 20 June 1709.
- v.   Benjamin, b. about 1678; d. in 1749; m. (1) Laura Sampson, daughter of Caleb Sampson, 2 Jan. 1705; m. (2) Priscilla Delano 7 July 1715.
- vi.   Moses, b. in February 1680; d. 21 June 1761; m. 26 March 1718 Rachel Sampson.
- vii. Joseph, b. in 1683; d. 30 May 1761; m. 8 Feb. 1709 Mary Weston.
- viii. Rebecca, b. in 1685; m. 10 Feb. 1714/15 Constant Southworth.
- ix.   Joshua, b. in 1688; d. 15 Jan. 1774; m. 4 April 1728 Sarah Delano.

3. WILLIAM³ SIMMONS (John², Moses¹), born in Duxbury 24 Sept. 1672, died in LC in 1765.

He married in LC about 1696 ABIGAIL CHURCH, daughter of Joseph

and Mary (Tucker) Church, born about 1680, died in LC 4 July 1720.
Residence: LC. They lived on Simmons Hill, where he built a long house
in 1724.

His will, recorded book 2, page 59, made 8 March 1750 and proved
31 Aug. 1765: ". . . To son William Simmons, executor of this will, my
now dwelling house, westerly end of my orchard and blacksmith shop.
To son Joseph Simmons the east end of homestead farm from stone wall
to eastward of son John's house down to Long Highway. I confirm deed
of gift to son Joseph Simmons. To Simeon Simmons, son of my brother
Ichabod Simmons. . . To son John east end of my orchard he now improves
with remainder of homestead farm. To son Benjamin and Peleg. . . To
daughters Mary Bennett, Lydia Tillinghast, Abigail Palmer, Rebecca
Bagger and Mary Simmons five shillings each. . . "

       Children, all recorded in LC:

	i.	Mercy, b. 1 July 1697; d. in November 1768; m. 13 Sept. 1725 James Bennett of Roxbury, Mass.
4.	ii.	William, b. 30 Sept. 1699.
	iii.	Lydia, b. 15 Dec. 1700; m. 4 April 1723 Joseph Tillinghast of Newport.
5.	iv.	Joseph, b. 4 March 1702.
6.	v.	John, b. 14 Aug. 1704.
	vi.	Abigail, b. 14 July 1706; m. 8 Dec. 1736 Job Palmer of Norwich, Conn.
	vii.	Rebecca, b. 8 May 1708; m. 6 Jan. 1731 in Norwich, Conn., Nathal Badger.
	viii.	Mary, b. 15 Oct. 1709.
7.	ix.	Benjamin, b. 2 Feb. 1713.
	x.	Ichabod, b. 6 June 1715; m. 31 Aug. 1731 Experience Pearce.
8.	xi.	Peleg, b. 21 Dec. 1716.
	xii.	Sarah, b. 26 Aug. 1718; d. 26 Dec. 1718. Her inscription in cemetery 1 reads: "Here lyeth ye body of Sarah, ye daughter of William and Abigail Simmons, aged three months and her two brothers, one on ye right and one on ye left."

4. WILLIAM[4] SIMMONS (William[3], John[2], Moses[1]), born in LC
30 Sept. 1699, died there 8 Jan. 1774. Residence: LC. He owned what
was known as the Joseph Church land on the Great Highway in district
No. 2.

He married in LC 3 Dec. 1721 MARY PEARCE, daughter of George
and Alice (Hart) Pearce of LC, born 16 May 1700, died in LC 31 Jan.
1755. She is buried in the Old Commons cemetery.

His will, recorded book 2, page 255, dated 2 July 1772 and proved
1 Feb. 1774: ". . . To son Jonathan to be executor of this will. To son
Aaron the east end of my farm beginning at the brook, from the south-
ward of my farm. . . thence to extend west end of my little meadow with
all the buildings. To daughters Alice and Mary 20 dollars each. To
George and Adam, my other two sons, all my land at west end of above
mentioned line, to be divided equally. That my son George shall pay
my grandson Caleb Simmons 20 dollars and said Adam shall pay my
grandson Nathaniel Simmons 20 dollars. . . "

Children, recorded in LC:
    i.   Alice, b. 13 March 1723; m. 3 Nov. 1751 Isaac Sisson.
9. ii.   Isaac, b. 24 Feb. 1725.
    iii. William, b. 23 March 1727; d. 25 Dec. 1748.
    iv. Lydia, b. 5 Nov. 1729.
10. v.   George, b. 7 Oct. 1731.
11. vi. Adam, b. 11 Oct. 1733.
12. vii. Aaron, b. 24 March 1736.
    viii. Mary, b. 13 Sept. 1738; d. 18 Oct. 1832; m. (1) 10 Jan.
        1757 Nathaniel Ewing; m. (2) 12 April 1760 David
        Stoddard.

    5. JOSEPH[4] SIMMONS (William[3], John[2], Moses[1]), born in LC 4
March 1702, died there 17 July 1778. Residence: LC.
    He married in LC 28 March 1726 REBECCA WOOD, daughter of
Jonathan and Elizabeth (Thurston) Wood, born in LC 26 Dec. 1704.
    His will, recorded LC Wills, book 2, page 402, dated 25 April
1776 and proved 4 Aug. 1778: ". . . In the 16th year of the reign of
George 3d of Great Britain. I Joseph Simmons of LC, gentleman. . .
To wife Rebecca one bed with all furniture, any bed in my house, and
my son Ephraim to find her all necessities of life. To son Edward 10
dollars. To son Jonathan 10 dollars. To Jeremiah, son of my son
John Simmons, deceased, one dollar. To daughters Abigail and Betty
five dollars each. To Susannah, my daughter, all household stuff to
make her equal with my daughters who are married. To daughter
Rebecca 5 dollars. To son Ephraim all the remainder, both real and
personal. . . "

Children, recorded in LC:
13. i.   John, b. 29 Jan. 1727.
    ii. Abigail, b. 7 Dec. 1728; m. in LC 7 Aug. 1752 Benjamin Pitman.
14. iii. Edward, b. 16 March 1730.
    iv. Betsey, b. 8 March 1733; m. in LC 12 Nov. 1755 Samuel
        Pearce, son of James and Martha (Wilbore) Pearce.
15. v.   Jonathan, b. 20 Aug. 1736.
16. vi. Ephraim, b. 29 June 1739.
    vii. Susanna, b. 8 July 1742; m. 11 Jan. 1774 John Pratt of Hingham,
        Mass.
    viii. Rebecca, b. 7 Feb. 1746; m. (--) Miller.
17. ix. Joseph, b. in 1748.

    6. JOHN[4] SIMMONS (William[3], John[2], Moses[1]), born in LC 14 Aug.
1704, died there 8 March 1774. He married there 6 April 1728 COMFORT
SHAW, daughter of Israel and (--) (Tallman) Shaw, born in LC 9 Aug.
1709, died in May 1785. His will, recorded book 2, page 266 LC Wills,
dated 3 March 1774 and proved 19 March 1774: ". . . To wife Comfort
best bed and furniture and high case of furniture and great round table.
To daughters, Sarah, Deborah, Comfort, Elizabeth, and Rachel, 12
dollars each. To Phebe and Lydia, my daughters, all household movables.
To Rachel, aboved named, a two year old heifer. To daughter Phebe,
improvement of my store bedroom. To two sons, John and Zarah
Simmons, all my land in LC and buildings. . . "

Her will, recorded book 3, page 109, made 3 Feb. 1785 and proved 7 June 1785: ". . . To daughter Sarah Pearce, widow, my oldest great wheel. To daughter Deborah Davenport my largest pewter platter. To daughter Lydia Little, widow, my case of drawers and my chest. To sons John and Zarah I give little as they had so much by my husband's will. To daughter Rachel Brownell my gown. To daughter Elizabeth Manchester my best striped linnen gown. To granddaughter Cynthany Slocum, daughter of my daughter Comfort Slocum, my small table. To grandson John Pearce my grandbedstead. To grandson Ichabod Pearce my other bed. To daughter Comfort Slocum my foot whell. My son-in-law Thomas Davenport to be executor. . . "

Children, recorded in LC:

i.	Phebe, b. 28 Dec. 1728; d. 24 April 1730.
ii.	Sarah, b. 26 Jan. 1730; m. in LC 14 Sept. 1749 James Pearce, son of James and Martha (Wilbore) Pearce.
18. iii.	Zarah, b. 13 Sept. 1731.
iv.	Ichabod, b. 28 Nov. 1732; d. 8 Feb. 1756.
v.	Deborah, b. 13 Oct. 1736; d. 8 Jan. 1809; m. in LC 31 Dec. 1761 Thomas Davenport.
vi.	Ezekiel, b. 25 July 1740; d. in Duxbury 23 Nov. 1827.
19. vii.	John, b. 27 Aug. 1741.
viii.	Comfort, b. 28 Oct. 1743; m. (--) Slocum.
ix.	Elizabeth, b. 14 Oct. 1747; m. in LC 23 Nov. 1769 Godfrey Manchester.
x.	Rachel, b. 30 Nov. 1751; m. (--) Brownell.
xi.	Lydia, b. 1 March 1753; m. 1 Jan. 1782 Joseph Little, son of Fobes and Sarah Little.

7. BENJAMIN[4] SIMMONS (William[3], John[2], Moses[1]), born in LC 2 Feb. 1713, died there 16 March 1788.

He was married in LC 27 Nov. 1734 by Richard Billings, justice, to MERCY TAYLOR, daughter of Peter and Hannah (Wood) Taylor, born in LC 24 Feb. 1717, died there 3 Oct. 1796. Residence: LC. They probably lived on Long Highway at the James N. Pearce place.

Children, recorded in LC:

20. i.	Peter, b. 19 May 1735.
ii.	Capt. Cornelius, b. 15 March 1737; d. 28 Dec. 1775. In his will, recorded LC Wills, book 2, page 334, made 27 Sept. 1775 and proved 5 Dec. 1775: ". . . To my brother Ivory all my wearing apparel and my artillery. To wife Mary all rest and residue real and personal. . . "
21. iii.	Benjamin, b. 2 Dec. 1739.
22. iv.	Samuel, b. 24 July 1742.
v.	Hannah, b. 21 Feb. 1745; d. 24 Jan. 1821; m. in November 1766 in LC Ichabod Burgess, son of Jacob and Susanna (Williston) Burgess, b. 5 Feb. 1741, d. 19 Oct. 1821.
vi.	Abigail, b. 25 Feb. 1748; m. in LC 7 May 1780 Redford (Richard) Dennis.
23. vii.	Ivory, b. 17 Oct. 1750.
viii.	Mercy, b. 31 July 1753; m. in LC 20 April 1777 Caleb Simmons.
24. ix.	Ichabod, b. 10 July 1756.

8. PELEG[4] SIMMONS (William[3], John[2], Moses[1]), born in LC 21 Dec. 1716, died 4 Jan. 1807. He was married there 19 Dec. 1739 by Richard Billings, justice, to MARY BROWNELL, daughter of Thomas and Mary (Crandall) Brownell, born in LC 15 July 1717. Residence: LC.

Children, all recorded in Tiverton, some also recorded in LC:

25. i.   Thomas, b. 9 Sept. 1740.
    ii.   Moses, b. 16 Jan. 1743; perhaps m. 31 Oct. 1765 Wait Borden; m. 21 Sept. 1797 Susannah Tabor, daughter of Paul and Sarah Tabor.
26. iii.   Capt. Gideon, b. 14 Dec. 1744.
    iv.   Mary, b. 13 Jan. 1747.
    v.   Phebe, b. 21 April 1749.
    vi.   Rhoda, b. 2 May 1751; m. (--) Sanford.
    vii.   Unis, b. 24 March 1753.
    viii.   Peleg, b. 7 May 1755; d. 3 Dec. 1828. He served in the Revolutionary War and afterwards settled in Tiverton and was known as Capt. Peleg. He may have m. (1) Martha (--) and m. (2) Elizabeth (--).
27. ix.   Benjamin, b. 7 Nov. 1757.
    x.   Joseph, b. 31 Oct. 1760; m. 7 May 1780 Redford Dennis, daughter of John and Hannah Dennis of Tiverton.

9. ISAAC[5] SIMMONS (William[4], William[3], John[2], Moses[1]), born in LC 24 Feb. 1725, died there 4 Sept. 1758. Residence: LC.

He was married in LC 25 March 1748 by Richard Billings, justice, to MARY CHURCH, daughter of Caleb and Deborah (Woodworth) Church, born in LC 6 Jan. 1728, died 3 Sept. 1815. Both are buried in Old Commons cemetery. She married second Seth Pope of Dartmouth, son of Lemuel and Elizabeth Pope of LC.

Children, recorded in LC:

28. i.   William, b. 24 Feb. 1749.
29. ii.   Nathaniel, b. 10 June 1751.
30. iii.   Caleb, b. 23 Jan. 1754.
    iv.   Mary, b. 1 Dec. 1755; m. in LC 20 Oct. 1774 Joseph Simmons, son of Joseph and Rebecca Simmons.
    v.   Priscilla, b. 24 April 1758.

10. CAPT. GEORGE[5] SIMMONS (William[4], William[3], John[2], Moses[1]), born in LC 7 Oct. 1731, died there 26 March 1809. He lived on Peckham Road near the head of Willow Avenue, marked Pearce on the map of 1870. He was a captain in the Revolutionary War.

He was married first in LC 18 Dec. 1753 by Joseph Wood, justice, to DEBORAH TAYLOR, daughter of Philip and Comfort (Dennis) Taylor, born in LC 22 Sept. 1729, died there 18 July 1765. Both are buried in the Old Commons cemetery. He married second about 1766 LUCY DAVIS, daughter of Fobes and Sarah (Baker) Little and widow of Aaron Davis, born in 1734, died in LC 9 Jan. 1806. He married third in LC 21 June 1807 SARAH (CARR) WILBOR, daughter of William and Abigail (Dring) Carr and widow of William Wilbore, born in LC 23 July 1757, died there 29 March 1825.

Children by second wife, recorded in LC:
i.   Deborah, b. 19 Nov. 1767; m. in LC 2 Oct. 1791 Benjamin
      Tompkins, son of Michael and Sarah Tompkins.
31. ii.   Davis, b. 20 Oct. 1769.
iii. Mary, b. 15 Dec. 1772.
iv.   Sarah, b. 21 Dec. 1775; m. in LC 1 Sept. 1799 Godfrey
      Pearce, son of Wright and Anstress Pearce.

11. DEACON ADAM[5] SIMMONS (William[4], William[3], John[2],
Moses[1]), born in LC 11 Oct. 1733, died there 21 Aug. 1803.
      He was married in LC 27 Nov. 1755 by the Rev. Jonathan Ellis
to DEBORAH CHURCH, daughter of Caleb and Margaret (Torrey)
Church of LC, born there 10 Aug. 1736, died there 6 April 1826.
Both are buried in the Old Commons cemetery.
      He was a deacon of the Congregational Church. They lived on
the placed owned by Thomas White 1870-1890, on the Ware Main
Road in district No. 2.
      His will, recorded book 4, page 138 LC Wills, made 20 March
1802 and proved 7 Sept. 1803: ". . . To wife Deborah all personal
estate and use of all real estate. To daughter Elizabeth Taylor one
fourth of all real estate and one half of pew in the Congregational
Meeting House. To daughter Sarah Coe one fourth of all real estate
and one half of pew. To daughter Lucy Richmond one fourth of real
estate. To grandchildren, children of Isaac Simmons, Betsey, Lurany,
Deborah and Mary Simmons, one fourth of all real estate. To granddaughter Deborah Church Simmons my loom. To my poore and beloved Isaac Simmons my blacksmith shop and tools. My wife Deborah
to be executrix. . . "
      Her will, recorded book 6, page 174, made 19 Dec. 1822 and
proved 8 May 1826: ". . . To son Isaac Simmons one dollar. To
daughter Lucy Richmond two dollars. To granddaughter Betsey Wood
one great iron pot. To granddaughter Mary Simmons six of my best
towels. To granddaughter Lydia Southworth Simmons five dollars. To
daughter Sarah Coe the rest and residue of both real and personal.
Grandson Ezra Coe to be executor. . . "

      Children, recorded in LC:
i.   Elizabeth, b. 9 June 1758; d. in November 1821; m. 22 Jan.
      1789 Philip Taylor, son of Philip and Comfort (Dennis)
      Taylor.
ii.   Sarah, b. 23 Sept. 1759; d. in 1834; m. in LC 13 Jan. 1780
      Benjamin Coe.
iii. Lucy, b. 16 April 1761; m. in LC 14 Sept. 1784 Thomas
      Richmond.
32. iv.   Isaac, b. 28 Aug. 1764.

12. AARON[5] SIMMONS (William[4], William[3], John[2], Moses[1]),
born in LC 24 March 1736, died there in January 1802 ae 66.
      He was married in LC 30 Nov. 1757 by the Rev. Jonathan Ellis
to ABIGAIL CHURCH, daughter of Caleb and Margaret (Torrey)
Church, born in LC 29 Sept. 1737.
      Residence: LC. They lived near Clapp's corner, perhaps on
Peckham Road.

Children, recorded in LC:
i.   Margaret, b. 2 Feb. 1759; m. in LC 8 Oct. 1780 George
      Pearce, son of Nathaniel and Sarah Pearce.
ii.   Ruth, b. 3 March 1761; m. 7 April 1782 Ichabod Simmons,
      son of Benjamin and Lucy Simmons.
iii. Abigail, b. 23 Aug. 1762.
iv.   Abel, b. 3 Nov. 1765; m. in LC 29 Aug. 1791 Ruth Wood,
      daughter of George and Desire Wood.
v.   Aaron, b. 18 April 1768.
vi.   Adam, b. 12 July 1770.
vii. Lydia, b. 3 Sept. 1774; m. 8 Dec. 1791 William Barstow.
viii. Gamaliel Church, b. 18 March 1779.
ix.   Mehitable, b. 18 July 1781.

13. JOHN[5] SIMMONS (Joseph[4], William[3], John[2], Moses[1]), born
in LC 29 Jan. 1727. Residence: LC and Easton, Mass.

He was married in LC 13 July 1746 by William Richmond, justice,
to LYDIA GRINNELL, daughter of George and Mercy (Sanford) Grinnell,
born in LC 7 Dec. 1726.

Children, first two recorded in LC:
33. i.   Capt. Jeremiah, b. 8 April 1747.
    ii. Joseph, b. in LC 23 March 1749.
34. iii. Benoni, b. 4 Aug. 1755.
    iv. John, d. in Easton, Mass.; m. 1 Feb. 1786 Ruth Mitchell,
         b. in 1762, d. in Easton 8 Aug. 1843. He was a soldier of
         Revolution.
    v.   Isiah.
    vi. Ruth, m. 22 Jan. 1775 Barnabus Clapp, son of Elisha and
         Elizabeth Clapp.
    vii. Elizabeth, d. unmarried in Easton.

14. EDWARD[5] SIMMONS (Joseph[4], William[3], John[2], Moses[1]),
born in LC 16 March 1730. He married AMEY COGSWELL. Residence: LC and Newport.

Children, only the first recorded in LC:
i.   James, b. 26 May 1780; m. (--) Cone.
ii.   Jonathan, d. at Newport.

15. JONATHAN[5] SIMMONS (Joseph[4], William[3], John[2], Moses[1]),
born in LC 20 Aug. 1736.

He was married in LC 5 May 1759 by the Rev. Jonathan Ellis to
ABIGAIL BAILEY, daughter of William and Comfort (Billings) Bailey,
born in LC 27 Oct. 1736. Residence: LC and Newport.

Children, recorded in LC:
i.   Sarah, b. 19 May 1761; m. in LC 2 Nov. 1784 Timothy Chace,
      son of James and Huldah Chace.
ii.   Rebecca, b. 6 April 1763; m. (--) Raymond.
iii. Edward, b. 26 July 1766. Residence: Madison, N.Y.
iv.   Ephraim, b. 18 Jan. 1769.
v.   Betsey, b. 23 May 1772; m. John Pierce.

vi.   William, b. 22 Jan. 1775. Residence: Madison, N.Y.
vii. Joseph, b. 4 March 1779; m. 23 Oct. 1809 Comfort Grinnell,
      daughter of Billings and Comfort Grinnell.

16. EPHRAIM[5] SIMMONS (Joseph[4], William[3], John[2], Moses[1]),
born in LC 29 June 1739, died about 1825.
    He married in LC 11 Sept. 1777 MARY RICHMOND, daughter of
Perez and Deborah (Loring) Richmond, born in Dartmouth 26/7 Aug.
1749, died 7 Nov. 1816. Residence: LC and Fairhaven, Mass.
    In 1794 Ephraim Simmons and his wife Mary sold to the Rev.
Mase Shepard 47 acres, bounded north by Thomas Wilbur, deceased,
east on the highway, south on Gamaliel Tompkins and Robert Taylor,
west on land of William Taylor and Nathaniel Church. This became
the Joshua Richmond place on the road south of the Commons.

17. JOSEPH[5] SIMMONS (Joseph[4], William[3], John[2], Moses[1]), born
in LC in 1748, died there in December 1803.
    He was married in LC 20 Oct. 1774 by the Rev. Jonathan Ellis to
MARY SIMMONS, daughter of Isaac and Mary (Church) Simmons, born
in LC 1 Dec. 1755. Residence: LC.

      Children, all recorded in LC:
i.   Elizabeth, b. 9 Jan. 1775.
ii.   Deborah, b. 9 Oct. 1776.
iii. Susanna, b. 20 May 1778.
iv.   Ezra, b. 22 Feb. 1780.
v.   Abigail, b. 11 Jan. 1782.
vi.   Andrew, b. 10 March 1784.

18. ZARAH[5] SIMMONS (John[4], William[3], John[2], Moses[1]), born
in LC 13 Oct. 1731.
    He was married first in LC 1 Nov. 1770 by the Rev. Jonathan Ellis
to PHEBE BROWNELL, daughter of Stephen and Edith (Wilbor) Brownell,
born in LC 4 Sept. 1747. He was married second in LC 28 Aug. 1789 by
the Rev. Mase Shepard to SUSANNAH STODDARD, daughter of Israel and
Elizabeth (Brownell) Stoddard, born in LC 17 June 1750.
    A carpenter, he lived in LC in the big house (Pearce) on Peckham
Road. In 1812 he apparently sold his home to Stephen Simmons and
moved to Madison, Madison County, N.Y.

      Children by first wife, recorded in LC:
i.   George, b. 27 Oct. 1771; m. 23 March 1794 Ruth Head,
      daughter of Jonathan and Ruth Head.
ii.   Elizabeth, b. 22 April 1774; m. 15 Sept. 1799 Jacob
      Manchester, son of Archer and Lavina Manchester.
iii. Abigail, b. 18 Feb. 1776.
iv.   Abigail, b. 18 Jan. 1778; m. in LC 3 Dec. 1797 Isaac Seabury,
      son of Constant and Susannah Seabury.
v.   Edith, b. 11 Oct. 1782.
vi.   Ezekiah, b. 18 Nov. 1783.
vii. Stephen, b. 25 Nov. 1785.
viii. Edith, b. 11 Aug. 1788.

Children by second wife:
ix.   Thomas, b. 21 Jan. 1791; m. (--) Woodman, daughter of Pardon
       and Elizabeth (Brown) Woodman.

19. JOHN[5] SIMMONS (John[4], William[3], John[2], Moses[1]), born in LC
26 Aug. 1741. He was married there 22 Jan. 1767 by Jeptha Pierce,
justice, to HANNAH BRIGHTMAN, daughter of Henry Brightman of
Dartmouth.

His will, recorded book 6, page 41 of LC Probate, made 1 Jan. 1816
and proved 13 Dec. 1824: ". . . To wife Hannah securities and everything
that came to her in the will of her father Henry Brightman and sister
Christian Brightman. Also the use of all real estate. To son Stephen
150 dollars. To son John 100 dollars. . . " He left to his daughters,
Rhoda, Lucy and Phebe, and to son Pardon each a fourth of his estate.

Her will, recorded book 8, page 14, made 25 Nov. 1826 and proved
11 March 1833: ". . . being sane in mind though debilitated in body and
in view of my approaching dissolution. . . To son Pardon 1 bed, blanket
and one sheet. To son Stephen eight dollars. To son John my low blue
chest, one coverlid and blue blanket, both of which belonged to my sister
Christian Brightman. To my daughter Rhoda Bliffins my warming pan.
To granddaughter Sarah Sanders, one suit of wearing apparel. To three
daughters, Rhoda Bliffins, Lucy Pearce and Phebe Meeson the rest
and residue. . . "

Children, recorded in LC:
i.   Rhoda, b. 16 Aug. 1767; m. (--) Bliffins.
35. ii.   Pardon, b. 24 Sept. 1768.
iii.   Lusanna (Lucy), b. 20 March 1771; d. 26 Nov. 1859; m. 3
        Dec. 1789 Ichabod Pierce.
36. iv.   Stephen, b. 25 March 1773.
v.   John, b. 9 Feb. 1777; d. 28 June 1851; m. (--) Negus.
vi.   Phebe, b. 10 May 1785; m. 12 July 1814 Edward Meeson.

20. PETER[5] SIMMONS (Benjamin[4], William[3], John[2], Moses[1]),
born in LC 19 May 1735.

He was married in LC 6 Oct. 1760 by the Rev. Jonathan Ellis to
REBECCA ROUSE, daughter of George and Hannah (Horswell) Rouse,
born in LC 17 Jan. 1744. They lived in Tiverton until 1790 when they
moved to Galloway, N.Y.

Children, recorded in LC:
i.   Hannah, b. 12 Sept. 1761.
ii.   Eliphal, b. 26 April 1763.
iii.   Deborah, b. 5 Oct. 1765.
iv.   George, b. 13 Dec. 1766.
v.   Mary b. 16 March 1769.
vi.   Benjamin, b. 3 Jan. 1771.
vii.   Lemuel, b. 22 Sept. 1773.
viii. Rouse, b. 11 Aug. 1775.
ix.   Isaac, b. 15 March 1778.
x.   Deborah, b. 8 May 1781.
xi.   Peter, b. 16 Oct. 1783.

21. BENJAMIN⁵ SIMMONS (Benjamin⁴, William³, John², Moses¹),
born in LC 2 Dec. 1739. He married MARY (--).

      Children, recorded in LC:
i.   Loring, b. 27 Jan. 1765.

22. SAMUEL⁵ SIMMONS (Benjamin⁴, William³, John², Moses¹),
born in LC 24 July 1742, died there 4 Feb. 1821.

He married first about 1766 PHEBE MANCHESTER. He married
second in Tiverton 7 Oct. 1802 SARAH COE, daughter of John and
Rebecca (Taylor) Coe, born in LC 11 Feb. 1756.

Residence: LC. He lived on Long Highway on what was in 1890
the James Pearce place.

His will, recorded LC Wills, book 5, page 220, made 15 Jan.
1814 and proved 13 March 1821: ". . . To wife Sarah Simmons one
maple desk, my side saddle and loom. One half of real estate con-
sisting of dwelling house, out houses, grist mill and five acres of
land I bought of George Simmons. To daughter Eunice Knight, wife
of Philip Knight, remaining part of household goods and 300 dollars.
To son William Simmons my homestead farm where I now live and
salt meadow I bought of John Wilbor. To two grandsons, Samuel
Simmons, son of my son William Simmons and Samuel Knight, son
of Philip Knight all wearing apparel. My wife to be sole executrix.
To wife Sarah that lot of land that I bought of Dr. Benjamin Richmond. . . "

      Children by first wife, born in LC:
37. i.   William, b. 7 Dec. 1767.
    ii.   Eunice, m. Philip Knight.

23. IVORY⁵ SIMMONS (Benjamin⁴, William³, John², Moses¹),
born 17 Oct. 1750 in LC. He was married in Tiverton 1 Feb. 1781
by the Rev. Jonathan Ellis to SARAH BORDEN, daughter of John and
Patience Borden of Tiverton. Residence: LC.

      Children, recorded in LC:
i.   Cornelius, b. 2 Oct. 1781.
ii.   Borden, b. 14 Dec. 1782.
iii.   Humphrey, b. 23 Feb. 1785.
iv.   Samuel, b. 27 Sept. 1786; m. (1) 26 Jan. 1809 in LC Amy
         Beal; m. (2) 17 Oct. 1813 Hannah Wilbor, daughter of
         Isaac Wilbor of Troy, Mass.
v.   Amaziah, b. 11 April 1788.
vi.   Malinda, b. 3 April 1790.
vii.   Benjamin, b. 28 May 1792.
viii. Layton, b. 1 July 1794.
ix.   Ruth Borden, b. 10 July 1796.
x.   Thurston, b. 12 April 1799.
xi.   Tillinghast, b. 6 Oct. 1801.
xii.   Sarah, b. 5 Nov. 1803.
xiii. Almira, b. 22 Oct. 1806.

24. ICHABOD⁵ SIMMONS (Benjamin⁴, William³, John², Moses¹),

born 10 July 1756 in LC, died 1841. He was married in LC 7 April
1782 by the Rev. Jonathan Ellis to RUTH SIMMONS, daughter of Aaron
and Abigail (Church) Simmons, born 3 March 1761 in LC.
> Residence: Paris, Herkeimer County, N.Y., in 1797.

> Children, recorded in LC:
> i.   Dianna, b. 28 Oct. 1782.
> ii. George Pearce, b. 2 Jan. 1785.
> iii. Caleb, b. 3 April 1787.

25. THOMAS[5] SIMMONS (Peleg[4], William[3], John[2], Moses[1]), born
in LC 9 Sept. 1740, died in Tiverton 12 June 1833.

He married first in Tiverton 25 Feb. 1761 MARTHA HART of
Tiverton, daughter of Jonathan and Mercy (Tripp) Hart.   He married
second in Tiverton 5 Feb. 1769 ELIZABETH MANCHESTER, daughter
of Edward Manchester. Residence: Tiverton.

> Children, born in Tiverton:
> 38. i.   Ichabod, b. 20 Sept. 1761.
> ii. Abner, b. 22 Sept. 1762; m. (1) (?); m. (2) 1 May (?) Ruth
>   (--).
> iii. Pardon, b. 5 Sept. 1769.
> iv. John, b. 28 Sept. 1770.
> v.   Thomas, b. 13 July 1780; m. in Tiverton 5 July 1801 Polly
>   Church, daughter of Seth and Lois Church of LC.
> vi. Edward.
> vii. Amasa.
> viii. Stephen.
> ix. George.
> x.   Hannah.
> xi. Ruth, m. Joseph Albert.
> xii. Rachel, m. (--) King of Westport.

26. CAPT. GIDEON[5] SIMMONS (Peleg[4], William[3], John[2], Moses[1]),
born in LC 14 Dec. 1744.

He was married first in LC 27 June 1771 by the Rev. Jonathan Ellis
to PATIENCE ELLIS, daughter of the Rev. Jonathan and Patience Ellis,
born about 1747, died in LC 13 Oct. 1792. He married second in LC
9 April 1797 RUTH STODDARD, daughter of Benjamin and Phebe (Brownell) Stoddard, born in LC in 1759.

He was a captain of one of the companies of militia for the town
of LC during the Revolutionary War. A pensioner, he lived at one
time in Easton, Madison County, N.Y. He and William Church moved
from LC to New York State, driving an ox team containing their
personal belongings. In 1795 he was living in Paris, N.Y., and in
1796 he was in Hamilton, N.Y. In 1811 he was living in Madison,
Madison County, N.Y.

> Children, all recorded in LC:
> i.   Thomas Brownell, b. 16 Aug. 1772; m. in LC 6 Sept. 1797
>   Susanna Brown, daughter of Thomas and Priscilla Brown.
> ii. Jonathan Ellis, b. 1 March 1775. Residence: Providence.
> iii. Charles Lee, b. 2 Jan. 1777.

iv.   William Pitts, b. 27 Sept. 1780; m. Susannah Durfee.
v.   Eunice, b. 10 Nov. 1782.
vi.   Mary, b. 7 Oct. 1784.
vii. Benjamin Clapp, b. 11 Oct. 1788.

27. BENJAMIN⁵ SIMMONS (Peleg⁴, William³, John², Moses¹),
born in LC 7 Nov. 1757, died 4 Jan. 1829.
He was married in LC 1 May 1783 by the Rev. Jonathan Ellis to
SUSANNA BRIGGS, daughter of Cornelius and Mary (Brownell) Briggs,
born in LC 22 March 1766. Residence: Madison, Madison County, N.Y.,
in 1822.

        Children, all recorded in LC:
i.   Cornelius, b. 1 Oct. 1783.
ii.   Mary, b. 1 Nov. 1785.
iii. Lucy, b. 6 Dec. 1787.
iv.   Joseph, b. 22 April 1790.
v.   Judith, b. 1 April 1792.

28. WILLIAM⁶ SIMMONS (Isaac⁵, William⁴, William³, John²,
Moses¹), born in LC 24 Feb. 1749.
He married in LC 1 July 1770 ANNA RICHMOND, daughter of
Ephraim and Elizabeth (Cook) Richmond, born in LC 14 Dec. 1749,
died in Schoharie, N.Y., in 1815. Residence: LC and Schoharie, N.Y.

        Children, recorded in LC:
i.   William, b. 21 Jan. 1771.
ii.   Isaac, b. 27 Oct. 1772.
iii. Richmond, b. 2 Oct. 1774; m. Anna Brownell, daughter of
        James Brownell.
iv.   Hannah Gray, b. 24 Nov. 1776.
v.   Anna, b. 15 Oct. 1778.
vi.   Mary Pope, b. 18 Sept. 1780.

29. NATHANIEL⁶ SIMMONS (Isaac⁵, William⁴, William³, John²,
Moses¹), born in LC 10 June 1751.
He married in LC 21 Dec. 1777 MARY WOOD, daughter of Joseph
and Mary (Brownell) Wood, born in LC 31 Jan. 1748. Residence: LC.
They lived on the West Main Road in district No. 2, on the place marked
E. Palmer on the map of 1870.

        Children, not recorded in LC:
i.   Charlotte.
ii.   Zella, b. 26 Oct. 1783.
39. iii. Lindal, b. 18 Aug. 1783.
iv.   Ruth, b. 17 Aug. 1789.
v.   Perez, b. 6 March 1781.

30. CALEB⁶ SIMMONS (Isaac⁵, William⁴, William³, John², Moses¹),
born in LC 23 Jan. 1754.
He was married in LC 20 April 1777 by the Rev. Jonathan Ellis to
MERCY SIMMONS, daughter of Benjamin and Mercy (Taylor) Simmons,
born in LC 31 July 1753. This family must have moved away from LC.

In 1797 he was living in Paris, Herkeimer County, N.Y.

> Children, recorded in LC:
> i.   Nancy, b. 30 July 1777.
> ii.   Mary, b. 10 March 1779.
> iii. Mercy, b. 17 July 1784.
> iv. Margaret, b. 17 March 1787.
> v.   Elizabeth, b. 24 April 1791; m. 29 Nov. 1811 William Winsor.
> vi. Isaac, b. 21 March 1793.

31. DAVIS[6] SIMMONS (George[5], William[4], William[3], John[2], Moses[1]), born in LC 20 Oct. 1769.

He was married first in Tiverton 28 Nov. 1792 by Elder Peleg Burroughs to ELIZABETH COOK, daughter of Walker and (--) Cook of Tiverton. He married second in Newport 26 Aug. 1802 MARY COOK.

> Children, recorded in LC:
> i.   Walter Cook, b. 19 May 178-.
> ii.   James Fowler, b. 11 Sept. 1795; d. 4 May 1862 in LC; m. twice
>   and had four sons by each wife. One was Samuel Randall
>   Simmons, whose portrait is owned by the Little Compton
>   Historical Society, the grandfather of Margaret Bailey, the
>   author. Residence: Johnston, R.I. He was a United States
>   Senator.
> iii. Eliza Hall, b. 21 Sept. 1796; d. in LC 4 May 1862; m. there 2
>   Nov. 1815 Jonathan Brownell.

32. ISAAC[6] SIMMONS (Adam[5], William[4], William[3], John[2], Moses[1]), born in LC 28 Aug. 1764, died there 25 March 1848.

He was married there 25 May 1788 by the Rev. Mase Shepard to ABISHAG BRIGGS, daughter of Cornelius and Mary (Brownell) Briggs, born in LC 16 March 1768. Residence: LC.

Her will, recorded in LC Wills, book 6, page 197, made in August 1822, proved 9 July 1827: ". . . To four daughters. . . all my wearing apparel. To said Lydia my side saddle, etc. because she cannot inherit my property of which her honored grandfather, Adam Simmons, died seized of. To the said Mary and Lydia Simmons use of all real estate, and they to be executors. . . "

> Children, all recorded in LC except the last two:
> i.   Betsey, b. 4 April 1789; d. in LC 24 Feb. 1847; m. Capt.
>   Charles Wood.
> ii.   Lurana, b. 3 Aug. 1791; m. in LC 28 Feb. 1808 Jonathan
>   Brownell Taylor.
> iii. Deborah Church, b. 14 Aug. 1793; d. 26 Oct. 1819.
> iv. Mary Brownell, b. 3 Sept. 1800; m. (intention 27 Sept. 1834)
>   in Westport Osmond Brownell, son of Nathaniel Brownell.
> v.   Lydia, m. (--) Tenney (?).
> vi. Henrietta, b. in 1806; d. 27 Oct. 1819.
> vii. Susanna, m. in LC 28 Feb. 1808 Jonathan Brownell, son of
>   Samuel and Lydia Brownell.

33. CAPT. JEREMIAH[6] SIMMONS (John[5], Joseph[4], William[3], John[2], Moses[1]), born in LC 8 April 1747.

SAMUEL
RANDALL
SIMMONS

This portrait is
owned by the
Little Compton
Historical Society.

He was the son of
James Fowler Simmons
and the grandfather
of the novelist,
Margaret Bailey.

A United States Senator,
he made his home
in Johnston, R. I.

He evidently moved to Philadelphia as a young man, for he appears as lieutenant of Proctor's Company of Pennsylvania Artillery,
promoted to captain 24 Feb. 1776; he served as such until 1 Oct. 1776,
when he joined "Arnold's Floating Battery" of the "Pennsylvania State
Navy," serving as captain on the armed ship Warren under command
of Commodore John Hazlewood. These boats sought to prevent the
British from coming up the Delaware River to relieve the troops in
and around Philadelphia, and they took part in the battles of Red Bank
and Mud Fort (October-November, 1777). Captain Simmons appears
to have served until the end of November 1778, when it was found
necessary to destroy the boats. It is probable that this little fleet on
the Delaware carried the first flag displayed by marine forces of the
United States, made especially for these ships by Mrs. Elizabeth Ross
of Philadelphia.

After his active service as above, Captain Simmons was master
of at least two armed ships which received letters of marque as follows:
Letters dated 9 March 1780: "Morning Star," Pennsylvania ship. Guns,
18; crew, 100. Master, Jeremiah Simmons. Mate, Enoch Stillwell of
Philadelphia. Bond, 20,000 dollars. Bonders, Hugh Lennox of Philadelphia, and Jeremiah Simmons of Philadelphia. Owners, Frances Gurney

and Co., Philadelphia. Letters dated 14 Dec. 1781: "Mayflower,"
Connecticut schooner. Guns, 6; crew, 12. Master, Jeremiah Simmons.
Bond, 20,000 dollars. Bonders, Jeremiah Simmons of Philadelphia,
Levinus Clarkson, Philadelphia and John Hallam, New London. Owners,
Levinus Clarkson and Co., Philadelphia.--from "Naval Records of the
American Revolution," Washington, Government Printing Office, 1906.

He married, 3 Dec. 1778, ELIZABETH CROSSMAN, at Christ
Episcopal Church, Philadelphia, the ceremony being performed by the
rector, the Rev. William White, later a well known bishop of the church.
A statement of this marriage, with names and date, in the bishop's own
writing, is to be found with the pension papers. The church records
also verify this marriage, but show no further Crossman entries,
except the burial of a Rebecca Crossman, 28 Feb. 1804, in St. Peter's
churchyard (at that time within the same parish as Christ Church). A
search of the St. Peter's Church index of old records yielded no
Crossman entry.

Captain Simmons evidently lived in Philadelphia for some years:
his name appears in an old Philadelphia directory of 1785, and in 1793
a "Captain Simmons," with no given name, is listed, who may easily
be the same person. He died 16 Jan. 1798; place uncertain, possibly
Easton, Mass.

The only child of whom we have positive record is Julia Ann
Simmons, born in Philadelphia 19 Aug. 1787; died in Woodbury, N.J.,
16 Sept. 1853; married at Philadelphia 21 May 1805, Samuel Pote
Watkins, born in Salem, Mass., 14 Sept. 1778; died in Mobile, Ala.,
about 1837.

Mrs. Elizabeth Simmons, the widow of Captain Simmons, evidently had no need of a pension for many years after her husband's
death, (a Philadelphia directory of 1823 lists an Elizabeth Simmons
as a "dealer," some sort of business woman), but later she was in
need, and with the help of her grandson, Samuel Pote Watkins, Jr.,
she applied for a pension in papers dated 3 Sept. 1838, over 40 years
after she became a widow; she was then living in Philadelphia, aged
78. Pension payments were begun the next year and continued until
her death (16 July 1849), the payment being at first 500 dollars per
year, later increased to 552 dollars per year.

34. BENONI[6] SIMMONS (John[5], Joseph[4], William[3], John[2], Moses[1]),
born in Portsmouth 4 Aug. 1755, died in LC 15 June 1835.

He was married in LC 19 Dec. 1784 by the Rev. Jonathan Ellis to
NANCY BAILEY, daughter of Cornelius and Mary (White) Bailey of LC,
born there 14 Feb. 1767, died 21 Oct. 1855.

He served in the Navy during the Revolution and was a pensioner.
They lived in district No. 1, on land south of the place marked L.
Sisson on the map of 1870 and later owned by Marian Baldwin.

In her will, recorded LC Wills, book 11, page 64, made 15 Nov.
1837 and proved 10 Dec. 1855, she left 750 dollars to her son Valentine,
10 dollars each to her son John and to her grandchildren, and the rest
and residue to her three daughters, Lydia Austin, Mary Almy and
Comfort Sisson.

Children, born in LC:

    i.   Cornelius, b. 19 Sept. 1785; d. in LC 5 Oct. 1822; m. (1)
           Margaret Lord; m. (2) Eliza Bradford.
    ii.   Lydia, b. 19 Aug. 1787; m. Joseph Austin of Boston.
    iii.   Jeremiah, b. 30 Nov. 1789; d. 12 March 1790 ae 3 months.
    iv.   Mary, b. 1 Feb. 1791; m. in LC 20 Dec. 1814 Capt. Frederick
           Almy, son of Sanford and Lydia Almy.
    v.   George Washington, b. 9 Sept. 1793; lost at sea 9 Sept. 1814.
40. vi.   John, b. 30 Oct. 1796.
41. vii.   Valentine, b. 19 April 1802.
    viii. Comfort, b. 7 July 1803; m. 16 Nov. 1826 Lemuel Sisson.

     35. PARDON[6] SIMMONS (John[5], John[4], William[3], John[2], Moses[1]),
born in LC 24 Sept. 1768, died there 11 March 1841.
     He married first in LC 28 Sept. 1794 HANNAH PALMER, daughter
of John and Mercy (Mary) Palmer of Westport. He was married second
in Tiverton 4 Feb. 1814 by the Rev. Benjamin Pearce to BETSEY CHURCH,
daughter of Constant Church of Westport.
     He is buried in Simmons cemetery on Peckham Road near the Long
Highway. He is listed in the will of his wife's sister as a goldsmith.
     His will, recorded LC Probate, book 9, page 10, made in November
1833 and proved 10 May 1841: ". . . To the Congregational Church of LC
50 dollars, the interest of which is to be used alone. To daughter Eliza
Ann Church, 5 dollars. To sister Rhoda Bliven, 6 silver teaspoons.
To sister Phebe Meeson, wife of Edward Meeson, 50 dollars. To brother
Stephen Simmons, 100 dollars. To brother John Simmons, wearing apparel. To Ichabod Pearce's three daughters, Clarinda Wilbor, Cinderella Brown and Cynthia Pearce, three feather beds under beds, cords
and bedsteads. To brother Stephen Simmons's three daughters, Lydia
Simmons, Sarah Simmons Slocum and Julia Ann Simmons, 10 dollars
each. To Sarah Saunders, wife of Joseph Saunders, 20 dollars. To
Charles Simmons, son of brother John Simmons, 10 dollars. To Hannah
Simmons, daughter of John Simmons, 15 dollars. To Jonathan Pearce,
son of Ichabod Pearce, rest and residue. . . "

     36. STEPHEN[6] SIMMONS (John[5], John[4], William[3], John[2], Moses[1]),
born in LC 25 March 1773, died 7 July 1861 ae 88.
     He was married in Westport 29 Nov. 1798 by William Almy, justice,
to PRISCILLA HEAD, daughter of John and Elizabeth Head, born 8
March 1777, died in LC 27 Feb. 1875 ae 98.
     Children:
    i.   Sarah, m. in LC 26 Jan. 1832 Solomon Slocum of Dartmouth,
           son of Charles Slocum.
    ii.   Julia Ann, d. 21 Aug. 1815 ae 9.
    iii.   Julia A., b. in LC 17 Aug. 1817; d. in Newport 4 Dec. 1891; m.
           (1) in LC 10 Aug. 1836 Job Slocum, son of Charles and
           Jane Slocum of South Dartmouth, Mass.; m. (2) John Dyer.
42. iv.   Henry Brightman, b. 11 June 1800.
    v.   Lydia, b. 31 Dec. 1804; m. in LC 4 Dec. 1833 Francis Zeray
           of Dartmouth. They had a daughter, Lydia Frances, b.
           in LC 21 Aug. 1836.

37. WILLIAM[6] SIMMONS (Samuel[5], Benjamin[4], William[3], John[2], Moses[1]), born in LC 27 Dec. 1767, died there 20 Jan. 1853 ae 85.

He married 18 Nov. 1791 REBECCA SOULE, daughter of Jacob and Meribah (Lewis) Soule of Tiverton and Blenheim, N.Y., born 18 Nov. 1771 and died in LC 7 Feb. 1862 ae 90. They lived on the James N. Pearce place (1890) on the Long Highway.

Children, recorded in LC:
    i.   Samuel, b. 5 Aug. 1795.
43. ii.   Benjamin, b. 29 Feb. 1796; m. 12 Jan. 1822 Martha Simmons.
    iii. Phebe, b. 22 March 1798; m. in LC 19 Feb. 1821 George Woodman, son of William and Priscilla Woodman.
    iv.   Abraham, b. 23 Oct. 1800.
    v.   Lewis, b. 5 May 1804; m. 26 Feb. 1823 in LC Nancy Davis of Westport, daughter of Philip and Clarisa Davis.
    vi.   Abigail Dennis, b. 14 Sept. 1807.
44. vii. Elisha, b. 2 May 1810.

38. ICHABOD[6] SIMMONS (Thomas[5], Peleg[4], William[3], John[2], Moses[1]), born in Tiverton 20 Sept. 1761, died there 17 Oct. 1841 ae 80.

He married ANNA THOMAS of Newport, daughter of Burgess Thomas, born in 1764, died in Tiverton 30 Nov. 1846 ae 82.

They lived and are buried on the east side of Stafford Road in Tiverton, later the David Wilbur place. He served for seven years as a soldier in the Revolutionary War, and was a body guard to George Washington.

His will, recorded in Tiverton, book 11, page 231, made 26 May 1841 and proved 6 Dec. 1841: ". . . To wife Anna my homestead farm for life, interest in livestock and all household goods. To my five daughters. . . all furniture at decease of their mother. To son William all my real estate not already given. To all my children and grandchildren the use of my burying yard. To son Pardon Simmons. . . To son Abel Simmons 80 dollars. . ."

Children, born in Tiverton:
    i.   Mahalah, b. 23 June 1787; m. (--) King.
    ii.   Burgess Thomas, b. 30 Aug. 1788.
    iii. Pardon, b. 1 Sept. 1791.
45. iv.   Abel, b. 27 Feb. 1794.
    v.   Martha, b. 21 Dec. 1794; m. Benjamin Simmons, son of William and Rebecca (Sowle) Simmons of LC, b. 29 Feb. 1796.
    vi.   Phebe, m. Pardon Hart.
    vii. Anna, m. (--) King.
    viii. Permilla (Pamelia), m. 16 March 1823 David Wilbor of LC, son of Hezekiah and Alice (Palmer) Wilbor.
46. ix.   William L., b. 6 July 1809.
    x.   Ichabod, d. 11 Nov. 1831 ae 28 in Tiverton; m. Bathsheba Albert, widow of his brother William, b. 6 May 1810.

39. LINDALL[7] SIMMONS (Nathaniel[6], Isaac[5], William[4], William[3], John[2], Moses[1]), born in LC 26 Oct. 1783, died there 5 Sept. 1866.

He was married first in LC 23 Jan. 1806 by the Rev. Mase Shepard
to MARY TAYLOR, daughter of Philip and Mary (Gray) Taylor, born
in LC 27 Jan. 1775, died 19 March 1844. He was married second in
LC 30 Sept. 1844 by the Rev. Daniel Webb to LYDIA (PALMER) CHURCH,
daughter of Job and Lydia Palmer, born in LC 1796, died there 23 May
1857. All are buried in the Union cemetery.

They lived on the place in district No. 2 marked A.S. Simmons on
the map of 1870.

His will, recorded LC Wills, book 11, page 437, made 10 Dec. 1860
and proved 8 Oct. 1866: "... To children of Alden Simmons, Philip
Simmons, Mary S. Wilbor, Nathaniel Simmons and Eliza T. Church, all
household furniture except my desk. To son Alden Simmons my desk.
To son Nathaniel Simmons my wearing apparel. To son Philip Simmons
wood lot I bought of son Nathaniel. To heirs of wife Lydia C. Simmons,
deceased, 700 dollars. To her daughter Lydia C. Knapp 200 dollars and
daughter Elizabeth T. Coggeshalle 500 dollars and her granddaughter,
Maria D. Knapp, 50 dollars and grandson Joseph C. Coggeshalle 50 dollars.
To children of Alden Simmons, Mary C. Wilbor, Daniel Simmons and
Eliza Church, 250 dollars. To son Philip Simmons my homestead farm
and rest and residue... "

The will of Lydia Simmons, recorded book 11, page 116, made
7 Jan. 1857 and proved 13 July 1857: "... To daughter Lydia Knapp
my bureau given to me by George Briggs. To granddaughter Maria
Knapp a bed and bedstead. To grandson Joseph Coggeshalle my secretary
and nine teaspoons. To grandson Joseph Church, son of Nathaniel, my
Cottage Bible. To daughter Elizabeth Coggeshalle rest and residue of
all personal estate... "

Children by first wife, recorded in LC:

46. i.   Alden Southworth, b. 20 Dec. 1809.
    ii.   Mary, b. 21 Nov. 1811; m. (1) 5 Dec. 1727 Thomas K. Weston,
        b. 20 Feb. 1795; m. (2) 25 March 1835 Isaac Wilbor of
        Newport.
    iii.   Philip, b. 3 Jan. 1814; m. Abby H. (--).
    iv.   Nathaniel, b. 1 Jan. 1816; m. Annie H. (--). Residence:
        Newport.
    v.   Eliza Taylor, b. 23 Jan. 1818; d. in LC 16 March 1897; m.
        there 2 May 1741 Deacon George Church.

40. JOHN⁷ SIMMONS (Benoni⁶, John⁵, Joseph⁴, William³, John²,
Moses¹), born in LC 30 Oct. 1796, died there 30 Aug. 1870.

He married in Boston 29 Oct. 1818 ANN SMALL of Provincetown,
Mass., born 1 Sept. 1797, died in Boston 30 May 1861. He was the
founder of Simmons College of Boston, where he made his home.

Children, born in Boston:

    i.   Mary Ann, b. 4 Oct. 1819; d. 17 April 1887 in Wasladen,
        Germany; m. (1) George L. Ditson; m. (2) William Arnold
        Buffum.
    ii.   John, b. 14 Nov. 1820; d. 4 April 1846; m. 22 May 1843 Martha
        Vinton.
    iii.   Lorenzo, b. 3 April 1822; d. 9 Feb. 1841.

Infant portrait of

JOHN SIMMONS

Founder of Simmons College

The painting is in the Wilbor House
of the Little Compton Historical
Society, a gift of Mr. and Mrs.
P. B. Simonds (Sr.), who were
owners of the old Simmons homestead
on the West Road.

iv. Alvina, b. 11 Feb. 1824; d. 4 April 1886; m. Edward White,
     d. 13 May 1891.
v. Theodore Augustus, b. 10 April 1828; d. 8 Feb. 1829.
vi. Theodore, b. 22 March 1829; d. 13 May 1858; m. 6 Jan. 1850
     Harriet W. Jackson.

41. VALENTINE[7] SIMMONS (Benoni[6], John[5], Joseph[4], William[3],
John[2], Moses[1]), born in LC 19 April 1802, died there 22 Sept. 1885.
    He married first in LC 20 Aug. 1826 MARY ANN LOMBARD,
born 14 Nov. 1809, died in LC 23 March 1843. He married second in
LC 29 Aug. 1844 LYDIA BAILEY, daughter of William and Susanna
Bailey, born in LC 17 Dec. 1804, died there 18 May 1893. They are
buried in the New Wilbor cemetery or Seaconnet Cemetery.

    Children by first wife:
i. Benonie, b. 4 Dec. 1828; d. 20 May 1850.
ii. Peter Lombard, b. 9 May 1831; m. 11 Jan. 1858 Annie M.
     Stearns.
iii. Helena Antoinette, b. in Boston 16 June 1833; m. in LC 5
     November 1855 Francis T. Church, son of Nathal and
     Sarah Church.
iv. Mary Ann, b. 7 Aug. 1835; d. in Providence 21 Feb. 1863;
     m. in LC 5 Nov. 1855 George R. Drowne, son of Henry
     and Julia Drowne, b. 14 May 1835, d. 19 May 1902.
v. Valentine, b. 19 Feb. 1838; d. in LC 28 Dec. 1843.
48. vi. Frank Wells, b. 9 Sept. 1839.
vii. Josephine Alvina, b. in LC 1 Aug. 1841; d. in Newton, Mass.,
     6 Nov. 1916; m. in LC 25 Nov. 1868 George R. Drowne,
     son of Henry and Julia Drowne.

Children by second wife:
viii. Anna Kempton, b. 16 Sept. 1845; d. 15 May 1917; m. 25 Dec.
      1875 Isaac B. Cowen, son of Jesse H. and Ann Cowen, b.
      in Canadaigua, N.Y. 16 March 1853, d. in LC 23 March
      1886.
ix.   Valentine, b. 19 Dec. 1847; d. 24 July 1890; unmarried.

42. HENRY BRIGHTMAN[7] SIMMONS (Stephen[6], John[5], John[4],
William[3], John[2], Moses[1]), born in LC 11 June 1800, died 12 May
1888 ae 87.
   He was married first in LC 18 Nov. 1821 by Thomas Burgess,
justice, to SARAH SEABURY, daughter of Gideon and Betsey Seabury,
born in LC 4 July 1794, died there 21 March 1850. He married second
LOUISE V. MacLANE, daughter of Thomas and Sarah MacLane, died
in LC 25 Oct. 1860 ae 54. He married third PHEBE M. DOW of
Nantucket, Mass., born 20 June 1827, died 12 May 1895. All are buried
in the New Commons cemetery.

      Children:
i.   Lurana, b. 22 June 1822; d. 28 Feb. 1850.
ii.   Eliza B., b. 5 Jan. 1825; d. in LC 9 Sept. 1902; m. there 19
      May 1851 Henry T. Brown, son of Christopher and Deborah
      Brown. He was postmaster of LC.
iii. Frederic S., b. 29 March 1827; d. in LC in June 1866; m. there
      5 Sept. 1849 Caroline Copland of Tiverton.
iv.   Henry, b. 30 Dec. 1829. Residence: Fall River.
v.   Stephen, b. 19 May 1834.
vi.   Betsey, b. 11 July 1837; m. in LC 19 Feb. 1861 William Mason
      of Fall River, son of J. B. and Mary Mason, b. in 1822.
vii. Charlotte, b. 24 June 1840; m. Henry Weeks.

The grave of

VALENTINE
SIMMONS

and his family
in the
Wilbour Cemetery
on the West Road.

43. BENJAMIN[7] SIMMONS (William[6], Samuel[5], Benjamin[4], William[3], John[2], Moses[1]), born in LC 29 Feb. 1796, died in Fall River 4 Jan. 1842.

He married in LC 12 Jan. 1822 MARTHA SIMMONS, daughter of Ichabod and Anna (Thomas) Simmons of Tiverton, born in Tiverton 29 Dec. 1794, died in LC 11 June 1849. Residence: LC and Fall River.

Children, recorded in LC:
- i.   William Taylor, d. 21 May 1822; d. 16 Dec. 1824.
- 49. ii.   William Taylor 2d, b. 4 June 1825.
- iii.   George Clarke, b. 24 April 1827; d. in LC 2 Aug. 1905; m. Ida A. Mosher, daughter of Caleb and Mary (Crosby) Mosher.
- 50. iv.   Henry, b. 13 May 1830.
- v.   Hannah Wilbor, b. 8 April 1837; m. Thomas Grinnell.

44. ELISHA[7] SIMMONS (William[6], Samuel[5], Benjamin[4], William[3], John[2], Moses[1]), born in LC 2 May 1810. He married there 1 Dec. 1834 MERCY SIMMONS, born in Fairhaven, Mass., 15 July 1810.

Children, recorded in LC:
- i.   Elisha, b. 30 Nov. 1835.

45. ABEL[7] SIMMONS (Ichabod[6], Thomas[5], Peleg[4], William[3], John[2], Moses[1]), born in Tiverton 27 Feb. 1794, died in LC 1 July 1856.

He married in LC 5 Dec. 1819 LYDIA C. PEARCE, daughter of Isaac and Susanna (Stoddard) Pearce, born in LC 22 Dec. 1794, died there 15 March 1862. Both are buried in the Old Commons cemetery.

Residence: LC. They lived on Willow Avenue, called Pudding Bag Lane in 1850.

In his will, recorded in LC Probate, book 11, page 95, made 5 Aug. 1854 and proved 11 Aug. 1856, he left to his wife Lydia all estate both real and personal.

Her will, recorded LC Probate, book 11, page 291, made 1 Aug. 1861 and proved 14 April 1862: ". . . To son Albert Simmons, note which I hold against him and 100 dollars. To son Frederic Simmons, note I hold against him. To grandson Walter Simmons 200 dollars. To the Congregational Church 50 dollars, to remain in perpetual fund. To four children, Orin Simmons, Alexander Simmons, Jane Brownell and Susan Wilbor, the rest and residue. . . "

Children, born in LC:
- i.   Walter, b. 29 Jan. 1813; d. 3 Nov. 1845; unmarried.
- 51. ii.   Orin Wheaten, b. 3 July 1815.
- 52. iii.   Alexander, b. 5 May 1817.
- iv.   Jane, b. 4 Sept. 1819; m. Frederic Brownell.
- v.   B. Wilson, b. 15 Feb. 1822; d. 18 Dec. 1842; unmarried.
- vi.   Andrew, b. 24 Dec. 1824; d. 26 Oct. 1845; unmarried.
- 53. vii.   Albert, b. 13 May 1827.
- viii.   Susan, b. 28 Dec. 1832; d. 7 Feb. 1883; m. 14 May 1857 William Andrew Wilbor, son of Clark and Luranna

(Taylor) Wilbor.
ix.   Frederic H.

46. WILLIAM L.[7] SIMMONS (Ichabod[6], Thomas[5], Peleg[4], William[3], John[2], Moses[1]), born 6 July 1809, died 12 May 1885, buried in Pleasant View cemetery.

He married BATHSHEBA ALBERT, widow of his brother Ichabod, born 6 May 1810, died 25 July 1894. Residence: Tiverton.

Children, born in Tiverton:
i.   James, m. Phebe Tabor.
ii.   William B., b. in 1832; m. Cornelia Grinnell.
iii.   Cynthia M., b. 6 May 1834; d. in LC 9 Sept. 1908; m. Cornelius
        King Jr., son of Cornelius and Deborah (Dennis) King, d.
        in May 1907.
iv.   Ichabod, b. 1 Oct. 1838; d. 27 April 1852.
v.   Anna, b. 4 Dec. 1840; d. 4 Oct. 1870.
vi.   Permilia M., d. in LC 3 Feb. 1905; m. Philip J. Gray.
vii.   Martha, m. Charles H. Tripp.
54. viii. David, b. in 1842.
ix.   Zillah, m. Job Herbert Wilcox.

47. ALDEN SOUTHWORTH[8] SIMMONS (Lindall[7], Nathaniel[6], Isaac[5], William[4], William[3], John[2], Moses[1]), born in LC 20 Dec. 1809, died there 16 Dec. 1883.

He married first ELIZA T. BARTLETT, born 31 July 1811 in Plymouth, died 1 May 1864 in Newport. He and his first wife are buried in the Union cemetery. He married second RUTH S. (--), born in 1816. They lived on the place marked A.S. Simmonson on the map of 1870, later owned by Stuart Carton.

Children, recorded in LC:
i.   Mary, b. in 1838; d. in 1924; m. (1) 25 Nov. 1866 George
        Briggs Wilbor, b. 27 Aug. 1836, d. 12 April 1879; m.
        (2) 13 March 1882 Nelson B. Hinckley.

48. FRANK WELLS[8] SIMMONS (Valentine[7], Benoni[6], John[5], Joseph[4], William[3], John[2], Moses[1]), born in LC 9 Sept. 1839, died there 22 March 1884.

He married first LIZZIE GAY. They had no children. He married second in LC 11 Sept. 1872 HARRIET MILFORD TAYLOR, daughter of George Milford and Sarah J. (Dean) Taylor, born in LC 5 May 1850.

Residence: LC. They lived on the place in district No. 2 marked F. W. Simmons on the map of 1870.

Children by second wife, recorded in LC:
i.   Josephine Taylor, b. in LC 22 June 1873; m. there 12 June
        1895 Lysander W. Manchester, son of Forbes and Rhoda
        Manchester.
ii.   Minnie Church, b. in LC 20 Oct. 1875; m. there 26 Oct. 1897
        Alfred Huntington Burnham, son of Henry F. and Sophia
        (Bennet) Burnham, b. in Norwich, Conn.
iii.   Hattie Frank, b. 2 Sept. 1877; d. in LC 31 May 1879 ae 1.

iv.   Valentine, b. in LC 21 June 1880; m. (1) 17 Nov. 1909 Ruth
        Anna Roberts; m. (2) in LC 27 June 1942 Louise Howard,
        daughter of George T. and Julianna (Peckham) Howard,
        b. in LC 1 June 1884.
v.   Helena Antoinette, b. 12 Dec. 1882; d. 14 May 1886 ae 3.

49. WILLIAM TAYLOR[8] SIMMONS (Benjamin[7], William[6], Samuel[5],
Benjamin[4], William[3], John[2], Moses[1]), born 4 June 1825, died in LC 15
March 1904, buried in Pleasant View cemetery.

He married in LC 21 Dec. 1850 SARAH WILBOR DYER, daughter
of John and Hannah (Wilbor) Dyer, born in Westport 26 July 1827, died
in LC 24 Sept. 1883.

Residence: LC. They lived at Clapp's Corner on the place marked
W. T. Simmons on the map of 1870.

Children, recorded in LC:
i.   Martha Jane, b. 31 Jan. 1852; m. in Tiverton 3 Jan. 1872
        Thomas Frank Manchester, son of Thomas and Catharine
        Manchester.
55. ii.   William Taylor Jr., b. 9 July 1855.
iii.   Evelyn Josephine, b. in LC 10 Sept. 1857; d. 15 Oct. 1948; m.
        in LC 14 March 1877 William Clarke Wilbor, son of
        Ichabod and Deborah (Brownell) Wilbor.
56. iv.   Benjamin Herbert, b. 9 May 1859.
v.   George Arthur, b. 21 Jan. 1861; d. 25 March 1863 ae 2.
vi.   Frank Ellsworth, b. 27 March 1862; d. in 1897; m. Annie H.
        Palmer. Residence: Fall River.
vii.   Abbie Hannah, b. 16 Dec. 1865; m. (1) Warren Corey; m. (2)
        in Providence Herbert Thompson of Providence.

50. HENRY L.[8] SIMMONS (Benjamin[7], William[6], Samuel[5], Benjamin[4],
William[3], John[2], Moses[1]), born in LC 13 May 1830, died in 1925. He
married SUSAN M. DYER, born in 1838, died in 1928. Residence: Westport.

Children:
i.   Charles Leander, b. in Westport 3 June 1851; d. in LC 6 June
        1915; m. 11 Aug. 1897 Bertha Hoxie Wilbor, daughter of
        George Henry and Georgianna (Wilbor) Wilbor, b. 22 Oct.
        1880.
ii.   Richmond M., b. 24 May 1859 in Westport; d. in LC 14 Nov.
        1927.
iii.   Martha S., b. in 1865; may have m. George W. Hubbard.

51. ORIN WHEATON[6] SIMMONS (Abel[7], Ichabod[6], Thomas[5],
Thomas[4], William[3], John[2], Moses[1]), born in LC 3 July 1815, died
there 18 April 1915, ae almost 100.

He married first in LC 4 April 1838 PRISCILLA BROWNELL,
daughter of Christopher and Sarah (Taylor) Brownell, born in LC 3
Feb. 1816, died 20 April 1858. He married second 8 Jan. 1863 MARY
B. TAYLOR, daughter of John and Elizabeth Taylor and widow of David
Shaw, born in LC 24 Feb. 1819, died in Providence 17 Feb. 1899. All
are buried in the Old Commons cemetery.

Residence: LC. They lived on the place marked O. W. Simmons
on the map of 1870, on the road south of the Swamp Road to Shaw Road.

Children by first wife, born in LC:
i.   George B., b. in 1839; d. 28 April 1859; unmarried.
ii.   James Pearce, b. in LC 28 July 1840; d. 15 Feb. 1932 ae 91;
      unmarried.
iii. Maria W., b. in LC 19 March 1842; d. 21 April 1898; m. in
      LC 15 Sept. 1863 Thomas E. White, son of David and
      Patience (Brown) White.
iv.   Harlan P., b. 27 Jan. 1843; lost at sea 2 Dec. 1865; unmarried.
v.   Franklin H., b. 28 May 1847; d. ae 10 months.
vi.   Oliver Emerson, b. 15 March 1848; d. 12 Jan. 1906; unmarried.
vii. Mary S., b. 16 Sept. 1850; d. 14 Sept. 1851.
57. viii. Abel Brownell, b. 15 Aug. 1852.

52. ALEXANDER C.[8] SIMMONS (Abel[7], Ichabod[6], Thomas[5], Peleg[4],
William[3], John[2], Moses[1]), born in LC 5 May 1817, died there 23 Oct.
1894.
      He was married 25 Dec. 1842 in LC by the Rev. Alfred Goldsmith to
CLARINDA BURGESS, daughter of Peter T. and Permelia (Bailey)
Burgess, born in LC 12 Nov. 1820, died 11 Nov. 1898. Both are buried
in the Union cemetery.

Children, last two recorded in LC:
i.   Edward Wilson, b. 25 June 1844; m. Adelaide (--). Residence:
      Jamaica Plain, Mass., in 1899.
58. ii. Charles Leonard, b. 26 Aug. 1846.
iii. Mary Jane, b. 22 June 1853; m. in LC 19 Dec. 1876 Frank Newman
      Brownell, son of Oliver C. and Ann (Bailey) Brownell, b. 28
      March 1851.
iv.   Clara Permelia, b. in LC 2 Sept. 1858; d. there 13 Sept. 1928;
      m. there 1 Dec. 1897 Henry Augustus Groth, son of Charles
      Augustus and Rose (Seamon) Groth, b. in New York City 5
      Jan. 1858, d. in LC 14 Dec. 1936.

53. ALBERT[8] SIMMONS (Abel[7], Ichabod[6], Thomas[5], Peleg[4], William[3],
John[2], Moses[1]), born in LC 13 May 1827, died there 3 Oct. 1901.
      He married first SARAH TOLLES. He married second in LC 19
June 1872 DIANNA BROWNELL, daughter of Charles and Susan (Gifford)
Brownell, born in LC 8 April 1839, died there 14 March 1895. He and
his second wife are buried in the New Commons cemetery. Residence:
LC.

Children by first wife, recorded in LC:
i.   Francis, b. in LC 8 Sept. 1855.

Children by second wife:
ii.   Susan Brownell, b. in LC 4 Dec. 1874.

54. DAVID[8] SIMMONS (William[7], Ichabod[6], Thomas[5], Peleg[4],
William[3], John[2], Moses[1]), born in Tiverton 12 Aug. 1852, died there
3 Feb. 1942. Residence: Tiverton.
      He married first GRACE A. GRINNELL, born in 1846, died in

1899. He married second LILLY E. TERRY, born in 1866.

Children by first wife:

i.   Lottie Gertrude, b. in 1866; d. in Tiverton 3 March 1932;
      m. 9 May 1894 Frank Sylvanus Wilbor, b. 29 June 1852,
      d. 13 Nov. 1936.

ii.   Frederick Almy, b. 5 Nov. 1876; m. 10 Nov. 1897 Hattie
      Lucia Cook, b. 28 Dec. 1877, d. 6 Aug. 1951.

iii. Philip G., b. 11 Aug. 1882; m. 17 March 1919 Dora
      Mason (Jason) Allen of Tiverton, daughter of Alonso
      and Dora (Mason) Jason, b. in New Bedford 23 May
      1892.

iv.   Lester, m. Daisy Manchester of Milford.

v.   Alice B., m. William Allen of Westport.

vi.   Permilia G., m. Clifton Hart of Tiverton.

vii. Clara Edna, m. Frederick B. Whiting of Fall River.

viii. Helen Richards, b. in 1876 (?); m. 9 Nov. 1910 Stewart
      F. Pierce of Tiverton.

Children by second wife:

ix.   Evelyn Young, b. 25 July 1902; m. 9 Nov. 1924 Roger G.
      Hart, b. 28 March 1904.

x.   (?), m. Warren H. Waite.

55. WILLIAM TAYLOR[9] SIMMONS (William[8], Benjamin[7], William[6]
Samuel[5], Benjamin[4], William[3], John[2], Moses[1]), born in LC 9 July 1855,
died there 9 March 1921.

He married in Tiverton 10 Dec. 1876 LUCY FULLER GRINNELL,
daughter of Stephen and Rosella (Fuller) Grinnell of Tiverton, born
in Tiverton 31 Jan. 1860, died in Fall River 27 Aug. 1941. They lived
at Clapp's Corner in LC.

Children, born in LC:

59. i.   William Taylor 3d, b. 2 Oct. 1878.

ii. Sadie Ethel, b. in February 1880; d. in LC 21 March 1901;
     m. 11 Sept. 1898 William Borden Manchester, son of
     Owen and Sarah (Borden) Manchester.

60. iii. George Franklin, b. 25 May 1882.

iv. Roscoe Emerson, b. 18 Aug. 1884; m. (1) 8 Oct. 1907
     Florence Irene (Harrington) Barker, daughter of Samuel
     and Sophia (Lake) Harrington, b. in Leavenworth, Kan.;
     m. (2) in LC 9 Sept. 1940 Annis Smith, daughter of John
     and Elizabeth (Corbishley) Smith, b. 2 Oct. 1890, d. in
     Cranston 21 April 1953.

v.   Esther Louise, b. in 1886; m. 14 June 1906 William Hall
     Wood, son of George and Alice (Hall) Wood, d. in Fall
     River.

vi. Susan Morand, m. 14 Oct. 1906 in Tiverton Nathaniel Levi
     Sisson of Westport, son of John and Susan (Dring) Sisson.

vii. Royal Kenton, b. in LC 7 Feb. 1894; m. Rita Sousa.

viii. Icie, b. in LC 13 March 1896; m. in LC Robert Smith.

ix. Mattie Frank, b. in LC 8 Dec. 1896; m. (1) in LC 14 Aug.
     1917 Edward LeRoy Manchester, son of Ernest and Lizzie

(Wilbor) Manchester, b. in LC 9 May 1894, d. there 28
June 1925; m. (2) (--) Fuller.
x.   Son, b. 8 Dec. 1899.

56. BENJAMIN HERBERT[9] SIMMONS (William[8], Benjamin[7],
William[6], Samuel[5], Benjamin[4], William[3], John[2], Moses[1]), born in LC
9 May 1859, died there 18 Aug. 1943.
He married HULDA ANN WILBOR, daughter of Solomon and
Esther (Palmer) Wilbor, born in LC 18 Dec. 1865, died there 14 Sept.
1941. Residence: LC.

Children, recorded in LC:
i.   Cora Belle, b. in LC 11 Oct. 1887; d. there 12 April 1924;
      m. Isaac Cowen Bliss, son of Adniram and Mary (Hathaway)
      Bliss, b. 11 Jan. 1882.
ii.   Harold Stephen, b. 5 Feb. 1891 in LC; m. in Putnam, Conn.,
      29 Aug. 1927 Lillian Etta Carter, daughter of William
      and Mary Etta (Henry or Hedley) Carter, b. in 1891.

57. ABEL BROWNELL[9] SIMMONS (Orin[8], Abel[7], Ichabod[6], Thomas[5],
Peleg[4], William[3], John[2], Moses[1]), born in LC 15 Aug. 1852, died there
12 June 1937.
He married in LC 22 Nov. 1878 HARRIET ELIZABETH LITTLE,
daughter of Benjamin and Sarah (Lawton) Little, born in Westport 5
Jan. 1861, died in LC 9 Aug. 1906.
Residence: LC. They lived on the place formerly owned by his
father, Orin Simmons, and marked on the map of 1870 as the O. W.
Simmons place. The road leads from Swamp Road to Shaw Road.

Children, born in LC:
61. i.   George Harlan, b. in LC 21 March 1881; d. in LC 31 March
         1952; m. in LC 18 Sept. 1907 Lottie Annie Wilcox, daughter
         of Peleg and Lizzie Pierce (Dodge) Wilcox.

58. CHARLES LEONARD[9] SIMMONS (Alexander[8], Abel[7],
Ichabod[6], Thomas[5], Peleg[4], William[3], John[2], Moses[1]), born in LC 26
Aug. 1846. Residence: Fall River.
He married in LC 25 Dec. 1872 GEORGIANNA AMELIA WILBOR,
daughter of Ezra and Mary Tew (Marble) Wilbor, born in LC 23 May
1848.

Children:
62. i.   Leonard Wilbor, b. in LC 1 Oct. 1877; d. in Fall River 1947/8;
         m. 2 July 1921 Susan Sanford Taber, daughter of Cornelius
         and Cynthia Tompkins (Case) Taber.

59. WILLIAM TAYLOR[10] SIMMONS 3d (William[9], William[8],
Benjamin[7], William[6], Benjamin[5], Samuel[4], William[3], John[2], Moses[1]),
born in LC 2 Oct. 1878. He married in Tiverton 19 Sept. 1897
HARRIET WEBB MANCHESTER, daughter of Owen and Sarah
(Borden) Manchester, born in LC 12 Aug. 1876, died there 16 Nov.
1920.

Children, recorded in LC:

i.   Ruth Bailey, b. in LC 20 April 1898; m. George Pearson.
ii.   Raymond, b. 22 June 1900; m. 14 June 1930 in Westport
      Mildred Nickeson of Westport, daughter of Ahira and
      Sara (Sabrius) Nickeson.
63. iii. Colson Orville, b. 22 Sept. 1903.
64. iv.   Howell William, b. 27 Nov. 1905.
    v.   Melba Alice, b. 17 May 1908; m. in LC 5 March 1931
          Samuel Sowle West, son of William and Lottie (Sowle)
          West, b. in LC 15 Feb. 1905.
    vi.   Hazel Ethel, b. 8 Dec. 1910; m. Charles Borden.
65. vii. Thornton Owen, b. 24 May 1913.
    viii. Harriet Fuller, b. 1 May 1916; m. Wallace Dinsmore.

60. GEORGE FRANKLIN[10] SIMMONS (William[9], William[8],
Benjamin[7], William[6], Samuel[5], Benjamin[4], William[3], John[2], Moses[1]),
born in LC 25 May 1883, died in Cranston 21 April 1953.

He married first in LC 18 Oct. 1908 ALICE WHALLEY, daughter
of William and Ann (Riding) Whalley, born in Tiverton 4 May 1878,
died in LC 9 June 1925. He married second in LC 6 Aug. 1925
MILDRED CELIA ALBRO, daughter of Henry and Margaret (Cohen)
Albro of Fall River, born in Fall River 1 Feb. 1906.

Children by first wife, born in LC:

66. i.   Myron Franklin, b. 29 Oct. 1908.
    ii. Lois Dorance, b. in LC 26 May 1912.
    iii. Marjorie Alice, b. in LC 18 April 1917.

Children by second wife:

    iv. Edmund F., b. 7 April 1927 in Fall River.
    v.   Shirley Margaret, b. in Fall River 27 May 1933; m. in LC
         3 Feb. 1951 George Silvia Medeiros, son of Jose S. and
         Mary (Mello) Medeiros, b. in LC 17 Sept. 1925.

61. GEORGE HARLAN[10] SIMMONS (Abel[9], Orin[8], Abel[7], Ichabod[6],
Thomas[5], Peleg[4], William[3], John[2], Moses[1]), born in LC 21 March
1881, died there 31 March 1952.

He married 18 Sept. 1907 LOTTIE ANNIE WILCOX, daughter of
Peleg and Lizzie Pierce (Dodge) Wilcox of Tiverton, born in Tiverton
6 Aug. 1883. Residence: LC. They lived on the place marked O. W.
Simmons on the map of 1870.

Children, recorded in LC:

i.   Doris Elizabeth, b. in LC 14 July 1910.

62. LEONARD WILBUR[10] SIMMONS (Charles[9], Alexander[8], Abel[7],
Ichabod[6], Thomas[5], Peleg[4], William[3], John[2], Moses[1]), born in LC
1 Oct. 1877, died in Fall River in 1947/8.

He married in LC 2 July 1921 SUSAN SANFORD TABER, daughter
of Cornelius and Cynthia (Tompkins) (Case) Taber, born in LC 29
April 1886. Residence: Fall River.

Children:

i.   Charles Leonard, b. 20 March 1923.
ii.   Edward Taber, b. 20 April 1924.

63. COLSON ORVILLE[11] SIMMONS (William[10], William[9], William[8], Benjamin[7], William[6], Benjamin[5], Samuel[4], William[3], John[2], Moses[1]), born in LC 22 Sept. 1903. He married in Tiverton 15 Sept. 1928 GLADYS IRENE PECKHAM, daughter of William E. and Wedie (Stanbrige) Peckham, born in New Bedford 26 May 1910. Residence: LC.

Children:
i.   Norma Jean, b. in Fall River 24 Oct. 1932.
ii. Colson Orville Jr., b. in Fall River 25 April 1938.

64. HOWELL WILLIAM[11] SIMMONS (William[10], William[9], William[8], Benjamin[7], William[6], Benjamin[5], Samuel[4], William[3], John[2], Moses[1]), born in LC 27 Nov. 1905. He married there 5 March 1931 ELIZABETH M. BURKE. Residence: LC.

Children:
i.   Howell William Jr., b. in Fall River 7 Jan. 1943.

65. THORTON OWEN[11] SIMMONS (William[10], William[9], William[8], Benjamin[7], William[6], Benjamin[5], Samuel[4], William[3], John[2], Moses[1]), born in LC 24 May 1913. He married in Swansea 4 July 1939 GERTRUDE L. MURPHY, daughter of Charles Reed and Cora (Ryan) Murphy. Residence: LC.

Children:
i.   Thornton Jr., b. 28 Jan. 1943.
ii. (?), b. 24 Sept. 1945.

66. MYRON FRANKLIN[11] SIMMONS (George[10], William[9], William[8], Benjamin[7], William[6], Samuel[5], Benjamin[4], William[3], John[2], Moses[1]), born in LC 29 Oct. 1908. He married there 24 Feb. 1926 MARY CARRAVALHO OLIVEIRA, daughter of Jose A. and Rosa (Medeiras) Oliveira, born in Fall River 10 Oct. 1906. Residence: LC.

Children, recorded in LC:
i.   Alice, 15 Jan. 1927 in Fall River; d. 22 Feb. 1927.
ii.   Doris May, b. 5 May 1928; m. in LC 28 Sept. 1946 Harold
      Arthur Sawyer, son of Harold and Bridgett (Tobin) Sawyer,
      b. in Yonkers, N.H., 19 Aug. 1916.
iii. Ethel Louise, b. 17 July 1929; m. in LC 15 May 1948 Antone
      Rodriges, son of Zalmiro and Emelinda (Barbosa)
      Rodriges, b. 2 Aug. 1925.
iv.   Ellen, b. in LC 23 June 1931.
v.   Phillis Jane, b. 26 Aug. 1932 in LC; m. there 11 Oct. 1952
      George Lewis Mello, son of Joseph and Gloria Dutra
      (Mello), b. in Fall River 17 Feb. 1926.
vi.   Jeanette Delores, b. in LC 2 April 1935; m. 10 Oct. 1953
      Leo Wilfred Gagne Jr., son of Leo and Annie (Hall) Gagne
      of Fall River.
vii. Myron Franklin Jr., b. in Fall River 29 Aug. 1939.
viii. Betty A., b. in Fall River 2 April 1945.
ix.   Elizabeth A.

. . . .

PERRY SIMMONS, son of Peleg and Eliphal, born in 1783, died in
LC 17 Oct. 1853. He married there 1 April 1804 LYDIA STODDARD,
daughter of Brownell and Hannah Stoddard, born 12 Feb. 1780, died 30
May 1868. Residence: Tiverton and LC.

Her will, recorded book 11, page 516, made 18 Nov. 1859 and
proved 1 June 1868: ". . . To daughter Hannah S. Gifford a small bureau
and my earrings; to above daughter and granddaughter Sarah J. Deplick
all my wearing apparel; to grandson Benjamin Simmons, son of Brownell,
one chest; to Charles H. Turner one bed; to son Perry Simmons all
real estate; to son Philip all real and personal estate at death of son
Perry and he to have rest and residue. . . "

Children:

i.   Philip, b. in 1815; d. 15 Aug. 1881.
ii.   Brownell, b. in 1817.
iii.   Perry, b. in 1820; m. 27 Aug. 1857 Eliza Clarke, daughter
        of Daniel and Sarah (Davis) Clarke, widow of (--) Pearce.
iv.   Hannah S., m. (1) (--) Records; m. (2) 27 Aug. 1857 George
        W. Gifford, son of Ebenezer and Susan Gifford of Westport.

Other records of the Simmons family include Philip and Dianna
Simmons, parents of Diantha B. Simmons, born in 1860, married in
LC 2 May 1885 Thomas Gibbs, son of George and Mary Gibbs, born
in 1856.

There are gravestones in the cemetery at the Old Stone Church for
Emeline Simmons, who died 11 Dec. 1847 in her 40th year, and her
husband, Philip Simmons, who died 15 Aug. 1881 ae 74-1-23.

An Amy Simmons of LC was the mother of James Simmons, born
26 May 1780.

Benjamin Simmons, died 21 April 1862 ae 51-11-21. He married
Nancy (--), who died 12 Dec. 1895 ae 95-1-15.

Children:

i.   Flora Helena, d. 28 Dec. 1800 ae 17-2-17.
ii.   Eliza J., m. (--) Wood.
iii.   Otis B.
iv.   Joseph.
v.   Albert.
vi.   Giles H.

THE SISSON FAMILY

See Representative Men Old Families of Southeastern Massachusetts, page 1655.

1. RICHARD[1] SISSON, born in 1608, died in 1684, married MARY (--), died in 1692. Residence: Portsmouth and Dartmouth.

2. JAMES[2] SISSON (Richard[1]), born in 1662, died in 1734. He married LYDIA HATHAWAY, daughter of John and Sarah (Cook) Hathaway, died in 1714. Residence: Dartmouth.

3. RICHARD[3] SISSON (James[2], Richard[1]), born 19 Feb. 1682, died in 1704. He married in 1704 MEHITABEL (--). Residence: Dartmouth.

4. RICHARD[4] SISSON (Richard[3], James[2], Richard[1]), born 17 July 1705, died in Dartmouth 20 June 1790. He married first ALICE SOULE, daughter of William and Hannah (Brewster) Soule, born 15 Feb. 1705, died 1 Feb. 1731. He married second 15 Nov. 1739 ELIZABETH TAYLOR, daughter of John and Joanna (Wilbor) Taylor, born in LC 5 Jan. 1717. Residence: Dartmouth.

5. PHILIP[5] SISSON (Richard[4], Richard[3], James[2], Richard[1]), born 24 March 1740. He married 1 May 1763 HOPE ANTHONY of Dartmouth.

6. PELEG[6] SISSON (Philip[5], Richard[4], Richard[3], James[2], Richard[1]), born 23 June 1773, died in Westport 25 Oct. 1826. He married in Dartmouth 12 June 1793 HANNAH BROWNELL, daughter of George and Rhoda (Milk) Brownell, born in Westport in 1771.

7. GREENE BRADFORD[7] SISSON (Peleg[6], Philip[5], Richard[4], Richard[3], James[2], Richard[1]), born in Westport 9 Nov. 1796, died in LC 3 Aug. 1854. He married 26 March 1815 HOPE POTTER, daughter of Edward and Betsey Potter of Westport, born in Westport 18 July 1798, died in Pawtucket, R.I., 24 Sept. 1886. Residence: Westport and LC.

. . . .

1. RICHARD[1] SISSON, born in 1608, died in 1684. He married MARY (--), died in 1692. He was surveyor of the highways. Residence: Portsmouth and Dartmouth.

His will, made 18 Oct. 1683 and proved 26 Feb. 1684: ". . . To wife Mary my house and movables during her life. To son James all my housing and land in Dartmouth with reservations for wife, land near Pogansett Pond. To daughter Ann Tripp and her husband Peleg land near Pogansett. To son John all my land and a house in Portsmouth. To son George five pounds in money. To daughter Elizabeth Allen, wife of Caleb Allen, five pounds. To Indian servant Samuel a two year old mare. To grandchild Mary Sisson three cows and a bed. . . one pewter flagon, and brass kettle which was her Aunt Mary's. . . "

The will of his wife Mary is listed in Austin's Dictionary.

Children:
2. i.   George, b. in 1644.
    ii.   Elizabeth, m. 8 April 1670 Caleb Allen, son of George and
          Hannah Allen.
    iii. James, d. in 1734; m. Lydia Hathaway, daughter of Arthur
          and Sarah (Cook) Hathaway, b. in 1662, d. 23 June 1714.
    iv.   John, d. about 1687; m. Mary (--).
    v.   Anne, d. after 1713; m. Peleg Tripp, son of John and Mary
          (Paine) Tripp, b. about 1642, d. 13 Jan. 1714.
    vi.   Mary, d. in 1674; m. Isaac Lawton, son of Thomas Lawton,
          b. 11 Dec. 1650; d. 26 Jan. 1732.

2. GEORGE² SISSON (Richard¹), born in 1644, died 7 Sept. 1718.
He married in Portsmouth 1 Aug. 1667 SARAH LAWTON, daughter of
Thomas Lawton, died 5 July 1718. Residence: Dartmouth and Portsmouth.
     His will, made 30 Aug. 1718 and proved 20 Sept. 1718: ". . . To
eldest son Richard about 80 acres in northerly part of my farm where
I dwell, also 17 acres in Solentary Hole and all land in Warwick. To
son George farm now possessed by him in Swansea. To son Thomas
land in Newport. To son John land in Tiverton with housing, he paying
to daughters. . . certain moneys. To son James the remainder of all
lands in Portsmouth. To granddaughter Jane, daughter of son John. . .
To son James land in Portsmouth and he to fence in the burial place
which is hereby preserved for my posterity. To him old Negro man
Abraham and his wife Lucy. . . My grindstone to be shared by my sons
James and Richard Sisson. To five daughters equally all silver money
and plate. To granddaughter Sarah Clarke a feather bed and 10 pounds. . ."

          Children, born in Portsmouth:
    i.   Elizabeth, b. 18 Aug. (Oct.?) 1669; m. Jeremiah Clarke.
    ii.   Mary, b. 18 Oct. 1670; d. 18 June 1698.
    iii. Ann, b. 17 Dec. 1672; d. 19 March 1749/50; m. Philip Weeden.
    iv.   Hope, b. 24 Dec. 1674; m. in Portsmouth 26 Jan. 1699
          William Sanford.
3. v.   Richard, b. 10 Sept. 1676.
    vi.   Ruth, b. 5 May 1680; m. (--) Tew.
    vii. George, b. 23 March 1683.
    viii. Abigail, b. 23 March 1685; m. in Portsmouth 16 March 1707/8
          William Tew.
    ix.   Thomas, b. 10 Sept. 1686.
    x.   John, b. 26 June 1688.
    xi.   James, b. 26 July 1699; m. in Portsmouth 17 April 1712
          Deborah Cook, daughter of Joseph and Susanna (Briggs)
          Cook.

3. RICHARD³ SISSON (George², Richard¹), born in Portsmouth 10
Sept. 1676, married there 17 July 1701 ANN CARD, daughter of Joseph
and Jane Card of Portsmouth. Residence: Portsmouth.

          Children, born in Portsmouth:
4. i.   George, b. 30 March 1702. (See page 608).
    ii.   Sarah, b. 1 Oct. 1703; d. 11 Feb. 1736; m. in Portsmouth 19

> June 1729 Thomas Sherman.
5. iii. Joseph, b. 27 Jan. 1705. (See page 608).
    iv. Jane, b. 5 July 1706 (?).
6. v.   Richard, b. 25 Feb. 1707/8.
    vi. Job, b. 28 Oct. 1711; d. young.
    vii. Mary, b. 10 Sept. 1717; d. young.
    viii. Isaac, b. 25 Oct. 1719.
    ix. Elizabeth, b. 19 Feb. 1722/3; m. in Portsmouth 24 Nov. 1751 Joseph Sherman.

6. RICHARD[4] SISSON JR. (Richard[3], George[2], Richard[1]), born in Portsmouth 25 Feb. 1707/8, died there 30 May 1753.

He married in Portsmouth 2 Aug. 1741 DELIVERANCE TALLMAN, daughter of Benjamin and Patience (Durfee) Tallman, born 4 Feb. 1715, died about 1753. Residence: Portsmouth.

Children, born in Portsmouth:
    i.   William, b. 7 Nov. 1742.
7. ii. Mary, b. 10 Sept. 1743.
    iii. Anne, b. 10 May 1745.
    iv. Richard, b. 11 May 1747.
    v.   Job, b. 5 April 1749; d. in LC 2 Sept. 1824, according to an article in the Providence Journal. His estate was settled by his nephew, Lemuel Sisson.
    vi. Isaac, b. 20 June 1750.

7. MARY[5] SISSON (Richard[4], Richard[3], George[2], Richard[1]), born 10 Sept. 1743, married JOHN SISSON (?). Residence: Portsmouth.

Children, born in Portsmouth:
8. i.   Lemuel, b. 21 April 1769.

8. LEMUEL[6] SISSON (Mary[5], Richard[4], Richard[3], George[2], Richard[1]), born in Portsmouth 21 April 1769, died in LC 20 April 1849.

He married in Portsmouth 19 Sept. 1793 SUSANNA LAKE, daughter of David Lake, born 28 April 1775, died in LC 29 Feb. 1826 ae 51.

Residence: Portsmouth, Newport and LC. In 1812 they moved from Portsmouth to Newport and in 1816 to LC at Seaconnet Point. He was a tenant on the Roach estate.

In 1820 he started Methodist meetings which were held at his home. The Rev. Daniel Webb was the first minister. He baptized 7 July 1821 Job Sisson, uncle of Lemuel; he baptized second Lemuel Sisson and then his wife and son, John, and daughters, Mary and Anna. A lot for the church was purchased from Sylvester Brownell at the head of Meeting House Lane and the first church building was put up in 1825, directly south of the Frederick R. Brownell place. The second building was what is now the Odd Fellows Hall and a third building was built on land given by the town and was directly west of the Old Commons cemetery.

The farm that Lemuel Sisson bought was the one owned first by Colonel Benjamin Church and later by his grandson, Thomas Church.

After 1800 a windmill was placed on the hill where the Gardiner cottage was afterwards built.

His children, on 12 Sept. 1853, signed over the farm to their brother, David Sisson. In that deed the place is called the White farm. It is the land where the stone house stands today at Seaconnet Point. His house, on the west side of the road to Warren's Point was later torn down. It was in the area more recently known as the Orchard.

The deeds at Portsmouth show that he engaged in buying and selling land with his uncles, Richard and Job Sisson. He owned land bordering theirs.

Children, all born in Portsmouth except the last two:
	i.	Mary, b. 1 Oct. 1793.
9.	ii.	John, b. 23 Jan. 1796.
	iii.	Eleanor, b. 25 Nov. 1797; d. in LC 1 March 1883.
	iv.	Ann, b. 26 Feb. 1799; d. in LC 1 March 1887; unmarried.
10.	v.	Joseph, b. 12 Feb. 1801.
11.	vi.	David, b. 14 Feb. 1803.
12.	vii.	Lemuel, b. 27 May 1805.
13.	viii.	Levi, b. 19 March 1807.
	ix.	Susanna, b. 10 March 1809; d. in LC 24 June 1886; m. Henry Burlingame, son of Henry and Nancy Burlingame, b. in North Kingstown, R.I., in 1808, d. 18 April 1894.
14.	x.	James P., b. 24 June 1812.
	xi.	Sarah Ann, b. 9 Jan. 1814; m. Thomas Ely.
	xii.	William H., b. 19 Jan. 1818; d. 26 March 1826 ae 8.
	xiii.	Harriet, b. 19 Jan. 1818; m. 16 April 1876 the Rev. Philip Crandon, b. in January 1810, d. in Pennsylvania. Residence in 1850: Warwick.

9. JOHN[7] SISSON (Lemuel[6], Mary[5], Richard[4], Richard[3], George[2], Richard[1]), born in Portsmouth 23 Jan. 1796, died in LC 20 Nov. 1879.

He married MARY BROWNELL, daughter of Edmund and Polly (Bailey) Brownell, born in LC 10 May 1800, died there 6 Jan. 1881. Both are buried in the New Commons cemetery. Residence: LC.

Children, born in LC:
i.	Ephraim Bailey, b. 4 Feb. 1821; d. in LC 27 Dec. 1905; m. (1) Harriet E. Shaw, daughter of Jediah and Rhoda (Manchester) Shaw, b. in LC 25 Dec. 1820, d. there 4 June 1902. They had Mary Bailey Sisson, d. 25 March 1844 ae 3 months. He m. (2) Eliza R. Robinson.

10. JOSEPH[7] SISSON (Lemuel[6], Mary[5], Richard[4], Richard[3], George[2], Richard[1]), born in Portsmouth 12 Feb. 1801, died in LC 21/7 Oct. 1876.

He married first in LC 20 Aug. 1827 PATIENCE T. WILBOR, daughter of Governor Isaac and Hannah (Tabor) Wilbor, born in LC 27 May 1798, died 14 June 1842. Both are buried in the New Commons cemetery. He married second in LC 19 Oct. 1843 HARRIET (WEBB) ALLEN, daughter of the Rev. Daniel and Eliza Webb and widow of John Allen, born 2 Nov. 1817, died 25 July 1894. She was known in LC as Aunt Harriet. They lived on the John Sisson Road, the very short road running from the Long Highway or Bixby Road, west to the Wilbor Sisson Boulevard, or the road that in 1962 ran to the South Shore.

    Children, born in LC:
15. i. John, b. 23 Oct. 1846.

  11. DAVID[7] SISSON (Lemuel[6], Mary[5], Richard[4], Richard[3], George[2], Richard[1]), born in Portsmouth 14 Feb. 1803, died in LC 22 Feb. 1874, buried in New Commons cemetery.

  He married SARAH ANN BAILEY, daughter of Tillinghast and Ann (Briggs) Bailey, born in LC 10 Aug. 1805, died there 26 June 1895.

  Residence: First LC, then Fall River and finally LC again. They lived in the large stone house at Seaconnet Point, which they built in 1836 from stones used to build the first breakwater, which was under construction at that time.

    Children, born in LC:
 i. William Henry, b. 12 July 1828; d. in LC 2 Nov. 1829 ae 1.
16. ii. Henry Tillinghast, b. 20 Aug. 1831.

  12. LEMUEL[7] SISSON JR. (Lemuel[6], Mary[5], Richard[4], Richard[3], George[2], Richard[1]), born in LC 27 May 1805, died there 1 Feb. 1874.

  He married there 16 Nov. 1826 COMFORT SIMMONS, daughter of Benoni and Nancy (Bailey) Simmons, born in LC 7 July 1803, died 14 April 1878. Both are buried in the New Commons cemetery.

  Residence: LC. They lived in district No. 1 near the stone house, across from Valentine Simmons.

  His will, made 22 May 1873 and proved 16 March 1874, recorded LC book 11, page 681: ". . . To wife Comfort household goods and 300 dollars. To her the use and improvement during her life and reversion after her decease to my daughter Mary Ann Tallman. New part of house and southeast corner bedroom in the old part with privilege in the kitchen and porch in old part. Use of milk room, also meadow land bordered by the west main road, north James H. Bailey, east and south by Valentine Simmons. To her also 4569 dollars, that is to Mary Ann Tallman.

  To daughter Susan E. Seabury, except what I have given granddaughter Henrietta, all homestead estate, two pastures on south of road leading out of neck. Also Coe lot. . . To children Marion S. Tallman and Henrietta Tallman 100 dollars. To son-in-law Edwin T. Seabury my gun and boat. To daughter Susan Seabury the rest and residue and all personal estate not already given. . . "

    Children:
 i. Mary Ann, b. 23 Oct. 1830; d. 2 Jan. 1892; m. (1) in LC 20
    Nov. 1856 George C. Tallman, son of John and Elizabeth
    H. Tallman; m. (2) 26 Aug. 1879 Stephen Russell Howland,
    son of William and Innocent Howland.
 ii. Susan E., b. in LC 16 March 1836; d. there 15 June 1910; m.
    31 Dec. 1867 Edwin Tompkins Seabury, son of Benjamin
    and Elizabeth Brownell (Tompkins) Seabury, b. in LC 7
    April 1840, d. 23 April 1911.

  13. LEVI W.[7] SISSON (Lemuel[6], Mary[5], Richard[4], Richard[3], George[2],

Richard[1]), born in Portsmouth 19 March 1807, died in LC 1 Nov. 1880.

He married 2 Feb. 1837 MARY TABOR, daughter of Elnathan Tabor of Fairhaven, born 19 April 1813, died 28 Nov. 1889. Both are buried in the New Commons cemetery. Residence: LC. They lived at the South Shore.

Children, born in LC:

17. i.   William Henry, b. 24 Dec. 1837.
    ii.   Elizabeth T., b. 22 May 1839; d. in LC 30 March 1885; unmarried.
    iii.   Rachel D., b. 20/30 Oct. 1840; d. 15 Sept. 1921 in Waltham, Mass.
    iv.   Mary F., b. 30 Sept. 1845; d. 27 April 1902; unmarried.
18. v.   Lemuel, b. 8 Feb. 1849.
    vi.   Levi W., b. 9 Dec. 1852; d. 5 May 1908 in LC; unmarried.

14. JAMES PHILIPS[7] SISSON (Lemuel[6], Mary[5], Richard[4], Richard[3], George[2], Richard[1]), born in Portsmouth 16 June 1815, died in East Greenwich, R.I., 8 May 1861.

He married MARY TEW, daughter of Philip and Silence (Mason) Tew, born 2 Feb. 1815, died in East Greenwich 27 July 1885.

They were living in LC in 1850, and later moved to East Greenwich. He evidently owned land near the No. 1 school house in district 1, for his children signed a deed in LC on 17 June 1861. The census of LC in 1850 lists his entire family.

Children:

    i.   James L., b. in 1837. Residence: Providence.
    ii.   Mary, b. in 1840; perhaps m. James Burlingame.
19. iii.   Joseph P., b. in 1842.
    iv.   Harriet E. C., b. in 1843; m. 8 Jan. 1918 Thomas Allen Congdon.
    v.   David, b. in 1845.
    vi.   Sarah Ann, b. 15 Dec. 1847; m. 12 June 1872 John Jay Hicks, son of John and Caroline B. (Almy) Hicks, b. in Duxbury 13 Aug. 1833, d. in New Bedford 4 April 1909. They had no children.

15. JOHN[8] SISSON (Joseph[7], Lemuel[6], Mary[5], Richard[4], Richard[3], George[2], Richard[1]), born in LC 23 Oct. 1846, died there 2 June 1913.

He married there 31 Dec. 1868 MARY EUDORA ALMY, daughter of John S. and Lidora (Sisson) Almy, born in LC 25 Sept. 1846, died there 27 Jan. 1924. Residence: LC. They lived near the South Shore on the farm with a stone barn.

Children, born in LC:

20. i.   William Northupp, b. 1 Sept. 1871.
    ii.   Lydora Almy, b. in LC 24 May 1882; m. 15 June 1904 Frederick Richmond Brownell, son of Frederick R. and Annie D. Coggeshalle.

16. COL. HENRY TILLINGHAST[8] SISSON (David[7], Lemuel[6], Mary[5], Richard[4], Richard[3], George[2], Richard[1]), born in Fall River 20 Aug. 1831, died in Providence 19 Oct. 1910.

Statue of

HENRY
TILLINGHAST
SISSON

(1830-1910)

Colonel of the
5th R. I. Regiment

Lieutenant Governor
of Rhode Island

The statue in
Union Cemetery
was unveiled by
Calvin Coolidge,
who was at the time
acting Governor
of Massachusetts.

He married first 14 March 1864 at New Berne, N.C. NETTIE WALWORTH, daughter of Gilbert H. Walworth, born 9 Oct. 1845, died 23 March 1868. He married second in LC 30 June 1870 EMILY JOSEPHINE BROWNELL, daughter of Joseph and Christiana Durfee (Manchester) Brownell, born in LC 27 Jan. 1851, died 26 July 1902 in East Providence. She also called herself Josephine Emily Sisson.

Residence: LC and Fall River. A soldier in the Civil War, he became lieutenant governor of Rhode Island from 1875 to 1881.

Children by second wife, born in LC:
i.   Nettie Walworth, b. 5 Aug. 1873; d. in Worcester, Mass., 11 Feb. 1918; m. 9 April 1917 Bessie Irene Doolittle, daughter of James R. Doolittle of East Providence.
ii.   David, b. in LC 12 May 1875.
iii.   Henry Tillinghast Jr., b. 15 May 1876; d. of pneumonia 20 May 1900 ae 24.
iv.   Frank Harris, b. 3 Jan. 1885.

17. WILLIAM HENRY[8] SISSON (Levi[7], Lemuel[6], Mary[5], Richard[4], Richard[3], George[2], Richard[1]), born in LC 24 Dec. 1837, died there 17 Aug. 1922. Residence: LC.

He married first in LC 4 April 1866 JUDITH GRAY WILBOUR, daughter of Jonathan and Maria G. (Taylor) Wilbour., born in LC 10 Oct. 1840, died 29 Jan. 1886. Both are buried in the New Commons cemetery. He married second ALICE M. BIERCE.

Children by first wife, recorded in LC:
i.   Fannie Maria, b. in LC 20 March 1867; m. 22 Nov. 1893 Wilfred B. Jones, son of William Phelps and Catharine (Brown) Jones, b. 23 Sept. 1859.

    ii.   Alice Mary, b. 9 March 1868; d. 20 July 1896; unmarried.
    iii.   James Phillips, b. in LC 9 Sept. 1875.

    18. LEMUEL[8] SISSON (Levi[7], Lemuel[6], Mary[5], Richard[4], Richard[3], George[2], Richard[1]), born in LC 8 Feb. 1849, died there 25 Sept. 1924. Residence: LC.
    He married in LC 5 April 1894 LAURA FRANCES PECKHAM, daughter of Albert and Charlotte (Brightman) Peckham, born in Westport 27 Feb. 1864, died in Swansea 8 Feb. 1946.

        Children, born in LC:
    i.   Levi Walker, b. 9 Jan. 1895; d. in LC 23 April 1896.
    ii.   Albert Peckham, b. 11 Feb. 1897.
    iii.   Sidney, b. 2 Feb. 1900.
    iv.   Alice Teele, b. 10 March 1902; m. in LC 1 Oct. 1927 Charles
           Allen Buxton of Pascoag, R.I., son of Charles A. and Ada
           (Taft) Buxton, b. in Pascoag 21 Sept. 1901.
    v.   Ida May, b. 30 Sept. 1904; d. in Burrillville, R.I., 2 Sept. 1947.
    vi.   Thomas, b. 24 Dec. 1906; d. in Cranston 19 April 1944; m. in
           Tiverton 18 Nov. 1943 Joanna Moriarty.

    19. JOSEPH P.[8] SISSON (James[7], Lemuel[6], Mary[5], Richard[4], Richard[3], George[2], Richard[1]), born in LC in 1842 (?). He married ELLEN HOLDEN, born in Oregon.

        Children:
    i.   Charles Furneaux, b. in Hilo, Hawaii, 4 Oct. 1886; m. in LC
           11 May 1929 Bessie Maria Hunt, daughter of John and
           Phebe (Hambley) Hunt, b. in Tiverton 25 Sept. 1888.

    20. WILLIAM NORTHUPP[9] SISSON (John[8], Joseph[7], Lemuel[6], Mary[5], Richard[4], Richard[3], George[2], Richard[1]), born in LC 1 Sept. 1871, died there 4 July 1936.
    He married in LC 5 Nov. 1897/99 LYDORA LOUISE PECKHAM, daughter of Albert and Charlotte (Brightman) Sisson, born in LC 2 Sept. 1872.

        Children, born in LC:
    i.   Charlotte Peckham, b. 21 June 1902; m. in LC 26 Sept.
           1923 Sidney Mayo Wordell, son of Gershom and Emma
           F. (Potter) Wordell, b. in LC 26 July 1897.
    ii.   Mary, b. in LC 23 Aug. 1914; m. (1) 16 Jan. 1937 in
           Harrisville, R.I., John Bishop Wilcox, son of John Wilcox
           of Tiverton; m. (2) (?).

        . . . .

    4. GEORGE[4] SISSON (Richard[3], George[2], Richard[1]), born in Portsmouth 30 March 1702. He married in Portsmouth 5 March 1723/4 ELIZABETH SHERMAN, daughter of Peleg and Alice (Fish) Sherman. Residence: Portsmouth.

    5. JOSEPH[4] SISSON (Richard[3], George[2], Richard[1]), born in Portsmouth 27 Jan. 1704/5, died there 20 Sept. 1737. He married RUTH (--).

21. PELEG[5] SISSON (George[4], Richard[3], George[2], Richard[1]),
born in Portsmouth 31 May 1726, died perhaps 2 Oct. 1802. He married
in Portsmouth 7 Dec. 1749 RUTH SHERMAN, daughter of John and
Grizzell (Fish) Sherman, born 9 July 1727, died 5 Sept. 1822. Residence: Portsmouth.

22. RICHARD[6] SISSON (Peleg[5], George[4], Richard[3], George[2],
Richard[1]), born in Portsmouth 16 Sept. 1750, died there 29 April
1831. He married there 10 Dec. 1772 PHILADELPHIA BROWNELL,
daughter of Joseph and Rebecca (Tripp) Brownell, born 17 May 1752.
Residence: Portsmouth.

23. JAMES[7] SISSON (Richard[6], Peleg[5], George[4], Richard[3], George[2],
Richard[1]), born in Portsmouth 16 Sept. 1788, died 3 May 1857. He
married in 1813 ANNA GARDINER WOODMAN of Albany, N.Y.

24. JAMES MANNING[8] SISSON (James[7], Richard[6], Peleg[5], George[4],
Richard[3], George[2], Richard[1]), born 18 Nov. 1824, died in New Bedford
26 Aug. 1911. He married VILROY ANN DEAN.

25. CHARLES DEAN[9] SISSON (James[8], James[7], Richard[6], Peleg[5],
George[4], Richard[3], George[2], Richard[1]), born in Dartmouth 11 July
1851, died in LC 4 March 1932.
He married in LC 23 Dec. 1884 ABBY SOPHIA PECKHAM, daughter
of Nathaniel C. and Abbie G. (Browne) Peckham, born in LC 23 Dec.
1862, died in New Bedford 24 Sept. 1911.
Residence: LC until about 1907. They lived on the place which
formerly belonged to Nathaniel C. Peckham, and was opposite the
Coval Osborn place or Sherrer place, later occupied by Louise (Kelly)
Manchester.

      Children, born in LC:
i.   Son, b. 19 Dec. 1887.
ii.   Edward R., b. 4 May 1889.
iii.   Irene Hope, b. 16 May 1891; d. in LC 27 Aug. 1891.
iv.   Philadelphia Brownell, b. in April 1893.
v.   Daughter, b. 13 Feb. 1896.
vi.   Melville W., b. 31 Aug. 1898.
vii.   Edith, b. 9 Nov. 1902.

26. BARNEY (BARNARD)[5] SISSON (Joseph[4], Richard[3], George[2],
Richard[1]), born about 1772, died 19 Aug. 1809. He married in Portsmouth 17 Dec. 1797 BARBARY (BARBARA) SISSON, daughter of Richard
and Sarah (Fish) Sisson, born in 1772, died in April 1829. Both are
buried in the Portsmouth cemetery on Vanderbilt land.

27. JABEZ[6] SISSON (Barney[5], Joseph[4], Richard[3], George[2], Richard[1]),
born 24 Nov. 1799, died in Tiverton 10 Nov. 1873. He married in Portsmouth 24 Dec. 1828 ELIZABETH B. WARD, daughter of Selathiel Ward,
born in 1806, died 15 May 1881.

28. JOHN E.[7] SISSON (Jabez[6], Barney[5], Joseph[4], Richard[3], George[2],

Richard[1]), born in Portsmouth 12 Nov. 1845, died 29 Aug. 1884. He
married first SUSAN J. DRING, daughter of Thomas and Abby Dring,
born in LC 14 July 1846, died 16 Nov. 1894. He married second in Fall
River 1 Nov. 1877 BETSEY JACKSON, daughter of James and Mary
Jackson, born in England in 1845. No records have been found concerning his first marriage.

29. NATHANIEL LEVI[8] SISSON (John[7], Jabez[6], Barney[5], Joseph[4],
Richard[3], George[2], Richard[1]), born in Tiverton 23 May 1886, the son of
John and Susan J. (Dring) Sisson. He married before 1908 SUSIE MORAND
SIMMONS, daughter of William T. and Lucy (Grinnell) Simmons, born in
LC. He was living in Westport at the time of his marriage.

     Children:
i.   William Sisson, b. 3 Jan. 1911.
30. ii.   Nathaniel L., b. 11 May 1913 in Westport.

30. NATHANIEL LEVI[9] SISSON (Nathaniel[8], John[7], Jabez[6], Barney[5],
Joseph[4], Richard[3], George[2], Richard[1]), born in Westport 11 May 1913.
He married in Tiverton 28 March 1932 BEATRICE ANN MANCHESTER
of LC, daughter of Albert S. and Lillian (Wimer) Manchester, born in LC
7 Nov. 1914. Residence: LC.

     Children:
i.   Richard Levi, b. 26 July 1932 in Fall River; m. 1 July 1952
        Carolyne Eileen Blanchette, daughter of Alfred and Eileen
        (Burns) Blanchette, b. in Fall River 20 Sept. 1934.
ii.   Beatrice Anna, b. in Fall River 19 Feb. 1936; d. 2 Dec. 1950
        ae 14.
iii.   Robert A. or Roger A., b. in Fall River 17 Sept. 1940.
iv.   Russell L., b. 24 Aug. 1944.

     . . . .
The following information from the New Bedford Public Library:

GREEN BRADFORD[7] SISSON (Peleg[6], Philip[5], Richard[4], Richard[3],
James[2], Richard[1]), born in Westport 9 Nov. 1796, the son of Peleg and
Hannah (Brownell) Sisson, died in LC 3 Aug. 1854.

He married in Westport 26 March 1815 HOPE POTTER, daughter
of Edward and Betsey Potter, born in Westport 18 July 1798, died in
Pawtucket, R.I., 24 Sept. 1886. Residence: LC.

     Children:
i.   Charles R.
ii.   Andrew F.
iii.   Philip G., b. in 1820.
iv.   Lidora V., b. in 1820; d. in LC 18 Aug. 1882; m. 21 Dec.
        1843 John S. Almy, son of Frederick and Mary (Simmons)
        Almy.
v.   Peleg H., b. in 1829.
vi.   William B.
vii.   Mary M., b. in 1835.
viii. Sanford, b. in 1837.
ix.   Elizabeth H., b. in 1840.
x.   Hope E.

THE SLOCUM FAMILY

From the Slocum Genealogy (1882) by Dr. Charles E. Slocum, and other records.

1. GILES[1] SLOCUM, married JOAN (--). His will was proved 12 March 1683. Residence: Portsmouth.

2. ELEIZER[2] SLOCUM (Giles[1]), born in Portsmouth 25 Dec. 1664, died in Dartmouth 1727. He married ELIPHAL FITGERALD, died in 1748. His will was probated in Dartmouth 30 July 1727. Residence: Portsmouth and Dartmouth.

3. ELEIZER[3] SLOCUM (Eleizer[2], Giles[1]), born in Dartmouth 20 Jan. 1693/4. He married 20 July 1716 DEBORAH SMITH, daughter of Deliverance and Mary Smith of Dartmouth, born 13 July 1695, died in 1738/9. His will was proved 18 Jan. 1738/9. Residence: Dartmouth.

4. JOHN[4] SLOCUM (Eleizer[3], Eleizer[2], Giles[1]), born in Dartmouth 4 Aug. 1717. He married there 25 Dec. 1738 DEBORAH ALMY, daughter of John and Deborah Almy. Residence: Dartmouth.

5. JOHN[5] SLOCUM (John[4], Eleizer[3], Eleizer[2], Giles[1]), born in Dartmouth 6 Oct. 1746. He married there 9 Oct. 1767 RHODA BRIGGS. Residence: Dartmouth and Nashewana Island, now Dukes County, Mass.

6. CHARLES[6] SLOCUM (John[5], John[4], Eleizer[3], Eleizer[2], Giles[1]), born on Nashewana Island 2 Jan. 1779, died there 11 Sept. 1850. He married first 22 Dec. 1801 in Dartmouth MARY DAVOL, daughter of Daniel and Sarah (Bowditch) Davol, born 4 Jan. 1772, died in 1809. He married second 7 Aug. 1810 JANE HASKIN of Dartmouth. He was a seaman in the War of 1812.

7. SOLOMON[7] SLOCUM (Charles[6], John[5], John[4], Eleizer[3], Eleizer[2], Giles[1]), born in Dartmouth 1 May 1805, died in LC 22 March 1886.
He was married first in LC 26 Jan. 1832 by the Rev. Emerson Paine to SARAH PIERCE SIMMONS, daughter of Stephen and Priscilla (Head) Simmons, born in LC 11 Sept. 1811, died there 24 March 1867. He married second in LC 13 Oct. 1870 SARAH HOWLAND GIFFORD, daughter of Charles and Phebe (Davol) Gifford, born 2 Aug. 1822. She married second in LC 12 Oct. 1888 Charles Davoll, son of John and Diana Davoll. They are buried in the cemetery on Adamsville Hill.
They lived on or in the vicinity of Peckham Road in the census of 1880.

Children by first wife, recorded in LC:
i.   Charles, b. in LC 4 April 1832; d. there 18 Sept. 1853; unmarried.
ii. Job Stephen, b. 7 Oct. 1833; m. in LC 21 May 1865 Emily Tompkins, daughter of Joseph Tompkins of Newport.
iii. Priscilla Head Simmons, b. 7 May 1840; d. 30 April 1858.

8. JOB[7] SLOCUM (Charles[6], John[5], John[4], Eleizer[3], Eleizer[2], Giles[1]), born 5 March 1813, died in LC 22 May 1851.

He married in LC 10 Aug. 1836 JULIA ANN SIMMONS, daughter of Stephen and Priscilla (Head) Simmons, born in LC 17 Aug. 1817, died in Newport 4 Dec. 1891. Both are buried in the Simmons cemetery on Simmons Hill. She married second Deacon John Dyer of LC, son of John and Christian (Brightman) Dyer.

He was a seaman and died of consumption.

His will, recorded LC Probate book 10, page 435, made 2 Jan. 1845 and proved 9 June 1851: ". . . To Job Slocum, son of my brother Solomon Slocum, ten dollars. To wife Julia Ann Slocum the rest and residue of both real and personal and she to be executrix. . . "

THE SMITH FAMILY

1. ROBERT AMES SMITH, born in New Bedford in 1891. He married ICIE DORRANCE SIMMONS, daughter of William Taylor and Lucy Fuller (Grinnell) Simmons, born in LC 13 March 1896. Residence: LC.

Children, recorded in LC:

2. i. Royal Kenton, b. 30 Aug. 1915; m. Mary E. Cummings.
    ii. Rosella, b. 25 June 1917.
    iii. Evelyn, b. 17 Oct. 1921 in New Bedford; m. (1) 25 June 1941 Charles Kenyon LeValley, son of William A. and Mary (Kenyon) LeValley, d. 4 July 1915; m. (2) 6 May 1951 Reginald Arthur Vokes.
    iv. Mattie Louise, b. in LC 17 Oct. 1923; m. there 25 July 1942 Richard Edward Cooper, son of Edward and Mabel Cooper of Hillsdale, Mich., b. in Hillsdale 5 Sept. 1920.
    v. Lorraine, b. 15 June 1932.
    vi. Robert Ames Jr., b. 9 June 1936 in Fall River.

2. ROYAL KENTON[2] SMITH (Robert Ames[1]), born in LC 30 Aug. 1915. He married MARY E. CUMMINGS. Residence: LC.

Children, recorded in LC:

i. Judith M., b. in Fall River 31 Aug. 1941.
ii. Peter K., b. in Fall River 17 March 1944.
iii. Linda V., b. in Fall River 11 Sept. 1945.

. . . .

THOMAS SMITH of Newport, married in Portsmouth 27 May 1738 SUSANNA WOOD of Newport. Residence: LC.

Children, recorded in LC:

i. Mary, b. 28 May 1738; m. in LC 12 Oct. 1769 Elisha Peckham, son of William and Phebe (Barker) Peckham of LC.

JOHN SMITH, born in 1669. He came from Durham, N.H. and lived in LC.

Children, recorded in LC:
i.   Mary, b. in LC 3 Aug. 1697.

CLINTON SMITH, married MARY L. PECKHAM, born in Adamsville. Residence: LC.

Children, recorded in LC:
i.   Elaine May, b. in Fall River 26 Oct. 1924.
ii. Clinton Jr., b. 25 Sept. 1926.

JAMES ALPHONSUS SMITH, son of James H. and Margaret (Corcoran) Smith, born in Fall River 2 Aug. 1917. He married in LC 18 Aug. 1944 ALTHEA MAUDE DAVIS, daughter of Edward Homer and Margaret Emeline (MacDonald) Davis, born in LC 26 Nov. 1922.

Children, recorded in LC:
i.   Terry P., b. 31 May 1946.

LORENZO SMITH of Tiverton, son of Pardon and Judith (Cook) Smith of Tiverton, born 28 May 1815, died in LC 22 April 1886, buried in the Hillside cemetery in Tiverton. His father, Pardon, was the son of Daniel and Johanna Smith of New Bedford.
    He was married in LC 16 July 1846 by the Rev. Richard Davis to LYDIA LOUISA LADD, daughter of Jesse and Robey (Wilbor) Ladd of LC, born in LC 1 Sept. 1824, died 14 Aug. 1886, buried in Hillside cemetery. Residence: LC.

Children:
i.   Pardon H., b. in Tiverton in 1847.
ii.   Clifford H., b. in LC 7 Dec. 1848; d. 1 Oct. 1929.
iii. Joseph W., b. in LC 15 Aug. 1852.
iv.   Russell J. W., b. in 1853; m. in LC in October 1896 Emma
        Houseman of Fall River, daughter of Francis and
        Elizabeth Houseman.
v.   Robey, b. 23 Sept. 1854; d. 13 Dec. 1927; m. 26 Nov. 1885
        John Charles Cook, son of Charles and Abby Cook.
vi.   Geneva E., b. in LC 1 July 1858; m. 1 Jan. 1886 Edward F.
        Hambly, son of Edwin and Eliza Hambly of Tiverton.

THE SNELL FAMILY

From the history of Bridgewater, New England Genealogical
Register, page 100, vital records of Bridgewater and LC.

1. THOMAS[1] SNELL, born about 1625, died 25 Jan. 1724/5 ae 99.
He married MARTHA HARRIS, daughter of Arthur Harris of Bridgewater,
Mass.

He probably came to this country with his uncle, Samuel Edson, who
may have been from Whitacre in Warwickshire, England. He arrived in
Salem, Mass., about 1650 and was a large land owner in Bridgewater from
1668 to the time of his death. In Bridgewater there are some portions of
the town named after him, such as Snell's Meadows.

In his will dated 10 May 1724 he named nine surviving children. The
will was contested by the eldest son.

Children, recorded in Bridgewater:
	i.	Martha, b. 26 Oct. 1669; d. young.
	ii.	Thomas, b. 1 Feb. 1671; m. in Mansfield, Mass., 3 Sept. 1702 Abigail Kinsley of Milton, Mass.
	iii.	Josiah, b. in Duxbury 5 May 1674; m. there (1) 21 Dec. 1699 Anna Alden, daughter of Zachariah Alden of Duxbury; m. (2) Faith Fish.
2.	iv.	Samuel, b. 6 Jan. 1676.
	v.	Amos, b. 18 May 1678; m. in Bridgewater 2 May 1700 Mary Packard.
	vi.	John, b. 23 Sept. 1680; d. in Bridgewater 20 Jan. 1767; m. there 1 Feb. 1714/15 Susannah Packard.
	vii.	Joseph, b. 22 Feb. 1683; d. in Bridgewater 15 Aug. 1736; m. there 3 Dec. 1712 Hannah Williams.
	viii.	Anna, b. 24 Feb. 1685; m. in Bridgewater 3 Aug. 1708 Nicholas Byram.
	ix.	Mary, b. 1 Jan. 1689; m. (1) Nathaniel Reynolds; m. (2) David Ames.
	x.	Martha, b. 8 Oct. 1692; m. in Bridgewater 22 April 1714 Ephraim Fobes.

2. SAMUEL[2] SNELL (Thomas[1]), born in Bridgewater 6 Jan. 1676.
He was married in Newport 13 Dec. 1705 by Giles Slocum to MARY
ALMY, daughter of Job and Mary (Unthank) Almy, died in 1760.

Residence: Newport and Tiverton. He was called a tanner. In
1705 he sold land in East Bridgewater to Joseph Shaw.

Children, recorded in Tiverton:
3.	i.	Samuel, b. 19 Sept. 1708.
	ii.	Job, b. 30 June 1710.
	iii.	Martha, b. 21 March 1712/3; d. 24 Feb. 1725/6; m. (--) Salisbury.
	iv.	Mary, b. 22 Feb. 1715/16.
	v.	Anthony, b. 20 March 1718/19.

3. SAMUEL[3] SNELL (Samuel[2], Thomas[1]), born in Tiverton 19 Sept.
1708. He was married in LC 20 Nov. 1728 by Richard Billings, justice,

to MARY HEAD, daughter of·Henry and Elizabeth (Palmer) Head of LC, born there 16 April 1711. Residence: LC, Tiverton and Newport.

       Children, recorded in Tiverton:
	i.	Samuel, b. 12 March 1730/31.
4.	ii.	Isaac, b. 16 Jan. 1732.
	iii.	Anthony, b. 5 Nov. 1738.
5.	iv.	Benjamin, b. 25 Dec. 1745/6.
6.	v.	Pardon, b. 18 Aug. 1747.
	vi.	Job.

    4. ISAAC[4] SNELL (Samuel[3], Samuel[2], Thomas[1]), born in Tiverton 16 Jan. 1732, died in LC. He married SARAH (--).
    A cordwainer, he lived in LC. His estate was administered there by his son, Michael Crawford Snell, 2 Feb. 1779.

       Children, recorded in LC:
i.	Michael Crawford, b. 21 June 1755; m. probably 22 Nov. 1778 Susannah Grinnell, daughter of Daniel and Grace (Palmer) Grinnell. His estate was administered by his wife in LC 3 Aug. 1784.
ii.	Deborah, b. 16 Aug. 1757; m. William Seabury.
iii.	Sarah, b. 30 Dec. 1759; d. 18 July 1737; m. in LC 7 Jan. 1781 Nathaniel Tompkins, son of Michael and Sarah (Dring) Tompkins.
iv.	Isaac, b. 12 Aug. 1762.
v.	Phebe, b. 17 Dec. 1765.
vi.	Job, b. 7 July 1767.
vii.	Frizeweed, b. 2 Dec. 1769; m. in LC 18 Dec. 1788 Jabez Manchester, son of Archer Manchester.
viii.	Anthony, b. 27 May 1772. His estate was administered by his mother, Sarah Snell, 13 Nov. 1801.
ix.	Samuel, b. 11 July 1774; m. in LC 18 Aug. 1799 Kezia Grinnell, daughter of Malachi and Lydia (Coe) Grinnell.
x.	Mary, b. 24 Aug. 1776.

    5. BENJAMIN[4] SNELL (Samuel[3], Samuel[2], Thomas[1]), born in LC 25 Dec. 1745. He was married there 6 Nov. 1774 by the Rev. Jonathan Ellis to PHEBE HEAD, daughter of Joseph and Bathsheba (Palmer) Head of LC. Residence: LC and Westport.

       Children, born in LC and Westport:
i.	Phebe, b. 29 April 1776.
ii.	Mary, b. 2 Dec. 1778.
iii.	Lydia, b. 24 March 1782.
iv.	Deborah, b. 6 April 1785.
v.	John, b. 9 July 1787.
vi.	Obed, b. 20 April 1791.
vii.	Hannah, b. 7 May 1793.

    6. PARDON[4] SNELL (Samuel[3], Samuel[2], Thomas[1]), born in Tiverton 14 Jan. 1746. He was married in LC 22 April 1770 by Jeptha Pearce, justice, to ALICE GRINNELL, daughter of Daniel and Grace

(Palmer) Grinnell, born in LC 10 Jan. 1746. Residence: LC.

 Children, recorded in LC:
 i.   Mary, b. 14 Oct. 1770.
 ii.   Nancy, b. 18 Jan. 1773.
 iii.   Isaiah, b. 20 June 1775.
 iv.   Grace, m. (--) King.
 v.   Moses, b. 7 April 1780.
 vi.   Michael Crawford, b. 29 March 1782; m. Mary Brownell.
7. vii. Joseph Crandall, b. 4 Oct. 1784.

 7. JOSEPH CRANDALL[5] SNELL (Pardon[4], Samuel[3], Samuel[2], Thomas[1]), born in LC 4 Oct. 1784. He married first PRISCILLA BROWNELL. He married second MARY BROWNELL.

 Children:
 i.   Nancy.
8. ii.   Isaiah, b. 17 Dec. 1810.
9. iii. George Washington, b. 1 March 1812.
 iv.   Thomas, b. in April 1816 in Portsmouth.
 v.   Maybe Sarah Stoddard, b. (?) in Tiverton.

 8. ISAIAH[6] SNELL (Joseph[5], Pardon[4], Samuel[3], Samuel[2], Thomas[1]), born in Tiverton 17 Dec. 1810, died in LC 25 Nov. 1892.
 He was married in LC 18 May 1834 by the Rev. Emerson Paine to HANNAH C. WILBOR, daughter of Wright and Hannah (Gray) Wilbor, born in LC 14 Aug. 1815, died there 10 July 1893. Both are buried in Union cemetery. Residence: LC. They lived on the south side of Snell Road where the late Ephraim C. Palmer lived.

 Children:
10. i.   Brownell Wright, b. 29 July 1835.

 9. GEORGE WASHINGTON[6] SNELL (Joseph[5], Pardon[4], Samuel[3], Samuel[2], Thomas[1]), born in LC 1 March 1812, died there 21 Aug. 1882.
 He was married in LC 6 Dec. 1841 by George C. Bailey to SARAH E. PEARCE, daughter of Benjamin and Sarah (Pearce) Pearce, born in LC 3 Nov. 1820, died there 14 Sept. 1896. He is buried in the Old Commons cemetery. Residence: LC.

 Children:
 i.   Sarah E., b. in 1844.
11. ii. George V., b. 16 April 1848.

 10. BROWNELL WRIGHT[7] SNELL (Isaiah[6], Joseph[5], Pardon[4], Samuel[3], Samuel[2], Thomas[1]), born in LC 29 July 1835, died there 5 Feb. 1907. Residence: LC.
 He married in LC 7 Jan. 1855 HARRIET L. ALMY, daughter of John Edwin and Levina (Manchester) Almy of LC, born there 28 Aug. 1833, died there 4 Dec. 1891. Both are buried in the Almy cemetery at Windmill Hill.

 Children, recorded in LC:
 i.   Son, b. 29 June 1859.

12. ii.   William Otis, b. 29 Nov. 1860.
    iii.   Mary Louisa, b. 26 Dec. 1862; d. 27 June 1913; m. in LC
           21 Nov. 1883 Jere Bailey Wilbur, son of Ezra and Mary
           T. (Marble) Wilbur.
    iv.   Charles, b. 22 July 1864; d. ae 3 days.
    v.   Harriet Brownell, b. 5 Nov. 1866; d. 17 April 1949; m. in
           LC 10 April 1890 Charles M. Andrews of Dartmouth.

   11. GEORGE V.[7] SNELL (George[6], Joseph[5], Pardon[4], Samuel[3],
Samuel[2], Thomas[1]), born in LC 16 April 1848, died there 15 Feb.
1928. Residence: LC. They lived on the south side of Snell Road.
   He married NORAH MOSHER, daughter of Caleb Seekel and Mary
(Crosby) Mosher of LC, born there 8 Jan. 1858, died there 11 Jan.
1940.

        Children:
    i.   Elliot Richmond, b. 23 Feb. 1884; d. 13 Sept. 1933; m. 19
           April 1907 Ethel May Wilbour, daughter of Daniel and
           Hannah (Soule) Wilbour, b. 10 May 1889, d. in March
           1924.
13. ii.   Herman A., b. 5 April 1885.
    iii.   George Winnifred, b. 3 Dec. 1897.

   12. WILLIAM OTIS[8] SNELL (Brownell[7], Isaiah[6], Joseph[5], Pardon[4],
Samuel[3], Samuel[2], Thomas[1]), born in LC 29 Nov. 1860, died there 26
Oct. 1918.
   He married first in LC 30 April 1885 EDITH M. DENNIS, daughter
of Edward W. and Lucy (King) Dennis of Tiverton, born in 1869 in
Tiverton, died in 1951. He married second BETSEY DENNIS.

        Children:
    i.   Ethel May, b. in LC 10 Oct. 1885.
    ii.   Louise Rider, b. in LC 27 Jan. 1889; d. in 1940.
    iii.   Edward Brownell, b. in LC 15 Aug. 1893.
    iv.   Emeline, b. 31 Jan. 1898; m. 15 Jan. 1931 Hervey M. Wilbour.

   We have record of a William B. Dennis, son of Betsey Dennis and
grandson of Edward W. and Lucy (King) Dennis, born in 1893, died in
1936.

   13. HERMAN A.[8] SNELL (George[7], George[6], Joseph[5], Pardon[4],
Samuel[3], Samuel[2], Thomas[1]), born in LC 5 April 1885. He married
ELIZABETH C. McSHANE, born 23 Dec. 1881. Residence: LC.

        Children, recorded in LC:
    i.   Eleanor Claire, b. 10 Nov. 1908; m. 14 Feb. 1925 Elmer Z.
           Brayton, son of Elmer and Eudora (Palmer) Brayton.
    ii.   Leah May, b. 30 May 1911.
    iii.   Paul Aubrey, b. 27 Feb. 1914.

                    . . . .

GEORGE W. SNELL, married EMMA L. (--), born in Fall River.
Residence: LC.

    Children, recorded in LC:
i.   Mary Emma, b. 22 Jan. 1869.
ii.   Charles Edward, b. 17 March 1871.

WILLIAM T. SNELL, married LUCY (--).

    Children, born in LC:
i.   Mabel Louisa, b. 10 Oct. 1885.

JOB SNELL, son of Samuel Snell, was married in LC 8 June
1769 by Aaron Wilbor, justice, to RUTH DAVENPORT, daughter of
Eliphalet and Ann (Devoll) Davenport. Residence: LC.

    Children, recorded in LC:
i.   Judith, b. 29 Oct. 1769; d. 9 June 1849.
ii.   Edmund, b. 14 Oct. 1771.
iii. Michael Crawford, b. 31 Dec. 1773.
iv. Ruth, b. 10 April 1776.
v.   Ruby, b. 26 July 1780.
vi. Job, b. 28 Sept. 1782.
vii. Isaac, b. 22 July 1786.
viii. Shadrach, b. 12 Dec. 1793.

ISAAC SNELL, born in 1804, married CYNTHIA (--). They lived
on Snell Road in LC.

    Children:
i.   Samuel, b. about 1830.
ii.   Sarah, b. about 1830.
iii. Mary, b. about 1834.
iv. Pardon, b. about 1836.
v.   Moses, b. about 1838.
vi. William H., b. about 1840.
vii. Margaret H., b. about 1842.
viii. Job, b. in 1845.

ARTHUR C. SNELL, married EDITH CHASE. Residence: LC.

    Children, recorded in LC:
i.   Ronald A., b. in LC 19 Jan. 1943.
ii.   Judith, b. in Fall River 5 Oct. 1944.
iii. Laura J., b. in Fall River 12 Dec. 1946.

THE SNOW FAMILY

See Families of Southern Massachusetts, page 1440.

ROBERT[8] SNOW (Lowm[7], Loami[6], Mark[5], Jonathan[4], Nicholas[3], Mark[2], Nicholas[1]), born in New Bedford about 1854, died 15 Nov. 1905.
 He married 16 Nov. 1881 SARAH GORDON HUNT, daughter of John B. and Abby G. (Taber) Hunt, born 25 April 1860. Residence: New Bedford and LC.

   Children, born in New Bedford:
 i. Constance, b. 26 Aug. 1883.
 ii. Agatha, b. 13 July 1886.
 iii. Edith, b. 6 June 1891.
 iv. Robert, b. 13 May 1898; m. Dorothy Clarke.

ROBERT[9] SNOW (Robert[8], Lowm[7], Loami[6], Mark[5], Jonathan[4], Nicholas[3], Mark[2], Nicholas[1]), born 13 May 1898, married DOROTHY D. CLARKE. Residence: New Bedford and LC.

   Children:
 i. Deborah, b. 30 Aug. 1921; m. in LC 16 Sept. 1941 Lt. Clarke
   Simonds, son of Philip B. and Persis (Godfrey) Simons, b.
   in Providence 1 May 1917.
 ii. Willard Clarke Snow, b. in Hartford, Conn., 28 Dec. 1922;
   m. in Providence 15 May 1948 Carolyn Fries of Haverford,
   Pa., b. in Bryn Mawr, Pa., 23 Aug. 1927.
 iii. Susanne, b. in Hartford, Conn., 3 Sept. 1926; m. in LC 3
   Sept. 1949 Albion Gibbs Davis, son of Albion and Ada
   (Holland) Davis, b. in New Bedford 4 Feb. 1925.

THE SOULE FAMILY

1. GEORGE[1] SOULE, who came in the Mayflower in 1620, died in Duxbury, Mass., in 1679/80. He married MARY BECKET, who came in the Anne, and who died in Duxbury in December 1676.
 He was a servant of Edward Winslow of Plymouth, probably indentured for seven years. He served as a volunteer for the Pequot War (1637).
 According to Francis R. Stoddard in "The Truth About The Pilgrims" page 150, "George Soule came as a servant of Edward Winslow. He was the 35th signer of the Mayflower compact. He was born about 1600 and is credited to the London contingent. He was the son of John Soule of Eckington, Worcestershire, England. Robert Soule of the family was a London salter. Droitwich, where Edward Winslow was born, was a salt mining place and connected with the salters company of London. This last may have brought George Soule and Edward Winslow together. George Soule married Mary Becket before 1627. His autograph has been preserved."

The will of George Soule, taken from The Mayflower Descendants:
"In the name of God Amen, I George Soule Senr of Duxbury in the
Colonie of New Plymouth in New England, being aged and weake in
body but of a saine mind and memory, God be praised for same doe
make this my last will and testament. First I have alreddy and formerly by deeds under my hand and seale given unto my two sonnes,
Nathaniel and Gorge all my lands in the township of Dartmouth. Item.
I have formerly given unto my daughters Elizabeth and Patience all
my lands in the township of Middleberry. Item. I give and bequeath
unto my daughters Susannah and Mary 12 pence a peece to be payed by
my executor hereafter named after my decease and for as much as my
eldest son John Soule and his family hath in my extreme old age and
weakness bin tender and carefull of mee and very healpfull to mee: and
is likely soe to be while it shall please God to continew my life heer,
therefore I give unto my said son, all the remainder of my housing
and lands whatsoever to him, his heires and assigns forever.

"Item. I give and bequeath to my son John Soule all my goodes
and chattles what soever. Item. I nominate and appoint my son John
Soule to be my sole executor of this my last will and testament and
lastly I doe make null and voyde all other and former wills and testa-
ments by mee att any time made, in witness whereof I the said George
Soule have hereunto sett my hand and seale this eleventh day of August
in the yeer of our Lorde, one thousand six hundred and seaventy and
seaven. George Soule and a seale. Nathaniel Thomas. The marke D.
T. of Deborah Thomas.

"Item. The 20th day of September 1677, I the above named Gorge
Soule, doe heerby further declare that it is my will that if my son
John Soule or any of my heires shall disturbe my daughter Patience
or her heirs in peacable possession or enjoyment of the lands I have
given her at Namassakett allie Middleberry and recover the same
from her or her heires that then the gift to my son John Soule shall
be voyd and then my daughter Pateince shall have all my lands at
Duxberry and she shall bee my sole executrix. . . "

The will was probably probated in the month of January since
his inventory was taken 1 Feb. 1680.

Children:

12. i.   George, b. about 1624; m. Deborah (--). His will was proved
           30 June 1704.

    ii.   John, b. about 1633; d. in 1707; m. (1) Rebecca Simmons,
           daughter of Moses and Sarah Simmons; m. (2) in 1678
           Esther Nash, daughter of Lt. Samuel Nash and widow of
           Samuel Sampson, b. 6 March 1638.

    iii.   Mary, b. in Plymouth or Dartmouth about 1642; m. in 1665
           John Peterson. He died between 27 April 1718 and 26 March
           1720.

    iv.   Elizabeth, m. before 1663 Frances Walker.

2. v.   Nathaniel, b. in Duxbury, Mass.

    vi.   Susanna, m. Francis West.

    vii.   Benjamin, b. in Plymouth or Duxbury; killed by Indians
           at Pawtucket 26 March 1676.

    viii. Patience, b. in Plymouth or Duxbury; d. 11 March 1705/6;

m. in January 1666 John Haskell, d. 15 May 1706 ae 66.
ix.   Zachariah, m. Margaret Ford.

2. NATHANIEL² SOULE (George¹), born in Duxbury or Plymouth,
died in Dartmouth in 1699. He married ROSE (THORNE)?.
Residence: Duxbury and Dartmouth. He lived in the section which
later became Westport.
Administration of his estate was granted to his wife Rose 12 Oct.
1699. Three years later, the estate was divided among his four sons
and his widow (10 Sept. 1702). The three eldest sons were instructed
to care for their brother Miles, who was an idiot.

Children:
3. i.   Nathaniel, b. 31 Oct. 1687 (?).
    ii.   Jacob, b. after 1688; m. in Dartmouth 22 Jan. 1709/10
          Rebecca Gifford. He died before 12 Aug. 1747, when his
          will was proved. Residence: Dartmouth.
    iii. Sylvanus.
    iv.   Miles, b. in Dartmouth; probably died young.

3. LT. NATHANIEL³ SOULE (Nathaniel², George¹), born in Dartmouth 12 Jan. 1681 (?), died there in 1766.
He married first in Dartmouth 20 July 1708 MERIBAH GIFFORD,
daughter of Christopher and Deborah (Perry) Gifford, born 21 Oct.
1689. He married second in Dartmouth 13 Feb. 1732/33 HANNAH
MACOMBER, daughter of William and Elizabeth (Randall) Macomber,
born in Dartmouth 8 Nov. 1703.
Much of his land lay on the west side of the Occoaxet River and
on land which later became Westport. He lived not far from the LC
line in the neighborhood of the Gifford family.
His will was made 12 March 1764 and proved 30 June 1766.

Children by first wife:
i.   Meribah, b. 10 June 1709.
ii.   Jonathan, b. 3 March 1711.
iii. Henry.

Children by second wife:
4. iv.   Weston, b. about 1729.

4. WESTON⁴ SOULE (Nathaniel³, Nathaniel², George¹), born
about 1729, died shortly after 21 March 1825 at the age of 96.
He married first (intention 22 Sept. 1753) in Dartmouth RUHAMMAH
HIX, daughter of William and Anna (Durfee) Hix, born 18 Feb. 1735/6,
died 25 May 1771, according to her gravestone in Westport. He married
second in LC 10 Dec. 1772 SARAH WILBORE, daughter of Aaron and
Mary (Church) Wilbore of LC, born there 25 Dec. 1748, died there 22
Oct. 1825 (?). He married third in Westport 16 Aug. 1803 (?) PHILENA
MANCHESTER, born about 1751, died in LC 15 Oct. 1846, buried on the
old Aaron Wilbor place, afterwards the John Soule place. She was the
sister of Charles Manchester of LC who married Priscilla Brownell and
so must be the daughter of John and Mary (Brownell) Manchester of
Westport (that is, if she was not a half sister) for she was named in
the will of Charles Manchester as his sister.

He was a seaman, remembered for his great physical strength.

His will, made in Westport 29 Sept. 1804 and proved 26 July 1825, mentions his daughters, Mary Allen, wife of Gershom Allen; Elizabeth Earle, wife of James Earle, and her daughter Hannah; granddaughter Ruhamma Robinson, daughter of his daughter, Ann Wood, deceased; grandsons Joseph, Abner, Silvester and Weston Soule; granddaughter Elizabeth Austin; and daughter Barbara Davis. He left to his wife Philena Soule use of all lands and buildings in Westport "which I hold by virtue of a lease given me during my natural life and after my death Philena Manchester, during her natural life, if she survives me unmarried, which lease was given me by Hiram S. Manchester, 7 March 1797." There is also a codicil to the will, dated 6 Oct. 1810: "All that was for Elizabeth Earle in my will to her daughter Hannah. To grandson William my handsome volume. . . To Jacob Soule of Westport, wife Abigail, three sons, Stephen, Avery and Elisha. . . "

Children by first wife, recorded in Westport:

i.   Anna, b. 7 Sept. 1757; m. 28 May 1778 William Wood Jr.
ii.   Barbara, b. 2 Aug. 1759; m. 5 Oct. 1781 Ichabod Davis of Freetown, Mass.
iii.   James, b. 25 May 1761; m. in Westport 6 Dec. 1789 Patience Macomber, daughter of William Macomber. He settled in Danby, Vt.
iv.   Elizabeth, b. 13 Oct. 1763; m. 6 Dec. 1789 James Earle, son of Caleb Earle.
v.   William, b. 9 July 1765; m. (intention 11 July 1789) Sylvia Aiken. He settled in Danby, Vt.
vi.   Mary, b. 25 May 1767; m. Gershom Allen.

Children by third wife:

5. vii.   Hiram Manchester, b. 6 Dec. 1774.

Weston Soule made a deed to his son, Hiram Soule Manchester, as follows: "I, Wesson Soule of Westport, gentleman, considering ye love and affection that ye said Wesson Soule have unto Hiram Soule Manchester, son of Philena Manchester of said Westport, for maintenance and support of him, my homestead farm in Westport of fifty acres, bounded north on Nathaniel Soule, east by Gideon Cornell, south by Gideon Cornell and Christopher Cornell and west on the highway and a sedge flat that my father, Nathaniel, gave to me in his last will and testament, 5 March 1797. . . "

On 12 Jan. 1826 Philena Soule and others of Westport and LC made a deed to William Macomber of the Wesson Soule farm, bounded north by Isaac Corey, east by Gideon Cornell, south by Gideon Cornell and Serviah Wing and west on the highway, sixty (?) acres excepting a burial place of two rods square. This deed was signed by Charles S. Manchester, Ann S. Manchester, Priscilla S. Manchester, Ephraim Manchester and Lydia S. Manchester, as guardian.

Several of this family are buried in the cemetery on the John Soule farm, formerly the Aaron Wilbore place on the Long Highway on the east side near south end. They are: Philena Soule, died 15 Oct. 1846 ae 95. Priscilla Earl, died 30 May 1840 ae 91. Lydia, wife of Hiram Soule, died 23 July 1852 ae 72. Patience Wood, died

4 Oct. 1850 ae 73. Mary D., wife of John Soule, died 15 Feb. 18 67 ae 57. Hiram Soule, died 19 Oct. 1822 ae 48. Ann Soule, died 4 June 1846 ae 40.

5. HIRAM MANCHESTER[5] SOULE (Weston[4], Nathaniel[3], Nathaniel[2], George[1]), born in Westport 6 Dec. 1774, died in LC 19 Oct. 1822. Residence: Westport and LC.

He married in Westport 24 June 1798 LYDIA EARLE, daughter of John and Priscilla (Hilliard) Earle, born 3 Sept. 1780, died in LC 23 July 1852. Both are buried on the Aaron Wilbor or John Soule place on the south end of the Long Highway.

He sometimes went by the name of Hiram Soule Manchester and at other times by the name of Hiram Manchester Soule. His gravestone says Hiram M. Soule. His will, made under the name of Hiram Soule Manchester, book 5, page 106-12: ". . . To son Charles Soule Manchester my best hat, best boots and my case of bottles. To daughter Betsey Soule Manchester my new fall leaf table and set of luster ware and hymn books. To my daughter Amy Soule Manchester my chest with feet. To son John Soule Manchester my gun and bayonet and one share in the school house which I own. To daughter Priscilla Soule Manchester my large Bible. To son Ephraim Soule Manchester one share in the school house that I own. To grandson Hiram, for his name, one sheep at the age of 7 years. To wife all the rest and residue and to sell the farm in Westport and my wife Lydia to be sole executrix. . . " His will was made 10 Nov. 1820 and proved 11 Nov. 1822.

Children, all recorded in Westport except Ephraim:

  i.   Charles, b. 29 May 1801; m. in LC 28 June 1818 Sophia Brownell, daughter of James and Hannah (Manchester) Brownell.
  ii.   Betsey, b. 15 July 1803; m. in LC 14 May 1822 Reuben Davis, son of Philip Davis of Westport.
  iii. Anna, b. 9 July 1806; d. in LC 4 June 1846; unmarried.
6. iv. John, b. 23 Aug. 1809.
  v.   Priscilla, b. 2 May 1812.
7. vi. Ephraim M., b. 1 Dec. 1818.

6. JOHN[6] SOULE (Hiram[5], Weston[4], Nathaniel[3], Nathaniel[2], George[1]), born in Westport 23 Aug. 1809. He married in New Bedford 22 April 1832 MARY D. WOOD, born in 1810, died in LC 15 Feb. 1867.

Residence: New Bedford, LC and (perhaps) Boston. They lived on the Long Highway on the place called the John Soule place on the map of 1870. She is buried there. He went away and became very well to do, but the money was eventually lost and he became bankrupt. He had gone back to LC and built the house there with the cupola. There was also another much older house at the north of the newer one which in 1776 belonged to Aaron Wilbore. It was burned about 1910/20 while in the possession of Walter Bullock.

Patience Wood, ae 70, was living with them in 1850, according to the census.

Children, not recorded in LC:
8. i.   Henry W., b. in 1833.

    ii.   Lydia A., b. in Massachusetts in 1842.
    iii.   John, b. in New Bedford 10 Oct. 1843.

    7. EPHRAIM M.[6] SOULE (Hiram[5], Weston[4], Nathaniel[3], Nathaniel[2], George[1]), born in LC 1 Dec. 1818, died there 31 Oct. 1885.

He married LYDIA ALMIRA PALMER, daughter of Wilbor and Hannah (Snell) Palmer, born in LC 22 May 1816, died there 23 Nov. 1877. Both are buried in the Old Commons cemetery. He married second in LC 14 April 1878 LOUISA M. (TOWN) DUNBAR, widow, daughter of Charles and Mary Town, born in 1832 in Providence, died in LC 24 March 1890. It was her third marriage.

Residence: LC. They lived on the north side of Snell Road, at the west end. The house has since been torn down.

    Children, born in LC, but not recorded there:
    i.   Hannah Borden, b. 2 May 1839; d. in LC 9/10 Jan. 1939 ae
           99-8-8; m. in LC 31 Jan. 1860 James Edmund Peckham,
           son of James Davis and Harriet Byron (Brownell) Peckham.
9. ii.   John Earle, b. 25 Dec. 1840.
    iii.   Ephraim W., b. 13 March 1842; d. in LC 26 Jan. 1925; un-
           married.
    iv.   Mary Wood, b. in LC 29 May 1843; d. 21 Jan. 1933; m. in
           Tiverton 11 July 1864 Isaac Clarke, b. in Newport 21
           March 1835, d. 4 Feb. 1905.
    v.   Charles, b. in LC 18 Oct. 1844; d. 21 Dec. 1913, probably
           in Newport; m. 22 March 1864 Alice Elizabeth Bennett,
           b. in Westerly, R.I., 31 March 1844, d. 20 Feb. 1914.
    vi.   Lydia, b. in LC 3 Feb. 1846; d. there 17 June 1866 ae 20.
10. vii. Samuel Palmer, b. 21 Aug. 1853.

    8. HENRY W.[7] SOULE (John[6], Hiram[5], Weston[4], Nathaniel[3], Nathaniel[2], George[1]), born in New Bedford in 1833. He married ROSINA S. (--), born in Massachusetts in 1840. Residence: LC.

    Children, recorded in LC:
    i.   Henrietta, b. 12 Dec. 1859.
    ii.   Herbert F., b. 19 Aug. 1862.
    iii.   Mary Adams, b. 24 April 1868.
    iv.   Alice Wood, b. 28 Oct. 1870.

    9. JOHN EARLE[7] SOULE (Ephraim[6], Hiram[5], Weston[4], Nathaniel[3], Nathaniel[2], George[1]), born in LC 25 Dec. 1840, died 12 Dec. 1916.

He married in LC 27 Feb. 1871 MARY ELLA WILBOR, daughter of Solomon and Esther (Palmer) Wilbor, born in LC 30 July 1852, died there 8 Jan. 1943. Residence: LC. They lived on Crosby Lane, and are buried in Pleasant View cemetery.

    Children:
    i.   Lydia Esther, b. 10 Aug. 1871; d. in LC 23 March 1933; m.
           there 13 Nov. 1894 James Edmund Pearce, son of Wright
           and Julia (Francis) Pearce, b. in 1867, d. in 1941. He
           m. (2) 18 Oct. 1933 Abby Elizabeth (Soule) Sawyer, daughter
           of Zoeth and Julia M. (Dyer) Soule.
11. ii.   George Walter, b. 28 May 1876.

10. **SAMUEL PALMER[7] SOULE** (Ephraim[6], Hiram[5], Weston[4], Nathaniel[3], Nathaniel[2], George[1]), born in LC 21 Aug. 1853, died there 22 Feb. 1932.

He married in LC 16 Sept. 1874 ELLEN GRAFTON CROSBY, daughter of John Luce and Sarah A. (Cowen) Crosby, born in LC 4 June 1855, died there 1 March 1938. They lived on the Long Highway in LC.

Children, born in LC:

i. Lottie H., b. 21 July 1880; d. in LC 19 July 1885.

ii. Lottie H., b. 24 June 1886; m. (1) in LC William E. West, son of William E. and Pamelia (Luther)West; m. (2) William Richmond Mosher, son of William and Emma L. (Manchester) Mosher, b. 5 Aug. 1873 in LC; d. 13 July 1947.

iii. Annie Ellen, b. in LC 5 April 1888; m. in LC 24 Oct. 1907 Arthur Everett Wilbor, son of George Henry and Georgianna (Wilbor) Wilbor.

11. **GEORGE WALTER[8] SOULE** (John[7], Ephraim[6], Hiram[5], Weston[4], Nathaniel[3], Nathaniel[2], George[1]), born in LC 28 May 1876, died there 24 June 1953. Residence: LC.

He married first in LC 9 May 1906 MARY LOUISE BROWNELL, daughter of Robert G. and Mary Etta (Palmer) Brownell, born in LC 8 Feb. 1878, died there 1 Jan. 1934. He married second 16 Dec. 1935 in Newport MABEL FRANCES CRANDALL, daughter of Charles S. and Minnie G. (Alger) Crandall, born in Newport 24 Dec. 1891.

Children by first wife, born in LC:

i. Walter Earl, b. 9 Feb. 1907; d. in LC 4 Sept. 1906 ae 6 months.

12. **GEORGE[2] SOULE** (George[1]), married DEBORAH (--).

13. **WILLIAM[3] SOULE** (George[2], George[1]), married HANNAH (--). Residence: Dartmouth.

14. **JONATHAN[4] SOULE** (William[3], George[2], George[1]), born 15 Dec. 1710, died in 1779. He married 12 Feb. 1736 LYDIA SISSON, born 8 Sept. 1714, died in 1779. Residence: Dartmouth.

15. **JOSEPH[5] SOULE** (Jonathan[4], William[3], George[2], George[1]), born 1 Sept. 1733 in Westport, died there in April 1828. Residence: Dartmouth.

He married in Tiverton 25 Feb. 1762 RUTH TRIPP, daughter of Benjamin[4] (Joseph[3], Joseph[2], John[1]), and Martha (Luther) Tripp of Dartmouth, born in 1746, died in Westport in 1812. The will of her father Benjamin, recorded book 46, page 322, lists grandsons: James Tripp, Asa Tripp, Preserved Tripp, Abner Tripp, and leaves to his daughter one third of his estate. Her brother Preserved married 14 April (?) in Dartmouth the daughter of Jonathan and Lydia (Sisson) Soule.

Children (from the letter of Jethro Soule, grandson):

    i.   Jethro, b. in 1763; d. in 1797; m. 25 Dec. 1789 Sylvia
           Ricketson.

    ii.   David, b. in 1766; d. in March 1800; m. (1) 22 July 1790
           Phebe Kirby of Westport; m. (2) 13 Jan. 1799 Mary
           Russell, daughter of Prince and Sabiah Russell.

    iii.   Susannah, b. in 1767; d. 2 March 1853 in New Bedford; m.
           in Westport 27 July 1791 Zadock Maxfield.

    iv.   Benjamin, b. in June 1771; d. 26 July 1859; m. in Westport
           in July 1807 Mary (Russell) Soule, daughter of Prince
           and Sabiah (Howland) Russell.

    v.   Mary, b. in 1774; d. in 1815; m. 3 Jan. 1793 David Maxfield.

    vi.   Thankful, b. in 1777; d. in 1814; m. in Westport 12 May 1796
           Abner Kirby.

16. vii.   Jonathan, b. 16 July 1782.

17. JETHRO[7] SOULE (Jonathan[6], Joseph[5], Jonathan[4], William[3],
George[2], George[1]), born in Westport 8 Aug. 1818, died in Vineland,
N.J., 13 Jan. 1902. He married 26 Feb. 1846 MARY GRINNELL, born
in LC 8 Sept. 1825, died in November 1892. Residence: LC and Vineland, N.J.

    Children:

    i.   Eliza M., b. in New Bedford 7 Sept. 1849; m. in Vineland 21
           Oct. 1880 Henry Wilbur.

    ii.   Amy G., b. in 1851; d. in LC in 1860.

    iii.   Lydia M., b. 17 July 1854; m. Andrew Hoeson at Millville,
           N.J.

    iv.   Hannah, b. in LC 1 Dec. 1856; m. 7 Nov. 1882 Daniel Wilbour,
           b. in LC 3 April 1838, d. there 14 Sept. 1909.

    v.   Jethro Jonathan, b. 4 Aug. 1859 in LC; d. in Vineland in 1863.

    vi.   Annie M., b. 24 Nov. 1868; m. in Vineland George C. Gifford.
           They had two children, a daughter and a son, Chester.
           The family moved to Texas.

    vii.   Benjamin Grinnell, b. in LC 18 May 1862; m. in Nebraska
           (--) Hartsook (?). He had two children, Andrew and Annie.

. . . .

GIDEON[1] SOULE, married in Westport 16 Sept. 1828 PATIENCE[7]
HOWLAND (Capt. Zoeth[6], Prince[5], Stephen[4], Henry[3], Zoeth[2], Henry[1]).

    Children:

    i.   Gideon, lost at sea.

    ii.   Zoeth Howland, b. 8 July 1838.

    iii.   James H., m. Betsey Dyer, daughter of Warren Dyer of West-
           port.

    iv.   Louisa, m. (--) Mason.

    v.   Jethro.

ZOETH HOWLAND[2] SOULE (Gideon[1]), born in Westport 8 July
1828, died in Fall River 22 Oct. 1921, buried in Pleasant View cemetery.
    He married in Tiverton 1 Jan. 1861 JULIA MARIA DYER, widow
of Charles Dyer and daughter of Warren and Eliza (Manchester) Dyer,

born in Westport 10 July 1842, died in LC 7 Jan. 1912.

He was a cooper and lived in LC in 1865 in that part which is called Pottersville.

Children:

   i.   Caroline, b. 23 April 1865 in Westport; m. in LC 26 Dec.
        Edward Athington, son of William and Mary (Hargraves)
        Athington.

  ii.   Abbie Elizabeth, b. 11 June 1870 in East Greenwich, R.I.;
        d. in LC 10 March 1943; m. (1) (?); m. (2) 29 Oct. 1933
        James Edmund Pearce, son of Wright and Julia (Francis)
        Pearce.

THE SOUTHWORTH FAMILY

From the Southworth Genealogy.

1. EDWARD[1] SOUTHWORTH, born probably about 1590, died about 1621. He married 28 May 1613 ALICE CARPENTER, daughter of Alexander Carpenter of Wrington, Somersetshire, England, born about 1590, died in Plymouth, Mass., 26 March 1670. She married second in Plymouth 14 Aug. 1623 William Bradford, governor of Plymouth.

Ed. Note: Edward Southworth was a sill worker in Leyden and one of the Pilgrim exiles who formed the Rev. John Robinson's church. It is not known what part of England he came from but in my journey to England in 1923 I visited Wellam in Notts and found the baptisms of an Edward Southworth with brothers Robert and Thomas. I have an idea that they came from this town but it has not been proven. He died in London about 1621.

After his death Governor Bradford of Plymouth sent for his widow, Alice Carpenter, whom he had known in England and married her in New England. There is much more on Edward Southworth given in the Southworth genealogy by Samuel G. Webber, but let it be understood that up to this time it has never been proved that he came from the celebrated Southworth family of Lancashire, although much work has been done on this family in England--BFW.

Children:

2. i.   Constant, b. in Leyden, Holland, in 1615.

  ii.   Thomas, b. in Leyden, Holland, in 1616; d. in Plymouth,
       Mass., 8 Dec. 1669.

2. CONSTANT[2] SOUTHWORTH (Edward[1]), born in Leyden, Holland, in 1615, died in Duxbury, Mass., 10 March 1679. He married 2 Nov. 1637 ELIZABETH COLLIER of Duxbury, daughter of William Collier, merchant of Duxbury.

Besides the land that he owned in Duxbury, he had land in Tiverton and LC. From his position as treasurer he had an opportunity to know

what land was of value and opportunities to select his land. He came to
LC with William Pabodie at its settlement and surveyed much of the
land there. His will, made 27 Feb. 1678 and proved in March 1678/9:
". . . To wife Elizabeth Southworth during her terme of live this
dwelling house with out-housing and mill belonging and all uplands
and meddowes lying within the town of Duxburrow or Marshfield for
her support and comfort. To son Edward Southworth after the decease
of my aforesaid wife my aforesaid dwelling house with out-housing
and mill. Also twelve pounds in money. To son Nathaniel Southworth
the one halfe share of lands that lyeth neare Taunton by name of
Ffreeman's lands. To three daughters Marcye Ffreeman, Allice Church
and Mary Alden, my other one half share of the Ffreeman's lands. To
my daughter Elizabeth Southworth my next best bed and furniture, provided she doe not marry William Fobbes but if she doe then to have five
shillings. To daughter Prissila Southworth my next best bed and furniture. Unto my son William Southworth my next best bed. To my grandson Constant Ffreeman and all those lands and meddows that I have at a
place called Pawomett in the town of Eastham. To my cosen Elizabeth
Howland, my brother Thomas his daughter five pounds. All the rest
and residue to my beloved wife, and she to be sole executrix. . . "

      Children:
- i.   Mercy, b. about 1638; d. 25 Nov. 1712; m. 12 May 1758
  Samuel Freeman.
- ii.   Edward, d. about 1727; m. Mary Pabodie, daughter of William[2]
  and Elizabeth (Alden) Pabodie.
- iii.   Alice, b. in 1646; d. 5 March 1719; m. 26 Dec. 1667 Col.
  Benjamin Church, the celebrated Indian fighter of King
  Philip's War.
- iv.   Nathaniel, b. in 1648; d. 14 Jan. 1711.
- v.   Mary, b. probably about 1650; d. in 1719; m. about 1670
  David Alden, son of John and Priscilla (Mullins) Alden.
- vi.   Elizabeth, m. about 1679 Lt. William Fobes, son of John
  and Constant (Mitchell) Fobes, b. in 1649, d. 6 Nov.
  1712. This was the man to whom her father objected
  in his will.
- vii. Priscilla, m. (1) in Bristol, R.I., 1 March 1678 Samuel.
  Talbot (?).
3. viii. William, b. in 1659.

3. CAPT. WILLIAM[3] SOUTHWORTH (Constant[2], Edward[1]), born
in Duxbury in 1659, died in LC 25 June 1719. He married first in 1680
REBECCA PABODY, daughter of William and Elizabeth (Alden) Pabody,
born in Duxbury 16 Oct. 1660, died in LC 23 Dec. 1702. Her mother
was the daughter of John and Priscilla Alden of Plymouth. Both are
buried in a tomb in the Old Commons cemetery. He married second
in Saybrook, Conn., 14 Nov. 1705 MRS. MARTHA (KIRTLAND) BLAGUE,
born about 1667, died 7 Feb. 1737/8. She was also known as Blaque and
Blake.
    He lived in Duxbury, LC and Bristol, R.I. He was a deputy in
Duxbury 1654-63 and 1671-82, a selectman there 1672-75 and 1683-85.
He owned much land in LC and was there in 1686. He lived on Swamp

Road on the place known as the Franklin C. Southworth place. All of
his children are entered on the records of the Church of Christ in
Bristol, as baptized 29 June 1709.

He gave land to his sons Samuel, Thomas, Stephen, Benjamin and
Andrew; and to Gideon he gave his dwelling house, orchard and land.
With his wife Martha he gave Joseph and his wife Mary Blague a dwelling
house, orchard and 26 acres of upland, with a sawmill standing upon the
cornmill stream with 42 acres of upland on the west side of that stream
and 20 acres of upland adjoining the land of Reynolds Marvin, with 10
acres meadow known by the name of the Fresh Meadow. In his will, recorded in Taunton, made 8 May 1719 and proved 24 Aug. 1719, he left
to his wife Martha "her third as the law allows"; 20 pounds each to sons
Joseph, Edward, Thomas and Gideon; to son Samuel 5 pounds; to son
Nathaniel 400 pounds; to son Benjamin 10 shillings; to daughter Elizabeth
60 pounds; to daughter Alice 70 pounds; to son Stephen one half of his
Negro man called Cuff and one cow, and to son Andrew the other half
of his Negro man called Cuff. He also mentioned his grandsons William
and Constant Southworth. He named his friend Lt. John Wood to be one
of his executors along with his sons Joseph and Samuel. An inventory
of his estate lists one Negro man called Cuff, one Negro woman called
Sue and one Negro woman called Kate, two houses and one hundred acres
of land with 2000 pounds, with the estate totaling 2593 pounds.

In her will his widow left 5 shillings each to her sons Joseph Blague
and Samuel Blague, ". . . To sons Gideon Southworth and Andrew Southworth the rest and residue. To son Andrew my Negro girl named Kate
and my silver tankard, to daughter Mary Southworth my wearing apparel,
to grandson William Southworth my young heifer that came of that cow I
had of Stephen Wilcox, to granddaughter Mary Blague my satinet gown
and short apron. . . " Her son-in-law Joseph Southworth was named sole
executor.

In 1689 he was commissioned a lieutenant and later became known
as Captain Southworth.

Children by first wife, recorded in LC:

4. i.   Benjamin, b. 16 April 1681.
5. ii.   Joseph, b. in February 1683.
6. iii.   Edward, b. 23 Nov. 1684.
    iv.   Elizabeth, b. 23 Sept. 1686; m. in LC 2 Dec. 1703 David
           Little.
    v.   Alice, b. 14 July 1688; d. 25 April 1770; m. in LC 25 May
           1709 John Cook.
    vi.   Samuel, b. 26 Dec. 1690; d. in Stratford in 1758; m. Abigail
           (--). Residence: Bristol, R.I., and Lyme, Conn.
    vii.   Nathaniel, b. 31 Oct. 1692; m. Mary Torrey.
    viii. Thomas, b. 13 Dec. 1694; m. 21 Feb. 1723 in LC Patience
           Thurston, daughter of Jonathan Thurston. Residence:
           Bristol, R.I. and Mansfield, Conn.
    ix.   Stephen, b. 31 March 1696.

    Children by second wife:
8. x.   Gideon, b. 21 March 1707.

xi.   Andrew, b. 12 Dec. 1709; m. 27 Dec. 1731 Temperance
       Kirtland. Residence: Saybrook and Chester, Conn.

4. BENJAMIN[4] SOUTHWORTH (William[3], Constant[2], Edward[1]),
born in LC 16 April 1681.
    He married first in LC 18 Dec. 1701 ELIZABETH WOODWORTH,
daughter of Walter Woodworth, born in 1678, died 18 June 1713. He
married second 14 March 1717 ALICE CHURCH, daughter of Joseph
and Grace (Shaw) Church, born in LC 8 Feb. 1695, died there 14 Feb.
1718. He married third in LC 18 July 1722 SUSANNA (PALMER)
BLACKMAN, daughter of William and Mary (Richmond) Palmer, born
12 Oct. 1692. She was the widow of Jonathan Blackman, who married
her as a second wife and not Sarah, as given in Arnold's Vital Records.
The first two wives are buried in the Old Commons cemetery. He and
his third wife are probably buried there but have no stones.
            Children by first wife, recorded in LC:
i.   William, b. in October 1703.
ii.   Oliver, b. 7 Dec. 1705; m. 15 Sept. 1740 Ann King. Residence:
        Hingham, Mass.
iii.   Mary, b. 5 March 1713; m. 3 May 1755 Edward[4] (John[3], Joseph[2],
        Richard[1]) Church.

            Children by third wife:
iv.   Elizabeth, b. 13 Sept. 1723.
v.   Benjamin, b. 29 July 1725; d. in 1784.
vi.   Isaac, b. 31 Oct. 1727.
vii.   Patience, b. 1 Jan. 1730.

5. CAPT. JOSEPH[4] SOUTHWORTH (William[3], Constant[2], Edward[1]),
born in LC 1 Feb. 1683, died there 20 April 1739.
    He married there 20 April 1710 MARY BLAKE or BLAGUE, daughter
of Joseph and Martha (Kirtland) Blague, born in 1691, died in LC 29 Oct.
1770. Both are buried in the Old Commons cemetery.
    He was town clerk of LC for nine years: 1725-30 and 1732-36. He
lived on Swamp Road on the place later owned by Franklin C. Southworth
and owned in 1890 by William Tweed Peckham.
    Her will, proved 4 Dec. 1770: ". . . To son Constant my loom and
Willard's Body of Divinity. One small pair of stilliards. To son Joseph
15 shillings. To daughter Elizabeth Corey three pewter platters and four
plates. To daughter Sarah Lawton my best bed and two silver spoons. To
daughter Mary Wilbor one iron pot, two silver spoons and three pounds
five shillings lawful money. To daughter Abigail Woodworth one looking
glass and three pounds five shillings. Rest and residue to three daughters.
My son-in-law Daniel Wilbour to be my executor. . . "

            Children, recorded in LC:
i.   Elizabeth, b. in Lyme, Conn., 13 April 1712; d. 7 May 1773;
        m. in LC 6 July 1757 Caleb Corey.
9. ii.   Constant, b. 21 April 1715.
iii.   William, b. 30 June 1719; d. in March 1754.
iv.   Sarah, b. 7 Sept. 1721; m. in LC 20 Feb. 1746 William Lawton.
v.   Nathaniel, b. 27 March 1724; baptized in LC 2 July 1724.
vi.   Joseph, b. 28 June 1726; baptized in LC 21 Aug. 1726.

vii.   Mary, b. 30 Dec. 1728; baptized in LC 27 April 1729; d. 18
April 1799; m. in LC 22 March 1753 Daniel Wilbur.

viii. Samuel, b. 1 Oct. 1731.

ix.   Abigail, b. 11 June 1734; baptized in LC 25 Sept. 1734; d. 14
Jan. 1805; m. (1) 13 Dec. 1753 Hezekiah Woodworth; m.
(2) (--) Church.

x.   John, b. 1 June 1737; baptized in LC 2 Aug. 1737.

xi.   Susanna.

6. EDWARD[4] SOUTHWORTH (William[3], Constant[2], Edward[1]),
born in Duxbury, Mass., 23 Nov. 1684. Residence: LC.

He married 17 March 1708 MARY FOBES, daughter of William
and Martha (Pabodie) Fobes, born in 1689, died in LC 29 Feb. 1712.
He married second in LC 11 Oct. 1716 ELIZABETH PALMER, daughter
of John and Elizabeth (Richmond) Palmer of LC, born there 17 Nov.
1691, died in Lebanon, Conn., 13 Oct. 1784.

Children by first wife, recorded in LC:

i.   Rebecca, b. 22 Dec. 1708; m. in 1733 Benjamin Seabury,
son of Joseph and Phebe Seabury.

10. ii.   Fobes, b. 1 Sept. 1710.

Children by second wife, recorded in LC:

iii.   Thomas, b. 7 June 1718 in LC.

iv.   Alice, b. 24 Nov. 1720; m. in March 1745 Aaron Brownell,
son of Jeremiah and Deborah Brownell.

v.   Edward, b. 27 Feb. 1724.

vi.   Elizabeth, b. 29 Dec. 1725.

vii.   Esther, b. 25 Sept. 1727.

viii. Beriah, b. 28 May 1729; d. in 1811 in Lebanon, Conn.;
m. there in 1755 Rebekah Williams.

ix.   Mary, b. 15 July 1732.

x.   William, b. 28 Dec. 1735.

7. STEPHEN[4] SOUTHWORTH (William[3], Constant[2], Edward[1]),
born in LC 31 March 1696. Residence: LC and Freetown, Mass.

He married in LC 27 Jan. 1725/6 LYDIA WARREN, daughter of
Joshua and Rebecca (Church) Warren, born 3 Nov. 1696.

Children, recorded in Freetown, Mass.:

i.   Rebecca, b. 7 Oct. 1726; bapt. in LC 28 May 1727.

ii.   Thomas, b. 5 Sept. 1728; m. 13 Nov. 1753 Mrs. Sarah Ward,
widow, of Plymouth. Residence: Freetown, Mass.

iii.   Stephen, b. 12 Jan. 1731; d. before 1670; m. 27 Sept. 1753
Hannah Sibley of Sutton, Mass.

8. GIDEON[4] SOUTHWORTH (William[3], Constant[2], Edward[1]), born
in LC 31 March 1707, died in 1772 in Rochester, Mass. Residence:
LC and Rochester.

He married in LC 25 Sept. 1728 MARY WILBORE, daughter of
John and Sarah (Palmer) Wilbore of LC, born there 13 April 1711.
She was baptized there 3 May 1730.

In 1719 his father gave him a dwelling house, orchard and land

in LC. He graduated from Yale University with an AB degree in 1727,
and in 1732 he left LC for Rochester, where he was a school master.
In 1751 records place him in Coventry, Conn., but he soon returned to
Rochester where he died.

Children, first three recorded in LC:

11. i.   Isaac, b. 31 July 1729.

    ii.   Parnel, b. in LC 31 July 1729; bapt. there 3 May 1730; d.
19 June 1821; m. in LC 5 Feb. 1749 William Church.

    iii.   Wilbur, b. in LC 22 Feb. 1730; bapt. there 2 May 1731; d.
in Rochester 27 Feb. 1807; m. 26 March 1775 Lois
(Winslow) Roper.

    iv.   Sarah, b. in Rochester 29 Dec. 1732; bapt. in LC 1 April
1733; d. 25 Jan. 1775; m. 8 March 1752 Joseph Hawkins.

    v.   Elizabeth, b. in Rochester 7 March 1734; bapt. in LC 6 June
1736.

    vi.   Charles, b. in Rochester 14 Feb. 1736; d. same day.

    vii.   Mabel, b. in Rochester 28 Dec. 1737; bapt. there 25 Oct.
1741; m. 12 Jan. 1772 William Wiltshire of Rochester.

    viii.   Rachel, b. in Rochester 24 Jan. 1739; m. Daniel Lyman.

    ix.   Lois, b. in Rochester 10 Jan. 1741; m. (intention 18 Oct.
1765) John Aulden of Dartmouth.

    x.   Ebenezer, b. in Rochester 16 Jan. 1743.

    xi.   Alice, b. in Rochester 21 Feb. 1745; d. 3 May 1807; m. 8
Feb. 1770 Luther Burgess.

    xii.   William, b. in Rochester 3 May 1747.

    xiii.   Andria, b. in Coventry, Conn., 27 July 1751.

    xiv.   Hannah, b. in Rochester in April 1755; d. in August in 1841;
m. 4 July 1776 Ebenezer Drew.

9. CAPT. CONSTANT[5] SOUTHWORTH (Joseph[4], William[3], Constant[2],
Edward[1]), born in LC 21 April 1715, died there 24 Nov. 1791.

He married there 15 Aug. 1751 REBECCA RICHMOND, daughter of
Sylvester and Elizabeth (Talbot) Richmond, born in LC 12 Feb. 1723,
died there 22 Dec. 1803. Both are buried in Old Commons cemetery.

He was a resident of LC when his father died in 1739. In 1745 he
was living on the Franklin C. Southworth place and later lived in Dighton,
Mass. He united with the church in LC in 1740. He was captain of a
company at the seige and capture of Louisburg.

In his will, recorded in LC, made 21 Feb. 1785 and proved 7 Feb.
1792, he left to his sons William, Nathaniel and Samuel Southworth all
real estate equally with livestock, and to his daughter Mary Southworth
one half of household goods.

Children, recorded in LC:

12. i.   William, b. 27 July 1753.

    ii.   Nathaniel, b. 6 June 1755; lived and died a bachelor. In
early life he was attracted to his cousin, Mary Wilbour,
the daughter of Daniel and Mary (Southworth) Wilbour
(who lived on what was later the Benjamin F. Wilbour
place). Friends objected to the marriage as they were
first cousins so that he and she remained single for 50
years, he visiting her every week. He lived with his

brother, William Southworth, in the house across the
way, on the swamp corner, which later was the house
of Charles Edwin Wilbour.

iii.   Mary, b. 11 April 1757; m. in LC 1 Jan. 1787 Judge William
       Wilbor.
iv.   John, b. 7 May 1759; d. 29 July 1782; m. 6 Dec. 1762 Elizabeth
       Wightman.
v.   Joseph, b. 30 March 1761.
vi.   Hannah, b. 6 April 1763; d. 1 Dec. 1765.
vii.   Samuel, b. 20 March 1767; d. by drowning 6 June 1801.

10. FOBES[5] SOUTHWORTH (Edward[4], William[3], Constant[2],
Edward[1]), born in LC 1 Sept. 1710.
    He married first in LC 27 Oct. 1732 SUSAN WINCHESTER of
Barrington, Mass. He married second in LC 19 Oct. 1738 MARY
SEABURY of Tiverton, daughter of Arnold Joseph and Phebe (Smith)
Seabury, born 17 April 1715.

       Children, not recorded in LC:
i.   Priscilla, b. in March 1740; bapt. in LC 6 July 1740.
ii.   Rebecca, b. in May 1841; bapt. in LC 24 May 1741.
iii.   John, b. 4 Jan. 1743; bapt. in LC in April 1743; d. in Rochester,
       N.Y., 30 Nov. 1832; m. (1) 6 Dec. 1762 Elizabeth Weightman;
       m. (2) Hannah Rundel.

11. ISAAC[5] SOUTHWORTH (Gideon[4], William[3], Constant[2], Edward[1])
born in LC 31 July 1729; bapt. there 3 May 1730; died before 1790. Resi
dence: LC.
    He married there 13 Dec. 1753 ABIGAIL PABODY, daughter of John
and Rebecca (Gray) Pabodie, born in LC 16 Jan. 1735, died there 14 Jan.
1805.

       Children, only the first recorded in LC:
i.   Ruth, b. 12 June 1754.
13. ii. Alden, b. 6 Aug. 1758.
iii.   Ephraim, b. 27 July 1760; d. in 1828; m. 8 May 1788 Rebecca
       Simmons of Dighton, Mass. Residence: Dighton, Providence
       and New York State.
iv.   Rebecca, b. 30 Sept. 1762.
v.   Elizabeth, b. 26 April 1767.
vi.   Luther, b. 13 Dec. 1769; m. 12 Oct. 1804 Mrs. Eunice (Simmons)
       Boynton. Residence: Madison, N.Y.
vii.   Oliver, d. in infancy.
viii. Jeremiah, d. in infancy.

12. MAJOR WILLIAM[6] SOUTHWORTH (Constant[5], Joseph[4],
William[3], Constant[2], Edward[1]), born in LC 27 July 1753, died in Milton,
now Genoa, N.Y., 30 Oct. 1808.
    He married 12 Sept. 1782 MARY THROOP of Bristol, R.I., daughter
of Thomas and Hannah (Morton) Throop, born 25 Dec. 1760, died 5 Sept.
1828.
    In 1775 he was ensign of Ninth Company, Army of Observation of
Rhode Island and Providence Plantations; in 1777 ensign of company

formed out of Alarm List of Little Compton; in 1779 lieutenant of the
Trained Band of Little Compton; in 1781 major of Second Battalion.

In 1807 he sold his home in Little Compton to his brother Nathaniel and moved to Milton, now Genoa, Cayuga County, N.Y. He owned
a place later owned by the heirs of Franklin Chester Southworth on
the Swamp Road, owned in 1890 by William T. Peckham. The Southworth place was at one time very large and went from the present
farm to the main road. The Swamp Road was, before 1812, a driftway and this driftway ran through the middle of the Southworth farm.
The old Southworth house was a little to the north of the present barn.

> Children, recorded in LC:
>
> i.   Clarissa, b. 15 May 1784; d. in 1838.
> ii.   Joseph, b. 1 June 1784/5; bapt. in LC in 1785; d. in York 11
>   April 1841.
> iii. Hannah, b. 8 Oct. 1786; d. in LC 11 Oct. 1819; m. Charles
>   Wood.
> iv.   Harriet, b. 13 Oct. 1788; bapt. 14 Dec. 1788; d. 16 July 1866;
>   m. 17 Jan. 1808 Ira Tilliotson.
> v.   Eliza S., b. 10 Jan. 1790; d. in August 1822; m. William Rufus
>   Commons.
> vi.   Dr. William Throop, b. 12 July 1791; bapt. 13 June 1790; d.
>   20 Jan. 1857; m. (1) 25 Feb. 1818 Harriet Montague; m.
>   (2) in Ithaca, N.Y. in 1826 Clarissa Parsons.
> vii. Sarah, b. 22 Nov. 1792; d. 28 Sept. 1843; m. (1) 25 Dec. 1813
>   Thomas Wilbur; m. (2) in October 1817 (--) Reed; m. (3)
>   in August 1826 Lewis Scout.
> viii. Mary, b. 22 July 1794; m. (1) about 1819 (--) Evens; m. (2)
>   in 1836 Levi Kirkham.
> ix.   Abigail, b. 2 Jan. 1796; d. 20 Oct. 1815; unmarried.
> x.   Rebecca, b. 27 Sept. 1797; d. 26 Oct. 1809.
> 14. xi. Constant, b. 27 Sept. 1797.
> xii. Charlotte, b. 26 Oct. 1799; d. 23 May 1842; m. in April
>   1818 Isaac Beers.
> xiii. Lucy, b. 28 July 1801; d. 10 Dec. 1850; m. William R. Collins.
> xiv. Lydia, b. in January 1803; d. 2 Feb. 1805.

13. ALDEN[6] SOUTHWORTH (Isaac[5], Gideon[4], William[3], Constant[2],
Edward[1]), born in LC 6 Aug. 1758, died in November 1794. Residence:
LC.

He married there 24 Nov. 1790 LYDIA TAYLOR of LC, daughter of
Philip and Mary (Gray) Taylor, born in LC 20 June 1767, died 24 Aug.
1794.

In the Revolutionary War, he served in 1778 as a sergant with a
guard boat of the Rhode Island Forces, commanded by Col. Israel Angell.
On 7 Jan. 1779 he was discharged by sentence of court marshall, the
reason not given. He was a seafaring man, and in August 1794 he sailed
in the ship Washington, Captain Hicks, master. He did not return home
and his fate is unknown.

> Children, recorded in LC:
>
> i.   Richmond, b. 24 July 1791; bapt. in LC 4 Oct. 1795; d. 31
>   March 1831; m. (1) in March 1814 Laura Gridley; m. (2)

9 Dec. 1828 Elizabeth Coburn. Residence: Clinton,
Oneida County, N.Y.

14. CONSTANT[7] SOUTHWORTH (William[6], Constant[5], Joseph[4],
William[3], Constant[2], *Edward[1]), born in LC 27 Sept. 1797, died 11 Dec.
1855 (?) in New York State. He married ALMIRA SEARS, daughter of
Joshua and Martha (Parsons) Sears.

When he was nine years old his parents moved to Genoa, Cayuga
County, N.Y. He moved to Locke, Cayuga County, and in 1863 to North
Collins, Erie County, N.Y. He was a successful farmer.

Children:
15. i.   Nathaniel Chester, b. 19 May 1827.

15. NATHANIEL CHESTER[8] SOUTHWORTH (Constant[7], William[6],
Constant[5], Joseph[4], William[3], Constant[2], Edward[1]), born in Locke, N.Y.,
19 May 1827, died in Forestville, N.Y., 7 Nov. 1900. Residence:
Villenova, N.Y.

He married 12 Jan. 1860 CHLOE RATHBONE, daughter of Damercus
and Amanda (Hills) Rathburn, born 17 June 1829.

In 1836 he moved to North Collins, Erie County, N.Y. In 1874 he
moved to Forestville, N.Y.

Children, born in North Collins, N.Y.:
i.   Effie Almira, b. 29 Oct. 1860; m. in Forestville 1 Jan. 1896
       Professor Volney Morgan Spalding, Ph.D., son of Frederik
       Austin and Almira (Shaw) Spalding, b. in Ontario, N.Y., 29
       Jan. 1849.
ii.   Franklin Chester, b. 15 Oct. 1863.
iii.   Ward Rathburn, b. 10 May 1866; d. in June 1878.
iv.   Angia Lina, b. 23 May 1868; m. 5 Sept. 1893 Carlton S. Dye,
       son of Thomas and Amy (Smith) Dye, b. 12 March 1868 in
       Villenova, N.Y. Residence: Saybrook, Ohio.
v.   Charles Wilson, b. 23 Nov. 1870. He received his M.D. degree
       from the University of Buffalo. Residence: Buffalo, N.Y.

16. REV. FRANKLIN CHESTER[9] SOUTHWORTH (Nathanial[8], Constant[7],
William[6], Constant[5], Joseph[4], William[3], Constant[2], Edward[1]), born in
North Collins, N.Y., 15 Oct. 1863, died in LC 20 May 1944.

He married 5 Sept. 1893 ALICE A. BERRY, daughter of James Hervey
and Abba Sophia (Dix) Berry, born in Forestville, N.Y., 15 Oct. 1863.
She graduated from Vassar College with an AB degree and was an instructor in Greek and Latin at Rockford Seminary, Rockford, Ill., 1885-
92. The following year she was an instructor in Latin at Vassar.

He received his AB degree from Harvard in 1887, and graduated
from Divinity School in 1892. He was settled first in Duluth, Minn., over
the first Unitarian Church from 1892 to 1897. Then he settled over the
third Unitarian Church in Chicago. In 1902 he was chosen president of
the Meadville Theological School in Pennsylvania.

He bought back from William T. Peckham his ancestral home in LC,
first owned by his ancesters, William Southworth (who married Rebecca
Pabodie) and Joseph Southworth (who married Mary Blague). In his last
years he made his home in LC.

Children:
i.   Constant, b. 12 Aug. 1894; m. Evelina Prescott Kean.
ii. William Berry, b. 28 May 1896; d. in 1927.
iii. Dr. Franklin Chester Jr., b. 28 June 1898; m. in 1925
     Margaret Boynton of Framingham, Mass. His son,
     Franklin Chester 3d of New Haven, m. Jose Clesse,
     daughter of M. and Mme. Willy Clesse of Luxemburg
     and granddaughter of Dr. Richard W. Boynton of Buffalo,
     N.Y.

೧೪൭

THE SPRINGER FAMILY

1. LAWRENCE[1] SPRINGER of Tiverton, born about 1655, married
MARTHA HICKS, died in 1704. Residence: LC and Tiverton.

His will, probated in Taunton book 2, page 33, made 4 Sept. 1701
and proved 24 Feb. 1701/2: ". . . To Martha Springer my wife use of
whole estate during her life, housing, lands, goods and chattels and
after her death to my two sons Thomas and Edward Springer who shall
have all housing and lands, goods and chattels equally. . . To daughter
Mary's eldest daughter called Ann Dier and daughter Joanna's eldest
son Jeremiah a yearling calf between them. . ." He also left five pounds
to each of his five sons and 40 shillings to each of his three daughters.

Children, the first recorded in LC:
i.   Edward, b. in March 1685.
ii.   Thomas, b. about 1685.
2. iii. John, b. about 1671.
iv.   Jonathan, b. about 1672.
v.   Joseph, m. 19 June 1718 in LC Mary Knight, daughter of
      Richard[2] Knight.
vi.   Benjamin.
vii. Henry.
viii. Mary, m. (--) Weaver; had Ann, called Ann Dier.
ix.   Waddy (?).
x.   Joanna. Her son, Jeremiah, mentioned in her father's will,
      was also mentioned in the will of William Briggs 3 April
      1716 as his servant, to live with him until age 21.
xi.   Martha.

2. JOHN[2] SPRINGER (Lawrence[1]), probably born in LC or Tiverton,
married ELIZABETH (--).

Children:
i.   James, b. 18 June 1698 and recorded in LC.
3. ii. Lawrence.

3. LAWRENCE[3] SPRINGER (perhaps John[2], Lawrence[1]), perhaps
married ESTHER (--). Residence: Tiverton and LC.

Children, first three recorded in LC, last five recorded in Tiverton:
- i.   Joseph, b. 11 July 1750.
- ii.   Richmond, b. 25 July 1752.
- iii. Isaac, b. 28 June 1755.
- 4. iv.   John, b. 11 Dec. 1759.
- v.   Elizabeth, b. 17 Dec. 1759 (?).
- vi.   Gamaliel, b. 27 April 1762.
- vii. Peleg, b. 11 Dec. 1766.

4. JOHN⁴ SPRINGER (Lawrence³, perhaps John², Lawrence¹), born in LC 11 Dec. 1759, died there 23 Aug. 1846. Residence: LC. He was a soldier of the Revolution.

He married in LC 28 Dec. 1787 RHODA STODDARD, daughter of David and Mary (Simmons) Stoddard of LC, born there 24 Nov. 1767, died there 3 Nov. 1857.

Children:
- i.   Rhoda, b. in LC 27 Sept. 1800; d. there 13 March 1886; m. 27 Dec. 1819 Hezekiah Woodworth, son of Elisha and Edith (Wilbor) Woodworth.

THE STAPLES FAMILY

1. GEORGE W.² STAPLES, son of George¹ and Eliza Staples of Temple, Maine, born 2 Sept. 1820, died in LC 17 July 1875. Residence: LC. They lived on the West Road opposite Fred Sherman's place and Simeon Wonderly lived with them.

He was married in LC 9 March 1847 by the Rev. Philip Crandon to RUTH D. WHITE, daughter of David and Patience (Brown) White, born in LC 15 May 1827, died 5 July 1866.

Children:
- i.   Eliza Emma, b. in Tiverton in 1850; m. in LC 4 Oct. 1870 Frederick Hoffer Jr., son of Frederic and Catharine Hoffer, b. in Buffalo, N.Y.
- ii.   Lena, b. in LC 8 Nov. 1853.
- iii. Ruth White, b. in LC 25 June 1866.

2. CHARLES A.² STAPLES, son of George¹ and Eliza Staples of Temple, Maine, born in Temple in June 1832, died in LC 14 Aug. 1892. Residence: LC.

He married ELIZABETH W. WHITE, daughter of David and Patience (Brown) White, born in LC 13 Jan. 1835, died in March 1903. They are buried in the Union cemetery.

Children:
- i.   Charles H., b. in July 1863.

THE STODDARD FAMILY
From the Stoddard Book (1912).

1. JOHN[1] STODDARD, born in Hull, England, died in Hingham, Mass., 19 Dec. 1661. Residence: Hingham.

He married in England HANNAH (--). His will was made 20 Nov. 1661 and proved 31 Jan. 1661.

Children:
i. John, b. 20 Dec. 1608 (?); m. 13 Dec. 1665 Hannah Bryant, daughter of John and Mary (Lewis) Bryant of Scituate, Mass.
ii. Hannah, m. Gershom Wheelock, son of Ralph Wheelock of Medford, Mass.
iii. Elizabeth, b. in England; d. 14 Sept. 1658; m. 28 Feb. 1648/9 John Low of Medford, Mass., d. 25 Jan. 1696/7.
iv. Daniel, b. in 1633; m. 27 Dec. 1665 Abigail Lane, daughter of Andrew and Triphany Lane of Hingham.
2. v. Samuel.

2. SERGEANT SAMUEL[2] STODDARD (John[1]), baptized at Hingham, Mass., 14 June 1640, died 16 Sept. 1731 ae 91. Residence: Hingham, Mass., where they lived at the corner of Main Street and Elm.

He married first in January or February 1666/7 ELIZABETH GILL, daughter of Thomas and Hannah (Otis) Gill, baptized in Hingham in June 1647, died in Hingham 8 May 1693. He married second 12 Jan. 1698/9 MRS. MARTHA (BEAL) CHUBBUCK, daughter of Nathaniel and Martha Beal and widow of John Chubbuck, baptized in Hingham 2 Aug. 1646.

Children by first wife, all recorded in Hingham, Mass.:
i. Elizabeth, b. 1 Dec. 1667; m. 6 March 1694 Thomas Joy.
ii. Tabitha, b. 1 Dec. 1667; d. ae 2 weeks.
iii. Samuel, b. 11 Aug. 1670; d. in Scituate, Mass., 25 July 1762. Residence: Scituate.
iv. Mary, b. 30 Aug. 1672; m. 28 May 1700 Israel Whitcomb of Scituate.
v. Stephen, b. 18 Sept. 1674.
3. vi. Thomas, b. 19 Dec. 1676.
vii. Simon, b. 17 Feb. 1678/9.
viii. Rachel, b. 9 March 1680/81; m. 22 May 1707 William Curtis, son of John and Miriam (Brooks) Curtis of Scituate.
ix. Jeremiah, b. 3 Nov. 1683.
4. x. Jonathan, b. 1 May 1686.
xi. David, b. 9 July 1688; d. ae 10 days.
xii. David, b. 19 March 1692/3; d. 5 Sept. 1748.

3. THOMAS[3] STODDARD (Samuel[2], John[1]), born in Hingham, Mass., 19 Dec. 1676. Residence: Hingham and LC.

He was married in LC 19 Oct. 1704 by Joseph Church, justice, to RUTH NICHOLS, daughter of Israel and Mary Nichols of Hingham, born there 23 Nov. 1687, died in LC 7 Oct. 1731.

His will, recorded in Book 1, LC Wills, page 202, made 19 Oct. 1754 and proved 7 Dec. 1756: ". . . To son Israel Stoddard all that part

of my land that he now improves and fenced with his land and all my now
dwelling house. To son Ichabod 5 shillings. To son Nathaniel all that
part of homestead farm that he now improves with all housing. To son
Noah 5 shillings. To son Joshua 200 pounds. To son Benjamin part of
homestead farm he now improves. To daughter Elizabeth Briggs 50
pounds. To grandson Thomas Stoddard, son of my son Thomas, deceased,
40 pounds. To granddaughters Ruth Taylor, Susannah and Sarah Stoddard,
20 pounds each. . . To sons Nathaniel and Benjamin all right I have in
housing and lands that were formerly of the Rev. Richard Billings, equally
. . . "

Children, recorded in LC:

	i.	Thomas, b. 5 March 1706.
5.	ii.	Israel, b. 14 Nov. 1707.
	iii.	Elizabeth, b. 28 Oct. 1709; m. (intention 29 June 1740) in LC Job Briggs.
	iv.	Samuel, b. 22 Feb. 1712; d. 25 Dec. 1714.
	v.	Gideon, b. 7 Aug. 1714; probably died young.
6.	vi.	Ichabod, b. 31 March 1717.
7.	vii.	Nathaniel, b. 25 June 1719.
8.	viii.	Noah, b. 25 April 1721.
	ix.	Joshua, b. 19 April 1723.
9.	x.	Benjamin, b. 23 Aug. 1725.
	xi.	William, b. 23 March 1729; probably d. young.
	xii.	Ruth, b. in 1731; m. in LC 8 Feb. 1753 Joseph Taylor, son of Philip and Comfort (Dennis) Taylor.

4. JONATHAN³ STODDARD (Samuel², John¹), born in Hingham,
Mass., 1 May 1686, died in LC 4 Nov. 1774. He was a blacksmith in
Hingham and LC.
    He married about 1724 MARY DRING, daughter of Thomas and
Mary (Butler) Dring, born 23 April 1699, died in May 1786 in LC.
    Her will, recorded book 3, LC Probate, made 17 May 1779 and
proved 6 June 1786: ". . . under decay of nature. . . To three sons
Salisbury, David and Jonathan, 4 shillings each. To three daughters
Hannah Dring, Ruth Dring and Mary Crandall my wearing apparel. To
daughter Ruth Dring my best bed and bedstead. To daughter Mary Crandall
my other bed and bedstead, my two wheels and my washing tub. To son
David Stoddard an iron bar, axe and retchell. Rest and residue to my
three daughters. My son Salisbury to be executor. . . "

Children, recorded in LC and Hingham:

	i.	Elijah, b. 24 Sept. 1725; d. in LC September 1732.
	ii.	Hannah, b. 15 May 1727; m. in LC 19 Oct. 1749 Benjamin Dring.
10.	iii.	Salisbury, b. 17 June 1730.
	iv.	Mary, b. 31 Aug. 1732; d. 4 Oct. 1732.
	v.	Ruth, b. 1 Oct. 1733; m. in LC 19 Dec. 1751 Philip Dring, son of Thomas and Sarah (Searles) Dring.
11.	vi.	David, b. 13 May 1736.
	vii.	Mary, b. in June 1739; m. in LC 20 March 1760 Thomas Crandall.
	viii.	Jonathan, b. 4 May 1741.

5. ISRAEL[4] STODDARD (Thomas[3], Samuel[2], John[1]), born in LC
14 Nov. 1707, died there in November 1781. Residence: LC, near the
Westport line.

He married in LC 31 March 1737 ELIZABETH BROWNELL, daughter
of George and Mary (Thurston) Brownell, born in LC 15 Sept. 1717.

His will, recorded in book 3, page 10 LC Probate, made 18 July
1781 and proved 4 Dec. 1781: ". . . To wife Elizabeth my lower room
at west end of house and my two daughters to live with her, namely
Ruth and Susannah Stoddard together with all household stuff. To son
Zebedee Stoddard, my executor, two shares of all land I possess and
the remainder to my three sons, Israel, Cornelius and Thomas, to be
equally divided. They to pay to their sisters 50 Spanish milled dollars
each. I also give my daughter Mary Palmer one old fashioned chest.
All farming utensils and stock to sons Zebedee and Cornelius. My son
Zebedee to be executor. . . "

Children, first six recorded in LC:

i.   Mary, b. 30 July 1737; m. (intention 7 Nov. 1767) in Dartmouth
        John Palmer.
ii.   Samuel, b. 30 Sept. 1739.
iii.   Gideon, b. 9 June 1742.
iv.   Zebedee, b. 30 Dec. 1743.
v.   Ruth, b. 5 Feb. 1747.
vi.   Elizabeth, b. 29 April 1748; probably died before 1781.
vii.   Susannah, b. in 1750; m. in LC 28 Aug. 1789 Zarah Simmons,
        son of John and Comfort (Shaw) Simmons.
viii.   Israel, b. about 1752.
ix.   Cornelius, b. about 1754; d. in July 1818.
x.   Thomas, b. in July 1756; d. in June 1781.

6. ICHABOD[4] STODDARD (Thomas[3], Samuel[2], John[1]), born in LC
31 March 1717. Residence: LC and Dartmouth. He married about 1750
DEBORAH (--).

Children, first three recorded in LC:

i.   William, b. 6 June 1751.
ii.   Alice, b. 17 May 1753.
iii.   Elizabeth, b. 20 Jan. 1756, also recorded in Dartmouth.
iv.   Innocent, b. 19 March 1759, recorded in Dartmouth.

7. NATHANIEL[4] STODDARD (Thomas[3], Samuel[2], John[1]), born in
LC 25 June 1719, died there 19 Feb. 1803. Residence: LC.

He was married there 5 Dec. 1748 by Joseph Wood, justice, to
EMLIN WILBORE, daughter of Joseph and Emlin (Champlin) Wilbore,
born in LC 31 June 1729, died there 10 Jan. 1733.

Children:

i.   Hannah, b. 16 Aug. 1750, recorded in LC; d. 19 Dec. 1756.
ii.   Lydia, b. 19 Oct. 1752; d. 23 Dec. 1756.
iii.   Emlin, b. 13 March 1755; d. 31 Dec. 1756.
iv.   Joseph, b. 27 Oct. 1756; d. 4 Nov. 1756.
v.   Comfort, b. 27 Oct. 1757; recorded in LC; d. 11 Aug. 1823.
vi.   Susannah, b. 9 March 1760; d. 27 March 1825; m. 1 Aug. 1784

Isaac Pierce, son of Jepthah and Elizabeth (Rouse) Pierce.
vii. Elizabeth, b. 2 March 1763; d. 10 June 1765.
viii. Martha, b. 1 April 1765; d. 20 Feb. 1848; m. in Westport
      (intention 12 March 1797) Elijah Davis, son of Stephen
      and Reliance Davis.
ix.   Ruth, b. 12 Sept. 1767; d. 7 Dec. 1848; m. 3 May 1787 John
      Sawyer.
12. x. Thomas, b. 13 July 1770.

8. NOAH⁴ STODDARD (Thomas³, Samuel², John¹), born in LC 25
April 1721, died there in July 1766. Residence: LC.
    He married in Portsmouth 24 Sept. 1746 SARAH THURSTON JR.,
daughter of Edward and Sarah (Carr) Thurston, born in LC 14 July
1725, died there in February 1767.
    Her will, recorded LC Probate, book 3, page 96, made 10 Jan.
1767 and proved 19 March 1767: ". . . To three daughters, Phebe,
Ruth and Sarah, my wearing apparel. The land lying in LC to be sold
by my executor and estate divided amongst my six sons, Edward, Noah,
Jeremiah, Nichols, Henry and Samuel Stoddard, and my three daughters,
Phebe, Sarah and Ruth Stoddard. My trusty loving brother-in-law
Christopher White of LC to be sole executor. . . "

Children, all recorded in LC except last two:
i.   Thomas, b. 17 Aug. 1748.
ii.   Edward, b. 4 Aug. 1750.
iii. Phebe, b. 29 April 1752.
iv.   Sarah, b. 5 Nov. 1753.
v.   Noah, b. 17 Feb. 1755.
vi.   Jeremiah, b. 27 Oct. 1756.
vii. Nicholas, b. 12 Sept. 1758.
viii. Henry, b. 25 July 1760.
ix.   Samuel, b. in 1762.
x.   Ruth, b. in 1764.

All of these children probably moved from town.

9. BENJAMIN⁴ STODDARD (Thomas³, Samuel², John¹), born in
LC 23 Aug. 1725, died there in June 1819 ae 94. Residence: LC.
    He married there 5 Oct. 1752 PHEBE BROWNELL, daughter of
Charles and Mary (Wilbore) Brownell, born in LC 22 Sept. 1730.
    His will, recorded LC Probate, book 5, page 137, made 29 June
1818 and proved 12 July 1819: ". . . Of advanced age. . . To son
Brownell all my real estate. To daughter Mary Stoddard a comfortable
home support as long as single. Son Brownell Stoddard to be executor. . ."
He also left 14 dollars each to his grandchildren: Phebe Stoddard Butler,
Brownell Stoddard Simmons, Prudence Wilbor, Phebe Stoddard Wilbor,
Russ Wilbour, Susannah Wilbour, Lydia Wilbour. To his granddaughter
Lydia Simmons he left 14 dollars and one turkey feather bed.

Children, only the first recorded in LC:
i.   Brownell, b. 22 Dec. 1756; d. 11 June 1843; m. 26 Feb. 1780
      Hannah Sawdry, daughter of Peleg and Lydia Sawdry.
ii.   Ruth, b. about 1759; m. (1) in LC 2 May 1787 John Sawyer,

son of Josiah Sawyer; m. (2) Gideon Simmons.
iii.   Prudence, b. about 1763. (one of these girls m. (--) Butler)
iv.   Patience, b. about 1766.
v.   Mary, b. in 1767; d. unmarried.
vi.   Phebe, b. about 1770; d. 15 Feb. 1804; m. 3 Oct. 1790 Walter
        Wilbore, son of Walter and Catharine (Davenport) Wilbore,
        b. 22 Feb. 1766, d. 26 Nov. 1839.

10. SALISBURY[4] STODDARD (Jonathan[3], Samuel[2], John[1]), born in
LC 17 June 1730. He moved from LC to Middletown.
He married in LC 20 Sept. 1750 HANNAH DRING, daughter of
Thomas and Sarah (Searl) Dring, born in LC 14 Sept. 1732.

Children, the first recorded in LC, the others in Middletown:
i.   Thomas, b. 13 June 1751.
ii.   Rachel, b. 4 Feb. 1754.
iii.   Isaac, b. 26 March 1757.
iv.   Hannah, b. 1 June 1760.
v.   Ruth, b. 11 March 1765.
vi.   Salisbury, b. 19 May 1767.
vii.   Samuel, b. 19 April 1769; m. in Middletown 22 June 1794
        Elizabeth Crandall, daughter of Thomas Crandall.

11. DAVID[4] STODDARD (Jonathan[3], Samuel[2], John[1]), born in LC
13 May 1736, died there 23 Jan. 1818.
He married there 12 April 1760 MARY (SIMMONS) DRING, daughter
of William and Mary (Pearce) Simmons and widow of Nathaniel Dring,
born in LC 13 Sept. 1738, died there 18 Oct. 1822. Both are buried in
the Old Commons cemetery.
They lived in LC in the east part of town near the Westport line.
David Tabor lived at the north of his house.
His will, recorded Book 5, page 105, made 29 Dec. 1817 and
proved 2 March 1818: ". . . To wife Mary use of all real estate.
To daughter Abigail Manchester, wife of Barzilla Manchester, four
silver dollars. To daughter Molly Stoddard the land I bought of
Christopher White, two acres and she to be executrix. To grandson
Jonathan Stoddard Carr my farm that was given me by my father
Jonathan, deceased, after the decease of my wife. To granddaughter
Lydia Carr one feather bed. . . " He also left one dollar each to his
daughters Rhoda Springer, wife of John Springer; Lydia Wilbor, wife
of Isaac Wilbor; Betsey Peckham, wife of John Peckham; Elizabeth
Stoddard, widow of Arnold Stoddard.

Children, recorded in LC:
i.   Abigail, b. 16 April 1764; m. in LC 13 March 1783
        Barzilla Manchester.
13. ii. Arnold, b. 9 April 1766.
iii.   Rhoda, b. 24 Nov. 1767; m. in LC 28 Dec. 1787 John Springer,
        son of Lawrence and Esther Springer.
iv.   Lydia, b. 10 Nov. 1773; d. 9 Feb. 1862; m. Isaac Wilbore, son
        of Samuel and Phebe (Gray) Wilbore.
v.   Mary, b. 10 Nov. 1773.

vi.   Betsey, b. 24 Aug. 1777; m. John Peckham.

One of his daughters married (--) Carr and had Jonathan Stoddard Carr and Lydia Carr.

12. THOMAS[5] STODDARD (Nathaniel[4], Thomas[3], Samuel[2], John[1]), born in LC 13 July 1770. Residence: LC.

He married in Tiverton 17 Dec. 1799 SARAH WOOD, daughter of Abner and Mary Wood. Ed. Note: I cannot find an Abner and Mary Wood. -- BFW.

       Children, recorded in LC:
i.   Christianna, b. 28 Sept. 1798; m. 22 Nov. 1818 Alfred Brownell, son of Nathan and Sarah Tompkins Brownell.
ii.   Phebe, b. 10 May 1801.
iii. Hannah, b. 11 Dec. 1802.
iv. Betsey, b. 21 Feb. 1807.
v.   Matilda, b. 5 Jan. 1811; m. Alexander Forbes.

13. ARNOLD[5] STODDARD (David[4], Jonathan[3], Samuel[2], John[1]), born in LC 9 April 1766, married ELIZABETH (--). Residence: LC.

       Children (Persilla and David recorded in LC, last child recorded in marriages):
i.   Persilla, b. 13 March 1786.
ii.   David, b. 13 Nov. 1787.
iii. Elizabeth, m. in LC 24 July 1825 Clark Brown, son of John Brown.

THE SYLVIA FAMILY

1. MANUEL L. SYLVIA, son of Manuel and Rose Sylvia, born 12 May 1865 in the Azores and landed in New Bedford in 1878. He came to LC the same year. He was naturalized at the Common Pleas division of the Supreme Court in Providence 21 June 1902. He died in LC 12 July 1908 of heptic cancer and is buried in the Hillside cemetery, Tiverton Four Corners. He was a carpenter.

He married ELIZA HENDERSON BOEN, born in LC 26 July 1872, died there 11 Feb. 1956. She was the daughter of Charles and Isabella Henderson (Taylor) Boen, and the granddaughter of Samuel and Elizabeth (MacDowell) Boen of Stranraer, County Wigtown, Scotland. She married second Frank C. Penny or Pennie, died 18 Dec. 1912, buried in the Hillside cemetery at Tiverton Four Corners. They had one daughter, Catharine Christina Pennie, b. 3 July 1911, m. 4 July 1935 John Walker Pennington, son of John W. and Cora L. (Brownell) Pennington. He was born in New Bedford 13 April 1911.

       Children, born in LC:
2. i.   Manuel Lopes, b. 17 May 1889.

ii.   Leonard Henderson, b. 22 Feb. 1891; d. 25 July 1958 in LC;
      m. (1) 28 Sept. 1929 Vida May Hambly, daughter of Otis F.
      and Emma (Henderson) Hambly of Tiverton, b. 26 July 1900,
      d. 7 Sept. 1954; m. (2) Lois Wilbur, daughter of Lester E.
      and Lillian (Dunbar) Wilbur.
iii. Charles B., b. in LC 17 May 1893. He had a daughter Evelyn.
iv.   Eliza Henderson (Lila), b. in LC 25 April 1896; m. (1) 27 May
      1912 Calvin Arthur Field, son of Samuel S. and Elizabeth
      R. (Mosher) Field; m. (2) John Beastey.
v.   Euphemia, b. 1 Nov. 1902; m. Thomas Truesdale.
vi.   Fannie Isabella.

2. MANUEL LOPES[2] SYLVIA (Manuel[1]), born in LC 7 May 1889,
died there 24 June 1952. Residence: LC.
   He married 3 June 1915 MILDRED CHARLOTTE GRINNELL,
daughter of Louis I. and Lottie (Chase) Grinnell, born in Tiverton 4
July 1893.

      Children:
i.   Evelyn Mildred, b. 11 Jan. 1916; m. 26 Nov. 1934 Charles
      Patrick Ryan.
ii.   Charlotte, b. 8 June 1917; m. 17 Oct. 1941 Joseph Stanley
      Hermidas Gendreau.
iii. Charles Clifton, b. 26 Nov. 1919; d. 27 Aug. 1920.
iv.   Manuel Lopes, Jr., b. 11 Sept. 1921.

. . . .

   1. JOSEPH F. SYLVIA, born in 1846, married ELLEN T. KELLY,
daughter of Benjamin and Margaret (Lynch) Kelly, born in Ireland in
1848, died in LC 6 Sept. 1911. Residence: LC.

      Children, recorded in LC:
i.   Joseph, b. 8 Feb. 1875; d. 15 Feb. 1875.
ii.   William Henry, b. in December 1876.
iii. Son, b. 15 July 1879.
iv.   Margaret, b. 9 Aug. 1882.
v.   Anna Theressa, b. 18 July 1885.
2. vi.   Jerry, b. in LC 10 Nov. 1888.

   2. JERRY[2] SYLVIA (Joseph[1]), born in LC 10 Nov. 1888. Residence:
LC.
   He married in Portsmouth 8 Oct. 1913 ALICE MAY HOWARD,
daughter of George T. and Julianna (Peckham) Howard, born in LC 5
May 1888, died in 1938.

      Children, recorded in LC:
i.   Geraldine, b. in LC 10 May 1916.
ii.   George Howard, b. in Fall River 11 July 1921.

. . . .

MANUEL SYLVIA, born in 1840, married ROSA MADELEIN, born in 1840. Residence: LC.

    Children, recorded in the census of 1880:
i.   George J., b. in 1863.
ii.   Mary Madeleine, b. 1 Aug. 1866 in Troy, N.Y.; d. in LC 24 Nov. 1940; m. there 1 Jan. 1887 George F. Chase.
iii.   Frederic J., b. in 1869.
iv.   Walter J., b. 23 Jan. 1878.

VICTOR² SYLVIA JR. (Victor¹), married ROSE CARDOZA. Residence: LC.

    Children, recorded in LC:
i.   George A., b. in Fall River 23 Sept. 1926.

ന്ദ

THE TABOR FAMILY

See the Tabor Genealogy by Albert and Anna A. Wright.

1. PHILIP¹ TABER, born in 1605, died after 1672 in Tiverton. He married first 21 Dec. 1639 LYDIA MASTERS, daughter of John and Jane Masters of Cambridge, Mass. He married second JANE LATHUM, born in 1605, died after 1669.
    He was living in Plymouth, Mass., in 1630; in Watertown, Mass. in 1634; in Yarmouth in 1640; Portsmouth in 1654; in Providence in 1659; and in Dartmouth in 1667. At the time of his death he was in Tiverton.

    Children:
i.   Lydia, m. (1) 16 April 1664/5 Pardon Tillinghast, b. in Seven Cliffs, England, in 1622, d. 20 Jan. 1718; m. (2) 4 Nov. 1718 Samuel Mason.
ii.   John, b. in 1640; d. young.
iii.   Philip, b. in 1642; bapt. in February 1646; d. about 1693; m. Mary Cooke, d. after 1694.
2.   iv.   Joseph, bapt. in 1646.
3.   v.   Thomas, bapt. in 1646.
    vi.   Esther, m. (--) Mayhew.

2. JOSEPH² TABOR (Philip¹), baptized in 1646. Residence: Tiverton. He married first (?). He married second HANNAH (--). He married third MARY GLADDEN, died in New London, Conn., in 1734/5.

    Children:
i.   Philip, b. in 1682; d. in 1750; m. 1 Oct. 1724 in New London, Conn., Elizabeth Tillinghast, daughter of

Pardon and Lydia Tillinghast.
4.   ii.   John, b. in 1690.
5.   iii.   Ebenezer, b. in 1693.
      iv.   Thomas, d. in 1728; m. in 1723 Martha Morey.
      v.   Amon, b. in 1706; d. in 1785/6; m. Mary Brown. Residence:
             Long Island.
      vi.   Elizabeth, m. in Portsmouth 13 Dec. 1703 Daniel Pearce
             of Prudence Island.
      vii.   Mary, m. in 1729 Joseph Prescott.

   3. THOMAS[2] TABER (Philip[1]), baptized in Yarmouth, Mass.,
in February 1646, died 11 Nov. 1730.
   He married first about 1667 ESTHER COOKE, daughter of John
and Sarah (Warren) Cook, born in Plymouth 16 Aug. 1650. He married
second in June 1672 MARY THOMPSON, daughter of John and Mary
(Cooke) Thompson, born about 1650, died in 1723.
   His will, made 15 June 1723 and proved 20 March 1733: ". . . To
wife Mary south half of homestead with all housing while widow and to
her all personal. To six daughters what ever is left of personal at
death of wife. To son Thomas one eighth of a share of upland swamp
at death of wife, he paying ten pounds to his sisters. To son Joseph
and son John, farm where they now dwell, they paying ten pounds to
their sisters. To son Jacob north half of homestead, he paying 14
pounds to sisters. To son Philip south half of homestead with housing
and orchard except privilege to wife above. To daughter Esther Perry
and her husband certain land and six pounds. To daughter Lydia Kinney
certain land and six pounds. To daughter Sarah Hart and her husband
land and six pounds. To daughter Mary Morton land and 20 pounds.
To daughter Rebecca Blackwell land and six pounds. To daughter Abigail
Tabor 20 pounds. To former man servant Simeon Spooner 20 acres. . . " .

      Children:
      i.   Thomas, b. 29 Oct. 1668; d. young.
      ii.   Esther, b. in Dartmouth 17 April 1671; m. in Sandwich, Mass.,
             23 Oct. 1689 Samuel Perry, son of Ezra and Elizabeth
             (Burgess) Perry.
      iii.   Lydia, b. in Dartmouth 8 Aug. 1673; m. John Kinney.
      iv.   Sarah, b. in Dartmouth 28 Jan. 1674; d. after 1735; m. in
             Dartmouth 1 Dec. 1702 William Hart, son of Richard and
             Hannah (Keene) Hart.
      v.   Mary, b. in Dartmouth 18 March 1677; m. Manasseh Morton,
             son of George and Joanna (Kempton) Morton.
6.   vi.   Joseph, b. 8 March 1679.
      vii.   Thomas, b. in Dartmouth 22 Feb. 1681; d. there before 1724;
             m. there 4 July 1700 Rebecca Harlow, daughter of Samuel
             and Priscilla Harlow.
      viii. John, b. in Dartmouth 22 Feb. 1681; d. after 1670; m. Phebe
             Spooner, daughter of John Spooner.
      ix.   Jacob, b. in Dartmouth 26 July 1683; d. there 4 April 1773;
             m. Sarah West, daughter of Stephen and Mary (Cooke)
             West.
      x.   Jonathan, b. 22 Sept. 1685; died in the woods, his mind im-

paired.
xi.   Bethia, b. in Dartmouth 2 Sept. 1687; d. in Rochester, Mass.,
         6 Aug. 1758; m. Caleb Blackwell.
xii.   Philip, b. in Dartmouth 7 Feb. 1689; m. Susannah Wilcox.
         Residence: after 1730 New Jersey.
xiii.   Abigail, b. 2 May 1693; m. Ebenezer Taber, son of Joseph
         Taber.

4. JOHN³ TABER (Joseph², Philip¹), born in 1690/1700, died
in Tiverton 22 Nov. 1756. His will, dated in November 1756, was
proved 6 Dec. 1756.
     He married first (intention 13 Jan. 1726/7 in Tiverton) MARY
SISSON of Dartmouth. He married second in Tiverton 8 May 1731
ABIGAIL LAKE, daughter of Thomas Jr. and Lydia (Fisher) Lake,
born in Tiverton 13 May 1713. She married second in Tiverton 18
Oct. 1761 Capt. Richard Hart.

        Children:
i.   Joseph, m. in Tiverton 1 June 1749 to Hannah Church
         by the Rev. Timothy Ruggles.
ii.   Amon, m. Lucretia Williston (Williamson?).
iii.   Constant, m. in Newport 3 Nov. 1747 Elizabeth Howland.
iv.   Ann.
v.   Elizabeth, m. in LC 3 July 1745 Nathaniel Gibbs, son of
         Warren and Abigail (Hilliard) Gibbs, b. in LC 13 Jan.
         1716.
vi.   Benedict, m. (1) in Newport 5 Aug. 1747 Rebecca Gladding;
         m. (2) Abigail Johnson.
vii.   Sarah, m. in Portsmouth 27 July 1749 Caleb Corey.
viii.   Hannah, m. in Tiverton 24 Jan. 1753 Walter Tabor, son of
         Ebenezer Tabor.
ix.   Stephen, b. about 1737; d. in LC in 1771; m. Ruth Briggs,
         daughter of Job and Elizabeth Briggs.
x.   Mary, m. in Portsmouth 21 Oct. 1759 Jonathan Albro
         (Joseph Wood?).
xi.   Gideon, m. Judith Records.
xii.   Daniel, m. (1) Hannah Tallman; m. (2) Sarah Wedley.
xiii.   Ruth, m. in Portsmouth 9 March 1766 Joseph Thomas Jr.
7.   xiv.   David.
xv.   Rebecca.
8.   xvi.   Philip, b. 6 Jan. 1747.
xvii.   Bridgett.
xviii. Noel, m. Mary (--).
xix.   Amey, m. 13-18 Dec. 1772 Joseph Hart, son of Stephen and
         Sarah (Taber) Hart. Residence: Tiverton.

     Also the children of John and Abigail Taber, according to M.L.T.A.:
xx.   Jabez, m. Abigail Toby.
xxi.   Deborah, b. in 1731; m. Elnathan Tobey.

5. EBENEZER³ TABOR (Joseph², Philip¹), born in Dartmouth in
1693. His will, made 19 Sept. 1765, was proved 5 Oct. 1772.

He married 1 Dec. 1715/16 ABIGAIL TABER, daughter of Thomas and Mary Taber, born in May 1693.

Children:
i.   Paul, b. 30 March 1716; m. 1 April 1739 Sarah Crandall.
ii.   Thomas, b. 28 Oct. 1717; m. Mary Crandall, b. 16 Jan. 1722.
iii.   Mary, b. 24 Aug. 1719; m. John Taber.
9.   iv.   Joseph, b. 21 Sept. 1721.
v.   Hannah, b. 13 Sept. 1723; m. (--) Hart.
vi.   Water, b. 4 Sept. 1725; d. 17 June 1730.
vii.   Lydia, b. 24 Oct. 1728.
viii.   Water 2d, b. 1 Oct. 1731; m. (1) Hannah Taber, daughter of John and Abigail Taber; m. (2) Martha (--).
ix.   Jacob, b. 2 Oct. 1735; m. 29 Sept. 1763 Susannah Davis.

6. JOSEPH[3] TABOR (Thomas[2], Philip[1]), born in Dartmouth 8 March 1679, died there in 1752.

He married in Dartmouth 12 Aug. 1701/2 ELIZABETH SPOONER, daughter of John Spooner, born in Dartmouth 19 June 1683, died there 14 July 1743 (34?). He married second in Sandwich, Mass., 30 Nov. 1738 LYDIA GIFFORD, widow of Jonathan Gifford.

Children, born in Dartmouth:
i.   Amos, b. 29 April 1703; d. in Dartmouth before 1753; m. there 13 June 1724 Elizabeth Lapham, daughter of John and Mary (Russell) Lapham; m. (2) 21 April 1730 Elizabeth Eastland.
ii.   Sarah, b. 2 March 1704/5 in Dartmouth; m. there 2 April 1727 Preserved Merihew.
iii.   Benjamin, b. 2 Dec. 1706; d. about 1782; m. in Dartmouth 5 Dec. 1729 Susan Lewis, daughter of John Lewis.
iv.   Mary, b. 6 June 1708 in Dartmouth; d. in Nantucket before 1735; m. in Dartmouth 30 April 1730 David Joy, son of Samuel Joy.
v.   Joseph, b. 15 Feb. 1709; d. in Dartmouth 1772; m. there 15 Nov. 1739 Mary Tinkham, daughter of John Tinkham.
vi.   Rebecca, b. 11 Oct. 1711 in Dartmouth; m. perhaps 10 April 1754 John Bennett Jr., son of William Bennett.
vii.   Eleanor, b. 28 March 1713 in Dartmouth; d. before 1738; m. in Dartmouth 24 May 1734 Peter Crapo, son of Peter and Penelope (White) Crapo.
10. viii.   John, b. 8 Aug. 1715.
ix.   Thomas, b. 20 Sept. 1717; d. in Dartmouth 14 July 1748; m. there 23 Jan. 1732 Ruth Bennett, daughter of William and Desire (Manchester) Bennett.
x.   Elizabeth, b. 2 Nov. 1718 in Dartmouth; m. there 5 Aug. 1704 Jonathan Brownell, son of George and Elizabeth (Devoll) Brownell.
xi.   Peter, b. 6 April 1721 in Dartmouth; d. before 1 Oct. 1793; m. Sarah Jenkins.
xii.   William, b. 15 March 1723 in Dartmouth; d. there 22 Oct.

1799; m. there 11 April 1751 Mary Wing, daughter of
Stephen and Margaret Wing.
  xiii.   Abigail, b. in Dartmouth 16 April 1725; m. there 1 Dec. 1747
       William (Jeremiah) Bennett Jr.

7. DAVID⁴ TABER (John³, Joseph², Philip¹), died 1 Oct. 1809.
He married first 9 Aug. 1767 ANN BRIGGS. He was married
second in Tiverton 8 Oct. 1769 by John Bowen, justice, to SARAH
WOODMAN, baptized in Tiverton 29 May 1774, died in LC 4 Dec.
1810. He perhaps married third MARY PEARCE.
    His will, recorded LC Wills, book 4, page 293, made 28 Aug.
1809 and proved 4 Oct. 1809: ". . . To wife Mary improvement of all
estate both real and personal. To son John my sedge flat lying in
Brant Channell so-called. To son William Taber 100 dollars. To
son Cornelius house where I now live with lot it stands on beginning
at Stephen Brownell's wall at west end of said lot east to Mill Brook,
and one other lot at south of my lot where my corn now stands and
extending south to David Stoddard's and north to Edward Manchester's.
To son Benjamin south part of my pasture. To son Robert Taber 50
dollars. To son Samuel Taber 50 dollars. To daughters Rebecca
Albro and Anstress Gifford all the household furniture. To son William
rest and residue. . . "
           Children:
11. i.   John, b. in 1770/74.
     ii.   William.
12. iii.   Cornelius, b. 16 Oct. 1781.
     iv.   Benjamin, b. in 1782.
     v.   Robert, b. in 1788.
     vi.   Samuel, b. in 1790/1800.
     vii.   Rebecca, m. 8 Dec. 1790 James Albro, son of James Albro,
           b. in December 1771.
     viii. Anstress, m. in LC 2 Feb. 1804 Reuben Gifford, son of
           Deborah Gifford.

8. PHILIP⁴ TABER (John³, Joseph², Philip¹), born in LC 6 Jan.
1747, died in Lyons, N.Y., 14 May 1827.
    He was married in LC 1 July 1773 by Aaron Wilbor, justice,
to MARY GIBBS, daughter of Jabez and Mary (Gifford) Gibbs, born
in LC 22 March 1752, died 10 June 1848. They are buried in the Lyons
cemetery in Madison County, N.Y.
    They lived originally in LC. In 1816 they were living in Cazenovia,
N.Y. One son, Benjamin, remained in LC.
    He was a soldier of the Revolution and his pension papers are in
Washington.
           Children:
     i.   Amey.
     ii.   Judah.
     iii.   Lucy, d. 28 Sept. 1861 ae 74-0-10; m. Charles Simmons (?).
     iv.   David.
     v.   Elizabeth.
     vi.   Clark, b. 30 April 1790; d. 16 Jan. 1862; m. in Tolland, Mass.,

Mary Gibbs, b. 1 June 1796, d. 28 March 1858.
vii.   Peleg.
13.   viii. Benjamin, b. 14 Feb. 1774.
ix.   Nathaniel.
x.   Nancy.

9, JOSEPH⁴ TABER (Ebenezer³, Joseph², Philip¹), born in
Tiverton 13 Sept. 1723, married there 1 Nov. 1743 ABIGAIL SAWYER,
daughter of Josiah and Martha (Seabury) Sawyer. Residence: Tiverton.

Children:
i.   Judith, b. 6 March 1745.
14.   ii.   Lemuel, b. 30 Dec. 1748; m. 23 May 1771 Sarah Brightman.
iii.   Isaac, b. 13 Nov. 1750; m. Peace Tripp, daughter of John
and Penelope Tripp.
iv.   Ichabod, b. 11 March 1755.

10. JOHN⁴ TABER (Joseph³, Thomas², Philip¹), born in Dartmouth 8 Aug. 1715, died in 1787. Residence: Tiverton.
He married first (intention 10 Oct. 1741) in LC MARY TABER,
daughter of Ebenezer and Abigail (Taber) Taber, born 24 Aug. 1719,
died about 1751. He married second in Dartmouth 16 July 1753 SARAH
WALKER.

Children by first wife, recorded in Tiverton:
i.   Mary, b. 26 April 1742; m. Pardon Taber, son of Philip
Taber.
ii.   James, b. 13 Feb. 1745; m. 15 Jan. 1767 in Tiverton Judith
Macomber, daughter of Samuel and Mary (Tripp) Macomber.
iii.   Priscilla, b. 28 July 1746; m. Capt. Stephen Cunningham.
iv.   Ruth, b. 8 June 1749.
15.   v.   Jeremiah, b. 7 July 1751.

Children by second wife:
vi.   Phebe, b. 3 Feb. 1754.
vii.   Earle, b. in Tiverton 12 Feb. 1756; d. in East Aurora, N.Y.,
17 April 1735; m. in Tiverton 25 Jan. 1781 Susanna
Brightman, daughter of John and Hannah Brightman.
viii. Sarah, b. 18 Feb. 1759.
ix.   Elizabeth, b. 27 March 1762; d. 5 Nov. 1854.
x.   John, b. 4 Aug. 1764.
xi.   Tilly, b. 23 Nov. 1768.

In the printed records of Tiverton, John's first wife Mary is
credited only with the first child, and all the other children of John
are given to his wife Sarah. This is impossible as his wife Mary
lived until 1751, and his marriage to Sarah took place in 1753.

11. JOHN⁵ TABER (David⁴, John³, Joseph², Philip¹), born in
1770/2, died in LC 24 Aug. 1855. Residence: LC.
He was married in LC 7 Jan. 1795 by Enos Gifford, justice, to
MARY GIFFORD, daughter of Enos and Mary (Wilbor) Gifford and
widow of Gamaliel Brownell, born in LC 17 April 1767, died there 7
July 1850.

Children, recorded in LC:
i.   Mary, b. 15 May 1796; d. 22 Oct. 1821.
ii.   Abigail, b. 19 April 1798; d. 12 Oct. 1881; m. Pardon
      Brownell, b. in 1799.
iii. Otis, b. 9 April 1800.
iv.   Gamaliel, b. 12 Feb. 1802.
v.   Hannah, b. 16 Aug. 1806; m. (--) Brownell.
vi.   Sarah, b. 19 Nov. 1808; m. (1) (--) Gifford; m. (2) in LC
      26 Nov. 1868 Thomas Elliot, son of Thomas and Chloe
      Elliot, b. in Thompson, Conn.

12. CORNELIUS[5] TABOR (David[4], John[3], Joseph[2], Philip[1]),
born in LC 16 (?) October 1781, died there 16 Dec. 1856.
      He married DEBORAH SANFORD, daughter of George Sanford,
born in LC 31 Aug. 1789, died 19 Sept. 1867. Both are buried in the
Stone Church cemetery.
      Residence: LC. They lived on the east end of the Adamsville
Road near the end of the John Dyer Road. They were listed in the
census of 1850 and 1865.

Children, born in LC:
i.   Alexander, b. in 1825. He was a bricklayer.
ii.   Sarah C., b. in LC 23 Oct. 1828; d. there 23 March 1904;
      m. there 22 Oct. 1846 Philip Manchester, son of Abraham
      and Lydia (Shaw) Manchester.
iii. Susan S., b. in 1830; m. Leander Tabor, son of Christopher
      (?) Tabor. They were listed in the LC census of 1880,
      and had two sons, Cornelius, b. in 1848, and Frank, b.
      in 1864.

13. BENJAMIN[5] TABOR (Philip[4], John[3], Joseph[2], Philip[1]), born
in LC in 1774, died there 2 Nov. 1864.
      He was married in LC 20 March 1796 by William Almy, justice,
to ABIGAIL DYER of Westport, daughter of Zacheus and Ruth (Gifford)
Dyer, born in Westport 12 July 1777, died in LC 9 March 1835. They
are buried in the Hoxie-Tabor cemetery in LC. In 1850 they were
living on the east side of the John Dyer Road.

Children:
i.   Mary (Polly), b. in LC 27 March 1797; d. there 27 June
      1860; m. William Palmer, son of John Stoddard and
      Margaret (Macumber) Palmer.

14. LEMUEL[5] TABER (Joseph[4], Ebenezer[3], Joseph[2], Philip[1]),
born in Tiverton in December 1748, died in 1833 in Adams, Jefferson
County, N.Y.
      He married in Tiverton 23 May 1771 SARAH BRIGHTMAN of
Dartmouth, died in 1822.
      He was a soldier of the Revolution. He and his family were
living in Tiverton at the time the census was taken in 1790, and moved
thereafter to New York State.

Children, recorded in Tiverton:

       i.   Judith, b. 23 Sept. 1771; d. in Tiverton 15 Feb. 1774.
      ii.   Priscilla, b. 18 April 1773; d. 2 April 1852; m. 24 June
            1792 Isaac Manchester, son of Archer and Elizabeth
            Manchester, b. in 1768/9, d. in Westport 13 Feb. 1860.
     iii. Thomas, b. in 1775; d. in 1777.
     iv. Joseph, b. 20 Jan. 1777.
16.   v.   Christopher, b. 25 Dec. 1778.
     vi. Sarah, b. 18 Sept. 1781.
    vii. Lemuel, b. 14 Nov. 1783; d. in Tiverton 20 Nov. 1785.
   viii. Cynthia, b. 28 Nov. 1785; m. William Chase of LC; may
            have m. Borden or Lake.
     ix. Clarissa, b. 29 Jan. 1788.
      x.   Lemuel, b. in January 1790.
     xi. Elizabeth, b. 20 Dec. 1791.
    xii. Isaac Manchester, b. 27 Aug. 1794.
   xiii. Mary, b. in August 1796.
   xiv. Cornelius Manchester, d. in July 1798.

     15. JEREMIAH[5] TABOR (John[4], Joseph[3], Thomas[2], Philip[1]),
born in Tiverton 7 July 1751, died after 1716. Residence: Tiverton.
He married in Tiverton 7 Nov. 1773 RUTH DANFORTH.

        Children, all recorded in Tiverton except Gideon:
      i.   Phebe, b. 28 March 1774.
      ii.   Restcome, b. 6 Feb. 1776; d. young.
     iii. Sarah, b. 18 Aug. 1777; d. in Dartmouth 24 Jan. 1798.
     iv. Peleg, b. 6 Aug. 1780.
      v.   Restcome 2d, b. 7 May 1782; d. in Providence in 1836;
            m. (1) in Nantucket in November 1804 Mary Swain; m.
            (2) 30 Aug. 1821 Nancy Richmond.
     vi. Gideon, b. in Westport in 1784; d. in Woodstock, Conn.,
            26 May 1862; m. (1) 28 Dec. 1800 Nancy Macomber,
            daughter of Humphrey and Phebe (Brightman) Macomber;
            m. (2) in 1836 Nancy Richmond.
    vii. John, b. 23 Jan. 1785; d. in Nantucket in April 1839; m.
            19 Feb. 1809 in Nantucket Lucretia Swain.
   viii. Elizabeth, b. 6 Aug. 1788.
17. ix. Ellery, b. 13 Dec. 1791; d. in LC 22 Nov. 1839; m.
            Abigail Carr, daughter of John and Mary (Wilbor)
            Carr. She married second Ezra Brownell.
      x.   Elsie, b. 22 June 1794.
18. xi. James Harvey, b. 8 June 1797.

     16. CHRISTOPHER[6] TABER (Lemuel[5], Joseph[4], Ebenezer[3],
Job[2], Philip[1]), born in Tiverton 25 Dec. 1778.
     He married in LC 25 July 1805 RHODA BROWNELL, daughter
of George and Elizabeth (Peckham) Brownell, born in LC 6 Jan. 1781,
died there maybe 27 Jan. 1823.

        Children, born in LC:
      i.   Harriet Byron, b. 19 Aug. 1805.
      ii.   Sarah, b. 7 June 1807.
     iii. Rachel Brownell, b. 3 April 1808.

iv.   Barton, b. 10 Nov. 1809.

17. ELLERY[6] TABER (Jeremiah[5], John[4], Joseph[3], Thomas[2], Philip[1]), born in Tiverton 13 Dec. 1791, died in LC 22 Nov. 1839. Residence: LC and Tiverton.

He married ABIGAIL CARR, daughter of John and Mary (Wilbor) Carr, born 5 Jan. 1795, died in LC 30 Oct. 1876. She married second Ezra Brownell. They are buried in the Stone Church cemetery.

Children:
i.   Jeremiah, b. in 1818; d. in Tiverton 21 Dec. 1855; m. 10 April 1842 Hannah W. Borden, daughter of Richard and Sarah (Chace) Borden. She married second Benjamin Chase.
ii.   Mary, d. in New Bedford before 1860; m. 2 Oct. 1841 Adoniram Merrick.
iii.   Sarah, b. 12 Jan. 1820 in Westport; d. in New Bedford 19 May 1896; m. there 9 June 1844 James Porter Prior, son of Joseph and Sally (Winsor) Prior.
19. iv.   Clarke, b. 25 April 1824.
20. v.   Leander, b. 6 Jan. 1828.
      vi.   Phebe, m. James Simmons.
      vii.   Judith Wood, b. 7 Sept. 1830; d. in Revere, Mass., 21 April 1898; m. in New Bedford 8 Oct. 1846 Richard Peckingham Walsh, son of Peter and Sarah Walsh.
      viii. Lucy C., b. in LC 18 June 1833; d. in New Bedford 12 March 1890; m. in Tiverton 11 Nov. 1849 Philip Harrison King, son of Philip and Mahala (Simmons) King.

18. JAMES HARVEY[6] TABOR (Jeremiah[5], John[4], James[3], Thomas[2], Philip[1]), born in Tiverton 8 June 1797, died in LC 25 March 1876.

He married in LC 20 Oct. 1819 NANCY PALMER, daughter of John Stoddard and Margaret (Macumber) Palmer, born in LC 28 Sept. 1797, died there 23 Feb. 1882.

Residence: LC. According to the census of 1865, they lived in Pottersville.

Children, recorded in LC:
i.   John, b. 22 Jan. 1821.
ii.   Anna, b. 27 Jan. 1823; d. in Dartmouth 1 Dec. 1899; m. in Tiverton 7 Aug. 1849 Christopher H. Manchester, son of Peleg and Fannie (Hoxie) Manchester.
21. iii.   Alexander, b. 28 Oct. 1824.
      iv.   William Harvey, b. 26 Jan. 1827 in LC; d. there 21 Aug. 1895; m. (1) in Providence 8 June 1852 Louisa Lewis, daughter of Hiram and Mary Pearce (Macomber) Lewis, b. in Bristol 14 Sept. 1835, d. in Mt. Vernon, N.Y., 1 April 1895; m. (2) 3 May 1878 Susan M. Wilbor, daughter of Solomon W. and Esther (Palmer) Wilbor, b. 18 Dec. 1848, d. 11 May 1904.

    v.   Sarah, b. in LC 1 April 1829; m. 5 April 1852 John Taylor.
    vi.   Oliver Restcomb, b. 1 Sept. 1831 in LC; d. in New Bedford
          27 Dec. 1912; m. (1) Bethana M. Manley, daughter of
          John and Emily Manley; m. (2) 23 Feb. 1865 Ellen O.
          Reynolds, daughter of Elias and Ann Reynolds.
    vii. Horatio D., b. 6 Sept. 1833; d. in New Bedford 25 Feb. 1886;
          unmarried.
    viii. Nancy M., b. 29 Sept. 1835; m. in New Bedford 5 March 1854
          Thomas B. Manchester, son of Lewis and Mary Man-
          chester.
    ix.   Harriet P., b. 13 Nov. 1836 (?); m. 30 Dec. 1860 Charles E.
          Briggs, son of Charles and Joanna Briggs.

    19. CLARKE[7] TABER (Ellery[6], Jeremiah[5], John[4], Joseph[3],
Thomas[2], Philip[1]), born in LC 25 April 1824, died there 3 June 1891.
    He married in Tiverton 22 March 1849 RUTH ANN ALBERT,
daughter of Joel and Ruth (Simmons) Albert, born in Tiverton 24 May
1830, died in LC 10 May 1906.
    Residence: LC and Tiverton. They were named in the census
listings of 1865 and 1880. They lived on the Stone Church Road going
north from Adamsville.

          Children, recorded in Tiverton:
22. i.   Theodore Clark, b. 10 March 1851.
    ii.   Harriet Maria, b. 8 April 1855; m. 23 Dec. 1875 in LC
          Oliver Palmer Head, son of Abraham and Nancy
          (Grinnell) Head.
    iii.   Jeremiah Borden, b. 1 Nov. 1860; d. in New Bedford 25
          May 1912; m. 25 Dec. 1883 Mercy B. Tabor, daughter
          of Samuel H. and Elizabeth (Beden) Tabor.
    iv.   Ellery.
    v.   Abigail.
    vi.   Nellie Frances, b. in LC 8 Jan. 1868; d. there 20 Feb.
          1944; m. there 20 Oct. 1884 George A. Lemunyon, son
          of George and Sarah (Austin) Lemunyon.
    vii.   Abbie Augusta, b. in LC 20 May 1869; d. 15 Feb. 1870.
23. viii. Edward Waldo, b. 20 Nov. 1870.

    20. LEANDER S.[7] TABOR (Ellery[6], Jeremiah[5], John[4], Joseph[3],
Thomas[2], Philip[1]), born in LC 6 Jan. 1828; died there 24 April 1895.
    He married MARY W. CARR, born in 1838. Residence: LC.
They lived near Adamsville on High Hill Road.

          Children, recorded in LC:
    i.   Charles R., b. 30 June 1858.
    ii.   Thomas W., b. 16 Dec. 1860.
    iii. Emma Brownell, b. 5 Feb. 1868; m. Charles Chase.
    iv.   Laura J., b. 18 Sept. 1875.

    21. ALEXANDER[7] TABER (James[6], Jeremiah[5], John[4], Joseph[3],
Thomas[2], Philip[1]), born in LC 18-28 Oct. 1824, died there 15 Sept.
1906. Residence: LC.

He married in LC 13 Feb. 1849 SUSAN SANFORD TABER, daughter of Cornelius and Deborah (Sanford) Taber, born in LC 26 May 1831, died 22 Nov. 1904, buried Pleasant View cemetery.

Children:
24.   i.   Cornelius, b. 15 Sept. 1848.
      ii.   John Sanford, b. 15 May 1848 (?); m. in Portsmouth 3 Jan. 1876 Ella Frances Cornell, daughter of Joshua and Angeline Cornell.
      iii.   Franklin H., b. 28 Aug. 1863.
      iv.   Frank Herbert, b. 4 Aug. 1864; m. 28 Aug. 1886 Patience Lillian Soule, daughter of James and Betsey (Dyer) Soule.

22. THEODORE CLARK[8] TABER (Clark[7], Ellery[6], Jeremiah[5], John[4], Joseph[3], Thomas[2], Philip[1]), born 10 March 1851 in Tiverton, died in LC 28 Sept. 1926, buried in Pleasant View cemetery.

He married in Tiverton 27 Oct. 1875 BETSEY ROUNDS HART, daughter of Peleg and Mary (Manchester) Hart, born in Tiverton 18 Oct. 1848, died in LC 19 Aug. 1927.

Children, born in LC:
      i.   Lillian May, b. 18 Dec. 1874/5; d. in 1945; m. in LC 20 Dec. 1892 Gideon B. Peckham, son of Albert and Charlotte (Brightman) Peckham, b. 30 Oct. 1866, d. in 1950.
      ii.   Ruth Ann, b. 18 Oct. 1876/7; m. in LC 26 Feb. 1899 Lester LeRoy Wordell, son of Joshua and Harriet (Wordell) Wordell, b. in 1872, d. in 1922.
      iii.   Ida Louise, b. 5 Dec. 1881; m. in LC 31 Dec. 1919 Harold (?) Ellsworth Cory Soule, son of James H. and Betsey (Dyer) Soule, b. 7 Oct. 1885 in Westport.

23. EDWARD WALDO[8] TABER (Clark[7], Ellery[6], Jeremiah[5], John[4], Joseph[3], Thomas[2], Philip[1]), born in LC 20 Nov. 1870. Residence: LC.

He married in LC 17 July 1890 WINONA MINERVA GRINNELL, daughter of William T. and Ellen (Hindle) Grinnell, born in 1870.

Children:
      i.   Elsie W., b. in LC; m. (intention in Westport 1 July 1909) Herbert S. Gray, son of Herbert and Hattie M. Gray.
      ii.   Lois Edward, b. 7 Feb. 1904 (?).

24. CORNELIUS[8] TABER (Alexander[7], James[6], Jeremiah[5], John[4], Joseph[3], Thomas[2], Philip[1]), born in LC 15 Sept. 1848, died there 12 Dec. 1917. Residence: LC.

He married in LC 1 Oct. 1885 CYNTHIA TOMPKINS CASE, daughter of William and Frances (Wilbor) Case, born in LC 12 June 1868, died there 3 April 1920.

Children:
      i.   Susan Sanford, b. 28 April 1886; m. 2 July 1921 Leonard Wilbor Simmons, son of Charles L. and Georgianna

(Wilbour) Simmons.
ii.   Florence Priscilla, b. 10 Jan. 1889; m. 20 April 1918
       William Thomas Nickerson.
iii.   Emma Lavina, b. 25 Jan. 1891; m. 9 Nov. 1912 William
       Tongue.
iv.   Beatrice Gertrude, b. 3 Jan. 1894; m. Samuel Soule.
v.   Sarah Althia, b. 8 Aug. 1896; m. Daniel Lewis.
vi.   Helen Bartlett, b. 7 July 1900; m. 20 Nov. 1919 Harold
       Waite.
vii.   Marion Case, b. 23 Dec. 1904.
viii. Alexander Francis, b. 17 May 1910.

. . . .

Miscellaneous records concerning the Taber family in LC:

William Earl Tabor, son of Joseph and Mary Tabor, born in LC
in 1811, died in Providence 31 Dec. 1863 ae 52-6-5. He was a merchant.
Alphonso Taber, born in LC to William and Louisa Taber, died
in Providence 15 May 1853.
Pardon Taber, son of Joseph and Mary Taber, born in LC, died
in Providence 24 Dec. 1857 ae 56-10-0.
Deacon Joseph Tabor and Mary Tabor, daughter of Thomas,
were married in LC 12 Nov. 1788 by Enos Gifford, justice.

THE TALLMAN FAMILY

1. HENRY[1] TALLMAN of Hamburg, Germany, probably born at
Schleswid, Holstein, Germany, about 1586. He was living in the parish
of St. Nicholas, Hamburg, Germany, 24 March 1619.

    Children:
    i.   Anna Maria, bapt. in St. Nicholas 20 Sept. 1616.
    ii.   Elizabeth, bapt. in St. Nicholas 24 March 1619.
2. iii. Peter (probably) b. about 1623.

2. PETER[2] TALLMAN (Henry[1]), born about 1623, probably at
Hamburg, Germany, died in 1708. See details in the Genealogical
Register, volumn 85, page 69.
He married first in the parish of Christ Church in the Barbados
2 Jan. 1649 ANN HILL, daughter of Phillip and Ann Hill of Christ
Church, Barbados. He married second JOAN BRIGGS of Taunton,
Mass., died about 1685. He married third about 1686 ESTHER (--).
He was admitted a burgher of Hamburg 14 Aug. 1646. Two years
later he had settled in Christ Church, Barbados. By 18 Nov. 1651 he
was an apothecary in Newport, R.I. He soon moved to Portsmouth,
and also purchased land in Dartmouth.
    Children by first wife:

i.   Mary, b. about 1651; d. in 1720; m. in 1668 John Pearce,
     son of Richard and Susannah (Wright) Pearce from
     Portsmouth. They had eight children.

ii. Elizabeth, b. about 1654; d. 20 May 1701; m. 3 March
     1674 Isaac Lawton, son of Thomas Lawton of Ports-
     mouth.

iii. Ann, b. about 1656; m. 8 March 1679 Stephen Brayton,
     son of Francis and Mary Brayton of Portsmouth.

iv. Peter, b. 22 March 1658; d. 6 July 1726; m. 7 Nov. 1683
     Ann Walstone, daughter of Benjamin and Jane Walstone.

v.   Joseph, b. about 1660.

vi. Susanna, b. about 1662; m. (--) Becket.

vii. Daughter, m. about 1684 William Wilbor, son of William
     and Martha Wilbor of Portsmouth.

     Children by second wife:

viii. Jonathan, b. about 1666; m. Sarah (--).   Residence: Dart-
      mouth.

ix. James, b. about 1668; d. in 1724; m. (1) 18 March 1689 Mary
     Davol, daughter of Joseph and Mary (Brayton) Davol; m.
     (2) 14 Sept. 1701 Hannah Swain, daughter of John and
     Mary (Wyer) Swain. He was a physician.

x.   Daughter, b. about 1670; m. William Potter of Flushing, N.Y.

xi. John, m. Mary (--). Residence: Flushing, L.I., N.Y.

xii. Daughter, b. about 1674; m. in 1689 Israel Shaw, son of
     Anthony and Alice (Stonard) Shaw of LC.

xiii. Benjamin, b. 28 Jan. 1684; d. 20 May 1759; m. (1) 23 Sept.
      1708 Patience Durfee, daughter of Thomas and Deliverance
      (Hall) Durfee; m. (2) 7 June 1724 Deborah Cook, daughter
      of John and Mary Cook. Residence: Warwick, R.I.

     Children by third wife:

xiv. Samuel, b. 14 Jan. 1688.

DARIAS TALLMAN, born 3 Feb. 1690. He married in LC 10
Dec. 1728 SARAH[3] WILBOR (William[2], William[1]), born 10 Sept. 1702.

     Children:

i.   Britain, b. in LC 23 Dec. 1729.

GEORGE C. TALLMAN, son of John and Elizabeth Tallman, born
in Portsmouth in 1834. Residence: LC.

He married first in LC 20 Nov. 1856 MARY ANN SISSON, daughter
of Lemuel and Comfort (Simmons) Sisson, born in LC 23 Oct. 1830,
died there 2 Jan. 1892. She married second 26 Aug. 1879 Stephen Russell
Howland, son of William and Innocent (Wilbor) Howland.

     Children:

i.   Marion Simmons, b. 22 Oct. 1859; d. in LC 20 July 1944;
     m. Edward I. Chase, son of Joseph and Julia Chase, b.
     in Providence 27 Oct. 1857, b. there 1 Dec. 1937.

ii. Henrietta T., b. in LC 10 March 1862; m. there 6 Nov. 1882
     Joseph Edwin Cornell, son of Alexander and Mary Cor-
     nell, b. in Fall River in 1856.

THE TAYLOR FAMILY

1. ROBERT[1] TAYLOR, died in Newport 13 Jan. 1688. He married in Scituate in November 1646 MARY HODGES, daughter of John and Mary (Miller) Hodges of Scituate. Her grandfather, John Miller, came from Carne Dorsetshire, England, married Ann, daughter of Giles Winterhay.

Residence: Scituate and Newport. He was a rope maker and also was appointed by the General Assembly 29 Oct. 1673 to be prison keeper in Newport.

As most of the people of Scituate came from Kent County, England, it is likely that he came from there also. He owned a farm in Sachuest Meadows. There is a point of land once called Taylor's point, now called Ochre Point, between Shepard Avenue and Ruggles Avenue, and the Taylor farm was located there from the time of the settling of the Island according to Peterson's History of Rhode Island, page 59. This place was owned by William B. Lawrence after 1850, and was later named the Breakers.

Another first settler by the name of William Taylor (of Barnstable Devonshire, England) settled in Portsmouth and married Ann Goodfellow 4 Oct. 1722. He was probably not related to the above Robert Taylor.

A record of the marriage of Robert Taylor and Mary Hodges is found in the Friends Society records of Newport. From Arnold: "Died at Newport, Robert Taylor of Scituate, Mass., 13 Jan. 1688." On 5 Nov. 1658 Robert Taylor of Newport conveyed to Edward Smith of Newport his share of Quinanquit and Dutch Islands.

Children, recorded in Newport:

    i.   Mary, b. in November 1647; m. in 1664 George Hulate.
    ii.   Ann, b. 12 Feb. 1650.
    iii. Margaret, b. 30 Jan. 1652.
    iv.   Robert, b. in October 1653; d. 12 June 1707; m. Deborah
          Peckham, daughter of John Peckham.
2. v.   John, b. in June 1657.
3. vi.   Peter, b. in July 1661.
    vii. James (perhaps), b. 7 Oct. (?); m. Catharine (--), b. in
          1660, d. 15 Sept. 1690.

2. JOHN[2] TAYLOR (Robert[1]), born in Newport in 1658, died in LC 9 June 1747.

He married first ABIGAIL (--), born in 1660, died in LC 16 Sept. 1720. He married second SARAH (--), died in LC in 1764.

Residence: LC. They lived on what was called the Alexander S. Carton place in 1890.

His will, recorded LC Probate, book 1, page 12, made 24 April 1745 and proved 7 July 1747: ". . . To wife Sarah all goods she brought with her, one mare called her mare, one cow and use of my now dwelling house with leanto. To son John Taylor Jr., executor with brother Robert Taylor, 35 acres of land, part of my homestead farm already mentioned in a deed of gift to son John, and part of my farm that I bought of Edward Richmond and the west end thereof from the great highway east to a heap of stones or south side of said farm with buildings thereon. (This

is on the north of Meeting House Lane.) To son Robert 30 acres, part
of homestead, the east end, deed of gift all remaining land lying to the
eastward of the great brook that runs across my homestead farm, excepting
what land I gave to Philip Taylor which he has by deed of gift and all
remainder of part of land I bought of Edward Richmond. To two grandsons, Joseph and Philip Taylor, sons of Philip Taylor deceased, I confirm the deed of 35 acres, part of homestead land called the Little
Pasture, part of homestead with all the buildings and all. To daughter
Margaret Woodman 50 pounds. To daughter Lydia Cook 50 pounds.
To grandson Job Taylor 20 pounds. To grandson Samuel Irish 50
pounds. To granddaughter Comfort Taylor remaining household goods.
To grandson Jesse Irish . . . To three granddaughters Comfort Taylor,
Hannah Vinero and Ann Irish 10 shillings. To three granddaughters
Susannah Palmer, Abigail Taylor and Deborah Taylor each 10 shillings.
To three great grandsons, Joseph, George and Jonathan Wilbor, 10
shillings each. To three great granddaughters, children of daughter
Priscilla Wilbor, deceased, Job, Abner and Ann Wilbor. . . "

> Children, recorded in LC:
> i.   Mary, b. 25 Oct. 1682; m. in LC about 1702 Jonathan Irish,
>   son of John and Elizabeth Irish.
> ii.   Anna, b. in September 1686.
> iii.   Margaret, b. in July 1688; m. about 1710 Edward Woodman,
>   son of John and Hannah (Timberlake) Woodman.
> iv.   Lydia, b. in April 1891; m. in LC 17 Jan. 1712 Thomas
>   Cook.
> 4.   v.   John, b. 7 Jan. 1694.
> 5.   vi.   Robert, b. in December 1695.
> 6.   vii.   Philip, b. 13 May 1697.

3. PETER² TAYLOR (Robert¹), born in July 1661.

He married first ELIZABETH PECKHAM, daughter of John
and Mary (Clarke) Peckham, died in LC 24 May 1714 ae 45. He was
married second in LC 1 Nov. 1715 by Benjamin Church, justice, to
HANNAH WOOD. She was probably related to the Wood family which
lived on lot number 31 of the great lots. Peter Taylor lived on lot
number 32, next north to the Wood family, on land which he had purchased 4 Dec. 1688 from Col. Benjamin Church. He owned from the
bay to the road south of the Commons, as lot number 32, which is
north of Taylor's Lane, ran across the road. According to tradition
Peter Taylor stood in his orchard with a gun when the first settlers
wanted to put the main road through his land. He later gave Taylor's
Lane to the town.

He is buried in the Old Commons cemetery, where the Taylor
stones were moved after being taken from Taylor's Lane by Sarah
Soule Wilbour. The cemetery was on the corner of the lot at the
south of the yard of the homestead, north of the lane from the road.
His first wife is buried at the Quaker Meeting House yard.

His will, recorded Taunton Probate, book 8, page 407, made
13 May 1730 and proved 13 Oct. 1736: ". . . To wife Hannah one half
stock, improvement of my dwelling house in which I now dwell and
profits of one half of my land, one half interest money which I give

to my four youngest daughters until they come of age to receive the principle. She to be executrix. To son Peter Taylor the house he now dwells in, one half my orchard, two thirds of rest of my lands and use of whole until my son William comes of age, also other half of my stock. To son William the dwelling house I now dwell in, one half of my orchard, one third of rest of land. To daughter Elizabeth Davenport, wife of John Davenport, 50 pounds. To daughter Mary eight pounds. To daughter Mercy Taylor 50 pounds at 18. To daughter Hannah Taylor 50 pounds at 18. To daughter Anna Taylor 50 pounds at 18. The rest and residue to my five youngest children, Viz, those I had by my present wife. . . " Inventory of the estate, taken 6 Oct. 1736: 9 cows, 2 oxen, 3 yearling cattle. . . total of inventory 974 pounds.

Children by first wife, recorded in LC:

7.   i.   Peter, b. 20 Oct. 1697.

ii.   Elizabeth, b. 4 Jan. 1701; m. in LC 15 June 1726 John Davenport, son of Jonathan and Hannah (Maynard) Davenport.

iii. Mary, b. 30 Dec. 1703.

Children by second wife:

iv.   Mercy, b. 24 Feb. 1717; m. in LC 27 Nov. 1734 Benjamin Simmons, son of William and Abigail (Church) Simmons.

v.   Rebecca, b. 4 Jan. 1719; m. in LC 10 Dec. 1741 John Coe Jr., son of John and Sarah (Peabody) Coe.

vi.   Hannah, b. 12 April 1721; m. (intention 17 Dec. 1737) in LC Thomas Burgess Jr., son of Thomas and Martha (Closson) Burgess.

8.   vii. William, b. 30 April 1724.

viii. Anna, b. 13 Feb. 1726; m. in LC 5 Aug. 1745 Jeremiah Briggs, son of Job and Mary (Tallman) Briggs.

4. JOHN[3] TAYLOR (John[2], Robert[1]), born in LC 7 Jan. 1694, died there in June 1762.

He was married first in LC 31 May 1716 by Richard Billings, justice, to SARAH HORSWELL, daughter of Peter and Elizabeth Horswell, born in LC in July 1693, died there 18 Dec. 1719. He was married second in LC 29 Dec. 1719 by Thomas Church, justice, to JOANNA (HANNAH) WILBOR, daughter of Samuel and Mary (Potter) Wilbor, born in LC 8 June 1700.

His will, recorded book, page 333, made 17 June 1762 and proved in July 1762: ". . . To son David Taylor all my homestead farm on which my dwelling house stands. To son Job the farm that he now lives on. To son Humphrey the farm that he now lives on with all the buildings. To sons John, David, Peter and Reuben, all woodland. Rest and residue to son David Taylor. . . "

They evidently lived on the south end of the road south of the Commons in LC.

Children, recorded in LC:

i.   Elizabeth, b. 5 Jan. 1717; m. in LC 15 Nov. 1739 Richard Sisson.

      ii.   Job, b. 6 Sept. 1720.

9.   iii.   David, b. 31 March 1722.

      iv.   Phebe, b. 26 Aug. 1723; m. in LC 2 Dec. 1745 John Irish.

      v.   John Jr., b. 24 July 1725; m. 3 Dec. 1747 Jemima Grinnell, probably the daughter of George and Mercy (Sanford) Grinnell.

      vi.   Margaret, b. 20 April 1727; m. in LC 31 Dec. 1758 Aaron Grinnell.

      vii. Sarah, b. 14 Feb. 1728; m. in LC 28 Jan. 1748 John Lawton.

      viii. Humphrey, b. 9 Jan. 1730; m. in LC 19 Feb. 1751 Martha Wood, daughter of John and Mary (Burgess) Wood.

      ix.   Mary, b. 8 Oct. 1732; m. in LC 8 Oct. 1752 Giles Slocum of Middletown, R.I.

      x.   Samuel, b. 4 Aug. 1734.

      xi.   Peter, b. in 1736; m. in LC 1 Dec. 1771 Hannah Pearce, daughter of Giles and Mercy (Rouse) Pearce.

      xii. Reuben, b. in 1738.

     5. ROBERT[3] TAYLOR (John[2], Robert[1]), born in LC in December 1695, died there in July 1770.

     He was married first in LC 15 Oct. 1719 by Richard Billings, justice, to DEBORAH TAYLOR, probably the daughter of Robert and Deborah (Peckham) Taylor. He was married second in LC 21 May 1732 by Justice Billings to REBECCA ROUSE, daughter of James and Joanna (Fisher) Rouse, born in LC 29 Nov. 1705.

     Residence: LC. They lived on the road south of the Commons, possibly the place which afterwards belonged to Deacon Richmond.

     His will, recorded LC Wills, book 2, page 165: ". . . To wife Rebecca improvement of great room in my now dwelling house, with rent of one third of real estate. To son Robert my homestead farm, dwelling house, allowing son James and daughter Joanna to remain as long as single. To son Gideon a tract of land containing 40 acres which adjoins his own land where he lives and one third of shop tools and one third farming tools. To son James 10 acres of homestead on north side and shall sell same to Robert. To daughter Eunice Brownell two silver spoons. To daughter Joanna Taylor a cow. All of my indoor movables to daughters Eunice, Rebecca, Marcy and Joanna. Rest of real estate to sons Robert, Gideon and James. . . "

           Children by first wife, recorded in LC:

      i.   Abigail, b. 25 May 1720; d. young.

      ii.   Eunice, b. 12 March 1723; m. (intention in LC 18 Sept. 1742) Thomas Brownell, son of Thomas and Mary (Crandall) Brownell.

10. iii.   Robert, b. 13 May 1726.

11. iv.   Gideon, b. 15 May 1729.

           Children by second wife:

      v.   James, b. 3 Feb. 1733; d. 27 Aug. 1736.

      vi.   Deborah, b. 9 Feb. 1736.

      vii. Rebecca, b. 9 Feb. 1736.

12. viii. James 2d, b. 21 Jan. 1739.

ix.   Joanna, b. 21 Jan. 1739; m. in LC 22 July 1787 Abiah
       Tripp of Tiverton.
x.   Mary, b. 18 May 1743; m. in LC 7 Dec. 1777 Peter
       LeBarbier Duplessis Esq., son of John Francis and
       Margaretta Angelia Duplessis.

6. PHILIP[3] TAYLOR (John[2], Robert[1]), born in LC 13 May 1697,
died there 10 Oct. 1739.
       He was married in LC 9 June 1723 by Thomas Church, justice,
to COMFORT DENNIS, daughter of Robert and Susannah (Briggs)
Dennis, born in LC 12 March 1703.
       Residence: LC. In her accounting of the estate of her husband,
his widow Comfort listed ". . . for digging grave one pound five shillings.
Paid George Thurston for doctor's stuff 14 pounds. Paid for recording
of children's names one pound nine shillings. Rum and sugar one pound
nine shillings ten pence. Paid Dr. Richmond 14-10-0. . . "

       Children, recorded in LC:
i.   Susannah, b. 30 March 1724; m. 25 (?) 1745 in LC Moses
       Palmer, son of John and Sarah (Blood) Palmer.
ii.   Abigail, b. 4 March 1726; m. 8 Sept. 1745 Thomas Burgess,
       son of Edward and Elizabeth (Coe) Burgess.
iii.   Deborah, b. 22 Sept. 1729; d. in LC 18 July 1765; m. there
       18 Dec. 1753 Capt. George Simmons, son of William
       and Mary (Pearce) Simmons.
13. iv. Joseph, b. 3 Dec. 1731.
     v.   Comfort, b. 28 May 1735; m. in LC 28 May 1735 George
          Wood, son of Joseph and Mary (Brownell) Wood.
14. vi. Philip, b. 10 July 1737.

7. PETER[3] TAYLOR (Peter[2], Robert[1]), born in LC 20 Oct.
1697.
       He was married first in LC 27 Oct. 1720 by Thomas Church,
justice, to ELIZABETH IRISH, daughter of David and Martha (Nelson)
Irish, born in 1669. He was married second in LC 25 Dec. 1734 by
Richard Billings, justice, to BRIDGET WOOD.

       Children by second wife, recorded in LC:
i.   Elizabeth, b. 14 Feb. 1739/40; d. 11 Sept. 1758.
ii.   Hannah, b. 14 Dec. 1743.

No children are recorded for his first wife.

8. DEACON WILLIAM[3] TAYLOR (Peter[2], Robert[1]), born in
LC 30 April 1724, died there 28 Jan. 1810.
       He was married in LC 15 Oct. 1747 by Richard Billings, justice,
to DEBORAH GRAY, daughter of Lt. Samuel and Hannah (Kent) Gray,
born in LC 26 Nov. 1730, died there 28 Jan. 1825. They are buried
in the Old Commons cemetery.
       Residence: LC. They lived in district number 2 on the place
owned by Alexander Simmons in 1890. It is probable that he also
lived on the place north of Taylor's Lane on the north side, of the
Long Lane, known at one time as the Hall place.

His will, recorded LC Wills, book 4, page 299, proved 7 March 1810: ". . . To wife Deborah use of all lower rooms in my dwelling house that I now live in and a privilege of the cellar. To son Jonathan that house and lot of land that I own to the westward of the great highway. To son John Taylor all my land lying to the eastward of the great highway with buildings thereon standing. To son Peter Taylor 25 cents. To sons Joseph, William and Dan Taylor 25 cents each. To children of my son Benjamin Taylor 25 cents. To the children of my daughter Susannah Wood 25 cents. To daughter Elizabeth Church 10 dollars. To daughter Deborah Willbur 10 dollars. To daughter Hannah Richmond Taylor 50 dollars and after my wife's decease three fourths of the household goods. To the children of my son Samuel Taylor 25 cents. . . "

Children, recorded in LC:

	i.	Simeon, b. 7 July 1749 (?).
	ii.	Peter, b. 31 July 1751.
15.	iii.	Jonathan, b. 18 Feb. 1753.
	iv.	Susannah, b. 20 Dec. 1754; m. in LC 21 April 1779 Isaac Wood, son of Joseph and Mary (Brownell) Wood.
	v.	Samuel, b. 6 Sept. 1756; d. 18 Sept. 1756.
16.	vi.	Samuel, b. 17 Oct. 1757.
	vii.	Benjamin, b. 8 Jan. 1761; m. in LC 23 Dec. 1784 Elizabeth Grinnell, daughter of Aaron and Margaret (Taylor) Grinnell.
	viii.	Elizabeth, b. 17 Jan. 1763; m. 15 Sept. 1793 Joseph Church, son of Ebenezer and Hannah (Wood) Church.
	ix.	William, b. 6 Feb. 1765; m. in 1789 Elizabeth Andrews. Residence: Providence.
	x.	Josiah, b. 4 March 1767.
	xi.	Dan, b. 1 Feb. 1769.
	xii.	Deborah, b. 20 Dec. 1770; d. 22 April 1850; m. in LC 30 May 1790 Daniel Wilbour, son of Daniel and Mary (Southworth) Wilbour.
17.	xiii.	John, b. 3 Jan. 1773.
	xiv.	Hannah Richmond, b. 16 July 1776; d. in LC 28 May 1854; unmarried.

9. DAVID[4] TAYLOR (John[3], John[2], Robert[1]), born in LC 31 March 1722.

He was married first in LC 16 July 1746 by William Richmond, justice, to ELIZABETH LAWTON. He was married second in LC 3 Feb. 1753 by Joseph Wood, justice, to ELIZABETH GIBBS, born 3 Feb. 1733.

Residence: LC. He received the homestead farm of his father, John Taylor. This family must have left town.

Children, recorded in LC:

	i.	Thomas, b. 14 June 1748; d. 14 Aug. 1748.
	ii.	Lois, b. 10 Sept. 1749.

Children by second wife:

	iii.	Jude, b. 10 Oct. 1753.
	iv.	Elizabeth, b. 15 Aug. 1760.

    v.   Samuel, b. 7 March 1763.

    10. ROBERT[4] TAYLOR (Robert[3], John[2], Robert[1]), born in LC 13 May 1726, died there in December 1802.
    He was married first in LC 14 Feb. 1754 by the Rev. Jonathan Ellis to ANNA WHEATON. He married second about 1764 ABIGAIL (--), born in LC 18 April 1741, died there in May 1817. She may have been a Jameson or a Richmond, as "Abigail Taylor" is mentioned in the will of those two families.
    His will, recorded LC Probate, book 6, page 296, made 19 March 1800 and proved 5 Feb. 1803: ". . . To wife Abigail one half of my personal and use of my real estate, all that I own in this world, as long as she is my widow. To daughter Anna Pearce all the real estate that I own in this world after her mother. To grandson Robert Taylor Pearce 50 dollars. . . "
                Children by second wife, recorded in LC:
    i.   Gilbert, b. 8 June 1765.
    ii.   Anna, b. 22 Nov. 1773; m. in LC 7 Feb. 1793 John Pearce, son of James and Deborah (Hunt) Pearce.

    11. DEACON GIDEON[4] TAYLOR (Robert[3], John[2], Robert[1]), born in LC 15 May 1729, died there 11 July 1790.
    He married in LC 18 Jan. 1753 MARY BROWNELL, daughter of George and Sarah (Bailey) Brownell, born in LC 8 Aug. 1735, died there 15 March 1815. Both are buried in the Old Commons cemetery.
    He was a deacon of the United Congregational Church. They lived in LC at what was the Edmund Peckham place on Meeting House Lane. This place was owned by the first John Taylor in town, son of Robert, and also owned by Robert Taylor, father of Gideon. Her family lived in Westport Harbor at the Barker Peckham place.
                Children, recorded in LC:
    i.   George, b. 27 June 1754.
    ii.   Eunice, b. 1 May 1756.
    iii.   Abigail, b. 12 Nov. 1758; d. in Paris, N.Y., 28 Oct. 1856; m. 18 Feb. 1776 in LC Stephen Pearce, son of James and Sarah (Simmons) Pearce, b. in LC 20 Dec. 1753, d. in Paris, N. Y., 4 May 1843.
    iv.   Deborah, b. 20 Oct. 1760; d. in LC 10 Sept. 1807.
18.   v.   Andrew, b. 18 Nov. 1763.
    vi.   Mercy, b. 28 Oct. 1767; d. in LC 3 Dec. 1847; m. there 31 Aug. 1794 Uriah Tompkins, son of Michael and Sarah (Dring) Tompkins.
    vii.   Robert, b. 13 Feb. 1771.
19.   viii. Simeon, b. 7 May 1774.

    12. JAMES[4] TAYLOR (Robert[3], John[2], Robert[1]), born in LC 21 Jan. 1739. Residence: LC. This family must have left town.
    He was married in LC 7 July 1768 by the Rev. Jonathan Ellis to LYDIA SISSON, daughter of Isaac and Alice (Simmons) Sisson.

Children, recorded in LC:
i.   Isaac, b. 29 June 1772.
ii.   Rebecca, b. 1 Sept. 1774.
iii. Abigail, b. 25 Nov. 1776; d. in August 1778.
iv.   Sisson, b. 30 Sept. 1778; m. in LC 17 Feb. 1805 Mary
      Palmer, daughter of Thomas and Phebe (Shaw) Palmer.
v.   Betsey, b. 25 Nov. 1780.
vi.   William, b. 27 March 1783.
vii. Lydia, b. 3 July 1785.
viii. Anna, b. 6 May 1787.
ix.   Deborah Wheaton, b. 10 Sept. 1789.

13. JOSEPH[4] TAYLOR (Philip[3], John[2], Robert[1]), born in LC
3 Dec. 1731. Residence: LC. This family must have moved away.
    He married in LC 8 Feb. 1753 RUTH STODDARD, daughter of
Thomas and Ruth (Nichols) Stoddard, born about 1731.

Children, recorded in LC:
i.   Jeremiah, b. 19 Sept. 1754.
ii. Dennis, b. 20 Dec. 1756.

14. PHILIP[4] TAYLOR (Philip[3], John[2], Robert[1]), born in LC 10
July 1737, died there 5 March (or February) 1819.
    He was married first in LC 18 July 1760 by the Rev. Jonathan
Ellis to MARY GRAY, daughter of Samuel and Hannah (Kent) Gray,
born in LC 5 July 1739, died there 30 Oct. 1786. He was married
second in LC 22 Jan. 1789 by the Rev. Mase Shepard to ELIZABETH
SIMMONS, daughter of Adam and Deborah (Church) Simmons, born
in LC 9 June 1758, died there 5 Dec. (or November) 1821.
    Residence: LC. They lived on the place owned in 1890 by
Alexander Carton on the West Main Road, district number 2.
    His will, recorded LC Probate, book 5, page 123, made 8 May
1815 and proved 13 March 1819: ". . . To wife Elizabeth Taylor, all
household goods, all securities, one cow and great Bible, use of one
third of homestead farm and use of real estate, and then to daughter
Mary Simmons until my son Nathaniel deceases. Then all real estate
to daughter Lois Brown and Mary Simmons, they paying my grandson
Richmond Southworth two hundred dollars. To son Nathaniel wearing
apparel, farming utensils and use of all real estate not mentioned. To
daughters Lois Brown and Mary Simmons one half the pew in the
Congregational Meeting House. To son Philip Taylor 25 dollars. To
grandson Richmond Southworth 50 dollars. To granddaughter Mary
Brown one bedstead, a cow, best chest. To daughter Mary Simmons
my great Bible when wife dies and remainder of books. I do in this
my will reserve the land in meadow where the graves are, a family
burial plot, say three rods of land east and west and two rods north
and south. . . "
    The will of Elizabeth Taylor, recorded LC Probate, book 5,
page 275, made 10 Sept. 1821 "in the 45th year of American independence" and proved 10 Dec. 1821: ". . . So as to have my house in
order. . . To cousin Elizabeth Wood, wife of Charles Wood, one bed
and great silver spoon. To cousin Elizabeth Coe, daughter of Saray

Coe, the bed that she has in her possession. To cousin Deborah,
daughter of my sister Lucy Richmond, one bed and great silver
spoon. To Lindall Simmons, my chaise. To Eliza Simmons, daughter
of Lindall Simmons, 20 dollars. To Lois Brown, wife of John Brown
Esq., 10 dollars. To Richmond Southworth my gold necklace. To
Saray Coe, my sister, part of pew in the Congregational Meeting
House. To cousin Mary Simmons, daughter of Isaac Simmons, my
silver teaspoons. To Abishag Simmons, formerly the wife of my
brother Isaac Simmons, the rest and residue. . . "

> Children, recorded in LC:
> i.   Comfort, b. 9 Oct. 1761.
> ii. Nathaniel, b. 23 Sept. 1763; d. in LC 21 Dec. 1844; m.
>   5 Sept. 1821 Comfort Church, daughter of William
>   and Parnell (Southworth) Church, died 23 March 1844
>   ae 74. Her estate was administered 13 May 1844 by
>   her husband. See his will below.
> iii. Lois, b. 30 Aug. 1765; d. in LC 9 June 1853; m. there 11
>   July 1784 John Brown, son of William and Elizabeth
>   (Thomas) Brown.
> iv. Lydia, b. 20 June 1767; m. 24 Nov. 1790 in LC Alden South-
>   worth, son of Isaac and Abigail (Peabody) Southworth.
> v.   Philip, b. 16 June 1769.
> vi. Mary, b. 27 Jan. 1775; d. in LC 19 Nov. 1844; m. there 23
>   Jan. 1806 Lindall Simmons, son of Nathaniel and Mary
>   (Wood) Simmons.

He had no children by his second wife.

The will of Nathaniel Taylor, son of Philip, recorded LC Wills,
book 9, page 231, made 2 July 1844 and proved 10 Feb. 1845: ". . . To
Alden Simmons my silver watch and chest and one half wearing apparel.
To Nathaniel Simmons 20 dollars, small brass kettle, pewter basin,
porringer and wood lot at Cole Brook woods. To Philip Simmons one
half wearing apparel. To Mary S. Wilbor, wife of Isaac of New Bedford,
one feather bed. . . To Eliza T. Church, wife of George W. Church, one
half pew in the Congregational Meeting House. Houselot and buildings
to be sold one year after my death. To Deborah C. Richmond, wife of
Barton Richmond of Nashville, Tenn., my gold necklace. To the Little
Compton Congregational Society 125 dollars in trust. To the American
Home Mission Society founded in 1826, one third of my securities and
one third of buildings. To the Bible Society one third of same. To
Nathaniel Simmons, the son of Lindall Simmons, the rest and residue. . . "

15. JONATHAN[4] TAYLOR (William[3], Peter[2], Robert[1]), born in
LC 18 Feb. 1753, died there 20 March 1809.

He was married in LC 8 June 1783 to MARTHA BRIGGS, daughter
of William and Abishag (Records) Briggs, born in LC 29 Dec. 1759,
died there 11 Sept. 1842. Both are buried in the Old Commons cemetery.

He was a soldier of the Revolution. He lived in LC at the place
owned by his father, William Taylor, on Taylor's Lane, and given to
him in his father's will. His daughter Rhoba was living there in 1850
with Thomas Wilbor 2d and his wife, Dorcas.

Children, recorded in LC:
i.   Rhoba, b. 20 Dec. 1783; d. in LC 22 Jan. 1853; unmarried.
ii.   Sarah (Sally), b. 5 March 1785; d. in LC 8 June 1856; m.
        there 11 Jan. 1808 Christopher Brownell, son of James
        and Hannah (Manchester) Brownell.
iii.   Samuel, b. 21 Jan. 1787.
iv.   Jonathan, b. 8 June 1788.
v.   John Briggs, b. 28 March 1789.
vi.   Abishag, b. 29 May 1791; d. 10 July 1838; unmarried.
20.   vii.   Mase, b. 13 March 1793.
viii.   Deborah, b. 29 Aug. 1795; d. 17 Feb. 1886; m. in LC 3
        March 1817 Thomas Brownell, son of James and Hannah
        (Manchester) Brownell.
ix.   William, b. 5 March 1798; d. in LC 25 Aug. 1806.
x.   Lurana, b. 1 Feb. 1800; d. in LC 2 Dec. 1860; m. there
        6 Nov. 1817 Clarke Wilbor, son of Jonathan and
        Priscilla (Wilbor) Wilbor.
xi.   Elizabeth, b. 14 Sept. 1805.

16. SAMUEL[4] TAYLOR (William[3], Peter[2], Robert[1]), born in
LC 17 Oct. 1757, died there 5 April 1785.

He was married in LC 14 Jan. 1779 by the Rev. Jonathan Ellis
to LYDIA BROWNELL, daughter of Jonathan and Elizabeth (Richmond) Brownell, born in LC 7 Nov. 1755, died there 14 Aug. 1788.

His estate was administered in LC by his father, William Taylor,
20 April 1785. He lived in LC, probably in the house of his father,
for according to the census records he was living next to his father.
That place was owned by Alexander Simmons in 1890.

Children, recorded in LC:
i.   Simeon, b. 5 Sept. 1779.
ii.   Ruth, b. 9 May 1782; d. in LC 19 July 1818; m. there 17
        July 1803 Thomas Burgess, son of Ichabod and Hannah
        (Simmons) Burgess.
iii.   Jonathan Brownell, b. 17 Feb. 1784; perhaps married
        Susannah and had Philip, b. in LC 11 Dec. 1809.

17. JOHN[4] TAYLOR (William[3], Peter[2], Robert[1]), born in LC
3 Jan. 1773, died there 10 Sept. 1851.

He was married in LC 5 Nov. 1797 by the Rev. Mase Shepard
to ELIZABETH BAILEY, daughter of Ephraim and Mary (Briggs)
Bailey, born in LC 3 March 1778, died there 21 April 1855. Both
are buried in the Old Commons cemetery.

His estate was administered in LC 10 Nov. 1851. He lived in
LC in the house owned by Alexander Simmons on the map of 1870.
His will, recorded LC Probate, book 10, page 468, made 17 Feb.
1844 and proved 8 Dec. 1851: ". . . To wife Elizabeth use of all real
estate except that part of dwelling house which I shall give to my
single daughters and use of all my farming tools. To son William
5 dollars. To five married daughters. . . 5 dollars each. To daughter
Sally Taylor 50 dollars. To daughter Hertilla Taylor 25 dollars. To
single daughters Sally and Hertilla use and improvement of the west

room. To two sons, John and Edwin, all the real estate at the decease
of my wife. . . "

Children, recorded in LC:

i.   Fanny, b. 15 Oct. 1798; d. in LC 20 Oct. 1846 Elkanah
       Palmer, son of Jonathan D. and Deborah (Wood) Palmer.
ii.   Galen, b. 21 May 1801; d. 19 Jan. 1829. He is buried in the
       Old Commons cemetery and his gravestone reads: "Mr.
       Galen Taylor who was drowned by the upsetting of the
       ferry boat while passing from Rhode Island to Little Comp-
       ton, died 19 Jan. 1829 in the 29th year of his age."
iii.   Maria Sevey, b. 1 June 1804; d. in LC 3 Oct. 1847; m. there
       3 Dec. 1826 Jonathan Wilbor, son of Jonathan and Pris-
       cilla (Wilbor) Wilbor.
iv.   John Pope, b. 28 July 1806; d. 4 March 1875. He was an
       inventor and lived in Providence.
v.   William P., b. 17 June 1808.
vi.   Harriet, b. 18 March 1810; m. in LC 6 Jan. 1839 Robert L.
       Thurston of Providence.
vii.   Juliann, b. 31 Oct. 1811; d. in Marion, Mass., 6 Feb. 1875;
       m. 3 Nov. 1834 Joseph Coe of Boston, son of Ezra and
       Sarah (Bailey) Coe.
viii. Sally, b. 27 Sept. 1814; d. in LC 22 Sept. 1852.
ix.   Edwin Walles, b. 20 June 1816.
x.   Mary Burr, b. 24 Feb. 1819; d. in LC 17 Feb. 1899; m.
       (1) David Shaw, son of David and Sarah E. (Shaw) Shaw;
       m. (2) 8 Jan. 1863 in LC Orrin W. Simmons, son of
       Abel and Lydia (Pierce) Simmons.
xi.   Hertilla B., b. 17 July 1822; d. in LC 29 Oct. 1901; m.
       there 31 March 1845 James Hubbard Bailey, son of
       William and Susanna (Bailey) Bailey.

18. CAPT. ANDREW[5] TAYLOR (Gideon[4], Robert[3], John[2],
Robert[1]), born in LC 18 Nov. 1763, died in Providence 10 Sept. 1835.
He married ELIZABETH FIELD of Providence.

Residence: LC and Providence. He was a merchant and had
a store at one time at the Edmund Peckham place on Meeting House
Lane. Later he had a store in the house owned in 1890 by Nathaniel
Church.

A manuscript listing his descendants is on file at the Rhode
Island Historical Society Headquarters in Providence.

Children:

i.   Abbie Field, b. 26 April 1789; d. 14 July 1853; m.
       Sylvester Brownell, son of Sylvester and Mercy
       (Church) Brownell of LC, b. in 1785, d. in 1863.
ii.   Allen Field, b. 27 Dec. 1790; d. in Westerly 8 Nov. 1865.
iii.   Julia Ann, b. 31 Oct. 1794; d. 3 May 1883; m. John A.
       Field.
iv.   Eliza, b. 23 Dec. 1796; d. in November 1853; m. Amasa
       Manton.
v.   George Washington, b. 28 Feb. 1798; d. 26 April 1862;
       m. Mary T. Pope.

vi.   Benjamin Franklin, b. 13 Jan. 1799; d. 14 Nov. 1863; m.
       Jane Cushing of Chicago.
vii.   Joseph W., b. 10 Oct. 1800; d. 20 Sept. 1876; m. Elizabeth
       Dean.
viii. Robert, b. 27 Dec. 1800 (?); d. 21 May 1873.
ix.   Mary Brownell, b. 16 Nov. 1802; unmarried.
x.   Sophia Field, b. 14 Jan. 1805; d. 22 April 1883; m. Walter
       Paine Jr.
xi.   Maria, b. 26 July 1807; d. 14 March 1808.

19. SIMEON[5] TAYLOR (Gideon[4], Robert[3], John[2], Robert[1]), born
in LC 7 May 1774, died there 16 June 1835.

He was married in LC 13 Oct. 1799 by the Rev. Mase Shepard to
MARY ANN JONES, daughter of George and Phebe (Bevans) Jones of
Haverfordwest, Pembrokeshire, Wales, born in Haverfordwest 25
May 1775, died in LC 4 April 1867. Her father and grandfather were
both saddlers.

Both are buried in the Old Commons cemetery. They lived in
LC on the West Road in the house owned in 1890 by J. Follen Beebe.
His estate was administered by Hezekiah Woodworth 13 July 1835.

       Children, recorded in LC:
i.   Keziah, b. 4 Oct. 1801; d. 7 March 1891 in Poplar Ridge,
       N.Y.; m. 16 March 1825 Thomas Boucher, son of Henry
       Boucher.
ii.   John Bevans, b. 31 Oct. 1803; d. in Oakland, Calif.; m.
       6 Oct. 1829 Mary Barker, daughter of Deacon Joshua
       and Aurelia (Sherman) Barker, b. in New Bedford 5
       April 1807, d. in Oakland 13 Dec. 1879.

JOHN BEVINS TAYLOR and MARY (SYLVIA) CHACE
at the well on the George Arnold Gray place (Middendorf)

      iii.   Mary Ann, b. 2 Nov. 1805; d. young.
      iv.   Alexander Lloyd, b. 26 Aug. 1807; d. in LC 3 Dec. 1807.
      v.   Francis Malbone, b. 31 March 1809; d. young, perhaps
             26 July 1849.
      vi.   Abby Maria, b. 26 Feb. 1811 in LC; d. there 11 Feb. 1887;
             m. there 30 Sept. 1827 Benjamin Franklin Wilbour, son
             of Daniel and Deborah (Taylor) Wilbour.
      vii.   Alexander Wellington, b. 15 May 1815; d. 6 June 1836.
21. viii. George Milford, b. 15 Sept. 1817.

      20. MASE[5] TAYLOR (Jonathan[4], William[3], Peter[2], Robert[1]),
born in LC 13 March 1793, died there 19 March 1823. Residence: LC.
      He was married in LC 1 Feb. 1818 by the Rev. Mase Shepard
to ABIGAIL TAYLOR PEARCE, daughter of John and Ann (Taylor)
Pearce, born in LC 15 Dec. 1793.
      His estate was administered 1 April 1823 by Clarke Wilbor,
and her estate was administered by John Pearce 2d.

      Children:
      i.   William, b. 2 Nov. 1818.

      21. GEORGE MILFORD[6] TAYLOR (Simeon[5], Gideon[4], Robert[3],
John[2], Robert[1]), born in LC 15 Sept. 1817, died there 14 Feb. 1872.
      He married 30 Oct. 1844 SARAH JANE DEAN, daughter of Capt.
Joseph and Sarah (Tew) Dean, born in Berkely, Mass., 29 March
1823, died in LC 9 Dec. 1911.
      His middle name was taken from Milford Haven in Wales, the
port from which his mother had sailed. He lived in LC in district
number 10 on the road at the east end of Shaw Road. Earlier he had
lived at Onegan, in district number two on West Road.
      In his will, recorded book 11, page 639, made 10 Feb. 1872
and proved 13 May 1872, he named his wife sole executrix and left
to her all property both real and personal.

      Children, recorded in LC:
22. i.   George Francis, b. 2 Dec. 1845.
      ii.   Josephine Elizabeth, b. 17 Feb. 1848; d. 6 July 1864.
      iii.   Harriet Milford, b. 5 May 1850; m. 11 Sept. 1872 in
             LC Frank Wells Simmons, son of Valentine and Mary
             Ann (Lombard) Simmons.
      iv.   Mary Jane, b. 29 July 1853; d. in LC 5 Oct. 1940; m.
             there 18 Oct. 1869 Thomas Warren Kempton, son
             of Ephraim Warren and Susan Amanda (Grinnell)
             Kempton, d. 16 Nov. 1899.
      v.   Elmira Dean, b. 20 May 1855; m. in LC 24 Nov. 1875
             George D. Hubbard.
23. vi.   Andrew Simeon, b. 18 July 1859.
      vii.   John Bevans, b. 4 Aug. 1863; d. in LC 15 Dec. 1928;
             m. Susan Marion Marble, daughter of Samuel H. and
             Susan Marble, b. in Southbridge, Mass. 10 Feb. 1866,
             d. in LC 7 March 1946.
24. viii. Albert Joseph, b. 5 June 1866.

22. GEORGE FRANCIS[7] TAYLOR (George[6], Simeon[5], Gideon[4], Robert[3], John[2], Robert[1]), born in LC 2 Dec. 1845. He married there 25 Dec. 1869 SARAH AUGUSTA BROWNELL, daughter of George Taylor and Rhoda Ann (Shaw) Brownell, born in LC 22 May 1846, died there 1 Sept. 1921. They lived in LC on Shaw Road, and in New Bedford.

Children, recorded in LC:
i. Harriet Augusta, b. 21 Sept. 1873.
ii. Mabel, b. 25 Oct. 1882; m. Louis Gidley.

23. ANDREW SIMEON[7] TAYLOR (George[6], Simeon[5], Gideon[4], Robert[3], John[2], Robert[1]), born in LC 18 July 1859, died there 21 Jan. 1892. He married there 25 Nov. 1889 MARY PRISCILLA WHITE, daughter of Thomas E. and Maria W. (Simmons) White, born in LC 21 Dec. 1868. Residence: LC.

Children, born in LC:
i. Minnie White, b. in LC 18 Oct. 1890; m. there 23 June 1934 Harlan Harvey York of Philadelphia, son of Pleasant M. and Elizabeth (Hornaday) York, b. in Plainfield, Ind., 8 Sept. 1875.

24. ALBERT JOSEPH[7] TAYLOR (George[6], Simeon[5], Gideon[4], Robert[3], John[2], Robert[1]), born in LC 5 June 1866, died there 9 Feb. 1943. He married SARAH JANE CARTON, daughter of Alexander S. and Nancy (McFarland) Carton, born in LC 16 Jan. 1873, died there 11 May 1936. They lived in LC on the north side of Taylor's Lane, on the former Otis Brown place.

Children, born in LC:
i. Child, b. 23 June 1911, d. same day.
ii. Dorothy, b. in Fall River 28 Sept. 1913; m. in LC 22 May 1940 Guerdon William Brockson, son of Joseph and Martha (Rouse) Brockson, b. in Waukegan, Ill., 24 June 1909.

. . . .

Miscellaneous records of the Taylor family in LC:

GALEN TAYLOR, son of Jonathan Taylor, married MEHITABLE (--). Residence: LC. They had a daughter, Lydia C., who died 12 July 1828 ae 14 months, 9 days. She is buried in the Old Commons cemetery.

ABBY TAYLOR, given in the LC census of 1850. The name of her husband was not given. She may have married a son of John and Elizabeth (Bailey) Taylor.

Children, as given in the census of 1850:
i. Cornelia, b. in 1834.
ii. Galen, b. in 1836.
iii. Edwin F., b. in 1839.

PETER G. TAYLOR married ANN (--). They had a son, Pardon M., born in April 1824.

THE B. F. WILBOUR WINDMILL ABOUT 1880.
Notice the two barns in back of the house, the small size of
the trees at the road, and the old house of Albert T. Seabury.

This windmill was
placed on the east side
of the road where
the present Wilbor
cemetery is, then
was moved to the
west side of the road
and eventually
down into the fields
so that horses
would not be scared.

The old mill was
converted into
a home by the
Rev. T. R. Sleicer
and is now the
Herbert A. Taylor
house.

THE THOMAS FAMILY

ARNOLD THOMAS, born in 1813, died in LC 25 July 1877. He married 27 Jan. 1848 MARTHA BRIGGS BROWNELL, daughter of Thomas and Deborah (Taylor) Brownell, born in LC 5 May 1822, died 3 Jan. 1892. Residence: LC.

    Children:
i.   Isabella M., b. in 1851, d. 24 Sept. 1856.
ii.   Susan M., b. in 1854; d. in 1923.
iii.   Deborah E., b. in Fall River 6 Dec. 1857; d. in LC 1 Nov. 1923.

THE THOMPSON FAMILY

JOHN E. THOMPSON, born in 1845, married ANN E. (--). They were listed in the census of 1880.

    Children:
i.   Eliza A., b. in 1869.
ii.   Reliance M. (Son), b. in 1872.

ARNOLD THOMPSON, born in 1814, died in LC 16 May 1895. He married RELIANCE DAVIS, born in 1806. Residence: LC.

    Children:
i.   Mary A., b. 18 Feb. 1844 in LC; d. there 2 May 1919; m. 2 Jan. 1873 in Tiverton George F. Dyer, son of Canaan and Abigail (Palmer) Dyer.
ii.   Martha Reliance, d. 21 Jan. 1921 ae 80-10-11 in LC.

They also had in their family Maude L. Jackson, a niece from Fall River, Mass.

THE THURSTON FAMILY

From the Thurston Genealogy by Brown Thurston.

1. EDWARD[1] THURSTON, born in 1617, died in Newport 1 March 1707. He married in June 1647 ELIZABETH MOTT, daughter of Adam Mott, born in 1629, died 2 Sept. 1694. Residence: Newport.

He must have come to this country some time previous to 1647, at least, in order to attend the preliminaries of his marriage, which is the third marriage on the record of the Society of Friends in Newport. He was a freeman in 1655, a commissioner and assistant deputy

1663 to 1690. On 26 Aug. 1686 he, with others, signed an address from the Quakers of Rhode Island to the King.

His will, made 11 Jan. 1704 and proved 12 March 1707, named a grandson, Edward, son of his son Edward; sons Jonathan, Daniel, Samuel and Thomas; a granddaughter, Elizabeth, daughter of Jonathan; sons-in-law Weston Clarke and Ebenezer Slocum. His will is in very bad condition and practically unreadable.

Children, born in Newport:
i. Sarah, b. 10 March 1648.
ii. Elizabeth, b. in February 1650.
iii. Edward, b. 1 April 1652; m. Susanna Jeffrey, daughter of William and Mary (Gould) Jeffrey. Residence: Newport.
iv. Eleanor, b. in March 1655; m. in 1674 George Havens, son of William and Dionis Havens.
v. Mary, b. in February 1657; m. the Rev. Ebenezer Slocum, son of Giles and Joan Slocum.
2. vi. Jonathan, b. 4 Jan. 1659.
vii. Daniel, b. in April 1661; d. in 1712; m. Mary Easton, daughter of John and Mehitable (Gaunt) Easton. Residence: Newport.
viii. Rebecca, b. in April 1662; d. 16 Sept. 1737; m. (1) Peter Easton, son of Peter and Ann (Coggeshalle) Easton; m. (2) 25 Nov. 1691 Weston Clarke, son of Jeremiah and Frances (Latham) Clarke.
ix. John, b. in December 1664; d. 22 Oct. 1690; m. Elizabeth (--). Residence: Newport. Both are buried in the Clifton burial ground.
x. Content, b. in June 1667.
xi. Samuel, b. 24 Aug. 1669; d. 26 Oct. 1747; m. Abigail Clarke, daughter of Latham and Hannah (Wilbor) Clarke. Residence: Newport.
xii. Thomas, b. 8 Oct. 1671; d. 22 March 1730; m. Mehitable Tripp, daughter of Peleg and Ann (Sisson) Tripp.

2. JONATHAN[2] THURSTON (Edward[1]), born in Newport 4 Jan. 1659, died in 1740. He married about 1678 SARAH (--).

Residence: First Newport, LC next, and finally Dartmouth. He lived on the Main Road of LC on the next place north of the Amasa Gray place. In 1870 it belonged to George Brown. He was the appraiser of the estate of John Dye in 1715, and took inventory of that estate in 1728. The Dye family lived directly south of him.

His will, recorded Taunton Probate, book 9, page 390, made 22 Aug. 1735 and proved 15 April 1740: ". . . Jonathan Thurston of LC, yeoman, now resident and living in Dartmouth. . . To son Edward 10 shillings. To son Jonathan 140 pounds and he to be sole executor. To son Joseph 150 pounds. To son Job 150 pounds. To daughter Mary Brownell 30 pounds. To daughter Content Wood 30 pounds. To daughter Abigail White 30 pounds. To daughter Susannah Carr 30 pounds. To grandson Lovit Peters 30 pounds and that which belongs to his mother Eleanor. To granddaughter Rebecca Southworth 20 pounds and household stuff that belonged to Patience, her mother. Ten shillings each

to all daughters of Elizabeth Wood's children. To daughter Sarah
Sawday's children 10 shillings. To two youngest sons, Joseph and
Job, all household goods not otherwise disposed of . . . "

Children, recorded in LC:

3. i.   Edward, b. 18 Oct. 1679.
    ii.   Elizabeth, b. 29 Nov. 1682; m. in LC 6 Jan. 1703 Jonathan
           Wood, son of Col. Thomas and Rebecca Wood.
    iii.   Mary, b. 20 March 1685; m. in LC 6 July 1706 Lt. George
           Brownell, son of Thomas and Mary (Pearce) Brownell
           of LC.
4. iv.   Jonathan, b. 5 July 1687.
    v.   Rebecca, b. 28 Nov. 1689; m. 6 May 1711 Edward Rich-
           mond, grandson of John Richmond of Taunton and New-
           port, and son of Edward and Sarah Richmond.
    vi.   Content, b. 18 Aug. 1691; m. in LC 14 Sept. 1815 Henry
           Wood.
    vii.   Sarah, b. 9 Nov. 1693; m. in LC 26 June 1712 Benjamin
           Sawdy.
    viii. John, b. 12 July 1695; d. before 1735.
    ix.   Eleanor, b. 26 Nov. 1696; m. (--) Peters.
    x.   Hope, b. 26 Nov. 1698; d. in February 1716.
    xi.   Abigail, b. 7 May 1700; m. in LC 2 Oct. 1729 William
           White.
    xii.   Patience, b. 16 Feb. 1702; m. 21 Feb. 1723 Thomas South-
           worth.
    xiii. Amey, b. 29 Jan. 1705; d. before 1735.
    xiv.   Peleg, b. 8 July 1706; d. before 1735.
    xv.   Jeremiah, b. 8 Aug. 1710; d. before 1735.
    xvi.   Susannah, b. 20 Aug. 1712; m. (--) Carr. She was bapt.
           at Trinity church in Newport.
5. xvii. Joseph, b. 25 April 1714.
    xviii. Job, b. 1 July 1717.

3. EDWARD[3] THURSTON (Jonathan[2], Edward[1]), born in LC 18
Oct. 1679. Residence: LC.
    He was married first in LC 19 Dec. 1706 by Joseph Church,
justice, to SUSANNAH PEARCE, daughter of George and Alice (Hart)
Pearce, born 21 Aug. 1688, died in LC 5 Aug. 1711. He was married
second in LC 15 Oct. 1712 by Richard Billings, justice, to SARAH
CARR, daughter of Ezek and Susanna Carr, born in LC 14 July 1685.
    His will, recorded LC Probate, book 9, page 206, made 20
March 1738 and proved 15 Jan. 1739: ". . . To wife Sarah 140 pounds
and all household goods, my Indian boy named Isaac. To son George
49 acres of land south side of my farm adjoining Samuel Gray's land
in breadth to make 49 acres and the house he now dwells in, one
acre more where house stands next to 49 acres. To five daughters,
Mary Brownell, Elizabeth White, Ruth Thurston, Sarah Thurston
and Hope Thurston, all remaining part of my land and housing. To
wife Sarah the use of farm tools and cart, use of my house where I
now dwell and all land I gave to son George until youngest daughter
comes of age. My wife and friend Samuel Gray executors. . . "

Children:
6. i.   George, b. 4 Nov. 1709.
    ii.   William, b. 13 April 1711; d. 13 March 1712.
    iii.   Mary, b. 16 May 1714; m. in LC 2 July 1733 John Brownell
           (Margaret³, Robert², Thomas¹).
    iv.   Elizabeth, b. 24 Sept. 1719; m. 4 March 1739 Christopher
           White, son of William and Sarah (Cadman) White.
    v.   Ruth, b. 3 Oct. 1722; m. in LC 7 Feb. 1740 Pearce Brownell,
           son of Jeremiah and Deborah (Burgess) Brownell.
    vi.   Sarah, b. 14 July 1725.
    vii.   Hope, b. 8 Sept. 1727; m. in LC 26 Dec. 1751 Ichabod Potter,
           son of Ichabod and Eleanor Potter.

4. JONATHAN³ THURSTON (Jonathan², Edward¹), born in LC 5
July 1687, died in 1740. He married HANNAH (--), born 2 Oct. 176-,
ae 88. Residence: LC.

Children:
    i.   Edward, b. in 1719; m. in Newport 8 April 1753 Elizabeth
           Crocum.
    ii.   Jonathan, b. about 1721.
    iii.   Mary, b. about 1723.
    iv.   Content, b. about 1727.
    v.   Abigail, b. about 1727.
    vi.   Susanna, b. about 1729.

5. JOSEPH³ THURSTON (Jonathan², Edward¹), born in LC 25
April 1714. He was married there 1 June 1738 by Richard Billings,
justice, to MERCY BURGESS, daughter of Thomas and Patience
Burgess, born in LC 22 Feb. 1722. Residence: LC and Newport.

Children, recorded in LC:
    i.   Mary, b. 2 Dec. 1741.

6. GEORGE⁴ THURSTON (Edward³, Jonathan², Edward¹), born
in LC 4 Nov. 1709. He was married first in LC 11 Dec. 1729 by Thomas
Church, justice, to KEZIAH THURSTON. He married second (--)
GREENE.

He lived on the place called the George Brown place, next north
of the Amasa Gray place. He sold his farm in LC to John Brown, son
of Tobias Brown, about 1740 and moved to Hopkinton, R.I. He may
have been a doctor as the estate of Philip Taylor, husband of Comfort,
mentions "for doctor's stuff from George Thurston".

Children, first five recorded in LC:
    i.   Susanna, b. in January 1730.
    ii.   William, b. 17 Jan. 1733; m. Ruth Stetson.
    iii.   Hannah, b. 10 Jan. 1735; m. (--) Greene.
    iv.   Mary, b. 27 Aug. 1737.
    v.   Edward, b. 16 May 1740; m. Thankful Main.
    vi.   George, b. in 1741; m. (1) Dolly Cottrell; m. (2) Sarah
           Rathbun.
    vii.   Nabby, b. in 1753; m. Nathaniel Main.

viii. Gardner, b. in 1760; m. Lydia Taylor.
ix. Joseph, m. Sarah Taylor.

THE TIMBERLAKE FAMILY

1. HENRY[1] TIMBERLAKE, married MARY (--), died in LC
10 Sept. 1705. Residence: Newport and LC. The inventory of her
estate was taken in LC by John Woodman, her son-in-law, 3 July
1706.

     Children:
i. William, d. in 1678; m. Mary (--). He lived in Newport
     and Boston, and had a daughter, Mrs. Mumford.
ii. Henry, m. Sarah (--). He had a son Henry and two daughters.
2. iii. Joseph.
iv. John, d. after 1706; m. Mary (--). He had three daughters,
     Elizabeth, Mary and Hannah.
v. Elizabeth, m. 24 Dec. 1670 John Coggeshalle, son of John
     and Elizabeth (Baulston) Coggeshalle.
vi. Hannah, b. in 1656; d. in LC 3 May 1713; m. John Woodman.

2. JOSEPH[2] TIMBERLAKE (Henry[1]), married about 1683 MARY
(EARLE) CORY, daughter of Ralph and Joan Earle and widow of
William Cory, died 22 March 1718. Residence: Portsmouth and LC.
He was a cordwainer, licensed in 1688. On 23 June 1691 in LC,
he entered into an agreement before marriage with Mary Cory, widow
of William Cory, carpenter of Portsmouth, to whom she was sole
executrix. It was agreed that said Mary should, after marriage, have
full liberty to improve and dispose of all her former husband's estate.
Joseph Timberlake, to confirm above, delivered an instrument to
Edward Moss and to George Bunnell, giving them "power of her
estate while widow and for bringing up of her children. . . reserving
only to myself a mare, four neat cattle, four hogs, four sheep." He
gave up all of his own estate, also house, land, etc., he being free
of all debts.

THE TOMLIN FAMILY

JOHN TOMLIN, died in May 1761. He married MARY SMITH, born 3 Aug. 1697. Residence: LC.

        Children, recorded in LC:
- i.   Alfeah, b. 15 July 1720.
- ii.   Sarah, b. 27 Dec. 1723.
- iii. Mary, b. 29 Nov. 1725.
- iv. John, b. 29 Dec. 1727.
- v.   Lydia, b. 14 Feb. 1729.
- vi. William, b. 14 Dec. 1731.
- vii. Eunice, b. 16 June 1735.
- viii. Gideon, b. 1 July 1736.

THE TOMPKINS FAMILY

RALPH TOMPKINS married KATHERINE FOSTER at Bucks in the parish of Edlesborough, England.

        Children:
- i.   John, b. in 1610; d. 23 June 1684; m. (1) Margaret Goodman at Edlesborough, d. 18 May 1672; m. (2) Mary Read.
- 1. ii.   Nathaniel, b. about 1612, appeared in Providence in 1620.
- iii. Samuel, b. in 1613; d. in 1676; m. 11 Oct. 1639 Lettice Forster.
- iv. Micah, b. about 1615; m. Mary (--). Residence: Newark, N.J.
- v.   Elizabeth.
- vi. Marie or Mary, b. in 1621; d. in 1656; m. John Foster.

1. NATHANIEL[1] TOMPKINS, son of Ralph and Katherine (Foster) Tompkins, born about 1612, probably at Edlesborough, Buckinghamshire, England. Residence: Providence.

        Children:
- 2. i.   Nathaniel, b. in 1650.

2. NATHANIEL[2] TOMPKINS (Nathaniel[1]), born in 1650, died 15 Feb. 1732. He married 15 Jan. 1671 ELIZABETH ALLEN, daughter of John and Elizabeth (Bacon) Allen, born in July 1651, died 24 March 1714. Residence: Newport and LC.

His will, made 30 May 1719 and proved 19 May 1724: ". . . To son Nathaniel 15 pounds. To son Samuel all lands not already given him by deed. To daughter Elizabeth, wife of William Ladd, a cow. To daughter Mary Tompkins, 30 shillings and a bed and 4 pounds borrowed by her. To daughter Mercy, wife of William Bowditch, a ewe sheep. To daughter Priscilla, wife of William Lyndon, a cow.

To daughter Sarah, wife of Benjamin Gifford, a cow. To daughter
Rebecca Tompkins, a cow and a bed. To daughter Hannah, wife of
Timothy Gifford, a cow. To son Samuel's three sons, Joseph, John
and Christopher, any estate remaining..."

Children:
- i. Elizabeth, b. in 1675; d. in 1729; m. in LC 17 Feb. 1696
  William Ladd, son of Joseph and Joanna Ladd.
- ii. Nathaniel, b. 31 Dec. 1676; d. in 1748; m. in 1696 Elizabeth
  Ladd.
- iii. Mary, b. 16 Sept. 1677.
- iv. Priscilla, b. 24 May 1679; d. 11 Dec. 1732; m. in July
  1703 Samuel Lyndon, son of Josias Lyndon.
3.   v. Samuel, b. 24 May 1681.
- vi. Mercy, b. 20 Oct. 1685; m. William Bowditch of Dartmouth.
- vii. Rebecca, b. in 1685; d. in 1688.
- viii. Sarah, m. Benjamin Gifford, son of Robert and Sarah
  (Wing) Gifford.
- ix. Robert, d. young (before 1724).
- x. Hannah, b. in 1689; m. in LC 18 April 1717 Timothy Gifford,
  son of Robert and Sarah (Wing) Gifford.

3. SAMUEL[3] TOMPKINS (Nathaniel[2], Nathaniel[1]), born in LC
24 May 1681, died there in May 1760. He married there 24 Jan. 1712
SARAH COE, daughter of John and Sarah (Pabodie) Coe, born in 1690,
died in LC 2 Jan. 1749. Residence: LC.

His will, recorded LC Probate, book 1, page 275, proved 3
June 1760: "... To son Joseph 40 pounds and he to be executor. To
sons Gideon and Micah all my real estate in LC with buildings. To
son Benjamin 5 pounds. To son William 50 pounds and the privilege
of living in my house as long as he is single. To daughters Elizabeth
and Abigail 30 pounds. To four grandchildren, children of my son
John, deceased, 5 pounds each at the age of 21 for males and 18 for
females..."

Children, recorded in LC:
4. i. Joseph, b. 26 Oct. 1712.
5. ii. John, b. 14 Sept. 1714.
- iii. Elizabeth, b. 8 Dec. 1715; m. George Heiter.
6. iv. Christopher, b. 8 Dec. 1715.
- v. Abigail, b. 28 Jan. 1717.
- vi. Nathaniel, b. 19 Nov. 1719; d. 20 Jan. 1724.
- vii. Gideon, b. 19 Nov. 1720; drowned in March 1774 in the
  bay at LC.
7. viii. Micah, b. 20 Jan. 1722.
8. ix. Benjamin, b. 26 Jan. 1723.
- x. Augustine, b. 19 March 1725; d. 16 Feb. 1747.
- xi. Priscilla, b. 6 June 1726; d. 18 Aug. 1739.
- xii. William, b. 17 Oct. 1730; d. in November 1768. See his
  will below.

The will of William Tompkins, son of Samuel, recorded LC
Wills, book 2, page 126, made 9 Nov. 1768 and proved 6 Dec. 1768:

". . . I, William Tompkins of LC, laborer, being very weak and low
. . . To brother Gideon Tompkins 200 pounds and he to be executor.
My best velevet britches trimmed with silver and silver shew buckles.
To the Rev. Othnial Campbell, pastor of Christ Church, Tiverton, two
dollars. To the Rev. Jonathan Ellis of the Church of Christ of LC two
dollars. To my friend Mary Burden of Tiverton, widow of George
Burden, deceased, two dollars. To brother Christopher Tompkins
a peace of blew broad cloth. To brother Micah Tompkins my new
thick jacket and my old great coat. To nephew John Tompkins, son
of my brother Micah, my silver headed cane marked on top I.T. To
nephew Benjamin Tompkins, son of brother Micah, my guns. To
nephew Elijah, son of brother Joseph Tompkins, my silver knee
buckles. To Martha Tompkins, wife of brother Joseph, two dollars.
To my sister Abigail Tompkins 100 pounds. . . "

    4. JOSEPH⁴ TOMPKINS (Samuel³, Nathaniel², Nathaniel¹),
born in LC 26 Oct. 1712. Residence: LC.
    He was married in LC 20 March 1741 by Richard Billings,
justice, to MARTHA PEARCE, daughter of James and Martha (Wilbore)
Pearce of LC, born in LC 14 Aug. 1717.

        Children, recorded in LC:

	i.	Priscilla, b. 8 Aug. 1743; d. in LC 28 March 1744.
	ii.	Elijah, b. 7 April 1745; m. 6 Jan. 1771 Elizabeth Pratt.
9.	iii.	Nathaniel, b. 25 Feb. 1748.
	iv.	Oliver, b. 11 May 1749.
10.	v.	Gilbert, b. 4 April 1751.
11.	vi.	Deacon Gamaliel, b. 4 April 1751.
	vii.	Gilbert (?), b. 24 May 1753; d. 1 Oct. 1835; m. (1) in LC 4 July 1784 Lucy Brownell, daughter of Samuel and Ruth (Burgess) Brownell, b. 6 Feb. 1766; m. (2) in LC 5 Feb. 1789 Mary Brownell, b. 8 July 1770, d. 10 May 1844. Residence: Madison, N.Y. He was a sergeant of the marines during the Revolution. It is said he served under Paul Jones, and was captain of a sloop on the Hudson.
12.	viii.	James, b. 22 Jan. 1757.
	ix.	Phebe, b. 8 June 1759; m. Samuel Brownell.
13.	x.	Gideon, b. 25 Dec. 1761.

    5. JOHN⁴ TOMPKINS (Samuel³, Nathaniel², Nathaniel¹), born
in LC 14 Sept. 1714, married about 1741 BRIDGET SANFORD, born
30 March 1720. Residence: LC. This family must have moved out
of town.

        Children, recorded in LC:

i.	Catherine, b. 20 March 1740.
ii.	Henry, b. 12 Nov. 1741.
iii.	Sanford, b. 13 Sept. 1744.
iv.	Eliphal, b. 20 July 1746.

    6. CHRISTOPHER⁴ TOMPKINS (Samuel³, Nathaniel², Nathaniel¹),

born in LC 8 Dec. 1715, married 3 Aug. 1751 SARAH LUSSE.

Children, recorded in LC:
i.   Lucy, b. 8 Aug. 1752.
ii.   Abigail, b. 11 Aug. 1754.
iii. Priscilla, b. 27 Oct. 1755.

7. MICAH[4] TOMPKINS (Samuel[3], Nathaniel[2], Nathaniel[1]), born in LC 20 Jan. 1722, died there in May 1771. He married about 1755 SARAH DRING, died 9 May 1827. Residence: LC.

Children, recorded in LC:
14. i.   Benjamin, b. in October 1755/58.
15. ii.   Nathaniel, b. 15 Dec. 1756.
16. iii. John, b. 2 Dec. 1760.
    iv.   Sarah, b. 14 April 1763; d. in LC 24 March 1856; m. there 25 March 1790 Nathaniel Brownell, son of George and Sarah (Bailey) Brownell.
    v.   Mary, b. 14 April 1763; d. in October 1855; m. in LC 26 March 1782 Gilbert Manchester, son of Thomas Manchester of Westport.
    vi.   David, b. in 1765; d. 14 April 1840. See his will below.
17. vii. Uriah, b. 17 Aug. 1767.
    viii. Rhoda, b. in 1769; d. 15 July 1840; m. (intention 14 June 1805 in Westport) John Knight, son of Waldron Knight.

The will of David Tompkins, son of Micah, recorded LC Wills, book 8, page 190-2, made 27 Jan. 1837 and proved 11 May 1840: "... To the Congregational Church of Tiverton 1200 dollars and the interest alone to be used. In case the church becomes extinct then to care for the ministers in LC and Fall River. To sister Rhoda... To Lucy Brownell, daughter of Nathaniel of Westport, deceased, 80 dollars and furniture except that cupboard that my sister Rhoda has. To brother Uriah my wearing apparel, ladder and cart and horse. To sister Mary Manchester, widow, 20 dollars. To Arnold Levere, son of Rhoda Levere, widow, my shoe bench, shoe making tools, lasts and all appurtenances. To sister Rhoda Waldron a cupboard in her possession, then to Rhoda Clark, daughter of Gilbert Manchester, deceased. To the Congregational Church of Tiverton Four Corners, rest and residue. To Job Lake and wife a seat in my pew in the Meeting House at Four Corners, Tiverton. Friend Gideon Almy sole executor... "

8. BENJAMIN[4] TOMPKINS (Samuel[3], Nathaniel[2], Nathaniel[1]), born in LC 27 Jan. 1723, died there in March 1774. He married about 1759 SUSANNA DEAN. Residence: LC.

Children:
i.   Benjamin, b. in 1756; d. 4 Aug. 1844; m. about 1792 Susannah Brightman.
ii.   Gilbert, b. in 1770; d. 19 Feb. 1812; m. Martha Schryver, daughter of Johanes and Neltenjen (Van Benschoten) Schryver, b. 9 July 1775, b. 15 April 1857. Residence: Clinton, N.Y.

iii. Michael, b. 14 March 1772; d. 14 Sept. 1841; m. Rachel
      Schryver, b. 4 Oct. 1777, d. 2 July 1856. Residence:
      Clinton, N.Y.

9. NATHANIEL⁵ TOMPKINS (Joseph⁴, Samuel³, Nathaniel²,
Nathaniel¹), born in LC 25 Feb. 1748, died 22 March 1775. He married
in LC 16 Jan. 1774 PHEBE PEARCE, daughter of Nathaniel and Sarah
(Rouse) Pearce of LC, born there 21 March 1752. Residence: LC.

          Children, recorded in LC:
18. i.   Nathaniel, b. 5 May 1775.

10. GILBERT⁵ TOMPKINS (Joseph⁴, Samuel³, Nathaniel²,
Nathaniel¹), born in LC 4 April 1751, died 6 Jan. 1853.
   He was married first in LC 4 July 1784 by the Rev. Jonathan
Ellis to Lucy Brownell, daughter of Samuel and Ruth (Briggs)
Brownell, born in LC 6 Feb. 1766. He was married second in LC
5 Feb. 1789 by the Rev. Mase Shepard to MARY BROWNELL, daughter
of Samuel and Ruth (Briggs) Brownell of LC, born there 8 July 1770.
Residence: LC and Westport. They moved to Madison, N.Y.

          Children by first wife, recorded in LC:
     i.   Brownell, b. 17 Nov. 1785.

          Children by second wife, first five recorded in LC and
          the others in Westport:
     ii. William, b. 4 Nov. 1789.
     iii. Isaac, b. 16 June 1791.
     iv. Samuel, b. 11 April 1793.
     v.   Maria, b. 23 Feb. 1795.
     vi. Ruth, b. 10 June 1797.
     vii. James, b. 28/29 April 1799.
     viii. Phebe, b. 23 Oct. 1802.
     ix. Philip, b. 29 March 1804.
     x.   Lucy, b. 18 Nov. 1806.

11. DEACON GAMALIEL⁵ TOMPKINS (Joseph⁴, Samuel³,
Nathaniel², Nathaniel¹), born in LC 4 April 1751, died there 18 Feb.
1822. Residence: LC.
   He married in LC 14 March 1776 MARY CHURCH, daughter
of Ebenezer and Hannah (Wood) Church, born in LC 30 Dec. 1754,
died there 4 Oct. 1844. They are buried in the New Commons cemetery.
   He was a second lieutenant during the Revolutionary War.
   His will, recorded LC Wills, book 5, page 62, made 14 June
1815 and proved 11 March 1822: ". . . Gamaliel Tompkins of LC,
far advanced in years and laboring under many bodily infirmities. . .
To wife use of all real and personal estate. To son Nathaniel my
desk. To three daughters, Betsey C. Tompkins, Lucy Tompkins and
Mary Tompkins, use of all chambers in my house except one half
of porch chamber and one half of cellar as long as they are single.
To children Ellery Tompkins, Priscilla Brownell, Patty Hicks,
Abel Tompkins, Betsey Tompkins, Lucy Tompkins, Nathaniel

Tompkins, Hannah Nichols, Samuel Tompkins and Mary Tompkins,
the rest and residue at the decease of their mother. . . "

Children, all recorded in LC except James, Thomas,
Samuel and Gideon:

i.   Priscilla, b. 20 Oct. 1776; d. 13 Oct. 1821; m. 4 May 1800
        Isaac Brownell, son of Joseph and Deborah Brownell.
ii.   Martha (Patience), b. 27 Aug. 1778; m. (intention 26 Oct.
        1805 in Westport) Benjamin Hicks.
iii.   John Ellery, b. 20 Dec. 1780; m. 13 Dec. 1803 Mercy Taber.
iv.   Gideon, b. in 1781; d. in 1837; m. Maria (--). Residence:
        Rensselaerville, N.Y. (according to Tompkins book.)
v.   Betsey, b. 16 March 1783; d. in LC 15 Aug. 1821.
vi.   Samuel (according to Tompkins book).
vii.   Lucy, b. 30 March 1786; d. 11 Sept. 1860.
19.   viii.   Abel, b. 5 March 1788.
ix.   Hannah, b. 18 April 1790; d. in December 1850; m. (--)
        Nichols.
20.   x.   Col. Nathaniel, b. 27 Dec. 1792.
xi.   Thomas, bapt. in 1793 (according to Tompkins Genealogy.)
xii.   Rev. Lemuel, b. 19 July 1795; d. 2 May 1860.
xiii.   Mary, b. 16 Sept. 1797; m. 2 Oct. 1825 in LC Zina Y. Paine
        of Lebanon, Conn., son of Abial and Cynthia (Robinson)
        Paine.
xiv.   James J., bapt. in 1799 (according to Tompkins book).

12. JAMES[5] TOMPKINS (Joseph[4], Samuel[3], Nathaniel[2], Nathaniel[1]),
born in LC 22 Jan. 1757, died there 20 March 1832.

He was married in LC 13 June 1784 by the Rev. Jonathan Ellis
to MARY RICHMOND, daughter of Ephraim and Elizabeth (Cook) Richmond, born in LC 22 Sept. 1765, died there 20 June 1847. He was a
soldier of the Revolutionary War. Residence: LC.

His will, recorded LC Wills, book 8, page 1, made 19 March
1827 and proved 14 May 1832: ". . . To son Ichabod my watch at
decease of my wife. To two sons Gilbert and William all my wearing
apparel. To two daughters Susannah and Sarah my two best beds. . .
To daughters Anna Hazard, Matilda Tompkins, Susannah Tompkins,
Harriet Ruggles and Sarah W. Tompkins . . . To wife Mary Tompkins
all estate both real and personal, not mentioned in this will, she to
be executrix. . . "

Children, recorded in LC except last three:

i.   Ephraim, b. 6 Jan. 1785; went to sea and never returned.
ii.   Cook, b. 21 Aug. 1786; d. young.
iii.   Calista, b. 21 Oct. 1788; d. young.
iv.   Matilda, b. 2 Dec. 1790; m. (1) about 1840 Deacon Nathaniel
        Tompkins; m. (2) Brownell Tompkins.
v.   Anna, b. 16 March 1793; d. in LC 29 March 1851; m. Perry
        Hazard, son of Oliver and Abby Hazard, b. in LC 24 July
        1854.
vi.   Isaiah, b. 17 Feb. 1796; d. in December 1822. He went to sea
        and, while on a voyage, was stabbed and killed by Spaniards

in the West Indies, having been mistaken for a cousin who
was on the same ship and who had quarrelled with the
Spaniards.
vii. Susannah, b. 23 Feb. 1798; d. 11 Jan. 1850.
viii. Ichabod, b. 26 May 1800; d. at sea.
ix.   Sarah Walker, b. 26 June 1802; m. 20 Dec. 1829 John
      Ruggles.
x.   Gilbert.
xi.   Harriet, b. in 1804; d. 25 April 1829; m. the same John
      Ruggles as above.
xii. William Richmond, b. in 1809; d. in 1882; m. Elizabeth
      Yelverton, b. in 1809; d. in 1898. Residence: Pough-
      keepsie, N.Y.

13. GIDEON[5] TOMPKINS (Joseph[4], Samuel[3], Nathaniel[2],
Nathaniel[1]), born in LC 28 Dec. 1761, died there 3 Jan. 1837. Residence: LC.
    He married there 2 June 1791 CYNTHIA BROWNELL, daughter
of Joseph and Deborah (Briggs) Brownell, born in LC 14 Dec. 1769,
died there 1 Nov. 1828. Both are buried in the Old Commons cemetery.
    He was a soldier in the Revolutionary War. His will, recorded
LC Wills, book 8, page 169, made 31 Dec. 1836 and proved 20 March
1837: ". . . To sons Pierce and Silas 200 dollars each. To sons
Tillinghast, Joseph and Edwin 10 dollars each. To son Gideon my
watch and 50 dollars. To four daughters, Cynthia Case, Hulda Hicks,
Elizabeth Seabury and Deborah Tompkins, 50 dollars each. To daughter
Lydia Tompkins 150 dollars and use of the east room in my house and
use of kitchen. To son Thomas all estate both real and personal not
before disposed of. . . "

        Children, all recorded in LC except Silas:
    i.   Pearce, b. 28 Feb. 1792; m. (intention 27 April 1816) in
          Westport Meribah Manchester, b. 12 Feb. 1792. Resi-
          dence: Rochester, N.Y.
    ii.   Deborah, b. 8 Dec. 1793; d. 12 Oct. 1796.
    iii. Pardon Tillinghast, b. 13 Oct. 1795; d. 15 Jan. 1860; m.
          (1) Susan Drew; m. (2) 25 Dec. 1833 Charlotte Merriell.
    iv.   Cynthia, b. 30 Aug. 1797; m. 8 Oct. 1818 in Westport Abner
          Case.
    v.   Dr. Silas, b. 8 Oct. 1799; d. 21 Dec. 1853.
    vi.   Joseph, b. 28 June 1801; m. 9 Nov. 1822 Angelina Nelson,
          daughter of Paule and Grace (Wood) Nelson, b. in 1801,
          d. 27 Feb. 1827.
    vii. Hulda, b. 1 March 1803; m. Isaac Hicks.
21. viii. Thomas Green, b. 11 Jan. 1805.
    ix.   Elizabeth Brownell, b. 14 March 1807; d. in LC 24 Sept. 1893;
          m. 9 Feb. 1830 Capt. Benjamin Seabury Jr.
    x.   Deborah Brownell, b. in LC 28 Jan. 1808; d. in 1890.
    xi.   Lydia Brownell, b. 2 Sept. 1809; m. (intention 24 Dec. 1836)
          in Westport William A. Davis.
    xii. Edwin, b. 12 April 1812; m. Mary J. Stanton, daughter of
          Leonard R. and Ann (Seaman) Stanton.

xiii.   Gideon, b. 3 July 1814; m. Elizabeth Brownell.

14. BENJAMIN[5] TOMPKINS (Micah[4], Samuel[3], Nathaniel[2],
Nathaniel[1]), born in LC in October 1755/8, died there 4 Aug. 1841/4.
He was married in LC 2 Oct. 1791 by the Rev. Mase Shepard to
DEBORAH SIMMONS, daughter of Capt. George and Lucy (Davis)
Simmons, born in LC 19 Nov. 1767, died there 31 Dec. 1834.
Residence: LC. He was a justice of the peace and a Revolution-
ary War pensioner.

Children, recorded in LC:
i.   George Simmons, b. 3 March 1792; m. 14 Dec. 1815
       Penelope Myrrick.
ii.   Mary (Mercy), b. 28 Dec. 1793; m. Thomas Wilbor, son
       of Benet and Mary (Shaw) Wilbor.
iii.   Lucy, b. 20 Oct. 1795; d. in LC 12 Nov. 1864. See her
       will below.
iv.   Sarah, b. 9 Oct. 1797; d. in LC 20 Sept. 1879 Clark Brownell,
       son of William and Betsey (Grinnell) Brownell.
v.   Capt. Isaac, b. 28 May 1799. He was a sea captain and with
       his brother Davis he sailed for Antigua with the brig
       Mary Elizabeth 24 Aug. 1826. No further word was ever
       received from them.
vi.   Eliza T., b. 13 April 1803; d. in 1896; m. Benjamin Peck-
       ham, son of Isaac·and Phebe (Wilbor) Peckham.
vii.   David, b. 19 Feb. 1801; d. in 1813 (?).
viii. Saressa, b. 6 April 1805; m. in LC 13 Aug. 1849 Easton
       Peabody of Middletown.
ix.   Davis S. (or David), b. 29 Jan. 1807.

The will of Lucy Tompkins, daughter of Benjamin, recorded
book 11, page 378, made 8 Nov. 1864 and proved 9 Jan. 1865: ". . .
To sisters Eliza and Saressa 25 dollars each; to Hannah Tompkins,
wife of my brother David, 10 dollars; to sisters Sarah Brownell and
Mary Wilbor 10 dollars each; to Etta and Lilla Fisher, daughters of
my niece Mary Ann Fisher, deceased, 10 dollars; to niece Charlotte
A. Sisson 10 dollars; to Adelbert Peckham, son of Isaac Peckham 10
dollars; to Belle Sisson, daughter of Richard W. and Charlotte Sisson,
10 dollars; to niece Deborah Wilbor, wife of Ichabod Wilbor, 10 dollars;
daughter of brother David Tompkins, 6 silver spoons; to sister
Saressa Peabody two feather beds and use of all real estate and after
her decease, to nephew Isaac D. Peckham all real estate; James
Pearce of LC to be executor. . . "

15. NATHANIEL[5] TOMPKINS (Micah[4], Samuel[3], Nathaniel[2],
Nathaniel[1]), born in LC 15 Dec. 1756. He married there 7 Jan. 1781
SARAH SNELL, daughter of Isaac and Sarah (--) Snell, born in LC
30 Dec. 1759, died 18 July 1837. Residence: LC. He was a soldier
of the Revolutionary War.

Children, recorded in LC:
i.   Micah (Michael), b. 18 March 1781.
ii.   Gilbert, b. 7 Dec. 1782.

22. iii. Lindall, b. 16 Sept. 1784.
     iv. Permella, b. 20 Feb. 1786; d. 27 Nov. 1846.
     v.   Carolina, b. 3 Feb. 1788.
     vi. Henrietta, b. 15 Oct. 1789.
     vii. Sarah Crawford, b. 3 June 1791.
     viii. Deacon Samuel, b. 24 Oct. 1792. He moved to Illinois.
     ix. Fritzweed (twin), b. 2 Oct. 1795.
     x.   Fidelia, b. 2 Oct. 1795; m. 4 March 1817 Donald Lake.
     xi. Mary, b. 27 July 1799.
23. xii. Thomas Jefferson, b. 23 Oct. 1800.
     xiii. Ann Almy (Nancy), b. 22 Aug. 1803; m. 13 Nov. 1825
           Ransom Hicks.

16. JOHN[5] TOMPKINS (Micah[4], Samuel[3], Nathaniel[2],
Nathaniel[1]), born in LC 2 Dec. 1760, died there 14 Sept. 1834.
     He married in LC 1 Jan. 1786 COMFORT SEABURY SOULE,
daughter of Abner and Dorcas (Seabury) Soule, born in Tiverton
14 Oct. 1767, died in LC 18 Jan. 1853.
     Residence: LC. He was a pensioner of the Revolutionary
War.
     His will, recorded book 8, page 77, made 19 Dec. 1833
and proved 8 Dec. 1834: ". . . To wife Comfort Tompkins, the east
half of my dwelling house from garret to cellar and east part of corn
house. . . also my cyder mill. To son Nathan all my homestead farm
where I now live except what wife has and one ten acre lot of land
bounded south by Thomas Pearce, west by Sanford Almy, north and
east on David Tompkins. Ten dollars each to sons William, Joseph,
Abner, Cornelius, Seabury, John and Clarke; to daughters Eliphal
Pearce, wife of Thomas Pearce, and Clarissa Potter, wife of Henry
Potter; and to granddaughter, daughter of Peleg S. Tompkins, deceased,
ten dollars. To granddaughter Angeline Tompkins, daughter of son
Joseph Tompkins, my wood lot called Bailey Wood Lot. To son Nathan
the rest and residue and he the sole executor. . . "
     The will of his widow, recorded book 10, page 644, made 28 June
1848 and proved 14 March 1853: ". . . To sons William and Joseph 10
dollars each. . . To Minerva Tompkins, daughter of my son Joseph,
one bed and bedding. To son Cornelius 5 dollars. To son Clarke two
beds and to be executor. To Anna Tompkins, widow of my son John,
one black silk dress. To Alfrida Tompkins, widow of Abner, one red
cloak. To Eliza Tompkins, wife of Clarke, all wearing apparel. To
grandchildren, children of my son Seabury, namely Cecelia, Edmund
and Nancy, remainder of household goods. To son Nathan one dollar.
To daughter Eliphal Pearce, widow of Thomas Pearce, one dollar.
To Clarinda Potter, ten dollars and brass warming pan. To Eliza
Tompkins, widow of Peleg, 5 dollars. To son Cornelius rest and
residue. . . "

          Children, born in LC:
     i.   William, b. 12 May 1786; m. 28 Jan. 1816 Elizabeth
          Davenport. She is called Freelove in the journal of
          Abner Soule Tompkins, written in 1838, but the vital
          records list her as Elizabeth.

ii. Joseph, b. 26 Dec. 1787; d. 5 Jan. 1854; m. in LC in
    October 1813 Susan Grinnell, daughter of Owen and
    Rhoda (Bailey) Grinnell of LC.

iii. Eliphal, b. 15 March 1790; d. 1 Feb. 1868; m. in LC
     26 Feb. 1811 Thomas Pearce, son of Wright and
     Antrace (Sawyer) Pearce.

24. iv. Abner Soule, b. 22 Feb. 1792.

25. v. Seabury Soule, b. 7 March 1794.

vi. Nancy, b. 7 June 1796; d. 28 Nov. 1796.

vii. Cornelia Soule, b. 1 Nov. 1797; d. 18 April 1868; m. in
     1835 Maria Carpenter, daughter of Peter and Patience
     (Rogers) Carpenter.

viii. Clarrissa, b. 15 May 1800; m. Henry Potter.

ix. John Almy, b. 20 Jan. 1803; d. 15 Dec. 1838; m. 5 Nov.
    1829 Anne Russell Tillinghast, daughter of Charles
    and Dulcena (Nelson) Tillinghast. He was a second
    lieutenant in the Fayette Rifle Corps of LC.

x. Peleg, b. 13 May 1806; d. 9 March 1833; m. 22 July 1828
   Eliza Gay, daughter of Ebenezer and Rebecca (Smith)
   Gay.

xi. Clark, b. 10 July 1808; d. in 1876; m. Eliza Ann Cook 5
    Aug. 1827. In 1840 he was in Cohoes, N.Y., and in
    1846 was in Troy. He later moved to California.

xii. Nathan Jenks, b. 26 May 1811; lived on the homestead of
     his father.

17. URIAH[5] TOMPKINS (Micah[4], Samuel[3], Nathaniel[2],
Nathaniel[1]), born in LC 17 Aug. 1767, died there 15 Nov. 1848. Residence: LC.

He married there 31 Aug. 1794 MERCY TAYLOR, daughter of
Gideon and Mary (Brownell) Taylor, born in LC 28 Oct. 1767, died
there 3 Dec. 1847.

His will, recorded LC Wills, book 10, page 121, made 2 Feb.
1841 and proved 8 Jan. 1849: ". . . To daughter Fanny, wife of Bradford
Pearce, one dollar and a small lamb. One dollar each to daughter
Lydia, wife of Allen Gifford; Abby, wife of Elias Barstow; Mary, wife
of James Wilbor. To son Andrew Taylor Tompkins 35 dollars and one
small silver teaspoon. To wife all household furniture. To son Robert
T. Tompkins my clock, one good bed, carpenter tools, all real estate
and he to be sole executor. . . "

Children, recorded in LC with the exception of the last
three, which were added by the Tompkins Genealogy:

i. Fanny, b. 18 Jan. 1796; m. in LC 22 Jan. 1818 Bradford
   Pearce, son of Rouse and Mary (Brownell) Pearce.

ii. Gideon Taylor, b. 7 Jan. 1798.

iii. Lydia, b. 16 Nov. 1799; m. (intention 3 Jan. 1826) in
     Westport John A. Gifford.

iv. Andrew Taylor, b. 23 Dec. 1801; d. young.

v. Abby, b. 7 Nov. 1804; m. Elias Bastow.

vi. Mary, b. 27 Nov. 1806; d. in 1866; m. 23 March 1834 James
    Wilbor, son of Hezekiah and Alice (Palmer) Wilbor.

	vii.	Andrew Taylor, b. 17 Feb. 1808; m. 25 Feb. 1841 Elizabeth Allen Sanford, b. 20 Nov. 1816.
26.	viii.	Robert Taylor, b. 30 May 1812.
	ix.	Gideon, b. in 1814; d. young.
	x.	Nanny, m. Bradford Brownell.
	xi.	James, b. 7 March 1819; d. 21 Feb. 1900; m. 3 Dec. 1838 Sarah Pearce, daughter of John and Lydia (Palmer) Pearce.

18. NATHANIEL[6] TOMPKINS (Nathaniel[5], Joseph[4], Samuel[3], Nathaniel[2], Nathaniel[1]), born 5 May 1775.

He married first 1 Nov. 1795 ELIZABETH PIERCE, who died in 1805.
He married second 21 July 1805 MEHITABEL SIMMONS, who died in 1810.
He married third 1 Jan. 1811 LUCRETIA HENRY, who died in 1827.
He married fourth 2 March 1828 CLARISSA HENRY, who died in 1838.
He married fifth 29 Jan. 1840 MATILDA TOMPKINS, the daughter of James and Mary (Richmond) Tompkins, born 25 May 1775.

		Children by his first wife:
	i.	Phebe, b. 8 Jan. 1798.
	ii.	Lydia, b. 17 Dec. 1799.
	iii.	Sarah, b. 21 Aug. 1800.
	iv.	John, b. in 1803.
		Children by his second wife, born in Paris, N. Y.
	v.	Elizabeth, b. 27 Oct. 1806.
	vi.	Naomi, b. 9 Sept. 1808; d. 10 Dec. 1813.
	vii.	Nathaniel, b. 23 Aug. 1810; d. 23 March 1842.
		Children by his third wife:
27.	viii.	Henry, b. 10 Sept. 1811.
	ix.	Joshua, b. 22 Dec. 1814; d. 3 March 1891; m. Angelina Pearce 21 Aug. 1836.
	x.	Mary Ann, b. 23 Oct. 1816.
	xi.	William, b. 3 Aug. 1818.
	xii.	Mehitable, b. 3 Aug. 1821.

19. ABEL[6] TOMPKINS (Gamaliel[5], Joseph[4], Samuel[3], Nathaniel[2], Nathaniel[1]), born in LC 5 March 1788, died there 28 Dec. 1822. He married 3 Sept. 1809 MARY SWEET, born 28 March 1789, died 7 Jan. 1852.

		Children:
28.	i.	Abel (Albert?), b. 12 June 1810.
	ii.	John Shepard, b. in 1814; m. Lydia Brownell. Residence: Cambridge, Mass.
	iii.	William Church, b. 2 May 1816; d. 16 Aug. 1875; m. Jane Baldwin, daughter of Joseph Baldwin.
	iv.	Mary Elizabeth, b. in 1821; d. in 1821.
	v.	Mary 2d, b. in 1822.

20. COLONEL NATHANIEL[6] TOMPKINS (Gamaliel[5], Joseph[4], Samuel[3], Nathaniel[2], Nathaniel[1]), born in LC 27 Dec. 1792, died there

1 Jan. 1861. Residence: LC.

He married in Westport 21 Nov. 1817 BETSEY HICKS, daughter
of Barney and Sally (Cook) Hicks, born in Westport 9 Feb. 1798, died
in LC 29 Jan. 1874. They are buried in the Union cemetery.

Children:
29. i.   John H., b. 20 June 1829.

21. THOMAS GREENE⁶ TOMPKINS (Gideon⁵, Joseph⁴, Samuel³,
Nathaniel², Nathaniel¹), born in LC 12 Jan. 1805, died there 24 March
1876. Residence: LC.

He married in Rochester, Mass., 6 May 1832 SUSAN LEWIS
BATES, daughter of Thomas and Olive (Bartlett) Bates, born in
Kingstown, Mass., 28 Dec. 1810, died in Denver, Colo., 16 Aug. 1888.
They are buried in the Old Commons cemetery.
Above information from the William Shurtleff Genealogy.

Children, all recorded in LC except the first:
i.   Charles Thomas, b. in New Bedford 4 Aug. 1833; d. in
      San Diego, Calif., 23 Nov. 1900; m. in Boston 8 March
      1858 Melissa Lavina Frizzell, b. in Essex County, Vt.,
      24 Feb. 1830.
ii.   Cynthia Brownell, b. 18 Jan. 1835; d. in Westport 25 Nov.
      1869; m. 27 Nov. 1857 Horatio Horonzo Brownell, b. in
      LC 6 June 1830.
iii. Susan Melissa, b. 24 Aug. 1836; m. in New Bedford 23
      July 1855 Ichabod Tompkins Hazard, b. 12 May 1831 in
      Westport.
iv.   Albert Green, b. 30 Aug. 1838; d. in LC 15 July 1858; un-
      married.
v.   Olive Bartlett, b. 21 Oct. 1840; d. in LC 18 July 1857; un-
      married.
vi.   Gideon Franklin, b. 1 Jan. 1843; d. in Fall River 15 Dec.
      1884; m. in New Orleans, Ala., 12 Feb. 1880 Florence
      (Cooney) Tomes, b. in New Orleans 28 March 1846.
vii. Mary Elizabeth, b. 23 April 1845; m. in New Bedford 25
      Dec. 1872 Charles Bradford Belt, b. in Hartford, Conn.,
      16 Sept. 1847.
viii. Maria Amanda, b. 19 Oct. 1847; d. in New Bedford 1 April
      1886; m. 31 Dec. 1867 George Andrew Jenks, b. in Fall
      River 5 Aug. 1844.
ix.   Eleanor Louise, b. 13 Oct. 1852; m. in Denver, Colo., 16
      March 1887 William Harper Walker, b. in Providence
      16 March 1853.

22. LINDALL⁶ TOMPKINS (Nathaniel⁵, Michah⁴, Samuel³,
Nathaniel², Nathaniel¹), born in LC 16 Sept. 1784. He married 10
July 1810 REBECCA PINKHAM, daughter of Charles and Mary
(Coffin) Pinkham, born 9 June 1790. Residence: LC.

Children, not recorded in LC:
i.   Lucy, b. 22 July 1811.
ii.   Nathaniel, b. 7 April 1812.

iii.   Gilbert, b. 9 March 1814.
iv.   Andrew, b. 10 June 1816.
v.   Daniel, b. 2 Aug. 1818.
vi.   Lydia Ann, b. 2 Dec. 1820.
vii. George Washington, b. 16 Sept. 1823.

23. THOMAS JEFFERSON[6] TOMPKINS (Nathaniel[5], Michah[4], Samuel[3], Nathaniel[2], Nathaniel[1]), born in LC 23 Oct. 1800. He married 14 Nov. 1826 CHARITY S. DAVIS.

    Children, born in LC but not recorded there:
i.   Franklin P., b. in 1833; d. 4 Feb. 1896; m. 28 May 1854 Elizabeth Sumner, d. 2 Aug. 1876 ae 33.
ii.   William H., b. in 1835; d. 25 June 1897.

24. ABNER SOULE[6] TOMPKINS (John[5], Michah[4], Samuel[3], Nathaniel[2], Nathaniel[1]), born in LC 22 Feb. 1792, died 15 July 1838. He married 6 May 1815 ALFREDA J. WILLIAMS, daughter of Jabez Williams, born 27 Jan. 1793.
Residence: LC. He was a first lieutenant of the LC Rifle Corps. His journal has been preserved.

    Children:
i.   Mary Pitcher, b. 21 Sept. 1817; m. in 1839 Albert Carlisle Jenks.
ii.   Delia Eliza, b. 22 Oct. 1819; m. 14 June 1840 Joseph Alger Allen.
iii. Susan Greenhill, b. 9 Aug. 1822; d. 18 April 1823.
iv. Abner Soule, b. in 1832; d. 2 Aug. 1907 Josephine Tompkins, daughter of Seabury Soule and Temperance (Manley) Tompkins.
v.   Maria, m. (--) Taylor.
vi. Cordelia W., b. in 1835; m. 23 Feb. 1860 William W. Reed, son of Alvin O. and Martha J. Reed.
vii. Albert W., b. 7 Oct. 1836; d. 30 Dec. 1920; m. Sarah McIntyre.

25. SEABURY SOULE[6] TOMPKINS (John[5], Michah[4], Samuel[3], Nathaniel[2], Nathaniel[1]), born in LC 7 March 1794, died 17 June 1841. Residence: LC.
He married in LC 15 June 1816 TEMPERANCE TURNER MANLEY, daughter of William and Judith (Snell) Manley, born in LC 11 May 1798, died 7 June 1845.

    Children (from Tompkins Genealogy), not recorded in LC:
i.   Cecelia, b. 27 July 1817; d. 6 April 1876; m. (1) 2 Sept. 1839 Horatio N. Chase; m. (2) James Arnold.
ii.   Edmund Cooley, b. 6 Aug. 1820; d. 1 July 1886; m. 19 April 1843 Polly Tingley, daughter of Elias Tingley. Residence: Wrentham, Mass.
iii. John, b. 6 June 1823; d. in September 1859.
iv. Nancy, b. 1 March 1825; d. 14 June 1902; m. 6 May 1849 Simeon Allen.
v.   Susan, b. 30 Dec. 1828; d. 1 Feb. 1832.

vi.   Temperance, b. 22 Dec. 1830; d. 22 Nov. 1900; m. Albert
       Manchester.
vii.   Seabury Soule, Jr., b. 13 Feb.1832; d. 10 April 1894; m.
       29 Dec. 1850 Julia Frances Perrin, b. 9 June 1830.
viii. Josephine M., b. 14 March 1834; d. 13 Aug. 1905; m. Abner
       Soule Tompkins.
ix.   Cordelia, b. 7 July 1837; d. 30 Aug. 1858; m. William
       McGrath in October 1857.
x.   Clarissa Richmond, b. 9 Jan. 1840; d. 25 July 1918; m.
       26 Nov. 1863 Robert M. McQuiston, b. 31 Oct. 1837,
       d. 25 May 1904.

26. ROBERT TAYLOR[6] TOMPKINS (Uriah[5], Michah[4], Samuel[3],
Nathaniel[2], Nathaniel[1]), born in LC 30 May 1812, died there 6 Feb.
1867. Residence: LC.
He married EMILY BROWNELL, daughter of James and Lydia
(Church) Brownell of LC, born there 14 Dec. 1820. They are buried
in the Union cemetery.

       Children, recorded in LC:
i.   James Brownell, b. 22 June 1841; d. 26 April 1875.
ii.   Joseph R., b. in LC 9 Aug. 1846; d. in Providence 21 Feb.
       1908.
iii.   Horatio A., b. 18 April 1850; d. 11 Aug. 1871.
iv.   Mary Elizabeth, b. 27 Aug. 1852; m. 28 June 1877 Jeremiah
       D. Blossom, son of Barney and Nancy Blossom, b. in
       Somerset, Mass., in 1857. Residence: New Bedford.

27. HENRY M.[7] TOMPKINS (Nathaniel[6], Nathaniel[5], Joseph[4],
Samuel[3], Nathaniel[2], Nathaniel[1]), born in Paris, N.Y., 10 Sept. 1811.
He married ANNA BROWNELL GRAY, daughter of Loring and Ruth
(Richmond) Gray, born in LC 1 Sept. 1810.
He spent his early years in Paris, N.Y. He eventually returned
to LC, the birthplace of his father, where he was town clerk for many
years.

       Children, born in Paris, N.Y., according to Tompkins
       Genealogy:
i.   Helen A. She was a school teacher in LC.
ii.   Clara, b. 8 Nov. 1842; d. in LC 21 July 1852.
iii.   Dr. Albert Henry (M.D.). He had a son, Ernest, who had
       two daughters.
iv.   Nathaniel Richmond.
v.   Clarence G., b. 13 Sept. 1858; d. 28 May 1924; m. Nina W.
       (--) of Palomar Park, Calif.

28. ABEL (ALBERT?)[7] TOMPKINS (Abel[6], Gamaliel[5], Joseph[4],
Samuel[3], Nathaniel[2], Nathaniel[1]), born in LC 12 June 1810, died 7
April 1862. Residence: Boston.
He married first 4 Sept. 1838 LUCY ANN EATON, born 20 Nov.
1816, died 3 Nov. 1839. He married second in LC 23 Sept. 1843
ELIZABETH TAYLOR CHURCH, daughter of Col. John and Prudence

(Simmons) Church of LC, born in LC 29 March 1820, died 26 April 1838.

Children by first wife:
30.   i.   William Abel Eaton, b. 9 Oct. 1839.

Children by second wife:
   ii.   Elizabeth Church, b. in Boston 2 June 1845; d. 8 Aug. 1912; m. Alexander Granville Bowditch, son of Alexander and Sarah Ann (Hobart) Bowditch, b. 1 Nov. 1839.

29. JOHN H.[6] TOMPKINS (Nathaniel[5], Gamaliel[4], Joseph[3], Samuel[2], Nathaniel[1]), born in LC 20 June 1829, died there 22 May 1897.

He married MARY J. LEARY of Tiverton, daughter of Timothy and Ruth Leary, died in LC 12 Aug. 1884 ae 48. They are buried in the Union cemetery.

Children, recorded in LC:
   i.   Emeline M., b. 22 Oct. 1854.
   ii.   Eudora M., b. in 1855; d. 21 March 1931.
   iii. Lester, b. in LC 18 Aug. 1860; m. in LC 4 Nov. 1874 Carrie Macomber, daughter of Thomas and Mary Macomber.
   iv.   Mabel, b. 28 Oct. 1862.
   v.   Betsey, b. 30 July 1873.
   vi.   Mary H., b. 6 May 1875.

30. WILLIAM ABEL EATON[8] TOMPKINS (Abel[7], Abel[6], Gamaliel[5], Joseph[4], Samuel[3], Nathaniel[2], Nathaniel[1]), born 9 Oct. 1839, died 22 Feb. 1893. He married 28 Nov. (April?) 1870 HETTIE MARIA MEARS, born 26 Nov. 1848, died 23 Feb. 1909.

Children, born in New York City:
31.   i.   John Stuart.

31. JOHN STUART[9] TOMPKINS (William[8], Abel[7], Abel[6], Gamaliel[5], Joseph[4], Samuel[3], Nathaniel[2], Nathaniel[1]), married 14 June 1899 MARY WILLARD CRANE. Residence: New York City and LC.

Children:
   i.   Henrietta Frances, b. 6 March 1903 in New York City; m. 24 Aug. 1928 James Rowlands (?) Todd, son of Thomas D. and Edith (Wells) Todd, b. in New York City 15 Jan. 1898.
   ii.   Stuart Willard, m. in 1929 Elizabeth Frazier, daughter of Charles Russell Frazier. Residence: Honolulu.
   iii. Allerton DeCormis, m. Honor Marjorie Paul, daughter of Stephen Paul.
   iv.   Elizabeth Church.

LINEAGE OF HENRIETTA (TOMPKINS) TODD

1. I am the Child of John Stuart Tompkins and Mary Willard Crane, m. June 14 1899.

2. The said John Stuart Tompkins is child of William Abel Eaton Tompkins, b. 9 Oct. 1839, d. 22 Feb. 1893, m. 28 April 1870 Henrietta Maria Mears, b. 26 Nov. 1848, d. 23 Feb. 1909.

3. The said William Abel Eaton Tompkins is the child of Abel Tompkins, b. 22 June 1810, d. 7 April 1862, and Lucy Ann Eaton, b. 20 November 1816, d. 3 Nov. 1839, m. 4 Sept. 1838.

4. The said Abel Tompkins is the child of Abel Tompkins, b. 5 March 1782, d. 22 Dec. 1822, and Mary Sweet, b. 25 March 1789, d. 7 Nov. 1852, m. 3 Sept. 1809.

5. The said Abel Tompkins is the child of Gamaliel Tompkins, b. in 1751, d. 18 Feb. 1822, m. Mary Church, b. 30 Dec. 1754, d. 4 Oct. 1844, m. 14 March 1776.

6. The said Gamaliel Tompkins is the child of Joseph Tompkins, b. 26 Oct. 1712, d. (?) and Martha Pearce, b. 4 Aug. 1717, d. (?).

7. The said Joseph Tompkins is the son of Sarah Coe, b. in 1690, d. 2 Jan. 1747 and Samuel Tompkins, b. in 1680, d. in May 1760.

8. The said Sarah Coe is the child of Sarah Pabodie, b. 7 Aug. 1660, d. 27 Aug. 1740, and John Coe, b. in 1658, d. 16 Dec. 1728.

9. The said Sarah Pabodie is the child of Elizabeth Alden, b. in 1623, d. 31 May 1717, and William Pabodie, b. in 1619, d. 13 Dec. 1707.

10. The said Elizabeth Alden is the child of Priscilla Mullen and John Alden, d. 12 Sept. 1687, (Mayflower).

11. The said Priscilla Mullen is the child of William Mullen, (Mayflower).

THE TRIPP FAMILY

1. JOHN[1] TRIPP, son of John and Isabel (Moses) Tripp of Northumberland County, England, born in 1610, died in Portsmouth, R.I., in 1678. He married MARY PAINE, daughter of Anthony Paine. Residence: Portsmouth.

2. JAMES[2] TRIPP, born in 1656, died in Dartmouth 30 May 1730. He married first in Portsmouth 19 Jan. 1682 MERCY LAWTON, daughter of George and Elizabeth Hazard Lawton, died in 1682. He married second LYDIA (--). He married third 12 Aug. 1702 ELIZABETH CUDWORTH. Residence: Dartmouth.

3. FRANCIS[3] TRIPP, born in Dartmouth 3 June 1705, died before 1 March 1779. He married first 22 April 1725 WAIT CHASE, daughter of Isaac and Elizabeth (Blither) Chase, born 24 April 1703 in Swansea. He married second in Dartmouth 30 June 1756 CONTENT GRIFFITH, daughter of Jeremiah and Mary Griffith. He married third 6 July 1758 DESIRE HOXIE. Residence: Dartmouth.

4. ISAAC[4] TRIPP, born in Dartmouth 29 July 1736, died after 1817. He married first (intention 21 Sept. 1757) in Dartmouth EDY RUSSELL. He married second in Westport (intention 15 Aug. 1804) RUTH JAMISON.

5. JOHN[5] TRIPP, born in Westport, died there 4 Aug. 1862. He married first 1 Nov. 1787 ELIZABETH TRIPP, daughter of Weston and Comfort (Potter) Tripp. He married second in Dartmouth 6 Nov. 1848 HANNAH (ROGERS) WHALON, daughter of Gideon and Sarah (Mosher) Rogers. Residence: Westport.

6. WESTON[6] TRIPP, born about 1792, died 12 Oct. 1848. He married in Westport 14 Jan. 1810 DEBORAH POTTER, daughter of Edward and Lydia Potter, died in Tiverton 13 March 1853. Residence: Westport.

7. URIAH[7] TRIPP (Weston[6], John[5], Isaac[4], Francis[3], James[2], John[1]), born in Tiverton 12 Feb. 1820, died in LC 11 Aug. 1846. Residence: LC.
He married in LC 20 June 1841 HANNAH BROWNELL, daughter of Thomas and Deborah (Taylor) Brownell, born in LC 25 Sept. 1818, died there 16 Jan. 1896. They are buried in the Old Commons cemetery.

Children:
i. Julia C., b. 12 April 1842; m. 26 Dec. 1861 Thomas M. Brown.
ii. Susan M., b. 31 Jan. 1844; d. in LC 7 June 1850.
iii. Helen M., b. 27 April 1845 in LC; d. in New Bedford 9 April 1881; m. 17 Aug. 1861 George H. Wood, son of John and Sarah Wood, b. in Woolwich, England. They had three children: Walter G., b. 5 Aug. 1870; Laura W., b. 19 Sept. 1872; Emma F., b. 17 Feb. 1879.

iv.   Uriah T., b. 20 Feb. 1847; m. in Fall River 4 June 1868
       Elizabeth A. Greenhalgh, daughter of Charles and
       Maria Greenhalgh, b. in Fall River 21 Jan. 1848, d.
       there 6 May 1922. They had three children: Ida B., b.
       24 Aug. 1869; Frank, b. 5 Jan. 1877; Albert, b. 21 Dec.
       1878, d. 30 April 1879.

8. JOHN³ TRIPP (James², John¹), born 3 Nov. 1685, died in Dartmouth. He married first in Dartmouth 13 Jan. 1712 REBECCA SPOONER,
died 9 March 1729. He married second 24 Oct. 1737 HANNAH DAVOL.
Residence: Dartmouth. He was descended from John and Isabel (Moses)
Tripp of Northumberland County, England.

9. GEORGE⁴ TRIPP (John³, James², John¹), born in Dartmouth
27 April 1714, married there 4 March 1735/6 ABIGAIL DAVIS. Residence: Dartmouth.

10. STEPHEN⁵ TRIPP (George⁴, John³, James², John¹), born in
Dartmouth 16 Jan. 1736, died before 1788. He married in Dartmouth
2 Feb. 1758 PATIENCE POTTER, daughter of Nathal and Serviah
(Cudworth) Potter, born in Dartmouth 8 Nov. 1740. Residence: Dartmouth.

11. GEORGE⁶ TRIPP (Stephen⁵, George⁴, John³, James², John¹),
born in Westport in 1760. He married SYLVIA DURFEE, daughter of
John and Phebe (Gray) Durfee, born in 1761, died in Dartmouth 3 Nov.
1851. Residence: Westport.

12. JOB⁷ TRIPP (George⁶, Stephen⁵, George⁴, John³, James²,
John¹), born in Westport in October 1794, died in LC 15 Dec. 1880.
Residence: Westport and LC.
       He married in Westport 5 Feb. 1812 PATIENCE (EARL) BROWNELL,
daughter of Christopher and Mary (Palmer) Earl of Westport, born in
Westport 13 Oct. 1787, died in LC 23 Aug. 1851. She married first 12
Sept. 1802 in Westport William Brownell, son of Prince and Mary Brownell.

       Children, born in Westport:
13. i.   William, b. 26 Feb. 1812.

13. WILLIAM⁸ TRIPP (Job⁷, George⁶, Stephen⁵, George⁴, John³,
James², John¹), born in Westport 26 Feb. 1812, died in LC 16 May
1891. Residence: LC.
       He married first ELIZA ANN SOULE, born in 1810, died 11 Oct.
1838. He married second REBECCA S. EARL, daughter of Jonathan
and Isabelle (Buffington) Earl, born in Swansea 29 Jan. 1819, died in
LC 11 July 1900. They are buried in Fall River in the Oak Grove cemetery.
       Residence: LC. He was the originator of the Rhode Island Red
hen.

       Children by first wife, born in LC:
       i.   Patience E., b. in 1833; m. 26 Aug. 1848 Thomas S. Crosby,

son of John and Elizabeth (Pearce) Crosby.

14. ii.   Benjamin E., b. in 1836.

          Children by second wife:
      iii.   Rebecca Williams, b. in LC 20 Sept. 1854; d. there 14
            Nov. 1931; unmarried.
      iv.   Patience, b. 20 Sept. 1854; d. in LC 21 Sept. 1854.

     14. BENJAMIN E.[9] TRIPP (William[8], Job[7], George[6], Stephen[5], George[4], John[3], James[2], John[1]), born in 1836. Residence: LC and Fall River.

He married first in Tiverton 9 Dec. 1859 MERCY S. BRAYTON, daughter of Preserved Brayton, born in February 1835, died in Fall River 15 Nov. 1871. He married second HELEN MOORE.

          Children:
      i.   Arthur R., b. 7 Dec. 1859.
      ii.   Edgar Benjamin, b. 18 March 1865; d. in Fall River 17
            April 1865.

. . . .

     COOK G. TRIPP, married ELLEN (--). (There is no Cook Tripp listed in the Tripp Genealogy.)

          Children, recorded in LC:
      i.   Anna King, b. in LC 10 June 1867.
      ii.   Benjamin F., b. in LC 22 Aug. 1869.

     ABIAL TRIPP of Tiverton, married in Westport 26 Dec. 1793 PHEBE R. SNELL.

          Children, recorded in LC:
      i.   Mary A., b. in 1803; d. 8 May 1886.
      ii.   Susan, d. 20 April 1882 ae 67-2-3.
      iii.   Ann, b. in 1817.

THE VERAY FAMILY

FRANCIS VERAY, son of Francis and Sarah Veray of the Azores, born in the Azores in February 1803, died in LC 23 Nov. 1868. He married in LC 4 Dec. 1833 LYDIA H. SIMMONS, daughter of Stephen and Priscilla (Head) Simmons, born in LC 31 Dec. 1804, died there 16 April 1885.

It is said that he was a minister. He lived in LC in the house on the south side of Simmons Hill, directly opposite the Simmons cemetery on the north side of the road.

          Children, born in LC:
      i.   Lydia Frances, b. in LC 21 Aug. 1836; m. 14 Nov. 1868
            Alexander J. Lewis, son of John and Elizabeth Lewis.

THE WARDEN FAMILY

DR. FRANK RYAN WARDEN, M.D., son of James M. and
Joanna C. (Carmer) Warden, born in Manontan, West Virginia, 6 Dec.
1861, died in LC 28 May 1947. Residence: LC (Adamsville).

He married first KATE COLEVILLE, born 27 Oct. 1872, died
in Fall River 21 May 1928. He married second MARION E. HUTTON,
daughter of William Adams and Mary Ida (Earle) Hutton, born 17 Jan.
1899. She married second 20 July 1949 Roy E. Durkee.

   Children:
 i. Donald Wallace, b. in LC 22 Jan. 1914.

THE WARREN FAMILY

1. RICHARD[1] WARREN of the Mayflower, died before 1628 in
Plymouth, Mass. He married ELIZABETH (--), born about 1563 in
England, died in Plymouth, Mass., 2 Oct. 1673. Residence: Plymouth.

See the New England Register volume 7, page 177. He came from
London in the Mayflower in 1620 and settled at Plymouth. Some say he
was born or lived in Greenwich, County Kent, England. His wife
Elizabeth and children came in the ship Ann in 1623. According to
Winthrop, he was "an useful instrument and bore a deep share in the
difficulties and troubles of the settlement." It was his grandson, Nathaniel
Warren, who came to LC before 1680 and settled on Warren's point,
which was named for him.

   Children, born in England:
  i. Mary, m. Robert Bartlett.
  ii. Ann, m. Thomas Little.
  iii. Sarah, m. John Cooke Jr.
  iv. Elizabeth, m. Richard Church.
  v. Abigail, m. Anthony Snow.
2. vi. Nathaniel, b. in 1624.
  vii. Joseph, b. before May 1627; d. in 1689; m. 1651/2 Priscilla
    Faunce.

2. NATHANIEL[2] WARREN (Richard[1]), born in 1624, died in
Plymouth in 1667. He married 19 Nov. 1645 SARAH WALKER, granddaughter of William Collier, died in Plymouth 24 Nov. 1700.

Residence: Plymouth. His home was on the Eel River and he had
land on Summer Street in Plymouth. He was a member of the militia
there in 1643, and a selectman in 1667.

His will was executed 29 June 1667, and was copied in The Mayflower Descendants, Vol. 2. ". . . Nathaniel Warren Sr. of Plymouth,
being weake in body and ill at ease but of disposing memory. . . Wife
Sarah executrix. To her 15 pounds in goods and chattels. . . Unto my

children (without naming same) each of them at marriage 3 pounds. To wife my best bed and bedstead with curtains and valances belonging to it, and with two pillowes, with two pair of pillowe beers and two pair of sheets, also best rugg. . . " Will proved 30 Oct. 1667.

Children, born in Plymouth:
i.   Richard, b. in 1646; d. 23 Jan. 1697; m. Sarah (--).
ii.   Jabez, b. in 1647; drowned at sea 17 April 1701.
iii.   Sarah, b. 29 Aug. 1649; m. John Blackwell of Sandwich.
iv.   Hope, b. 7 March 1651.
v.   Jane, b. 31 Dec. 1652; d. 27 Feb. 1683; m. 19 Sept. 1672 Benjamin Lombard.
vi.   Elizabeth, b. 16 Sept. 1654; m. William Green of Plymouth.
vii. Alice, b. 2 Aug. 1656; m. 23 Dec. 1674 Thomas Gibbs.
viii. Mercy, b. 20 Feb. 1657/8; m. 26 Feb. 1678 Lt. Jonathan Delano.
ix.   Mary, b. 9 March 1660.
3.   x.   Nathaniel, b. 19 March 1662.
xi.   John, b. 23 Oct. 1663; d. young.
xii. James, b. 7 Nov. 1665; d. 29 Jan. 1715; m. Sarah Doty.

3. NATHANIEL[3] WARREN (Nathaniel[2], Richard[1]), born in Plymouth 19 March 1662, died there 29 Oct. (?). He married PHEBE MURDOCK. She married second Thomas Gray of Plymouth. Residence: Plymouth, LC and Newport.

He bought land in LC which was named for him, and which has continued throughout the years since then to be called Warren's point. He later moved to Newport, as shown by the deeds of his sales of land in LC, and afterwards lived in Plymouth, where he made his will. He left no descendants.

THE WATTS FAMILY

LOTT WATTS, son of John and Mary Watts of Leeds, Yorkshire, England, born in Leeds in 1872. He married in LC 1 Feb. 1893 ANN WHALEY, daughter of William and Ann (Brooks?) Whaley of England, born in England in 1872, died in LC 23 Aug. 1909. Residence: Tiverton and LC.

Children:
i.   Jessie, d. in LC 11 Dec. 1897.
ii.   Ida May, b. in LC 10 Jan. 1901.
iii.   John William, b. in LC 30 June 1907.

There is record of a John Watts, son of Godfrey and Louise Watts, who died 4 Oct. 1899 ae 61-10-3.

THE WEST FAMILY

WILLIAM WEST, married ABIGAIL (--).

Children, recorded in LC:
i.   Thomas, b. 27 May 1723.
ii.   Dorothy, b. 31 July 1725.
iii. Joseph, b. 6 Sept. 1727.

WILLIAM E. WEST JR., son of William E. and Parmilla (Luther) West, born in Warren, R.I., 27 Aug. 1870, died in Cranston 7 Oct. 1916. Residence: LC.

He married first LOTTIE H. SOULE, daughter of Samuel P. and Ellen (Crosby) Soule, born in LC 24 June 1886. She married second William Richmond Mosher.

Children, born in LC:
i.   William Everett, b. in LC 21 Nov. 1902; m. in Westport 18 Oct. 1930 Sylvia Borden DeAzvedo, daughter of Manuel and Lydia Almira (Palmer) DeAzvedo. They had a son, William E. 4th, b. in LC 23 June 1943.
ii.   Samuel Soule, b. in LC 15 Feb. 1905; m. in Tiverton 5 March 1931 Melba Alice Simmons, daughter of William Taylor and Harriet W. (Manchester) Simmons, b. in LC 17 May 1908. They had a son, Samuel Jr., b. in Fall River 25 Nov. 1939.
iii. Earl Luther, b. in LC 30 Jan. 1912; m. there 16 Aug. 1940 Helen May Case, daughter of George H. and Emma (Davis) Case, b. in LC 24 March 1921.

THE WHALLEY FAMILY

WILLIAM WHALLEY, son of John and Jane (Waring) Whalley, born in England 8 July 1838, died in LC 19 Sept. 1912, buried in Pleasant View cemetery.

He married ANN RIDING, daughter of Richard and Ann (Spencer) Riding, born in Lancaster, England, 8 Feb. 1842, died in LC 30 Jan. 1922. Residence: LC.

Children, recorded in LC:
i.   Jane, b. 28 June 1868 in Barnafurnace, England; d. 13 Jan. 1938; m. in LC 8 Nov. 1884 Charles Ellery Briggs, son of Charles F. and Ann (Manchester) Briggs.
ii.   Alice, b. 4 May 1878; d. 9 June 1925; m. 18 Oct. 1906 in LC George Franklin Simmons, son of William T. and Lucy F. (Grinnell) Simmons, b. in 1882.

THE WHEELER FAMILY

STAFFORD ANDREW WHEELER, born in Brooklyn, N.Y. He married LYDIA MARIA MANCHESTER, daughter of Philip and Sarah C. (Tabor) Manchester, born 20 March 1848, died in LC 1 Oct. 1880. Residence: Adamsville, LC.

        Children, recorded in LC:
i.   Philip Manchester, b. 3 Nov. 1876; d. 5 Dec. 1945.
ii.   Agena Villette, b. 27 Feb. 1878; m. Dr. Roger H. Dennett. They had two children: Alice, b. in LC 10 June 1906, and William, b. in 1916, d. in 1916, buried in Pleasant View cemetery.

LT. STAFFORD MANCHESTER WHEELER (U.S.N.M.C.), was killed in action in Zenica, Yugoslavia, 13 April 1945. He was born in LC 11 July 1910.

☙❧

THE WHITE FAMILY

1. WILLIAM[1] WHITE, who came to this country on the Mayflower, born about 1592, died in 1621 in Plymouth, Mass. He married 11 Feb. 1612 in Leyden, Holland, SUSANNA FULLER, sister of Deacon Samuel of the Mayflower, died in October 1680. She married second in Plymouth in 1621 Edward Winslow Jr., of Droitwich, England. This was the first marriage in New England.
Residence: Plymouth. He came with his wife and one son, Resolved. His other son, Peregrine, was born on the Mayflower. He brought two servants, William Holbeck and Edward Tompson. He was the eleventh signer of the Mayflower compact and was one of the Leyden Contingent. He died during the first general sickness at Plymouth. He brought with him the family Bible to which we are indebted for many early family records.

        Children:
i.   Resolved, b. in Leyden, Holland, in 1614; m. 8 April 1640 Judith Vassall.
2. ii.   Peregrine, b. on the Mayflower in Cape Cod Harbour 20 Nov. 1620.

Ed. Note: Above taken from The Descendants of Peregrine White by Roscoe White, and also from an article on William White of the Mayflower by George Andrews Moriarty in the American Genealogist, number 17, page 193. This line to Christopher White's brother has been approved by The National Society of Mayflower Descendants. -- BFW.

2. PEREGRINE[2] WHITE (William[1]), born on the Mayflower 20 Nov. 1620, died 30 July 1704. He married SARAH BASSETT, daughter

of William Bassett, died 22 Jan. 1710/11.

Residence: Duxbury and Bridgewater, Mass., and Marshfield, Mass. He went to Green Harbor with the family of his step father, Governor Edward Winslow, after 1632. His will was made 14 July 1704 and proved 14 Aug. 1704.

William Bassett died in Bridgewater in 1667, leaving to his son-in-law, Peregrine White, his valuable collection of books, which formed a large library for that period.

Children:

      i.   Daniel, b. about 1649; d. 6 March 1724; m. 19 Aug. 1674 Hannah Hunt. Residence: Marshfield.

3.   ii.   Silvanus.

    iii.   Jonathan, b. 4 June 1658; m. (1) 2 Feb. 1682/3 Hester Nickerson, d. 8 Feb. 1702/3; m. (2) Elizabeth (--). Residence: Yarmouth.

    iv.   Peregrine, b. about 1661; bapt. in Brattle Street Church of Boston 16 Feb. 1723 ae 62; m. Mary (--). She m. (2) 19 Dec. 1728 Cornelius Judewine. Residence: Weymouth, Boston and Concord.

    v.   Sarah, b. in October 1663; m. in Scituate in January 1688/9 Thomas Young.

    vi.   Marcy, m. 3 Feb. 1697/8 William Sherman.

3. SILVANUS[3] WHITE (Peregrine[2], William[1]), married DEBORAH (--). Residence: Marshfield and Scituate, Mass. Administration of his estate was taken 30 June 1688 by his father.

Children:

4.   i.   William, b. about 1683.

4. WILLIAM[4] WHITE (Silvanus[3], Peregrine[2], William[1]), born about 1683. He married about 1707 ELIZABETH CADMAN, daughter of George and Hannah (Hathaway) Cadman of Dartmouth, descended from Francis Cooke of the Mayflower.

Residence: Dartmouth, Mass., where he was a blacksmith. In his will, made in Dartmouth 6 Jan. 1768 and proved there 3 Oct. 1780, he named his daughters, Sarah Brown, Hannah Tabor, Elizabeth Slocum, deceased, and Susannah White; his sons, William, Roger, George, Christopher, Thomas, Oliver and Abner; and ten grandchildren, children of his son George: Israel, Peleg, William, Sylvanus, Abner, Ruth, Sarah, Hannah, Mary and Unice.

Children:

      i.   Sarah, m. in LC 23 May 1726 John Brown, son of Tobias and Alice (Burrington) Brown.

    ii.   William, m. in LC 2 Oct. 1729 Abigail Thurston, daughter of Jonathan and Sarah Thurston.

    iii.   George C., m. in LC 18 Feb. 1730 Deborah Shaw, daughter of Israel (?) and (--) (Tallman?) Shaw.

    iv.   Roger, m. in LC 24 April 1736 Rebecca Grinnell, daughter of Richard and Patience (Emery) Grinnell.

    v.   Elizabeth, m. in LC 24 April 1737 Benjamin Slocum.

vi.   Abner, m. in LC 14 April 1746 Ruth Brownell of LC, daughter of Charles and Mary (Wilbor) Brownell.

vii.   Oliver, m. 21 Jan. 1747 Mary Harmon, d. 28 Nov. 1811.

viii. Thomas, m. 25 Aug. 1751 in Dartmouth Elizabeth Jenney of Dartmouth. Residence: Freetown.

ix.   Hannah, b. 22 Aug. 1732; m. 27 Dec. 1750 in Dartmouth William⁴ Taber (Philip³, Philip², Philip¹) and Margaret (Wood) Taber.

5.   x.   Christopher.

      xi.   Susanna.

5. **CHRISTOPHER⁵ WHITE** (William⁴, Silvanus³, Peregrine², William¹), born in Dartmouth, Mass. Residence: LC.

He was married in LC 4 March 1739 by Richard Billings, justice, to ELIZABETH THURSTON, daughter of Edward and Sarah (Carr) Thurston, born in LC 29 Sept. 1719. He married second SARAH (--).

Children by first wife, all recorded in LC:

i.   Sarah, b. 28 Sept. 1740; m. in LC 28 Feb. 1759 Isaac Hilliard, son of Oliver and Sarah (Wilbor) Hilliard.

ii.   Thurston, b. 28 Oct. 1741.

iii.   William, b. 26 May 1742.

iv.   Mary, b. 28 May 1744.

6.   v.   Noah, b. 26 March 1745.

7.   vi.   Peregrine, b. 19 Nov. 1748.

      vii.   Susanna, b. 11 Aug. 1751.

      viii. Elizabeth, b. 27 Feb. 1753; d. 22 Jan. 1844; m. George Brown.

      ix.   Lucy, b. 24 Jan. 1755.

      x.   Pardon, b. in 1755; d. in July 1789.

Children by second wife:

8.   xi.   Thomas, b. about 1757.

6. **NOAH⁶ WHITE** (Christopher⁵, William⁴, Silvanus³, Peregrine², William¹), born in LC 26 March 1745. Residence: LC and Newport.

He was married in LC 16 March 1777 by the Rev. Jonathan Ellis to RHODA SHAW, daughter of Benjamin and Elizabeth Shaw of LC, born there 1 Jan. 1756.

Children, recorded in LC:

i.   William, b. 15 July 1777; d. in Newport 22 Feb. 1855; m. (1) (?); m. (2) Sarah Lawton, daughter of Robert Lawton, b. in 1776, d. 15 March 1860 in Newport. Residence: Newport, where he was a blacksmith.

ii.   Elizabeth, b. 28 March 1779.

7. **PEREGRINE⁶ WHITE** (Christopher⁵, William⁴, Silvanus³, Peregrine², William¹), born in LC 19 Nov. 1748, died there in September 1832.

He was married first in LC 19 Feb. 1782 by the Rev. Jonathan Ellis to ABIGAIL (WHITE) SOULE, widow. She married first in Newport 6 July 1764 Gideon Soule. He probably married second 23 Dec. 1804

PATIENCE TABOR of Westport. Residence: LC.

      Children, recorded in LC:
   i.   Gideon Soule, b. 21 April 1783; m. in Tiverton 4 Jan. 1807
           Hannah Gray, daughter of William Gray of Tiverton.
  ii.   George, b. 1 Aug. 1785; m. in Tiverton 14 Feb. 1808 Hannah
           Woodman, daughter of Robert and Hannah (Howland)
           Woodman.

8. THOMAS[6] WHITE (Christopher[5], William[4], Silvanus[3],
Peregrine[2], William[1]), died in LC 7 Dec. 1844. Residence: LC.
    He married in LC 11 Oct. 1789 RUTH DURFEE, daughter of
David Jr. and Mary (Gifford) Durfee of Tiverton, born there 23 Oct.
1765.
    His will, recorded LC Probate, book 9, page 231, made 27
Oct. 1844 and proved 10 Feb. 1845: ". . . To grandson Gideon White,
my south lot or Thurston Farm at 25 years of age. (This Thurston
Farm is the one opposite the Frederick Sherman place on the map of
1890.) To my son Thomas my Irish lot or farm at age 25. To grandson Benjamin White my Ichabod Wood farm after the death of my son
David. To Sarah B. Grinnell 80 dollars. To Simeon Wonderly a home
in the family of my son David D. White. To son David the rest and
residue and he to be sole executor. . . " He also left two hundred
dollars to each of his granddaughters: Ruth D. White, Harriet A. White,
Mary C. White, Elizabeth White and Martha L. White.

      Children, recorded in LC:
     i.   Christopher, b. 13 Aug. 1796.
9.   ii.   David Durfee, b. 11 Oct. 1799.

9. DAVID DURFEE[7] WHITE (Thomas[6], Christopher[5], William[4],
Silvanus[3], Peregrine[2], William[1]), born in LC 11 Oct. 1799, died there
20 July 1849. Residence: LC.
    He married in LC 12 May 1825 PATIENCE BROWN, daughter of
Benjamin and Patience (Davol) Brown of Portsmouth, born there 9
Sept. 1804, died in LC 11 March 1895. Both are buried in the Union
cemetery.
    The census of 1850 names their family and also Simeon Wonderly,
who was living with them at the time. Their children were named as
his heirs at law in the record of 13 Aug. 1849.

      Children, recorded in LC:
10.   i.   Christopher, b. 22 March 1826.
    ii.   Ruth D., b. 15 May 1827; d. 5 July 1866; m. 9 March 1847
           in LC George W. Staples, d. 17 July 1875 ae 54-10-15.
   iii.   Harriet Atwell, b. 10 March 1829; m. (1) in LC 28 Oct. 1849
           George W. Pierce, son of Jonathan D. and Hannah P.
           (Head) Pierce, b. 12 Feb. 1826, d. at sea 26 Oct. 1851;
           m. (2) 2 Oct. 1853 Isaac M. Rogers, son of John and Ann
           Rogers.
   iv.   Mary Cooper, b. 8 Feb. 1831; m. (--) Dean.
    v.   Benjamin Brown, b. 29 Jan. 1833; d. in LC 14 May 1835.
   vi.   Elizabeth W., b. 13 Jan. 1835; d. in March 1903; m. Charles

A. Staples, b. in June 1832, d. in August 1892. They had
a son, Charles H. Staples.

11. vii. Thomas Ely, b. 5 Nov. 1836.
12. viii. Benjamin Brown, b. 22 Jan. 1838.
     ix. Martha Lovis, b. 8 Jan. 1840; d. 5 April 1852.
     x. Pardon Brown, b. 9 March 1842; d. 19 Oct. 1865. He was
          a soldier in the Civil War.
     xi. Susan F., b. 5 March 1843; m. Edward Lawton.
     xii. Charles Green, b. 19 May 1846; m. Lucy Pierce (?).

10. CHRISTOPHER THOMAS[8] WHITE (David[7], Thomas[6], Christopher[5], William[4], Silvanus[3], Peregrine[2], William[1]), born in LC 22 March 1826, died in Hudson, N.H., 25 Feb. 1904.

He married first 21 Jan. 1850 MARY G. BROWNELL of New Bedford, daughter of Pardon and Abigail (White) Brownell, born in 1832 in Westport, died 11 Oct. 1853. He married second 25 Dec. 1854 MARY H. CRANSTON, daughter of William S. and Elizabeth R. Cranston, born in Newport, died there 1 Nov. 1874. He married third in Hudson, N.H., 10 March 1877 ELIZABETH BROWN (STALL) GILMORE, daughter of Isaac and Charlotte Stall and widow of James W. Gilmore.

He was a soldier of the Civil War, enlisted 18 Sept. 1862 and discharged 29 July 1863 in Providence: He was a corporal in company D, 12th regiment, Rhode Island Volunteers.

Children:
i. Susan A., b. 19 Jan. 1851; m. Amos H. Armington.
ii. Child, b. 7 June 1753; m. (--) Prentice.

11. THOMAS ELY[8] WHITE (David[7], Thomas[6], Christopher[5], William[4], Silvanus[3], Peregrine[2], William[1]), born in LC 5 Nov. 1836, died 16 May 1898.

He married in LC 15 Sept. 1863 MARIA WILLIAMS SIMMONS, daughter of Orrin W. and Priscilla (Brownell) Simmons, born in LC 19 March 1842, died there 21 April 1898. Both are buried in the Union cemetery.

Residence: LC. They lived in district number 2 on the place owned in 1774 by Deacon Adam Simmons. This family was listed in the census of 1865.

Children, recorded in LC:
i. Harriet Maria, b. 30 Aug. 1864; m. in LC 17 July 1890
     Edward L. Hunt, son of Samuel and Lucy H. (Borden)
     Hunt.
ii. Mary Priscilla, b. 21 Dec. 1868; m. in LC 25 Nov. 1889
     Andrew Simeon Taylor, son of George Milford and
     Sarah Jane (Dean) Taylor, b. 18 July 1859, d. 21 Jan.
     1892.
iii. Grace Williams, b. 1 April 1882; d. 1 March 1900.
iv. Minnie S., b. 6 June 1870; d. 29 Dec. 1878.
13. v. Thomas Elbert, b. 4 June 1872.

12. BENJAMIN BROWN[8] WHITE (David[7], Thomas[6], Christopher[5],

William[4], Silvanus[3], Peregrine[2], William[1]), born in LC 22 Jan. 1838.
He married first PATIENCE ROGERS, born in 1838. He married second
(--).
　　　Residence: Portsmouth. He was a plumber in Fall River.

　　　　　Children by first wife:
　i.　　Joseph.
　ii.　 Frank Bennet, b. in LC 22 Oct. 1864.

　　　　　Children by second wife:
　iii.　Benjamin (twin).
　iv.　 Edmund (twin).
　v.　　Thomas.

　　　13. THOMAS ELBERT[9] WHITE (Thomas[8], David[7], Thomas[6],
Christopher[5], William[4], Silvanus[3], Peregrine[2], William[1]), born in
LC 4 June 1872, died in Fall River 26 April 1946.
　　　He married in LC 3 May 1898 MARY HICKS TOMPKINS, daughter
of John H. and Mary (Leary) Tompkins, born in LC 6 May 1875, died
there 22 April 1937. They are buried in Union cemetery.
　　　Residence: Adamsville, LC. They lived on the place in Adams-
ville formerly owned by her father, John H. Tompkins.

　　　　　Children, recorded in LC:
　i.　　Gertrude, b. 5 April 1900; m. in Fall River Fergus Ferguson.
　ii.　 Helen, b. 6 Feb. 1902; m. in LC 24 Feb. 1926 Albert Lee
　　　　　Percell, son of Robert L. and Anna (Walker) Percell, b.
　　　　　in Portsmouth 4 Nov. 1908.
　iii.　Richard Simmons, b. 7 Feb. 1907; m. (1) June Davenport.
　　　　　He had a son, Richard White.

　　　　　. . . . .

　　　DR. GEORGE F. S. WHITE, son of William and Cynthia (Cornell)
White of Dartmouth, born (according to the death record) 6 Aug. 1818 in
Dartmouth, died in LC 5 May 1881, buried in Beech Grove cemetery,
Central Village, Mass.
　　　He married in Fall River 24 April 1845 MARY C. COREY, daughter
of Isaac and Mercy (Brownell) Corey, born in Westport 31 Dec. 1821,
died in LC 7 Jan. 1903. Residence: Adamsville, LC and Westport. He
was a manufacturer of a well known diphtheria cure.

　　　　　Children:
　i.　　William, b. in Westport 27 Sept. 1846. Residence: New
　　　　　York City.
　ii.　 Julia B., b. 22 Jan. 1851; d. in LC 11 Nov. 1929; unmarried.
　iii.　George Frederick, b. in LC 29 June 1852; d. 17 Sept. 1943;
　　　　　unmarried.

　　　MARY E. WHITE, daughter of Edward and Elizabeth White, died
in LC 22 Feb. 1885 ae 24-6-17.

THE WHITNEY FAMILY

SOLOMON WHITNEY JR., son of Solomon and Sybil W. Whitney, born in 1832 in Whitingham, Vt. He married in LC 4 April 1852 SARAH (CHACE) MARBLE, daughter of Thomas and Ruth (Devol) Chace and widow of Adniram Marble, born in 1829. Residence: LC.

Children, recorded in LC:

i.   Daughter, b. 29 Jan. 1853.
ii.   Harriet E., b. 13 April 1855.
iii. Williard A., b. 5 Oct. 1857.
iv.   Geneveive, b. 25 June 1859.

BESSIE GRAY WITH THE SHEEP

THE WILBOR FAMILY

1. WILLIAM[1] WILBORE, cousin of Samuel Wilbore of Boston
and descendant of John, Joseph, Nicholas and maybe Thomas Wilbore,
born about 1630 in Braintree, Essex County, England, died in Portsmouth, R.I., in 1710. He married MARTHA (--).

He was called cousin several times in the will of Samuel Wilbore
Jr., the son of Samuel Wilbore of Boston, who was born in Braintree,
England, the son of Nicholas and Elizabeth Wilbore of Sible Heddingham, Essex County, England, and grandson of Nicholas and Ann Wilbore of Colchester, Essex County, England.

He first appeared in the legal records when his cousin Samuel of
Boston transferred to him a piece of land in Portsmouth, 10 July 1654.
He also owned land touching the land of Samuel Sr. and also of Samuel
Jr. in Portsmouth, on the west road there near the coal mines. He
lived on the farm which later became the Burrington Anthony farm, on
the road that leads to the ferry, bound on the south by Freeborne Street.

Besides owning land in Portsmouth, he bought much land in LC
and about 1690 four of his sons settled there--Samuel, William Jr.,
John and Joseph. He had two other sons, Daniel who settled in Swansea, and Benjamin who settled in Dartmouth.

Samuel owned what is now the Oliver H. Wilbor Place, Joseph
settled on what was later the Isaac W. Howland place on the road south
of the Commons, John settled on the place later owned by Walter Bullock on the Long Highway, and son William owned what was afterwards
the Ephraim Sisson place near the South Shore.

In the will of William Wilbore of Portsmouth, recorded there,
dated 1 March 1710 and proved 15 Aug. 1710, he gives as follows: ". . .
To son John Wilbore's two children, John and Mary Records, 30 pounds;
to son Daniel Wilbore all land in the first division, great neck in Swansea; to son Samuel 43 pounds which he owes me; to daughter Mary
Mowrey money that she owes me and then to her children; to son Joseph
Wilbore 100 pounds in money; to son John Wilbore 20 pounds in money;
to son Benjamin Wilbore the money which is due me from Daniel Wilcox; to daughter Martha Sherman 10 pounds and to daughter Joan 10
pounds; to four sons, John, William, Joseph and Samuel, all my lands
that I now have in the township of LC equally divided between them. . . "

Children, recorded in Tiverton although William lived in
Portsmouth:

	i.	Mary, b. in 1654; d. 17 April 1720; m. in 1671 Joseph Mowry, son of Roger and Mary Mowry.
2.	ii.	Joseph, b. in 1656.
3.	iii.	John, b. in 1658.
	iv.	Thomas, b. in 1659; m. Mary (--).
4.	v.	William, b. in December 1660.
	vi.	Martha, b. in 1662; m. 12 May 1681 William Sherman, son of Peleg and Elizabeth (Lawton) Sherman.
5.	vii.	Samuel, b. in 1664.
6.	viii.	Daniel, b. in 1666.
	ix.	Joanna, b. in 1668; d. in 1759; m. in 1688 Nathaniel Potter, son of Nathaniel (Stokes) Potter.

   x.   Benjamin, b. in 1670; d. in 1729; m. (1) 22 June 1700 Mary
        Kinnicut, daughter of Roger and Joanna Kinnicut; m. (2)
        2 Nov. 1710 Elizabeth Head, daughter of Henry and
        Elizabeth Head.

   2. JOSEPH² WILBORE (William¹), born in Portsmouth in 1656,
died in LC 4 May 1729. He married in LC 4 May 1683 ANN BROWNELL,
daughter of Thomas and Ann (Bourne) Brownell, born in Portsmouth
in 1654, died in LC 2 April 1747.

   They lived on the road south of the Commons on the place owned in
1890 by Otis Wilbor's widow in 1870, and in 1920 by Mrs. Isaac Howland.
He and his wife were buried in the Old Wilbore cemetery south of the
house. The original house was over the wall east of the present house.

   In his will, made in LC 11 Jan. 1728 and proved 5 June 1729, he
bequeathed to his wife Anna all household stuff, money, debts, etc.,
and improvement of the biggest room in the house for life and 10 dollars
per year; to son William certain land and buildings; to son John 25 acres
of land; to son Thomas his homestead farm and dwelling house; to sons
Benjamin and Stephen 5 shillings each; to daughters Ann Wood, Mary
Eldridge and Abigail Wilbore 50 pounds each; to grandson Joseph Clossen
15 acres of land and 40 pounds; to son-in-law Thomas Burgess 5 shillings;
to nine children all the rest of his estate.

   The will of his widow was made 12 Dec. 1739 and proved 7 April
1747.

           Children, recorded in LC:
   i.   Martha, b. 20 Aug. 1684; m. (1) 16 June 1702 Timothy Clossen;
          m. (2) 24 Oct. 1707 Thomas Burgess, son of Thomas and
          Lydia Burgess.
   ii.   Ann, b. 8 May 1686; m. 4 Dec. 1717 George Wood, son of
          William and Martha (Earl) Wood.
7. iii.   William, b. 25 March 1688.
8. iv.   Joseph, b. 30 Dec. 1689.
   v.   John, b. 15 Dec. 1691; d. 13 Dec. 1783; unmarried.
9. vi.   Thomas, b. 14 Jan. 1693.
   vii.   Mary, b. 4 Jan. 1696; m. 19 Sept. 1716 William Eldred, son
          of Thomas Eldred.
10. viii. Benjamin, b. 20 June 1699.
11. ix.   Stephen, b. 20 March 1701.
   x.   Abigail, b. 27 Aug. 1703; m. 4 Sept. 1734 Joseph Rathbun Jr.

   3. JOHN² WILBORE (William¹), born in Portsmouth in 1658,
died in LC, married in 1682 HANNAH (--).

   He lived in LC on the place owned by John Soul in 1850 on the Long
Highway and later owned by Walter Bullock. They are probably buried
in the burying ground on the place.

           Children, not recorded in LC:
12. i.   John, b. in 1683; d. in 1747.
   ii.   Mary, b. in 1686; d. in 1771; m. 28 Feb. 1705 Jonathan
          Records, b. in 1684, d. 1 June 1742.

   4. WILLIAM² WILBORE (William¹), born in Portsmouth in December

-708-

1660, died in LC in 1738. He married first (--) Tallman, daughter of
Peter and Ann (Hill) Tallman. He married second JOAN BRIGGS. He
lived on what was in 1890 the Ephraim Sisson place near the South Shore.

In his will, recorded in Taunton, made in December 1732 and
proved 20 June 1738, he left to son Joseph all housing and lands in
LC, household goods, barns and rest of estate not mentioned; five shil-
lings each to his daughters Hannah Lippincott, Abigail Hilliard, Jane
Dennis, Sarah Tallman and Phebe Shaw; 10 shillings each to sons
William and Jeremiah, and to the heirs of son Samuel, deceased.

Children, recorded in LC:
i.   Mary, b. in 1685; m. 3 May 1706 Samuel Crandall, son of
    Samuel and Sarah (Celley) Crandall.
13. ii.   William, b. 8 Aug. 1687.
iii.   Hannah, b. 17 June 1689; m. 1 May 1710 William Lippincott,
    son of Remembrance and Margaret (Barber) Lippincott.
iv.   Samuel, b. 17 Feb. 1691; m. (1) Penelope Parker, daughter
    of Peter Parker; m. (2) Hannah Parker, daughter of
    Peter Parker.
v.   John, b. 1 May 1693.
14. vi.   Joseph, b. 26 May 1695.
vii.   Abigail, b. 1 April 1697; m. 13 May 1716 Jonathan Hilliard,
    son of William and Deborah Hilliard.
viii.   Joan, b. 7 Nov. 1698; m. (--) Dennis.
ix.   Jedediah, b. 5 Nov. 1700.
x.   Sarah, b. 10 Sept. 1702; m. 10 Dec. 1728 Darius Tallman.
xi.   Phebe, b. 1 Oct. 1704; m. 1 April 1725 Jeremiah Shaw, son
    of Israel Shaw.
15. xii.   Jeremiah, b. 17 Dec. 1706.

5. SAMUEL[2] WILBORE (William[1]), born in Portsmouth in 1664,
died in LC in 1740. Residence: LC.

He married in 1689 MARY POTTER, daughter of Nathaniel and
Elizabeth (Stokes) Potter. They are buried in the cemetery laid out
by him in his will. They lived on the place owned by Oliver H. Wilbor
in 1890. The original house was built about 1690, that is the east
half with ell. The west half was built later, probably about the time
of the Revolution.

His will, recorded in Taunton, made in 14 Jan. 1729/30 and
proved 17 June 1740: ". . . I give to son Samuel his now dwelling
house and all my lands that lie to the eastward of the Cole Brook line
and 100 pounds. To son William Wilbore my now dwelling house and
the rest of my land where it now standeth, that is to say the west half
of all my homestead farm (later the Oliver H. Wilbor place). To son
Isaac Wilbor one half of my homestead farm, the east end thereof
(this is the land off the Swamp Road opposite the Woodworth place,
owned by Robert G. Wilbor in 1870). To daughters Martha Pearce,
Johanna Taylor, Mary Brownell, Thankful Irish and Elizabeth Peckham, 40 pounds each. And my will is that whereas I have a burying
place on the south side of the land that I have given my son William,
my will is there be a piece of land four rods square allowed for a
burying place and also a driftway to use and no other forever, never

to be sold and put away, so that my family may have liberty to bury
in it. (This is the old cemetery on the Oliver Wilbor place.). . . "

Children, recorded in LC:
i.   Martha, b. 22 Oct. 1690; d. 22 Sept. 1760; m. 5 March 1712
      James Pearce, son of George and Alice (Hart) Pearce.
16. ii.   Samuel, b. 7 Nov. 1692.
17. iii. William, b. 6 Jan. 1695.
iv.   Mary, b. 29 Oct. 1697; m. 6 July 1717 Charles Brownell,
      son of Thomas and Mary (Pearce) Brownell.
v.   Joanna, b. 8 June 1700; m. 29 Dec. 1719 John Taylor, son
      of John and Abigail Taylor.
vi.   Thankful, b. 8 June 1700; m. 10 May 1720 John Irish, son
      of John and Elizabeth Irish.
vii. Elizabeth, b. 23 Dec. 1702; m. 5 Nov. 1723 Joseph Peckham,
      son of John and Mary Peckham.
viii. Thomas, b. 29 Dec. 1704.
ix.   Abial, b. 27 May 1707; m. 5 April 1742 Thomas Palmer, son
      of William and Mary (Richmond) Palmer.
x.   Hannah, b. 9 Feb. 1709; m. 6 Jan. 1731 John Dennis, son of
      Robert and Susanna (Briggs) Dennis.
18. xi.   Isaac, b. 24 Aug. 1712.

6. DANIEL[2] WILBORE (William[1]), born in 1666, died in Swansea
28 Nov. 1741. He married in 1692 ANN BARNEY, died in 1741. He
was the first Wilbore settler in Swansea.

Children:
19. i.   William, b. 2 March 1694.
ii.   Peleg, b. 30 Aug. 1695; m. 13 March 1721 Anna Anthony,
      daughter of William and Mary (Coggeshalle) Anthony.
iii. Daniel, b. 31 March 1697; d. 8 June 1759; m. 24 July 1743
      Ann Mason, daughter of Joseph and Elizabeth (Barney)
      Mason.
iv.   Ann, b. 20 Oct. 1698; m. 20 June 1723 Job Carpenter, son
      of Benjamin and Renewed Carpenter.
v.   Martha, b. 25 Sept. 1700; m. 6 March 1730 Peleg Chase,
      son of William and Sarah (Gardner) Chase.
vi.   Lydia, b. 30 Nov. 1702; m. 3 Jan. 1722 Richard Sherman,
      son of Peleg and Alice (Fish) Sherman.
vii. Elizabeth, b. 14 June 1705; m. 1 Feb. 1727 Robert Luther,
      son of Hezekiah and Martha (Gardner) Luther.
viii. John, b. 19 July 1706; d. young.
ix.   Thomas, b. 22 Oct. 1708; m. 28 Oct. 1733 Mary Bowen,
      daughter of James and Elizabeth (Gansey) Bowen.
x.   Samuel.

7. WILLIAM[3] WILBORE (Joseph[2], William[1]), born in LC 25 March
1688, died there 7 April 1775. Residence: LC.
He married in 1712 JANE CRANDELL, daughter of Samuel and
Sarah (Celley) Crandell, born in LC 23 Aug. 1692, died there 20 Jan.
1782. Both are buried on his father's homestead farm in the old
cemetery.

His will, recorded in LC, dated 27 March 1775 and proved 18 April 1775: ". . . in the 15th year of the reign of King George 3d. . . To true and faithful wife Jane Wilbore the interest on 750 dollars. To son William all my wearing apparel, all farm and carpenter tools and livestock, and use of all my real estate, and then to his eldest son. To daughter Sarah Hilliard 62.50. To William, son of Anna Cole, deceased, and her husband John Cole, 25 dollars. To Mary Jane and Anna, daughters of Anna Cole, deceased, 12.50 each. To daughter Mary Palmer 62.50. To Joseph, son of my daughter Martha, deceased, and Joseph her husband, 18.75. To William, son of daughter Martha, 25 dollars. To Martha, daughter of my daughter Martha, deceased, 18.75. To children of my daughter Phebe Brown, deceased, and Samuel Brown her husband, 62.50. To William, son of daughter Elizabeth Brown and Walter, her husband, 25 dollars. To other children of Elizabeth Brown, deceased, 32.50 to be equally divided. To William, son of daughter Edy Brownell, deceased, and Stephen her husband. . . To George, Stephen, Abigail, Phebe, Edy and Mary, children of daughter Edy Brownell, 37.50. To daughter Abigail Brown. . . "

Children, recorded in LC:

i. Sarah, b. 28 Feb. 1712; m. 18 Nov. 1731 Oliver Hilliard, son of David and Joanna (Andros) Hilliard.
ii. Anna, b. 11 Sept. 1715; m. 22 May 1734 John Cole.
iii. Martha, b. 8 Jan. 1718; m. 1 March 1743 Joseph Cole.
20. iv. William, b. 2 July 1721.
v. Mary, b. 29 June 1723; m. 12 May 1748 Thomas Palmer.
vi. Edith, b. 11 July 1725; d. 28 April 1726.
vii. Edith 2d, b. 22 April 1727; d. in March 1766; m. 5 Jan. 1747 Stephen Brownell.
viii. Phebe, b. 23 Feb. 1728; m. 12 May 1748 Samuel Brown.
ix. Elizabeth, b. 17 March 1730; m. 3 Jan. 1754 Walter Browne.
x. Abigail, b. 7 Sept. 1734; d. 31 Oct. 1822; m. 10 March 1756 Abraham Brown, son of Abraham and Saray (Cory) Brown.

8. JOSEPH[3] WILBORE (Joseph[1], William[2]), born in LC 30 Dec. 1689, died there 1 May 1754. Residence: LC.

He married in 1721 EMLIN CHAMPLIN, daughter of Jeffrey and Susanna (Eldred) Champlin, born 30 Jan. 1701, died in LC in 1736. They are buried in the cemetery on the homestead of his father, Joseph Wilbore, on road south of Commons.

Children, recorded in LC:

21. i. Walter, b. 24 Oct. 1722.
ii. Susannah, b. 24 May 1724; d. in March 1773; unmarried.
iii. Martha, b. 26 March 1727; d. in June 1757; m. 4 Jan. 1753 Jonathan Davenport.
iv. Emlin, b. 31 Jan. 1728; d. 10 Jan. 1823; m. 5 Dec. 1748 Nathaniel Stoddard, son of Thomas and Ruth (Nichols) Stoddard.
v. Hannah, b. 18 July 1731; d. 10 Jan. 1822; m. 28 Sept. 1748 William Wilbor, son of William and Esther (Burgess) Wilbor.

9. THOMAS³ WILBOR (Joseph², William¹), born in LC 14 Jan.
1693, died there in September 1783.

He married first 5 Oct. 1721 SUSANNAH IRISH, daughter of
Jonathan and Mary (Taylor) Irish, born in 1703, died in LC 18 April
1729. He married second in LC 18 Dec. 1737 SUSANNAH CARR,
daughter of Ezek Carr, born in LC 20 Sept. 1700, died there in November
1790.

In his will, recorded in LC, dated 9 July 1770 and proved 7 Oct.
1783, he left to his sons George and Jonathan land in LC, east of the
highway, bounded south by Henry Wood, west by John Irish. ". . . To
son Joseph Wilbor, land west of above. To son Thomas the house and
land I now live in lying both sides of the highway. To son Job one silver
spoon and 50 dollars. To my kinswoman Susannah Clossen a bed with
furniture belonging. To wife Susannah 8 onces of silver, one half household goods. . . "

Her will, made 23 June 1785 and proved 7 Dec. 1790: ". . . To son
Thomas one silver dollar. To grandsons Job and George Wilbor. . . To
granddaughter Hannah Wilbor my bed and bedstead. To granddaughter
Elizabeth Wilbor my looking glass. To granddaughter Susannah Wilbor
my black silk gloves. To cousin Susanna Clossen my wearing apparel,
gold necklace of beads. . . "

Children by first wife, recorded in LC:
22. i.   George, b. 28 Sept. 1722.
    ii.   Jonathan, b. 12 Dec. 1724; d. 11 Dec. 1804; m. Sarah Fones.
23. iii.   Joseph, b. 19 Nov. 1728.

Children by second wife:
    iv.   Thomas, b. 20 Sept. 1738; d. in December 1791; m. 13 Nov.
           1768 Judith Head, daughter of William and Elizabeth
           (Manchester) Head.
24. v.   Job, b. 2 April 1740.

10. BENJAMIN³ WILBORE (Joseph², William¹), born in LC 20
June 1699. Residence: LC and Westerly, R.I.

He was married first in LC 9 Nov. 1724 by Thomas Church, justice,
to DEBORAH GIFFORD, daughter of Christopher and Deborah (Perry)
Gifford, born 2 Feb. 1709. He married second RUTH (PENDLETON)
SMITH, widow of Benonie Smith.

He made his will in Westerly, 19 March 1772. It was proved 20
April 1772. He bequeathed ". . . To son Christopher silver spoons
marked B.W. To wife Ruth money left to her by her first husband. . .
To son John Wilbor my farm in Westerly and one half part of land I
purchased of James Babcock. To son Joseph Wilbor one half part of
land I purchased of James Babcock. To son David Wilbor the land I
purchased of son Joseph Wilbor. . . To grandchildren Benjamin Coon,
Jeremiah, Joseph and John Coon, and granddaughters Sarah and Ann
Coon. . . To daughter Judith Hall. . . "

Children, born in LC:
    i.   Christopher, b. 23 Dec. 1762; d. in 1821; m. 7 Dec. 1746
           Sarah Vaughn.
    ii.   Lydia, b. 3 May 1729; m. Mathew Coon.

iii. Judith, b. 23 Nov. 1730; m. in May 1748 David Hall.
iv. John, b. 31 Jan. 1733; d. 24 Aug. 1811; m. 28 March 1761
      Elizabeth Larrabie.
v. Joseph, b. 23 Sept. 1736; m. 25 March 1758 Sarah Hall.
vi. Joseph, b. in September 1738; d. in 1826/7; m. 27 April
      1765 Hannah Pendleton, daughter of James Pendleton.

11. STEPHEN[3] WILBORE (Joseph[2], William[1]), born 22 March
1701 in LC, died in Scituate, R.I., 23 July 1760.
    He was married first in LC 3 Jan. 1725 by Thomas Church, justice,
to PRISCILLA IRISH, daughter of Jonathan and Mary (Taylor) Irish,
born in 1707, died in 1732. He married second 13 Nov. 1738 MARY
(BAKER) FONES, daughter of Benjamin Baker and widow of Samuel
Fones.
    He moved from LC to Westerly, R.I., and later to Scituate, R.I.,
where he died in 1760. A deed dated 3 April 1747, whereby he sold
land in LC, showed him to have been in Scituate at that time.
    In his will, dated at Scituate 14 July 1760: ". . . To wife Mary
the use of one half of household goods, excepting my plate during her
natural life. To son Job 5 shillings old tenor. To son Abner 5 shillings
and my old gun. To son Jonathan the sum of 20 pounds. To son Samuel
one half of all stock of creatures of all sorts. To daughter of Anne
Rathbone 10 pounds. To granddaughter Priscilla Rathbone, daughter of
the above said Anne Rathbone, one feather bed and furniture belonging
to same. Rest and remainder of estate to three sons, Samuel, Stephen
and John. . . "

        Children, only the first recorded in LC:
i. Anne, b. 7 July 1726; m. 25 Sept. 1745 Thomas Rathbone.
ii. Job, b. in 1728; d. 1 Feb. 1778; m. about 1752 Lurana Knight,
        daughter of Joseph and Mary Knight.
iii. Abner, b. in 1730; d. 3 March 1814; m. 8 Feb. 1753 Sarah
        Rathbone, daughter of Ebenezer and Sarah (Berry) Rathbone,
        b. 27 March 1728.
iv. Jonathan, b. in 1730; m. 7 Nov. 1765 Hannah Tompson,
        daughter of William and Ruth Tompson.
v. Samuel, b. 2 Nov. 1739; d. 27 Oct. 1735; m. (1) Mary Knight,
        daughter of Jonathan and Zilpha (Bucklin) Knight.
vi. Stephen, b. 25 Oct. 1741; d. in 1816; m. 14 Dec. 1769 Sarah
        Jenckes, daughter of Jeremiah Jenckes.
vii. John, b. 13 March 1746; d. 18 April 1836; m. 17 Jan. 1779
        Sarah Millard, daughter of Noah Millard, b. 2 Aug. 1752,
        d. 9 Jan. 1822.

    12. JOHN[3] WILBORE (John[2], William[1]), born in 1683, died in LC
in 1747. Residence: LC.
    He married first MARGARET[3] BROWNELL, daughter of Robert[2]
and Mary Brownell and granddaughter of Thomas[1]. He married second
in LC 22 June 1710 SARAH PALMER, daughter of John and Elizabeth
(Richmond) Palmer, born 29 Sept. 1689.
    His will, made in LC 25 June 1747 and proved 27 Nov. 1747: ". . .
To wife Sarah a feather bed and furniture. To son John 15 pounds; to

son Aaron all lands and housing in LC; to son Constant 200 pounds; to
son Isaac 200 pounds; to daughter Sarah Shaw 5 pounds; to daughters
Mary Southworth, Elizabeth Hammond and Sarah Shaw all my household goods. To Parnell Southworth. . . "

      Children by first wife, recorded in LC:

  i.   John, b. 14 April 1706; m. 2 July 1733 Mary Thurston.

      Children by second wife:

  ii.   Joanna.

  iii.   Mary, b. 13 April 1711; m. 25 Sept. 1728 Gideon Southworth,
         son of William and Martha (Kirtland) Southworth.

  iv.   Elizabeth, b. 1 June 1713; d. in 1808; m. 8 Oct. 1737 Israel
         Hammond, son of Benjamin Hammond.

  v.   Sarah, b. 22 June 1715; d. in 1785; m. 1 June 1740 Israel
         Shaw, son of William and Content (Irish) Shaw.

25. vi.   John, b. 11 May 1717.

  vii.   Gideon, b. 8 June 1719.

26. viii. Aaron, b. 24 May 1724.

  ix.   Constant, b. 16 Dec. 1728; d. 25 Sept. 1815 in Newport; m.
         30 Jan. 1753 Judith Greenhill.

  x.   Isaac, b. 26 May 1733.

13. WILLIAM³ WILBORE (William², William¹), born in LC 8 Oct.
1687, died there 7 April 1775. Residence: LC.

He married in LC 3 May 1711 ANNA RICHMOND, daughter of
Edward and Sarah Richmond, born in LC 2 Jan. 1692.

      Children, recorded in LC:

  i.   Hannah, b. 11 Feb. 1711; m. 13 May 1734 Jonathan Heath.

  ii.   Richmond, b. 16 Feb. 1714.

  iii.   Samuel, b. 3 March 1716.

  iv.   Uzziah or Isaiah, b. 25 Jan. 1718.

  v.   William, b. 17 Jan. 1724.

14. JOSEPH³ WILBORE (William², William¹), born in LC 26 May
1695, died in LC in January 1775. Residence: LC.

He married there 12 Aug. 1729 MARTHA RECORDS, daughter of
Jonathan and Mary Records, born in LC 23 April 1709.

His will, dated 14 Oct. 1772 and proved 7 Feb. 1775: ". . . To son
Joseph Wilbore all my real estate in LC. (This place near the South
Shore was owned in 1890 by Ephraim B. Sisson.) To son John 100 silver
dollars; to daughters Judith Briggs and Ruth Woodworth two silver dollars each; to daughters Phebe Wilbor and Mary Wilbore all household
goods. . . "

      Children, recorded in LC:

  i.   Owen, b. 21 May 1731; d. 3 Feb. 1751.

  ii.   Judith, b. 25 June 1733; m. 11 March 1756 Enoch Briggs,
         son of William and Deborah (Church) Briggs.

  iii.   Ruth, b. 19 Oct. 1735; m. Stephen Woodworth, son of Elihue
         Woodworth.

  iv.   Phebe, b. 11 Dec. 1737; d. in 1792.

27. v.   Joseph, b. 20 Feb. 1742.

vi.   John, b. 31 May 1748; d. in 1823; m. 18 March 1773 Mary
        Head, daughter of Benjamin and Judith (Waite) Head.
vii. Abigail.
viii. Mary, b. 7 May 1754.

15. JEREMIAH³ WILBOR (William², William¹), born in LC 17 Dec.
1706. Residence: LC and Groton, Conn.
He married in LC 20 June 1728 HANNAH RECORDS, daughter of
Jonathan and Mary (Wilbor) Records, born in LC 24 Nov. 1706.

        Children:
i.   Jedediah, b. 10 Feb. 1729; d. 31 Oct. 1815; m. (1) 12 Oct.
        1752 Deborah Pollard; m. (2) 3 Aug. 1769 Abigail Plummer.
ii.   Elam, b. 20 Oct. 1730.
iii. Adin, b. in June 1733; d. 9 May 1779.
iv.   Uriah, b. 30 Aug. 1735; d. 13 April 1818; m. Abigail Burrows.
v.   Hannah, b. in 1737; m. 13 Sept. 1761 John Burrows.
vi.   William, b. 28 March 1742; d. 24 Jan. 1822; m. 24 Dec. 1778
        Sarah Sawyer.

16. SAMUEL³ WILBORE (Samuel², William¹), born in LC 7 Nov.
1699, died there 28 April 1752. He married there 24 Dec. 1713
ELIZABETH CARR, daughter of Ezek and Susannah Carr.
He lived in LC on the west road on the place owned in 1870 by
Isaac G. Wilbour and later by his son Philip.
His will, dated 27 Feb. 1749/50 and proved 30 May 1752: ". . . To
wife Elizabeth use of all my lands, housing, orchard and meadows in
LC. To son Robert all my lands, housing·and orchard in the town of
Dartmouth, Mass., where he now dwells. To son Thomas 50 pounds;
to son Abishag 750 pounds; to daughters Susannah Tripp, Mary Davol
and Elizabeth Moseher 50 pounds apiece; to daughters Ruth and Joanna
each 60 pounds and a feather bed with furniture; one fourth of all my
land in LC to each of my four sons Ezek, Samuel, Ebenezer and David. . ."

        Children, recorded in LC:
i.   Robert, b. 4 Feb. 1715; d. in 1782; m. 12 July 1737 Freelove
        Duval.
ii.   Thomas, b. 14 Sept. 1716; d. in 1799; m. 24 Nov. 1737 Deborah
        Closson.
iii. Susannah, b. 10 June 1718; m. 28 Jan. 1741 Timothy Tripp.
iv.   Mary, b. 14 March 1719; m. 3 Oct. 1744 Silas Duval.
v.   Abishag, b. 22 Nov. 1721; d. in 1786; m. 20 Oct. 1751 Ruth
        Strange.
vi.   Elizabeth, b. 23 July 1723; m. 26 Nov. 1749 Caleb Mosther.
vii. Martha, b. 11 March 1725; m. 11 July 1766 Canaan Gifford,
        son of Enos and Phillis (Allen) Gifford.
viii. Ruth, b. 20 Oct. 1726.
ix.   Ezek, b. 22 Dec. 1728; d. in 1781; m. (1) 7 Feb. 1751 Rachel
        Gifford, daughter of Enos and Philip Gifford; m. (2) 7
        March 1765 Rebecca Taber.
x.   Samuel, b. 10 Oct. 1730; m. 15 Dec. 1751 Susannah Wilcox.
xi.   Joanna, b. 29 May 1732; m. 15 July 1751 Benjamin Church,
        son of Joseph and Lydia (Randall) Church, d. 6 Dec. 1831

ae 91 in Washington, N.Y.
xii.   Ebenezer, b. 3 Sept. 1735; m. 1 Sept. 1763 Ruhammah Kirby,
daughter of Ichabod and Rachel (Allen) Kirby.
xiii.   David, b. 31 July 1740; d. 13 Sept. 1793; m. (1) 10 April
1760 Mary Kirby.

17. DR. WILLIAM³ WILBORE (Samuel², William¹), born in LC
6 Jan. 1695, died there in September 1774.

He married there 20 June 1717 ESTHER BURGESS, daughter of
Thomas and Esther (Richmond) Burgess, born in LC in 1696, died
there in 1760.

A doctor of physic, he lived on the farm given to him by his
father Samuel (the Oliver H. Wilbor place).

His will, recorded in LC, made 21 May 1772 and proved in 1774:
". . . To son Thomas six pounds; to son Samuel all my land I bought
of Joseph and William Pabodie (the Philip H. Wilbour place); to son
William my homestead farm (the Oliver H. Wilbor place); to son
Daniel the farm he now lives on, which I bought of Thomas Church
Esq., bounded as follows: easterly on highway, southerly on Thomas
Burgess's land, westerly on the sea or sound and northerly on Pardon
Gray's land (later the Benjamin F. Wilbour place); to son Charles the
farm or tract of land I bought of Jeremiah Shaw, the one whereon my
said son Charles now lives (this is the John A. Seabury place in District
No. 10, the birth place of Gov. Isaac Wilbor); to daughters Mary Brownell
and Esther Gifford one silver dollar each; to my granddaughters Esther
Tucker and Lydia Tucker one hundred dollars each; to son William the
rest and residue . . . "

Children, recorded in LC:
28. i.   Thomas, b. 1 May 1718.
    ii.   Mary, b. 7 Sept. 1719; d. in March 1817; m. 24 Feb. 1741
          Richard Brownell.
   iii.   Esther, b. 8 May 1721.
    iv.   Lydia, b. 16 April 1723.
29. v.   Samuel, b. 10 Dec. 1725.
30. vi.   William, b. 24 July 1727.
31. vii. Daniel, b. 1 June 1729.
32. viii. Charles, b. 22 Aug. 1732.
    ix.   Esther 2d, b. 18 Nov. 1733; d. 17 March 1710; m. (1) 11
          May 1755 Ephraim Gifford; m. (2) James Chase Jr.
    x.   Lydia 2d, b. 2 Nov. 1735; m. 17 Nov. 1757 John Tucker,
          son of Joseph and Mary (Howland) Tucker.
    xi.   Deborah, b. 29 Aug. 1738; d. 21 Feb. 1791; m. 15 Oct.
          1761 Elijah Gifford, son of Enos and Phillis Gifford.
    xii. Clarke, b. 1 Nov. 1742.

18. ISAAC³ WILBORE (Samuel², William¹), born in LC 24 Aug.
1712, died there in September 1793. Residence: LC, in the east
part of the town near Pottersville.

He married in LC 10 March 1735 MARY BROWNELL, daughter
of John and Mary (Carr) Brownell, born in LC 11 Sept. 1719.

Children, recorded in LC:

33. i.   John, b. 2 Oct. 1738.
    ii.   Mary, b. 30 May 1740; m. 13 March 1760 Enos Gifford,
            son of Enos and Phillis (Allen) Gifford.
34. iii.   Samuel, b. 28 Sept. 1742; d. in October 1806; m. (1) 22 Nov.
            1761 Elizabeth Wood; m. (2) 17 July 1771 Phebe Gray.
    iv.   Deborah, b. 24 Feb. 1744; m. (1) 10 Oct. 1776 Lemuel
            Palmer; m. (2) 17 June 1784 Benedict Palmer, son of
            Thomas and Abial (Wilbor) Palmer.
    v.   Elizabeth, b. 27 July 1751; d. 30 July 1829; unmarried.
    vi.   Susannah, b. 29 May 1754; m. 24 Nov. 1803 Enos Gifford.
35. vii.   Brownell, b. 15 Dec. 1755; d. 20 Dec. 1830; m. 1 Sept. 1776
            Esther Wilbor, daughter of William and Hannah Wilbor.
    viii.   Hannah, b. 24 July 1759; m. (1) Elisha Wilbor; m. (2) 19
            Jan. 1791 Caleb Church, son of Joseph and Lydia (Randall)
            Church.

    19. WILLIAM³ WILBORE (Daniel², William¹), born in Swansea,
Mass., 2 March 1694. Residence: LC and Swansea.
    He married first COMFORT (--). He married second 14 Feb.
1732 REBECCA GRAY.

            Children by first wife:
    i.   Phebe, b. 21 Jan. 1724; m. in 1754 Joseph Wilbor, son of
            Thomas and Susannah (Irish) Wilbor.
    ii.   Elisha, b. 3 Aug. 1726; d. in 1813; m. 7 Jan. 1770 Lydia How-
            land.
    iii.   Elizabeth, b. 3 Aug. 1726; m. 10 May 1753 Isaac Palmer.
    iv.   Daniel, b. 15 Jan. 1728; d. 30 May 1807; m. 13 Dec. 1750
            Ruth Smith.

            Children by second wife:
    v.   Joshua, b. 30 Dec. 1733; m. 6 Nov. 1755 Phebe Howland.
    vi.   Caleb, b. 10 Nov. 1735; m. 23 Aug. 1769 Elizabeth Trafton.
    vii.   Content, b. 12 March 1739; m. 15 Dec. 1763 Benjamin Tripp.
    viii.   William, m. (intention 27 April 1771) Rebecca Read.

    20. WILLIAM⁴ WILBOR (William³, Joseph², William¹), born in LC
2 July 1721; died there 22 Dec. 1818. Residence: LC and Westerly, R.I.
    He married in LC 17 April 1745 MARY BABCOCK, died in Westerly
18 Aug. 1806 ae 79.

            Children, recorded in LC:
    i.   Mary, b. 14 March 1746.
36. ii.   William, b. 17 May 1747.
    iii.   Anna, b. 13 May 1748.
    iv.   Susannah, b. 22 Oct. 1749; m. 4 Feb. 1779 Thomas Ormsby,
            son of Daniel and Martha Ormsby.
    v.   Martha, b. 25 May 1751.
    vi.   George, b. 23 Sept. 1753; m. 5 Nov. 1778 Anna Freeborn,
            daughter of Henry and Sarah Freeborn.
    vii.   Martha, b. 28 March 1755; d. in 1852; m. Benjamin Cornell.
37. viii.   Samuel, b. 29 Sept. 1758.
38. ix.   Hezekiah, b. 22 Aug. 1763.

21. **WALTER[4] WILBOR** (Joseph[3], Joseph[2], William[1]), born in LC 24 Oct. 1722, died there 16 Jan. 1792. Residence: LC.

He married there 28 Dec. 1748 CATHERINE DAVENPORT, daughter of Eliphalet and Hannah Davenport, born in LC in 1728, died there in 1806.

He lived on the family place given to him by his father and they are buried in the cemetery there. This place is south of the Commons and was the property of the first Joseph, son of William.

His will, dated 2 Jan. 1792 and proved 21 Feb. 1792 in LC: ". . . To wife Catherine Willbur a decent and comfortable maintenance out of my estate and homestead. To sons Chaplin and Walter Willbur Jr. a part of my estate called Salisbury plain containing tan yard with buildings thereon standing, the land bounded partly on the highway westerly and north and east by Hezekiah Woodworth and south partly by Benjamin Stoddard. To daughter Lydia Willbur a comfortable living in my house while she remains single. To two sons Joseph and Simeon Willbur all remainder of real estate. . . " He also left one cow and 15 dollars to each of his daughters, Emblim Palmer, Hannah Willbur and Susannah Hilliard.

       Children, recorded in LC:

i.	Emlin, b. 17 Nov. 1749; d. 2 Oct. 1843; m. 28 Dec. 1769 Elkanah Palmer, son of Thomas and Abial Palmer.
ii.	Hannah, b. 16 Sept. 1752; d. 11 Feb. 1820; m. (1) 23 Dec. 1773 Job Wilbor, son of Thomas and Susannah (Carr) Wilbor.
iii.	Lydia, b. 26 May 1756; d. 9 Dec. 1847; unmarried.
39. iv.	Joseph, b. 26 June 1758.
40. v.	Champlin, b. 27 Sept. 1760.
vi.	Susannah, b. 5 Oct. 1762; d. 30 Jan. 1846; m. 2 June 1782 Jonathan Hilliard, son of David and Ann Marcy (Irish) Hilliard.
vii.	Simeon, b. in September 1764; d. 20 Oct. 1810; unmarried.
41. viii.	Walter, b. 22 Feb. 1766.

22. **GEORGE[4] WILBORE** (Thomas[3], Joseph[2], William[1]), born in LC 28 Sept. 1722, died in Scituate, R.I., in 1781. Residence: LC and Scituate.

He married ELIZABETH SWEET.

In his will, made in Scituate 28 Nov. 1781 he bequeathed as follows: ". . . To wife Elizabeth one third rents and profits of real estate, one bed and furniture with household goods suitable to keep house, one cow and also four large rooms with fuel brought to the door. To sons Simeon and Thomas certain land. To daughter Susannah, furniture and a cow. . . "

       Children:

i.	Susannah, b. 25 July 1747; m. Peter Pearce.
ii.	Thomas, b. 15 April 1759; d. 31 July 1827; m. 3 July 1773 Anna Wood, daughter of George and Sarah (Devol) Wood.
iii.	Simeon, b. 20 Aug. (?); m. 17 May 1776 Phebe Wood, daughter of George and Sarah (Devol) Wood.
iv.	Elizabeth, b. in July 175-; d. 13 Oct. 1830; m. Jonathan Saunders.
v.	Martha, m. (--) Wilcox.

23. JOSEPH[4] WILBOR (Thomas[3], Joseph[2], William[1]), born in LC 19 Nov. 1728, died in Johnston, R.I., 5 Feb. 1811. Residence: LC, Newport and Johnston.

He married about 1754 PHEBE WILBOR, daughter of William and Content Wilbor, born 21 Jan. 1724.

Children:
i. Daniel, m. (1) in 1786 Phebe Slack, daughter of Benjamin Slack; m. (2) 18 July 1804 Polly Horton.
ii. Thomas, m. Elizabeth Warner, daughter of Daniel and Jemima Warner.
iii. Elisha.
iv. Susannah.
v. Phebe, b. in 1761; d. 10 Aug. 1855; m. 26 Sept. 1787 the Rev. Michael Eddy, son of Michael Eddy.

24. JOB[4] WILBOR (Thomas[3], Joseph[2], William[1]), born in LC 2 April 1740, died there in March 1785. Residence: LC.

He married there 25 Dec. 1773 HANNAH WILBOR, daughter of Walter and Catherine (Davenport) Wilbor, born in LC 16 Sept. 1752, died there 11 Feb. 1820. She married second Reuben Wood.

Children, recorded in LC:
i. George, b. 22 Aug. 1774.
ii. Hannah, b. 29 April 1777.
iii. Job, b. 27 April 1783; d. young.

25. JOHN[4] WILBOR (John[3], John[2], William[1]), born in LC 11 May 1717. Residence: LC.

He married there 12 Dec. 1746 HANNAH HILLIARD, daughter of David and Joanna (Andros) Hilliard, born in LC 11 Oct. 1721.

Children:
i. Gideon, b. 25 June 1749; d. 14 Oct. 1773.
ii. Abigail, m. 30 March 1775 Joseph Soul, son of Joseph and Alice Soul.
iii. John.
iv. Deborah.

26. CAPT. AARON[4] WILBOR (John[3], John[2], William[1]), born in LC 24 May 1724, died there in 1802. Residence: LC.

He married first in LC 31 March 1748 MARY CHURCH, daughter of Thomas and Sarah (Horswell) Church of LC, born there 2 Jan. 1724, died there 17 May 1762. She is buried on the George Bixby place, on the farm formerly part of the Aaron Wilbor place. He married second in LC 4 July 1779 RUTH HUNT, daughter of William and Elizabeth Hunt, born in LC 3 Feb. 1735, died there 14 Dec. 1821.

He served as captain in the Revolutionary War and had five sons, all soldiers in the Revolution. He served at or near Boston for eight months, was in the Battle of Rhode Island, and many times guarded the shores of the town. He served in the town council of LC beginning in 1775. He lived on the Long Highway in the eastern part of the town, on the farm owned in 1870 by John Soule and later owned by Adolphus

Allen. His will, made 7 April 1802 and proved 3 Nov. 1802: ". . . To
wife Ruth the east part of my dwelling house. To son Benjamin two
dollars. To son Aaron three silver dollars, wearing apparel except
silver buttons and buckles. To son Francis all his lands in LC. To
son Thomas two silver dollars and case of drawers of black walnut.
To son John two silver dollars. To daughter Sarah Soule one silver
dollar. To daughter Ruth Palmer one cow. . . "

Children by first wife, recorded in LC:
i.   Sarah, b. 25 Dec. 1748; d. 22 March 1825; m. 10 Dec. 1772
        Weston Soul, son of Nathaniel and Hannah Soul.
ii.   Benjamin, b. 22 Oct. 1750; d. about 1852; m. 5 Dec. 1774
        Betsey Hammond.
iii.   Aaron, b. 22 July 1753; d. 21 July 1831; m. 26 March 1778
        Elizabeth Manchester, daughter of Thomas and Dorcas
        (Gifford) Manchester.
iv.   Francis, b. 4 Aug. 1755.
42. v. Thomas Church, b. 23 Sept. 1756.
vi.   Edith, b. 15 June 1760; d. 16 Dec. 1841; m. 23 Feb. 1783
        Daniel Cole, son of Ebenezer Cole.
43. vii. John, b. 4 May 1762.

Children by second wife:
viii.   Ruth, b. 17 Aug. 1780; m. 15 March 1801 Rescum Palmer,
        son of Rescum and Hope Palmer.

27. JOSEPH⁴ WILBOR (Joseph³, William², William¹), born in LC
20 Feb. 1742. Residence: LC.
      He married first about 1765 RACHEL BAILEY, daughter of Thomas
and Abigail (Lynd) Bailey. He married second in LC 8 Feb. 1782 RUTH
BROWNELL, daughter of Jonathan and Elizabeth (Richmond) Brownell,
born in LC 24 Nov. 1753, died there 14 Jan. 1793.
      He owned a farm which belonged to his grandfather, William Wilbor,
and which he deeded in 1793 to his son Owen. This became the William
N. Sisson place near the South Shore.

Children, recorded in LC:
i.   Martha, b. 28 Jan. 1766; m. 22 July 1788 in LC Hezekiah
        Wilbore, son of William and Mary (Babcock) Wilbor.
ii.   Owen, b. 25 April 1770; d. 13 Sept. 1821; m. in LC 30 Jan.
        1790 Sarah Pearce, daughter of James and Deborah
        (Hunt) Pearce.
44. iii. Bennett, b. 4 Oct. 1773.

Children by second wife:
iv.   Elizabeth Brownell, b. 2 Feb. 1783.
v.   Samuel Taylor, b. 4 July 1785.
vi.   Prudence Brownell, b. 21 March 1789.

28. DR. THOMAS⁴ WILBORE (William³, Samuel², William¹), born
1 May 1718 in LC, died in Hopkinton, R.I., 5 March 1787. Residence:
LC and Hopkinton.
      He was married 9 March 1790 in LC by Thomas Church, justice,
to EDITH WOODMAN, daughter of John and Elizabeth (Briggs) Wood-

man, born in LC 20 Dec. 1719. He married second 27 July 1761 MARY
HOXIE, daughter of Solomon and Mary (Davis) Hoxie, born 9 Sept. 1736;
died 4 July 1827. She married second Jabez Wing.

Children:
i. Enock, b. 6 March 1741, recorded in LC.
ii. Elizabeth, b. in 1743; d. 16 April 1799; m. 8 Dec. 1763
Barnabus Hoxie.
iii. Woodman, b. 13 Oct. 1743; d. 24 July 1825; m. (1) 6 April
1769 Dorcas Sheffield, daughter of Nathan and Dorcas
Sheffield; m. (2) 15 Sept. 1771 Elizabeth Sheffield, daughter
of Nathan and Dorcas Sheffield; m. (3) 8 Dec. 1803 Catherine
Kenyon, daughter of George and Martha Kenyon.
iv. Clark, d. in May 1801; m. 7 Feb. 1771 Sarah White.
v. Gideon, m. Hannah Babcock.

Children by second wife:
vi. Thomas, b. 7 April 1762; d. 8 Aug. 1796; m. 15 Jan. 1784
Sarah Sheffield, daughter of William and Lois Sheffield.
vii. William, b. 10 June 1765; d. 26 March 1821; m. 3 June 1790
Anna Bragg, daughter of Nicholas and Sarah Bragg.
viii. Solomon, b. 11 Feb. 1768; d. 17 May 1779.
ix. Esther, b. 17 Feb. 1769.
x. Isaac, b. 2 June 1771; d. 2 Nov. 1825; m. 15 Oct. 1794
Susannah Wilcox, daughter of Elijah and Elizabeth
(Knowles) Wilcox.
xi. Mary, b. 9 Nov. 1772; d. 21 Feb. 1858; m. 14 Oct. 1790
Abel Collins, son of Amos Collins .
xii. John, b. 17 July 1774; d. 1 May 1856; m. 17 Oct. 1793
Lydia Collins, daughter of Amos and Thankful Collins.

29. SAMUEL[4] WILBORE (William[3], Samuel[2], William[1]), born
in LC 10 Dec. 1725, died there in May 1791. Residence: LC.
He married there 15 Dec. 1748 ELIZABETH SHAW, daughter
of Anthony and Rebecca (Wood) Shaw, born in LC 10 Jan. 1728, died
there in January 1804.
His will, recorded LC Probate book 3, page 213, made 6 Sept.
1789 and proved 7 June 1791: ". . . To Elizabeth my wife all south
end of my dwelling house I now live in with privilege in the milk
room. . . To son Silvanus all that lot of land that I bought of David
Taylor with the buildings thereon. To son Clark the north part of
my homestead farm bounded north by William Wilbur, east on the
highway, south on the little meadow, west on wall and sea. To son
Anthony south part of homestead farm bounded east by the highway, south by Pardon Gray, west on the sea and north on the land I
gave my son Clark. To two sons Clark and Anthony all notes of hand,
they to be executors. . . "
The place he gave his son Anthony became known as Onegan and
was the south part of the farm owned by Isaac C. Wilbour in 1890. The
farm he gave his son Silvanus was owned in 1890 by George L. Burgess,
at the east of Taylor's Lane and east of the west road.

Children, recorded in LC:

45. i.   Sylvanus, b. 18 Aug. 1749.
46. ii.   Clarke, b. 30 May 1752.
47. iii.   Anthony, b. 24 July 1759.

30. WILLIAM⁴ WILBOR (William³, Samuel², William¹), born in
LC 24 July 1727, died there in September 1796. Residence: LC.
     He was married there 22 Sept. 1748 by Richard Billings, justice,
to HANNAH WILBOR, daughter of Joseph and Emlin (Champlin) Wilbor,
born in LC 18 July 1731, died there 10 Jan. 1822. Her mother was a
descendant of Ann (Marbury) Hutchinson.
     His will, recorded LC wills, book 3, page 338, dated 6 June 1786
and proved 4 Oct. 1796: ". . . To wife Hannah one third of household
goods, two cows and one horse. To son Joseph land that I purchased
of John Wood with buildings. To sons William and Jonathan my homestead farm with buildings. William to have the north side and Jonathan
to have the south side. To son Benjamin, as he will not ever be capa-
ble of looking out for himself, William and Jonathan to care for him.
To daughter Esther 100 silver dollars. To five others daughters,
Mary, Lois, Deborah, Emlin and Hannah, all household furniture not
given away except two large meat tubs, loom and tackling. . . To wife
Hannah the use of one half of my dwelling house as long as she remains my widow. To sons William and Jonathan the rest and residue.
To my five daughters if unmarried the use of certain real estate. . . "
     His homestead farm is the place in district No. 2, on the east
side of the main road, which belonged to Oliver H. Wilbor in 1900.
The place he gave to his son Joseph was probably the one which bordered
on Taylor's Lane and was four lots long from the road to the shore and
one lot wide.

          Children, recorded in LC:
     i.   Mary, b. 15 Feb. 1749.
     ii.   Lois, b. 28 June 1752; d. 17 Sept. 1844; unmarried.
     iii.   Esther, b. 10 Dec. 1754; d. 17 June 1829; m. in LC 1 Sept.
              1776 Brownell Wilbor, son of Isaac and Mary (Brownell)
              Wilbor.
48. iv.   Joseph, b. 25 May 1757.
49. v.   William, b. 1 Jan. 1760.
50. vi.   Jonathan, b. 4 March 1762.
     vii.   Deborah, b. 5 Nov. 1764; d. in 1813.
     viii.   Emlin, b. 18 Feb. 1767; d. 1 April 1825; unmarried.
     ix.   Benjamin, b. 20 July 1769.
     x.   Hannah, b. 28 Nov. 1770; d. 9 April 1825; unmarried.

31. DANIEL⁴ WILBUR (William³, Samuel², William¹), born in LC
1 June 1729, died there in April 1803.
     He was married there 22 March 1753 by Joseph Wood, justice,
to MARY SOUTHWORTH, daughter of Joseph and Mary (Blague) Southworth, born in LC 30 Dec. 1728, died there 18 April 1799.
     Residence: LC. They lived on what was formerly the Col.
Benjamin Church place west of main road and near Swamp Corner.
     His will, recorded book 4, LC Probate, page 113, made 21 Jan.
1800 and proved 2 May 1803: ". . . To son Joshua my homestead farm

with buildings. To son Daniel lands and buildings I bought of Elizur
Chase which layeth west on the highway, part of little meadow which
I bought of Ezra Chase lying south of ye barn. Land at east of road,
six rods wide and 40 rods long. To son Philip land I bought of Ezra
Chase in 1794 with buildings and privilege of spring water in corner
of meadow which I bought of Ezra Chase. To sons Daniel and Philip
land I bought of James Chase called the pound and also land I bought
of Isaac Wilbur. To daughters Lydia and Mary 500 silver dollars
apiece. To three sons equally my stock... and they to be executors. . . "

He was a member of the General Assembly of Rhode Island 1775-
76 and 1783-84, and for several years was a member of the town
council. His wife Mary was a descendant of John Alden, the Pilgrim.

He owned several farms, as shown by his will. The place that
he left to his son Philip was in the possession of his descendant Ezra
Wilbor who held it in 1870. The place left to son Joshua was held in
1870 by Benjamin F. Wilbour. The place left to Daniel was in possession of Daniel Wilbour in 1870.

        Children, recorded in LC:
    i.   Joshua, b. 23 Sept. 1754; d. 22 Aug. 1820.
    ii. Lydia, b. 15 Sept. 1758; d. in April 1803; unmarried.
51. iii. Daniel, b. 15 Feb. 1761.
    iv. Sarah, b. 19 Oct. 1763; d. in November 1799.
    v.   Mary, b. 4 May 1766; d. 24 Oct. 1845; unmarried.
52. vi. Philip, b. 5 Feb. 1771.

32. CHARLES⁴ WILBOR (William³, Samuel², William¹), born in
LC 22 Aug. 1732, died there 17 Feb. 1810. He married first 17 Nov.
1757 at the Friends Meeting House in Tiverton HANNAH BORDEN,
daughter of John and Hannah (Russell) Borden of Dartmouth, born 5
July 1735, died in LC in August 1779. He married second in LC 23
Nov. (or March) 1780 HANNAH SISSON, daughter of Jonathan and Mary
Sisson.

Residence: LC. They lived on the south of the Swamp Road on the
place that belonged to John A. Seabury in 1890, near the end of the road
that goes south of the Commons.

        Children, recorded in LC:
    i.   Ruth, b. 20 Aug. 1758; d. in September 1793; m. 21 Jan. 1779
          Reuben Wood, son of Peleg and Ruth (Shaw) Wood.
53. ii.   Borden, b. 12 Dec. 1759.
    iii. Hannah, b. 2 Dec. 1761; m. 21 June 1779 William Shaw, son
          of Israel and Sarah (Wilbor) Shaw.
54. iv.   Isaac, b. 25 April 1763.
    v.   Phebe, b. 28 Dec. 1764; d. 29 Nov. 1827; m. 29 Sept. 1785
          Isaac Peckham, son of John and Mary (Wood) Peckham.
    vi.   Charles, b. 22 Aug. 1766; d. 14 Jan. 1830; m. in August 1794
          Sarah Handy.
    vii. Lydia, b. 3 Oct. 1768; m. Aaron Simmons, son of Aaron
          Simmons.
    viii. Edith, b. 3 March 1771; d. 30 Sept. 1839; m. 11 Nov. 1790
          Elisha Woodworth, son of Hezekiah and Abigail (South-
          worth) Woodworth.

ix.   Rachel, b. 29 Nov. 1772; m. 12 Dec. 1793 Ephraim Gifford,
      son of Joseph and Judith (Gifford) Gifford.
x.   Elizabeth, b. 2 Aug. 1774.
xi.   Innocent, b. 22 Nov. 1777; d. 12 March 1856; m. 23 April 1800
      William Howland, son of Thomas and Elizabeth Howland.

      Children by second wife:
xii. Mary, b. 8 Sept. 1781; m. 31 Jan. 1798 Joseph Gifford, son
      of Timothy and Maria Gifford.

33. JOHN⁴ WILBORE (Isaac³, Samuel², William¹), born 2 Oct.
1738, died in 1812.
He married first 12 Nov. 1760 ELEANOR TRIPP, daughter of
George Tripp. He married second 20 Dec. 1787 MARGARET WEEDEN.

      Children by first wife:
i.   Rebecca, b. 21 Aug. 1761; m. in October 1780 Samuel
      Eldred, son of Thomas and Hannah (Congdon) Eldred,
      b. 8 May 1757, d. 17 Dec. 1836.
ii.   Isaac, b. 26 Sept. 1763; m. (--) Simmons, daughter of John
      Simmons.
iii. Abigail, b. 27 May 1766; d. 24 July 1852; m. 28 May 1801
      Zebedee Shaw, son of Mary Shaw, b. 25 July 1759, d. 23
      Dec. 1826.
55. iv. George, b. 10 Feb. 1768.
v.   John, b. 10 Jan. 1770; d. 11 Feb. 1826; m. Lucy Durfee,
      daughter of Wing and Hannah (Brownell) Durfee.

34. SAMUEL⁴ WILBOR (Isaac³, Samuel², William¹), born 28
Sept. 1742 in LC, died there in October 1806.
He was married there 22 Nov. 1765 by Nathaniel Searl, justice,
to ELIZABETH WOOD, daughter of Peleg and Ruth (Shaw) Wood, born
in LC 3 Oct. 1737, died there in May 1770. He was married second
17 July 1771 to PHEBE GRAY, died in LC in February 1821. They
lived in LC in the east part of town, near Pottersville.

      Children by first wife, recorded in LC:
i.   Elizabeth, b. 28 April 1770; d. in 1778.

      Children by second wife:
56. ii. Isaac, b. 12 Oct. 1775.
57. iii. William, b. 12 Oct. 1775.

35. BROWNELL⁴ WILBOR (Isaac³, Samuel², William¹), born in
LC 15 Dec. 1755, died there 20 Dec. 1783.
He was married there 1 Sept. 1776 by Aaron Wilbor, justice, to
ESTHER WILBOR, daughter of William and Hannah (Wilbor) Wilbor,
born in LC 10 Dec. 1754, died there 17 June 1829.
Residence: LC. They lived on what became the Oliver C. Wilbor
place in the east part of the town, which was owned in 1870 by John
Gray Wilbor.
His will, recorded LC wills, book 6, page 232, made 29 June
1829 and proved 14 Feb. 1831: ". . . To son Wright all real estate in
LC and Westport, he to maintain my sister Elizabeth. To daughter

Martha Palmer 125 dollars. To daughter Hannah Brownell 125 dollars.
To daughter Nancy Durfee and her children Brownell W. Durfee,
Addison Durfee and Hannah Durfee 125 dollars. To granddaughter
Deborah Brownell 25 dollars. To Esther Brightman's children 125
dollars. To daughter Phebe Woodman's children 125 dollars equally.
To daughter Lois Woodman's child named Esther B. Woodman 125
dollars. To daughters and daughters' children. . . all household goods.
To son Wright Wilbor my desk and one case of bottles, also the rest
and residue both real and personal and he to be sole executor. . . "

       Children, recorded in LC:
- i.   Nancy, b. 31 Aug. 1777; d. 4 Feb. 1803; m. 1 Dec. 1796
  William Durfee, son of Wing and Hannah (Brownell)
  Durfee.
- ii.   Martha, b. 11 June 1779; m. 6 Nov. 1803 Dudley Palmer,
  son of John Palmer.
- iii. Thankful, b. 21 Dec. 1781; d. 5 Jan. 1804; m. (intention 2
  Sept. 1804) Dennis Records, son of William and Judith
  (Brownell) Records.
- 58. iv. Wright, b.19 May 1783.
- v.   Esther, b. 4 Oct. 1786; d. in March 1829; m. 27 Nov. 1803
  John Brightman, son of Israel Brightman.
- vi.   Phebe, b. 6 Nov. 1788; d. 30 May 1829; m. 6 Dec. 1807
  Enoch Woodman, son of William and Priscilla (Brownell)
  Woodman.
- vii. Hannah, b. 15 Aug. 1793; m. William Brownell, son of
  William and Betsey (Grinnell) Brownell.
- viii. Isaac.
- ix.   Lois, b. 11 Dec. 1795; m. Ucal Woodman, son of William
  and Priscilla (Brownell) Woodman.
- x.   Mary, b. 17 Feb. 1799; d. 27 March 1820; m. 24 Aug. 1817
  Job Woodman, son of William and Priscilla (Brownell)
  Woodman.

    36. WILLIAM⁵ WILBOR (William⁴, William³, Joseph², William¹),
born in LC 17 May 1747; died there in March 1805. Residence: LC.
He was married there 29 Jan. 1778 by the Rev. Jonathan Ellis to
SARAH CARR, daughter of William and Abigail (Dring) Carr, born in
LC 23 July 1757, died there 29 March 1825. She married second 21
June 1807 George Simmons.

       Children, recorded in LC:
- i.   Abigail, b. 8 Jan. 1779; m. 9 March 1797 Isaac Gifford, son
  of Enos and Mary (Wilbor) Gifford.
- ii.   William, b. 24 March 1781.
- iii. Sally, b. 19 July 1784; d. 16 June 1835; m. 11 Dec. 1808 Owen
  Records, son of William and Judith (Brownell) Records.
- iv.   Jesse, b. 8 Aug. 1787.
- 59. v. Nathan, b. 15 March 1791.
- vi.   Hannah, b. 20 Nov. 1794; m. 12 Feb. 1817 John Dyer, son of
  John and Bethenia Dyer.

    37. SAMUEL⁵ WILBOR (William⁴, William³, Joseph², William¹),

born in LC 29 Sept. 1758, died there 23 March 1844.

He was married there 30 Oct. 1791 by the Rev. Mase Shepard to CHARLOTTE SEARLS, daughter of James and Mary Searls, born in 1771, died in LC 25 June 1799. He was a soldier and pensioner of the Revolutionary War.

His will, recorded LC Probate, book 9, page 161, made 8 Dec. 1842 and proved 10 June 1844: ". . . That slate gravestones decently lettered be set up at my grave and also at the grave of my first wife and daughter Betsey, and also graves of my father and mother. That the burial ground on my estate be kept as a burying ground and kept in good order. To Cynthia Gifford, wife of David Gifford and daughter of Isaac Wilbor, 40 dollars. To Ruth Palmer one cow. To Hezekiah Wilbor and Ruth Palmer all rest and residue. That in the division of the land east of the road that Hezekiah Wilbor have the south half and Ruth Palmer have the north half. That the land west of the highway be sold but if they prefer to pay legacies than to sell, they are to do so. Alexander Brownell to be sole executor. . . " In a codicil to the will dated 12 April 1843, he left to Ruth Palmer, his housekeeper, all personal estate.

Children, recorded in LC:
i. Elizabeth, b. 8 Dec. 1792; d. young.
ii. Betsey.

38. HEZEKIAH[5] WILBOR (William[4], William[3], Joseph[2], William[1]), born in LC 22 Aug. 1763, died there 14 April 1839.

He was married first in LC 22 July 1788 by the Rev. Mase Shepard to MARTHA WILBOR, daughter of Joseph and Rachel (Bailey) Wilbor, born in LC 28 Jan. 1766. He was married second 13 Dec. 1792 by William Davis, justice, to ALICE PALMER, daughter of John and Mary (Stoddard) Palmer. According to the records he was married in LC, but other information indicates he was married in Westport.

He was a soldier of the Revolutionary War. He lived on the east side of the Long Highway near the south end of district No. 9, on the place owned in 1850 by William Tripp and in 1900 by Samuel Jennings.

Children by second wife, recorded in LC:
60. i.   Benjamin, b. 14 March 1793.
61. ii. George, b. 19 Dec. 1794.
62. iii. David, b. 16 Sept. 1796.
    iv. Martha, b. 28 June 1798; d. 11 May 1882; unmarried.
    v.   Harriet, b. 30 May 1800; d. 27 Dec. 1882; unmarried.
    vi. James, b. 21 July 1804; d. 1 March 1851; m. 23 March 1834
         Mary L. Tompkins, daughter of Uriah and Mary (Taylor)
         Tompkins.
    vii. Tillinghast, b. 15 Aug. 1806; m. Joanna Woodward, daughter
         of Samuel and Nancy Woodward.
63. viii. Hezekiah, b. 3 Sept. 1808.

39. JOSEPH[5] WILBOR (Walter[4], Joseph[3], Joseph[2], William[1]), born in LC 26 June 1758, died there 9 Jan. 1838.

He was married 19 Dec. 1790 in LC by the Rev. Mase Shepard to HANNAH BROWN, daughter of Thomas and Priscilla (Head) Brown, born in LC 14 Sept. 1771, died there 16 Feb. 1830.

Residence: LC. They lived on the road south of the Commons on the place which was owned by the first Joseph Wilbor in town. That place was owned in 1870 by B. Wilbor and in 1890 by Catherine Wilbor. Both are buried in the Wilbor Commons cemetery which is located at that place.

His will, recorded in LC Probate book 8, page 125, made 12 March 1830 and proved 12 Feb. 1838: "...To daughter Rhody Woodman one high case of drawers, three banister backed chairs. To granddaughter Lydia Ladd 20 dollars at 18. To daughter Priscilla Peckham my great spinning wheel and one foot wheel and three banister backed chairs and one cow. To daughter Susannah Wilbor all her mother's wearing apparel, household goods and nine silver spoons. To sister Lydia Wilbor all legacy given her by her father Walter Wilbor's will. To son George 5 dollars. To son Otis one good feather bed. To sons Thomas and Otis the 25 acre lot lying west of the highway called the Burgess lot and all my dwelling house. To son Walter my great iron kettle and my hetchels on condition that he let my children use said hetchels, also my side saddle and pillion for my daughter Susannah the use of. To son Walter the rest and residue. Reserving forever the burying ground as a privilege for all the relatives to bury their dead. . . "

Children, recorded in LC:

	i.	Rhoda, b. 19 Nov. 1791; d. 31 Dec. 1798.
64.	ii.	Walter, b. 1 Sept. 1793.
65.	iii.	Thomas, b. 17 March 1795.
	iv.	George, b. 25 Feb. 1797; d. 27 Oct. 1835.
	v.	Rhoda 2d, b. 12 March 1799; d. 7 May 1843; m. (1) 16 March 1822 Jesse Ladd; m. (2) in LC 10 Feb. 1830 Humphrey Woodman, son of Edward and Priscilla (Negas) Woodman.
	vi.	Priscilla, b. 9 March 1801; d. 22 March 1874; m. in LC 13 Nov. 1824 Wilbor Peckham, son of Peleg and Lucy (Palmer) Peckham.
	vii.	Otis, b. 12 Jan. 1803; d. 15 Jan. 1859; m. in LC in November 1837 Mary Shaw, daughter of Zebedee and Abigail (Wilbor) Shaw, b. 19 July 1807, d. 2 Aug. 1882. He had no children. For many years he was town clerk of LC. He was very interested in family history and genealogy and we owe a great deal to him in his preservation of the town records. He also made a copy of the births, marriages and deaths in LC, connecting the families by putting down the birth and death dates of the parents when a child's birth date was given. One comes across examples of his interest in genealogy at many times. He lived at one time in the house which is now the Village Improvement Society headquarters.
	viii.	Susannah, b. 13 Nov. 1805; d. 23 Jan. 1881; m. John S. Palmer.
	ix.	Catharine, b. 5 Feb. 1807; d. 22 Sept. 1808.
	x.	Jonathan H., b. 10 June 1810; d. 16 July 1811.

40. CHAMPLIN[5] WILBOR (Walter[4], Joseph[3], Joseph[2], William[1]), born in LC 27 Sept. 1760. Residence: LC.

He was married there 24 Feb. 1785 by Aaron Wilbor, justice, to

RUTH RECORDS, daughter of Jonathan and Mary (Briggs) Records.

Children:
i.   Walter.
ii.   William.
iii. Rhoda, b. 19 June 1785.
iv.   Lois, b. 19 June 1785.
v.   Susannah, b. 14 March 1787; m. Jesse Sellick.
vi.   Simeon, b. 15 Feb. 1789.
vii. Mary.

Only Rhoda, Susannah and Simeon are recorded in LC. It would seem that this family moved away.

41. WALTER[5] WILBOR (Walter[4], Joseph[3], Joseph[2], William[1]), born in LC 22 Feb. 1766, died there 26 Nov. 1839. Residence: LC.

He was married there 3 Oct. 1790 by the Rev. Mase Shepard to PHEBE STODDARD, daughter of Benjamin and Phebe (Brownell) Stoddard, born in 1770, died in LC 15 Feb. 1804. He was married second in LC 31 March 1805 by the Rev. Benjamin Peckham to LYDIA COOK, daughter of Peleg Cook, born in 1763, died in 1815. They are buried in the Wilbor cemetery on the road south of the Commons.

Children, recorded in LC:
i.   Prudence, b. 21 Jan. 1792; m. 27 March 1825.
ii.   Phebe Stoddard, b. 13 March 1794; m. 18 April 1819 John
          Bussey.
iii. Ruth, b. 7 May 1794; d. 23 July 1796.
iv.   Ruth 2d, b. 12 Jan. 1798; m. 26 Sept. 1819 Joseph Underwood.
v.   Susannah, b. 21 Jan. 1800.
vi.   Lydia, b. 27 June 1802.
vii. Lucy Mary, b. 9 Oct. 1804.

Children by second wife:
viii. Sarah Cook, b. 13 March 1806.
ix.   Catharine, b. 7 Aug. 1813.

These children seem to have married out of town.

42. THOMAS CHURCH[5] WILBOR (Aaron[4], John[3], John[2], William[1]), born in LC 23 Sept. 1756, died there 13 Sept. 1840, as given in his Revolutionary pension record.

He married first in LC 29 Dec. 1791 ZILPHA HUNT, daughter of Adam and Ruth (Jameson) Hunt, born in LC 20 Dec. 1773. He married second in LC 17 Dec. 1797 RUTH HUNT, daughter of Adam and Ruth (Jameson) Hunt, born in LC 29 Dec. 1777, died there 22 March 1862.

His estate was administered by his son, Thomas Church Wilbor, 12 Oct. 1840. His wife applied for a pension for his services in the Revolution on 12 March 1849. He lived on the Long Highway on the place where his son Thomas Wilbor was living, according to the map of 1850, and owned in 1890 by Horace Bixby.

Children, recorded in LC:
i.   Susanna, b. 29 Sept. 1792; d. in LC 12 Oct. 1872; m. (1)
          24 Dec. 1812 Walter Brownell, son of William and Betsey
          (Grinnell) Brownell; m. (2) Samuel Broadbent.

  ii. James Hammond, b. 3 Jan. 1794; d. young.
  iii. Elizabeth, b. 7 Aug. 1795; d. 15 July 1820.
  iv. Zilpha, b. 6 Dec. 1796; d. young.
  v. Simeon, b. 14 April 1798; d. 4 Oct. 1877; m. 7 March 1820
     Electra Bly.
66. vi. William Hunt, b. 22 June 1799.
67. vii. James Hammond, b. 11 May 1800.
  viii. Sarah, b. 5 Dec. 1801.
  ix. John Bunyan, b. 26 Jan. 1803.
68. x. Thomas Church, b. 2 June 1804.
  xi. Angeline, b. 28 Oct. 1805; d. 25 March 1821.
  xii. Zilpha, b. 2 July 1807; m. Gilbert Millter.
69. xiii. Andrew T., b. 5 April 1809.
  xiv. Lydia, b. 14 June 1810; d. young.
  xv. Betsey, d. young.
  xvi. Dewitt Clinton, b. 14 Jan. 1812; d. 29 Nov. 1890; m. 30 June
     1863 Harriet Cowen, daughter of Stephen and Wealthy Cowen.
  xvii. Abigail, b. 8 Jan. 1814; m. 8 Nov. 1835 John Andrews.
  xviii. Lydia Ann, m. (1) 12 Oct. 1831 Edwin Luce; m. (2) Frederick
     Kempton; m. (3) Samuel Spooner.
  xix. Frederick Plummer, b. 8 Oct. 1818; d. 13 Jan. 1889; m. 5
     May 1845 Joanna Potter Mosher, daughter of Isaac and
     Rebecca (Briggs) Mosher.

  43. JOHN[5] WILBOR (Aaron[4], John[3], John[2], William[1]), born in LC
4 May 1762, died in Nantucket, Mass., 9 Jan. 1851.
  He married 6 March 1785 MERCY GRINNELL, daughter of Malachi
and Lydia (Coe) Grinnell, born in 1761, died 22 July 1854.
  Residence: LC and Nantucket. He was a soldier of the American
Revolution.

     Children, born in LC:
  i. Mary Church, b. 21 Jan. 1785; m. 2 July 1809 Samuel
     McNeal.
70. ii. Owen G., b. 19 Oct. 1787.
  iii. John, b. 1 Sept. 1788; d. in June 1834; m. 17 July 1817
     Maria Macy, daughter of Nathaniel Jr. and Elizabeth
     (Brock) Macy.
  iv. Lydia, b. in 1790; d. 22 June 1811.
  v. Diana Green, b. 14 March 1793; m. Charles Ray, son of
     John and Judith (Marshall) Ames.
  vi. Kezia, b. 7 Sept. 1795; m. 25 March 1819 George Allen,
     son of John and Amy (Swain) Allen.
  vii. Hannah, b. 23 Feb. 1798; m. 12 Jan. 1823 William Burdett,
     son of Edward and Parnell (Russell) Burdett.
  viii. Sanford, b. 4 Aug. 1800; d. 13 Sept. 1862; m. (1) 8 June
     1824 Mary Hussey, daughter of Cyrus and Nancy (Butler)
     Hussey; m. (2) 6 Sept. 1831 Mary G. Wilson, daughter of
     Elihue and Mary (Gardner) Wilson.
  ix. Elizabeth P., b. in 1804; m. 19 June 1825 William Swain, son
     of Peletiah and Lucinda (Russell) Swain.
  x. Sarah, b. in 1809.

44. BENNET[5] WILBOR (Joseph[4], Joseph[3], William[2], William[1]),
born in LC 4 Oct. 1773.
    He was married in LC 16 Aug. 1792 by the Rev. Mase Shepard
to MARY SHAW, daughter of Pierre and Lydia (Briggs) Shaw, born
in LC 2 Dec. 1770, died there 2 June 1852. Both are buried in the
Old Commons cemetery.

        Children, born in LC but not recorded:
- i.   Briggs, b. 4 Sept. 1793; d. 24 July 1831; m. Jedida Coffin,
  daughter of Simeon and Polly (Whipley) Coffin, b. in
  1797, d. in 1842. She married second William Tucker-
  man.
- ii.   David, bapt. 19 Sept. 1799.
- iii. Peleg, b. in 1797; d. 23 Dec. 1840; m. Maria DeLos Angeles
  Navarre.
- 71. iv. Thomas, b. 4 Sept. 1798.
- v.   Lydia, bapt. 5 April 1805; m. Waterman Irons.
- 72. vi. Bennet, b. 5 July 1805.

45. SILVANUS[5] WILBOR (Samuel[4], William[3], Samuel[2], William[1]),
born in LC 18 Aug. 1749, died 12 May 1812.
    He was married in LC 20 Jan. 1771 by Daniel Wilbor, justice, to
SYLVIA CHASE, daughter of James and Huldah (Winslow) Chase, born
in LC 20 Sept. 1751, died 8 May 1847.
    In May 1793 he sold his farm in LC (the Solomon place near Taylor's
Lane) to his brother Anthony and, with his wife and eleven children and
the families of Philip Irish and Isaac Wood, moved to Hyde Park, N.Y.,
settling on the farm that his grandchildren now own. These Rhode
Islanders embarked for their emigration from a point on the Seaconnet
River.

        Children, recorded in LC:
- i.   Hulda, b. 1 June 1771; m. 18 Oct. 1789 Philip Irish, son of
  Ichabod and Ruth (Cook) Irish.
- ii.   Elizabeth, b. 16 July 1772; d. 15 Sept. 1827; m. 10 Dec. 1805
  William Warner, son of Gilbert and Sarah (Ellis) Warner.
- iii. James, b. 5 Sept. 1774; d. 29 Aug. 1834; m. 23 Sept. 1799
  Abigail M. Manning, b. 17 March 1782; d. 23 Sept. 1836.
- iv.   Rhoda, b. 22 Sept. 1775.
- v.   Sarah, b. 16 March 1778; m. Daniel Baker.
- vi.   Abner, b. 16 July 1780; d. 15 April 1866; m. in 1805 Margaret
  Doty, daughter of Stephen and Mary (Carey) Doty.
- vii. Alse, b. 1 Nov. 1781.
- viii. Silvanus, b. 1 Aug. 1783; d. 6 July 1867; m. 14 Dec. 1808
  Caroline Schriner.
- ix.   Clark, b. 1 Aug. 1786; m. (1) (?); m. (2) Jane E. (--).
- x.   Cynthia, b. 29 Dec. 1788.
- xi.   Oliver, b. 1 Aug. 1791; d. 24 July 1864; m. 15 Jan. 1817
  Maria Hoffman, b. 18 March 1798; d. 26 Dec. 1887.
- xii. Samuel, not recorded in LC.

46. CLARKE[5] WILBOR (Samuel[4], William[3], Samuel[2], William[1]),
born in LC 30 May 1752, died there 25 April 1822.

He married there 24 Feb. 1774 JUDITH BRIGGS, daughter of
William and Abishag (Records) Briggs, born 19 Aug. 1754. Residence:
LC.

His will recorded LC, book 5, page 77, made 20 Feb. 1822 and
proved 6 May 1822: ". . . To daughter Priscilla 500 dollars, bed
spread and eight banister chairs. To granddaughter Abigail 300 dollars.
To granddaughter Elizabeth 300 (30?) dollars. To daughter-in-law
Deborah 500 dollars, also my horse, cow, loom and machinery and
all household goods if she remains a widow until my youngest son
Silvanus arrives at the age of 21 years, and if she be reduced to
proverty he to assist her until 1834. If my executors are removed
by death then my grandsons Clark and Peleg Wilbour, the sons of
Daniel, are appointed. To grandsons Cornelius and Job Wilbor 150
dollars each. To grandson Joshua Wilbor 130 dollars. To grandson
John G. Wilbor 110 dollars. To grandson Sylvanus Wilbor 100 dollars.
To five grandsons before named the rest and residue. . . "

        Children, recorded in LC:
i.   Priscilla, b. 5 Nov. 1774; d. 13 March 1838; m. 1 Jan. 1792
       Jonathan Wilbor, son of William and Hannah (Wilbor)
       Wilbor.
73. ii.   Samuel, b. 28 Dec. 1778.
iii.   Thomas, b. 8 Sept. 1789; d. 11 Sept. 1815.

47. JUDGE ANTHONY[5] WILBOR (Samuel[4], William[3], Samuel[2],
William[1]), born in LC 24 July 1759, died in Newport 27 July 1826.
Residence: LC and Newport, where he was judge of the court of
common pleas.

He married in LC 8 Nov. 1778 GRACE SHAW, daughter of Peter
and Sarah (Brown) Shaw, born in LC 25 Dec. 1759, died 20 May 1837.

His will, made 15 April 1822 and proved 4 Sept. 1826: ". . . To
son Arnold the farm partly in Middletown and partly in Newport where
he now lives, known by name as the Bliss farm (near Bliss Road). To
son Edwin my dwelling house in Newport on Spring Street and he is to
take care of my son Samuel. To Abigail Wilbor, wife of my son Arnold
Wilbor. . . To daughter Content Hazard, wife of George. . . To daughter
Nancy. . . To daughter Elizabeth Peckham. . . To daughter Emma Gillet,
wife of Baraliel Gillet, physician. . . To daughter Elizabeth Peckham,
wife of Thomas J. Peckham, certain money. To all relatives the right
to burial on the farm given to my son Arnold. . . "

        Children, only the first recorded in LC:
i.   Thomas, b. 8 Oct. 1780.
ii.   Content, b. 18 Oct. 1780 (?); d. 16 Jan. 1833; m. in September
      1800 George Hazard, son of Simeon and Abigail (Mumford)
      Hazard.
iii. Arnold, b. 12 Feb. 1784; d. 15 Oct. 1867; m. 19 March 1812
      Abigail Congdon, daughter of Thomas R. and Betsey Congdon.
iv. Nancy, b. 14 June 1786; d. 24 June 1849; unmarried.
v.   Emma, b. 29 Dec. 1788; m. Baraliel Gillet.
vi. Samuel, b. 8 July 1791; d. 17 March 1850; unmarried.
vii. Betsey, b. 23 Aug. 1793; m. (intention 6 Jan. 1818) Thomas
      J. Peckham of Newport.

viii.   Matilda, b. 16 May 1798; m. in 1822 Augustus Peckham.
ix.   Edwin, b. 10 March 1802; d. 17 Nov. 1864; m. 20 Dec. 1830
        Ann Maria Lyon, b. 19 June 1806, d. 28 Aug. 1866.

48. JOSEPH[5] WILBOR (William[4], William[3], Samuel[2], William[1]),
born in LC 25 May 1757, died in Newport where his will was proved
14 Sept. 1832. Residence: LC and Newport.
        He was married in LC 25 Sept. 1779 by the Rev. Jonathan Ellis
to ABIGAIL WOOD, daughter of John and Eunice (Shaw) Wood, born
in LC 25 Sept. 1757, died 13 Feb. 1810.

        Children:
i.   Eunice, b. 27 Dec. 1780; m. 29 Dec. 1804 Solomon Boyce.
ii.   Elijah, b. 13 July 1783; m. Elizabeth (--).
iii.   Ruth, b. 11 July 1785; d. 17 Aug. 1786.
iv.   Richard, b. 16 July 1787; d. 24 March 1811.
v.   Ruth, b. 24 Dec. 1789; d. 4 April 1799.
vi.   Ephraim, b. 25 May 1792.
vii.   John, b. 21 March 1795; d. 3 July 1859; m. in 1821 Phebe
        Armstrong.
viii.   Sarah, b. 7 Sept. 1797; m. Benjamin Austin.
ix.   William, b. 12 July 1800; m. 15 April 1827 Elizabeth
        Hazard, daughter of George and Content (Wilbor) Hazard.

49. JUDGE WILLIAM[5] WILBOR (William[4], William[3], Samuel[2],
William[1]), born in LC 1 Jan. 1760, died there 21 March 1843.
        He married first 1 Jan. 1787 MARY SOUTHWORTH, daughter of
Constant and Rebecca (Richmond) Southworth, born in LC 11 April
1757. He married second 5 Jan. 1833 DEBORAH CHASE, born in
1788, died 13 Oct. 1866.
        Residence: LC. They lived at Onegan, the place next north of
the so-called Betty Alden place.
        His will, recorded book 9, page 105 LC Probate, made 12 Feb.
1834 and proved 8 May 1843: ". . . To wife Deborah, horse, chaise
and harness and use of my farm to the west of the road with the buildings
and use of clock as long as she remains my widow. To nephew Clark
Wilbor all farm and buildings at west of road and land east of the road
called Coe Lot. At decease of my wife. Also to him all land and buildings
I bought of Ezra Brownell for seven years and my part of west end of
house. To John and William Wilbor, the sons of brother Joseph, all
that tract of land I bought of Ezra Brownell with rights to buildings
equally. To Eunice Boyce and Sarah Austin, daughters of brother
Joseph Wilbor, one hundred dollars. To Martha Palmer, wife of Dudley
Palmer, and Hannah Brownell, wife of William Brownell, 80 dollars.
To widow Priscilla Wilbor 40 dollars. To niece Abigail T. Wilbor 100
dollars and best bed and furniture. Rest and residue of household goods
to all granddaughters of Brownell Wilbor except to Esther Brownell,
wife of Amasa Brownell, and Lucy Brownell, wife of Ezra Brownell.
To Clarke Wilbor rest and residue. . . "

        Children by first wife:
i.   Andrew, d. young.

50. JONATHAN[5] WILBOR (William[4], William[3], Samuel[2], William[1]),
born in LC 4 March 1762, died in LC 8 March 1822.

He married first in LC 8 Nov. 1787 ESTHER WOODWORTH,
daughter of Hezekiah and Abigail (Southworth) Woodworth, born in
1759. He married second in LC 1 Jan. 1792 PRISCILLA WILBOR,
daughter of Clarke and Judith (Briggs) Wilbor, born 5 Nov. 1774,
died 14 March 1838.

       Children by first wife:

i.   Esther, b. 14 June 1789; m. Amasa Brownell, son of James
       and Hannah (Manchester) Brownell.

       Children by second wife:

ii.   Lucy, b. 26 Sept. 1792; m. 8 Feb. 1814 Ezra Brownell, son of
       George and Elizabeth (Peckham) Brownell.

iii.   Huldah, b. 4 Nov. 1794; m. 27 Oct. 1816 John Gifford, son of
       Enos and Mary (Wilbor) Gifford.

74. iv. Clarke, b. 20 Aug. 1796.

v.   Judith, b. 2 March 1798; d. 10 Oct. 1840; m. 13 July 1823
       Willard Gray, son of Job and Judith (Briggs) Gray.

75. vi. William Bartlett, b. 14 Nov. 1800.

76. vii. Jonathan, b. 21 Feb. 1804.

51. DANIEL[5] WILBOR (Daniel[4], William[3], Samuel[2], William[1]),
born in LC 15 Feb. 1761, died there 11 Feb. 1841. He lived in LC
on what later became the Benjamin F. Wilbour place.

He married in LC 30 May 1790 DEBORAH TAYLOR, daughter of
William and Deborah (Gray) Taylor, born in LC 20 Dec. 1770, died
there 22 April 1850.

His will, recorded LC Probate, book 8, page 206, made 22 March
1839 and proved 8 March 1841: ". . . To wife Deborah use of keeping
room, closet and bedroom adjoining in east end of my dwelling house
where my son Daniel now lives and use of chamber in southeast corner
of said house. Use of east half of kitchen and right to porch and wood-
house and right to draw water from the well. . . and my large Bible.
To son Peleg land which I purchased of William Southworth and the
widow Fallee Briggs with all buildings. Carting 80 loads of seaweed
on shore formerly belonging to the Joshua Wilbour farm yearly. Also
my Sears woodlot and sons Peleg, Benjamin and Daniel to pay Mary
Wilbour her yearly stipend. To son Benjamin that tract of land lying
to the west of the road, part of the Joshua Wilbor farm and privilege
of carting all seaweed except such as also given away in this will.
Also my salt meadow and my desk. To son Daniel that tract of land
lying eastward of the road bounded north by Thomas Burgess and Philip
Chase, east on the creek Philip Chase and Peleg Wilbour and the salt
meadow which I gave to my son Benjamin and land of Philip Chase and
Philip Wilbor and west on Philip Chase and Philip Wilbor and Thomas
Burgess. Also all that tract of land on the west of the road bounded
east on the main road, south of Philip Wilbor, north on Thomas and
Peter Burgess with all buildings and 50 loads of seaweed from the
Chase shore so-called yearly and my loom in my house. Also the
privilege from the Joshua Wilbour farm of 30 loads of seaweed yearly.
To two sons Rowland and Edwin 1200 dollars equally. To son Edwin

Wilbor 20 loads of seaweed from the Joshua Wilbour shore. To daughter
Sophia Brown 5 dollars. To daughter Philena Briggs 300 dollars and
improvement of keeping room, closet, bedroom in the east part of my
house where my son Daniel now lives, if she remains single after her
mother's death. To grandson Hervey J. Wilbour 300 dollars at age 21.
To daughter-in-law Prudence Wilbour my silver bowed spectacles and
two books entitled Imitation of Christ and Valley of Lilies and use of
rooms she now occupies until her son Hervey is 21. To grandchildren
Daniel and Deborah Brown six dollars each. To sons Peleg, Benjamin
and Daniel all the rest and residue. . . "

Children, recorded in LC:

	i.	Sophia, b. 11 Feb. 1791; m. 11 Feb. 1810 Pardon Browne, son of George and Elizabeth (White) Browne.
77.	ii.	Hervey, b. 11 Feb. 1793.
	iii.	Philena, b. 13 March 1795; d. 16 June 1845; m. 26 May 1816 Taylor Briggs, son of Thomas and Lucy (Shaw) Briggs.
78.	iv.	Peter, b. 8 Aug. 1797.
	v.	Peleg, b. 26 June 1799; d. 24 Dec. 1858; m. 4 Nov. 1830 Elizabeth Gifford, daughter of Noah and Martha (Hathaway) Briggs.
79.	vi.	Benjamin Franklin, b. 30 Jan. 1802.
80.	vii.	Daniel, b. 25 Sept. 1804.
	viii.	Rowland Greene, b. 2 Oct. 1809; d. 22 July 1884; m. Hannah Godding, b. 22 Nov. 1817, d. 9 July 1897.
81.	ix.	Edwin, b. 10 Jan. 1813.

52. PHILIP[5] WILBOR (Daniel[4], William[3], Samuel[2], William[1]),
born in LC 5 Feb. 1771, died there 22 Feb. 1846. He lived on the
place given on the map of 1870 as belonging to Ezra Wilbor, on West
Road in district No. 1.

He was married 4 Nov. 1804 by the Rev. Mase Shepard to MERCY
BURGESS, daughter of Ichabod and Hannah (Simmons) Burgess, born
in LC 13 Dec. 1776, died there 17 Oct. 1848. They are buried in the
New Wilbor or Seaconnet cemetery.

His will, recorded book 9, page 334, made 29 March 1841 and
proved 9 March 1846: ". . . To wife Mercy Wilbour improvement of
south room and south bedroom. Privilege to bake in oven. . . My
clock and one third of furniture and one third of books. I further
order that nine rods of land in the corner of my little orchard meadow,
where my two daughters and one grandchild now lie, be set apart as a
burial place for myself and family and their posterity forever. To son
Charles 500 dollars and all rest and residue. To sons Henry and Ezra
. . . and they to be executors. In case sister Mary survives me my
residuary legatees must find her yearly stipend secured to her by my
father's will. . . "

Children, recorded in LC:

82.	i.	Charles, b. 15 Aug. 1805.
	ii.	Eliza, b. 29 July 1807; d. 16 Dec. 1827.
	iii.	Lydia, b. 3 Dec. 1808; d. 10 Sept. 1832.
83.	iv.	Henry, b. 12 April 1811.
84.	v.	Ezra, b. 2 Feb. 1813.

53. BORDEN[5] WILBOR (Charles[4], William[3], Samuel[2], William[1]),
born in LC 12 Dec. 1759, died in Talmadge, Ohio, 21 Sept. 1818.
Residence: LC and New Hartford, N.Y.
   He was married in LC 1 May 1783 by the Rev. Jonathan Ellis to
LYDIA GRAY, daughter of Samuel and Deborah (Peck) Gray, born in
LC 27 Jan. 1761, died 8 March 1853.

   Children, the first two recorded in LC:
   i.   Simeon Gray, b. 29 July 1783; d. 23 July 1825; m. 29 Dec.
         1807 Sally Henry, daughter of William and Persis
         (Hayden) Henry, b. 22 Dec. 1787, d. 12 Aug. 1850.
   ii.   John Borden, b. 1 Sept. 1785; d. 31 May 1860; m. Elizabeth
         Lester Stanton.
   iii. Deborah Peck, b. 6 March 1795; d. 20 Oct. 1820; m. 26 Oct.
         1815 Joseph Plumb.
   iv.   Hannah Borden, b. 29 Dec. 1798; d. 5 Nov. 1897; m. 14 April
         1817 Horace Butler, born in 1792.

   54. GOVERNOR ISAAC[5] WILBOUR (Charles[4], William[3], Samuel[2],
William[1]), born in LC 25 April 1763, died there 4 Oct. 1837.
   He was married 17 May 1786 by William Davis, justice, to
HANNAH TABOR, daughter of Capt. Philip Tabor, born 22 March
1767, died in LC 13 Aug. 1836.
   He was one of Little Compton's most influential citizens. He was
born there on the farm of his father, Charles Wilbour, owned by the
heirs of John Alden Seabury, at the end of the road leading south from
the Commons. In early life he moved to the place which was later owned
by his heirs or Philip H. Wilbour and is in district No. 2, owned according
to the map of 1890 by Isaac C. Wilbor.
   He served as a member of congress from 1807 to 1809 and the
following year was elected lieutenant governor of Rhode Island. He
was acting governor of the state 1806-1807.
   In 1801 he became a member of the Rhode Island Assembly and
again in 1805 when he was made Speaker of the House. In that year
the people of the north part of Glocester petitioned to be set off into a
separate town, but the political feeling existing resulted in a tie vote,
whereupon Speaker Wilbour cast his vote in favor of the bill. Action
in the Senate was adverse and when in 1806 the bill came up again with
a tie Isaac Wilbour gave the decisive vote. The petitioners were anxious
to give his name to the new town but, he being unwilling, it was called
Burrillville in memory of James Burrill.
   In 1818 he was appointed Associate Justice of the Supreme Court
and soon through the retirement of the Hon. James Fenner, became
Chief Justice, an office he held until 1826 when he retired because of
ill health.
   He was much interested in the Quaker faith, with was the religion
of his father. He and his family are buried in the New Wilbor or
Seaconnet cemetery in LC.
   An interesting anecdote is told of Mr. Wilbour. It occurred between
the close of the Revolution and the War of 1812. The scene, Tiverton
Four Corners, R.I., where quite a hubbard is going on. A terrified
woman is bound to an upright stake. For some misdemeanor the court

has sentenced the woman to be flogged. Governor Wilbour is attending the execution of the court's sentence. The women of the town are surging about him in violent protest. They inquire as to the law and he reads from the statue: "The condemned shall be tied to an upright post and flogged according to the sentence of the court." Another rebellious outcry is followed by an expectant hush as His Excellency suggests: "But ladies, if it happened that there was no upright post, how could the law be carried out?" Whereupon a hundred willing hands unite in overthrowing, not for the occasion, but for all time the offensive instrument of public castigation; since then no woman has been publicly flogged in Rhode Island.

        Children, recorded in LC:

    i.   Taber, b. 25 Oct. 1787; d. 12 May 1788.

    ii.   Eliphal, b. 12 March 1789; d. 20 June 1832; m. 24 April 1806 William Humphreys, b. 26 Nov. 1784.

    iii.   Hanah Borden, b. 4 Feb. 1793; d. 20 May 1839; m. 1 Jan. 1810 Nathan Crary Brownell, son of Abner and Hannah Brownell.

85. iv.   Philip, b. 12 July 1895.

    v.   Patience T., b. 27 May 1798; d. 14 Jan. 1842; m. 20 Aug. 1827 Joseph Sisson, son of Lemuel and Susannah (Lake) Sisson.

    vi.   Sarah Soule, b. 9 May 1804; d. 17 May 1891; m. 19 Aug. 1827 Charles Wilbor, son of Philip and Mercy (Burgess) Wilbor.

SARAH SOULE WILBOUR
1804 - 1891

55. GEORGE[5] WILBOR (John[4], Isaac[3], Samuel[2], William[1]), born in LC 10 Feb. 1768, died there 11 March 1837. Residence: LC and Westport. He was married first in LC 14 Jan. 1802 by the Rev. Mase Shepard to NANCY ROBINSON, daughter of William and Mary Robinson. He was married second 13 March 1806 by the Rev. Mr. Shepard to SUSANNAH BAILEY, daughter of (--) and Abigail Bailey, born in 1783, died in LC 4 Oct. 1848.

His will, recorded LC Probate, book 8, page 178, made 12 Feb.
1836 and proved 10 April 1837: ". . . To son Abraham one dollar. To
son Abel my wearing apparel and gun. To daughter Susannah 30 dollars.
To daughter Hannah 30 dollars and use of home and dooryard. To daughter
Eleanor 50 dollars and use of house and dooryard. To wife Susannah
use of all estate both real and personal. The rest and residue to Abel,
Susannah, Hannah and Eleanor. Wife Susannah to be executrix. . . "

       Children, recorded in LC:
86. i.   Abraham, b. 29 July 1803.

       Children by second wife:
  ii.   Abel, b. 11 July 1807; d. 16 Aug. 1836.
  iii.   Nancy Robinson, b. 16 Jan. 1812; m. (intention 2 June 1832)
       Henry Brightman.
  iv.   Susannah, b. 12 Sept. 1814; d. 5 Jan. 1892; m. (1) 30 April
       1844 Charles M. Gifford, son of William and Lydia
       (Palmer) Gifford; m. (2) in LC 27 March 1852 Richard
       Reynolds, son of Humphrey and Sarah Reynolds.
  v.   Hannah, b. 28 June 1818; d. 28 June 1854; m. Hezekiah Wilbor,
       son of Hezekiah and Alice (Palmer) Wilbor.
  vi.   Eleanor, b. 13 Oct. 1824; d. 20 May 1855; m. 1 Jan. 1836
       James Rodney Longley, son of Obadiah and Elizabeth
       (Woodcock) Longley.

56. ISAAC[5] WILBOR (Samuel[4], Isaac[3], Samuel[2], William[1]), born
in LC 12 Oct. 1775, died there 21 Feb. 1821. Residence: LC. He
married LYDIA STODDARD, daughter of David and Mary (Dring)
Stoddard, born in LC 10 Nov. 1773, died there 9 Feb. 1862.

       Children:
  i.   Mary M., b. 27 Feb. 1800; d. in LC 6 Dec. 1865; m. Otis
       Lake, son of Martin and Susannah (Springer) Lake.
  ii.   Lydia.
  iii. Maria.
  iv.   Clarinda, b. in 1810; d. 29 April 1884; m. Benjamin Palmer,
       b. in 1802, d. 9 Dec. 1849.
  v.   Addison, b. 10 Feb. 1827; d. in 1881.

57. WILLIAM[5] WILBOR (Samuel[4], Isaac[3], Samuel[2], William[1]),
born in LC 12 Oct. 1775, died in 1827. Residence: LC.
    He was married in LC 16 July 1795 by the Rev. Mase Shepard
to ABIGAIL PALMER, daughter of Joseph and Hannah (Briggs) Palmer,
born in LC 13 June 1768, died there 27 Dec. 1850. Both are buried in
the Old Commons cemetery.

       Children:
  i.   Phebe G., b. 2 March 1796; d. 5 April 1869; unmarried.
  ii.   Cory, b. in 1800; d. at sea 26 Sept. 1825.
87. iii. Robert Gray, b. 9 March 1802.

58. WRIGHT[5] WILBOR (Brownell[4], Isaac[3], Samuel[2], William[1]),
born in LC 19 May 1783, died there 20 Feb. 1851. Residence: LC.
    He married in LC 12 Dec. 1806 HANNAH GRAY, daughter of John

and Elizabeth (Church) Gray, born 2 March 1789, died in LC 18 July
1844. They are buried in the Wilbor Woodman Gifford cemetery on
their own farm, called in 1870 the Oliver C. Wilbor place.

        Children, recorded in LC:

i.	Sarah Ann, b. 23 April 1809; m. (--) Wilcox.
ii.	Abigail, b. 2 March 1811; d. 24 Feb. 1818.
iii.	Brownell, b. 2 Jan. 1813; d. 12 Feb. 1821.
iv.	Hannah C., b. 14 Aug. 1815; d. 10 July 1893; m. 18 May 1834 Isaiah Snell, son of Joseph C. and Mary (Brownell) Snell.
v.	John Gray, b. 24 Nov. 1817; d. 24 Feb. 1818.
88. vi.	John Gray 2d, b. 3 May 1819.
vii.	Abigail 2d, b. 11 Aug. 1821; m. Thomas Dring.
viii.	Brownell 2d, b. 9 Aug. 1823; d. 17 Jan. 1827.
ix.	Lois Mary, b. 26 Nov. 1825; m. Jabez Weaver.

59. NATHAN[6] WILBOR (William[5], William[4], William[3], Joseph[2],
William[1]), born in LC 15 March 1791, died in Fall River 9 Nov. 1853.
Residence: LC and Fall River.
    He married 12 Feb. 1817 PHEBE SIMMONS, born in 1799.

        Children:

89. i.	Solomon, b. in 1816.
90. ii.	William H., b. in 1820.
iii.	Philander, b. in 1826; d. 14 July 1864; m. 5 Sept. 1854 Abby Rogers, daughter of Joel and Sarah Rogers. He was a soldier of the Civil War.
iv.	James Addison, b. in October 1828; d. in Pawtucket, R.I., 7 June 1900; m. (1) 28 Oct. 1882 Elizabeth F. Manchester, daughter of Fred and Lucretia Manchester, b. in November 1856, d. 1 April 1891; m. (2) 27 Oct. 1892 Sarah B. (Cornell) Barker, b. in 1828.
v.	Sarah J., b. in 1831; m. (1) 3 Aug. 1851 Otis Hunt, son of Benjamin and Abigail (Brown) Hunt, b. 15 May 1827, d. in 1896; m. (2) 21 March 1860 James R. Lincoln, son of Ralph and Abbie B. Lincoln.
vi.	Andrew, d. 8 Sept. 1851.
vii.	George, d. 7 Nov. 1887.

60. BENJAMIN[6] WILBOR (Hezekiah[5], William[4], William[3], Joseph[2],
William[1]), born in LC 4 March 1793, died in Fall River 17 Jan. 1873.
Residence: LC and Fall River.
    He was married 17 Nov. 1819 by the Rev. Mase Shepard to NANCY
BROWNELL, daughter of George and Elizabeth (Peckham) Brownell,
born in LC 31 Aug. 1793, died 12 June 1879.

        Children:

i.	Elizabeth Alice, b. 6 March 1820; d. 26 Feb. 1911; m. 17 May 1846 William P. Cooke, son of Robert and Bethia Cooke, b. 27 Jan. 1809, d. 3 April 1882; m. (2) Nancy C. Gray, daughter of Thomas and Thankful Gray.
ii.	Mary Ware, b. 14 Dec. 1821; d. 17 Nov. 1900.
iii.	Hannah M., b. in 1831; m. 13 Sept. 1854 Hezekiah L. Drowne,

son of James and Ann Drowne.

61. GEORGE⁶ WILBOR (Hezekiah⁵, William⁴, William³, Joseph²,
William¹), born in LC 19 Dec. 1794. Residence: LC.
He was married there 5 Dec. 1819 by the Rev. Mase Shepard to
HANNAH PIERCE, daughter of Isaac and Susannah (Stoddard) Pierce,
died 1 Nov. 1824.

Children, recorded in LC:
i.   George Engs, b. 3 Sept. 1820; m. 3 Oct. 1841 Amey Hambly
      Chappell, daughter of Robert Chappell.
ii.   Caroline, b. 31 July 1822; m. Franklin Woodcock.

62. DAVID⁶ WILBOR (Hezekiah⁵, William⁴, William³, Joseph²,
William¹), born in LC 16 Sept. 1796.
He was married in LC 16 March 1823 by the Rev. Benjamin Peck-
ham to PAMELIA SIMMONS, daughter of Ichabod and Anna (Thomas)
Simmons, born in Tiverton in 1801, died 21 Sept. 1871.
Residence: LC and Tiverton. They probably lived on the Ichabod
Simmons place on Crandall Road in Tiverton opposite 1098 Crandall
Road, where the gravestones of some of their grandchildren may be
seem.

Children:
91. i.   David W.
    ii. Ann, m. Stephen C. Hart.
    iii. Mary, m. William Wilcox.
    iv. Sarah, m. Cyrenus Bliss.
    v.   Phebe, m. Cyrenus Bliss.

63. HEZEKIAH⁶ WILBOR (Hezekiah⁵, William⁴, William³, Joseph²,
William¹), born in LC 3 Sept. 1808, died 2 Feb. 1880, buried in Pleasant
View cemetery. Residence: LC.
He married HANNAH WILBOR, daughter of George and Susannah
(Bailey) Wilbor, born in LC 28 June 1818, died 28 June 1854.
They lived on the east side of the East Main Road, next north to
the old Peckham place or the Miranda Pierce place, later the Samuel
Jennings place, where there is a Wilbor cemetery.

Children:
i.   Nancy Robinson, b. 18 April 1841; d. 21 Jan. 1919; m. 18 June
      1962 Samuel Mosher Jennings, son of Jired and Sarah
      (Mosher) Jennings, b. 8 March 1858, d. 20 Dec. 1918.
92. ii. George Henry, b. 18 May 1847.
    iii. Hannah Brightman, b. 7 Nov. 1849; m. (1) 23 May 1868
         George F. Manchester, son of Charles and Comfort
         (Lake) Manchester; m. (2) William Manley.

64. WALTER⁶ WILBOR (Joseph⁴, Walter⁴, Joseph³, Joseph²,
William¹), born 1 Sept. 1793 in LC, died there 11 Nov. 1868.
He married in LC 14 Sept. 1820 LYDIA IRISH, daughter of John
and Nancy (Little) Irish, born in LC 18 March 1799, died there 15
Sept. 1877.

They lived in the house on the corner in front of the Congregational Church.

His will, recorded in LC Probate, book 11, page 529, made 28 Aug. 1865 and proved 11 Jan. 1869: ". . . To wife Lydia use of real estate and all buildings except burial ground which is to remain for use of all my connections. To wife and daughters Adeline and Mary charge of graveyard. To daughter Jane W. Brownell, wife of Isaac B. S. Brownell 100 dollars. To daughter Hannah B. Wilbor, wife of William B. Wilbor, 100 dollars. To daughters Adeline Wilbor and Mary Otis Wilbor all real estate after wife. To wife Lydia the rest and residue and she to be executrix. . . "

Children:

i.   Adeline Cornelia, b. 10 Aug. 1821; d. 29 March 1901; unmarried.
ii. Jane Helena, b. 15 Sept. 1823; d. 11 Dec. 1898; m. 8 Feb. 1848 Isaac S. Brownell, son of James and Lydia (Church) Brownell.
iii. Hannah Brown, b. 13 April 1831; d. 29 Aug. 1922; m. 6 Jan. 1853 William Wilbor, son of Abraham and Eliza Ann (Brown) Wilbor.
iv. Mary Otis, b. 31 Aug. 1836; d. 8 March 1895; unmarried.
v.   Joseph, b. 13 April 1843; d. 12 July 1844.

65. THOMAS[6] WILBOR (Joseph[5], Walter[4], Joseph[3], Joseph[2], William[1]), born in LC 17 March 1795, died there 12 Sept. 1853. Residence: LC.

He was married there 4 Oct. 1818 by the Rev. Mase Shepard to PRUDENCE SHERMAN, daughter of Daniel and Hannah Sherman, born in September 1795, died in LC 23 March 1889. Both are buried in the Wilbor cemetery south of the Commons.

Children:

i.   Albert Gallatin, b. 13 May 1820; d. 18 Dec. 1895; m. Elizabeth S. Grinnell, daughter of Brenton B. and Nancy (Brownell) Grinnell.
ii. Ardelia Maria, b. 26 Feb. 1822; d. 7 Jan. 1908; unmarried.
iii. Hannah Sherman, b. 10 Aug. 1824; d. 19 Nov. 1901; m. 25 Sept. 1844 William Simmons Church, son of John and Prudence (Simmons) Church.
iv. Alexander B., b. 3 March 1827; d. 27 April 1896; m. 29 July 1874 Ida Florence Littlefield, daughter of Rufus L. and Annette W. Littlefield, b. in 1853.
v.   Joseph Otis, b. 22 Nov. 1830; d. 21 April 1832.
vi. Caroline A., b. 13 March 1833; d. 13 Jan. 1905; m. 1 March 1857 Larkin C. Tolles, son of John and Elizabeth Tolles, b. in 1828.
vii. Mary J., b. in 1838; m. 19 Oct. 1859 William E. Tabor Jr., son of William and Charlotte Tabor.

66. WILLIAM HUNT[6] WILBOR (Thomas[5], Aaron[4], John[3], John[2], William[1]), born in LC 22 June 1799, died there 14 Dec. 1848. Residence: LC.

He was married there 10 Jan. 1831 by the Rev. Emerson Paine
to MARY ANN RICHARDSON HILLIARD, daughter of William and
Rhoda (Records) Hilliard, born in LC 30 July 1809, died there 20
Feb. 1892. Both are buried in the Old Commons cemetery.

      Children, recorded in LC:

i.   Child, b. 2 Dec. 1831.
ii.   Amanda Maria, b. 21 Jan. 1833; d. in LC 23 March 1904;
      m. 24 Jan. 1856 Borden Manchester, son of Ellery and
      Hannah Manchester.
iii. William Francis, b. 2 Jan. 1836; d. 30 April 1904; m. (1)
      26 Nov. 1862 Catherine P. Manchester, daughter of·
      Albert and Amelia Manchester; m. (2) 23 Sept. 1886
      Ruth Ann Easterbrooks, daughter of Gardner and Mary
      (Waldron) Easterbrooks, b. 19 June 1836, d. 2 Nov. 1927.
iv.   Horatio Nelson, b. 12 Oct. 1838; d. in 1906.
v.   Julius Wilson, b. 11 May 1841; d. 11 June 1847.
vi.   Mary Susan, b. 20 March 1843; d. 2 Feb. 1895; m. 19 Feb.
      1865 Albert Gray, son of John and Mercy Gray, b. in
      1829, d. 26 June 1865.
vii. Ira Wesley, b. 13 Sept. 1845; m. 22 Aug. 1870 Elizabeth M.
      Bolton, daughter of Joseph and Sarah (Hancock) Bolton.

      67. JAMES HAMMOND[7] WILBOR (Thomas[5], Aaron[4], John[3], John[2],
William[1]), born in LC 11 May 1800, died there 28 March 1881. Residence: LC.

He was married in LC 18 Sept. 1828 by the Rev. Emerson Paine
to EDITH BROWNELL, daughter of Stephen and Cynthia (Wilbor) Wilbor,
born in LC 24 July 1811, died there 18 Nov. 1895.

      Children, only the first recorded in LC:

93. i. Stephen Brownell, b. 5 Sept. 1830.
ii.   James Leander, b. 20 Feb. 1834; d. 23 July 1905; m. (1) 22
      July 1858 Lorinda M. Hathaway, daughter of David C. and
      Ann (Eldredge) Hathaway, b. 20 July 1842, d. 23 Sept.1911.
94. iii. Albert Cranston, b. 6 March 1841.
95. iv. Charles Frederick, b. 25 Aug. 1843.

      68. THOMAS CHURCH[6] WILBOR (Thomas[5], Aaron[4], John[3], John[2],
William[1]), born in LC 2 June 1804, died there 9 Feb. 1862. Residence:
LC.

He was married first in LC 6 Oct. 1830 to ORANGE W. BOSWORTH,
daughter of Ichabod and Lavina Bosworth, born 12 Dec. 1810, died in LC
14 April 1856. He married second 25 March 1858 JANET GILLIS,
daughter of Robert and Grace Gillis, born 10 June 1828.

In his will, recorded LC Probate book 11, page 283, he named his
wife executrix and ordered her to sell all real estate after his death,
with one half of the money received going to his wife and the remaining
estate to his two children, John and Georgia, at age 21.

      Children by first wife:

i.   Lucinda Bosworth, b. 2 Nov. 1837; d. 19 Aug. 1883; m. 2
      Jan. 1861 Arnold Brightman LeVarre, son of Epathridius
      and Rhoda LeVarre, b. 11 March 1820, d. 10 Feb. 1887.

ii. Cyrus Augustine, b. 1 Aug. 1841; d. 28 Oct. 1859.
iii. Sybil Tallman, b. 25 May 1847; d. 27 Sept. 1847.
iv. John Bunyan, b. 17 Dec. 1848; m. 1 March 1871 Elizabeth H.
     Wells, daughter of Nahum and Olive (Manuel) Wells.
v.   Georgia Anna, b. 7 March 1851; d. 19 May 1923; m. 4 Jan.
     1869 George Henry Wilbor, son of Hezekiah and Hannah
     (Wilbor) Wilbor.
vi. Edward Thomas, b. 23 July 1855; d. 8 April 1857.

Children by second wife:
viii. Katie Grace, b. 14 June 1861; d. 25 March 1863.

69. ANDREW T.[6] WILBOR (Thomas[5], Aaron[4], John[3], John[2],
William[1]), born in LC 5 April 1809. Residence: LC and Dartmouth.
He married 13 Nov. 1848 HANNAH SIMMONS, daughter of Benjamin and Peace Simmons, born in 1820, died 5 Oct. 1897.

Children:
i.   Abbie L., b. 27 July 1849; m. 27 Aug. 1865 Charles Hix,
     son of Jeremiah and Nancy Hix.
ii. Job Sampson, b. 15 Nov. 1852; m. (1) 26 May 1878 Emma
     J. Murdock, daughter of John J. and Anna P. Murdock,
     b. in 1851, d. 20 Oct. 1884; m. (2) 10 Dec. 1894 Adeline
     H. (Bentley) Bolles, daughter of Samuel and Emma W.
     (Westgate) Bentley.
iii. Andrew, b. 9 July 1856; m. 23 May 1887 Mary O'Neil
     Sullivan, daughter of John O'Neil and Joanna Sullivan.
iv. James Henry, b. 29 Oct. 1860; m. 1 June 1898 Lillian Pearl
     James, daughter of Frederic B. and Emeline M. James,
     b. 19 March 1878.
v.   Anthony S., b. 13 Oct. 1862; d. 3 Nov. 1916.

70. CAPT. OWEN G.[6] WILBOR (John[5], Aaron[4], John[3], John[2],
William[1]), born in LC 19 Oct. 1787, died there 23 Aug. 1853. Residence: LC.
He married first in LC 20 Oct. 1820 MARY BROWNELL, daughter
of Joseph and Deborah (Briggs) Brownell, born in LC 10 Jan. 1792,
died there 19 Sept. 1826. He married second in LC 9 Jan. 1831
ABIGAIL WOODWORTH, daughter of Elisha and Edith (Wilbor) Woodworth, born in LC 24 March 1797, died there 22 July 1877. Two of
the daughters and probably the rest of this family are buried in the
Brownell cemetery in district No. 10, east of the road that goes to
Ocean Echo and across the road from the William H. Briggs (Leslie
Coombs) place.
This family had the place owned in 1890 by Orrin W. Simmons
and in 1950 by George H. Simmons. He was probably a sea captain.

Children by first wife, recorded in LC:
i.   Elizabeth, b. 4 May 1821; d. 7 Sept. 1822.
ii. Hannah, b. 19 March 1823; d. 24 Feb. 1824.
iii. Mary E., b. 26 Sept. 1825; d. 5 Jan. 1826.
Children by second wife:
iv. George A., b. 5 March 1833.

-742-

v.   John, b. 23 April 183-; d. 2 July 1854.
vi.   Mary, b. 15 April 1836; d. 25 Feb. 1869.
vii. Charles B., b. 12 Oct. 1839. It was Charles B. Wilbor who,
      reportedly, after Orrin Simmons' son James had purchased
      a place, suddenly appeared from the west and made Mr.
      Simmons pay again.

71. THOMAS[6] WILBOR (Bennet[5], Joseph[4], Joseph[3], William[2],
William[1]), born in LC 4 Sept. 1798, died there 20 Sept. 1880.

He married first in LC 1 Jan. 1825 HANNAH SHAW, daughter
of Noah and Rhoda (Palmer) Shaw, born in LC 30 Oct. 1793, died
there 7 March 1839. He married second MARY TOMPKINS, daughter
of Benjamin and Deborah (Simmons) Tompkins, born in LC 28 Dec.
1793, died there 14 Jan. 1875.

Residence: LC. They lived on the east end of Shaw Road, on the
north side of the road, the place being owned in 1890 by his daughter
Anne Eliza Wilbour.

        Children, recorded in LC:
i.   Ann Eliza, b. 7 March 1883; d. 16 April 1921; m. 8 Nov. 1852
        in LC Henry Page Wilbour, son of Benjamin Franklin and
        Abby Maria (Taylor) Wilbour, b. 16 Jan. 1830, d. 20 March
        1908.

72. BENNET[6] WILBOR (Bennet[5], Joseph[4], Joseph[3], William[2],
William[1]), born in LC 5 July 1805, died there 5 Feb. 1882.

He married 25 Oct. 1828 in Westport MARY MANCHESTER, born
in January 1808, died 21 July 1896.

Residence: LC. They lived on the road south of the Commons
where in 1890 or 1900 lived Galen Brownell, his son-in-law.

            Children:
96. i.   David, b. in August 1829.
    ii.   Harriet Richmond, b. in 1831; d. 10 Oct. 1884; m. 31 May
            1855 Galen Taylor Brownell, son of James and Lydia
            (Church) Brownell.
    iii.   Amey Ann, b. 22 Jan. 1836; d. 2 Nov. 1881; m. 20 Jan.
            1856 Albert G. Brownell, son of James and Lydia (Church)
            Brownell.
    iv.   Mary S., b. 14 July 1842; d. 24 July 1909; m. 26 Jan. 1869
            Pardon C. Brownell, son of Oliver C. and Ann Bailey
            (Brownell) Brownell.

73. SAMUEL[6] WILBOR (Clarke[5], Samuel[4], William[3], Samuel[2],
William[1]), born in LC 28 Dec. 1778, died 4 April 1821. Residence:
LC and Newport.

He was married in LC 11 Dec. 1800 by the Rev. Mase Shepard
to DEBORAH WILBOR, daughter of Thomas and Judith (Head) Wilbor.

        Children, three of whom are recorded in LC:
i.   Job B., b. in LC 16 July 1802; d. 3 May 1873; m. 24 July
        1827 Amey Robinson Williams.
ii.   Cornelius B., b. 27 April 1804; d. 29 April 1870; m. 16 July
        1826 Mary Ann Dyer, daughter of Aaron Fisher and

Sarah (Lyon) Dyer.
iii.   Joshua, b. 11 July 1806 in LC; d.10 Oct. 1861; m. Margaret
       Locke Lloyd, daughter of John and Mary Lloyd, b. in
       1813, d. 12 March 1890.
iv.   Elizabeth, b. in LC 25 Nov. 1808; d. 3 July 1839; m. 12
       July 1837 Samuel Pratt.
v.   John G., b. 3 April 1811; d. 25 March 1840.
vi.   Sylvanus, b. 29 Sept. 1813; d. 2 March 1865; m. 1836 Mary
       Hopkins.

74. CLARKE[6] WILBOR (Jonathan[5], William[4], William[3], Samuel[2],
William[1]), born in LC 20 Aug. 1796, died there 17 Dec. 1855.
     He married there 6 Nov. 1817 LURANA TAYLOR, daughter of
Jonathan and Martha (Briggs) Taylor, born in LC 1 Feb. 1800, died
there 2 Dec. 1860.
     He was a school teacher in LC and taught in the northeast upstairs
room of the house built about 1690 by Samuel and Mary (Potter) Wilbor.
The west end of the house was built after the Revolution.
     His will, recorded LC Probate book 10, page 69, made 26 Sept.
1855 and proved 11 Feb. 1856: ". . . To wife Lurana my best cow,
horse, best wagon and harness, household goods and 250 dollars. My
wife to have the use of the east half of the lower story of my dwelling
house, the east porch and south and west chamber. . . To daughter
Deborah if unmarried use of the same after the decease of my wife.
To son Thomas the western third of pasture called Southworth's Swamp.
To daughters Maria Louisa Brownell and Mary Burgess 175 dollars
each. To son Alexander 300 dollars. To daughter Deborah Wilbor
one good bed and 225 dollars. To son Aldred 300 dollars. To son
George my woodlot I bought of William Wilbor and 300 dollars. To
son William my windmill with the yard in which it stands and that
part of homestead, south orchard meadow, long pasture and east and
west lower pasture. To my son Oliver that part of homestead, the
north orchard, north meadow, little pasture and Ward's plain meadow."

Children, recorded in LC:
97. i.   Thomas, b. 29 May 1818.
     ii.   Maria Louisa, b. 24 Feb. 1820; d. 10 March 1881; m. 8
           Sept. 1855 Charles M. Brownell, son of Christopher
           and Sarah (Taylor) Brownell.
     iii. Mary C., b. 2 March 1822; d. 10 Feb. 1882; m. 24 March
           1825 Thomas Burgess, son of Peter T. and Parmelia
           (Bailey) Burgess.
98. iv.   Alexander Clarke, b. 24 July 1824.
     v.   William Andrew, b. 7 March 1827; d. 22 May 1886; m. 14
           May 1857 Susan B. Simmons, daughter of Abel and
           Lydia (Pierce) Simmons.
     vi.   Deborah, b. 8 Feb. 1829; d. 8 Oct. 1903; unmarried.
     vii. Oliver Hazard, b. 20 Nov. 1830; d. 5 Aug. 1906; m. 23 Dec.
           1860 Abby H. Manchester, daughter of Wanton and Hannah
           (Brownell) Manchester.
99. viii. George Briggs, b. 27 Aug. 1836.
100. ix.   Alfred Goldsmith, b. 31 Aug. 1840.

75. **WILLIAM BARTLETT[7] WILBOR** (Jonathan[5], William[4], William[3], Samuel[2], William[1]), born in LC 14 Nov. 1800, died there 12 March 1873.

He married there 12 March 1823 CLARINDA PEARCE, daughter of Ichabod and Lucy (Simmons) Pearce, born in LC 23 March 1795, died there 12 June 1864.

Residence: LC. He lived on the west road in district no. 2, on the west side of the road (now called Onegan) later owned by Philip H. Wilbor, son of Isaac Wilbor.

Children, recorded in LC:

101.	i.	Ichabod Pearce, b. 13 April 1825.
	ii.	Jonathan, b. 14 Feb. 1827; d. 6 Nov. 1847.
102.	iii.	Charles H., b. 19 June 1828.
103.	iv.	Joseph G., b. 24 Feb. 1830.
	v.	Comfort, b. 12 March 1832; d. 23 Feb. 1858; m. 22 Feb. 1857 Stephen H. Shepard, son of Nathaniel and Ruth Shepard.
	vi.	William James, b. 27 April 1835; d. 19 Aug. 1897; m. (1) 19 March 1863 (?) Margaret Shaw, daughter of William and Margaret (McDowell) Shaw; m. (2) 10 Oct. 1889 Elizabeth Bailey, daughter of Wheaton and Deborah Bailey.
	vii.	Lydia C., b. 7 Nov. 1837; d. 3 Sept. 1838.
	viii.	Cynthia R., b. 2 Feb. 1841; m. 15 Dec. 1864 Joseph R. Pearce, son of Joseph and Phebe Pearce, b. 28 Aug. 1843.

76. **JONATHAN[6] WILBOR** (Jonathan[5], William[4], William[3], Samuel[2], William[1]), born in LC 21 Feb. 1804, died there 11 Dec. 1874.

He married first 3 Dec. 1826 MARIA G. TAYLOR, daughter of John and Elizabeth (Bailey) Taylor, born 1 June 1804, died 3 Oct. 1847. He married second ROSETTA CROWELL YOUNG, daughter of William and Rebecca Young, born 20 March 1818, perhaps in Fall River, died in LC 11 Jan. 1890.

Residence: LC. They lived on the West Road in district No. 1, on the west side of the road near Swamp Corner. He was a shoemaker and a Democrat, when there were very few of that party in town.

His will, recorded book 11, page 715: ". . . To wife Rosetta use of all real estate as long as she remains my widow and use of all buildings. Also the rest and residue of the personal property. To son James all real estate with buildings after the decease of my wife. To daughter Mary E. Woodruff, wife of Amos Woodruff, 25 dollars. To daughter Emma B. Carpenter, wife of Edward E. Carpenter, 75 dollars. To daughter Judith G. Sisson, wife of William H. Sisson, 100 dollars. To daughter Rosetta M. Wilbor 200 dollars. Son James Wilbor to be executor. . . "

Children by first wife:

i.	Mary E., b. in 1828; m. (1) John Amos Woodruff; m. (2) P.J. Kelley.
ii.	Lydia C., b. in 1829; d. 30 April 1836.
iii.	Emma Brown, b. 5 Oct. 1838; m. (1) 31 Dec. 1865 Edward

Everett Carpenter, b. 2 Oct. 1840; m. (2) John Morris.
iv.   Judith Gray, b. 10 Oct. 1840; d. 29 Jan. 1866; m. 4 April
       1886 William Henry Sisson, son of Levi and Mary Sisson,
       b. 24 Aug. 1837, d. 17 Aug. 1922.
104. v. James Henry, b. 9 Sept. 1846.

       Children by second wife:
vi.   Rosetta Maria, b. 29 Jan. 1853; d. 12 Sept. 1937; m. 10
       Nov. 1880 John Franklin Pierce, son of John and Sarah
       (Hathaway) Pierce.

77. HERVEY[6] WILBOR (Daniel[5], Daniel[4], William[3], Samuel[2],
William[1]), born in LC 11 Feb. 1793, died there 29 July 1827.
     He married in LC 26 Dec. 1822 PRUDENCE PEARCE, daughter
of John and Anna (Taylor) Pearce, born in LC 30 April 1798, died in
1878. He is buried in the Old Wilbor cemetery on the West Road near
the Seaconnet cemetery in district No. 2.
     Residence: LC and Minneapolis, Minn. He lived on the Benjamin
F. Wilbour place in the cottage, or the Colonel Church place.

       Children, born in LC:
i.   Hervey Joshua, b. 18 Jan. 1827; d. 3 Jan. 1899; m. 4 July
       1854 Mary O'Meara, daughter of Michael O'Meara, b.
       in 1827, d. in October 1906. He had one daughter,
       Lillian, b. 21 Jan. 1859; d. 26 June 1945; m. 16 Nov.
       1881 Frank Curtis Snyder, b. 7 Sept. 1857, d. 28 Aug.
       1928. He left his native town early in life and moved
       to Minneapolis, Minn., where he traded in furs with
       the Indians and reportedly made a great deal of money.

78. PELEG[6] WILBOR (Daniel[5], Daniel[4], William[3], Samuel[2],
William[1]), born in LC 26 June 1799, died there 24 Dec. 1858.
     He married 4 Nov. 1830 ELIZABETH GIFFORD, daughter of
Noah and Martha (Hathaway) Gifford, born 20 April 1802, died in
LC 28 Jan. 1859. They are buried in the New Wilbor or Seaconnet
cemetery.
     Residence: LC. They lived on the south side of Swamp Road.

       Children, born in LC:
i.   Abbie Elizabeth, b. 26 Jan. 1832; d. in December 1878;
       m. 7 Dec. 1853 Robert Steere, son of Shadrach and
       Mary (Fowler) Steere, b. 8 Aug. 1816, d. in 1880.
ii.   Noah Hervey, b. 8 June 1834; d. 6 May 1910; m. 17 Sept.
       1857 Adelaide V. Sherman, daughter of Edward W. and
       Mary (Davis) Sherman, b. 22 Feb. 1841.
105. iii. Arthur T., b. 17 May 1836.
iv.   Daniel Gifford, b. 26 July 1842; d. in 1861.

79. BENJAMIN FRANKLIN[6] WILBOUR (Daniel[5], Daniel[4], William[3], Samuel[2], William[1]), born in LC 30 Jan. 1802, died there 8 July
1877.
     He married there 30 Sept. 1827 ABBY MARIA TAYLOR, daughter
of Simeon and Mary Ann (Jones) Taylor, born in LC 26 Feb. 1811, died

there 8 Feb. 1887.
     Residence: LC. They lived on West Main Road near Swamp
Corner (the old Wilbor place, originally the Colonel Church place).
     His will, recorded LC Probate: ". . . To all persons to whom
these presents shall come, I Benjamin F. Wilbour of LC in the county
of Newport and state of Rhode Island, yeoman. . . I give to my beloved
wife Abby M. Wilbour the use of and improvement of all my real estate
(except a small woodlot hereafter given to my son Henry) during her
natural life, improvement of mansion house and yard. . . Also to her
all my household furniture. . . To son Henry my Cole Brook woodlot
of two acres adjoining Daniel Wilbour's woodlot, also a right to get
30 loads of seaweed annually on the Joshua Wilbor beach, whereever
I have a right to get seaweed. I also give him 1400 dollars in cash.
To daughter Mary Ann Austin 400 dollars. To daughter Abby M. Nobles
400 dollars. To daughter Evelyn C. Wilbour 500 dollars. I also give
the said Evelyn my Mary Wilbour house, dooryard and privilege to
get water at the well. I give to my grandson Philip H. Wilbour 25
dollars. I give to my granddaughter Dora J. Wilbour 25 dollars. I
give and devise to my son Benjamin F. Wilbour all the rest and residue of my estate of every name and description, including the Benjamin
F. Wilbour place, on condition that he shall pay all the cash legacies
beforenamed. I hereby appoint my aforesaid residuary legatee Benjamin F. Wilbour sole executor of this my last will and testament.
In testimony whereof I have hereunto set my hand and seal this ninth
day of January in the year of our Lord eighteen hundred and seventy
four. . ."
          Children, recorded in LC:
106. i.   Henry Page, b. 16 Jan. 1830.
     ii.   Mary Ann, b. 6 June 1832; d. 27 Aug. 1905; m. 28 Nov.

BENJAMIN F. WILBOUR SR.   ABBY MARIA WILBOUR

1850 John Simmons Austin, son of Joseph and Lydia
(Simmons) Austin, b. 2 Sept. 1829, d. 26 March (?).
iii. Deborah Josephine, b. 15 July 1834; d. 26 March 1865;
m. 5 Nov. 1854 Isaac Champlain Wilbour, son of Philip
and Eliza Penelope (Champlain) Wilbor.
107. iv. Benjamin Franklin, b. 31 Oct. 1840.
  v. Abby Maria, b. 9 Oct. 1845; d. 1 Oct. 1929; m. 26 Jan.
1870 Edwin Wilbour Nobles, son of Anson Carter and
Mary (Briggs) Nobles, b. 7 Aug. 1837, d. 25 Feb. 1891.
  vi. Evelyn Cushman, b. 22 Nov. 1852; d. 14 Nov. 1924; m. 23
Nov. 1887 George Herbert Brownell, son of George T.
and Rhoda Ann (Shaw) Brownell.

80. DANIEL[6] WILBOR (Daniel[5], Daniel[4], William[3], Samuel[2],
William[1]), born in LC 25 Sept. 1804, died in LC 9 Feb. 1881.
He married 1 April 1832 MARIA PEARCE, daughter of John
and Anna (Taylor) Pearce, born in LC 20 Jan. 1811, died there 13
June 1851. They are buried in the New Wilbor or Seaconnet cemetery.
Residence: LC. They lived on Main West Road in district No.
1, south of Swamp Corner, on the west and east side of the road.

  Children, born in LC:
i. Anna G., b. in 1834; m. (1) 10 April 1858 Sydney C. Clarke,
son of Jesse and Almira Clarke; m. (2) David Utely.
108. ii. Daniel, b. 3 April 1838.
  iii. Josephine Maria, b. 28 Sept. 1846; d. 11 April 1908; m. 25
Nov. 1871 George Henry Woodman.
109. iv. William Franklin, b. 19 March 1852.

81. EDWIN[6] WILBOR (Daniel[5], Daniel[4], William[3], Samuel[2],
William[1]), born in LC 10 Jan. 1813, died in Accushnet, Mass., 13
May 1878. Residence: LC and Accushnet.
He married 11 Dec. 1838 SALLY RICHMOND GRAY, daughter
of Loring and Ruth (Richmond) Gray, born in LC 10 Nov. 1813, died
in Accushnet 15 April 1897.

  Children:
i. Horatio, b. 12 Sept. 1839; d. 6 July 1914; m. 31 Oct. 1866
Mary Jane Palmer, daughter of Thomas and Deborah
(Gifford) Palmer.
ii. Edwin Richmond, b. in 1843; d. 25 April 1864.
iii. Sarah Cornelia, b. in 1849; d. 29 Feb. 1864.

82. CHARLES[6] WILBOUR (Philip[5], Daniel[4], William[3], Samuel[2],
William[1]), born in LC 15 Aug. 1805, died there 4 June 1882.
He married 19 Aug. 1827 SARAH SOULE WILBOUR, daughter of
Isaac and Hannah (Tabor) Wilbor, born in LC 9 May 1804, died there
27 May 1891. She was Governor Wilbour's daughter. She did a great
deal of historical and genealogical work.
Residence: LC. They lived at the corner of the Main West Road
and Swamp Road, on the place owned by Ezra Coe in 1850. It was at
one time part of the Southworth place, as the Swamp Road ran through
the middle of the Southworth farm.

Children, born in LC and recorded there:
i.   Elizabeth, b. 8 July 1829; d. 26 April 1832.
110. ii.   Charles Edwin, b. 17 March 1833.

83. **HENRY[6] WILBOR** (Philip[5], Daniel[4], William[3], Samuel[2], William[1]), born in LC 12 April 1811, died in Fall River 21 Dec. 1883.
He married 27 Nov. 1839 ABIGAIL DEAN, daughter of Joseph and Elizabeth Dean, born 28 March 1809, died 2 May 1883.
Residence: LC. They lived on the Benjamin F. Wilbour place in district No. 2, in the north part of the house which was built by Thomas Church Esq. in 1724.

Children, born in LC:
111. i.   Philip Henry, b. 3 Jan. 1843.
ii.   Elizabeth Dean, b. 2 July 1845; d. 20 Aug. 1855.
iii.   Lydia Rebecca, b. 12 Aug. 1847; d. 9 April 1875; m. 29
        Sept. 1874 Thomas A. Manchester, son of Albert and
        Frances Manchester.
iv.   John Parker Hale, b. 21 Sept. 1849; d. 28 July 1894; m.
        24 Nov. 1874 Hannah Palmer Brownell, daughter of
        James and Clarinda Richmond (Palmer) Brownell, d.
        12 June 1926.
v.   Abigail Dean, b. 26 May 1851; m. 26 May 1875 Oscar
        Lawrence, son of Leonard and Elizabeth (Lord) Lawrence,
        b. 24 May 1949, d. 25 Dec. 1917.

84. **EZRA[6] WILBOR** (Philip[5], Daniel[4], William[3], Samuel[2], William[1]), born in LC 2 Feb. 1813, died there 22 Feb. 1883. He lived in LC district No. 1, on the east side of main West Road.
He married 16 Nov. 1840 MARY T. MARBLE, daughter of James and Mary (Tew) Marble, born 26 Jan. 1821, died 19 April 1911.

Children, born in LC:
i.   Amanda Maria, b. 27 Feb. 1842; d. 30 April 1882; m. (1)
        8 March 1858 Benjamin Augustus Shaw; m. (2) 3 April
        1877 Louis Hayward.
ii.   Mary Eliza, b. 20 July 1844; m. 12 June 1889 William C.
        Brown, son of Otis L. and Caroline Chase (Wilbor)
        Brown.
iii.   Georgianna Amelia, b. 23 May 1848; m. 25 Dec. 1872 Charles
        Leonard Simmons, son of Alexander and Clarinda Sim-
        mons.
113. iv.   Jere Bailey, b. 31 Aug. 1860.

85. **PHILIP[6] WILBOR** (Isaac[5], Charles[4], William[3], Samuel[2], William[1]), born in LC 12 July 1795, died there 29 Jan. 1848. He lived in LC in what was later the Isaac C. Wilbour place in district No. 2, west of Main Road, bordered north on Taylor's Lane.
He was married in LC 8 Dec. 1823 by the Rev. Stephen Gano to ELIZA PENELOPE CHAMPLAIN, daughter of Daniel and Penelope (Allen) Champlain of Exeter, R.I., born in 1802, died in LC 20 Jan. 1848.
Children, born in LC:

      i.   Caroline Elizabeth, b. 8 May 1825; d. in 1862; m. Reuben
              Corey.
114. ii.   Isaac Champlain, b. 11 May 1831; d. in LC 19 Sept. 1899;
              m. (1) 15 Nov. 1854 Deborah Josephine Wilbor, daughter
              of Benjamin F. and Abby Maria (Taylor) Wilbour; m.
              (2) Amelia French, daughter of William S. and Rebecca
              (Coffin) French.

      86. ABRAHAM[6] WILBOR (George[5], John[4], Isaac[3], Samuel[2],
William[1]), born in Westport 29 July 1803, died in LC 24 Feb. 1889.
He lived in LC in the house on the corner of the road south of the
Commons and the Commons.
      He was married 21 Nov. 1824 in LC by the Rev. Emerson Paine
to ELIZA ANN BROWN, daughter of Thurston and Nancy (Pendleton)
Brown, born 8 Feb. 1806 in LC, died there 12 July 1878.

           Children, recorded in LC:
      i.   Nancy Robinson, b. 26 Jan. 1826; d. 28 July 1909; m. 12
              Jan. 1846 Enoch Fenno.
115. ii.   William Brown, b. 10 Aug. 1827.
      iii. Mary Elizabeth, b. 20 Jan. 1831; d. 15 Nov. 1922; m. 30
              Oct. 1848 Joseph Henry Lawton, son of Job W. and
              Frances Lawton.
      iv.   Emily Jane, b. 7 Aug. 1832; d. 20 May 1888; m. in August
              1858 Algenon Cook, son of Robert and Hope Cook.
      v.   Harriet Pendleton, b. 12 Nov. 1835; d. 31 July 1922; un-
              married.
      vi.   Catherine Matilda, b. 9 Oct. 1839; d. 26 April 1927; un-
              married.
      vii. George Thurston, b. 6 Nov. 1843; d. 4 Nov. 1903; m. 10
              Jan. 1864 Mary Ann Newell, daughter of Samuel and
              Mary Ann (Steiger) Newell.
      viii. Lydia Rose, b. 10 May 1846; d. 29 June 1907; m. 30 June
              1868 George Sisson, son of George and Frances Sisson.

      87. ROBERT GRAY[6] WILBOR (William[5], Samuel[4], Isaac[3], Samuel[2],
William[1]), born in LC 9 March 1802, died there 13 May 1882.
      He married first in LC 20 Aug. 1827 AMEY A. HAMMOND, daughter
of Humphrey Hammond, born 20 Aug. 1809, died 3 Nov. 1864. He
married second 17 Dec. 1865 MARY A. (SHEFFIELD) DEDMOND,
widow, daughter of Josiah and Martha (Mowrey) Sheffield, born in
1827, died 29 Oct. 1870. He married third 18 Sept. 1872 MARGARET
SCOTT, daughter of John and Catherine (Phalen) Scott, born in 1809,
died 25 Feb. 1895.
      Residence: LC. They lived a long way in from the Swamp Road,
opposite the Southworth place, at the north and quite near what used
to be the main village of Awashonks. The house house has been gone
sometime but the cellar is still there and maybe reached from the road
south of the Commons.

           Children, born in LC and recorded there:
      i.   Hannah Briggs, b. 23 Aug. 1828; m. 24 Nov. 1858 George
              F. Tallman, son of Abner and Sarah Tallman.

116. ii.   Samuel O., b. 24 Feb. 1830.
     iii.   Ray Palmer, b. 28 Oct. 1934; d. 3 Aug. 1855.
     iv.   Alma A., b. 2 Oct. 1836; d. 22 July 1837.
     v.   Charles Henry, b. 24 May 1839; d. 17 Dec. 1867; m. (1)
            17 March 1861 Mary E. Macomber, daughter of Abner
            and Nancy Macomber, b. in 1841, d. 16 Oct. 1861; m.
            (2) 24 March 1863 Augusta B. Pierce, daughter of
            Arnold and Susan Pierce.
     vi.   Theodore Francis, b. 24 July 1846.

     88. JOHN GRAY[6] WILBOR (Wright[5], Brownell[4], Isaac[3], Samuel[2],
William[1]), born in LC 3 May 1819, died there 22 Dec. 1902.
     He married SUSAN E. CROSBY, daughter of John and Elizabeth
(Pearce) Crosby, born in LC 10 Aug. 1822, died there 10 Sept. 1891.
     Residence: LC. They lived in the east part of town near Potters-
ville, where the Woodman Wilbor cemetery is located.

            Children, born in LC:
     i.   Mary E., b. in 1841; d. 1 Jan. 1916; m. 21 Oct. 1856 Noah
            M. Castinoe, son of John and Huldah Castinoe.
117. ii.   Oliver C., b. 20 Feb. 1843.
     iii.   Hannah Gray, b. 15 June 1845; d. 9 Sept. 1917; m. 21 Oct.
            1864 George Mowrey Potter, son of George and Sarah
            (Palmer) Potter, b. 13 Feb. 1839, d. 19 Dec. 1921.
     iv.   Frances Pitman, b. 28 March 1847; d. in April 1900; m.
            26 April 1867 William Albion Case, son of Abner and
            Cynthia (Tompkins) Case.
     v.   John R., b. 25 April 1852; d. 28 Aug. 1864.

     89. SOLOMON[7] WILBOR (Nathan[6], William[5], William[4], William[3],
Joseph[2], William[1]), born in 1816, died in LC 27 May 1876.
     He married in LC 21 May 1848 ESTHER W. (PALMER) BRIGHT -
MAN, daughter of Israel and Martha (Church) Palmer and widow of
Daniel Brightman, born 1828, died in LC 31 Dec. 1884.
     Residence: LC. They lived on the west side of the road which
goes to Westport from Pottersville.

            Children, born in LC:
     i.   Susan M., b. 18 Dec. 1848; d. 11 May 1904; m. 3 May 1878
            William H. Tabor, son of James and Nancy Tabor, b. in
            1827.
     ii.   Stephen, b. in October 1850; d. 23 March 1877; unmarried.
118. iii.   Mary Ella, b. 31 July 1852.
119. iv.   Nathan A., b. 17 March 1854.
     v.   George R., b. 9 Nov. 1856; d. 26 March 1897; unmarried.
     vi.   Charles, b. in December 1861; d. 6 Jan. 1885; unmarried.
     vii.   Huldah Ann, b. 18 Dec. 1865; d. 14 Sept. 1941; m. Benjamin
            Herbert Simmons, son of William T. and Sarah Wilbor
            (Dyer) Simmons, b. 9 May 1859.

     90. WILLIAM H.[7] WILBOR (Nathan[6], William[5], William[4], Wil-
liam[3], Joseph[2], William[1]), born in 1820, died in LC 27 Jan. 1892.
Residence: LC and New Bedford.

He married 29 March 1847 MRS. RHODA G. (SISSON) DYER, daughter of George and Nehala Sisson, born in 1817, died 25 Sept. 1881.

Children:

i.   Albert R., b. 4 Feb. 1848; d. 1 Aug. 1901; m. 28 April 1876 Hannah Wing, daughter of Leander and Melitha Wing.

ii.   Althea, b. 27 May 1855; m. 2 Jan. 1909 Daniel Gersthauer, son of Christopher and Katherine (Karcher) Gersthauer.

iii.   George William, b. in 1856; d. 26 Feb. 1912; m. (1) 4 Dec. 1882 Charlotte L. Mavis, daughter of William H. and Nancy E. Mavis; m. (2) Annie Chase Borden, daughter of James R. and Patience Borden.

iv.   Mary A., b. 2 July 1859; m. 24 Dec. 1880 Benjamin F. Gifford, son of Henry M. and Lydia A. Gifford.

v.   Arthur G., b. 5 Oct. 1860; d. 4 July 1880.

vi.   Lena M., b. 23 April 1863; m. 2 Jan. 1883 James W. Pettey, son of Potter and Abby Pettey.

91. DAVID W.[7] WILBOR (David[6], Hezekiah[5], William[4], William[3], Joseph[2], William[1]). He married HANNAH ROUNDS, daughter of Isaac and Phebe (Simmons) Rounds, born 18 April 1820, died 7 Feb. 1913. Residence: Tiverton.

Children:

i.   Victoria, b. in March 1843; d. 2 Oct. 1857.

120. ii.   David W., b. 6 April 1845.

iii.   Sylvanus, b. in 1847; d. 10 Sept. 1848 ae 14 months.

iv.   Cyrenus Bliss, b. 29 June 1847; d. 19 Sept. 1926; m. 18 Dec. 1879 Jane M. Simmons, daughter of William B. and Cornelia (Grinnell) Simmons.

v.   Ann Jeanette, b. in 1849; m. 6 Sept. 1868 William J. Cook, son of Darius and Louisa (Francis) Cook.

vi.   Frank Sylvanus, b. 29 June 1852; d. 13 Nov. 1936; m. (1) 9 May 1894 Lottie Gertrude Simmons, daughter of David and Grace A. (Grinnell) Simmons, b. in 1866, d. 3 March 1932; m. (2) Susan MacNulty.

92. GEORGE HENRY[7] WILBOR (Hezekiah[6], Hezekiah[5], William[4], William[3], Joseph[2], William[1]), born in LC 18 May 1847, died there 21 May 1915. Residence: LC.

He married there 4 Jan. 1869 GEORGIANNA WILBOR, daughter of Thomas C. and Orange Westgate (Bosworth) Wilbor, born in LC 7 March 1851, died there 19 May 1923.

Children, born in LC:

i.   Alice Westgate, b. 13 Feb. 1872; d. 13 June 1875.

ii.   Jennie Grace, b. 29 Sept. 1876; d. 15 July 1931; m. 23 Oct. 1902 Jirah Case, son of William and Frances P. (Wilbor) Case.

iii.   Son, b. in November 1879.

iv.   Bertha Hoxie, b. 22 Oct. 1880; m. (1) 11 Aug. 1897 Charles Leander Simmons; m. (2) 24 Oct. 1918 Arthur Truman Carter.

121. v.   Arthur Everett, b. 24 Oct. 1881.

93. STEPHEN BROWNELL[7] WILBOR (James[6], Thomas[5], Aaron[4], John[3], John[2], William[1]), born in LC 5 Sept. 1830, died in New Bedford 6 March 1907. Residence: LC, Fall River and New Bedford.

He married 30 June 1853 MARTHA ANN PEASE, daughter of Asa H. and Lydia (Brown) Pease, born in 1836, died 31 Jan. 1903.

Children:
i. Sarah Hammond, b. 23 April 1854; d. 1 Oct. 1854.
ii. Mary Anna, b. 4 May 1856; d. 15 Jan. 1902; m. 19 March 1878 Isaac C. Howland, son of Thomas and Judith Howland.
iii. James Herbert, b. 6 March 1858; m. 3 Oct. 1882 Esther Mellor, daughter of James and Jane C. Mellor, b. in 1862, d. 18 Jan. 1915.
iv. Fannie Cranston, b. 20 Feb. 1860; m. (1) 25 May 1881 George William Reed, son of Charles H. and Mary (Davis) Reed.
v. Son, b. 10 July 1875; d. 10 July 1875.
122. vi. Stephen Brownell, b. 11 May 1878.

94. ALBERT CRANSTON[7] WILBOR (James[6], Thomas[5], Aaron[4], John[3], John[2], William[1]), born in LC 6 March 1841, died in New Bedford 12 Sept. 1922.

He married first in LC 2 Dec. 1866 MARY JANE CHAPMAN, daughter of Alfred M. and Caroline F. Chapman. He married second 30 Dec. 1880 ANNIE MARIA HEAD, daughter of Abraham and Nancy S. (Grinnell) Head, born in 1860, died 6 Jan. 1903.

Residence: LC and New Bedford. He was a wheelwright and a soldier of the Civil War. He was living at LC Commons in 1890.

Children by first wife:
i. Carrie M., b. 5 Oct. 1867; d. 26 Jan. 1868.

Children by second wife:
ii. Walter C., b. 28 April 1884; d. 5 July 1911.

95. CHARLES FREDERICK[7] WILBOR (James[6], Thomas[5], Aaron[4], John[3], John[2], William[1]), born in LC 25 Aug. 1843, died 13 June 1904.

He married first in LC 22 Oct. 1870 HANNAH J. POTTER, daughter of Holder and Deborah G. (Tallman) Potter, born in 1852. He married second 15 Jan. 1884 MARY HANNAH (CROSBY) MANCHESTER, daughter of John Luce and Sarah (Cowen) Manchester, born 20 Sept. 1849, died in LC 19 June 1897.

Residence: LC. He was a soldier of the Civil War.

Children by first wife, born in LC:
i. Frederick Lee, b. 15 Oct. 1871; d. 28 March 1872.
ii. Emma Hammond, b. 3 June 1874; m. 5 May 1897 George E. Westgate, son of Dean P. and Mary (Philips) Westgate.

Children by second wife:
iii. Edgar H., b. 21 Dec. 1887; m. (1) 28 Nov. 1908 Mary E. Toomey, daughter of Peter and Kate A. (Noonan) Toomey;

m. (2) 24 Nov. 1917 Elizabeth (Martin) Carr, daughter
of John and Helen (Ladsborough) Carr.
123. iv. Everett Leander, b. 21 Dec. 1887.
      v.   Son, b. in August 1889.

96. DAVID[7] WILBOR (Bennet[6], Bennet[5], Joseph[4], Joseph[3], William[2],
William[1]), born in LC in August 1829, died there 12 Oct. 1896.
He married 28 Oct. 1882 HELEN DOUGHERTY, daughter of
James and Rosanna Dougherty, born in 1863.
Residence: LC and Fall River.

Children, born in LC:
i.   Olive Edna, b. 28 March 1884; d. 1 Sept. 1938; m. (1)
      8 Jan. 1898 George E. Briggs, son of Jeremiah and
      Phebe J. (Williston) Briggs; m. (2) Atwell F. Carter.
ii.   Maud L., b. 28 Feb. 1886; m. 10 Aug. 1905 Frederick S.
      Partington, son of James and Sarah A. (Brown)
      Partington.
iii. Mary Ann, b. 14 Sept. 1891; d. 15 Dec. 1891.
iv.   Lucia L., b. in 1893; m. 1 Oct. 1914 George E. Partington,
      son of James and Sarah A. (Brown) Partington.
v.   Raymond, b. in October 1896.

97. THOMAS[7] WILBOR (Clarke[6], Jonathan[5], William[4], William[3],
Samuel[2], William[1]), born in LC 29 May 1818, died there 29 April 1875.
He lived in LC in the first house on the north side of Taylor's Lane.
He married first 10 Jan. 1838 CAROLINE G. CHASE, daughter of
Ephraim and Clarissa Chase, born in 1818, died in LC 16 April 1839.
He married second DORCAS B. BURGESS, daughter of Peter and
Parmelia (Bailey) Burgess, born in LC 5 Nov. 1817, died there 14 Feb.
1895.

Children by first wife, born in LC:
i.   Caroline Chase, b. 9 April 1839; d. 9 April 1901; m. Otis
      Lake Brown, b. in Tiverton 30 Jan. 1837.

Children by second wife:
ii.   Albert C., b. in 1846 (?); d. 22 Sept. 1846.

98. ALEXANDER CLARKE[7] WILBOR (Clarke[6], Jonathan[5],
William[4], William[3], Samuel[2], William[1]), born in LC 24 July 1824,
died there 11 Dec. 1899.
He married there 16 Jan. 1850 ABBIE CATHERINE GRAY,
daughter of Willard G. and Judith (Wilbor) Gray, born in LC 11 June
1834, died there 31 March 1895. They are buried in the Old Wilbor
cemetery in district No. 2.
Residence: LC. They lived on the east side of West Road opposite the so-called Betty Alden place.

Children, born in LC:
i.   Florence Gray, b. 14 Oct. 1852; d. 1 Feb. 1915 in New
      Bedford.
ii.   Margaret W., b. 1 Feb. 1860; d. 24 Nov. 1860.
iii. Ethel Arnold, b. 2 June 1862; d. 29 April 1864.

99. GEORGE BRIGGS[7] WILBOR (Clarke[6], Jonathan[5], William[4], William[3], Samuel[2], William[1]), born in LC 27 Aug. 1836, died 12 April 1879. Residence: LC and New Bedford.

He married 29 Nov. 1866 MARY O. SIMMONS, daughter of Alden and Eliza (Bartlett) Simmons, born in 1838, died in 1924. She married second 13 March 1882 Nelson D. Hinckley.

Children:
i.   Eliza Lurana, b. 14 Nov. (?); d. 12 June 1883.
ii.   Martha Hathaway, b. 28 June 1874; m. 25 June 1904 Dr. Walter Edward Blaine, son of John A. and Mary (Carr) Blaine.

100. ALFRED GOLDSMITH[7] WILBOR (Clarke[6], Jonathan[5], William[4], William[3], Samuel[2], William[1]), born in LC 31 Aug. 1840, died in New Bedford 20 Feb. 1911. Residence: LC and New Bedford.

He married 9 Oct. 1862 LOUISA AUGUSTA KELLEY, daughter of Amasa and Louise (Lovejoy) Kelley, born in 1842, died 12 Jan. 1913.

Children:
i.   Herbert Clarke, b. 20 Aug. 1863 probably in New Bedford; d. 3 March 1917; m. Lulu May Keith.

101. ICHABOD PEARCE[7] WILBOR (William[6], Jonathan[5], William[4], William[3], Samuel[2], William[1]), born in LC 13 April 1825, died there 2 July 1888. He lived on the west side of Maple Avenue in LC.

He married in LC 21 Nov. 1848 DEBORAH ANN BROWNELL, daughter of Clarke and Sarah (Tompkins) Brownell, born in LC 20 Oct. 1829, died 11 Jan. 1870.

Children, born in LC:
i.   Cornelia M., b. 27 May 1852; d. 21 June 1932; m. (1) 25 June 1870 Adelbert H. Allen, son of Rodolphus H. and Mary Allen; m. (2) 27 Nov. 1878 William S. Wood, son of Nathan and Almira Wood.
ii.   William Clarke, b. 15 Dec. 1855; d. 25 Jan. 1912; m. 14 March 1877 Evelyne Josephine Simmons, daughter of William Taylor and Sarah Wilbor (Dyer) Simmons, b. 9 Sept. 1857.
124. iii.   Charles Richmond, b. 3 Oct. 1858.

102. CHARLES H.[7] WILBOR (William[6], Jonathan[5], William[4], William[3], Samuel[2], William[1]), born in LC 19 June 1828, died there 12 March 1897.

He married 22 April 1852 MARY A. DYER, daughter of Preserved and Annie (Durfee) Dyer, born 25 Nov. 1826, died 26 June 1904.

Residence: LC. They lived on the place south of the Meeting House Lane, opposite Christian Corner. It was the old Congregational Parsonage.

Children, born in LC:

i.   Elizabeth Alice, b. 8 Oct. 1860; d. 8 Nov. 1922; m. 18
       Nov. 1881 Clarence G. Wordell, son of Gardiner and
       Olive Wordell, b. 30 Nov. 1859, d. 30 July 1924.

103. JOSEPH G.[7] WILBOR (William[6], Jonathan[5], William[4],
William[3], Samuel[2], William[1]), born in LC 24 Feb. 1830, died there
18 Oct. 1871. Residence: LC and Tiverton.
       He married first 23 Dec. 1860 FRANCELIA AUGUSTA BURGESS,
daughter of Sylvester H. and Sally Almy (Briggs) Burgess, born in
November 1834, died in LC 2 Dec. 1866. He married second 4 Oct.
1868 CAROLINE M. COGGESHALLE, daughter of Abner and Elizabeth
(Albert) Coggeshalle, born 13 Oct. 1837, died 11 April 1922.

       Children, by first wife, born in LC:
i.   Emma Josephine, b. 6 April 1865; d. 21 March 1935; m. 19
       Nov. 1887 Frederick Lincoln Sherman, son of Walter A.
       and Phebe Sherman.
ii.   Francelia Burgess, b. 10 Nov. 1866; d. 28 Feb. 1869.

       Children by second wife:
iii.   Cora Elizabeth, b. in 1870; m. 16 May 1886 Alexander
       C. Nickerson, son of Alexander and Elizabeth (Chase)
       Nickerson.
iv.   Joseph G., b. in 1872; m. 8 Oct. 1899 Ida Stacy Bliss,
       daughter of Frank and Carrie A. (Hicks) Bliss, b.
       in 1876, d. 21 Jan. 1934.

104. JAMES HENRY[7] WILBOR (Jonathan[6], Jonathan[5], William[4],
William[3], Samuel[2], William[1]), born in LC 9 Sept. 1846, died in Fall
River 24 Sept. 1895. Residence: LC and Fall River.
       He married 15 Dec. 1870 SARAH A. BUSH, daughter of William
Dyer and Sarah Ann (Eltz) Bush, born in 1847. She married second
7 July 1903 Luther H. Hodges, son of Anton F. and Anna C. (Walters)
Hodges.

       Children:
i.   Minerva Louise, b. 26 July 1872; m. 16 Jan. 1897 Andrew
       Townley, son of Andrew and Mary (Broom) Townley.
ii.   Sarah Amelia, b. 28 Nov. 1874; m. 24 Aug. 1803 Clarence
       Gifford Straight, son of Charles T. and Ardelia H. (Hull)
       Straight.
iii.   James Henry, b. 18 May 1876; d. in November 1870.
iv.   Henry Bush, b. 12 Oct. 1878; d. in August 1879.
v.   Henry, b. 22 Oct. 1881; d. 23 Aug. 1882.
vi.   George Franklin, b. 24 Nov. 1884.

105. ARTHUR T.[7] WILBOR (Peleg[6], Daniel[5], Daniel[4], William[3],
Samuel[2], William[1]), born in LC 17 May 1836, died in Chelsea, Mass.,
14 July 1880.
       He married 1 Jan. 1855 CHARLOTTE PECKHAM, daughter of
Dr. James D. and Harriet Byron (Brownell) Peckham, born in LC 15
May 1834, died there 17 Feb. 1900.
       Residence: LC. They lived on the West Road in district No. 2
above Taylor's Lane at the place owned in 1890 by Frank W. Simmons.

Children, born in LC:

i.   Lillian, b. 19 Feb. 1856; d. 23 May 1920; m. (1) 25 Dec. 1875 Phineas Wordell, son of Eli and Lydia Wordell, b. 20 July 1854; m. (2) William Almy, son of William m. and Geneva Almy. The first marriage ended in divorce. Phineas Wordell m. (2) Stella Ann Wilbour, daughter of Henry and Ann Eliza Wilbour.

ii.   Harriet E., b. 28 March 1861; m. 10 March 1881 Lester N. Godfrey, son of Otis S. and Susan Lawrence (Shaw) Godfrey.

106. HENRY PAGE[7] WILBOR (Benjamin[6], Daniel[5], Daniel[4], William[3], Samuel[2], William[1]), born in LC 16 Jan. 1830, died there 20 March 1908.

He married in LC 8 Nov. 1852 ANN ELIZA WILBOR, daughter of Thomas and Hannah (Shaw) Wilbor, born in LC 7 March 1833, died there 16 April 1921. They are buried in the Wilbor or Seaconnet cemetery.

Residence: LC. They lived on the east end of Shaw Road in district No. 10.

Children, born in LC and recorded there with the exception of the last:

i.   Albert Thomas, b. 15 Aug. 1853; d. 14 Sept. 1853.

ii.   Albert Thomas 2d, b. 20 Nov. 1854; d. 31 July 1867.

125. iii.   John Charles Fremoht, b. 5 Dec. 1856.

iv.   Stella Ann, b. 24 Nov. 1858; d. 7 May 1952; m. 1 Sept. 1889 Phineas Wordell, son of Eli and Lydia (Tripp) Wordell, b. 20 July 1854, d. 28 Jan. 1914.

126. v.   Henry Frank, b. 18 May 1862.

vi.   Ellis Boyden, b. 1 Nov. 1868; d. 26 Jan. 1951; m. 1 May 1909 Josephine Taylor Fields, daughter of Charles H. and Julia (Leahey) Fields, b. 18 July 1875, d. in LC 21 Oct. 1923.

107. BENJAMIN FRANKLIN[7] WILBOUR (Benjamin[6], Daniel[5], Daniel[4], William[3], Samuel[2], William[1]), born in LC 31 Oct. 1840, died there 21 Jan. 1899.

He married in Providence 24 Nov. 1886 CLARA AUGUSTA BROWNE, born 21 March 1861 in Warwick, R.I., died 27 Feb. 1913 in Nashua, N.H. She was the daughter of Warren Bradford Knowles[8] Browne (Thomas[7], Benjamin[6], Jeremiah[5], Jeremiah[4], Samuel[3], Jeremiah[2], Chad[1]) and Maria Augusta (Bates) Browne.

Residence: LC. They lived in district No. 2 on the west side of the Main West Road on the Col. Benjamin Church place.

Children, born in LC and recorded there:

i.   Benjamin Franklin, b. 8 Sept. 1887; d. in Providence 18 July 1964.

127. ii.   Louise Retan, b. 30 Nov. 1891.

iii.   Ernest Warren, b. 9 July 1895; d. 13 May 1922 in Rutland, Mass.

CLARA BROWNE WILBOUR   BENJAMIN F. WILBOUR JR.
      1861 - 1913   1840 - 1899

BENJAMIN FRANKLIN
WILBOUR 3rd
born 8 September 1887

108. DANIEL[7] WILBOR (Daniel[6], Daniel[5], Daniel[4], William[3], Samuel[2], William[1]), born in LC 3 April 1838, died there 14 Sept. 1909.
He married first in LC 20 Dec. 1863 PHEBE E. GRINNELL, daughter of Benjamin and Lydia (Head) Grinnell, born in LC 17 Dec. 1834, died 2 April 1880. He married second 7 Nov. 1882 HANNAH B. SOWLE, daughter of Jethro and Mary (Grinnell) Sowle, born 1 Dec. 1856, died in LC 21 Nov. 1948. All are buried in the New Wilbor or Seaconnet cemetery.
Residence: LC. They lived in district No. 1 on both sides of Main Road.

Children by first wife, born in LC:
i.   Eleanor Maria, b. 8 April 1866; m. 25 May 1890 Louis K. Pierce, son of George and Julia Pierce, b. in 1868, d. in 1925.

Children by second wife:
ii.   Ethel May, b. 10 May 1889; d. in March 1924; m. 19 April 1907 Elliot R. Snell, son of George V. and Mora (Mosher) Snell, b. in 1884, d. in LC 12 Sept. 1933.
iii. Theodora Millicent, b. 4 Nov. 1895; m. 16 Dec. 1928 Rufus Brightman Peckham, son of Rufus Frank and Esther Idella (Hambly) Peckham, b. 1 June 1894.
iv. Daniel, b. 13 Nov. 1898.

109. WILLIAM FRANKLIN[7] WILBOUR (Daniel[6], Daniel[5], Daniel[4], William[3], Samuel[2], William[1]), born in LC 19 March 1852, died in Tiverton 9 Aug. 1929. Residence: LC and Tiverton.
He married in LC 23 Oct. 1879 BRUNETTE SANFORD HATHAWAY, daughter of William Henry and Adeline (Peets) Hathaway, born 24 March 1856.

Children:
i.   Daniel Nelson, b. 28 Feb. 1881; d. 7 Jan. 1910.
ii.   Addie Lincoln, b. 10 Jan. 1884; d. 18 June 1885.
iii. Addie Lincoln 2d, b. 18 Oct. 1885; m. 23 Nov. 1905 Eugene Warren Devol, son of Julius K. and Nancy Maria (Levalley) Devol, b. 2 Sept. 1881.
iv. Fred Stevens, b. 5 Aug. 1891; d. 12 Nov. 1891.
v.   Hervey Milton, b. 19 Jan. 1894; m. Emeline Snell.
vi. Richard MacKnight, b. 13 Jan. 1898; d. 25 Oct. 1898.

110. CHARLES EDWIN[7] WILBOR (Charles[6], Philip[5], Daniel[4], William[3], Samuel[2], William[1]), born in LC 17 March 1833; died in Paris, France, 17 Dec. 1896. Residence: LC and New York City.
He married 18 Jan. 1858 CHARLOTTE BEEBE, daughter of Edmund M. and Lucinda (Bidwell) Beebe, born 2 March 1833, died in New York City 25 Dec. 1914.
He was a famous Egyptologist and went to Egypt many times for exploration. Two very large rooms at the museum of the Brooklyn (N.Y.) Institute of Art and Sciences are filled with the treasures which he found there.

Children:

    i.   Evangeline, b. 1 Sept. 1858; m. Edwin Howland Blashfield.
   ii.   Theodora, b. 11 June 1860.
  iii.   Victor Hugo, b. 21 Oct. 1861; d. 17 May 1931; unmarried.
  iv.   Zoe, b. 18 Aug. 1864; d. 4 April 1885; unmarried.

    111. PHILIP HENRY[7] WILBOR (Henry[6], Philip[5], Daniel[4], William[3], Samuel[2], William[1]), born in LC 3 Jan. 1843, died in Fall River 26 May 1918.
    He married 29 Dec. 1864 SARAH ELIZABETH WINSLOW, daughter of Luther and Sally (Wilson) Winslow, born 23 Sept. 1842, died 22 March 1921.
    Residence: LC and Fall River. He lived on the Benjamin F. Wilbour place in the north side of the house before moving to Fall River.

        Children:
    i.   Harry Dean, b. 1 Aug. 1865; m. 3 Aug. 1893 Maude Evelyn Hall, daughter of Charles H. and Ledora S. (Cowen) Hall.
   ii.   Annie Evelyn, b. 9 April 1867; m. 10 Oct. 1888 Arthur Borden Brayton, son of Israel and Abby (Manchester) Brayton, b. 4 Nov. 1874.
  iii.   Grace Elizabeth, b. 16 July 1876; m. 24 April 1902 James Harrison Wilson, son of James Hathaway and Abby Maria (Bowen) Wilson.
  iv.   Charlotte Estelle, b. 17 Dec. 1879.

    112. JOHN PARKER HALE[7] WILBOR (Henry[6], Philip[5], Daniel[4], William[3], Samuel[2], William[1]), born in LC 21 Sept. 1849, died in Providence 28 July 1894. Residence: LC and Providence.
    He married 24 Nov. 1874 HANNAH PALMER BROWNELL, daughter of James and Clarinda Richmond (Palmer) Brownell, born in LC 6 Feb. 1845, died 12 June 1926.
        Children:
    i.   Florence Hale, b. 15 Feb. 1876; m. (--) Phettiplace.
   ii.   Fannie Brownell, b. 8 March 1878.

    113. JERE BAILEY[7] WILBOR (Ezra[6], Philip[5], Daniel[4], William[3], Samuel[2], William[1]), born in LC 31 Aug. 1860, died in LC 11 Aug. 1928.
    He married 21 Nov. 1883 MARY LOUISE SNELL, daughter of Brownell and Harriet (Almy) Snell, born in LC 26 Dec. 1862, died in LC 27 June 1913. Both are buried in the New Wilbor or Seaconnet cemetery.
    Residence: LC, where he was for many years a postman. They lived in district number one on West Main Road, across from the U.S. Fort, Fort Church.

        Children:
128. i.   Lester Emerson, b. 30 June 1886.

    114. ISAAC CHAMPLIN[7] WILBOUR (Philip[6], Isaac[5], Charles[4], William[3], Samuel[2], William[1]), born in LC 11 May 1831, died there 9 Sept. 1899.

He married first in LC 5 Nov. 1854 DEBORAH JOSEPHINE
WILBOUR, daughter of Benjamin F. and Abby Maria (Taylor) Wilbour,
born in LC 15 July 1834, died there 26 March 1865. He married second
AMELIA FRENCH, daughter of William S. and Rebecca (Coffin) French,
born 29 Oct. 1832, died in LC 20 April 1911.

Residence: LC. They lived on the west side of Main Road in
district number 2, on the Gov. Isaac Wilbor place, bounded north on
Taylor's Lane.

Children, born in LC:
129. i.   Philip Herbert, b. 25 Aug. 1855.
     ii.   Caroline Corey, b. 7 Nov. 1859; d. 13 March 1864.
    iii.   Elizabeth Champlin, b. 28 Oct. 1862; d. 14 March 1864.
    iv.   Deborah Josephine, b. 28 April 1864; d. in Providence in
            1950; m. 26 June 1884 Frederic Marcy Patten of Boston,
            son of David and Maria Patten.

Children by second wife:
     v.   William French, b. 1 May 1874; d. 7 Feb. 1937; m. 27 Dec.
            1906 Gertrude Holmes, daughter of John Holmes.

115. WILLIAM BROWN[7] WILBOR (Abraham[6], George[5], John[4],
Isaac[3], Samuel[2], William[1]), born in LC 10 Aug. 1827, died in South
Boston, Mass., 24 Oct. 1919.

He married 6 Jan. 1853 HANNAH BROWN WILBOR, daughter of
Walter and Lydia (Irish) Wilbor, born 13 April 1831, died in LC 29
Aug. 1922. They are buried in the Wilbor cemetery south of the Commons.

Residence: LC. They lived in the house on the Commons at the
corner of the road south of the Commons. He went to California in 1949
and brought back with him a flag with a bear on it, evidently a state flag.

Children:
     i.   Ella Louise, b. 2 Oct. 1854; d. 13 May 1922; m. 2 Oct. 1894
            Samuel W. Wileman, son of Samuel and Elizabeth (Wads-
            worth) Wileman.
130. ii.   George Walter, b. 17 Jan. 1856.
    iii.   William Champlin, b. 30 June 1859; d. 20 Nov. 1861.
    iv.   Fannie Winnifred, b. 21 July 1866; d. 6 Oct. 1871.
     v.   Florence Brown, b. 15 July 1875; m. 28 Oct. 1896 Joseph
            John Heath Oldfield, son of Joseph and Betsey Heath
            (Webb) Oldfield.

116. SAMUEL O.[7] WILBOR (Robert[6], William[5], Samuel[4], Isaac[3],
Samuel[2], William[1]), born in LC 24 Feb. 1830, died there 30 Dec. 1901,
buried in Pleasant View cemetery.

He married in LC 6 Aug. 1854 MARY ANN SHAW, daughter of
Jediah and Rhoda (Slocum) Shaw, born 7 June 1827, died in LC 30 Nov.
1891.

Residence: LC. They lived on the road running from Swamp
Road to the South Shore, the place facing the end of Shaw Road.

Children, born in LC:
     i.   Otis A., b. 25 May 1855; d. 26 May 1855.
    ii.   Harriet Letitia, b. 3 May 1859; d. 23 Oct. 1920; m. 28

March 1896 Benajah B. Gray, son of Joseph and
Deborah (Borden) Gray.

117. OLIVER C.[7] WILBOR (John[6], Wright[5], Brownell[4], Isaac[3],
Samuel[2], William[1]), born in LC 20 Feb. 1843, died there 5 March
1913.
     He married 2 Jan. 1864 MARY ANN FIELD, daughter of Henry
and Ann (Slocum) Field, born in Westport 14 Feb. 1842, died in LC
20 Dec. 1915.
     Residence: LC. They lived in the east part of town on Amesbury
Lane where the William Wilbor, Woodman cemetery is situated.

            Children, born in LC:
      i.   Lizzie Norah, b. 6 Nov. 1865; d. 11 Dec. 1926; m. 28 Oct.
            1889 Ernest L. Manchester, son of Silvester and Harriet
            Newell (Tripp) Manchester.
131. ii.   John Henry, b. 15 May 1867.
      iii. William Hazard, b. 17 Nov. 1870 in LC; d. there 9 Aug.
            1929; m. 25 Sept. 1898 Nellie Fuller Potter, daughter of
            George Morey and Hannah (Wilbor) Potter, b. in LC 17
            Sept. 1876, d. 30 July 1943.
      iv.   Frederick Clark, b. in September 1874; m. 31 Dec. 1905
            Martha Agnes Fraits, daughter of Emanuel Warren and
            Mary (Shorrocks) Fraits.

118. MARY ELLA[8] WILBOR (Solomon[7], Nathan[6], William[5],
William[4], William[3], Joseph[2], William[1]), born in LC 31 July 1852.
Residence: LC.
     She married 27 Feb. 1871 JOHN E. SOULE, son of Ephraim and
Lydia (Palmer) Soule, born 25 Dec. 1840, died 12 Dec. 1916.

            Children, born in LC:
      i.   Lydia Esther, b. 10 Aug. 1871; d. 23 March 1933; m. James
            E. Pearce.
      ii.   George Walter, b. 28 May 1877; m. (1) 9 May 1906 Mary
            Louise Brownell, daughter of Robert G. and Mary Etta
            (Palmer) Brownell, b. 8 Feb. 1878, d. 1 Jan. 1934; m.
            (2) 16 Dec. 1935 Mabel Frances Crandall, daughter of
            Charles S. and Minnie (Alger) Crandall, b. 24 Dec. 1891.

119. NATHAN ANDREW[8] WILBOR (Solomon[7], Nathan[6], William[5],
William[4], William[3], Joseph[2], William[1]), born in LC 17 March 1854,
died there 28 Feb. 1935.
     He married in LC 30 April 1891 CARRIE EMMA ROGERS, daughter
of Wilbor and Carrie (Shaw) Rogers, born in 1876.
     Residence: LC. They lived in the east part of town, on the road
that goes south from Pottersville to Westport.

            Children, born in LC:
      i.   Child, b. in November 1891; d. in November 1891.
      ii.   Esther, b. 6 Dec. 1892; d. 11 Aug. 1895.
135. iii. Nathan Andrew, b. 19 June 1896.
      iv.   Josephine, b. 15 June 1898.

120. DAVID W.[8] WILBOR (David[7], David[6], Hezekiah[5], William[4], William[3], Joseph[2], William[1]), born in Tiverton 6 April 1845, died in LC 16 Sept. 1922.

He married in Tiverton 17 Feb. 1870 ABBIE F. DYER, daughter of John and Hannah (Wilbor) Dyer, born 13 April 1839, died in LC 2 Dec. 1919. Both are buried in the New Wilbor or Seaconnet cemetery.

Residence: LC. They lived on the south side of Taylor's Lane in district No. 2, on the Isaac C. Wilbour place.

Children, born in LC:
i. Ernest L., b. 25 Dec. 1870; d. 29 Dec. 1870.
ii. Daughter, b. 1 June 1872; d. same day.
iii. Minnie Louisa, b. 7 March 1874; d. 4 Jan. 1885.

121. ARTHUR EVERETT[8] WILBOR (George Henry[7], Hezekiah[6], Hezekiah[5], William[4], William[3], Joseph[2], William[1]), born 24 Oct. 1881 in LC, died there 25 April 1946. Through his mother, Georgianna[8] (Wilbor) Wilbor, he was a descendant of Thomas[7], Thomas[6], Aaron[5], John[4], John[3], John[2], William[1].

He married 24 Oct. 1907 ANNIE ELLEN SOWLE, daughter of Samuel Palmer and Ellen (Crosby) Sowle, born in LC 5 April 1888. Residence: LC.

Children:
i. Irving Sowle, b. 4 June 1910; d. in LC in 1954; m. 8 Sept. 1934 Bessie Ella Grinnell, adopted daughter of Herbert A. and Lena (Gifford) Grinnell, and daughter of Allen Francis and Mabel (Fisher) Vickers, b. in Smithfield, R.I., 5 Jan. 1913.

122. STEPHEN BROWNELL[8] WILBOR (Stephen[7], James[6], Thomas[5], Aaron[4], John[3], John[2], William[1]), born in Fall River 11 May 1878, died in Cranston 18 Dec. 1941. Residence: LC.

He married in LC 26 Feb. 1898 SARAH ELIZABETH FIELD, daughter of Samuel Slocum and Elizabeth (Mosher) Field, born in LC 7 Nov. 1878, died 20 Nov. 1942 in LC.

Children:
133. i. Bernard Clinton, b. 12 July 1899.
ii. Mabel Irene, b. 17 Aug. 1900; m. (--) Burke.
134. iii. Ernest Carlton, b. 20 Nov. 1903.
135. iv. Kenneth Earl, b. 22 July 1909.

123. EVERETT LEANDER[8] WILBOR (Charles[7], James[6], Thomas[5], Aaron[4], John[3], John[2], William[1]), born in LC 21 Dec. 1887. Residence: LC and New Bedford.

He married 31 Aug. 1911 ADELLA L. LaPLANTE, daughter of Alphonso LePlante.

Children:
i. Douglas Leander, b. 29 July 1912.

124. CHARLES RICHMOND[8] WILBOR (Ichabod[7], William[6], Jonathan[5], William[4], William[3], Samuel[2], William[1]), born in LC 3

Oct. 1858, died there 9 Oct. 1914, buried in Pleasant View cemetery.
He married first 2 Jan. 1878 ESTELLA MARIA PEARCE,
daughter of Rouse and Comfort Maria Pearce, born 9 June 1858, died
in LC 27 Aug. 1884. He married second 7 March 1889 NANCY ANN
PEARCE, daughter of Joseph and Phebe (Pearce) Pearce, born in LC
15 May 1856, died there 20 Sept. 1938.

He lived on Maple Avenue on the west side of the road. He afterwards moved to the Commons and started a grocery business there,
which was later run by his son and daughter. It has been the main
grocery store in town for many years.

Children by first wife, recorded in LC:
i.   Arthur C., b. in LC 18 Sept. 1879.

Children by second wife, recorded in LC:
ii.   Ida Pearce, b. in LC 28 Jan. 1893; m. Frederick Smith.

125. JOHN CHARLES FREMONT[8] WILBOR (Henry[7], Benjamin[6],
Daniel[5], Daniel[4], William[3], Samuel[2], William[1]), born in LC 5 Dec.
1856, died there 19 Nov. 1936.
He married 28 April 1881 EMMA WESTON CHESSMAN, daughter
of John W. and Lizzie Amelia (Simmington) Chessman, born 10 Sept.
1858 in Hingham, Mass., died in LC 11 Feb. 1950. They are buried in
the Seaconnet cemetery.

Children, born in LC and recorded there:
i.   Herbert Francis, b. 12 Sept. 1884; m. 16 May 1913 Edith
       J. Webber, daughter of William L. and Edith (Cook)
       Wilbor, b. in 1882. They had two children, Francis W.,
       b. in 1914, d. 19 Aug. 1933; and a son, b. 2 Feb. 1922,
       d. same day.
ii.   Pearl Louise, b. 15 Jan. 1886; m. 24 June 1908 Francis
       Henry Hatton, son of Francis and Jane Hatton, b. 28
       July 1872.
iii.   LeRoy Chessman, b. 30 Aug. 1887.

126. HENRY FRANK[8] WILBOR (Henry[7], Benjamin[6], Daniel[5],
Daniel[4], William[3], Samuel[2], William[1]), born in LC 18 May 1862, died
in Pawtuxet, R.I., 15 March 1931.
He married 31 Oct. 1881 SARAH AGNES ROBERTSON, daughter
of George and Sarah (Brayton) Robertson, born 30 Aug. 1864, died 12
May 1926.
Residence: Adamsville and Pawtuxet. They lived on the north
side of the main road in Adamsville, the next place north of the Manchester store.

Children:
i.   Viola Ellis, b. 5 June 1882; d. 27 Aug. 1917.
136. ii. Benjamin Franklin, b. 9 Sept. 1884.

127. LOUISE RETAN[8] WILBOUR (Benjamin[7], Benjamin[6], Daniel[5],
Daniel[4], William[3], Samuel[2], William[1]), born in LC 30 Nov. 1891. Resi-
dence: Manchester, N.H.
She married in Corcord, N.H., 4 Oct. 1913 JOHN GUY NELSON,

son of Will Frank and Martha Jane (Thompson) Nelson, born in Rutland,
Vt., 18 July 1889.

Children (Nelson) born in Manchester, N.H.:
137. i.   Vivian Wilbour, b. 25 Sept. 1915; m. 4 Oct. 1938 Frederick
            Albert Wiese, son of John Philip and Louise Fredericka
            (Hendricks) Wiese, b. 24 Sept. 1908.
138. ii.   John Guy Jr., b. 24 Aug. 1916; m. 29 Oct. 1944 in San
            Francisco, Calif., Jean Kathryn Pinckney.
139. iii. Priscilla Alden, b. 14 May 1922; m. Robert Mason Estes,
            son of James M. and Margaret (Sullivan) Estes.

128. LESTER EMERSON[8] WILBOR (Jere[7], Ezra[6], Philip[5],
Daniel[4], William[3], Samuel[2], William[1]), born in LC 30 June 1886, died
6 Jan. 1945.
      He married in LC 2 Oct. 1907 LILLIAN ALICE DUNBAR, born
3 Nov. 1885.
      Residence: LC. They lived on the West Main Road in district
No. 1 on the place then owned by his father. He was Little Compton
town clerk for many years.

Children:
      i.   Philip Brownell, b. 14 Nov. 1915; m. in LC 25 June 1944
            Jacqueline Lorraine Manchester, daughter of Ronald A.
            and Florence T. Manchester.
      ii.   Lois, b. 2 Dec. 1918; m. Leonard Sylvia.

129. PHILIP HERBERT[8] WILBOR (Isaac[7], Philip[6], Isaac[5],
Charles[4], William[3], Samuel[2], William[1]), born in LC 25 Aug. 1855,
died there 3 Dec. 1933.
      He married 6 May 1885 GRACE FRANCES ROPES, daughter
of Ripley and Elizabeth (Graves) Ropes, born in Salem, Mass., 13
June 1848, died in LC 17 April 1925.
      Residence: LC. They lived on the place which once belonged
to his great great grandfather, Governor Isaac Wilbor, and belonged
to his father, Isaac C. Wilbor, in 1890.

Children, born in LC:
140. i.   Lincoln Ropes, b. 8 March 1886.
      ii.   Elizabeth Champlain, b. 22 March 1887; d. in March
            1888.
141. iii. Dorothy, b. 1 Jan. 1891.

130. GEORGE WALTER[8] WILBOR (William[7], Abraham[6], George[5],
John[4], Isaac[3], Samuel[2], William[1]), born in Wareham, Mass., 17 Jan.
1856.
      He married first 26 Sept. 1878 MARIA LOUISA MABERN, daughter
of James and Amanda (Macomber) Mabern, born 8 April 1856, died 12
Jan. 1898. He married second 18 Dec. 1907 HARRIET MERRIMAN
(BRYANT) NILES, daughter of Foster B. and Sarah (Burrows) Bryant,
born 8 May 1856, died 22 June 1918.

Children by first wife:
      i.   William James, b. 13 Sept. 1879; m. 4 June 1902 Bridie

Josephine Horan.
ii.   Alice Randall, b. 5 Sept. 1886; d. 2 May 1887.
iii.   Mildred Beatrice, b. 18 June 1894; d. 9 Sept. 1895.

131. JOHN HENRY[8] WILBOR (Oliver[7], John[6], Wright[5], Brownell[4], Isaac[3], Samuel[2], William[1]), born 15 May 1867, died 26 Jan. 1934. Residence: LC and Westport.

He married 8 Nov. 1889 LEILA E. BANNON, daughter of Alexander and Nancy Bannon.

Children:
i.   Alice Gertrude, b. 8 March 1890; m. 12 April 1908 Albert
        J. Jennings, son of Gilbert M. and Harriet (Gifford)
        Jennings.
ii.   Harriet Mildred, b. 11 Sept. 1891; m. 19 Sept. 1916 Albert
        M. Chase.
iii.   Ethel May, b. 2 May 1894; m. 5 July 1915 Harold A. White,
        son of Harry and Geneva (Higby) White.
iv.   Luella Gray, b. 1 March 1897; m. 29 March 1919 Joseph
        Sawyer Field.
v.   Edna Louisa, b. 25 Aug. 1898; m. 28 Nov. 1918 James Smith.
vi.   Viola Elizabeth, b. 29 Oct. 1902; m. 17 Nov. 1920 Floyd R.
        Purcells.
142. vii.   John Henry Jr., b. 11 Aug. 1905.
viii.   Doris Leila, b. 24 Oct. 1907; m. 23 Jan. 1929 Charles L.
        Dwelly, son of LeRoy E. and Annie (Dutton) Dwelly.
ix.   Marian Barrows, b. 5 Sept. 1910; m. 25 May 1929 Joshua
        Wimer Gifford, son of Charles H. and Grace (Wimer)
        Gifford.
x.   Prescott Linwood, m. Elizabeth N. Smith, daughter of
        Charles and Eva (Nimer) Smith.

132. NATHAN ANDREW[10] WILBOR JR. (Nathan[9], Solomon[8], Nathan[7], William[6], William[5], William[4], William[3], Joseph[2], William[1]), born 19 June 1896. Residence: LC.

He married first 1 June 1920 MAY ISABEL BARKER, daughter of Henry F. and Florence (Harrington) Barker, born in Newport 20 July 1900. He married second in Tiverton 9 Sept. 1941 BLANCHE ARDELIA WORDELL, daughter of LeRoy H. and Ethel (Palmer) Wordell, born 11 Dec. 1916.

Children by first wife, recorded in LC:
i.   Florence E., b. in Fall River 12 June 1923.
ii.   Nathan A. 3d, b. in Fall River 25 July 1930.

Children by second wife:
iii.   Faith E., b. in Providence 16 May 1949.

133. BERNARD CLINTON[9] WILBOR (Stephen[8], Stephen[7], James[6], Thomas[5], Aaron[4], John[3], John[2], William[1]), born in LC 12 July 1899. Residence: LC.

He married JANET GOODWIN, born 27 Dec. 1902.

Children:

-766-

i.   Bernard Jr., b. 30 May 1924 in Fall River; m. there 14
      Sept. 1946 Elizabeth Jeanette Wordell, daughter of Sidney
      M. and Charlotte (Sisson) Wordell, b. in Fall River 12
      Jan. 1925.
ii.   Paul, b. 19 July 1925; m. in Fall River Frances Elizabeth
      Wildes of LC, daughter of Theodore B. and Inez (Shaw)
      Wildes.

134. ERNEST CARLTON[9] WILBER (Stephen[8], Stephen[7], James[6],
Thomas[5], Aaron[4], John[3], John[2], William[1]), born in LC 20 Nov. 1903.
Residence: LC.
    He married there 27 April 1932 ELIZABETH LEWIS, daughter of
Manuel M. and Mary (Monis) Lewis, born in 1910.

      Children, recorded in LC:
i.   Caroll Elizabeth, b. in Fall River 11 Oct. 1939.
ii.   Carolyn J., b. in Fall River 30 Nov. 1941.

135. KENNETH EARL[9] WILBER (Stephen[8], Stephen[7], James[6],
Thomas[5], Aaron[4], John[3], John[2], William[1]), born 22 July 1909.
    He married 23 April 1932 LOUISE STELLA CARTER, daughter
of (--) and Edith S. Carter.

      Children:
i.   Kenneth Earl Jr., b. in Fall River 5 April 1933; m. Beverly
      Ann Sylvia, daughter of John L. and Merle (Mosher)
      Sylvia, b. in Fall River 6 June 1935. Residence: LC.
      They had one child, a daughter named Sandra Lee, b.
      in Fall River 7 Aug. 1953.

136. BENJAMIN FRANKLIN[9] WILBOR (Henry[8], Henry[7], Benjamin[6],
Daniel[5], Daniel[4], William[3], Samuel[2], William[1]), born in LC 9 Sept. 1884.
Residence: LC and Pawtuxet, R.I.
    He married 8 Jan. 1910 CAROLINE STOCKARD, daughter of James
Munroe and Caroline Stockard, born in 1884.

      Children:
i.   James Munroe, b. 24 Nov. 1910.
ii.   Vera Olive, b. 26 March 1912; m. 17 April 1937 David
      Frank Plumb, son of George C. and Marjorie (Scott)
      Plumb, b. 26 Aug. 1911.
iii. Sarah Roberton, b. 10 Feb. 1914; m. 18 Jan. 1936 George
      Herbert Goff, son of George Herbert and Anna (Lager-
      quist) Goff.
iv.   Benjamin Franklin, b. 16 Feb. 1922.

137. VIVIAN WILBOUR[9] NELSON (Louise R.[8] Wilbour, Benjamin[7],
Benjamin[6], Daniel[5], Daniel[4], William[3], Samuel[2], William[1]), born in
Manchester, N.H., 25 Sept. 1914. Residence: New Haven and Branford,
Conn.
    She married in Manchester 4 Oct. 1948 FREDERICK ALBERT WIESE,
son of John Philip and Louise Fredericka (Hendricks) Wiese, born 24
Sept. 1908.

Children (Wiese):
i.   Frederick Albert Jr., b. 22 April 1940.
ii.   Thomas Nelson, b. 22 March 1942.
iii. Carl Hendricks, b. 13 Sept. 1946.
iv.   Martha Thompson, b. 11 May 1948.
v.   Katharine Wilbour, b. 4 July 1950.
vi.   Richard Nelson, b. 27 Jan. 1953.

138. JOHN GUY[9] NELSON JR. (Louise R.[8] Wilbour, Benjamin[7],
Benjamin[6], Daniel[5], Daniel[4], William[3], Samuel[2], William[1]), residence:
Manchester, N.H.
    He married in San Francisco, Calif., 29 Oct. 1944 JEAN KATHRYN
PINCKNEY, daughter of Victor Harland Pinckney.

        Children, born in Manchester, N.H.:
i.   John Pinckney, b. 2 Oct. 1946.
ii.   Judith Wilbour, b. 1 April 1951.

139. PRISCILLA ALDEN[9] NELSON (Louise R.[8] Wilbour, Benjamin[7],
Benjamin[6], Daniel[5], Daniel[4], William[3], Samuel[2], William[1]), born in
Manchester, N.H., 14 May 1922. Residence: Manchester, Syracuse,
N.Y., and Fayetteville, N.Y.
    She married in Manchester 2 March 1947 ROBERT MASON ESTES,
son of James M. and Margaret (Sullivan) Estes of Manchester.
        Children:
i.   Mark Wilbour, b. 3 Aug. 1948.
ii.   Peter Mason, b. 26 May 1950.
iii. Carolyn Louise, b. 21 Jan. 1952.

140. LINCOLN ROPES[9] WILBOUR (Philip[8], Isaac[7], Philip[6],
Isaac[5], Charles[4], William[3], Samuel[2], William[1]), born in LC 8 March
1886. Residence: LC.
    He married 25 Nov. 1916 VICTORIA MAE WRIGHT, daughter
of George and Mary (Bolton) Wright.

        Children:
i.   Barbara, b. in New Bedford 2 Oct. 1918; m. 2 June 1940
      Roger Miller Wescott, son of Charles H. and Merriam
      (Thurston) Wescott, b. in Providence 25 Nov. 1916.
ii.   Grace Ellen, b. 8 Dec. 1920.
iii. Isaac Champlin, b. 15 Sept. 1923.
iv.   Waldo Ladd, b. 21 June 1929; d. young.

141. DOROTHY[9] WILBOUR (Philip[8], Isaac[7], Philip[6], Isaac[5],
Charles[4], William[3], Samuel[2], William[1]), born in LC 1 Jan. 1891.
Residence: LC. She married in LC 14 Oct. 1916 ADELBERT ALLEN
MARTIN, son of David Frank and Sarah Ann (Macomber) Martin, born
8 April 1888.

        Children, born in LC:
i.   Philip Wilbour, b. 9 Sept. 1918; m. in July 1941 Rita
      Hickey.
ii.   Adelbert Allen, b. 7 June 1920.

iii.   David Lincoln, b. 23 Feb. 1922.

142. JOHN HENRY[9] WILBOR (John[8], Oliver[7], John[6], Wright[5], Brownell[4], Isaac[3], Samuel[2], William[1]), born in LC 11 Aug. 1905. Residence: LC.
He married 2 Sept. 1928 CHARLOTTE LOUISE KNOWLTON, daughter of Mark W. and Annie (Rogers) Knowlton, born in Franklin, Mass., in 1910.

       Children, recorded in LC:
i.   Carol Leila, b. in New Bedford 31 May 1942.

. . . .

CAROLINE WILBOUR PATTEN, daughter of Frederick Marcy Patten of Boston and Deborah Josephine[8] Wilbour (Isaac[7], Philip[6], Isaac[5], Charles[4], William[3], Samuel[2], William[1]), born in LC 6 July 1885.
She married in LC 6 Sept. 1911 EUGENE BAILEY JACKSON of Boston, son of Fran A. and Adele (Howe) Jackson, born in 1880, died in 1936.

       Children (Jackson):
i.   Patten, b. 6 June 1912; d. in 1930.
ii.   Deborah, b. 18 Aug. 1915; m. Harry McIntosh McLeed of New York.
iii.   Anthony, b. in July 1923; m. 12 May 1950 Harriet Long Millikin, daughter of Dudley Long Millikin of Needham, Mass. Residence: Darien, Conn.

DAVID PATTEN, son of Frederick Marcy Patten of Boston and Deborah Josephine[8] Wilbour (Isaac[7], Philip[6], Isaac[5], Charles[4], William[3], Samuel[2], William[1]), born in Boston 12 April 1888. Residence: LC and Barrington, R.I.
He married 1 May 1912 MARTHA LOUISE FULLER of Danvers, Mass., daughter of John Robert and Henrietta (LeNatte) Fuller, born 10 Aug. 1889.

       Children:
i.   Dora, b. 13 Sept. 1913; m. George C. Vaughan. Residence: Redding, Conn.
ii.   Henrietta, b. 11 Aug. 1916; d. 7 Sept. 1916.
iii.   Davice, d. young.

THE WILCOX FAMILY

For additional information see the Wilcox Genealogy (1943) by Herbert A. Wilcox.

1. EDWARD[1] WILCOX. He was living in Aquidneck in 1638 and in Newport in 1639. In 1680 in Kingstown, a declaration was made by Randall Holden and John Greene that prior to Richard Smith's coming to Narragansett, a Mr. Wilcox was there. Afterwards, when Mr. Smith came there, he joined in partnership with Mr. Wilcox, whereby he much augmented his estate and had no occasion to spend anything, for the Indians would not let them have any land to improve nor suffer them to keep a beast there. It is assumed that Edward is the father of Stephen and Daniel Wilcox.

Children:
- i. Stephen of Portsmouth, b. about 1633; d. before 6 Feb. 1689/ 90 in Westerly, R.I.; m. in 1658 Hannah Hazard, daughter of Thomas and Martha Hazard.
2. ii. Daniel of Punketest, b. about 1635.

2. DANIEL[2] WILCOX (Edward[1]), born about 1635, died in Tiverton 2 July 1702. Residence: Portsmouth, Dartmouth and Tiverton.
He married 28 Nov. 1661 ELIZABETH COOK, daughter of John and Sarah (Warren) Cook, died in Tiverton 6 Dec. 1715.

Children by first wife:
- i. Daniel, b. about 1656/7; d. about 1692; m. Hannah Cook, daughter of John and Mary (Borden) Cook; m. (2) Enoch Briggs.
- ii. Samuel, b. about 1659; d. before July 1697 in Dartmouth.

Children, probably by second wife:
- iii. Mary, d. 1725 (35?); m. John Earle, son of Ralph and Dorcas (Sprague) Earle.
- iv. Sarah, d. in 1751; m. Edward Briggs, son of John and Hannah (Fisher) Briggs, d. 11 May 1718.
- v. Stephen, m. (1) 9 Feb. 1695 Susannah Briggs, daughter of Thomas and Mary (Fisher) Briggs; m. (2) Judith Briggs, daughter of John and Hannah Briggs.
3. vi. John, b. in 1670.
4. vii. Edward, b. in 1676.
- viii. Thomas, d. in Tiverton in 1712; unmarried.
- ix. Lydia, d. in 1727; m. (1) 26 May 1702 Thomas Sherman, son of Peleg and Elizabeth (Lawton) Sherman; m. (2) 8 Dec. 1720 Thomas Potter.
- x. Susannah, b. in 1680; m. in LC 7 Dec. 1704 Jonathan Head of LC, son of Henry and Elizabeth Head.

3. JOHN[3] WILCOX (Daniel[2], Edward[1]), born about 1670, died in LC in 1718. Residence: LC.
He married in 1698 REBECCA MOSHER, daughter of the Rev. Hugh and Rebecca (--) Mosher. Her father was the first pastor of the

Freewill Baptist Church in Tiverton.
    Inventory of his estate was filed 21 Feb. 1717/8 by his widow
Rebecca in LC.

          Children, recorded in LC:
      i.   Jacob, b. 14 Oct. 1699.
      ii.   Daniel, b. 25 Feb. 1701.
      iii. Elizabeth, b. 13 Dec. 1702; m. 13 Nov. 1718 Joseph Tripp.
      iv. John, b. 22 Sept. 1704; m. 20 Jan. 1729 Rebecca Mosher,
           daughter of Nicholas and Elizabeth Mosher.
5.   v.   Jabez, b. 21 March 1707.
      vi. Barjona, b. 23 Nov. 1708; m. 29 March 1744 Elizabeth Wait,
           daughter of Joseph Wait.
      vii. Rebecca, b. 14 Aug. 1711; m. 20 Jan. 1729 Nicholas Mosher
           Jr.

    4. EDWARD³ WILCOX (Daniel², Edward¹), born about 1675/76;
died in Tiverton 19 May 1718. Residence: Tiverton.
    He married in 1699 SARAH MANCHESTER, daughter of William
and Mary (Cook) Manchester.

          Children, recorded in Tiverton:
6.   i.   Josiah, b. 22 Sept. 1701.
      ii.   Ephraim, b. 9 Aug. 1704; m. 28 Oct. 1729 Mary Price of LC.
      iii. William, b. 26 Dec. 1706; d. in 1767/8; m. 16 Oct. 1733
           Priscilla Peabody, daughter of William and Judith Peabody.
      iv. Freelove, b. 18 Dec. 1709.

    5. JABEZ⁴ WILCOX (John³, Daniel², Edward¹), born 21 March
1707 in LC. Residence: Dartmouth.
    He married in LC 10 May 1736 HANNAH HART of Dartmouth.

          Children, recorded in Dartmouth:
      i.   Mary, b. 23 July 1737.
      ii.   Anstris, b. 3 Sept. 1738.
      iii. Thomas, b. 10 April 1740.
      iv. Rebecca, b. 21 Feb. 1742/3.
      v.   Sarah, b. 14 Aug. 1744.
      vi. Druzilla, b. 3 May 1746.
      vii. Hulda, b. 16 May 1748.
      viii. Eunice, b. 20 March 1750.
      ix. Jabez, b. 2 July 1753.
      x.   John, b. 3 Sept. 1754.
      xi. Stephen, b. 28 April 1757.

    6. JOSIAH⁴ WILCOX (Edward³, Daniel², Edward¹), born in
Tiverton 22 Sept. 1701, died there 1 March 1772.
    He was married first about 1718 to PATIENCE BORDEN CHASE,
daughter of Benjamin and Amey (Borden) Chase, born 16 April 1699.
He married second in Portsmouth 11 March 1745 MARY LAWTON,
widow.

          Children, born in Tiverton and recorded there:
      i.   Edward, b. 29 Oct. 1719.

    ii.   Thomas, b. 19 Dec. 1720.
   iii.   Gideon, b. 17 Dec. 1722; d. 27 April 1809; m. 11 Oct. 1772
            Phebe Davenport.
    iv.   Benjamin, b. 5 July 1725; d. 3 Jan. 1726.
     v.   Daniel, b. 6 Jan. 1727.
7.   vi.   Jeremiah, b. 1 Jan. 1729.
8.   vii.   William, b. 12 Feb. 1731.
   viii.   Sarah, b. 8 Sept. 1734.

    7. JEREMIAH[5] WILCOX (Josiah[4], Edward[3], Daniel[2], Edward[1]),
born in Tiverton 1 Jan. 1729. Residence: LC.
    He married in LC 10 Nov. 1756 SARAH BAILEY, daughter of
William and Comfort (Billings) Bailey, born in LC 4 Dec. 1734.

        Children, recorded in LC:
    i.   Sarah, b. 1 June 1757.
    ii.   Josias, b. 6 Jan. 1759.
   iii.   Borden, b. 3 Feb. 1761.
    iv.   William Bailey, b. 6 May 1764.
    v.   Jeremiah, b. 5 Aug. 1767.

    8. WILLIAM[5] WILCOX (Josiah[4], Edward[3], Daniel[2], Edward[1]),
born 12 Feb. 1731, died 30 Jan. 1813.
    He married in LC 25 May 1756 BETTY HORSWELL, daughter
of Peter and Mary (--) Horswell of LC, died there 11 Nov. 1801.

        Children, born in Tiverton:
    i.   Thomas, b. 28 Aug. 1757; d. 26 May 1843; m. 8 June 1782
            Keziah Bennet, daughter of Robert and Hannah Bennet
            of Tiverton.
    ii.   Abner, b. 5 May 1761; m. 17 Nov. 1779 Comfort Brownell,
            daughter of Charles Brownell.
9.   iii.   Pardon, b. 12 Jan. 1763.
    iv.   Sally, b. 6 Nov. 1765; m. (--) Lawton.
    v.   Nancy, b. 6 Jan. 1767; m. Elisha Estes.
    vi.   Ruth, b. 6 March 1775; m. (--) Albro.
   vii.   Borden, b. 27 Jan. 1780.

    9. PARDON[6] WILCOX (William[5], Josiah[4], Edward[3], Daniel[2],
Edward[1]), born in Tiverton 9 Jan. 1763, died there 22 Nov. 1854,
probably buried in the Old Presbyterian cemetery on Lake Road.
    He married HOPE CRANSTON, born in 1767, died in Tiverton
31 Aug. 1846.
    Residence: Tiverton. He lived at Four Corners, later occupied
by Oliver Wilcox. He received a Revolutionary War pension.

        Children:
    i.   Eliza.
    ii.   Maria, m. 22 July 1827 Frederic Tabor.
   iii.   Lurana, d. in Tiverton 7 Nov. 1834.
    iv.   Abraham, b. in April 1791; m. 10 July 1817 Sarah Pearce,
            daughter of Rouse and Mary (Brownell) Pearce.
    v.   Adley.

vi.   Adley 2d, b. 14 March 1799; d. 20 April 1857; m. Sarah B.
Cook, b. 5 Dec. 1812, d. 25 July 1890.

10. vii.   Cranston, b. 19 May 1800.

viii.   Allen.

ix.   Arlington, b. 4 Sept. 1810; d. 27 March 1889; m. 15 May
1836 Mary Ann Wilcox.

10. CRANSTON[7] WILCOX (Pardon[6], William[5], Josiah[4], Edward[3],
Daniel[2], Edward[1]), born in Tiverton 19 May 1800/1, died 24 Aug. 1880.

He married 2 Sept. 1823 BETSEY COOK, daughter of Samuel
Cook, born 18 Feb. 1803, died 2 July 1862.

Residence: LC. He owned a large fleet of whaling vessels and was
master of a ship called the Maria Theressa in 1828.

Children, recorded in LC:

i.   John Cranston, b. 19 July 1825; d. 6 Jan. 1843.

ii.   Pardon Tillinghast, b. 2 June 1832; d. 2 Aug. 1855.

iii. Ann Eliza, b. 18 April 1837; d. 20 May 1852.

. . . .

CHARLES OTIS[8] WILCOX, son of Charles and Priscilla (Gray)
Wilcox, born in Tiverton 4 Oct. 1845, died in LC 15 Sept. 1914, buried
in Hillside cemetery in Tiverton. He was the son of Charles[7] (Josiah[6],
Gideon[5], Josiah[4], Edward[3], Daniel[2], Edward[1]).

He married in LC 6 Dec. 1871 ANNIE LOUISE PECKHAM,
daughter of Cyrus and Mary A. Peckham, born in April 1852 in LC,
died in November 1918.

They were not listed in the Little Compton census of 1880.

Children, born in LC:

i.   Daughter, b. 20 Oct. 1872.

ii.   Mabel Louise, b. 6 June 1875.

JOHN SYLVESTER[8] WILCOX (Oliver[7], Josiah[6], Gideon[5], Josiah[4],
Edward[3], Daniel[2], Edward[1]), born 27 Aug. 1860 in Tiverton, died there
29 March 1941. Residence: Tiverton and LC.

He married THEORA M. TINGLEY, daughter of Agreen and Mary
(Bishop) Tingley of New Brunswick, born 28 Sept. 1871.

Children:

i.   Bertha May, b. 28 June 1891 in Tiverton.

ii.   Elsie Althea, b. 13 March 1895 in Providence.

iii. Ada Evelyn, b. 24 Aug. 1898 in Tiverton; d. 2 Aug. 1943.

iv. Alma Althea, b. 16 April 1901 in LC.

v.   Loring Sylvester, b. 11 Feb. 1904 in LC; d. 10 Feb. 1912.

vi. John Bishop, b. 22 Aug. 1907 in LC; m. (1) 16 Jan. 1938
in Harrisville, R.I., Mary Sisson, daughter of William
N. and Lidora L. (Peckham) Sisson; m. (2) 9 Feb. 1946
in LC Jeanette Mary Almy, daughter of Pardon and
Elizabeth (Carter) Almy; m. (3) 23 Dec. 1952 in Tiverton
Eleanor (Burchard) Toon, daughter of Roswell and Edith
Russell (Church) Burchard, b. 5 Jan. 1908. These mar-
riages ended in divorce.

THOMAS WILCOX, married in LC 13 April 1740 WAIT BRIGGS.

Children, recorded in LC:
i.   Phebe, b. 27 Sept. 1740.
ii.   Thomas, b. 17 Nov. 1742.
iii.   Rhoda, b. 30 Jan. 1744.

JOSEPH WILCOX, born in Tiverton in 1810, married RHODA
LAKE, born in 1812. Residence: LC.
There is record of a Joseph Wilcox, son of Borden Wilcox, who
died in LC 7 Feb. 1892 ae 87-7-10.

Children, recorded in the LC census of 1850:
i.   Adaliza, b. in 1832.
ii.   James, b. 18 June 1831 (?) in Tiverton; d. 7 April 1915.
iii.   Mary A., b. in 1838.
iv.   Joseph A., b. in Tiverton 21 Dec. 1840; d. 31 May 1910.
v.   John, b. in 1841.
vi.   William A., b. in 1843.
vii.   Anson, b. in 1850; d. in LC 27 Dec. 1903.

HORACE WILCOX, son of Peleg and Lydia (Tabor) Wilcox,
born in Tiverton 12 March 1824, died in LC 6 Sept. 1902. He was
living in LC at the time of the 1880 census taking.
He married PHEBE LEMUNYON, daughter of Arowitt and Phebe
(Manchester) Lemunyon, born in Tiverton 15 Oct. 1828, died in LC
3 Sept. 1906.

Children, only two recorded in LC:
i.   Herbert, b. 15 April 1855.
ii.   Mary W. or M., b. 21 Aug. 1857.
iii.   Foster (?) H.
iv.   Luther, b. in 1865.
v.   Arthur, b. in 1867.
vi.   Winnifred, b. in 1871; m. in LC 21 March 1892 Susan
        Florence Manchester, daughter of Owen and Sarah
        (Borden) Manchester.

WILLIAM ALBERT WILCOX, born in 1845, married EMELIN
L. SIMMONS, born in 1854. Residence: LC.

Children, all recorded in LC except one:
i.   Sarah E., b. 30 Aug. 1873.
ii.   Mary, b. 1 Sept. 1875.
iii.   William, b. in 1876.
iv.   Harry Philip, b. 15 Sept. 1884.

乀◉ᴖ

THE WILKIE FAMILY

JACOB WILKIE, born about 1669.

> Children, recorded in LC:
> i.   Thomas, b. 20 Feb. 1695.
> ii.   Jeremiah, b. 12 March 1697.
> iii. Thompson, b. 2 June 1699.
> iv.   Elizabeth, b. 2 April 1701.
> v.   Joan, b. in March 1703.
> vi.   Jacob, b. 2 March 1705.

BENJAMIN FRANKLIN WILKIE, son of William and Lucy Wilkie, born in Tiverton 25 March 1864, died in LC 27 June 1917. Residence: LC.

He married first ROSE M. KNOWLTON, daughter of Jackson and Catherine (Bowen) Knowlton, born in Rockport, Mass., 6 Dec. 1868, died in LC 9 April 1904. He married second in Westport 4 Feb. 1906 ADDIE BORDEN KIRBY, daughter of Pardon F. and Clarrissa (Hartwell) Kirby, born in 1890.

> Children by first wife:
> i.   Frank Lewis, b. 26 Aug. 1889 in Tiverton; m. 16 April 1911 in Providence Mary Catherine McDonald, daughter of Patrick and Margaret (Donnelly) McDonald, b. 7 Dec. 1889 in Roscommon, Ireland.
> ii.   Ernest H., b. in 1890; d. in LC in 1891.
> iii. Edna S., b. in 1892; d. in LC 29 Dec. 1898.
> iv.   LeRoy Harland, b. 20 Dec. 1893.
> v.   Alvin Knowlton, b. in LC 18 Dec. 1895; m. (1) 25 Oct. 1919 in LC Zoe Wilbour Cornell of Fall River, daughter of Joseph Edward and Henrietta (Tallman) Cornell, b. in Fall River 8 March 1886, d. in Cranston 3 May 1943; m. (2) in LC 27 June 1943 Eunice Helen Kaye, daughter of John Ward and Annie (Kirby) Kaye, b. in February 1911.
> vi.   Catherine, b. in LC 20 June 1900.
> vii. Lillian A., m. George Albert Davol, son of George A. and Cornelia Frances (Hitt) Davol.
> viii. Jessie Louise, b. 27 Aug. 1901 in LC; d. there 2 March 1903.
> ix.   Kenneth Jackson, b. in LC 20 Nov. 1902.
>
> Children by second wife:
> x.   Ernest, b. 20 Sept. 1907.
> xi.   Chester Raymond, b. 14 Oct. 1909.
> xii. Irving Benjamin, b. 30 Jan. 1912.
> xiii. Adelbert Earl, b. 7 Oct. 1915.
> xiv. Myrtle Annie, b. 13 May 1917.

CHESTER R. WILKIE, married INEZ CORNELL. Residence: LC.

> Children, recorded in LC:
> i.   Carlton, b. in Fall River 30 Sept. 1943.
> ii.   Caroline, b. in Fall River 30 Sept. 1943.

THE WILLISTON FAMILY

1. JOHN[1] WILLISTON. Residence: Boston and Milton, Mass.
He married in Milton 9 June 1676 ABIGAIL SALISBURY, probably the
daughter of William and Susannah Salisbury of Dorchester, born in 1651,
died in LC 15 Aug. 1736. She is buried in the Old Commons cemetery.

		Children, recorded in Milton, Mass.:
2.	i.	Ichabod, b. 16 Feb. 1676/7.
	ii.	William, b. 31 July 1679.
	iii.	Ebenezer, b. 12 Feb. 1681.
	iv.	Susannah, b. 16 Sept. 1684.

2. ICHABOD[2] WILLISTON (John[1]), born in Milton, Mass., 16
Feb. 1676, died in LC 11 Oct. 1736. Residence: Boston and LC.
He married in LC in August 1704 DOROTHY GARDNER, born
in 1679, died 11 Aug. 1764. They are buried in the Old Commons
cemetery.
Inventory of his estate, recorded book 8 Taunton Probate: Books
and spectacles 3-19-0. Indian servant boy 16 pounds. Pew in meeting
house ten pounds. Dwelling house with land 300 pounds. Farm in the
woods with housing and outhousing 600 pounds. Total inventory: 4114-
13-8.

		Children, recorded in Boston and LC:
	i.	Ruth, b. 16 Nov. 1700 in Boston; m. in LC 21 Jan. 1726 Robert Carter.
3.	ii.	John, b. 7 Sept. 1702.
	iii.	Dorothy, b. in Boston 11 Sept. 1707.
	iv.	Joseph, b. in LC 11 Aug. 1709.
	v.	Abigail, b. in LC 9 July 1713; m. there 28 July 1734 Thomas Stoddard.
	vi.	Phebe, b. in LC 10 May 1716; m. there 11 Sept. 1737 Ebenezer Vose.
	vii.	Susanna, b. in LC 28 March 1721; d. there 15 Nov. 1816; m. there in September 1739 Jacob Burgess, son of Thomas and Martha (Closson) Burgess.

3. JOHN[3] WILLISTON (Ichabod[2], John[1]), born in Boston 7 Sept.
1702.
He was married in LC 27 Aug. 1730 by Richard Billings, justice,
to HANNAH SAWYER of Tiverton, daughter of Josiah and Martha
(Seabury) Sawyer, born in Tiverton 27 Nov. 1710.

		Children, first two recorded in LC:
	i.	Seabury, b. 27 July 1731; d. in LC 14 Aug. 1733.
	ii.	Lucretia, b. 2 April 1732.
	iii.	Judith, b. in May 1733; d. in 1806.

တၛၟ

THE WIMER FAMILY

1. JACOB NOAH WIMER, son of Valentine and Hannah (Brooks) Wimer, born in Wisconsin 4 July 1858, died in LC 25 April 1935. Residence: LC.

He married there 25 Nov. 1884 GEORGIANNA BARLOW, daughter of William and Ellen Barlow, born in Fall River in 1867, died in LC 11 March 1920, buried in Pleasant View cemetery.

His sister, Lydia J. Wimer, born in Wisconsin in 1862, married in LC 9 Sept. 1881 Herbert E. Davis, son of Walter and Mary W. Davis, born in Westport.

Children, recorded in LC:
- i. Child, b. in LC 6 Aug. 1886.
- ii. Lillian Beatrice, b. in LC 22 Feb. 1888; m. 1 April 1909 Albert Francis Manchester, son of Albert G. and Frances (Briggs) Manchester, b. in Swansea.
- iii. Grace Florence, b. in LC 22 Feb. 1888; d. there 12 Dec. 1935; m. Charles Herbert Gifford.
- iv. Daughter, b. in LC 14 Oct. 1889.
- v. Ethel R., b. 26 April 1891; m. 22 April 1916 Bernard Milton Pearce, son of Bernard T. and Hattie (Negus) Pearce of Tiverton.
- 2. vi. Harold V., b. 8 Feb. 1894.
- vii. Vivian Louise, b. in LC 14 Nov. 1907; m. Jefferson Thomas Brooks. They had a daughter, Dorothy Ethel, born 4 Feb. 1934.

2. HAROLD V.[3] WIMER (Noah[2], Valentine[1]), born in LC 8 Feb. 1894, married MARGARET SULLIVAN. Residence: LC.

Children, recorded in LC:
- i. Catherine Theressa, b. 15 Jan. 1920 in LC; m. 11 Nov. 1947 Robert Perry Lake, son of Clement W. and Helen (Peckham) Lake.
- ii. Richard Vernon, b. in LC 1 March 1921; d. 5 May 1921.
- iii. Herbert Vernon, b. in LC 9 June 1922; m. in East Hartford, Conn., 11 Nov. 1948 Marilyn Catherine Hay, daughter of Robert H. and Helen (McCarty) Hay, b. in Providence. They had a daughter, Kathleen Anne, b. in Cranston 26 April 1950.

ೞ

THE WINSLOW FAMILY

CLARENCE EDWARD WINSLOW, son of John and Amanda F. (Buffington) Winslow, born in Fall River in 1877. Residence: LC.

He married first in LC 19 March 1906 EDITH M. DAVIS, daughter of Adelbert and Florence (Schoolcraft) Davis, born in 1890, died in LC 4 April 1909. He married second in Dartmouth BERTHA DAVIS, daughter of Adelbert and Florence (Schoolcraft) Davis, born in Masonville, Quebec. She married second in LC 25 Sept. 1927 Milton H. Wordell.

      Children by first wife:
- i.   Child, b. 14 April 1907; d. 12 May 1907.
- ii. Child, b. in LC 26 March 1909.

      Children by second wife:
- iii. Chester Alden, b. in LC 17 Aug. 1910.
- iv. Kenneth Edward, b. in LC 8 Aug. 1913.

THE WOOD FAMILY

1. JOHN[1] WOOD, died in Portsmouth in 1655. Residence: Portsmouth.

He married first (?). He married second ELIZABETH (--), died about 1655.

He died without leaving a will. Consequently on 17 March 1655 the town council chose as appraisers of his estate John Coggeshall, Thomas Cornell Jr., James Babcock and William Hall. The council disposed of the estate as follows: ". . . To John Wood land in his present possession, he paying his sister, Margaret Manchester, 8 pounds. To Thomas Wood the land that was his father's in Newport, 40 acres near William Weeden's farm. To William Wood 10 acres where widow now lives. To widow rest of land in her possession to improve for life, she paying eldest son of deceased four pounds. To two youngest children Susannah and Elizabeth eight pounds each at age 16. William Wood to have all land in the widow's possession at her decease, she being his mother-in-law (i.e. stepmother). . ."

      Children, as listed in Austin's Dictionary:
-     i.   George, untraced.
- 2. ii. John Wood Jr., b. in 1620.
- 3. iii. Thomas, b. in 1638.
- 4. iv. William, b. as early as 1640.
-     v.   Margaret, m. Thomas Manchester.
-     vi. Susanna.
-     vii. Elizabeth, m. in Swansea 5 Dec. 1677/8 Samuel Wheaton.

2. JOHN[2] WOOD JR. (John[1]), born in 1620, died in LC in 1704.

He married MARY PEABODY, daughter of John Peabody of Portsmouth. Residence: Newport.

In 1665 he was a freeman of Newport, and a deputy in 1673-4-5. In 1689 he and his wife Mary deeded to their son Thomas of LC two 50 acre lots with housing. According to the Wood Manuscript at the New England Genealogical Society, he may have been the father of Walter, Henry and William Wood of Newport.

Children:
5. i.   John, b. in 1664.
6. ii. Thomas, b. in 1666.
    iii. Jonathan.

3. COL. THOMAS² WOOD (John¹), born in 1638, died in 1703/4, married REBECCA (--). Residence: Portsmouth and Swansea. He was a freeman of Portsmouth in 1658.

Children:
i.   Thomas, b. in 1664; m. in 1690 Hannah Rider.
ii.   Abigail, b. in 1666.
iii. John, b. in 1668; m. Bethia Mason, daughter of Sampson and Mary (Butterworth) Mason.
iv. William, b. in 1670; d. 18 March 1734/5; m. Susannah Beckwith.
v.   George, b. 30 July 1679; m. Rebecca Dagget. His father deeded him land in Swansea.
7. vi. Jonathan, b. 20 Nov. 1681.
    vii. Hannah, b. 18 Feb. 1685; probably m. 1 Nov. 1715 Peter Taylor. According to the author of the Wood Manuscript she was his second wife.
    viii. Margaret, b. 1 March 1687; m. 21 May 1715 in Swansea John Page.
    ix. Sarah, b. 1 March 1687; m. 17 June 1714 John Baker. Another record says that he married Susannah Wood.

4. WILLIAM² WOOD (John¹), born as early as 1640. He married MARTHA EARLE, daughter of Ralph and Joan Earle, died 3 Feb. 1696. Residence: Dartmouth.

Children:
8. i.   William Jr., b. in 1652.
    ii. George, m. in LC 4 Dec. 1717 Ann Wilbore, daughter of Joseph and Ann (Brownell) Wilbore. Residence: Dartmouth.
    iii. Josiah, d. in 1711.
    iv. Daniel, m. (1) Elizabeth Ricketson; m. (2) Phebe Sherman.
    v.   Joseph.
    vi. John, b. in 1664; m. Mary Church, daughter of Joseph and Mary (Tucker) Church.
    vii. Mary, m. Thomas Mallets of New York.
    viii. Sarah.
    ix. Margaret.
    x.   Rebecca.

5. LT. JOHN³ WOOD (John², John¹), born in 1664, probably in
Newport, died in LC 22 Feb. 1740. Residence: LC.
   He married about 1688 MARY CHURCH, daughter of Joseph and
Mary (Tucker) Church, born about 1659, died in LC 11 Nov. 1748.
Both are buried in the Old Commons cemetery.
   On 6 April 1691 Joseph Church signed a marriage deed to John
Wood. Their farm went from the West Road to the shore along Taylor's
Lane and was one lot wide. It later became part of the farm of Isaac
C. Wilbour.
   Of their twelve children, one died in 1704 at age 11 months, and
six died in March 1711/12, when there seems to have been an epidemic.
Many people of LC died in that awful month. Another daughter died at
age 29, in 1730.

            Children, all recorded in LC:
   i.   John, b. 16 July 1689; d. 13 March 1711/12.
   ii.   Mary, b. 14 March 1691; d. 7 Oct. 1745; m. in LC 10 July
           1712 Thomas Bailey, b. in 1690, d. 4 Feb. 1741. Her
           husband is remembered for having given a silver cup
           to the church.
   iii.   Sara, b. 6 Nov. 1692; d. 8 March 1711/12.
   iv.   Deborah, b. 7 March 1694; d. 16 March 1711/12.
   v.   Margaret, b. 20 April 1696; d. 9 March 1711/12.
   vi.   Abigail, b. 26 Dec. 1697; d. 16 March 1711/12.
   vii.   Elizabeth, b. 6 Nov. 1699; d. 10 March 1712.
   viii.   Hannah, b. 7 Oct. 1701; d. 14 June 1730; m. in Bristol,
           R.I., 5 Jan. 1721 Jonathan Peck.
   ix.   Rebecca, b. 4 Nov. 1703; d. 3 Oct. 1704.
9. x.   Joseph, b. 23 Dec. 1705.
   xi.   Dorothy, b. 12 Dec. 1707; m. in LC 16 March 1727 Joseph
           Rogers.
   xii.   Thomas.

   6. THOMAS³ WOOD (John², John¹), born in 1666, died in LC 10
May 1729. He married CONTENT (--). Residence: LC.
   His will, recorded Taunton Probate, book 6, page 235, made 28
Aug. 1728 and proved 20 May 1729: ". . . To son Thomas all lands in
LC with housing thereon, all livestock, carpenter's tools . . . powdering
tubs. . . To son John 100 pounds. To daughters Elizabeth Phinney,
Content Shaw and Rebecca Shaw 5 shillings. To daughter Deliverance
Wood 20 pounds, great trunk and chest. To daughter Desire Wood 20
pounds, case of drawers and a cow. To granddaughter Content Sisson,
5 pounds. If son Thomas shall say so that John Wood my son shall have
the south 50 acres and son William Wood the north 50 acres. . . "

            Children, all recorded in LC:
   i.   Elizabeth, b. 22 May 1692; m. (--) Phinney.
   ii.   Content, b. 15 June 1694; m. William Shaw.
   iii.   Rebecca, b. 17 April 1696; m. in LC 14 Aug. 1718
           Anthony Shaw.
   iv.   Thomas, b. 26 Jan. 1698; d. in LC 20 Aug. 1729. In his
           will, recorded Taunton Probate, book 6, page 291,

made 20 Aug. 1729 and proved 16 Sept. 1729, he left
to his sister Rebecca and her husband Anthony Shaw
60 pounds of the bonds he held against them, to his
sister Desire he left two cows, to his sister Deliverence
all the brass he received from his father and two cows,
and to his brother John the rest and residue.

10.   v.   William, b. 7 Feb. 1700.
      vi.   Mary, b. 6 Feb. 1701/2; m. in LC 7 Feb. 1723 Jonathan
      .   Sisson.
      vii. Desire, b. 17 Aug. 1704; m. in LC 9 April 1732 John Irish.
11.   viii. John, b. 16 April 1707.
      ix.   Deliverance, b. 4 May 1711; m. in LC 2 June 1735 Henry
            Cuthbert.

7. JONATHAN³ WOOD (Thomas², John¹), born in Swansea 20
Nov. 1681, died in 1756 or 1759. Residence: LC.

He was married first in LC by Joseph Church, justice, 6 Jan.
1703 to ELIZABETH THURSTON, daughter of Jonathan and Sarah
Thurston of Newport, born 29 Nov. 1682, died in LC 27 Aug. 1717.
He was married second in LC 14 Aug. 1718 by Richard Billings,
justice, to ANNA CARR, daughter of Ezek and Susannah Carr, born
28 Feb. 1696, died after 1744. He left no will.

Children, all recorded in LC:
i.   Rebecca, b. 26 Dec. 1704; m. in LC 28 March 1726 Joseph
       Simmons.
ii.   Bridgett, b. 22 June 1706; m. in LC 25 Dec. 1734 Peter
       Taylor.
iii.   Elizabeth, b. 31 Jan. 1708; m. 1 April 1731 in LC Joseph
       Davenport.
iv.   Ruth, b. 7 Aug. 1710; d. 13 Aug. 17--.
v.   Susannah, b. 21 July 1712.
vi.   Jonathan Jr., b. 5 July 1714; m. in Newport 4 June 1759
       or 1769 Lydia Irish (?).
vii. Mary, b. 9 Jan. 1716; m. in LC 10 Oct. 1743 John Pitman.
viii. Margaret, b. 26 April 1719.
ix.   Ezek, b. 13 Nov. 1720; m. Sarah Tripp, daughter of Ichabod
       Tripp. Residence: Dartmouth.
x.   Job, b. 6 Dec. 1722; m. 16 Jan. 1752 Rest Gifford.
xi.   Sarah, b. 31 Jan. 1725; m. 30 Nov. 1757 Nathaniel Church.
xii. Robert, b. 4 Oct. 1727; m. in 1757 Rachel Howland, widow.
xiii. Martha, b. 1 Dec. 1729; m. in 1754 Timothy Cornell.
xiv. Hannah, m. in 1758 Joseph Allen Jr.

8. WILLIAM³ WOOD (William², John¹), born in 1652. He married
ANN CLARKE, daughter of Latham and Hannah (Wilbore) Clarke.

Children:
i.   Mary, d. in 1706.
ii.   Rachel, b. in April 1691.
iii.   William, b. in April 1691; m. (1) Elizabeth (--); m. (2)
       Keziah (--).
iv.   Hannah, b. in 1693; m. Nicholas Davis.

    v.   Isaac, m. Mary Potter.
    vi.   Jonathan, m. Peace Davis.
    vii.   Abigail.
    viii. Jedediah, m. Keziah Simmons.
    ix.   Meribah, m. (1) Moses Sherman; m. (2) John Rone (?).
    x.   Ruth, m. Abraham Stafford.
    xi.   Mary 2d, b. 7 March 1712.

    9. JOSEPH[4] WOOD ESQ. (John[3], John[2], John[1]), born in LC 23
Dec. 1705, died there 22 Jan. 1767. Residence: LC.

    He was married in LC 31 Aug. 1727 by Richard Billings, justice,
to MARY BROWNELL, daughter of George and Mary (Thurston)
Brownell, born in LC 9 Nov. 1709, died there 6 Oct. 1791. Both are
buried in the Old Commons cemetery.

    They lived on the west end of the 31st 100 acre lot of the great
lots, next north of Peter Taylor. This place was later owned by Ripley
Roaps about 1890 and is west of Main Road, near Taylor's Lane.

    His will, recorded book 2, page 88, made 16 Jan. 1767 and
proved 3 Feb. 1767: ". . . To wife Mary 1/3 of all household goods,
improvement of all buildings on my farm. To son John four 11 acre
lots on the highway that goes by William Taylor's to the sea. To son
George west end of 100 acre lot that I now live on from the highway
that crosses said lot to ye sea west and use of 1 of buildings for seven
years, he to have west end. To son Isaac east end of 100 acre lot that
I now live on from the highway that now crosses it with all buildings
when my wife ceases to be my widow. To daughters Hannah Church
and Sarah Church, 30 dollars each. To daughters Deborah Wood,
Ruth Brownell and Mary Wood, sixty dollars each. To three daughters,
Ruth, Mary and Deborah two thirds of household goods. . . "

    In her will, recorded LC Probate book 3, page 219, made 15 Nov.
1783 and proved 6 Dec. 1791, his widow left to her son John her great
Bible, to her son George her loom and all articles belonging to it,
to daughter Ruth a case of drawers, to daughter Mary a gold necklace,
to two daughters Hannah Church and Sarah Church two silver dollars
each, to son Isaac her desk and mare, and the rest and residue to her
four daughters.

           Children:
12. i.   John, b. 22 Dec. 1728.
13. ii.   George, b. 2 Nov. 1730.
     iii.   Paul, b. 19 Jan. 1733; d. 31 March 1734.
     iv.   Hannah, b. 22 Dec. 1734; d. 3 Feb. 1815; m. in LC 7 March
           1754 Ebenezer Church.
     v.   Sarah, b. 18 July 1737; d. 30 Dec. 1819; m. in LC 30 Nov.
           1757 Nathaniel Church.
     vi.   Deborah, b. 30 Nov. 1739; d. in January 1784. According to
           her gravestone, she died 25 July 1782. However, her will
           was made 15 July 1783 and proved 3 Feb. 1784. As recorded
           book 3, page 71, it reads ". . . To sister Hannah Church
           my best gown. To sister Susannah Wood my gold neck-
           lace. To brother Isaac Wood my bed and he not to take
           it until my mother's decease. To cousin Phebe Pierce,

daughter of my brother George Wood, my chest. To
sisters Hannah Church, Sarah Church, Marcy Simmons
and Deborah Brownell, ye daughter of my sister Ruth
Brownell, the rest of my wearing apparel. Rest and residue to brother Isaac Wood and he to be sole executor. . . "

vii.   Paul 2d, b. 5 Sept. 1741; d. 6 Oct. 1764.

viii.   Ruth, b. 25 Sept. 1743; m. (--) Cook or Brownell.

ix.   Mary, b. 26 Dec. 1745; d. young.

x.   Mary 2d, b. 31 Jan. 1748; m. 21 Dec. 1777 in LC Nathaniel
Simmons, son of Isaac and Mary Simmons.

14.   xi.   Isaac, b. 16 June 1752.

xii.   Rebecca, d. ae 11.

10. WILLIAM[4] WOOD (Thomas[3], John[2], John[1]), born 7 Feb. 1700.
Residence: Dartmouth.

He was married in LC 16 July 1794 by Richard Billings, justice,
to HANNAH SHAW, daughter of Israel and Ruth (?) (Tallman) Shaw,
born in LC 7 March 1699. He married second 22 June 1737 PATIENCE
(ELLIS) WING, widow.

Children by first wife, recorded in LC:

i.   Zilpha, b. 4 Aug. 1720.

ii.   Walter, b. 4 Feb. 1721; d. 14 Feb. 1726.

iii.   Antrace, b. 14 Sept. 1723; m. in 1741 Abraham Wing.
Residence: Oblong, N.Y.

iv.   Content, b. 10 Jan. 1726; m. Edward Wing. Residence:
Nine Partners, N.Y.

v.   Drucilla, b. 9 May 1729; m. Israel Howland, son of John
and Mary (Cook) Howland, b. 13 June 1713.

15.   vi.   Zerviah, b. 8 Jan. 1731.

vii.   Hannah, b. 20 Feb. 1733; m. (intention 19 Nov. 1758)
in Rochester, Mass., Caleb Mendol.

Children by second wife:

viii.   Rebecca, b. 6 Sept. 1737; d. 6 Sept. 1777; m. (intention 4
Nov. 1754) Sabathiel Eldridge.

ix.   John, b. 9 July 1742; d. before 1778; m. Sarah Russell.

11. JOHN[4] WOOD (Thomas[3], John[2], John[1]), born in LC 16 April
1707. He was married first in LC 7 May 1730 by Thomas Church,
justice, to MARY BURGESS, daughter of Thomas and Martha (Wilbor)
Burgess, born in LC 18 Sept. 1712. He was married second in LC 7
Feb. 1745 by Justice Church to SARAH HUDDLESTONE, died in LC
10 Dec. 1747. He married third JARUSHA (--).

He was a saddler. They lived on the farm owned in 1890 by
Philip Chase and George Seabury, on East of Main Road, south of
Swamp Corner.

His will, recorded LC Probate, book 3, page 180: ". . . To wife
Jarusha one cow, two small meat tubs, loom, side saddle and pillion.
To son Constant all my homestead farm with all buildings thereon. To
son Thomas six shillings. To son Jonathan land at Dartmouth I bought
of John Hunt adjoining Coaksett River and 50 dollars. To four daughters,
Martha Taylor, Abigail Irish, Mary Peckham and Avis Peckham, 16
silver dollars. Rest and residue to son Constant and he to be executor. . . "

Children, recorded in LC:
  i.   Martha, b. 28 Feb. 1731; m. in LC 19 Feb. 1751 Humphrey
       Taylor, son of John and Joanna (Wilbor) Taylor.
  ii. Abigail, b. 10 Nov. 1732; m. in LC 18 Oct. 1751 Charles
       Irish, son of John and Thankful (Wilbore) Irish.
  iii. Comfort, b. 13 Oct. 1734.
16. iv. Thomas, b. 12 April 1736.
17. v.   Constant, b. 4 July 1737.
  vi. Mary, b. 1 Feb. 1739; m. about 1760 John Peckham, son
       of Joseph and Elizabeth (Wilbor) Peckham.
  vii. Avis, b. 21 Aug. 1740; m. Samuel Peckham.
  viii. Jonathan, b. 29 Nov. 1747.
  ix. Joseph.

12. JOHN⁵ WOOD (Joseph⁴, John³, John², John¹), born 22 Dec.
1728. Residence: LC.
    He was married in LC 27 Nov. 1747 by William Hall, justice, to
EUNICE SHAW, daughter of Israel and Abigail (Palmer) Shaw, born
in LC 7 Oct. 1728, died there 13 Feb. 1810.
    They lived on, and owned, the farm which belonged to his father,
Joseph Wood, and his grandfather, John Wood. It later became part
of the Isaac Wilbour farm and bordered on Taylor's Lane.

Children, recorded in LC:
18. i.   Joseph, b. 18 May 1753.
  ii. Abigail, b. 25 Sept. 1757; m. in LC 26 Sept. 1779 Joseph
       Wilbore, son of William and Hannah (Wilbor) Wilbore.
19. iii. Benjamin, b. in LC 19 June 1760.
  iv. Meribah, b. 14 Oct. 1762.
  v.   Sarah, b. 6 May 1768.
  vi. Eunice, b. 19 Oct. 1770; m. Daniel Howland Jr.
  vii. Thirza, b. 8 March 1779.

13. GEORGE⁵ WOOD (Joseph⁴, John³, John², John¹), born in
LC 2 Nov. 1730, died there in June 1820.
    He was married first in LC 30 Dec. 1753 by Joseph Wood, justice,
to COMFORT TAYLOR, daughter of Philip and Comfort (Dennis) Taylor,
born in LC 28 May 1735. He was married second in LC 10 Feb. 1762 by
the Rev. Jonathan Ellis to DESIRE GRAY, daughter of Samuel and Hannah
(Kent) Gray, born in LC 7 July 1735, died there in March 1822.
    They lived in LC on the place that later belonged to Ripley Roaps
on the Main Road, at the west of the road, opposite the Frank Simmons
place of 1890.
    His will, recorded LC Wills, book 5, page 188, made 13 Dec.
1815 and proved 10 July 1820: ". . . To wife Desire all household furniture. To daughters Comfort Grinnell, Phebe Pearce, Sarah Barker
and Hannah Durfee, four dollars each. To daughter Lydia Seabury 20
dollars. To children of daughter Ruth Simmons, deceased, 7 dollars.
To four grandchildren, daughters of my son Gray, deceased, three
dollars each. To son John all my real and personal estate and he to be
my executor. . . "

Children by first wife, recorded in LC:

    i.   Comfort, b. 20 Aug. 1755; m. 2 March 1775 Billings
         Grinnell.

         Children by second wife:
    ii.   Phebe, b. 9 May 1763; m. in LC 3 July 1783 James Pierce.
    iii.   Sarah, b. 30/1 Dec. 1764; m. in LC 27 Nov. 1783 Hezekiah
         Barker.
    iv.   Hannah, b. 21 Nov. 1766; m. in LC 6 Feb. 1791 Gideon Dur-
         fee.
    v.   Lydia, b. 12 Dec. 1768; m. 7 Nov. 1790 in LC David Seabury.
    vi.   Ruth, b. 20 March 1771; m. in LC 29 Aug. 1791 Abel Simmons,
         son of Aaron and Abigail Simmons.
    vii. John, b. 14 Feb. 1773.
20. viii. Gray, b. 29 March 1775.

    14. ISAAC⁵ WOOD (Joseph⁴, John³, John², John¹), born in LC
16 June 1752.
    He was married in LC 21 April 1774 by the Rev. Jonathan Ellis
to SUSANNA TAYLOR, daughter of William and Deborah (Gray) Taylor,
born in LC 20 Dec. 1754.
    They lived in LC on the east of the Main Road, district number 2,
on the place owned in 1890 by Frank W. Simmons.

         Children, recorded in LC:
    i.   Comfort, b. 1 May 1775.
    ii.   Mary, b. 2 March 1778.
    iii.   Simeon, b. 10 July 1781.
    iv.   Deborah, b. 4 Dec. 1785.
    v.   Susanna, b. 4 Jan. (or July) 1788.
    vi.   Marietta, b. 30 Jan. 1791.

    15. ZERVIAH⁵ WOOD (William⁴, Thomas³, John², John¹), born
in LC 8 Jan. 1731. He married there 5 Aug. 1750 RHODA ELDREDGE.
Residence: LC.

         Children, recorded in LC:
    i.   Pearce, b. 7 Dec. 1751.
    ii.   Hannah, b. 4 May 1752; m. William Severance.
    iii.   Restcome, b. in May 1766.
    iv.   Isaiah.
    v.   Content, m. 5 June 1775 Amos Kelly.
    vi.   William, m. (intention 23 Oct. 1779) Mary Foster.
    vii. Elihue, m. Lydia Cushman.
    viii. Zerviah Jr., b. in Dartmouth 21 March 1772; d. in LC 30
         April 1862; m. in July 1798 Eunice Howland, b. 21 Sept.
         1776, d. 14 Oct. 1845.

    16. THOMAS⁵ WOOD (John⁴, Thomas³, John², John¹), born in
LC 12 April 1736. He was married there 15 May 1758 by the Rev.
Jonathan Ellis to LYDIA KIRBY. Residence: LC.

         Children, recorded in LC:
    i.   Lois, b. 6 June 1761.
    ii.   John, b. 22 June 1762.

    iii.   David, b. 12 Aug. 1764.
    iv.   Lemuel, b. 18 June 1766.
    v.   Joseph, b. 24 Nov. 1768.
    vi.   Thomas, b. 17 July 1771.
    vii. Comfort, b. 17 July 1771.

17. CONSTANT[5] WOOD (John[4], Thomas[3], John[2], John[1]), born in LC 14 July 1737. He married ELEANOR (--). Residence: LC. They lived on the Main Road south of Swamp Corner. They sold this place in 1793 to Philip Chase, and it probably became part of the George Seabury place.

    Children:
    i.   Elnathan, b. 19 Aug. 1767.
21. ii.   Mordecai, b. 15 March 1769.
    iii.   John, b. 8 June 1773.

18. JOSEPH[6] WOOD 2d (John[5], Joseph[4], John[3], John[2], John[1]), born in LC 18 May 1753.
He was married in LC 7 March 1776 by Philip Taylor, justice, to ELIZABETH CHURCH, daughter of Col. Thomas and Elizabeth Church of Bristol, R.I. Residence: LC.

    Children, recorded in LC:
    i.   Nancy, b. 6 Feb. 1777.
    ii.   Betsey, b. 8 March 1779.

19. BENJAMIN[6] WOOD (John[5], Joseph[4], John[3], John[2], John[1]), born in LC 19 June 1760. Residence: LC.
He was married 23 April 1780 by the Rev. Jonathan Ellis to SARAH TAGGART, daughter of William and Mary (Clarke) Taggart.

    Children, recorded in LC:
    i.   John, b. 17 Sept. 1780.
    ii.   William, b. 30 Aug. 1782.
    iii.   Paul, b. 22 Sept. 1784.

20. GRAY[6] WOOD (George[5], Joseph[4], John[3], John[2], John[1]), born in LC 29 March 1775, died there 17 Jan. 1808. Residence: LC.
He was married in LC 15 Dec. 1799 by the Rev. Mase Shepard to HANNAH HART, daughter of Joseph and Almy Hart, born in LC 22 March 1780.

    Children, recorded in LC:
    i.   Ruth, b. 13 Aug. 1801.
    ii.   Sarah C., b. 19 April 1803; d. in LC 9 Sept. 1855; m. there 30 Oct. 1825 Nathaniel Church, son of Joseph and Elizabeth (Taylor) Church.
    iii.   Mary Ann, b. 24 Feb. 1805; d. in LC 4 April 1885; m. there 27 April 1856 Hon. Nathaniel Church, son of Joseph Church 2d and Elizabeth (Taylor) Church.
    iv.   Hannah G., b. 6 Oct. 1807.

21. MORDECAI[6] WOOD (Constant[5], John[4], Thomas[3], John[2],

John[1]), born in LC 15 March 1769. He married there 23 Dec. 1787
MARY BAILEY, daughter of Thomas and Deborah (Carr) Bailey, born
in LC 13 July 1751.
   This family must have moved away from LC.

         Children, recorded in LC:
   i.   William, b. 11 April 1788.
   ii.   Mary, b. 22 Oct. 1790.
   iii. Lydia, b. 9 May 1793.

                 . . . .

      1. HENRY[1] WOOD. He was married in LC 14 Sept. 1715 by
Richard Billings, justice, to CONTENT THURSTON, daughter of
Jonathan and Sarah Thurston, of Newport, born 18 Aug. 1691.
      His will, recorded LC Probate, book 1, page 229, made 3 Feb.
1759 and proved 4 April 1758: ". . . To sons Henry and Peleg, my
executors, all real estate in LC. To wife Content use of whole house,
and piece of land for a garden, great looking glass, one half of pewter
. . . brass warming pan. To son Thomas 1200 pounds current money
of R.I. tenor. To daughters Sarah and Rebecca 120 pounds and the
use of the largest room in my house. . . "

         Children, recorded in LC:
2. i.   Henry Jr., b. 17 Nov. 1716.
   ii.   William, b. 7 Sept. 1720; d. 9 March 1724.
3. iii. Peleg, b. 20 March 1722.
   iv.   Sarah, b. 4 June 1726; m. in LC 31 July 1771 James Chace.
   v.   Rebecca, b. 15 Dec. 1727; d. in January 1797. In her will,
             made 10 May 1796 and proved 7 Feb. 1797, she left her
             wearing apparel and the rest and residue of her estate
             to her cousin, Ichabod Wood and his wife Elizabeth.
   vi.   Thomas, b. 3 March 1733.

      2. HENRY[2] WOOD (Henry[1]), born 17 Nov. 1716. He married
(intention 17 Aug. 1745) in LC SARAH POTTER, daughter of Ichabod
and Eleanor Potter of Dartmouth. In 1774 they were living in LC,
where he was a cordwainer.

         Children, born in LC:
4. i.   Ichabod, b. 14 March 1745.

      3. PELEG[2] WOOD (Henry[1]), born in LC 20 March 1722, died
there in January 1796.
      He was married in LC 18 Dec. 1746 by Richard Billings, justice,
to RUTH SHAW, daughter of Anthony and Rebecca (Wood) Shaw, born
29 Sept. 1723.
      He lived in LC where he was a weaver. He had received land
from his father, Henry Wood, who owned property across from
Redtop Farm.
      His will, recorded book 3, page 313, made 24 Oct. 1793 and
proved 3 Feb. 1796: ". . . To son Abner the house where he now lives.
To wife Ruth one half my household stuff, my great Bible. The other

half of my household stuff to my two sons, Reuben and Abner equally.
To son Abner all my wearing apparel. To grandson Peleg Wood a
silver spoon marked C.T. To sons Reuben and Peleg to be executors..."

Children, recorded in LC:
    i.   Elizabeth, b. 3 Oct. 1747; d. in May 1770; m. 22 Nov.
            1765 in LC Samuel Wilbore, son of Isaac and Mary
            (Brownell) Wilbore.
5. ii.   Reuben, b. 20 Feb. 1752.
6. iii.   Abner, b. 16 June 1758.

4. ICABOD³ WOOD (Henry², Henry¹), born 14 March 1745, died
in LC 4 Oct. 1817.

He married 15 March 1770 ELIZABETH BROWNELL, daughter
of Jonathan and Elizabeth (Richmond) Brownell, born in LC 12 June
1748, died there 20 Aug. 1827.

In 1790 he was living on his father's place, opposite Redtop
Farm, the next place south of John Hunt on the map of 1890. He administered his father's estate 6 Aug. 1776.

Children, recorded in LC:
    i.   Constant, b. 3 Oct. 1770.
    ii.   Content, (this maybe the Constant above) m. in LC 18 Dec.
            1791 Samuel Gray, son of Samuel and Deborah (Peck)
            Gray.
    iii.   Jediah, b. 23 Oct. 1772.
    iv.   Henry, b. 20 March 1781.

5. REUBEN³ WOOD (Peleg², Henry¹), born in LC 20 Feb. 1752,
died there in September 1810.

He was married first in LC 30 Dec. 1773 by the Rev. Jonathan
Ellis to ABIGAIL BROWNELL, daughter of Stephen and Edith (Wilbore)
Brownell, born in LC 15 March 1751. He was married second in LC
21 Jan. 1779 by Adam Simmons, justice, to RUTH WILBORE, daughter
of Charles and Hannah (Borden) Wilbore, born in LC 30 Aug. 1758, died
there in September 1793. She and her husband are buried in the Quaker
cemetery at the Friends Meeting House. He married third after 1793
HANNAH WILBORE, daughter of Walter and Catharine (Davenport)
Wilbore, born 15 Sept. 1752, died in LC 11 Feb. 1820.

They lived in LC near Peleg Wood, who, according to the census
of 1790, lived near Snell Road.

His will, recorded book 4, page 331, made in 1805 and proved
10 Oct. 1810: "...To son Charles all estate both real and personal
except as I shall bequeath my wife and daughter. To wife Hannah all
household goods she brought with her. To son Peleg 900 dollars. To
daughter Sarah household furniture and 20 silver dollars. To son Borden
120 silver dollars at the age of 21. To son Charles he to be sole executor. To son William 170 dollars..."

Children by first wife:
    i.   Peleg, b. 27 June 1774; d. young.

Children by second wife:
    ii.   Peleg, b. 24 Sept. 1779; m. Amy Palmer, daughter of

Lemuel and Deborah Wilbor Palmer, b. in LC 27 July 1779.

7.   iii.   Charles, b. 24 Dec. 1781.
     iv.   Sarah, b. 16 Nov. 1784; d. 31 Oct. 1857; m. in LC 28 Oct. 1804 Walter Grinnell, son of Billings and Comfort (Wood) Grinnell.
     v.   William, b. 21 April 1788.
     vi.   Borden, b. 18 Jan. 1791; d. 28 July 1870; m. 1 March 1818 Harriet Gray, daughter of Job and Judith (Wilbor) Gray.

6. ABNER^3 WOOD (Peleg^2, Henry^1), born in LC 16 June 1758. He was married there 31 May 1778 by the Rev. Jonathan Ellis to PHEBE POTTER, daughter of Stokes and Rebecca (Shaw) Potter.

Residence: LC and Tiverton. His land was bounded west by John Peckham, south by the road and north by John Bailey.

Children, recorded in LC:
i.   Royal, b. 26 Jan. 1779.
ii.   Ezra, b. 17 Sept. 1781; m. in Newport 4 Nov. 1804 Susannah Wilcox, daughter of John Wilcox of Portsmouth.
iii.   Content, b. 3 Jan. 1784; m. in LC 21 Aug. 1803 Hezekiah Irish, son of Thomas and Phebe Irish.
iv.   Elizabeth, b. 12 April 1787; m. in LC 28 Sept. 1800 Isaac Brownell, son of William and Elizabeth (Pearce) Brownell.
v.   Ruth, b. 25 March 1790.
vi.   Desire, b. 16 Sept. 1792.
vii.   Mary, b. 16 Oct. 1794.
viii. Thurston, b. 23 Jan. 1797.
ix.   Lucy, b. 3 Aug. 1799.

7. CHARLES^4 WOOD (Reuben^3, Peleg^2, Henry^1), born in LC 24 Dec. 1781, died there 13 April 1850.

He married BETSEY SIMMONS, daughter of Isaac and Abishag (Briggs) Simmons, born in LC 4 April 1789, died 24 Feb. 1847, buried in Old Commons cemetery.

Residence: LC. He lived on the place south of the John Church place on East of Main Road and alloted to him on the LC map of 1850. His estate was administered by John Church 13 May 1850.

Children:
i.   Charles Henry, d. 14 Nov. 1877 ae 60.
ii.   Hannah S., m. in LC by Alfred Goldsmith 25 Dec. 1842 to Samuel E. Irish, son of John and Nancy Irish.
iii.   Philip, b. in 1831.
iv.   Adaliza, b. in 1837.

The last two children listed above were given in the census of 1850 and were probably the children of Charles and Betsey Wood.

. . . .

JOHN WOOD, married LYDIA WOODMAN, daughter of John
and Jarusha (Dennis) Woodman, born in LC 26 July 1773. Residence:
LC.

   Children, recorded in LC:
i. Howland W., b. 24 Feb. 1799.

CHARLES R. WOOD, son of Robert E. and Malvina J. Wood,
born in 1869 in Westport. He married in LC 1 Jan. 1891 (?) ANNIE
L. COOK, daughter of George A. and Lydia (Coggeshall) Cook, born
in 1874. Residence: LC.
His father was born 13 June 1826 and his mother was born 31
Dec. 1832.

   Children, recorded in LC:
i. Ethel May, b. 21 Aug. 1891.
ii. Earl Howard, b. 18 May 1893.

WILLIAM S. WOOD of Westport, son of Nathan and Almira Wood,
married in LC 27 April 1878 CORNELIA M. ALLEN, daughter of Ichabod
and Deborah (Wilbor) Allen.

WILLIAM S. WOOD, son of Charles and Hannah Wood, born in
1815, according to the census of 1850. Residence: LC.
He was married in LC 21 Oct. 1835 by Samuel C. Colburn, justice,
to DIANNA C. GRAY, daughter of Nathaniel and Lydia (Coe) Gray, born
in LC 17 Aug. 1815.

   Children:
i. Theodore Dwight Weld, b. 31 Aug. 1836.

THE WOODMAN FAMILY

1. LT. JOHN[1] WOODMAN, born in 1636, died in LC 24 April
1713. Residence: LC.
He married about 1676 HANNAH TIMBERLAKE, daughter
of Henry and Mary Timberlake, born in LC in 1655, died there 3 May
1713. They are buried in cemetery number 20 on the homestead farm.
The cemetery is the Woodman cemetery east of the highway and south
of Windmill Hill, opposite (in 1952) the Philip W. Almy place.
He owned three of the great lots or hundred acre lots (numbers
7, 8 and 9). He was deputy to the General Assembly in 1682, '84 and
'86, general treasurer in 1685-86, and was overseer of the 1687
session.
His will, recorded Taunton Probate book 3, page 1, made 14
June 1709 and proved 2 June 1713: ". . . To eldest son Robert my
housing where I now live in LC with all land at the east of the great

highway, he quitting claim to my land in Newport. To son Edward
house and land in Newport. To son John lands at west of highway unto
the sea and my salt marsh I bought of Thomas Waite in Tiverton. To
daughter Hannah, wife of Nicholas Howland, 30 pounds. To four daughters,
Edith, Rebecca, Elizabeth and Silvia, each 100 pounds. Wife Hannah,
executrix, use of my house and land where I now live, with orchard,
and to sell the land that I bought of William Fobes. . . "
    Inventory of the estate of Lt. John Woodman, deceased, taken 15
June 1713: Total of the property 1905 pounds, 10 shillings, 2 pence.
He owned a great deal of land and was one of the wealthier men of LC.

            Children, recorded in LC:
2.   i.   Robert, b. 8 Sept. 1677.
     ii.   Hannah, b. 27 June 1679; m. in LC 26 Oct. 1697 Nicholas
            Howland of Dartmouth.
3.   iii.   John, b. 25 Feb. 1682.
     iv.   Edith, b. 7 Sept. 1685; d. in LC 3 June 1718; m. 16 April
            1712 Thomas Church Esq., son of Benjamin and Alice
            (Southworth) Church.
4.   v.   Edward, b. 17 March 1688.
     vi.   Rebecca, b. 10 Jan. 1690.
     vii.   Elizabeth, b. 31 May 1694.
     viii. Sylvia, b. 17 Sept. 1698; d. in LC 9 Feb. 1741.

    2. ROBERT[2] WOODMAN (John[1]), born in LC 8 Sept. 1677, died
there 27 Aug. 1757. He was married there 11 Nov. 1706 by Joseph Church,
justice, to DEBORAH PADDOCK.
    Residence: LC. They lived on the farm given him by his father,
which is on the east of the Main or Great Road south of Windmill Hill,
where the Woodman cemetery is situated.
    His will, recorded LC Wills, book 1, page 209, made 23 Dec.
1754 and proved 5 Sept. 1757: ". . . To eldest son John part of my
homestead farm. Northwest corner of orchard at wall by highway,
east by William Briggs' land, west on the Great highway. To son
Thomas 26 acres of land at easterly end of my homestead farm. To
daughter Hannah Sanford household stuff and a Negro girl called Peg.
To daughter Priscilla Woodman Negro girl called Prue. To son Constant
my dwelling house on the Great Highway and west of homestead farm,
he to be executor. To my daughter Hannah Sanford 30 pounds. To
daughter Priscilla 100 pounds and Negro boy called Tobey. . . "

            Children, recorded in LC:
5.   i.   John, b. 2 May 1708.
     ii.   Constant, b. 28 Aug. 1710 in LC; d. there 4 Dec. 1780;
            unmarried.
     iii.   Hannah, b. 22 April 1713; m. (1) in LC 19 Dec. 1734 Parker
            Hall; m. (2) in LC 30 Dec. 1750 William Sanford of
            Dartmouth.
     iv.   Joseph, b. 4 May 1716.
6.   v.   Thomas, b. 19 Sept. 1718.
     vi.   Priscilla, b. 1 July 1721; d. in LC 7 May 1791; m. there
            4 Feb. 1762 George Pearce.

3. JOHN² WOODMAN (John¹), born in LC 25 Feb. 1682, died there 8 May 1733.

He was married in LC 21 Oct. 1708 by Richard Billings, justice, to ELIZABETH BRIGGS, daughter of William and Elizabeth (Cook) Briggs, born 27 Dec. 1689, died in March 1763. She married first 17 July 1701 Richard Sisson. They are buried in the Woodman cemetery opposite the Philip W. Almy place.

Residence: LC. They lived on the land given him by his father, which was in 1890 the Philip Almy estate.

His will, recorded LC Wills, book 7, page 539, made 3 May 1733 and proved 15 May 1733: ". . . To wife Elizabeth use of new room in south end of new house, one hundred pounds and a milch cow. To eldest son Sylvester all my farm where I now live, bounded east on the highway, west on the salt water, north on Ward's land and south by the ministry lot about six score acres. Also the spring lot which lyeth to the south of my brother Robert Woodman's. West by the highway, north and east by brother Robert Woodman and south by the ministry lot. About seven acres which was given to me by my father's will, also land in Tiverton of 18 acres. To son Enoch Woodman 200 pounds and one half of my lands at Pocasset. To daughters Sarah, Elizabeth, Edith and Deborah Woodman, one hundred pounds and one silver spoon apiece. . ."

Inventory of the estate of John Woodman of LC, deceased: 22 May 1733. Six powdering tubs. 128 sheep, 9 lambs, 17 swine. All housing lands with the spring pasture. Total of whole inventory -- 3956 pounds, 3 shillings, 5 pence. One Negro man 75 pounds.

Children:
7. i.   Sylvester, b. 25 Jan. 1709.
    ii.   Mary, b. 3 Sept. 1710; d. 1 Sept. 1710/11.
    iii. Sarah, b. 3 April 1712.
    iv.   Elizabeth, b. 10 Sept. 1713; m. in LC 2 Nov. 1735 William
          Pearce, son of James and Martha (Wilbore) Pearce.
    v.   Enoch, b. 28 Jan. 1715; d. 14 July 1736.
    vi.   Edith, b. 20 Dec. 1719; m. (1) in LC 9 March 1739 Thomas
          Wilbor, son of William and Esther (Burgess) Wilbor.
8. vii. William, b. 27 May 1721.
    viii. Deborah, b. 21 Oct. 1726; d. in LC 30 March 1760; m. there
          25 Oct. 1750 George Pearce, son of James and Martha
          (Wilbore) Pearce.

4. EDWARD² WOODMAN (John¹), born in LC 17 March 1688.

He was married in LC in October 1708 by Joseph Church, justice, to MARGARET TAYLOR, daughter of John and Abigail (--) Taylor of LC, born there in July 1688.

Children, recorded in LC:
i.   John, b. 25 Jan. 1711.
ii.   Abigail, b. 23 Aug. 1714; m. in LC 22 Sept. 1734 Richard
      Billings Jr., son of Richard and Sarah (Little) Billings.

5. JOHN³ WOODMAN (Robert ², John¹), born in LC 2 May 1708, died there 19 Sept. 1798.

He was married in LC 30 Nov. 1735 by Richard Billings, justice,
to PATIENCE GRINNELL, daughter of Richard and Patience (Emery)
Grinnell, born in LC 24 April 1715.

Residence: LC. He lived on the farm he received from his father,
on the east side of the road near Windmill Hill, where the Woodman
cemetery is situated.

His will, recorded book 3 LC Wills, page 372, made 24 May 1790
and proved 3 Oct. 1798: ". . . To son Richard Woodman my salt meadow
and the feather bed that I sleep on. To son Robert one silver dollar. To
grandson Humphrey Woodman, son of my son John, deceased, one silver
dollar. To daughter Deborah Woodman, wife of John Woodman, five
silver dollars. To sons Richard, Edward and Robert Woodman, all
household goods. To son Edward Woodman all my homestead farm where
I now dwell. . . "

Children, recorded in LC:
	i.	Richard, b. 18 Aug. 1736.
9.	ii.	John, b. 26 Jan. 1740.
10.	iii.	Capt. Edward, b. 16 Oct. 1742.
	iv.	Deborah, b. 5 Sept. 1746; m. in LC 25 April 1790 John Woodman, son of Sylvester[3] (John[2], John[1]) Woodman.
11.	v.	Robert, b. 7 Jan. 1750.

6. THOMAS[3] WOODMAN (Robert[2], John[1]), born in LC 19 Sept.
1718. He was married in LC 11 Jan. 1747 by Richard Billings, justice,
to SARAH GRINNELL, daughter of Richard and Patience (Emory)
Grinnell, born in LC 6 May 1723, died before 26 April 1797.

Residence: LC. He received 26 acres of land at the east end
of the Woodman farm on the east of the main road, south of Windmill
Hill. He may have been facing on another road at the east.

Children, recorded in LC:
i.	Phebe, b. 22 Feb. 1747.
ii.	Isaac, b. in 1750; d. in April 1797. His estate was administered by his mother, Sarah Woodman, widow, 26 April 1797.

7. CAPT. SYLVESTER[3] WOODMAN (John[2], John[1]), born in LC
25 Jan. 1709, died there 4 March 1760.

He was married in LC 18 Dec. 1735 by Richard Billings, justice,
to BATHSHEBA DRING, daughter of Thomas and Mary (Butler) Dring,
born in LC 16 Aug. 1715, died there in March 1790.

Residence: LC. They lived on the Old Woodman place given him
by his father, on the west side of the Main Road, opposite the larger
of the two Woodman cemeteries.

In her will, recorded LC Wills, book 3, page 189, made 30 Dec.
1786 and proved 6 April 1790, his widow left to her son John her large
hand irons, to her daughter Comfort her small Bible, to her daughter
Mary one young cow, to Jeremiah Weeden, son of her daughter Eliphal,
deceased, 20 silver dollars, and to her daughter Ruth the rest and residue.

Children, recorded in LC:

      i.   Ruth, b. 3 Jan. 1737; d. 15 June 1806 in LC.
     ii.   Eliphal, b. 11 Sept. 1738; m. in LC 1 Dec. 1759 John Weeden.
    iii.   Mary, b. 26 May 1740; d. 15 Aug. 1798.
    iv.   Comfort, b. 26 June 1742; d. 3 April 1795.
12.   v.   John, b. 28 Sept. 1746.
    vi.   Rhoda, b. 2 Oct. 1751.

    8. WILLIAM³ WOODMAN (John², John¹), born in LC 27 May 1721, died there 2 Nov. 1761.

He was married in LC 23 March 1749 by Joseph Wood, justice, to MARY PEARCE, daughter of James and Martha (Wilbore) Pearce, born in LC 17 Oct. 1724, died there in January 1802.

His estate was administered by his widow 1 Dec. 1761, and her estate was administered 1 Feb. 1802.

          Children, recorded in LC:
      i.   Zilpha, b. 8 June 1752; m. in LC 24 May 1778 Job Manchester, son of Archer and Elizabeth Manchester.
     ii.   Betsey, b. 23 March 1755; m. in LC 2 Nov. 1777 Lemuel Sawyer, son of Josias and Sarah Sawyer.
13. iii.   William, b. 24 March 1757.
14. iv.   Sylvester, b. 23 March 1760.

    9. JOHN⁴ WOODMAN (John³, Robert², John¹), born in LC 26 Jan. 1740, died there 20 Aug. 1775.

He married about 1769 SUSANNA COOK. Residence: LC. His estate was administered by his widow 6 Feb. 1776.

          Children, recorded in LC:
      i.   Humphrey, b. 7 May 1770; d. 10 Feb. 1791. His estate was administered by his mother in 1791.

    10. EDWARD⁴ WOODMAN (John³, Robert², John¹), born in LC 16 Oct. 1742; died there 29 Aug. 1839.

He married in LC 13 Oct. 1782 PRISCILLA NEGUS, born in LC 11 Sept. 1746, died there 30 June 1827.

His will, recorded LC Probate book 8, page 163, made 26 June 1823 and proved 14 Oct. 1839: ". . . To wife Priscilla one undivided half part of my house, also a home in my house whereever she shall choose.. To daughter Sally Woodman 30 dollars and one feather bed. To daughter Rhoda Seabury, wife of Capt. William Seabury, twenty dollars. To daughter Carolina Seabury, wife of Mr. Robert Seabury, 20 dollars. To son Humphrey Woodman my homestead farm where I now live and right to salt meadow and beach lying between Quicksand Pond and the sea, my two guns, pistol and sword, quadrant charts. . ."

          Children, recorded in LC:
      i.   Sally, b. 15 April 1785.
     ii.   Rhoda, b. 11 Dec. 1786; m. in LC 12 April 1807 Capt. William Seabury, son of Constant and Susannah (Gray) Seabury. Residence: New Bedford.
    iii.   Caroline, b. 27 Sept. 1789; m. in LC 3 Jan. 1813 Robert Seabury, son of Constant and Susannah (Gray) Seabury.
15. iv.   Humphrey, b. 24 Sept. 1792.

11. ROBERT[4] WOODMAN (Maybe John[3], Robert[2], John[1]), died in LC 1835.

He married (intention 14 Feb. 1778) in Dartmouth HANNAH HOWLAND of Dartmouth. He married second in LC 30 June 1817 MERCY HUNT.

His will, recorded LC Wills, book 8, page 94, made 7 March 1832 and proved 9 Feb. 1835: ". . . To wife all estate both real and personal, except what I give to my daughters, namely, Deborah Grinnell and Hannah White, and to them one dollar each. . . "

> Children, recorded in LC:
> i.   Deborah, b. 11 Dec. 1779; m. in LC 6 Sept. 1797 Samuel Tillinghast Grinnell, son of William and Lydia Grinnell.
> ii.   Hannah, b. 9 June 1783; m. in Tiverton 14 Feb. 1808 George White, son of Peregrine and Abigail (Soule) White of LC.

12. JOHN[4] WOODMAN (Sylvester[3], John[2], John[1]), born in LC 28 Sept. 1746, died there 4 March 1831. Residence: LC.

He married about 1767 JERUSHA DENNIS, daughter of John and Hannah (Wilbor) Dennis, born in LC 17 March 1747, died there 28 June 1788. He was married second in LC 25 April 1790 by Enos Gifford, justice, to DEBORAH WOODMAN, daughter of John and Patience (Grinnell) Woodman, born in LC 5 Sept. 1746, died there 29 Jan. 1820. All are buried in the Woodman cemetery on the Philip W. Almy place on the west side of the road.

For further information see the Genealogical Register number 49, page 443.

His will, recorded LC Probate, book 6, page 34, made 6 June 1827 and proved 11 April 1831: ". . . To grandson John Woodman, son of my son Constant Woodman. . . All of the town of Madison, county same, of New York State, and all land and tenements in LC. Ten dollars each to son Sylvester Woodman, daughter Lydia Wood, son Constant Woodman, Silena Woodman, widow, Abby P. Woodman (daughter of Silena), Mary Woodman, Louisa Gray Woodman and Jarusha Clark Woodman. And that my family burial place be reserved for sacred purposes, forever, it to be six rods north and south and three rods east and west. All rest and residue to three children, Sylvester Woodman, Constant Woodman and Lydia Wood, the wife of John Wood. Tried and trusty John Tompkins sole executor. . . "

> Children by first wife, recorded in LC:
> i.   Sylvester, b. 25 Nov. 1768; d. 10 June 1845.
> ii.   Constant, b. 7 Jan. 1771; m. Irene (?). Residence: Madison, N.Y.
> iii. Lydia, b. 26 July 1773; m. John Wood.
> iv. Willard, b. 26 March 1776.
> v.   Philip, b. 23 Feb. 1779.
> vi. John, b. 25 Sept. 1782.
> 16. vii. Clarke, b. 11 Oct. 1785.

13. WILLIAM[4] WOODMAN (William[3], John[2], John[1]), born in LC 24 March 1757, died there 17 July 1838.

He was married in LC 4 Aug. 1782 (intention in Dartmouth 5

July 1782) by the Rev. Jonathan Ellis to PRISCILLA BROWNELL,
daughter of George and Sarah (Bailey) Brownell, born in LC 2 May
1754.

Children, recorded in LC:
i.   Nathaniel, b. 11 Dec. 1782; m. Sybil Palmer, daughter
        of Benedict and Deborah (Palmer) Palmer.
17.   ii.   Enoch, b. 21 April 1784.
       iii.   Sarah, b. 20 Jan. 1786.
       iv.   Lucy, b. 6 Feb. 1788.
       v.   Job, b. 24 Nov. 1790; m. 24 Aug. 1817 Mary Wilbore,
            daughter of Brownell and Esther (Wilbore) Wilbore.
18.   vi.   Ucal, b. 5 Nov. 1792.
19.   vii.   George, b. 28 April 1795.
       ix.   Elizabeth, b. 13 Sept. 1800; m. 16 Dec. 1821 Val Pierce,
            son of Joseph and Anna (Willard) Pierce, b. 14 Oct.
            1799, d. 21 Dec. 1852.

14. SYLVESTER[4] WOODMAN (William[3], John[2], John[1]), born
in LC 23 March 1760, died in Madison County, N.Y.
       He was married in LC 16 March 1786 by Enos Gifford, justice,
to MEREBAH BROWNELL, daughter of John and Luceanna Brownell.

Children, recorded in LC:
i.   William, b. 15 Nov. 1786.
ii.   Borden or Pardon, b. 12 June 1789; m. Elizabeth Brown,
        daughter of Joseph and Elizabeth Brown. Residence:
        Madison, N.Y.
iii.   Mary, b. 17 Feb. 1791.
iv.   Lucy, b. 16 Nov. 1792.
v.   Pearce, b. 24 June 1795.

15. HUMPHREY[5] WOODMAN (Edward[4], John[3], Robert[2], John[1]),
born in LC 24 Sept. 1792, died there 23 Feb. 1868.
       He married in LC 10 Feb. 1830 ROBY LADD, daughter of Joseph
and Hannah (Brown) Wilbor and widow of Jesse Ladd, born in LC 12
March 1799, died there 7 May 1843. Both are buried in the Woodman
cemetery opposite the Philip Almy place, south of Windmill Hill.
       Residence: LC. They lived on the homestead farm east of the
Main Road, opposite the Philip Almy place.
       His will, recorded in LC Wills, book 11, page 505, made 7 Sept.
1867 and proved 13 March 1868: ". . . To daughters Priscilla Peckham,
wife of Alanson W. Peckham, Hannah Maria Woodman and Georgia Ann
Woodman my homestead farm where I now live, bounded west by the
highway, north on Frederic Almy, east and south on Barney Hicks'
land I bought of him, also 40 acres adjoining said farm, also stock
of cattle. . . To Lydia Louisa Smith 15 acres that I bought of Barney
Hicks with buildings thereon bounded west by the highway, north on
homestead, east on other part of farm. To daughter Hannah Maria
Woodman 400 dollars. To daughter Georgia Ann Woodman 400 dollars.
To daughter Lydia Louisa Smith, wife of Lorenzo Smith, Priscilla
Peckham, wife of Alanson W. Peckham, Hannah Maria Woodman and
Georgia Ann Woodman all my real estate remaining. Alanson Peckham

and Lorenzo Smith executors. . . "

> Children, recorded in LC:
> i.   Priscilla, b. 21 May 1831; d. in LC 16 Sept. 1887; m. Alanson W. Peckham, son of Wilbor and Priscilla (Wilbor) Peckham.
> ii. Edward, b. 12 Nov. 1832; d. 7 Nov. 1833.
> iii. Hannah Maria, b. 22 Aug. 1834; d. 22 April 1877; unmarried.
> iv. Georgia Ann, b. 28 Dec. 1838; d. 30 Sept. 1878.
> v.   Lydia Louisa, m. Lorenzo Smith.

16. CLARKE[5] WOODMAN (John[4], Sylvester[3], John[2], John[1]), born in LC 11 Oct. 1785, died there 17 Feb. 1828.

He was married in Tiverton 14 June 1812 by the Rev. Benjamin Peckham to SILENA GRAY, daughter of Pardon Jr. and Sarah (Corey) Gray, born in Tiverton 30 April 1792. They are buried in the Woodman cemetery on the Philip Almy place. His estate was administered by Pardon Gray 13 April 1828.

> Children, recorded in LC:
> i.   Abby P., b. 14 April 1816.
> ii. Mary, b. 28 March 1824.
> iii. Louisa Gray, b. 15 Feb. 1826.

17. ENOCH[5] WOODMAN (William[4], William[3], John[2], John[1]), born in LC 21 April 1784, died there 14 Jan. 1857. He was married in LC 6 Dec. 1807 by the Rev. Mase Shepard to PHEBE WILBORE, daughter of Brownell and Esther (Wilbor) Wilbore, born in LC 6 Nov. 1788, died in Tiverton 30 May 1829. She is buried in cemetery 10 on the Oliver C. Wilbor place. He is buried in cemetery 10 or the Gifford cemetery. Residence: LC.

> Children, recorded in LC:
> i.   Nancy W., b. 28 Sept. 1808.
> ii. Priscilla H., b. 15 May 1814.
> iii. Temperance D., b. 9 April 1816.
> iv. Mary W., b. 7 July 1818; d. 23 Nov. 1834.
> v.   Brownell W., b. 25 Dec. 1820.
> vi. Job W., b. 27 March 1829.

18. UCAL[5] WOODMAN (William[4], William[3], John[2], John[1]), born in LC 5 Nov. 1792. He married LOIS WILBORE, daughter of Brownell and Esther (Wilbore) Wilbore, born in LC 20 Dec. 1796, died there 22 June 1829, buried in the Gifford cemetery number 10.

> Children:
> i.   Esther B.

19. GEORGE[5] WOODMAN (William[4], William[3], John[2], John[1]), born in LC 28 April 1795, died there 2 Jan. 1879.

He married first in LC 19 Feb. 1821 PHEBE SIMMONS, daughter of William and Rebecca (Soule) Simmons, born in LC 22 March 1798. He married second in LC 5 June 1842 MERCY SIMMONS, born in LC 14 July 1810, died there 14 June 1858. They lived in district number

5 near the Stone School house.

Children, born in LC and recorded there:
i. Phebe Minerva, b. 30 April 1826; d. in LC 22 Sept. 1852; m. there 17 June 1846 William Tillinghast Devol, son of Thurston and Margaret (Petty) Devol.
20. ii. George Henry, b. 22 Nov. 1843.
iii. Mary Ann, b. 15 Nov. 1846.

20. GEORGE HENRY[6] WOODMAN (George[5], William[4], William[3], John[2], John[1]), born in LC 22 Nov. 1843, died there 7 July 1921. Residence: LC.

He married in LC 25 Nov. 1871 JOSEPHINE MARIA WILBOUR, daughter of Daniel and Maria (Pearce) Wilbour, born in LC 28 Sept. 1846, died there 11 April 1908.

Children, recorded in LC:
i. Minerva Josephine, b. 13 June 1875; d. in 1951 in Taunton, Mass.; m. (1) in LC 19 May 1900 Charles Edson Wood, b. 2 June 1873; m. (2) (--) West.

THE WOODWORTH FAMILY

1. WALTER[1] WOODWORTH, born about 1610, probably in Kent County, England, died in 1685 in Scituate, Mass. Residence: Scituate.

He came from Kent County, England, to Scituate, Mass., in 1635 and was assigned a third lot on Kent Street at the corner of Meeting House Lane, where he built his house. In 1664 he was a member of the first church of Scituate. He made a purchase of 60 acres of land at Weymouth, Mass., in 1666. He also owned land in LC.

His will: ". . . Walter Woodworth of Scituate of New Plymouth in New England. . . I give and bequeath unto Thomas, my eldest son, upland containing acres lying in Scituate. To two sons Thomas and Joseph. . . Acres of marsh land equally in Scituate. To son Thomas one third part of my land that Seconet which I purchased. The other two thirds to sons Benjamin and Isaac Woodworth except two acres which I give to my son Joseph, ten of which I give to my daughter Martha, all the rest of my land at Seconet which is yet to be purchased I give unto my sons Thomas and Joseph equally. To son Benjamin my dwelling house, barn and other housing with all my land. Benjamin to pay 70 pounds to my son Joseph and my six daughters Sarah, Elizabeth, Mary, Martha, Mehitable and Abigail 10 pounds apiece. I herewith attach my hand and seal this 26th day of November 1685. . . " His will was proved 2 March 1865/6.

Children, given in his will but birth not given, with the exception of Mary and Mehitable:

2. i.   Thomas, b. in 1636.
    ii.   Sarah, b. in 1637.
    iii.   Benjamin, b. about 1638; m. in 1659 Deborah (--). He was killed in King Philip's War in Lebanon, Conn.
    iv.   Elizabeth.
3. v.   Joseph, b. about 1648.
    vi.   Mary, b. 10 March 1650; m. 24 Dec. 1677 in Scituate Aaron Symons.
    vii.   Martha, b. about 1656; m. in Scituate in June 1769 Zachariah Damon.
4. viii.   Isaac, b. about 1659.
    ix.   Mehitable, b. 15 Aug. 1662.
    x.   Abigail, b. about 1664; m. 24 Dec. 1695.
    xi.   Elizabeth, m. Benjamin Southworth, son of William and Rebecca (Pabodie) Southworth.

2. THOMAS[2] WOODWORTH (Walter[1]), born about 1636. He married in Scituate 8 Feb. 1666 DEBORAH DAMON, daughter of John Damon.

Residence: Scituate. He did not move to LC but he owned land there on Swamp Road which had been given him in the will of his father. It was held by his family for many years, and is next to the Southworth place. His brother Joseph must have moved to LC as he had two sons whose births are recorded there.

Children, born in Scituate and recorded there:
    i.   Deborah, b. 2 Jan. 1667; m. 1701 Eben Pincin.
5. ii.   Hezekiah, b. 5 Feb. 1670.
    iii.   Catharine, b. 5 Oct. 1673; m. in LC 20 July 1704 Thomas Davenport, son of Jonathan and Hannah (Maynard) Davenport of LC.
    iv.   Ebenezer, b. 25 May 1676; d. young.
    v.   Mary, b. 8 July 1678; m. 5 April 1704 in Scituate Stephen Vinal Jr.
    vi.   John, b. 31 Aug. 1683; m. Mary Rose.
    vii.   Hannah, b. 7 Sept. 1685; m. 20 Oct. 1713 Samuel Jackson.
    viii.   Jerusha, b. 1 Dec. 1688; m. (--) Randall.
    ix.   Ebenezer 2d, b. 10 Aug. 1690; m. in Scituate 16 Oct. 1712 Mary Wade.

3. JOSEPH[2] WOODWORTH (Walter[1]), probably born in Scituate. He married there 6 Jan. 1669 SARAH STOCKBRIDGE, daughter of Charles Stockbridge. Residence: Scituate.

See the American Genealogist (October 1955).

His will, recorded in Taunton, volume 4, page 110-112, made 3 Dec. 1712 and proved 26 April 1718: "...To wife Sarah...To my two sons Joseph and Benjamin...To six daughters Margaret, Sarah, Elizabeth, Eunice, Abigail and Ruth...To son Benjamin my property in Scituate. To son Joseph I give and bequeath all that my estate both housing and lands and meadows lying and being in LC, which he the said Joseph in now in the possession and improvement of, which said

. . meadows are particularly bounded as recorded. . . "

Children, probably born in Scituate:
6.   i.   Joseph, b. 19 March 1670.
     ii.   Margaret, b. 1673; m. Stephen Vinal.
    iii. Benjamin, b. in August 1676.
    iv. Sarah, b. in 1678.
     v. Elizabeth, b. in 1680; m. in Scituate in October 1707 Thomas Chittenden.
    vi. Eunice, b. in January 1682/3.
   vii. Abigail, b. 16 April 1685; m. in Scituate 7 Nov. 1711 Thomas Merritt.
  viii. Ruth, b. in May 1687; m. in Scituate 8 May 1718 Benjamin Sylvester Jr.

4. ISAAC² WOODWORTH (Walter¹), born in 1659, probably in Scituate, died in Norwich, Conn., in April 1714.

He married, probably in Scituate, LYDIA STOCKBRIDGE, daughter of Charles Stockbridge.

Residence: Scituate, LC and Norwich. He moved to LC where he was a proprietor in 1692. Soon after 1701 he moved to Norwich, Conn., where his brother Benjamin went at about the same time. He was a freeman of Norwich in 1705. See the New England Register, volumn 87, page 84.

Children:
     i. Lydia, b. in Scituate 1685; m. in New London, Conn., 13 Jan. 1717/8 William Menard (?).
    ii. Isaac, b. in 1687/8; m. in New London 5 Dec. 1711 Ruth Douglas, daughter of Robert Douglas.
   iii. Moses, b. in 1689, probably in Scituate; d. 21 Sept. 1745; m. 21 May 1730 in Norwich.

5. HEZEKIAH³ WOODWORTH (Thomas², Walter¹), born in Scituate 5 Feb. 1670, died in LC 25 Nov. 1716. Residence: LC.

He married in Scituate 23 Dec. 1697 HANNAH CLAPP, ·possibly the daughter of Samuel and Hannah (Gill) Clapp of Scituate, born 15 Jan. 1673, died in LC 10 Dec. 1734.

The Woodworth family records by Otis Wilbor are incorrect and so is the Woodworth Genealogy written about 1899 by William A. Woodworth (?). Hezekiah Woodworth of LC is not the son of Walter, for the births of Scituate plainly show that he is the son of Thomas Woodworth, and grandson of the first Walter.

His widow Hannah took inventory of his estate 17 Dec. 1716, recorded in Taunton, book 3, page 609: "Hannah Woodworth of LC, widow of Hezekiah Woodworth. Goods and chattels. Total 292 pounds 18 shillings and 8 pense."

Her will, recorded in Taunton Probate, book 7, page 190, made 17 June 1734 and proved 18 Feb. 1734: ". . . To four children, Elisha, Elihue, Naomie Hall and Hannah Jackson, all money and personal estate. To four grandsons, Thomas, William, Ebenezer and Nathaniel Church, when 21, four pounds each. To son Elisha use of a barn and all the rent he owes me for that part of the house he lives in. To son-in-law William Hall use of a barn of 40 pounds in consideration of his entertaining me in his house sundry times. To daughter Naomie Hall one third of household goods. To daughter Hannah Jackson one third of household goods. To granddaughters Priscilla and Mary Church one third of household goods. To son Elihue to be sole executor. . . " Inventory of her estate: 166 pounds-07 shillings-0 pense.

Children, recorded in LC:
7.   i.   Elisha, b. 1 Dec. 1698.
8.   ii.   Elihue, b. 24 July 1700.
    iii.   Naomie, b. 25 March 1701; d. in LC 23 May 1765; m. there 28 Dec. 1719 William Hall, b. 10 June 1695 in Wivescomb, Somersetshire, England, d. 24 Dec. 1766. He was a deacon of the Congregational Church in LC.
    iv.   Deborah, b. 17 Nov. 1703; d. 28 Aug. 1733; m. in LC 6 Dec. 1721 Caleb Church, son of Joseph and Grace (Shaw) Church.
    v.   Hannah, b. in LC 19 March 1706; m. there 15 Oct. 1724 Thomas Jackson.
    vi.   Mary, b. 4 March 1709 in LC; d. 22 July 1716.

6. JOSEPH³ WOODWORTH (Joseph², Walter¹), born in Scituate 19 March 1670, married REBECCA (--). Residence: LC and Lebanon, Conn.

On 23 Feb. 1733/4 Joseph Woodworth and his son Joseph Jr. both sold their homes to Nathaniel Searles Jr. of LC: land in LC containing 48 acres, the two 24 acre lots (22nd and 23rd in number) among the 24 acre lots and bounded west on highway, east upon Cole Brook line, north on land of Israel Shaw, south on the land of Mr. Richard Billings and partly on the land of Joseph Woodworth Jr., together with all housing and buildings.

Children:
·9.   i.   Joseph, b. 17 March 1696.
10.   ii.   Jedediah, b. 1 Dec. 1699.

7. ELISHA⁴ WOODWORTH (Hezekiah³, Thomas², Walter¹), born in LC 1 Dec. 1698, died there 20 April 1749.

He married first in Scituate 10 May 1722 JANE BAILEY, born in 1700, died in LC 6 Feb. 1729. He and his first wife are buried in the Old Commons cemetery. He married second ANN CLAPP.

They lived in LC at a place on the Swamp Road on the south of the road and east of the Southworth place, across from the main village of Queen Awashonks at the north.

His will, recorded book 1, page 62 LC Wills, made 11 Nov. 1748 and proved 6 June 1749: ". . . To wife Ann Woodworth, executrix, one half household goods, one half of livestock, 50 pounds and west room in my dwelling house. To son Hezekiah Woodworth all estate both real and personal, not otherwise disposed of. . . "

Children, recorded in LC:
11.   i.   Hezekiah, b. 1 Dec. 1732.

8. ELIHUE⁴ WOODWORTH (Hezekiah³, Thomas², Walter¹), born

in LC 24 July 1700, died there in September 1780.
    He was married in LC 6 March 1727 by Sylvester Richmond,
justice, to SILENCE STOUGHTON of Dartmouth.
    Residence: LC. They lived on the Swamp Road next to the
Southworth place and across from the principle village of Queen Awashonks.
    His will, recorded LC Probate, book 2, made 2 Feb. 1776 and
proved 3 Oct. 1780: ". . . To son Thomas 12 shillings of Rhode Island
currency. To son Stephen 10 shillings. To daughter Sible White 6
shillings. To daughter Deborah Smith 6 shillings. To daughter Sarah
Vose 6 shillings. To daughter Naomie Woodworth my land and all my
tackling. To grandson David Woodworth my gun, my cooper's tools
and all my glazing tools. To granddaughter Comfort Gifford 30 shillings.
To daughters Mary Woodworth and Naomie Woodworth all my real estate and rest and remainder of my estate. Grandson Joseph Gifford
to be my executor. . . "

                 Children, recorded in LC:
    i.   Mary, b. 30 Nov. 1727; unmarried in 1776.
    ii.   Hannah, b. 22 Jan. 1729; m. in LC 18 Nov. 1751 Constant
                Church.
    iii.   Sible, b. 25 Dec. 1731; m. (1) in LC 4 March 1752 Constant
                Hix, son of William and Anna (Durfee) Hix; m. (2) 2 Jan.
                1754 Israel White.
12. iv.   Thomas, b. 3 Aug. 1734.
    v.   Stephen, b. 16 July 1736; m. Ruth Wilbore, daughter of Joseph
                and Martha (Records) Wilbore.
    vi.   Deborah, b. 12 Nov. 1738; m. in LC 21 Aug. 1763 William
                Smith.
    vii.   Naomie, b. 21 Sept. 1741; unmarried in 1776.
    viii.   Sarah, b. 2 April 1744; m. (--) Vose.

    9. JOSEPH[4] WOODWORTH (Joseph[3], Joseph[2], Walter[1]), born in
LC 17 March 1696. Residence: LC and Lebanon, Conn.
    He was married in LC 17 Oct. 1723 by Richard Billings, justice,
to ANNA MANCHESTER.

         Children, the first four recorded in LC, others probably
         born in Connecticut:

    i.   Abner, b. 2 Aug. 1724; m. about 1748 Hannah Dyer. Resi-
                dence: Norwich, Conn.
    ii.   Judith, b. 4 Feb. 1726; m. 16 May 1745 Adams Pierce.
    iii.   Ruth, b. 23 Jan. 1728; m. 4 April 1747 Caleb Fitch.
    iv.   Sarah, b. 19 March 1729; m. 24 Oct. 1748 Samuel Goodwin.
    v.   Walter, b. in 1731; m. in 1755 Rachel French. Residence:
                Lebanon.
    vi.   Zebedee, b. in 1733.
    vii.   Lemuel, b. 25 June 1735; m. 10 Oct. 1757 Elizabeth Hunt.

    10. JEDEDIAH WOODWORTH (Joseph[3], Joseph[2], Walter[1]), born
in LC 1 Dec. 1699, married MARGARET (--).

Children, born in LC:
i.   Amey, b. 20 April 1725.

11. HEZEKIAH[5] WOODWORTH (Elisha[4], Hezekiah[3], Thomas[2], Walter[1]), born 1 Dec. 1732 in LC, died there 22 March 1761.

He was married in LC 13 Dec. 1753 by Joseph Wood, justice, to ABIGAIL SOUTHWORTH, daughter of Joseph and Mary (Blague) Southworth, born in LC 11 June 1734.

His estate was administered by his widow Abigail 7 April 1761. They lived on the Swamp Road on the place left to him by his father, Elisha Woodworth.

Children, only the first recorded in LC:
13. i.   Elisha, b. 30 May 1755.
     ii.   Samuel, b. in 1757; d. in January 1778. His estate was administered by his brother Elisha 2 Feb. 1779.
     iii. Esther, b. in 1759; m. in LC 8 Nov. 1787 Jonathan Wilbore, son of William and Hannah Wilbore.

12. THOMAS[5] WOODWORTH (Elihue[4], Hezekiah[3], Thomas[2], Walter[1]), born in LC 3 Aug. 1734, died there about or before 6 Dec. 1763.

He married first in LC 12 Sept. 1755 JUDITH BRIGGS, daughter of William and Deborah (Church) Briggs, born in 1735, died 4 April 1762 in Falmouth, Nova Scotia. He married second 12 June 1762 MARGARET McCURDY.

Children by first wife, first two recorded in LC:
i.   Job, b. 11 Feb. 1757.
ii.   Betsey, b. 2 Nov. 1759.

Children by second wife, born in Falmouth, N.S.:
iii. John, b. 22 Feb. 1764.
iv.   Paul, b. 3 Nov. 1765.
v.   Thomas, b. 12 May 1767.
vi.   Stephen, b. 11 Feb. 1769.
vii. Benjamin, b. 28 Nov. 1770.
viii. Joseph, b. 20 April 1772.
ix.   Mary, b. 12 Aug. 1774.
x.   Alexander, b. 6 May 1779.
xi.   Isaac, b. 14 Nov. 1781.

13. ELISHA[6] WOODWORTH (Hezekiah[5], Elisha[4], Hezekiah[3], Thomas[2], Walter[1]), born in LC 30 May 1755, died there 17 July 1827.

He was married in LC 11 Nov. 1790 by the Rev. Mase Shepard to EDITH WILBOR, daughter of Charles and Hannah (Borden) Wilbor, born in LC 3 March 1771, died there 30 Sept. 1839. Both are buried in the Old Commons cemetery.

His estate was administered by Hezekiah Woodworth 13 Aug. 1827. Her estate was administered by Hezekiah Woodworth 9 Dec. 1839.

They lived in LC on the Swamp Road next to the Southworth place, which the first Walter Woodworth owned in the mile square, at the settlement of the town.

Children, recorded in LC:
i.   Esther, b. in LC 14 July 1791; d. 16 Sept. 1822.
14. ii.   Hezekiah, b. 14 May 1793.
iii.   Anna, b. 28 Feb. 1794.
iv.   Abigail, b. 22 March 1797; d. 22 July 1877 in LC; m. there
        9 Jan. 1831 Owen Wilbor, son of John and Mercy (Grinnell)
        Wilbor.
15. v.   Samuel, b. 24 Jan. 1799.
vi.   Hannah, b. 18 June 1801; d. 25 Oct. 1831; m. Allen Gifford,
        son of Ephraim and Rachel (Wilbor) Gifford.
vii.   Lydia, b. 8 Nov. 1803; d. in LC 13 Jan. 1842; m. John Devoll.
viii.   Sarah, b. 8 Nov. 1803; d. 9 Nov. 1869.
ix.   Mary, b. 12 Oct. 1806; d. 17 Feb. 1846; unmarried.
16. x.   David, b. 27 Feb. 1808.
xi.   Rachel, b. 21 Nov. 1811.
xii.   Elihue, b. 7 May 1814; m. in New Bedford 22 June 1844
        Rosetta Crowell Young, daughter of William and Rebecca
        Young of Fall River. She married second Jonathan
        Wilbor.
17. xiii.   Elisha, b. 8 June 1817.

14. HEZEKIAH[7] WOODWORTH (Elisha[6], Hezekiah[5], Elisha[4],
Hezekiah[3], Thomas[2], Walter[1]), born in LC 14 May 1793, died there
11 Feb. 1863. Residence: LC.
        He was married there 27 Dec. 1819 by the Rev. Mase Shepard
to RHODA SPRINGER, daughter of John and Rhoda (Stoddard) Springer,
born in LC 27 Sept. 1800, died there 13 March 1886. Both are buried
in the Old Commons cemetery.

Children, all recorded in LC:
i.   John Q.A., b. 18 Oct. 1829. He moved to Providence in 1880.
ii.   Henry Staples, b. 29 Oct. 1835. He moved to Providence in
        1880.

15. SAMUEL[7] WOODWORTH (Elisha[6], Hezekiah[5], Elisha[4],
Hezekiah[3], Thomas[2], Walter[1]), born in LC 24 Jan. 1799, died there
5 Jan. 1860.
        He was married in LC 31 Dec. 1821 by Thomas Burgess,
justice, to ALMIRA WILBOR, daughter of Isaac and Lydia Wilbor,
born 4 Sept. 1804, died in LC 8 Feb. 1862. Both are buried in the
Old Commons cemetery.
        His will, recorded LC Probate, book 11, page 183, made 21
Oct. 1859 and proved 12 March 1860: ". . . To wife Almira use of all
my real and personal estate. Having made arrangements with my son
Charles I give him one dollar. To daughter Lydia a bed and bedstead.
. . To Albert Gray, son of John, formerly of LC and my daughter
Lydia A. Woodworth, all real and personal estate at decease of my
wife. My wife to be executrix. . . "
        They lived in LC on Maple Avenue, just south of the road going
east, opposite the home of Ichabod P. Wilbor.

Children, recorded in LC:
18. i.   Charles W., b. 26 Dec. 1824.

ii.   Lydia Ann, b. 26 April 1834; d. 1 April 1861; m. 1 April
       1861 (?) Albert Gray, son of John and Mercy T. Gray
       of Tiverton.

16. DAVID[7] WOODWORTH (Elisha[6], Hezekiah[5], Elisha[4],
Hezekiah[3], Thomas[2], Walter[1]), born in LC 27 Feb. 1808. He married
AMEY GIFFORD, daughter of Sylvester and Rhoda (Manchester) Gifford,
born in LC 26 June 1811. This family apparently moved away.

         Children:
i.   David Sylvester, b. in LC 5 Aug. 1830.

17. ELISHA[7] WOODWORTH (Elisha[6], Hezekiah[5], Elisha[4],
Hezekiah[3], Thomas[2], Walter[1]), born in LC 8 June 1817. Residence:
LC and Fall River.
         He was married in LC 10 Dec. 1834 by the Rev. Jonathan King
to LYDIA BROWNELL, daughter of Edward and Rebecca Brownell,
born in LC 29 Aug. 1821.

         Children:
i.   Lydia Maria.
ii.   Elisha Edward, b. 28 Oct. 1842.

18. CHARLES W.[8] WOODWORTH (Samuel[7], Elisha[6], Hezekiah[5],
Elisha[4], Hezekiah[3], Thomas[2], Walter[1]), born in LC 26 Dec. 1824.
         He married before 1850 CYNTHIA ANN POTTER, perhaps the
daughter of George and Sally (Palmer) Potter, born in 1829 (or 1825).
He perhaps had a second wife, SARAH (--).
         They are listed in the census of 1850 and lived on the east side
of Maple Avenue, next to the road that runs to the east. In the census
of 1865, they were in district No. 9.

         Children by first wife, all recorded in LC:
i.   Abby B., b. in 1850; d. in LC 8 Dec. 1851.
ii.   Ella R., b. 7 Dec. 1853; d. 17 Jan. 1928; m. William H.
       Gifford 3d of Dartmouth, son of William H. and Hannah
       (Gifford) Gifford, b. 20 Jan. 1851.
iii.   Carrie W., b. 25 June 1857.

         Daughter of Charles Woodworth and Sarah (--):
iv.   Lydia A., b. 24 April 1861.

                . . . .

ISAAC[3] WOODWORTH (Maybe Walter[2] and Walter[1]), born in 1676,
married (--).

         Children, not recorded in LC:
i.   David, b. in 1697 (?).
ii.   Grace, b. in 1699 (?).

THE WORDELL FAMILY

1. **WILLIAM[1] WORDELL**, died in 1693. He married MARY (--),
died 23 March 1676. Residence: Boston, Portsmouth and Tiverton.
His will was made 8 Sept. 1692 and proved 2 May 1693.

        Children:

    i.   Mary, b. in November 1640; m. Daniel Grinnell, son of
            Mathew and Rose Grinnell, b. about 1636, d. after 1703.

2. ii.   Gershom, b. 14 July 1642.

   iii. Sarah, b. in October 1644; d. 15 Dec. 1680; m. in October
            1662 Samuel Sanford, son of John and Elizabeth (Webb)
            Sanford, b. 14 July 1635, d. 18 May 1713.

   iv. Alice, b. 10 Feb. 1650; d. in 1734; m. 26 Dec. 1671 Abraham
            Anthony.

    v.   Frances, b. 6 July 1652; m. 23 Nov. 1669 John Anthony.

2. **GERSHOM[2] WORDELL** (William[1]), born in Portsmouth 14
July 1642. He married MARY TRIPP, daughter of John and Mary
(Paine) Tripp, born about 1646, died after 1716. She married second
5 March 1683 Jonathan Gatchell. Residence: Portsmouth.

        Children:

    i.   William, b. in 1663; d. 6 Jan. 1699; m. 10 Feb. 1681
            Ruth Lawton.

    ii.   Mary, d. 14 Jan. 1732; m. 16 Feb. 1681 Robert Lawton.

   iii. Elizabeth, d. in 1697; m. 13 Sept. 1684 Stephen Manchester.

   iv. Richard, d. in 1710; m. Susanna Pearce.

    v.   Return.

3. vi. Gershom.

   vii. Sarah, m. John Humery.

  viii. Innocent, m. Richard Borden.

3. **GERSHOM[3] WORDELL** (Gershom[2], William[1]), died 4 Sept. 1741
in Tiverton. He married SARAH MOTT, daughter of Jacob and Joanna
(Slocum) Mott, born 3 Feb. 1670, died after 1738.

His will, made 30 Dec. 1738 and proved 20 Oct. 1741: ". . . To
wife Sarah a third of income of all real estate while widow. To daughter
Ruth Phineas and to daughter Elizabeth a feather bed. To daughters
Patience Crandall, Alice Butts and Innocent Sherman 5 shillings each.
To son William the south half of homestead where I now dwell. To
son Gershom north half of homestead. Also to sons William and Gershom
a six score acre lot and all other lands in Tiverton. . . "

        Children:

    i.   William, b. 13 June 1702; m. 29 March 1732 Elizabeth Borden.

4. ii.   Gershom.

   iii. Elizabeth.

   iv. Ruth.

    v.   Patience.

   vi. Alice.

   vii. Innocent.

4. **GERSHOM⁴ WORDELL** (Gershom³, Gershom², William¹),
married in Freetown, Mass., 11 April 1743 MARY GAGE, daughter
of Thomas and Mary (Durfee) Gage, born there 7 Feb. 1720. Residence: Tiverton.

	Children:	
	i.	Susanna, b. 25 Oct. 1743.
5.	ii.	Gershom, b. 15 Jan. 1745.
	iii.	Mary, b. 23 Aug. 1747; d. in Sand Lake, N.Y.; m. Peleg Tabor.
	iv.	Sarah, b. 14 April 1749.
	v.	Elizabeth, b. 30 Aug. 1750.
6.	vi.	Phineas, b. in 1755.
	vii.	Thomas, b. in 1757; d. 23 May 1834; m. 29 Jan. 1784 Phebe Borden.
	viii.	Silas, b. in 1760; m. Ruth Borden.
	ix.	Lovina.
	x.	Constant, m. 19 Oct. 1786 Samuel Sherman.

5. **GERSHOM⁵ WORDELL** (Gershom⁴, Gershom³, Gershom²,
William¹), born in Tiverton 15 Jan. 1745. He married first HULDA
FOX. He married second in Dartmouth 12 Feb. 1784 RUTH MOTT,
daughter of Adam Jr. and Rachel (Ryder) Mott, born in 1763.

	Children by first wife, born in Tiverton:	
	i.	David, b. 7 June 1768; d. 11 May 1787.
	ii.	Hannah, b. 22 Nov. 1769; m. (--) Cook.
	iii.	Sarah, b. 14 June 1771; m. (intention 6 March 1789) in Westport Mathew Boomer.
8.	iv.	Gershom, b. 6 June 1773.
	v.	Eleazer, b. 25 Feb. 1775; d. 9 Dec. 1776.
	vi.	Hulda, b. 12 Oct. 1776; m. George Wordell.
	vii.	Elkanah, b. 3 April 1778; m. in Fall River 10 April 1803 Sarah Blossom.
	viii.	Abraham, b. 14 Jan. 1780; d. 24 Feb. 1853; m. Zilpha Stafford.

	Children by second wife:	
	ix.	Rebecca, b. 18 Feb. 1785; d. 27 July 1785.
	x.	Sylvia, b. 13 March 1786; d. 11 July 1787.
7.	xi.	David, b. 17 Oct. 1787.
	xii.	Rebecca, b. 14 May 1790; d. 11 May 1798.
	xiii.	Job, b. 22 Sept. 1792; m. in Dartmouth 10 Feb. 1814 Keziah Sampson.
	xiv.	Rachel, b. 27 Nov. 1794; m. 22 Nov. 1810 Capt. Jonathan Davis.
	xv.	Mary, b. in 1790 (?); d. in 1816; m. John Crapo.
	xvi.	Adam, b. 7 July 1800; m. Deborah Allen.
	xvii.	John, b. 23 Dec. 1802; d. in New Bedford 16 Dec. 1849; m. before 6 April 1827 Rebecca Smith.
	xviii.	Ruth, b. in 1805; m. in Fall River 27 March 1823 James Thurston.

6. PHINEAS⁵ WORDELL (Gershom⁴, Gershom³, Gershom²,
William¹), born in 1755, probably in Tiverton, died in Westport 23 Feb.
1821. He married 5 Jan. 1783 RHODA RYDER, daughter of William
and Abigail (Kirby) Ryder.

Children, born in Westport:
9. i.   Benjamin, b. 12 June 1783.
    ii.   Ruth, b. 14 Feb. 1787; m. in Westport 28 Feb. 1817 John
          Crapo.
    iii. Jonathan, b. 1 Oct. 1790; m. (intention 10 Nov. 1825) Sylvia
          Wordell.
    iv.   John, b. 23 Jan. 1795; m. 25 Nov. 1813 Sarah Brownell.
    v.   Peleg Tabor, b. 21 April 1797; m. 26 June 1818 Susan Pettey.
    vi.   Bradford, b. 29 Jan. 1801; m. (intention 8 Aug. 1823) Eunice
          Wordell.

7. DAVID⁶ WORDELL (Gershom⁵, Gershom⁴, Gershom³, Gershom²,
William¹), born 17 Oct. 1787, probably in Westport, but given in Tiver-
ton births.
   He married first REBECCA BRAYTON, daughter of Borden and
Mary Brayton. He married second INNOCENT BRAYTON, daughter of
Borden and Mary Brayton, born in February 1790, died 16 Dec. 1854.
Residence: Tiverton.

Children by first wife:
    i.   Thomas,
    ii.   David Brayton.

Children by second wife:
    iii. Innocent, b. 9 April 1817; m. (1) Rodney Durfee; m. (2)
          Isaac Crapo.
10. iv.   Job, b. 27 Dec. 1820.
11. v.   Borden, b. 6 Jan. 1823.
    vi.   Sarah Ann, d. young.
    vii. Rachell, b. in 1826; m. Gilbert Wordell.

8. GERSHOM⁶ WORDELL (Gershom⁵, Gershom⁴, Gershom³,
Gershom², William¹), born in Tiverton 6 June 1773, died 26 Jan. 1832.
   He married first in Dartmouth 27 July 1794 PEACE BORDEN,
daughter of Elijah and Sarah (Baker) Borden, born 18 April 1774,
died 15 Dec. 1812. He married second in Westport 18 Nov. 1813
SUSANNA (SOULE) WORDELL, daughter of Nathaniel and Deborah
(Gifford) Soule and widow of Richard Wordell, died 14 April 1869.
Residence: Westport.

Children:
12. i.   Abram, b. about 1795.
    ii.   Deacon Joshua, b. in December 1796; d. in Accushnet,
          Mass., 24 Feb. 1874; m. in Dartmouth 19 Jan. 1817
          Anna Cowen.
    iii. Patience, d. in 1879; m. Samuel Chace.
    iv.   Sarah, b. about 1801; d. in Fall River 18 Nov. 1863; m.
          in Dartmouth 2 Dec. 1819 Weston Gifford.

13. v.   Gershom, b. about 1803.
     vi.   Edmund, b. 9 May 1807; d. in Westport 28 Feb. 1873; m.
           in Dartmouth 6 Oct. 1834 Lucinda W. Tripp.
     vii. Rachel, b. in December 1809; m. Holder Wordell.
     viii. Elkanah, b. about 1811; d. in Westport 2 April 1853; m.
           Judith Gifford.
           Children by second wife:
     ix.   Richmond, b. in 1814; d. in Fall River 28 Dec. 1884; m.
           Susanna Hoyle.

9. BENJAMIN⁶ WORDELL (Phineas⁵, Gershom⁴, Gershom³,
Gershom², William¹), born in Westport 12 June 1783, died 3 Jan. 1850.
     He married in Westport 3 Feb. 1805 ELIZABETH SOULE,
daughter of Nathaniel and Rebecca (Gifford) Soule, born (according
to the death record) 18 March 1787, died 11 Dec. 1881.
           Children, born in Westport:
14. i.   Eli, b. 12 July 1805.
     ii.   Lovisa, m. Charles Wordell.
     iii. Almira, d. before 8 Nov. 1822.
     iv.   Dianna, d. in Fall River before 6 July 1827.
     v.   Rhoda.
     vi.   Samuel Egbert Henry, d. in Fall River 13 March 1870 ae 54;
           unmarried.
     vii. Benjamin Ryder, b. in December 1815.
     viii. Ruth Borden, b. in Fall River 2 July 1821.

10. JOB⁷ WORDELL (David⁶, Gershom⁵, Gershom⁴, Gershom³,
Gershom², William¹), born in Tiverton 27 Dec. 1820, died 26 Jan. 1907.
     He married 6 Oct. 1853 LYDIA ANN GRAY, daughter of Edward
Gray of Tiverton, born 7 Oct. 1823. Residence: Tiverton.

           Children:
     i.   Lydia Chase, b. 18 Aug. 1854; d. 6 Jan. 1876.
     ii.   Jane Hooper, b. 24 April 1856; m. Henry G. Douglas.
     iii. Maria Deborah, b. 2 Sept. 1854; m. Henry G. Douglas.
     iv.   Job Jr., b. 27 Feb. 1862; d. 31 July 1897.
     v.   James Gray, b. 11 Sept. 1863; m. Sarah Elizabeth Peckham,
           daughter of John P. and Sarah Elizabeth (Williston)
           Peckham.

11. BORDEN⁷ WORDELL (David⁶, Gershom⁵, Gershom⁴, Gershom³,
Gershom², William¹), born in Tiverton (or Westport) 6 Jan. 1823, died in
LC 24 Sept. 1921 ae 98.
     He married in LC MARY B. PECKHAM, daughter of Dr. James
Davis and Harriet Byron (Brownell) Peckham, born in LC 2 Nov. 1829,
died there 9 March 1891.
     He moved to LC and lived on the Main West Road on what is called
the Congregational Society lot.

           Children, born in LC:
     i.   John W., b. 14 March 1853.
     ii.   Harriet J., b. 20 Nov. 1858; d. in LC 13 Jan. 1922; m. 28

July 1877 William Baldwin.
iii. Lafayette Cook, b. 22 June 1864; d. 22 June 1925.
iv.   Mary M., b. in 1868; m. in Tiverton 10 July 1888 Emerson
      Fuller Ash.

12. ABRAM[7] WORDELL (Gershom[6], Gershom[5], Gershom[4],
Gershom[3], Gershom[2], William[1]), born about 1795, died in Fall River
5 Feb. 1860. He married (intention 15 Nov. 1813) HANNAH THURSTON.
      Children:
15. i.   Gardiner K., b. 20 May 1833.

13. GERSHOM[7] WORDELL (Gershom[6], Gershom[5], Gershom[4],
Gershom[3], Gershom[2], William[1]), born in Westport 16 July 1803, died
there 1 May 1882.
      He married in Dartmouth 16 Sept. 1827 SYLVIA MOSHER, daughter
of Gideon and Sarah Mosher, born (according to the death record) 19 Feb.
1806. Residence: Westport.
      Children:
     i.   Jethro, b. 2 Aug. 1828; d. 25 July 1897; m. 13 April 1851
          Nancy E. Terry, b. 7 April 1830.
16. ii. Gideon Mosher, b. 7 April 1830.
    iii. Sarah Ann, b. in Westport; m. in Fall River 6 June 1852
          Philip H. Sanford.
     iv. Gershom Abial, b. in Westport 21 March 1834; d. in Fall
          River 23 Feb. 1909; m. (1) in New Bedford 5 July 1857
          Mary Hicks; m. (2) Mary Grinnell.

14. ELI[7] WORDELL (Benjamin[6], Phineas[5], Gershom[4], Gershom[3],
Gershom[2], William[1]), born 12 July 1805, died in Westport 23 Oct. 1886.
      He married first in Fall River 28 April 1833 LYDIA TRIPP, died
in LC 21 Feb. 1861 ae 43. (According to the LC death records a Ruth
Wordell, daughter of Weston Tripp, died 26 Feb. 1861 ae 43-3-2.) He
married second in Fall River 26 Oct. 1868 LUCY AMANDA (BRIGHTMAN)
PEARCE, died in April 1875. He is buried in a private cemetery in
North Westport.
      Children:
     i.   Webster, b. 27 Jan. 1836; d. 25 Aug. 1862.
     ii. Uriah, b. 24 July 1839; d. in Taunton in 1902.
    iii. Eli, m. Emma (--).
     iv. Weston, m. Mary Jackson.
     v.   William.
     vi. Mary.
    vii. Edgar, b. in LC 15 July 1852; d. 28 Jan. 1914.
   viii. Phineas, b. in LC 20 July 1854; d. 28 Jan. 1914; m. (1)
          in Hampton, N.H. 25 Dec. 1875 Lillian A. Wilbor, daughter
          of Arthur T. and Charlotte (Peckham) Wilbor; m. (2)
          in LC 1 Sept. 1889 Stella Ann Wilbour, daughter of
          Henry Page and Eliza (Wilbour) Wilbour, b. 23 Nov.
          1858, d. in LC 7 May 1952.

15. GARDINER K.[8] WORDELL (Abram[7], Gershom[6], Gershom[5],

Gershom[4], Gershom[3], Gershom[2], William[1]), born in Fall River 20 May
1833.
  He married in Dartmouth 17 Dec. 1854 OLIVE KING, daughter
of Isaac and Peace (Hathaway) King, born 18 Aug. 1834 in Fall River,
died 22 April 1905 in New Bedford.
  For additional information, see the Wordell Manuscript, page
26, at the New Bedford Public Library.

          Children:
  i.   Abram, b. in New Bedford 4 Nov. 1857; d. in LC 8 April
          1936; m. Harriet J. (Peckham) Brownell, daughter of
          James Edmund and Hannah B. (Soule) Peckham and
          divorced wife of William B. Brownell, b. in LC 17 Feb.
          1863, d. 18 July 1946.
17. ii. Clarence G., b. 30 Nov. 1859.

  16. GIDEON MOSHER[8] WORDELL (Gershom[7], Gershom[6],
Gershom[5], Gershom[4], Gershom[3], Gershom[2], William[1]), born in
Dartmouth 7 April 1830, died in LC 30 May 1920.
  He married 10 Aug. 1851 SARAH GRINNEL, daughter of Gideon
and Sarah (Hart) Grinnel, born 5 Feb. 1834, died in LC 22 April 1912.

          Children, born in LC:
18. i.   Harriett, b. 15 Dec. 1851.
     ii.   Rodney Durfee, b. 22 Nov. 1856; m. (1) in Fall River 21
           May 1881 Lizzie Tripp Lincoln; m. (2) in December 1916
           Alberta Bernzen.
     iii. Gideon Frank, b. in LC 25 Feb. 1858; m. Abby Grinnell,
           b. 17 Dec. 1855, d. 11 April 1946.
19. iv.   Gershom, b. 19 April 1860.
20. v.   James McKenzie, b. 14 June 1863.
21. vi.   Charles A., b. 10 Feb. 1866.
22. vii. Nelson, b. 9 Sept. 1868.
     viii. Edmund, b. in 1875, d. in LC 13 May 1893.

  17. CLARENCE G.[9] WORDELL (Gardiner[8], Abram[7], Gershom[6],
Gershom[5], Gershom[4], Gershom[3], Gershom[2], William[1]), born in New
Bedford 30 Nov. 1859, died in LC 30 July 1924.
  He married in LC 18 Nov. 1881 ELIZABETH ALICE WILBOR,
daughter of Charles H. and Mary A. (Dyer) Wilbor, born in LC 9 Oct.
1860, died there 2 Nov. 1922.
  They lived in LC at the east end of Meeting House Lane on the
south side of the lane, up a long drive.

          Children:
  i.   Ethel Lincoln, b. in LC 15 June 1885; d. there 7 April 1912;
          m. in LC 25 Feb. 1908 Thomas Joseph Brennan, son of
          Michael F. and Sarah (Fay) Brennan, b. in Boston.
23. ii. Karl Francis, b. 7 Nov. 1888.

  18. HARRIETT[9] WORDELL (Gideon[8], Gershom[7], Gershom[6],
Gershom[5], Gershom[4], Gershom[3], Gershom[2], William[1]), born 15 Dec.
1851, died 3 Jan. 1930. She married JOSHUA N. WORDELL of New

Bedford.

        Children:
24. i.   Lester LeRoy Wordell, b. in 1872.

    19. GERSHOM⁹ WORDELL (Gideon⁸, Gershom⁷, Gershom⁶,
Gershom⁵, Gershom⁴, Gershom³, Gershom², William¹), born in LC
19 April 1860, died there 3 June 1952. Residence: LC.
    He married 22 June 1882 EMMA FRANCES POTTER, daughter
of George Morey and Hannah G. (Wilbor) Potter, born in LC 1 June
1865, died 10 Oct. 1950.

        Children, recorded in LC:
25. i.   Milton Herbert, b. 18 May 1883.
     ii.   Mabel Gray, b. 6 Jan. 1885; m. 23 Nov. 1902 Walter Everett
             Bixby, son of Horace and Jerusha (May) Bixby.
     iii. Maria Victoria, b. 1 Oct. 1886; m. Charles E. Pettey.
26. iv.   Everett Gershom, b. 6 July 1888.
27. v.   George Gideon, b. 25 March 1891.
28. vi.   LeRoy Harland, b. 20 Dec. 1893.
29. vii. Otho Edmund, b. 8 Aug. 1894.
     viii. Walter Clifford, b. 21 Sept. 1895; d. 2 July 1931.
30. ix.   Sidney Mayo, b. 26 July 1897.
31. x.   Glenwood Remington, b. 8 Oct. 1898.
     xi.   Warren Fulsom, b. 8 Sept. 1900; m. 8 Aug. 1929 (?) Fallee
             Helen Louise Brightman, b. in 1907, d. in 1934.
     xii. Frederic, b. 13 Nov. 1901; d. same day.
32. xiii. Harriett Emma, b. 1 June 1903.
     xiv. Francis Tripp, b. 27 Feb. 1908; m. in January 1935 Doris
             May Lindsey, b. in Fall River 2 May 1910.

    20. JAMES McKENZIE⁹ WORDELL (Gideon⁸, Gershom⁷, Gershom⁶,
Gershom⁵, Gershom⁴, Gershom³, Gershom², William¹), born in LC 14
June 1863, died in LC 20 Oct. 1946. Residence: LC.
    He married SARAH MARGARET ATHINGTON, daughter of William
and Mary (Hargraves) Athington, born in England 21 Sept. 1865, died
in LC 2 Dec. 1949. They are buried in Pleasant View cemetery.

        Children:
     i.   Alice H., b. in LC 7 July 1892; d. there 24 Aug. 1907.

    21. CHARLES A.⁹ WORDELL (Gideon⁸, Gershom⁷, Gershom⁶,
Gershom⁵, Gershom⁴, Gershom³, Gershom², William¹), born in LC 10
Feb. 1866. Residence: LC.
    He married in LC 11 Jan. 1891 CORA GERTRUDE GRINNELL,
daughter of Gideon and Emma M. (Hoxie) Grinnell, born in LC 19 Jan.
1871, died in 1938, buried in Pleasant View cemetery.

        Children, born in LC:
     i.   Mildred, b. in LC 10 Aug. 1897; m. 20 May 1931 Joseph
             Douglas Howard, son of Joseph W. and Esther H. (Hall)
             Howard of Fall River, b. in Fall River 18 April 1899.
     ii.   Louise Gertrude, m. in LC 13 Feb. 1937 Edmund Davis
             Carton, son of Alexander S. and Nancy (McFarland)

Carton, b. in LC 2 Oct. 1875, d. in Fall River 1 Dec. 1951.

22. NELSON[9] WORDELL (Gideon[8], Gershom[7], Gershom[6], Gershom[5], Gershom[4], Gershom[3], Gershom[2], William[1]), born in LC 9 Sept. 1868, died there 23 Aug. 1948. Residence: LC.
He married in Westport 28 Oct. 1896 IDA R. (B.?) MANCHESTER, daughter of Albert and Angenette (Borden) Manchester of Westport, born in Westport 18 Oct. 1874, died in LC 10 March 1935. They are buried in Beech Grove cemetery.

Children, born in LC:
33. i.   Albert Manchester, b. 19 June 1907.
     ii.   Son.
     iii. Anna Jeanette, b. in LC 7 Feb. 1913; m. there 24 July
           1936 Herbert Albion Case, son of George H. and Emma
           (Davis) Case, b. in LC 8 June 1916.

23. KARL FRANCIS[9] WORDELL (Clarence[8], Gardiner[7], Gershom[6], Gershom[5], Gershom[4], Gershom[3], Gershom[2], William[1]), born in LC 7 Nov. 1888, died there 5 July 1938. Residence: LC.
He married in LC 3 Oct. 1917 ETHEL MARIA BORDEN, daughter of Clarence and Maria (Wilkie) Borden, born 6 Aug. 1896, died in Westport. She married second in Henniker, N.H., 20 March 1942 Tinton Wight, son of Charles Tinton and Annie R. Wight, born in Wakefield, R.I., in 1893.

Children, recorded in LC:
     i.   Mary Elizabeth, b. 14 July 1919; m. (license 16 April 1938)
           Manuel Lewis Jr., son of Manuel and Mary (Moniz) Lewis.
34. ii.   Karl Francis Jr., b. 21 July 1922.

24. LESTER LeROY[10] WORDELL (Harriet[9], Gideon[8], Gershom[7], Gershom[6], Gershom[5], Gershom[4], Gershom[3], Gershom[2], William[1]), born in Westport in 1872, died in 1922. Residence: LC.
He married in LC 26 Feb. 1899 RUTHY ANN TABER, daughter of Theodore C. and Betty (Hart) Taber, born in LC in 1876, buried in Pleasant View cemetery.

Children:
     i.   Vernon LeRoy, b. in LC 23 Aug. 1911; m. there 19 Oct.
           1940 Elizabeth Frances Watters, daughter of Frank M.
           and Elizabeth A. (Hunt) Watters. They had a son, Robert
           E., b. 22 Jan. 1943.
     ii.   Merriell Earle, b. in LC 12 Nov. 1913; m. in Tiverton 29
           Oct. 1932 Dorothy Anna Simmons, daughter of Albert L.
           and Mabel (Coggeshalle) Simmons, b. in Westport 27 Nov.
           1914.

25. MILTON HERBERT[10] WORDELL (Gershom[9], Gideon[8], Gershom[7], Gershom[6], Gershom[5], Gershom[4], Gershom[3], Gershom[2], William[1]), born 18 May 1883.
He married first in LC 18 May 1904 CORA MAY BROWNELL,

daughter of George Herbert and Ida May (Bixby) Brownell, born in LC
23 Nov. 1883, died there 5 Jan. 1924. He married second 25 Sept. 1927
BERTHA M. (DAVIS) WINSLOW, daughter of Adelbert and Florence
(Schoolcraft) Davis.

Children by first wife:
- i. Harold Oscar, b. 15 Dec. 1904; m. 28 Aug. 1926 Doris Edna
  Macomber, daughter of Clarence R. and Lottie Devol
  Macomber, b. in Westport 17 Jan. 1904.
- ii. Herbert Francis, b. 17 April 1911; m. 9 April 1933 Beulah
  Velma Field of Pawtucket, daughter of Calvin and Lila
  (Sylvia) Field, b. 11 Aug. 1911.
- 35. iii. Winthrop Bixby, b. 5 April 1915.
- iv. Evelyn May, b. 1 July 1921; d. 1 July 1921.

26. EVERETT GERSHOM[10] WORDELL (Gershom[9], Gideon[8],
Gershom[7], Gershom[6], Gershom[5], Gershom[4], Gershom[3], Gershom[2],
William[1]), born in LC 6 July 1888/9.
He married 6 Nov. 1911 BELLBINA WOOD, daughter of Michael
and Bridget (Ivory) Wood, born 29 March 1887 in Nelson, New Brunswick.

Children, born in LC:
- i. Alice Helen, b. 2 Sept. 1912; d. young.
- ii. Louise.

27. GEORGE GIDEON[10] WORDELL (Gershom[9], Gideon[8],
Gershom[7], Gershom[6], Gershom[5], Gershom[4], Gershom[3], Gershom[2],
William[1]), born in LC 25 March 1891, died there 29 March 1953.
He married in Fall River 18 April 1915 MINERVA BORDEN,
daughter of Clarence and Maria (Wilkie) Borden, born in Tiverton
22 May 1893.

Children, born in LC:
- i. Emma Frances, b. 27 July 1916; m. 8 Sept. 1938 Vernon
  Alfred Anderson, son of Alfred A. and Ida M. (Pick)
  Anderson, b. 20 April 1916. They had a daughter,
  Eleanor F., b. in LC 5 July 1943.
- 36. ii. Edmund, b. 18 July 1919.
- 37. iii. Earl Borden, b. 19 July 1932.

28. LeROY HARLAND[10] WORDELL (Gershom[9], Gideon[8], Gershom[7],
Gershom[6], Gershom[5], Gershom[4], Gershom[3], Gershom[2], William[1]),
born in LC 20 Dec. 1893.
He married in LC 15 Oct. 1914 ETHEL VINCENT PALMER,
daughter of Jesse L. and Ardelia (Percey) Palmer, born 11 May 1892.

Children, born in LC:
- i. Blanche Ardelia, b. 11 Dec. 1916.
- ii. Lucile Audrey, b. 25 June 1922; m. in Tiverton 9 Sept. 1941
  Nathan Andrew Wilbor Jr., son of Nathan A. and Carrie
  E. (Rogers) Wilbor.
- iii. William R., b. 15 April 1929.

29. OTHO EDMUND[10] WORDELL (Gershom[9], Gideon[8],

Gershom[7], Gershom[6], Gershom[5], Gershom[4], Gershom[3], Gershom[2], William[1]), born in LC 8 Aug. 1894.
He married 5 July 1930 EDITH GERTRUDE PIERCE, daughter of Herbert W. and Sophie M. (Hilliard) Pierce, born 10 Nov. 1901.

Children:
i.   Robert Dana, b. in Fall River 14 March 1932; m. in LC 22 Aug. 1953 Ruth Arlene Dwelly, daughter of Charles and Doris (Wilbor) Dwelly, b. in Fall River 23 Oct. 1929.
ii. Roger Pierce, b. in Fall River 10 Jan. 1935.
iii. Russell (?), b. in LC in March 1945.

30. SIDNEY MAYO[10] WORDELL (Gershom[9], Gideon[8], Gershom[7], Gershom[6], Gershom[5], Gershom[4], Gershom[3], Gershom[2], William[1]), born in LC 26 July 1897.
He married in LC 26 Sept. 1923 CHARLOTTE PECKHAM SISSON, daughter of William Northupp and Lidora (Peckham) Sisson, born in LC 21 June 1902.

Children, born in LC:
i.   Elizabeth Janette, b. in Fall River 12 Jan. 1925; m. in LC 14 Sept. 1946 Bernard Wilbor Jr., son of Bernard and Janet (Goodwin) Wilbor.
ii. John Sisson, b. 6 Jan. 1929.
iii. David Gordon, b. 19 May 1933.

31. GLENWOOD REMINGTON[10] WORDELL (Gershom[9], Gideon[8], Gershom[7], Gershom[6], Gershom[5], Gershom[4], Gershom[3], Gershom[2], William[1]), born in LC 8 Oct. 1898.   Residence: LC.
He married 5 June 1927 RENA MAY BROWNELL, daughter of George P. and M. Mary Brownell, born 15 July 1898.

Children:
i.   Glenwood, b. 27 April 1929.
ii. Gladys Carman, b. 27 June 1931.
iii. Philip Brownell, b. 10 May 1935.
iv. Frederick Potter, b. 14 June 1937.

32. HARRIET EMMA[10] WORDELL (Gershom[9], Gideon[8], Gershom[7], Gershom[6], Gershom[5], Gershom[4], Gershom[3], Gershom[2], William[1]), born in LC 1 June 1903.
She married 17 June 1927 ARNOLD FORREST WARRING, son of Robert and Ellen (Forrest) Warring, born 10 Sept. 1901.

Children (Warring):
i.   Arnold Forrest Jr., b. 27 Dec. 1928.
ii. Richard Ivan, b. 27 July 1934.

33. ALBERT MANCHESTER[10] WORDELL (Nelson[9], Gideon[8], Gershom[7], Gershom[6], Gershom[5], Gershom[4], Gershom[3], Gershom[2], William[1]), born in LC 19 June 1907. Residence: • LC.
He married in Providence 26 April 1935 ISABEL SIMMONS KAYE, daughter of John W. and Annie (Kirby) Kaye, born in LC 28 April 1913.

Children:
i.   James C., b. in Fall River 27 Sept. 1940.
ii. Richard Albert, b. in Fall River 4 Feb. 1946.

34. KARL FRANCIS[10] WORDELL JR. (Karl[9], Clarence[8], Gardiner[7], Gershom[6], Gershom[5], Gershom[4], Gershom[3], Gershom[2], William[1]), born in LC 21 July 1922. Residence: LC.

He married in LC 8 June 1946 EDNA ABBIE LEWIS, daughter of Manuel and Mary (Moniz) Lewis, born in LC 24 Nov. 1920.

Children, recorded in LC:
i.   Karl Francis 3d, b. in Fall River 13 March 1947.
ii. Diane, b. in Fall River 4 July 1952.

35. WINTHROP BIXBY[11] WORDELL (Milton[10], Gershom[9], Gideon[8], Gershom[7], Gershom[6], Gershom[5], Gershom[4], Gershom[3], Gershom[2], William[1]), born in LC 5 April 1915. He married GLADYS M. LAWTON.

Children:
i.   Barbara, b. 5 Sept. 1942.
ii. Paul W., b. 20 Dec. 1944.
iii. Barry L., b. in Fall River 15 July 1949.

36. EDMUND[11] WORDELL (George[10], Gershom[9], Gideon[8], Gershom[7], Gershom[6], Gershom[5], Gershom[4], Gershom[3], Gershom[2], William[1]), born in LC 14 July 1919. He married MADELINE E. HAMLET, daughter of Clifford and Elvira (Field) Hamlet.

Children:
i.   Amey L., b. in Fall River 5 Oct. 1946.
ii. Ann, b. in 1953.

37. EARL BORDEN[11] WORDELL (George[10], Gershom[9], Gideon[8], Gershom[7], Gershom[6], Gershom[5], Gershom[4], Gershom[3], Gershom[2], William[1]), born 19 July 1932. He married MARY DOROTHY ETHIER.

Children:
i.   Theodore E., b. in Fall River 10 July 1951.
ii. (--), b. in Fall River 14 Aug. 1952.
iii. Donald Warren, b. in LC 1 Oct. 1953.

❧

THE YETTMAN FAMILY

FREDERIC YETTMAN, son of Patrick J. and Annie (Binn) Yettman of Nova Scotia, born in Milford, Mass., 7 Aug. 1899. Residence: LC.

He married in Providence 15 Feb. 1919 CAROLINE JOYCE BROWN, daughter of Walter and Catherine (Joyce) Brown, born in LC 6 Aug. 1902, died in Cranston 6 Sept. 1938.

      Children, recorded in LC:
- i.   Phillis Ann, b. in LC 26 July 1919.
- ii.   Irene Elizabeth, b. in LC 5 July 1920.
- iii.   Walter Brown, b. 2 Sept. 1921; m. in LC 14 Sept. 1946 Gladys Louise Hockler, daughter of Luther Lawrence and Susan (Thompson) Hockler, b. in Freebody, Ill., 6 Feb. 1922. This was her second marriage.

WILBOR HOUSE
Home of the Little Compton Historical Society

LITTLE COMPTON

FAMILIES

CORRECTIONS AND ADDITIONS

LITTLE COMPTON, RHODE ISLAND

1974

819

Page 6 — Line 11 should read "She was born 15 March 1763".

Page 10 — 12 Lines from bottom omit words "First to an Allen, secondly".

Page 11 — Philip W.[9] Almy, m. 9 July 1930 Dorothy Terry, b. 13 Dec. 1904 in Fall River, dau.. of George and Annie (Orton) Terry.

Page 13 — Line 9 should read "1717/19".

Page 19 — After Line 8 insert:

"Records of the BAILEY FAMILY" Providence 1895

1. WILLIAM[1] BAILEY, b. unknown, probably in London, a weaver, d. before 20 July 1670. He m. GRACE PARSONS, dau. of Hugh and Elizabeth Parsons of Portsmouth, R. I. She m. 2nd THOMAS LAWTON and d. after 1677. HUGH PARSONS, b. 1613, d. 1684; ELIZABETH PARSONS, b. about 1613, d. after 1684.

Children:

2. i. John, b. 1653, d. 13 Jan. 1736
   ii. Joseph, d. 16 Oct. 1702 (date of daughter's marriage)
       child: Sarah, m. 16 Oct. 1702 Samuel Dunn, son of Richard
   iii. Edward, d. 1712, M. Frances (--). Lived in Newport & Tiverton
        (4 children)
   iv. Hugh, d. 1724, m. 1st Anna, who d. Feb. 20-26, 1720/1. m. 2nd 30 May 1724 Abigail Williams of Voluntown. He died shortly thereafter. Resided in Newport, then East Greenwich. He and first wife had 5 children, mostly born in East Greenwich.
   v. Stephen,.b. 1665, d. 17 Oct. 1724, m. Susanna (--) b. 1673 d. 25 April 1723. They had 2 children.

2. JOHN[2] BAILEY (William[1]) m. (--) SUTTON. Lived in Portsmouth and Newport; d. 13 Jan. 1736.

Children: Sarah, William, John, Thomas, Abigail, Samuel, Mary and Ruth, all mentioned in "Records of BAILEY FAMILY". George probably one of William[3]'s children. Elizabeth may be from another family and Martha and Jane (mentioned in will) may be grandchildren.

Page 20 — WILLIAM[3] BAILEY. "BAILEY FAMILY" says he m. DOROTHY GRAVES, dau. of Richard and Dorothy Graves. She d. 26 Nov. 1771. (No authentification for either).

Page 21 — Lieut. THOMAS[3] BAILEY, b. 1690, d. 1741, m. 10 July 1712 Mary Wood. "BAILEY FAMILY" shows only 1 child Thomas[4] with same dates. Other children may be correct as to parentage and births — but other information obviously erroneous, such as

Date of death of William[4] and parenthood

Date of Death of Samuel[4] and marriage

(I cannot find references to them under any other generation or parentage).

Page 24 — 5. ii. Thomas Bailey b. 15 Mar. 1715
       v. Oliver Bailey b. 25 Sept. 1721
       viii. and ix. Incorrect

Page 26 — Line 1 should read "to SARAH CHURCH, daughter of Thomas[3] and Sarah (Horswell) Church."

— Line 16 should read "v. SARAH CHURCH, b. 23 Sept. 1749" etc.

Page 27 — Deborah Bailey Gray
        m. Philip Gray b. 6 Apr. 1738
Page 48 — Line 13 should read "b. 12 Feb. 1897 in Newport".

Page 51 — Omit "IV. CHARLES C." from children of ROBERT MASON[4] BONE.

— The picture is of HARBOR ROAD in Adamsville.

Page 53 — BENAJAH ALEXANDER[7] BORDEN, m. 1st Feb. 1845 in LC Elizabeth
A. Rossen. He m. 2nd 26 Feb. 1884 in LC Hannah B. (Palmer) Wordell, widow of
Jonathan Wordell.

— CLARENCE E. BORDEN's child Minerva m. George Gideon Wordell,
son of GERSHOM.

Page 55 — 1. THOMAS BRAYTON, b. 15 Feb. 1840 in Tiverton m. Mary N.
Borden, b. 15 May 1841 in Tiverton. He was son of Borden and Abby Brayton.
    Children:
    i.   George Henry, b. 12 Sept. 1863 in Westport, d. 22 May 1946 in Little
          Compton; m. Adelaide Potter, dau. of Abraham and Jane (Winslow)
          Potter, b. 11 Nov. 1854 in Dartmouth. She d. 7 Jan. 1931.
          Children: Henry P., Alden and Ruth — All of Westport
2. ii.   Elmer Zephaniah, b. 9 May 1866

— 2. ELMER Z.[2] BRAYTON (Thomas[1]) b. 9 May 1866 in Westport m.
1st ELIZABETH FLEMMING.
    Child:
    i.   Frank E., b. 26 May 1893, m. 29 Nov. 1917 Ethel Hart
          One child: Frank E. Brayton, Jr.
m. 2nd Eudora M. Palmer, b. 6 July 1880
    Children:
    ii.   Lillian E., b. 7 April 1901
    iii. Helen, b. 1902 Westport
3. iv.   Elmer Z., Jr. b. 8 Sept. 1906
    v.   John B., b. 18 Feb. 1910 ·

— 3. ELMER Z.[3] BRAYTON, Jr. (Elmer Z.[2], Thomas[1]) b. 8 Sept. 1906
m. 1st ELEANOR C. SNELL about 1924, dau. of Herman and Elizabeth (McChane)
Snell, who was b. 10 Nov. 1908.
    Children:
    i.   Dorothy E., b. 5 Feb. 1925 m. George Mosher. They had 3 children.
    ii.   Elmer Z., 3rd, b. 5 Aug. 1929, d. age 3 mos.
    iii. Arthur E., b. 2 May 1933
m. 2nd Susan E. Seabury, dau. of William H. and Josephine (Burlingame) Seabury,
b. 1 Nov. 1917 at LC. They were m. 10 June 1944
    iv.   Elmer Z., 3rd., b. 28 Jan. 1945, d. 9 July 1947

Page 61 — Last line "viii. Betsey, b. 23 March 1755 not married."

Page 62 — 12. JEREMIAH[4] BRIGGS m. Anna Taylor, dau. of Peter and Elizabeth
(Irish) Taylor.

Page 69 — Line 19 should read "CHARLES E.[4] BRIGGS (Charles E.[3], Charles F.[2],
Perry[1])".

821

— Line 23 should read "RAY THURSTON[4] BRIGGS (Charles E.[3], Charles F.[2], Perry[1])".

Page 73 — Nicholas[1] Brown, daughter Jane b. about 1647

Page 77 — Moses[5] Brown
see p. 81 for his children — No. 19 Abraham, No. 20 Robert

Page 85 — Line 11 should read "there 16 Nov. 1937 ae 92-8-23".

Page 89 — CAPT. THOMAS[3] BROWNELL m. Mary Crandall, dau. of Samuel and Sarah (Celley) Crandall.

Page 113 — RICHMOND[7] BROWNELL's wife Susan H. Allen d. 7 Aug. 1929.

Page 120 — 4 lines from bottom should read "1852, d. there 2 July 1934 ae 82".

Page 122 — Correct Spelling of FREDERICK RICHMOND[8] BROWNELL'S children:
Winthrop Sisson Brownell
Carlton Coggeshall Brownell

Page 123 — WALTER D[8] BROWNELL's child Seba, b. 19 Sept. 1908 d. young.

— Next to bottom line — eliminate ? mark.

Page 124 — HERBERT CARPENTER[9] BROWNELL's son Peter H. was b. 4 Aug. 1938 in Providence.

Page 129 — EDITH RUSSELL CHURCH BURCHARD d. 1942
Add another child: "vii. Caroline Corwin, b. 12 Dec. 1909"

Page 135 — PETER TAYLOR[6] BURGESS' child:
iv.   Benjamin, d. 23 Sept. 1862 ae 55, m. 4 Feb. 1831 Mary Hawes, who d. 16 Nov. 1862

Page 142 — EDWARD W. CANFIELD, b. 30 April 1874, son of Charles E. and Hannah. (Providence VR) m. 20 Nov. 1912 Hattie C. Manchester, (See Page 416)
Child Ernest Wentworth was b. 28 April 1913

Page 146 — FRANCIS J. CARROLL, Jr. was b. 28 March 1917.

Page 148 — ALEXANDER STEWART[3] CARTON, Jr. m. 2nd Mary G. DaCosta

Page 153 — ABNER BARTLETT[8] CASE m. 2nd Bessie Thomas (Snyder) Dewsnap.

Page 157 — Line 6. Benjamin Chase m. Amey Borden

Page 162 — PHILIP W.[8] CHASE. Omit child Sarah Ann. See below under Thomas W.[8].

Page 167 — Deborah[2] Church, b. 27 Jan 1646

Page 172 — Joseph[3] Church, m. Grace Shaw dau. of Anthony and Alice (Stonard) Shaw
Caleb[4], b. 11 Oct. 1701
John[3], b. 5 July 1668   822

Page 174 — THOMAS[3] CHURCH's child "x. Sarah, b. 15 May 1721 m. etc., died 5 Sept. 1762".

Page 178 — Child Number "vi. Mercy m. Deacon Sylvester Brownell".

Page 191 — THE CLARK FAMILY (Note spelling)
EDWARD LORD CLARK (son of Charles P. Clark) (See Page 388)
Children:
i.   Kempton, m. Janice (Cole) Dewey, widow of Homer Dewey
ii.   Susan, b. 28 May 1912, m. 23 March 1935 Henry Evans Stowell and
       had 3 children
iii.   Jane, b. 10 Jan. 1918, m. 16 Sept. 1940 Richard James Heer and had
       3 children (2 adopted)

Page 195— Children of Matthew[1] Coe
ii.   Sarah[2] Coe d. 29 May 1694
iv.   Abigail[2] and v. Martha[2] — dates may be reversed
viii. Elizabeth[2] Coe married Benjamin Tucker
2. John[2] Coe (Matthew[1])
i.   Lydia b. 26 Feb. 1682
ii.   Sarah b. 25 Feb. 1684/85

Page 196— Ruth Coe, d. of Hannah, m. Nov. 1745 Joseph Briggs, son of Job Briggs

Page 198— Benjamin[4] Coe, wife Sarah d. 1834

Page 199—
iv.   Harriet R. Coe m. Capt. Wm. A. Hussey, 14 Apr. 1859
v.   Jethro Briggs Coe b. 15 June 1826

Page 201 — Coggeshalle usually spelt Coggeshall

THE COGGESHALL FAMILY
(Reference: The Coggeshalls of America
Goodspeeds 1930)
1.   JOHN[1] COGGESHALL (John, John) Baptised Halsted, Co. Essex
9 Dec. 1601, died Newport, R. I. 27 Nov. 1647, m. in England MARY -- b. about
1604, d. 8 Nov. 1684 in Newport
Children:
2. i.   John (Major John) b. about 1620 Essex Co.
ii.   Ann, b. Essex Co. 1622, d. Newport, R. I. 6 Mar. 1688/9, m. 15 Nov.
       1643 Peter Easton, b. 1622, d. 12 Dec. 1693/4 son of Gov. Nicholas
       Easton and Ann (Clayton) Easton. They had 13 children (bad luck)
iii.   Mary, b. Essex Co. about 1624, living in 1645
iv.   Joshua, b. Co. Essex 1626
v.   James, b. England about 1628, living in 1645
vi.   Hananeel (Hannah) Bapt. Boston 3 May 1635, probably died young
vii.   Wayte (Wait) Bapt. Boston 11 Sept. 1636, m. 18 Dec. 1651 Daniel
       Gould, b. about 1625, d. 26 Mar. 1716, son of Jeremiah and
       Prescilla (Grover) Gould. They had 10 children
viii. Bedaiah, Bapt. 30 July 1637 in Boston. Probably died young.

2.   (Major) JOHN[2] COGGESHALL (John[1]) b. Essex Co. about 1620.
Emigrated with parents 1632, d. Newport, R. I. 1 Oct. 1708, buried Newport,
m. at Newport ELIZABETH BAULSTONE 17 June 1647. She was daughter of
William and Elizabeth Baulstone of Portsmouth, R. I. She was b. Aug. 1629, d. 1

Oct. 1700. They were divorced 25 May 1655. She married second Thomas Gould, brother of Daniel Gould above — no issue. JOHN[2] married second at Providence PATIENCE THROCKMORTON in Dec. 1655, daughter of John and Alice (Staut) Throckmorton of Providence. She was b. 1640, d. Newport 7 Sept. 1676 and buried in Coggeshall Cemetery, Newport. JOHN[2] married third MARY (HEDGE) STURGIS 1 Oct. 1679 in Yarmouth, Mass. She was daughter of Capt. William Hedge and widow of Samuel Sturgis. She was born in Yarmouth 1648, d. 22 Aug. 1731 at Newport.

Children by first wife correct

Children by second wife correct to

- vii.   Joseph, b. 30 May 1665, d. Newport 16 Sept. 1676
- viii.   Rebecca, b. Newport 20 June 1667, m. John Reynolds
- ix.   Patience, b. Newport 13 Aug. 1669, m. Newport 3 Nov. 1692 Samuel Rathbone, son of John and Margaret Rathbone. He was b. Newport 3 Aug. 1672, d. 24 Jan. 1757. They had 8 children
- x.   Benjamin, b. Newport 27 July 1672
- xi.   Content, b. Newport 28 Mar. 1674, d. 26 Sept. 1675
- xi.(A) Content, b. 10 May 1676, m. Samuel Morton

Children by third wife

- xii.   Joseph, b. 1680
- xiii.   Abraham, b. Newport about 1682
- xiv.   Samuel, b. about 1684, d. 24 July 1712 in London, Eng. Apparently did not marry.
- xv.   Elisha, b. Newport about 1687. Supposed to have married and had issue.

Page 202 — FREEGIFT[3] COGGESHALL

Children:

- i.   Patience, b. 6 Dec. 1685, d. 21 Dec. 1721, m. 23 Jan. 1705 Benedict Arnold 3rd (Benedict, Benedict). He was born 28 Aug. 1683, d. about 1739 in Newport. Had 12 children.
- ii.   Thomas, b. 17 Oct. 1687
- iii.   Freegift, b. 30 Sept. 1689
- iv.   Sarah, b. 20 Sept. 1691
- v.   Elizabeth, b. 4 Oct. 1693
- v. (A) William, b. Newport 24 June 1695
- vi.   Mary, b. 9 Oct. 1697 Newport, d. Rehoboth, Mass., about 1753, m. (intentions) 27 Jan. 1727 John Lyon
- vii.   Nathaniel, b. 19 April 1700, d. 22 Aug. 1701
- viii. Nathaniel (2) b. 28 Jan. 1702
- ix.   Rebecca, b. 26 Jan. 1703/4, d. 28 July 1714 Newport

Page 202 — Number 4 should read "(Deacon) NATHANIEL[4] COGGESHALL)"

Page 203 — (See Page 319 of COGGESHALL FAMILY book).
All John Coggeshall's children born in Tiverton, R. I.
Number vii. is spelled Jothran.
Most of Jothran's children born in Tiverton. Another child Number 5 (A) James, born in Tiverton.
Number 3 OTIS[3] COGGESHALL born in Tiverton

Page 204 — Lucy T. Collins d. 30 Mar. 1893.

Page 206 — Mary Cooke m. William Manchester

Page 212 — Correct spelling "THE CORY FAMILY"

Page 213 — Roy Earl Cory m. Miriam Armitage, daughter of George and Catherine (Allatte) Armitage
Etta Myrtle Cory was daughter of ARTHUR FOREST[9] CORY

Page 214 — ROBERT COZZENS of Newport was married 22 May 1735

Page 215 — William Crandall, b. 1711, m. Patience Wordell, daughter of Gershom and Sarah (Mott) Wordell

Page 216 — THE CRANDON FAMILY — Hattie omit "m. O.S. York" — (see Nellie)

Page 220 — Line 12 beside picture should be "Isaac C. Wilbour is credited . . . "

Page 221 — JAMES CROSBY d. 5 April 1923

Page 223 — THE DAVENPORT FAMILY — All entries of first 4 generations listed in NEHR have been carefully checked. Thomas Davenport's son Charles m. Waitstill Smith. THOMAS[1] married Mary --. It was THOMAS[2] who m. Mary Pitman. Child x. John m. Naomi (perhaps Foster).

Page 225 — EBENEZER DAVENPORT m. in Little Compton, Mary Pitman, who was born in 1693. Their son Jonathan was born in 1734

Page 226 — Line 1 should read "John, b. 18 Jan. 1735, d. 9 Nov. 1809, m. Sarah Weeden who was b. 5 Aug. 1754"

Page 226 — JOSEPH[3] DAVENPORT's children
William, b. 1 Aug. 1735 m. Elizabeth Briggs
Jeremiah, b. 10 Oct. 1738 m. Sarah Palmer
7. ELIPHALET[4] DAVENPORT died 1786 in Little Compton. He married in LC Hannah Phillips, d. of Seth and Abigail Phillips.

Page 227 — OLIVER[4] DAVENPORT m. Sarah Macomber of LC, m. 2nd Mary Devol of LC
JOHN[4] DAVENPORT m. Sarah Weeden, b. 5 Aug. 1754.

Page 231 — The name of CHARLES[8] DAVENPORT's fifth child was "Nathaniel Boomer" — per David Patten

Page 246— Nathaniel[3] Dring, wife Mary Simmons died 18 Oct. 1832

Page 247— 2. Henry Bernardin[5] Drowne
Page 248 — THOMAS[1] DURFEE's children:
  i.   Robert, b. 10 March 1665, d. 10 May 1718, m. 1687 in Portsmouth, Mary Sanford (see Page 533)
  ii.   Thomas, m. Ann Freeborn, b. 1669, d. 1729, dau. of William Freeborn of Portsmouth
  iii. Richard, d. 1700 in Portsmouth, m. Ann Almy, b. 29 Nov. 1667, dau. of Christopher & Elizabeth (Cornell) Almy

iv. William, b. 1673
v. Ann, m. William Potter of Portsmouth, son of Nathaniel and Elizabeth (Stokes) Potter, (see Page 504)
vi. Benjamin, d. 12 March 1733 in Portsmouth, m. Prudence Earle, dau. of William and Mary (Walker) Earle.
vii. Patience, m. in Portsmouth, 23 Sept. 1708 Benjamin Tallman (see Page 657)
viii. Deliverance, b. 1690 in Portsmouth, m. there 23 April 1724 William Cory of Tiverton, son of Wm. and Martha (Cook) Cory

Page 251 — Picture is of "United Congregational Church"

Page 259 — Line 5 — Abbie F. Dyer m. David Wilbor, son of David and Hannah (Rounds) Wilbor — (See Page 752)

Page 279 — Line 28 — The DAR accepted Enos Gifford

Page 293 — Children of Edward[2] GRAY:
v. Phebe, b. 6 Sept. 1699 m. John Manchester (see Page 407)
viii. Hannah, b. 3 Nov. 1707 (see Page 212)

Page 297 — Children of Job[5] Gray:
i. Sarah m. Peleg Bailey, son of Isaac and Sarah Bailey

Page 307 — See "ANCESTRY OF THE GRINNELL FAMILY" William M. Emery 1931 Correct Spelling is Matthew Grinnell

Page 308 — RICHARD[3] GRINNELL m. Patience Emery (or Amory)

Page 310 — RICHARD[4] GRINNELL m. 1st Alice Church 18 Nov. 1738. She was born 24 Jan. 1718, died 29 Sept. 1739

Page 315 — BAILEY[5] GRINNELL lived on the north side of Muddy Pond in Union, Maine, and then in Exeter

Page 339— ii. Samuel[3] Hicks Jr. probably was married 9 Jan. 1678/9
v. Margaret[3] Hicks possibly died 12 Dec. 1694

Page 342— ix. Mary[3] Hilliard d. L.C. 16 Feb. 1716

Page 349 — Picture — The Commons, Little Compton, Rhode Island (Main Street — There are West Main Road and East Main Road. The former was originally called The Great West Road — but no Main Street.)

Page 353— 2. ii. Benjamin Howland m. Judith Sampson

Page 369 — 6 lines from bottom — Phebe L. Hambly Hunt died 22 March 1929

Page 371 — Line 6 should read "From the Great Highway".

Page 379 — (Per David Patten) EUGENE BAILEY JACKSON, son of Frank and Adele (Howe) Jackson, born 6 Aug. 1880 in Woonsocket, R. I., died in Boston in 1936, m. 6 Sept. 1911 in LC, Caroline Wilbour Patten, daughter of Frederick M. and Dora J. (Wilbour) Patten, b. 10 July 1885 in LC.
Children:
i. Patten, b. 6 June 1912, d. 1930 while with William Beebe's scientific expedition in Bermuda. He was buried in the Seaconnet Cemetery on the Great West Road

ii.	Deborah, b. 20 Aug. 1915, m. 19 June 1934 Harry McIntosh McLeod of Chicago. He died in Nov. 1954 and was buried in the Seaconnet Cemetery.
Child (adopted) — Penelope, b. 21. Aug. 1940, m. in London, Eng., 22 May 1964 Richard B. Johnson of Norwich, Conn.
iii.	Anthony, b. 4 July 1923, m. 12 May 1950 Harriet Long Milliken dau. of Dudley Long Milliken and Eunice (Harriman) Milliken, m. 2nd 23 June 1956 Jane Lowe Arnold
Children:
i.	Diana, b. 20 March 1957
ii.	Patten, b. 17 Dec. 1959

Page 385 — EPHRAIM[2] KEMPTON (Ephraim[1])

Page 388 — THOMAS WARREN[9] KEMPTON m. Mary Jane Taylor who died 5 Oct. 1940
Child:
Mary Susan m. Edward Lord Clark, son of Charles P. and Caroline (Tyler) Clark. He died 1941.

Children: (See Page 191)
i. Kempton, b. 23 Sept. 1903
ii. Susan, b. 5/28/1912, m. 23 Mar. 1935 Henry Evans Stowell
iii. Jane, b. 10 Jan. 1918, m. 16 Sept. 1940 Richard J. Heer

Page 395 — CHARLES STERLING LAWTON was born 12 Feb. 1897. According to him he had no son — just daughter Deborah

Page 404 — LILA LADD McFADDEN died 23 Aug. 1928

Page 407 — Line 4 — Deborah Manchester m. Samuel Sanford (See Page 534)

Page 411 — JOHN[5] MANCHESTER m. Sarah Church Bailey (See Page 26)

Page 420 — AGNES GILETTE MANCHESTER m. Dr. R. H. Dennett

Page 428 — ADELBERT ALLEN MARTIN d. 27 April 1958 in Fall River. (See Page 768)

Page 429 — THE MIAS FAMILY
1.	NICHOLAS[1] MIAS m. Elizabeth Nicholes (or Nichols). He died 4 Nov. 1727. She was daughter of Richard and Phebe Nicholes of East Greenwich, R. I.
3.	OLIVER[2] MIAS (Nicholas)
Children:
i.	Elizabeth b. 12 Sept. 1736 Richmond, Kent County, R. I., m. Ephraim Howard 12 April 1764
ii.	Nicholas (2nd) b. about 1738 Richmond m. Elizabeth Hopkins 17 July 1781, daughter of Tibbets Hopkins. Nicholas died Feb. 1827
iii.	Mary, b. 6 April 1740 Richmond, m. Henry Bowers of Taunton, Mass. He was b. 1747

iv.	Ann, b. 20 Jan. 1742 Richmond, m. George Gardner of Pownal, Vermont. He was b. 3 June 1739

827

v. Hezakiah, b. about 1746 m. Elizabeth Gardner. Moved to Pownal, Vt., d. 2 Oct. 1798

vi. Alice, b. 19 March 1746 Richmond, R. I.

vii. Oliver, b. 18 March 1748 in LC, m. Elizabeth Niles 4 Dec. 1768 at West Greenwich. He died in Laurens, N. Y., in 1811

viii. Gideon, b. (c.) 1750, Kent County, R. I., m. Marcy (or Mary) - - . Moved to Pownal, Vt.

ix. Joseph, b. (c) 1752. Moved to Pownal, Vt.

Page 449— John[4] Palmer m. Mary Hilliard, b. 3 Apr. 1687; m. second Elizabeth Church 12 July 1717

Page 459 — JOHN STODDARD[7] PALMER, JR.'s child Hannah B. m. (1) Jonathan Wordell, m. 2nd Benajah A. Borden, b. in 1819.

Page 467—   v.   Mary[3] Pearce d. 31 Jan. 1755
JAMES[3] PEARCE m. Martha Wilbore, who d. 22 Sept. 1760, dau. of Samuel and Mary (Potter) Wilbore (See Page 709)

Page 497 — Laura Frances Peckham d. 8 Feb. 1946

Page 501 — BERNARD MAURICE[9] PECKHAM
Children:
i. Janice Johnson
ii. Nina Luthera b. 21 Aug. 1933 Fall River
iii. Rachel Emelia, b. 12 Oct. 1935 Fall River
iv. Jason Maxwell

Page 502 — PAUL FRANKLIN PERKINS m. AGNES LEEDS BURCHARD, daughter of Roswell etc.

Page 521— 15. Nathaniel[5] Richmond
Child No. iv., v. and vi. belong under Joshua[5] Richmond

15. Nathaniel[5] Richmond
add: By second wife—child Rebecca b. 17 Apr. 1793

Page 528 — (Insert) THE ROUNDS FAMILY
ISAAC ROUNDS and wife PHEBE SIMMONS (See Page 47)
Children:
i. Sarah, b. 1811, d. 17 Jan. 1839, m. Hon Cyrenus[10] Bliss
ii. Phebe, b. 5 Jan. 1818, d. 16 July 1883, m. (as his second wife) Hon. Cyrenus[10] Bliss
iii. Hannah, b. 18 April 1820, d. 7 Feb. 1913, m. David W.[7] Wilbor (See Page 752)
Also probably:
Ann, who m. Stephen C. Hart
Mary, who m. William Wilcox

Page 548   Martha[9] Seabury m. Francis B. Manchester, son of Giles Ernest and Etta (Hampton) Manchester

Pabe 552 — 1. ANTHONY[1] SHAW was probably the first Shaw of this family in America, although there is still some possibility he was the son of John Shaw. He was in Boston in 1653.

Children:

i.	William, b. 21 Jan. 1653*, d. 25 Jan. 1654* (Boston VR)
ii.	William (2nd), b. 24 Feb. 1654* (Boston VR)
iii.	Elizabeth, b. 21 May 1656 (Boston VR)
iv.	Mary, b. 17 Dec. 1658 (Boston VR)
v.	Israel, b. about 1660
vi.	Ruth, b. 10 Dec. 1660
vii.	Grace, b. 1666 Portsmouth, R. I., m. Joseph Church, d. 1 March 1739. Had 9 children

*One year later — new calendar

Page 552 — ISRAEL[2] SHAW

Children:

ii.	Mary (See Page 46) No children
iv.	Alice m. John Palmer, son of William Palmer and Mary (Richardson) Palmer of Taunton (See Page 445/7)
vi.	Hannah m. William Wood (See Pages 781/3)
viii.	Ruth m. Philip Tabor 21 Nov. 1721
xi.	Grace married Edward Church (See Page 176)
xii.	Comfort, b. 9 April 1709

Page 554 — ISRAEL[3] SHAW

Children:

vi.	Lillie
vii.	Meribah
ix.	Lois

Page 555— William Shaw m. Mary Hilliard dau. of Capt. David and Susanna (Luther) Hilliard

Page 558 PETER[4] SHAW

Children:

i.	Mary (See Page 730)
ii.	Ruth (See Page 115)
iii.	Jediah (his number should be 21A)
iv.	Prudence, b. 1 April 1782
vi.	Joseph m. Orpha Sutliff 26 April 1809. He d. 21 June 1854
vii.	Peleg m. Mary Delano 21 April 1811, d. 28 Dec. 1863

Page 559 — Children:

iii.	Sarah, who m. David Shaw (See Page 560)

Page 560 — JEDIAH[5] SHAW should be numbered 21A

Page 561 — Children:

vii.	George Wallace[7] Shaw m. 1st Charlotte F. Winsor. She died in Dec. 1875. They had one child Frank Harold[8]. He m. 2nd Mabel F. Harlow in 1877. They had 5 children. Descendants

Frank Harold[8]
George Frederick[9]
Peter Van Cleve[10]
Geoffrey Van Cleve[11] b. 25 Oct. 1970. He and his parents now
  living in Little Compton (1974)

Page 563/4 GEORGE M. SHAW, son of William and Margaret (McDowell) Shaw,
born in Combernaud, Scotland, 1845; died in LC 1915; married Anne Douglas
Shedden, b. Scotland 1851; after marriage lived for many years in LC; died in Providence 1940. They had one son, Robert Forrester Shaw, born 19 Jan. 1888 in LC
and long a resident of LC until he moved to Providence about 1916. Robert went
to school near head of Taylors Lane.

   ROBERT FORRESTER SHAW, son of George Main and Anne (Shedden)
Shaw, born LC 19 Jan. 1888; m. 18 Oct. 1916 Florence M. Nightingale of Chazy,
N. Y.
   Children:
   i.   Robert Forrester Shaw, Jr. (Lt. Col. U.S. Air Force Retired)
         b. 26 Aug. 1917 Providence, lives in Minneapolis
   ii.   Ruth Shaw Dyson, b. 7 Jan. 1921 Providence, lives in Albany, Ga.

Page 567 — JOSEPH FORREST SHERER m. Marion Osborn on 2 April 1902. He
died 4 July 1956, she 5 March 1937.
   Children:
   i.   Osborn, b. 14 June 1903, m. 11 Sept. 1937 Josephine Winifred
         Cassidy, who was b. 14 July 1903
   ii.   Jeannette Wesson, b. 21 April 1906, m. 24 Oct. 1925 Harold T.
         Merriman, who was b. 27 April 1902
   iii. Helene, b. 15 Jan. 1912, m. 2 April 1935 Channing S. Smith, who
         was b. 29 April 1904
   iv.   Joseph F., Jr., b. 17 Oct. 1918, m. 27 Dec. 1943 Mary Mackintosh,
         who was b. 5 April 1919
   v.   Charles T., 3rd, b. 2 July 1921, m. 5 Sept. 1942 Helen T. Rand,
         who was b. 31 Oct. 1922
   vi.   Edith O., b. 7 March 1926, m. 6 Aug. 1949 Thomson M. Whitin,
         who was b. 12 Jan. 1923

Page 571 — THE SIMMONS FAMILY — See "Moses Simmons and his descendants
1624—1930" (By no means complete)

Page 572 — MOSES[1] SIMMONS, d. Duxbury 1691
   Children:
   i.   Moses m. Patience Barstow
   iv.   Elizabeth was 2nd wife of Richard Dwelly

   — JOHN[2] SIMMONS, m. Nov. 16, 1669 Mercy Pabodie, who was b. Plymouth
   1649/1653, d. 1728

Page 574— William[4] Simmons
         child viii. Mary m. Nathaniel Dring

Page 575 — BENJAMIN[4] SIMMONS
    Children:
    i.   Peter, b. 19 May 1736
    v.   Hannah, d. 24 Jan. 1824

Page 576 — PELEG[4] SIMMONS
    Children:
    vii.   Eunice
    ix, x, xi — some confusion as to names and dates
    xi.   is indicated as Abigail

Page 577 — DEACON ADAM[5] SIMMONS, d. LC 21 Aug. 1807, age 74

Page 579 — EPHRAIM[5] (or Ephriam) SIMMONS
    Children:
    i.   Hannah, b. 1780
    ii.   Amy, b. 19 May 1782, m. Samuel Tripp

    — ZARAH[5] SIMMONS' Child III. Abigail, b. 18 Feb. 1776 died young

Page 580 — JOHN[5] SIMMONS
    Children:
    iii.   Probably Susanna
    vi.   Phebe, d. 19 Jan. 1862, m. Isaac Rounds, son of David and
          Hannah (King) Rounds, b. 24 June 1776, d. 19 April 1846

    — PETER[5] SIMMONS, b. LC 19 May 1736

Page 581 — IVORY[5] SIMMONS
    Children:
    iii.   Probably Sophronia, b. 27 Feb. 1785
    v.   Amaziah, m. Hannah Wilbor

Page 582 — THOMAS[5] SIMMONS — (Jane Wilbur, a descendant, says he had 3
wives and 18 children) m. 2nd Elizabeth Manchester, who died 14 Oct. 1798; m.
3rd 25 Aug. 1803 Susannah (Palmer) Macomber, widow of Job and dau. of John
and Mary (Stoddard) Palmer. She d. 6 Feb. 1820
    Children:
    vi.   Edward, b. 1783, d. 28 June 1867, m. Dillie Macomber
    vii.   Amasa, b. 6 June 1808, d. 9 Feb. 1895 m. Nancy King, dau. of
          Stephen
    xi.   Ruth, d. 22 Jan. 1853, aged 82, m. Joel Albert, b. 1783 son of
          John and Innocent (Crandell) Albert
    xii.   Rachel, m. Capt. Godfrey King, son of Stephen, of Westport

    — CAPT. GIDEON[5] SIMMONS — above referred to Genealogy says first
child was Moses

Page 583 — iv.   William Pitt
           vii.   Benjamin, b. 11 Oct. 1786

    — NATHANIEL[6] SIMMONS
    Children probably:

831

      i.   Sarah
      ii.   Priscilla, b. 6 March 1781
      iii.   Lindall (or Lindell), b. 26 Oct. 1783
      iv.   Ruth, b. 17 Aug. 1789

Page 584 — DAVIS[6] SIMMONS
    Child #1. Walter Cook, b. 19 May 1794, died young

    — ISAAC[6] SIMMONS
    Children:
      ii.   Probably Suvarry, b. 13 Aug. 1791 (See Page 667)
      iv.   Mary Brownell, b. 3 Aug. 1800

Page 586 — Note that CAPT. JEREMIAH[6] SIMMONS had one daughter — BFW says Julian Ann, Genealogy says Eliza Ann, b. Boston.

Page 587 — First Child of BENONI[6] SIMMONS, Cornelius, d. LC 5 Oct. 1832

Page 588 — Children of ICHABOD[6] SIMMONS
      i.   Mahalah, m. Philip King, b. 3 July 1786, son of Godfrey & Abigail (Macomber) King
      vii.   Anna, b. 1796, d. 3 May 1885, m. Joseph King, son of Godfrey & Abigail (Macomber) King
      x.   Ichabod, b. about 1806, d. 11 May 1834 in Tiverton, m. Bathsheba Albert, b. 6 May 1810, who later married his brother William.
           Children:
           i.   William B., b. 9 Nov. 1831, d. 17 July 1904, m. Cornelia Grinnell
           ii.   Cynthia M., b. 6 May 1834, d. 9 Sept. 1908, m. Cornelius King, Jr., son of Cornelius and Deborah (Dennis) King. He d. May 1907. They had 2 daughters.

Page 589 — Alden Southworth Simmons, b. 20 Dec. 1809 should be numbered 47.

Page 589 — JOHN[7] SIMMONS' first child, Mary Ann, probably died in Wiesbaden.

Page 590 — VALENTINE[7] SIMMONS' first child was Benoni.
    (He is the last member of the LC family to have a separate listing in the Simmons Genealogy).

Page 593 — WILLIAM L.[7] SIMMONS m. Mrs. Bathsheba (Albert) Simmons, widow of his brother Ichabod.
    Children:
      ii. and iii.   William B. and Cynthia were children of his brother Ichabod (See Page 588)

Page 595/6—DAVID[8] SIMMONS m. first Grace A. Grinnell, dau. of Gideon and Sarah (Hart) Grinnell. He m. 2nd Lilly E. Terry, b. 1866, d. 1957
    Children:
      iv.   Lester m. Daisy Almira Manchester, b. 11 Sept. 1880, d. 14 June 1940, dau. of William Horatio and Fannie Smith (Chase) Manchester

ix.   Evelyn Young m. Roger G. Hart, son of Roland and Ida (Smith) Hart

x.   Leah m. Warren Waite, son of Warren and Mabel (Wilkie) Waite

Page 607 — COL. HENRY TILLINGHAST[8] SISSON.
Children:
ii.   It was David who m. 9 April 1917 Bessie Irene Doolittle etc.

Page 609 — CHARLES DEAN[9] SISSON's residence opposite the Coval Osborn or Sherer Place, later occupied by Beatrice Kelley Manchester.

Page 619 — ROBERT[8] SNOW (Loum[7], Loami[6], etc.)

— ROBERT[9] SNOW (Robert[8], Loum[7], etc.) m. Dorothy D. Clark
    i.   Deborah, m. Clarke Simonds, son of Philip B. and Persis (Godfrey) Simonds

Page 636 — Children of Rev. Franklin Chester Southworth and Alice A. Berry Southworth
i.   Constant, b. 12 Aug. 1894, m. 15 Jan. 1927 Evalina Prescott Kean, dau. of Lancelot & Elizabeth (Prescott) Kean of Va. & La.
ii.   William Berry, b. 28 May 1896, d. 7 Aug. 1927
iii.   Dr. Franklin Chester, Jr., b. 28 June 1898, m. 30 June 1925 Margaret Boynton of Framingham, dau. of Dr. Richard M. Boynton of Buffalo, N. Y., d. 18 Sept. 1958.
Children:
i.   Richard Boynton, b. 16 May 1927, m. Anne Gregory 8 April 1966
ii.   Franklin Chester 3rd, b. 28 June 1929 m. Jose Clesse in 1952 and Joan Menchner 21 June 1966
iii.   Alice, b. 29 April 1932, m. Rev. Jacob Frank Schulman 19 June 1954
iv.   William Henry Boynton, b. 25 June 1933, m. Louise Dowd 18 Sept. 1959

Page 643 — MANUEL L. SYLVIA m. Eliza Henderson Bone (or Bowen)

Page 648— Ebenezer[3] Tabor
    child ix. Jacob m. Susannah Dennis (see p. 410)

Page 658 —   THE TAYLOR FAMILY
    Much of this material apparently came from the TAYLOR GENEALOGY by Geo. Taylor Paine in Manuscript at R. I. Historical Society Library. It does not go beyond the children of the members of the sixth generation. Generally we have limited ourselves to correcting mistakes and adding data on person listed.

— ROBERT[1] TAYLOR
Children:
i.   Mary, m. in April 1664
iv.   Robert, m. Deborah Peckham of Newport. Their daughter Margaret was b. 1689.
vii.   James, b. 7 Oct. 1660, d. 7 Oct. 1690, wife Catherine b. 1666, d. 15 Sept. 1690

— JOHN[2] TAYLOR, b. Newport June 1657, m. 1st in 1681 Abigail (- -)

Page 659 — Children:
  i.   Mary, b. 25 Oct. 1682, d. 1732, m. in LC about 1702 Jonathan
        Irish. He was b. 6 June 1678, d. 1732
  vii.   Philip, b. 13 May 1697, predeceased father

— PETER[2] TAYLOR (Robert[1]), b. July 1661, d. 1736. He married first
in 1696 Elizabeth Peckham, dau. of John and Mary (Clarke) Peckham, b. 1669, d.
in LC 24 May 1714, age 45. He m. second in LC 1 Nov. 1715 Hannah Wood, b.
18 Feb. 1685 dau. of Col. Thomas and Rebecca (- -) Wood. (See Page 779)

— Children:
  iii.   Mary, b. 30 Dec. 1703, d. 30 Oct. 1740
  viii. Anna, b. 13 Feb. 1726, d. 1777, m. 5 Aug. 1785 Jeremiah Briggs,
         son of Job and Mary (Tallman) Briggs, who was b. 1721, d.
         Sept. 1764
  (There is considerable confusion as to the Taylor Family, particularly in
  reference to Peter[2] and Peter[3] who were father and son. They each
  probably had two wives. Peter[2]'s children are authentically defined by
  his will, but some of them do not match the birth records of LC, including putative children of Elizabeth Irish Taylor, probably Hannah
  (4/12/1721), William (4/30/1724) and Anna (2/13/1726). However
  Peter[2] apparently had children with the names Hannah, William, and
  Anna also. BFW gives them the above dates.)

— JOHN[3] TAYLOR
Children:
  i.   Elizabeth, m. Richard Sisson, Jr. of Dartmouth, Mass.
  ii.   Job, m. 18 Nov. 1742 Sarah Munro (had 2 children)
  iii. David, m. 16 July 1746 Elizabeth Lawton (had 2 children)
  vi.   Margaret, m. Aaron Grinnell as his 2nd wife and had 6 children.
  vii. Sarah, b. 14 Feb. 1729, m. 27 Jan. 1748 John Lawton of Ports-
        mouth (7 children)
  viii. Humphrey (had 2 children)
  ix.   Mary, m. Giles Slocum. She d. 26 Jan. 1797 (4 children)
  x.   Samuel, died early
  xi.   Peter, m. Hannah Pearce (2nd wife). He d. 20 Sept. 1809
        (2 children)
  xii. Reuben, m. 12 Feb. 1761 Avis Slocum, b. 28 June 1739
        (4 children)

Page 661 — ROBERT[3] TAYLOR
Last sentence of will should read "to daughters Eunice, Rebecca, Mary
and Joanna".
Children by first wife:
  iii. Robert, d. 1 Dec. 1802
  iv. Gideon, d. 11 July 1790
Children by second wife:
  vi.   Deborah, d. before 1767, m. 18 Dec. 1753 George Simmons
  ix.   Joanna, m. 12 May 1771 Abiah Tripp, son of Rufus
  viii. James 2d, m. 7 Jan. 1768 Lydia, dau. of Isaac and Alice Sisson
  x.   Mary, m. Peter LeBarbier Duplessis, son of John Francis and
        Margaretta Angelica Duplessis

834

Page 662 — PHILIP[3] TAYLOR
    Children:
    i.   Susannah (had 7 children)
    ii.   Abigail, m. Thomas Burgess, who was b. 6 Sept. 1723
    iii. Deborah (See Page 576)
    v.   Comfort, m. 30 Dec. 1753 George Wood, who was b. 2 Nov. 1730
        d. June 1820 (1 child)

    — PETER[3] TAYLOR, b. LC 20 Oct. 1697, d. 31 March 1764, m. in LC
27 Oct. 1720 Elizabeth Irish, dau. of David and Martha (Nelson) Irish, who was b.
7 Oct. 1699, d. 11 Oct. 1733 (See Page 372). He m. second in LC 25 Dec. 1734
Bridget Wood, dau. of Jonathan and Elizabeth (Thurston) Wood, b. 22 June 1706
(See Page 781)
    Children:
    i.   Elizabeth, b. 14 Feb. 1739/40, d. 11 Sept. 1758
    ii.   Hannah, b. 14 Dec. 1743

Page 663 — Children:
    x.   Joseph, b. 4 March 1767
    xii. Deborah (See Page 773)

    — DAVID[4] TAYLOR
    Children by first wife:
    ii.   Lois, m. 11 April 1773 John Ross of Westerly
    Children by second wife:
    iii. Jude, d. 10 Dec. 1847 Westerly, m. Abigail Ross (7 children)
    iv. Elizabeth, m. 25 March 1779 Stephen Rathbun of Westerly
    v.   Samuel, m. 6 Jan. 1783 Rebecca Crandall of Westerly
        (14 children)

Page 664 — ROBERT[4] TAYLOR m. second 1764 Abigail Jameson

Page 665 — JOSEPH[4] TAYLOR also had children Lyndon, Phebe, Lydia and Ruth

Page 666 — Will of Nathaniel Taylor should read "Wood lot at Colebrook Woods".

Page 668 — CAPT. ANDREW[5] TAYLOR m. 6 July 1788 Elizabeth Field, dau. of
John and Abigail Field

Page 669 — SIMEON[5] TAYLOR m. Mary Ann Jones, dau. of George and Phebe
(Bevins) Jones, who was b. 25 May 1776
    Children:
    ii.   John Bevins
    v.   Francis Rathbun
    vi.   Abby Maria (See Page 746)
    vii. John Bevins

Page 670 — GEORGE MILFORD[6] TAYLOR lived at "Wunnegin" not Onegan
    Children:
    iv.   Mary Jane m. Thomas Warren Kempton, b. 21 Jan. 1847, d. 14
        Nov. 1899 (See Page 385)
    vii. John Bevins

Page 671 — ANDREW SIMEON[7] TAYLOR — (See Page 704)

Page 675 — "To all daughters of Elizabeth Wood's children, ten shillings a peace to all my daughter Rebecca Richmond's children. To daughter Sarah" etc.
> Children:
> v.   Rebecca m. Edward Richmond, son of John and Abigail (Rogers) Richmond.

Page 692 — JOHN STUART[9] TOMPKINS' Children:
> i.   Henrietta Frances m. James Rowlands Tod, son of Thomas and Edith (Wells) Tod

Page 693 — LINEAGE OF HENRIETTA (TOMPKINS) TOD

Page 704 — Mary Priscilla White (See Page 671)

Page 717 — WILLIAM[4] WILBOR m. Mary Babcock, daughter of George and Susannah (Potter) Babcock

Page 733 — DANIEL[5] WILBOR (See Page 663)

Page 739 — #91 David W. Wilbor — probably only child of David[6] Wilbor and Pamelia (Simmons) Wilbor

Page 746 — Benjamin Franklin[6] Wilbour (See Page 670) m. Abby Maria Taylor, who died 11 Feb. 1887

Page 752 — David W.[7] Wilbor (See Page 528)
> Children:
> iv.   Cyrenus Bliss Wilbor was father of Henry Lester Wilbur who m. Bess Louise Manchester (daughter of William Horatio Manchester and Fannie Smith (Chase) Manchester.) They had three daughters, including Jane Wilbur of Warren, R. I.

Page 761 — Line 7 — "Gov. Isaac Wilbour Place"

> Children:
> #143 iv.   Deborah Josephine d. 13 Sept. 1950 m. Frederick Marcy Patten, son of David and Marcia A. Patten

Page 765 — LESTER EMERSON[8] WILBUR

> PHILIP HERBERT[8] WILBOUR m. Grace Frances Ropes, who died in Providence 17 April 1925. Residence: LC. They lived on the place which once belonged to his great grandfather Governor Isaac Wilbour and to his father Isaac C. Wilbour".

Page 768 — DOROTHY[9] WILBOUR m. Adelbert Allen Martin, son of David Franklin. He was b. 8 April 1888, d. 27 April 1958 in Fall River. (See Page 428)

Page 769 — #143 Caroline[9] Wilbour Patten, d. of Frederick Marcy Patten and Deborah Josephine Wilbour b. LC 10 July 1885 m. Eugene Bailey Jackson, son of Frank A. and Adele (Howe) Jackson, who died 11 Nov. 1936. (See entries under Jackson Page 379)

Page 770 — DANIEL^2 WILCOX m. Elizabeth Cooke

Page 779 — JOHN^3 WOOD. There is some confusion as to his parents who were either John^2 and Mary (Peabody) Wood or William^2 and Martha (Earle) Wood. (See Page 780)

Page 780— Mary Church, wife of John Wood was b. 26 Mar. 1666/7

Page 784 — GEORGE^5 WOOD — (See Page 662)

INDIVIDUAL INDEX
(One Line)

Generation	Name of Ancestor	Spouse	Serial Number	Page
FIRST				
SECOND				
THIRD				
FOURTH				
FIFTH				
SIXTH				
SEVENTH				
EIGHTH				
NINTH				
TENTH				
ELEVENTH				
TWELFTH				

NOTES:

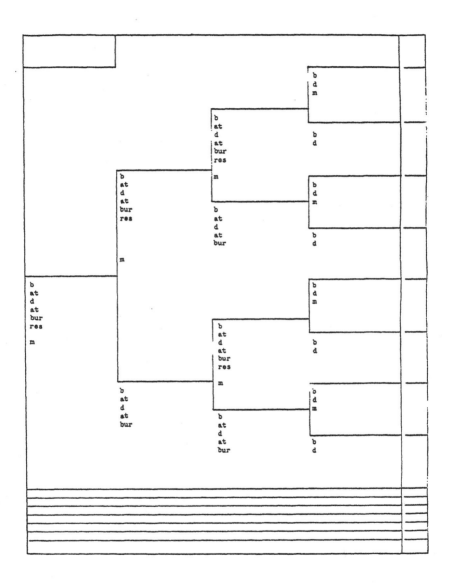